Embracing Democracy in Modern Germany

Embracing Democracy in Modern Germany

Political Citizenship and Participation, 1871–2000

Michael L. Hughes

BLOOMSBURY ACADEMIC
LONDON • NEW YORK • OXFORD • NEW DELHI • SYDNEY

BLOOMSBURY ACADEMIC
Bloomsbury Publishing Plc
50 Bedford Square, London, WC1B 3DP, UK
1385 Broadway, New York, NY 10018, USA
29 Earlsfort Terrace, Dublin 2, Ireland

BLOOMSBURY, BLOOMSBURY ACADEMIC and the Diana logo are
trademarks of Bloomsbury Publishing Plc

First published in Great Britain 2021
Paperback edition published in 2022

Copyright © Michael L. Hughes, 2021

Michael L. Hughes has asserted his right under the Copyright, Designs and
Patents Act, 1988, to be identified as Author of this work.

For legal purposes the Acknowledgments on p. viii constitute
an extension of this copyright page.

Cover image: Demos 1992 Berlin (© Photo by P/F/H/ullstein bild via Getty Images)

All rights reserved. No part of this publication may be reproduced or
transmitted in any form or by any means, electronic or mechanical, including
photocopying, recording, or any information storage or retrieval system,
without prior permission in writing from the publishers.

Bloomsbury Publishing Plc does not have any control over, or responsibility for,
any third-party websites referred to or in this book. All internet addresses given
in this book were correct at the time of going to press. The author and publisher
regret any inconvenience caused if addresses have changed or sites have
ceased to exist, but can accept no responsibility for any such changes.

Every effort has been made to trace copyright holders and to obtain their
permissions for the use of copyright material. The publisher apologizes for
any errors or omissions and would be grateful if notified of any corrections
that should be incorporated in future reprints or editions of this book.

A catalogue record for this book is available from the British Library.

Library of Congress Cataloging-in-Publication Data
Names: Hughes, Michael L., author.
Title: Embracing democracy in modern Germany :
political citizenship and participation, 1871-2000 / Michael L. Hughes.
Description: London ; New York : Bloomsbury Academic, 2021. |
Includes bibliographical references and index.
Identifiers: LCCN 2020035925 (print) | LCCN 2020035926 (ebook) |
ISBN 9781350153752 (hardback) | ISBN 9781350200111 (paperback) |
ISBN 9781350153769 (ebook) | ISBN 9781350153776 (epub)
Subjects: LCSH: Democracy–Germany–History. |
Political participation–Germany–History. | Germany–Politics and government–1871- |
Germany (West)–Politics and government. | Germany (East)–Politics and government.
Classification: LCC JN3971.A91 H84 2021 (print) |
LCC JN3971.A91 (ebook) | DDC 323/.0420943–dc23
LC record available at https://lccn.loc.gov/2020035925
LC ebook record available at https://lccn.loc.gov/2020035926

ISBN:	HB:	978-1-3501-5375-2
	PB:	978-1-3502-0011-1
	ePDF:	978-1-3501-5376-9
	eBook:	978-1-3501-5377-6

Typeset by Integra Software Services Private Limited

To find out more about our authors and books visit www.bloomsbury.com
and sign up for our newsletters.

For Gloria

Contents

Acknowledgments		viii
Introduction		1
1	Democratic Elements in an Authoritarian Regime: Enabling and Containing Political Participation in Imperial Germany, 1871–1918	9
2	Searching for Authority: Challenges to Parliamentary Democracy in the Weimar Republic, 1918–1933	33
3	Agency in a Total State: Compliance and Non-Compliance in the Third Reich, 1933–1945	57
4	Re-Imagining Democracy: Creating a Federal Republic in Postwar West Germany	79
5	Daring More Democracy: The Rise of Extra-Parliamentary Political Action in West Germany, 1968–1980s	103
6	Political Citizenship in a Dictatorship: Negotiating Agency in East Germany, 1945–1989	131
7	Coming to Fruition? Unification and Democracy in the Berlin Republic	155
Notes		172
Bibliography		236
Index		291

Acknowledgments

I have incurred many debts in the long process of writing this book.

I must thank the ILL staff at the Z. Smith Reynolds Library of Wake Forest University. The ZSR has impressive collections, but I have relied on James Harper and his colleagues to obtain the numerous books and articles I needed from around the United States and Germany. They have been tireless and efficacious in securing them for me.

I began thinking about democracy in Germany in graduate school in the 1970s. I have given innumerable talks at conferences in the United States and Germany and have benefited from feedback from many, many scholars. I would like particularly to thank the participants in the Social Science Research Seminar and the History Department Colloquium at Wake Forest, who have read and responded to many iterations of this material, and the participants in the Making Democratic Subjectivities Seminar at the 2015 German Studies Conference. Various individual scholars have read chapters and commented on them. I would particularly like to thank my colleague in German Politics, Helga Welsh, with whom I have been talking about these issues for decades and who read chapters intensely on my behalf. I would also like to thank Peter Caldwell, Moritz Föllmer, Barry Trachtenberg, and Maria Mitchell for their careful readings of various chapters. I must also thank Allison Brown of Henry Street Editing, as well as the anonymous readers for Bloomsbury Academic.

I need especially to thank Dr. Gloria J. Fitzgibbon, who has been challenging me intellectually for four decades and without whom I could not have written this work.

I am of course responsible for any errors or inadequacies.

Introduction

By 2000 a unified Germany was a stable democracy, and Germans seemed to have embraced democracy—quite a change from the authoritarian monarchy founded in 1871, the unstable Weimar Republic, or the dictatorial Third Reich and German Democratic Republic. But embracing "democracy" was always complex and could never be complete. Germans were never a national collective with a single mentality or character. Some Germans in the mid-nineteenth century already embraced democracy; some Germans (especially in the 1920s and early 1930s) used democratic means to undermine democracy, and only a minority voted for parties supporting the democratic Weimar Republic; some Germans, even in the twenty-first century, have never embraced it. Moreover, even Germans who embraced democracy have had widely varying conceptions of what "democracy" might entail—e.g., parliamentary democracy, leader democracy, party democracy, direct democracy, participatory democracy. Meanwhile, Hitler despised democracy but sought, in effect, democratic legitimacy through plebiscites, and East Germany's Communist dictatorship insisted it alone was the truly democratic German republic. This book seeks to illuminate the complexities and open-endedness of Germans' encounters with and embrace of "democracy," from 1871 to 2000—encounters that can illuminate debate on democracy more generally and that have recently taken on new relevance, as liberal democracy has come under increasing challenge, in Germany and elsewhere.

Democracy as Institution, Culture, and Practice

The rise of democracy in the modern period took on an aura of inevitability in the heady days after the collapse of Communism, as the number of "democracies" across the world grew. However, that rise was not inevitable. Understanding democratization requires looking at the specific circumstances that contributed to, hindered, or eroded democracy. Focusing on Germany, a complex and historically significant example, offers an illuminating case.[1]

Germany's democratization is a story of multiple pressures for and against democracy, pressures that played out amid contingent factors. History cannot be reduced to a simple theory or a simple narrative. It is always complicated. And because pressures and contingencies are ongoing, it never comes to a conclusion. Germany has experienced six regimes in 130 years because dramatic shifts proved possible—toward democracy and against it.²

Germany's movement toward democracy began in defeat. In 1806, Napoleon crushed the Prussian Army. As French troops approached Berlin, the city's Prussian commander issued a proclamation: "The king has lost a battle. The duty of the burgher is to remain calm." The people of Prussia were being told that *they* had not lost a battle and that *they* were to do nothing to defend the realm. After that defeat, Prussian officials—and their German successors—saw the French as dominating the European continent just because they had an engaged citizenry, a citizenry Prussia had lacked; they concluded that only by securing the people's engaged participation could their state defend itself against foreign enemies. In a striking example, Karl-August von Hardenberg's 1807 Riga Memorandum (for King Friedrich Wilhelm III) called for "democratic tenets in a monarchical government." Hardenberg did not seek a constitutional monarchy, let alone parliamentary democracy. ("Pure democracy," he added, "we must leave to the year 2440, if it is made for humans at all.") He was instead asserting the need for some role for public opinion and the people that would engage them enthusiastically in the state's affairs and its defense. Elites in Germany have insisted repeatedly on the need to secure citizen engagement, for defense of the realm and political stability, through democratic means—or the appearance of democracy.³

Pressure for democracy also came, decisively, from below. Despite stereotyping of Germans as unusually authoritarian in personality, significant numbers of Germans, in all regimes, have sought to secure agency—including democratic governance. They often resented what East German citizens characterized as "political infantilization" by elites. They hence repeatedly sought to influence government policy, even within dictatorships, and rebelled for democracy in 1918 and 1989. Increased education and affluence since the 1960s only strengthened and broadened these pre-existing desires. Political protest has characterized every German regime, though political organizing depended on the type of regime and the constraints it created. Albeit protest and organization could undercut, rather than advance, democratization. Crucially, the breadth and variety of agency and participation confute stereotypes of Germans as sharing some national character or as collectively inherently docile and subservient.

Pressures against democracy often came from governments and governing elites. Hardenberg spoke of "democratic tenets" while dismissing democracy until a far-distant future. Hitler could speak of his rule as "true democracy," and East German Communists insisted their regime was the only "German Democratic Republic (GDR)." As had Hardenberg, these two regimes saw a need for the appearance of democratic legitimacy but imposed draconian policies to prevent citizen agency. Moreover, even democratic leaders sought to limit popular agency. They might want popular input, but they seldom wanted citizens, individually or collectively, to have a substantive (let alone a predominant) role in making policy. Participation has meant for most German political elites either (1) popular engagement where citizens provide necessary information and enthusiastic support to maximize policy effectiveness and to defend the country or (2) at most a role in choosing their leaders—but with policy*making* firmly in elite hands.

As much as people may want influence over politics, for many if not most people outcomes matter. Polling on attitudes toward democracy does not always show a correlation between current economic conditions or personal economic circumstances and support for democratic regimes, though it sometimes does. And support for anti-democratic parties has risen in times of economic difficulty. More generally, people want a government that works. Perceptions that a regime, democratic or dictatorial, is not functioning effectively can call its legitimacy and sustainability into question.

Political cultures played a crucial role in democracy (and in this book), as institutions alone are insufficient to establish a stable democracy. Political culture refers to the values, attitudes, and practices within a society that structure the ways that people think about politics and the ways that they interact politically, with one another and with the state. It makes some ideas and actions possible and precludes others. Political scientists elaborated the concept to illuminate democracies' forms and stability, but the citizens of dictatorships have political values, attitudes, and actions, too. One may identify a political culture that seems predominant in a nation at a given moment, but that political culture is neither fixed nor universal nor determinant of all political action. Any nation at any moment has multiple political cultures because individuals never all agree with all or even some elements of any one political culture.

Germans have debated sharply over common interest versus individual interests. Parliamentary democracies have organized around the representation of individual and group interests. Yet many Germans, particularly before 1945, believed that a common interest of all Germans existed, one that should predominate over "egotistical" individual interests. That presumption could generate antipathy toward parliamentary government in general, but particularly its democratic form during the Weimar Republic. Arguably, only an acceptance of pluralism, that multiple interests do exist and deserve representation, makes stable parliamentary governance possible. And only in the Bonn Republic (West Germany) did majorities of Germans begin to accept pluralism over seeking a politics based on a putative common interest.

A single common interest implied a single set of values that should be determinative for political action. Political compromise then seemed a betrayal of values. Yet in practice it is difficult to find a majority for any specific policy position, certainly on complex issues but often even on straightforward ones. So governance in practice requires compromise. In democratic societies those compromises are more or less public. Many Germans, though, especially in the Weimar Republic, repudiated parliamentary governance as tawdry horse-trading over base material, egotistical, interests.

While it is misleading to see Germany as perpetually a nation of authoritarian personalities, some Germans could be deeply concerned with order (an attitude certainly not unknown among citizens of other nations); how many and how deeply did vary. They could associate order with certain types of regime, and disorder with other types. And seeing the Rechtsstaat (the rule of law) as orderliness and legal certainty could make democracy seem problematic.

Moreover, Germans disagreed about what democracy meant. They have argued, often vehemently, over how and how much the people should act politically.

Many Germans have been attracted to a leader democracy. The sociologist Max Weber asserted that democracy should mean that you vote every few years for your leaders, then go home and "shut up" until the next election, leaving the experts you had chosen to do their job. He, and others, doubted the masses were mature enough for more than that. And popular political engagement might be in pursuit of private interest—not the common interest that should prevail. Weber wanted Germany to have a parliamentary government, but one with limited popular input. Hitler, of course, offered a more extreme type of leader democracy, claiming to embody the popular will, so that checks and balances and parliament were unnecessary. And GDR Communists asserted that their Socialist Unity Party (SED) embodied the people's true interests, so that democracy equaled the rule of that party.

Parliamentary democracy has become normative. Support for direct democracy was significant in the November (1918) Revolution and has recurred since the 1960s. However, in 1918/19, Germans chose a constitution establishing a head of government responsible to a parliament of delegates with party-political bases. That government was going to make policy through negotiation and compromise among party leaders. The Bonn and Berlin (reunified German) Republics have also had parliamentary governance.

The early Bonn Republic had a party democracy with elements of Weber's notion of leader democracy. The first Chancellor, Konrad Adenauer, was the dominating political figure. Even after he left office, citizens were expected to vote but then to channel any concerns through leaders, that is, parties or certain large interest groups. Attempts to exercise influence through popular protest were denounced as "Nazi and Communist tactics" of "pressure from the streets." West Germany became a stable democracy by the mid-1960s, but many Germans found it too limited.

Increasing education and affluence, along with popular desires, then led to a participatory, but not direct, democracy by the 1980s, that is, one in which citizens expected to be able not only to vote but to participate through various forms of citizen agency. Citizens Initiatives (informal associations of citizens seeking to influence public policy implementation or legislation) sprang up. And popular protest blossomed. Citizens demanded—and secured the Constitutional Court's legitimation of—widespread popular input as central to German democracy. Understanding the unified Germany's democracy hence requires analysis of two forms of democracy in the Federal Republic of Germany (FRG).

Germans have also been in ongoing, often fierce disagreement as to who constituted the *demos*, the people, who should be allowed to participate. Almost always they have assumed citizens would be ethnically German. Moreover, in the German Empire, women lacked political rights and so were not full citizens, and various groups (e.g., Catholics, socialists) faced persecution or discrimination. The Third Reich redefined citizenship in "racial" terms, limited women's rights, and persecuted various groups and individuals. Even in the democratic Weimar, Bonn, and Berlin republics, Germans grappled with issues of citizenship for those who were not ethnically German. Democracy depends on tolerance, and difficulty in accepting non-ethnically German individuals as citizens (among most Germans until recently and many Germans still) is inherently problematic for democracy and has played a role in attacks on democracy—in the past and in the twenty-first century.

Each chapter here explicates, in one of Germany's political regimes, the institutional framework, political cultures, and concepts of political citizenship and participation. Institutions and events are discussed only as they are relevant to democratization, not comprehensively. The Bonn Republic gets two chapters because it arguably had two different forms of democracy. The work spans the period from 1871, when unification created Germany as a sovereign subject of political action, to 2000. The latter date allows an assessment of the development of a provisionally stable, predominantly democratic, widely accepted political culture in a unified Germany, while it also marked a significant, if still contested, redefinition of the *demos*, the German people, that was no longer de facto ethnic.

Scholars have worked diligently to analyze Germany's political cultures, but specifying exactly how many Germans at a given moment held particular political beliefs is impossible. No opinion-poll data exists before 1946. Scholars can only infer what people thought from what they said, what the organizations that they joined propounded, and what the candidates/parties they supported claimed to promote; they then assess numbers and impact. For the Third Reich and GDR, scholars must draw on indirect sources, including regime reports. And even post-1945 opinion-poll data have limits: Perhaps the response captures a respondent's opinion; but he may have only a fuzzy notion of the issue or one about which the question posed cannot elicit an accurate answer; she may say what she thinks she should say; and prior questions may prompt differing responses to a given question. Opinion-polling data does give us some sense of orders of magnitude for various views and development of views over time, but we can never be sure how accurately it reproduces respondents' actual opinions. Nonetheless, scholars have come to educated conclusions about political cultures and their weight in understanding historical developments.

Political citizenship and participation constitute the means through which citizens seek to exercise influence. Participation in nineteenth- and twentieth-century Germany took an enormous variety of forms. Making sense of citizen action and citizen influence in multiple regimes across decades requires attention to that variety.

The "political" must include whatever has political consequences, independent of the citizen's intent. We can never be *sure* of anyone's intent. Further, citizens, as individuals or collectives, frequently pursue private interests through political actions—overtly or covertly. And private actions without political intent can have substantial political effects. Moreover, would-be totalitarian regimes define as "political" actions that in most regimes would be purely private. So we must seek to identify both people's motives for political actions and the range of political consequences their actions might have independent of expressed intent.

Democracy and democratic are equivocal terms. "Democratic" in principle refers to actions or ideas that promote "democracy"—a substantive, effective role for the people in their own governance. Germans have held widely varying conceptions of what that might mean in practice. For political theorists it has required regular, competitive elections that empowered citizens to determine leaders and at least influence policy, equality of citizens (especially of adults in voting), and majority rule with protection of minority rights. Usually theorists have added an explicit renunciation of violence as a means of settling conflicts, recognition of pluralism and conflict as unavoidable, freedom of expression, checks and balances, and the Rechtsstaat. These criteria reflect representative democracy and theorists' perception of what is needed to guarantee continued democratic rights, but they leave open the degree and forms of the people's role and could apply to various forms of direct democracy. Nonetheless, we must recognize that not all Germans have accepted such criteria. For example, most Germans opposed pluralism and compromise before the 1960s and could accept only a democracy that would embody and implement a putative common interest. And often Germans wanted not liberal democracy's protections for minority rights but a system that would empower a leader to realize a putative univocal will of the real people. Hence, Hitler could characterize himself as representing "true democracy," and GDR Communists were certain that they understood the people's interests better than the people themselves.[4]

This book is written to be accessible to a broad audience, but with the hope that specialists will benefit from the overview of the complex literature that historians have developed and from a presentation and analysis of the sweep of developments across 130 years and six regimes.

One might recount the history of German democratization, 1871 to the present, as (in Hayden White's term) a romance—a story of democracy's struggles against adversity, culminating in its final triumph. Nonetheless, Germany's development from authoritarian monarchy through a failed democracy and two putatively totalitarian dictatorships to a stable, unified, participatory democracy was not steady evolution but fits and starts in a contested process. Democracy may have prevailed in Germany, with stable representative-democratic institutions and an overwhelmingly democratic, and a participatory, political culture, but conceptions of democracy remain contested and events may tilt the balance of pro- and anti-democratic forces. So, crucially, the story's outcome cannot be an ending, triumphant or otherwise, for the process will remain ongoing.[5]

From Subjects to Citizens

Rulers of the early nineteenth-century German states sought to turn subjects into *Staatsbürger*, into citizens of the state. Multifarious categories of subject in pre-Napoleonic Germany each had widely varying traditional rights and duties that constrained a ruler's ability to exercise direct power over each subject. Once everyone in a realm was a *Staatsbürger*, each would be equal before and immediate to the state/ruler, which could then implement laws and judgments directly and equally on everyone, increasing their power. Yet only with German unification in the last third of the nineteenth century would male Germans become formally equal *Staatsbürger*, as varying categories of subjects survived until then in different German states.[6]

As German rulers sought in the Napoleonic period and thereafter to engage and mobilize their populations, they sought a non-democratic but participatory citizenship. Before 1815, standing up to the French seemed to require developing among people in the German-speaking lands at least some commitment to the state, so that one could mobilize the population to defend the state. Participation by citizens then came to be seen by many as crucial for state survival. Even after Napoleon's defeat, staying competitive in a changing Europe seemed to require some popular commitment. Moreover, the post-Napoleonic German states needed to integrate the new territories they had gained through the 1814/15 Congress of Vienna, and they needed to manage the massive debts that decades of war had left. Hence, engaging the people, while denying them substantive political power, became a pressing issue.[7]

Nineteenth-century German political practice and constitutional theory rested on the "monarchical principle," the presumption that sovereignty (ultimate political authority) lay with the monarch. Monarchs might choose to issue a constitution, but did so as a favor, so they could in principle revoke and replace it at will. And a constitution would not limit the monarch's fundamental power but only its exercise. The limits did include the Rechtsstaat.[8]

After 1815 German states gradually introduced representative bodies—but what kind? The Germanic Confederation required its members to have a "*landständische* assembly," which could imply one based on representation for different orders or corporations within a realm, not the citizenry as a whole. Such divided representation would undermine most rulers' efforts to establish a unitary citizenship. Before and after the Revolutions of 1848, the German states introduced various types of representation, sometimes based on orders or corporations, sometimes not, though the number based on orders or corporations declined. No matter the type of assembly, no female and usually not every male *Staatsbürger* could vote, but only males who owned a specified amount of property or paid specified amounts of taxes. And voting was usually indirect (for electors who would then choose the parliamentary representatives). Participation beyond voting was usually limited to petitioning the ruler.[9]

For many nineteenth-century elites, a parliament was to have no political power. Many Germans were already suspicious of parliaments as representative of materialistic and divisive interests, so that rule by parliament was unacceptable. Instead, parliament would provide *limited* "participation" for the citizens. It could inform the rulers (monarchs and bureaucrats) about citizens' concerns, give rulers the benefit of broader perspectives on pressing problems, and serve as a transmission belt for the rulers to inform the citizens about policies and their logic. For much of the nineteenth century, political citizenship in German lands did not mean any substantive role in policy formation.[10]

The parliaments that were established did gradually secure some substantive powers, especially after the Revolutions of 1848 forced some concessions to the bourgeois citizens who had much of the economic power and most of the votes. A parliament's approval became generally required for the promulgation of laws, the imposition of at least direct taxes or the assumption of new state debt, and constitutional amendments. It could petition the monarch on the citizenry's behalf. However, the power to initiate bills was generally reserved to the monarch, and the parliament did not always have a vote on appropriations. As parliamentary powers increased, (some) citizens gained limited roles in the exercise of political power.[11]

The Revolutions of 1848 failed to establish democracy in the German lands but foreshadowed issues that would recur. Germans had already organized in innumerable associations before 1848, and many had engaged in various forms of protest. The Revolutions called up more organizational efforts and more protest—among liberals and democrats but also among conservatives suspicious of constitutional governance, let alone democracy. The predominant mood was for free and equal voting, though not all Germans agreed. And Germans were often suspicious of parliaments as representatives of egotistical interests instead of the communal interest, so many hesitated to grant parliaments "absolute power." Many Germans also came to find popular protest threatening. The Revolutions generated no majorities supporting a democratic republic, and lower-middle- to upper-class liberals ended up uniting with newly organized conservatives and ruling monarchs to establish constitutional governments that limited popular agency and left executive power in monarchs' hands. The Revolutions and their aftermath highlighted the presence in Germany of participatory and democratic forces but also of antidemocratic attitudes and groups. Both influenced the new unified Germany that came together in 1871.[12]

1

Democratic Elements in an Authoritarian Regime

Enabling and Containing Political Participation in
Imperial Germany, 1871–1918

In the German Empire (*Kaiserreich*), the labor movement (the Social Democratic Party (SPD) and the free trade unions) was the political force most committed to democracy, yet its leaders showed real doubts as to whether the working class was yet sufficiently mature to be trusted with democratic political citizenship. The debate over whether the movement should support the political mass strike focused on this issue. The editor of the printers' union periodical, for example, rejected the mass strike because "one must not put the knife in the hands of the children; then they will not be able to hurt themselves"—a notably dismissive attitude toward workers' democratic potential. Usually, though, worker leaders might argue, as did theorist Karl Kautsky, that the unorganized were "driven by mere instincts and needs" and so must be led by the "organized and superior elements" among the workers, that is, those under worker-movement tutelage. He and others did not share Lenin's insistence that only the professional revolutionaries could be trusted to exercise power initially, but even self-professedly democratic individuals often had significant doubts on how broadly democratic citizens could be allowed to act.[1]

The *Kaiserreich* was an authoritarian monarchy, and most Germans seem to have been content with that. The monarchy felt compelled to grant a constitution and a parliament with some substantive powers, to secure political stability and popular engagement in defense of the realm. Many Germans in the *Kaiserreich* did engage in political activities of various sorts. However, a majority of the electorate voted for parties that were not committed to democracy. Germans had an efficient government that had presided over decades of economic growth and increasing German political weight in the world. Many Germans feared that democratization might mean the eventual triumph of the socialists, as the SPD vote had increased from 3.2 percent in 1871 to 34 percent in 1912, with further growth expected. And even leaders of almost all parliamentary parties were uncomfortable with parliamentary government, which they dismissed as "parliamentary absolutism." Foreseeing a parliamentary government where they might never be in the majority, most parties, and apparently their voters, were content to work for some increase in parliamentary influence but with a strong monarchy as a check on democracy.

Parliamentary Power and Political Legitimacy in an Authoritarian Monarchy

The German Empire, created in 1871, had some strikingly democratic elements, but it remained an authoritarian monarchy until 1918. Rulers of the constituent states insisted on the "monarchical principle": Sovereignty (ultimate authority) lay with the monarchs; but they octroyed (graciously chose to grant) a constitution that constrained the *implementation* of the emperor's power. The constitution reflected the mix of authoritarianism and participation that had predominated in nineteenth-century German states. It reserved significant powers to the Emperor—over foreign affairs, the military, and the executive. But it did have a parliament (Reichstag) that citizens elected through universal, equal, secret, male suffrage and that had substantive powers over legislation, taxation, and appropriation. German political elites believed they needed an engaged citizenry, one committed wholeheartedly to supporting the state and its policies, to maintain sovereignty in a competitive and modernizing European state system, but they did not really want to surrender any more power than necessary to that citizenry. When Bismarck organized elections to a constituent Reichstag for the North German Confederation in 1867, he granted universal (male) suffrage to provide legitimacy, to recruit nationalist Germans to support the new federation despite the hesitancy of many regional elites, and in hopes lower-class, especially rural, Germans would vote against the liberals who had profited so greatly from the Prussian three-class voting system. Yet he had no intention of establishing democratic government for the Confederation or the subsequent *Kaiserreich*.[2]

The powers reserved to the monarchy were substantial. The King of Prussia, the largest and dominant state, was emperor, but he drew his legitimacy as emperor not from divine right or tradition but as the embodiment of German national unity. He appointed the Reich Chancellor, who was almost always also Minister-President of Prussia. The chancellor headed the federal government, had to countersign any imperial directives, and was "responsible"—though to whom was not constitutionally clear. In practice, though, the *Kaiserreich* had a ministerial government answerable only to the monarch—not a parliamentary government in which ministers were responsible to and served at the discretion of parliament. The *Kaiserreich* lacked its own civil service, so imperial officials were seconded from the Prussian civil service. The emperor/Prussian king hence effectively controlled the *Kaiserreich*'s executive branch. The monarch also controlled the *Kaiserreich*'s military forces. The military budget required Reichstag approval, which gave that body some leverage over military affairs. Yet because the military budget ran for several years and because Germany lay amid potentially hostile foreign powers, the Reichstag found it difficult to reject government demands to fund the military. The Reichstag had no effective control over the army's or navy's officer corps, manning, organization, or command, which lay entirely with the monarch. The monarch also controlled foreign policy.[3]

While Bismarck might have preferred a purely advisory parliament, he could not get away with that. By the 1850s almost all the German-speaking lands had parliaments whose approval was required for legislation, taxation, and, in some cases, appropriations. Bismarck had collected taxes without Prussian parliamentary approval from 1862 to 1866. Nonetheless, he had felt compelled, even after Prussia's great victories in the Austro-Prussian War, to agree to an Indemnity Bill from the parliament, to legitimate, if retrospectively, his actions. The *Kaiserreich* was going to have a parliament, and parliament was going to have some substantive powers.[4]

The parliament consisted of two houses, a Bundesrat, representing the governments of the empire's constituent states, and a Reichstag, elected by universal, equal, direct, secret, male suffrage. (Notably, it was liberals who added secret voting because they feared Bismarck intended to ape Napoleon III in manipulating the masses to establish dictatorial rule.) The constitution stipulated that members of the Reichstag "are representatives of the entire people and are not bound by orders or instructions." The parliament's powers extended to legislation, taxation, and appropriations. Legislation would only be valid with the approval of the Reichstag, Bundesrat, and emperor. Similarly, taxation and appropriation required parliamentary approval. Crucially, Germany was a rapidly changing country in a competitive state system; its need for legislation and regulation to manage change would make the Reichstag indispensable. The Reichstag could not impose its will on the monarchy, but the monarch could not rule on domestic affairs without Reichstag approval. So the Reichstag had significant powers. However, many areas of legislation were reserved to the states (e.g., education, health, police), and the implementation of federal laws was also often in the hands of state authorities.[5]

The judiciary was independent and implemented law relatively objectively, so the *Kaiserreich* was a Rechtsstaat. Even when Bismarck persecuted Catholics and socialists, he had to do so on the basis of law and due process—which set sufficient limits on government repression that the efforts failed. The *Kaiserreich*'s administrative courts provided substantive protection for citizens from arbitrary acts by individual bureaucrats. The judges, though, were conservative and monarchist. Moreover, no court could judicially review the constitutionality of laws.[6]

Historian Manfred Rauh argued that even before 1914 the *Kaiserreich* was moving toward parliamentary government, but scholars have not found his argument convincing. Rauh pointed to the fall of Chancellor Bernhard von Bülow in 1909 and to the establishment by 1913 of a right for the Reichstag to vote its loss of confidence in a chancellor. However, Bülow had already deeply antagonized the Kaiser, who hence had his own reasons to remove Bülow. And a 1913 vote of no-confidence in Chancellor Theobald von Bethmann Hollweg actually secured his position because replacing him would have looked like a monarchical surrender to parliament. Moreover, the bourgeois parties that expressed a lack of confidence in him denied that their votes meant they demanded he be responsible to parliament. Meanwhile, conservatives remained vehemently opposed to any steps toward parliamentary government, and their power in Prussia and the Bundesrat was considerable.[7]

Ultimately, even many non-conservatives, fearful of "parliamentary absolutism," were not sure they wanted a parliamentary government; instead they wanted a parliament that had a role in budget- and law-making and in raising issues with the government, but an executive branch independent of and a counterweight to parliament. Left liberals and even many Social Democrats were focused on first establishing universal equal suffrage for all German parliaments and increasing Reichstag supervision of the government, rather than establishing a parliamentary government chosen by the Reichstag. And neither the National Liberal nor (Catholic) Center Parties wanted parliamentary government because each feared that in such a system a coalition of its enemies would permanently exclude it from power. Absent the First World War, the *Kaiserreich* might eventually have evolved to parliamentary government, but such an evolution was very far from inevitable.[8]

Some Germans considered the constitution insufficiently democratic, but others who viewed it as too democratic periodically sought its fundamental revision. Because the *Kaiserreich* was based not on popular sovereignty but on monarchical sovereignty, some Germans emphasized that the constitution had been octroyed by the monarchs who came together to form the empire. So the possibility always remained of a *Staatsstreich*: those monarchs could revoke the 1871 constitution and replace it with another. Various political leaders toyed, repeatedly and occasionally publicly (seriously or as a tactical ploy), with the prospect of a *Staatsstreich* against the Reichstag suffrage. Crucially, German rulers never actually resorted to a *Staatsstreich*. The army was conservative and authoritarian; if so ordered, officers would have supported a *Staatsstreich* and the enlisted men most probably would have fired their weapons. Yet political elites still needed to legitimate the *Kaiserreich* and to secure some degree of popular support in the event of war. The *Kaiserreich*'s legitimacy rested in no small part on its reputation, among its citizens and abroad, as a Rechtsstaat, where one could trust in due process and certain rights. And the Reichstag, as arena of popular representation, had become central to securing that support. Moreover, the rulers of many federal states opposed such an action. Indeed, no one could know what forces one would unleash (e.g., civil war with the workers, secession by South German states) or what outcome would ultimately result from a *Staatsstreich*. Political elites were not happy with the citizen participation they had, but they were stuck with it.[9]

Rights and the Boundaries of Political Citizenship

Protecting minority rights is crucial for democracy, and the *Kaiserreich* had a mixed record. The imperial constitution lacked any protections for citizens' rights, though state constitutions guaranteed basic rights and due process. The *Kaiserreich*'s states did occasionally implement repressive measures. Governments often used lèse-majesté statutes and libel law to punish citizens whose statements could be construed as insulting to a monarch or politician. However, 1908 amendments to lèse-majesté legislation, and growing disrespect for Emperor Wilhelm II after the *Daily Telegraph* affair (where he gave a grossly indiscreet interview to a British journalist), resulted in a sharp decline in prosecutions.[10]

More significant was persecution of various minorities. Governing elites, starting with Bismarck, made a habit of declaring whole classes of individuals to be "enemies of the Empire." The government would seek to persecute such individuals, legally or otherwise. Catholics faced persecution in the 1870s under legislation passed during the *Kulturkampf*, a struggle by some Protestant- and liberal-dominated state governments against the Catholic Church. Socialists and working-class activists faced persecution from 1878 to 1890 under the anti-socialist laws, with sharp limits on their freedom of association, assembly, speech, and press. And even after those laws lapsed, official harassment and chicanery toward socialists continued (e.g., meetings were ordered dispersed on the slightest excuse; demonstrations were banned; journalists were slapped with libel suits). Ethnic minorities, especially Poles and Jews, also faced petty persecutions. Yet the *Kaiserreich* was not a dictatorship like the Third Reich and German Democratic Republic. Repression had some chilling effect on dissent, but an independent judiciary and the Rechtsstaat secured for citizens broad opportunities to participate in public life through expressions of opinion—even if they were from disdained minorities.[11]

The constitution established an imperial German citizenship, even as it continued citizenship in the separate states. Any subject or citizen of any state within the *Kaiserreich* would hold imperial German citizenship and be entitled to live, work, and enjoy the rights of any citizen within any German state. Localities could still determine who would be entitled to poor-relief and other benefits. The states controlled naturalization until 1913. Decisions about allowing it in each case could depend on the discretionary power (in practice the prejudices) of officials. Young German males who emigrated without meeting their military-service responsibilities could be prosecuted if they returned to Germany. Until 1913, individuals who left Germany for more than ten years would lose their citizenship, and it could be difficult to regain it.[12]

From 1885 Bismarck worked diligently to restrict further immigration by Jews and Poles and to expel any who were in the country "illegally." Such restrictions remained after he left office, as many officials shared his prejudices. Officials also systematized their policies, not only against ethnically undesirable but also against politically (usually socialist) and economically (potentially poor) undesirable immigrants. Yet when powerful landowners in the East objected to losing immigrant labor for their harvests, the government established a guest-worker program for Polish agricultural workers—not the only time in German history that the demand for labor by powerful interests would influence German immigration policies.[13]

The 1913 citizenship law reaffirmed the determination to deny citizenship to people who were not ethnically German, while encouraging all who were ethnically German to tie themselves to the *Kaiserreich*. Millions of people of ethnically German ancestry lived outside the *Kaiserreich*, scattered across Central and Eastern Europe and the Americas. Increasingly seeing itself as a world power, and spurred by pan-German radical nationalists, German policymakers saw these individuals as potential allies for Germany, either in influencing their governments or in supporting the *Kaiserreich*. So the 1913 law made it easier for ethnic German citizens living abroad to retain German citizenship (albeit, for male émigrés, only if they made themselves available for military service). Ethnic Germans who had never been citizens of the *Kaiserreich* could not automatically gain citizenship but could do so more easily. By granting the Bundesrat a veto over all naturalizations, the law effectively established Prussian control of naturalization, which allowed Prussia to impose nationally its anti-Polish and anti-Jewish immigration policies. The law also kept the internationally normative policy that upon marriage a woman automatically assumed her husband's citizenship, depriving women of any choice about their citizenship.[14]

Citizenship is about inclusion—but also about exclusion. German citizenship, in the immediate aftermath of unification (which excluded Catholic Austria), was rooted in Protestantism. After the 1870s, a combination of government action (e.g., universal education, conscription) and grassroots and commercial developments led to a widely shared sense of "Germanness" which came to include Catholics, grudgingly. Yet Jews and Polish-speakers and other ethnic minorities were never fully accepted. And socialists and other radicals were written out of true Germanness by many Germans and government officials (indeed, denounced as "louts without a fatherland" for their internationalism). Bismarck even proposed expatriating SPD leaders. As voters, all German males were, theoretically, equal political citizens—but only on the national level. At the *Land* (state) level, different German males had different voting rights and hence were unequal as political citizens. One cannot draw a straight line from 1870s/1880s to 1930s/1940s practices, but Germans had a tradition of writing some people in and some people out of the community of citizens.[15] Deciding who constitutes the *demos*, the people, is a central issue for any polity. Yet exclusionary practices are almost always freighted with prejudices and political motives.

Representing the National Interest

Germans did not share a single (let alone an authoritarian) mentality. Yet available sources show most Germans as repulsed by "egoistical" interests, committed to a putative single overriding national interest, and hence suspicious of parliamentary government and in conflict over the appropriate suffrage.

Crucially, most, though certainly not all, Germans in the nineteenth and early twentieth centuries preferred to see politics as a realm of ideals—not interests. Interests seemed to them corrupt and corrupting. When the North German Confederation was being formed, for example, one National Liberal said that one must exclude from the new Reichstag any hint of corruption by barring interest representatives, speculators, and representatives of the exchanges. Having rejected competing interests, many Germans rejected social conflict, especially if rooted in tawdry material concerns. Instead, many sought a politics that would emphasize national unity, community, and cooperation in pursuit of *the* national interest—which they assumed existed and could be identified. Indeed, the educated claimed a special role in politics by asserting that their education broadened them so that they were least tied to specific interests and hence best able to work for the good of the whole, for the national interest.[16]

Closely related to the belief in a single national interest was a desire for what Rudy Koshar calls "apoliticism." Many Germans, especially the Protestant and urban, expressed anxiety at the rise of mass politics, a rise that accompanied the development of powerful Catholic (the Center) and working-class/socialist (the Social Democratic) parties. They were also disturbed by the role of economic interests in politics (e.g., Agrarian League, Central Association of German Industrialists, trade unions) and by interest groups' active, often successful lobbying of the Reichstag and state parliaments, which they saw as tawdry horse-trading over base material interests. This disdain for the political was particularly strong at the municipal level. (As one mayor proclaimed, "Party politics have no place in city hall.") Liberals argued that knowledgeable individuals, independent because of their property ownership and education, could look beyond their own interests to the common good. This attitude could bolster reformist efforts by experts, but it left most Germans ill-disposed toward the rough and tumble of parliamentary democracy.[17]

Apolitical did not mean that politics were not involved. Liberals in German cities often set up "apolitical" entities to organize candidate selection for municipal elections. These groups claimed to represent all, so they usually did not proclaim platforms but emphasized the (superior) personalities they were supporting. The groups often had "Bürger" in their titles. This word could mean citizen and hence be all-inclusive. However, it could refer to the limited number of urban males with the wealth or status historically to have had full municipal citizenship rights and to count as deserving of a role in public life. And in practice, such Bürger associations were a means to mobilize the Protestant middling and upper classes electorally against the Center Party and the SPD.[18]

Modern citizenship is in theory equal, not least because the state wants equal access to, and control over, all within the polity—but imperial Germany remained in practice a deeply hierarchical society. For many Germans, that hierarchy was simply an expression of God-given or natural inequalities among individuals, so that citizens *should* participate unequally in political life. Even liberals, who generally believed in legal equality for all Germans, often emphasized that individuals were in practice unequal in their capabilities. They could believe in equal opportunity for all citizens but also that not all individuals would (or would even want to) secure equal outcomes—or an equal political role. Indeed, historian Fritz Stern saw a distinct "aesthetic-aristocratic bent," with "nothing egalitarian about it" in the individualism of many conservative and liberal Germans. The goal, rather, was to ensure that each individual had the freedom to develop as a person in the way appropriate to their (inherently differing) character and talents.[19]

Some inequalities might be inherent to the individual, but liberals and conservatives often identified differences in education as crucial. People obviously had varying degrees of access to education and took varying degrees of advantage of available opportunities. And *Bildung*, a mix of education and moral cultivation, was central to liberalism. For many liberals, politics was about enlightenment, and citizens could only be fully trusted to act politically after they had been enlightened. Lacking *Bildung*, the less well-educated were less prepared for participation in public life, so they ought to give way to the better-educated and better-qualified, indeed to "the best," certainly in positions of authority and responsibility but perhaps in voting as well.[20]

Voting was the most obvious form of political citizenship during the *Kaiserreich*, and for many Germans it was the only significant one. The *Kaiserreich* had universal, equal, direct, secret, male suffrage for the Reichstag—the most democratic element in the *Kaiserreich*; but many Germans actively opposed it or were at best ambivalent. And despite the relatively democratic suffrage for the Reichstag, Germans had numerous other unequal, indirect, public voting regimes at the municipal and state levels. Crucially, under the *Kaiserreich* more German states further restricted their suffrage than liberalized it. Saxony, Braunschweig, Lübeck, and Hamburg, for example, introduced more restrictive suffrages between 1896 and 1906, to prevent the SPD from ever coming to power (though Saxony introduced a somewhat more equitable but still unequal suffrage in 1909)—and the dominant state, Prussia, never reformed its unequal suffrage. Exercising political citizenship through voting was restricted significantly for most German males and completely for females.[21]

Debates about political participation and citizenship under the *Kaiserreich* were usually arguments about the purpose of and limits on suffrage. Germans deployed a range of arguments to justify existing or new restrictions. Socioeconomic status was the key criterion for the right to vote or the weight of one's vote. That status could be reflected in property ownership. It could be reflected in tax payments, notably in the Prussian three-class voting system, where *c.* 4 percent of the electorate (wealthy taxpayers who among them paid one-third of the direct taxes) had one-third of the votes; *c.* 14 percent of the electorate (middle-income taxpayers who among them paid one-third of direct taxes) had one-third of the votes; and *c.* 82 percent of the electorate (low-income taxpayers and non-taxpayers who among them paid the remaining one-third of direct taxes) had only one-third of the votes. The general argument here was threefold. Property ownership, or the economic wherewithal for high tax payments, was often seen as guaranteeing independence—and hence the ability to vote one's conscience and for the good of the whole. This argument was especially important given that voting in most non-Reichstag elections was a public act that subjected voters to considerable pressure from their employers and neighbors. Some argued that the right to vote should rest on one's achievements (*Leistung*) on society's behalf. Property ownership and tax payments were taken as reflecting accurately each individual's relative contribution. So the various suffrages usually denied the vote to anyone in receipt of poor-relief payments, on election day or in the recent past. Some also argued that property and high tax payments demonstrated competence, intellectual freedom, and maturity and hence the ability to identify the best man for the job.[22]

So-called plural voting systems, such as the one implemented in Saxony in 1909 or proposed by some to replace the existing Reichstag suffrage, gave extra votes to citizens based, putatively, on superior characteristics. The argument for an additional vote for older citizens was cast in terms of maturity but was clearly designed to reduce the chances of the SPD, whose vote was higher among younger voters. Conservatives and many liberals, with their emphasis on *Bildung* and marked confidence in their own intellectual superiority, argued that giving the vote to the masses lowered the intellectual level of governance, making more votes for the educated desirable. Defining what constituted proof of superior *Bildung* did prove controversial.[23]

Another suggested criterion for voting was military service. The Prussian Army had been the instrument of German unification, and the new German Army remained a central institution in the defense of a country surrounded by potential enemies. The *Kaiserreich* adopted the Prussian principle of universal conscription for men (albeit it never actually called up all who were eligible). So military service was a vital and widely experienced civic duty. In the *Kaiserreich*, liberals and conservatives proposed additional votes for veterans, nominally as a reward for their service but actually in the hope that their military service would have inculcated nationalist and anti-socialist values.²⁴

Imperial Germany's women's suffrage movement was small and fragmented. The SPD came out for women's suffrage early. One consequence, though, was that many Germans then associated women's suffrage with the radical socialists. Also, the worker movement was in practice more concerned to expand suffrage for men in state and municipal elections than to expand suffrage for women, with even most women in the movement agreeing that only the socialist revolution would create the circumstances for women's emancipation. Conservative women's suffrage supporters had chosen to become politically active, but they seldom favored *equal* suffrage for men or for women. The movement then splintered on class lines. And even proponents of women's suffrage often believed the time was not yet right for it.²⁵

A few states did expand their suffrages for males in the early twentieth century by introducing direct male suffrage. And proposals for further expansions were common. The fundamental purpose of suffrage concessions in the nineteenth and early twentieth centuries remained integrating the mass of the population into the *Kaiserreich*/nation—or at least not alienating them. Voting brought the masses into direct connection with the nation-state and engaged them with it. In the 1870s those masses were peasants and the lower-middle class, but increasingly they became workers. Despite fears of the growing SPD that led to efforts for more restrictive suffrages, opponents of such restrictions, including conservative ones, argued that one could not rule the country against the will of the majority. The perceived need for broad popular support in the event of war had driven the Napoleonic-era demands for broader political participation, and now many Germans feared suffrage restriction would drive the growing number of workers and perhaps others into the arms of would-be revolutionaries, weakening national defense. And even some German Conservative Party leaders resisted repressive measures to crush the SPD because they threatened efforts to make the Conservative Party a "people's" party.²⁶

Many Germans believed that the purpose of elections was to select the best people (in this period, men) for political offices. The *Kaiserreich* was a hierarchical society, so it could seem only appropriate that elite individuals dominate political leadership. Moreover, with most Germans seeing politics as a realm of ideals and not interests, they expected voters to choose based not on perceived self-interest or a candidate's platform but on which candidate could be trusted to best identify and promote the national welfare. Yet Germans were *not* yet explicitly promoting the idea that the point of elections was to legitimate rulers and their decisions. Given the predominance of the monarchical principle, legitimacy had, at least for most Germans in the *Kaiserreich*, other roots.²⁷

One reason to vote is certainly to advance one's own interests, as well as the society's interests. The worker movement sought a social revolution but also policies that would benefit workers. The appearance in the 1890s of the Agrarian League, peasant movements and parties, and antisemitic parties reflected desperate demands, amid an agricultural depression, for an agrarian party (i.e., one organized around a specific socioeconomic interest) and for a "'ruthless and uncamouflaged' pursuit of interest politics." And in the *Kaiserreich*, some citizens were willing to acknowledge that citizens would inevitably pursue their interests, as did, for example, social theorist and liberal politician Friedrich Naumann. Few commentators, though, shared this attitude, at least publicly.[28]

A major reason for voting, especially given the attenuated role of the Reichstag in the *Kaiserreich*, was to affirm one's identity or to protest. Germany's society was divided into milieus or camps, whose membership might be fluctuating but which clearly had significant cores of long-term members who organized their lives around milieu or camp. To vote for the SPD or Center or other party was then to affirm an identity. Many Germans clearly perceived this and acted on that basis. Or a vote could be an expression of protest against a status quo perceived as unjust or deleterious.[29]

Significantly, increasing numbers of Germans chose to exercise their citizenship by voting, affirming that citizenship and engaging with the state and its politics. Voter turnout at Reichstag elections grew from 50.7 percent in 1871 to 84.5 percent in 1912. And those elections became increasingly lively and contested expressions of political views. Increasing numbers of Germans—among males but among females as well—were becoming, to a degree, political agents.[30]

Political Parties and the Politics of Associational Life

Monarchical funerals offer an image of the kind of extra-parliamentary participation governmental elites preferred. In the later nineteenth century, European monarchies invested considerable energy in creating an attractive public image for themselves, and they did so because they needed continuing popular support in the face of growing challenges to their legitimacy. For the funerals of Kaiser Wilhelm I's father in 1840 and brother in 1861, the body lay in state in a small chapel inside a palace, with only aristocrats, military officers, and officials admitted; the funeral processions consisted entirely of aristocrats, military officers, and high officials; and army units lined the short funeral routes.[31]

By 1888, though, Wilhelm instructed that his body should lie in state in the large Berlin cathedral, where many could view it. And the dowager empress decreed that the lying-in-state would be open to anyone in mourning clothes, "without regard to person," an egalitarian reassertion that all were equal before the monarch (albeit one that the Court Marshall chose to ignore by providing privileged backdoor access to various elites). The *Spalier*, the formal line of people along the funeral route, comprised not soldiers but citizens. However, those citizens were members of carefully chosen groups (veterans, students, nationalist gymnasts, guild members, and workers from the state arsenal) who could be trusted to protect the cortege from unpleasantness. The liberal, Catholic, and conservative press generally welcomed the hundreds of thousands who, in bitter cold, stood in long lines to view the deceased emperor and who lined the funeral route behind the *Spalier*; although they muttered occasionally about "the mob," they mostly lauded the people for showing their love for the monarchy and the existing order. Governmental and social elites clearly wanted, if grudgingly, mass participation in the funeral obsequies to demonstrate broad popular support for the monarchy and the state—but in passive, orderly, hierarchical terms. Active political citizenship was only for elites, the only ones who could join the funeral cortege.[32]

German citizens, though, were not satisfied with purely passive citizenship, and across the span of the *Kaiserreich*'s existence, the number, participation levels, and assertiveness of associations increased. This burgeoning associational life took shape not only in recreational groups such as shooting societies, choirs, and bowling clubs but in an enormous range of organizations which engaged in lively discussion of and political action on all manner of issues of public policy. From the 1880s, key "patriotic" associations such as the Society for German Colonization, the Pan-German League, the Navy League, and the Army League appeared. Economic interest groups, such as the Agrarian League, various peasant associations, trade unions, and the General Union of German Artisans, also appeared. Most, like the Agrarian League and the patriotic societies, had elite leadership, but they reflected pressures from below for action, whenever the government and the political parties failed to meet citizens' expectations. They implicitly challenged the parties, which then quickly sought to co-opt such groups. The German Conservative Party, for example, developed close ties with the Agrarian League. Liberal parties sought to develop close ties with the Navy League and various *Mittelstand* and peasant organizations. Within the Catholic milieu, a range of organizations arose that cooperated, to varying degrees, with the Center Party. Catholic organizations vigorously resisted Bismarck's *Kulturkampf* against the Catholic Church, and they retained at least some political thrust thereafter. And Social Democratic and trade union organizations offered workers and others venues in which to stand up for alternative economic, social, and political visions.[33]

The constitution provided for a unified imperial law on rights of association and assembly, key elements in the exercise of political citizenship. The states, to retain their powers in this regard, fended off passage of such a law until 1908. Most state mandates had been restrictive: requiring associations to register with the authorities and often to provide membership lists; usually banning women's and youth's participation in political parties, organizations, and meetings; requiring registration with police of indoor "political" assemblies and a police presence at such assemblies; police permission necessary to hold an open-air assembly and police dissolution of "disorderly" or "subversive" assemblies. Citizens might be allowed to vote, but these laws actively discouraged them from any broader efforts at political discussion and input. Needing liberal support on certain issues, the imperial government finally promulgated, in 1908, a Reich Law on Association and Assembly. That law allowed German citizens to form associations without official permission and women across Germany to join political parties and associations; narrowed drastically the grounds for dissolving an association; required reporting to police of political associations' by-laws and leadership but not their membership. It ended requirements that indoor meetings be reported in advance to police, while easing reporting in advance of open-air meetings. The authorities could still ban open-air events if they threatened "disorder" and could dissolve any meeting if it became "disorderly." Opponents of reform focused on controlling youth participation in political associations and meetings (still banned for those under eighteen) and restricting partially the use of foreign languages, especially

Polish, at open-air meetings. They feared that, absent such restrictions, youth would be vulnerable to SPD proselytizing and the Poles would remain an unintegrated element in German society. Nonetheless, the law counted as progress. German women still could not vote; but with new rights to join associations and participate in political activities, they had acquired more elements of political citizenship. And all citizens had gained somewhat increased opportunities for political activity.[34]

Associational life was often dismissed at the time and since as marked by *Vereinsmeierei*, where all too many members focused excessively on associational life at the expense of other, more important, matters or were caught up in petty group politics at the expense of the group's actual goals. Yet that life could structure increasing political activism, and Thomas Kühne sees it as part of a "surge of democratization and participation" around 1900—even if those who joined were not always pro-democratic.[35]

A striking if malign form of social and political mobilization was the rise of antisemitic groups and political parties, an evil harbinger for the future. Germany's antisemitism began to take on a racist character from the 1870s, when Adolf Stöcker, a court chaplain, founded a Christian Social Party that embraced racial antisemitism. More strikingly, from the 1880s peasant movements began appearing in poorer agricultural areas devastated by economic change; they embraced antisemitism as the explanation of, and discriminatory policies as the solution for, their problems. These movements developed political parties and put up candidates, winning some seats in Reichstag elections. They were, however deplorable, genuine grassroots, mass movements. And they influenced other political parties to seek to broaden their appeal—but also to adopt more or less explicitly antisemitic platforms. Political elites would make repeated efforts to recruit such groups for their own purposes, but the groups reflected a vigorous challenge to traditional ruling elites' hierarchical claims to leadership.[36]

Organizational life in nineteenth-century Germany was theoretically egalitarian (anyone could join and participate equally)—but in practice usually was not. Organization requires inclusion and exclusion: Some belong to the group, some do not; and group membership in nineteenth- and early twentieth-century Germany tended to be divided along confessional and socioeconomic lines. A small city might have multiple shooting clubs or glee clubs or other groups, each drawing on a narrow socioeconomic or religious slice of the town's population. Even within groups, social status still strongly influenced or even determined leadership or claims to leadership. In terms of political culture, middle- and upper-class Germans saw the groups they founded as means for self-development as an individual but increasingly also as tools for educating citizens in personal, social, and political virtues. Many of these organizations had some political affiliation and, Stanley Suvall estimated, touched nearly a third of German voters.[37]

Recognizing both that bourgeois Germans deployed organizations to advance their interests and that bourgeois organizations mostly excluded workers, Social Democrats created their own, alternative organizational life, one that offered a full palette of organizations and that challenged traditional hierarchies. These organizations came to include millions of lower- and lower-middle-class Germans and constituted the *Kaiserreich*'s most striking example of political mobilization. Because

Bildung (education) was central to bourgeois claims to political predominance, the worker movement emphasized education, explicitly in *Bildungsvereine* (Educational Associations) but also in its other groups. Social Democrats also founded worker libraries and newspapers that offered workers access to knowledge. The goal was to provide an education that challenged bourgeois norms. Social Democrats had created for workers a space beyond the private sphere where they could discuss and be active in a public sphere. Notably, though, the SPD and the unions clearly thought only those workers who had accepted the tutelage of the labor movement could be trusted with political agency. They struggled for democracy but doubted all workers were ready for political citizenship just yet.[38]

Most German states forbade women to belong to political organizations until 1908, but women were mobilizing for social and political participation even before then. In Leipzig across the nineteenth century, 36 percent of philanthropic donors were women. Bourgeois women created a substantial range and number of social organizations. They included not only organizations to defend occupational and economic interests but everything from religious groups to anti-alcohol groups to suffragettes to athletic clubs. Even conservative women founded groups to promote conservative values. And Catholic women were particularly active, in the struggle against the *Kulturkampf* but in social action more generally. Bourgeois women's groups organized mass meetings and petitions that contributed to some improvements for women's rights in the new Civil Code, promulgated in 1896. The Social Democratic movement created its own palette of women's organizations, which extended to just about every issue the bourgeois women's groups addressed except religion. And SPD women were particularly active politically, in protest campaigns (e.g., the anti-grain tariff campaign of 1891) and in election campaigns. Women used their groups to comment and to work on "women's issues" (e.g., education, charity, welfare), but some women also chose to speak up on a broader range of issues.[39]

Officials sought to engage citizens to support specific government policies, though again not as independent agents. They expected members of the elite to organize groups supportive of the government and group members to follow their elite leaders' marching orders. The assumption also was that those leaders would take their cues from government officials. The groups would then act as transmission belts for official views and would mobilize popular support for the government's desires.[40]

Crucially, the new interest groups were not willing to serve merely as cat's paws for elites. *Mittelstand* interest groups, for example, sought to cooperate with liberal and conservative parties, but came to attack them bitterly when they did not secure desired policy changes. Peasant movements, David Blackbourn notes, were "disrespectful of authority." These groups expected the government to deliver. If the groups' members were "state-supporting," as they and the government often proclaimed, they expected the government to be *Mittelstand*-supporting. The groups often proved to have mobilized autonomous bases of individuals who acted as political citizens.[41]

Particularly striking in this regard are the patriotic societies, especially the Navy League and the Pan-German League. Elites founded these groups to support a radical-nationalist agenda. They were committed to hierarchy, discipline, and order in Germany's domestic affairs, as a firm base for aggressively asserting Germany's "rights" within the international system. Hence, they rejected parliamentary government and democracy. They initially sought to support the government and specific government policy initiatives that they believed necessary to secure Germany's future. The Navy League, not surprisingly, sought to foster support among the populace for building a large German navy that could challenge British command of the sea. The Pan-Germans supported, for example, aggressive government action in the Boer War and in the two Moroccan crises.[42]

However, these groups' leaders, convinced of the righteousness of their cause, came to assert that the good of the state and the will of the people were primary. They were convinced, not surprisingly, that they and their groups accurately expressed the good of the state—more accurately on some issues than the current government did. Crucially, they explicitly and repeatedly appealed to the will of the people as a legitimating basis for their actions. Their opposition to democracy and parliament was rooted in a belief that the masses could not be trusted properly to understand the good of the nation and that parliament reflected the clash of private interests and not a defense of the national interest. The people's will that they claimed to represent was not what a majority of Germans might think but what group leaders believed citizens should think and would think if they were properly informed and capable—a kind of de facto Rousseauian general will.[43]

Having grounded their legitimacy in the appeal to popular will, the groups proved willing to challenge government officials and even chancellors. Convinced that they truly understood the real interests of the German state and people, the leaders of these groups pushed the government to take more extreme actions, for example to seize territory in Africa despite French and other opposition or to build yet more battleships to challenge Britain. Conservative leaders might, as James Retallack pointed out, deplore the "'insubordinate posture' of most nationalist pressure groups," but those groups had become convinced that the government could no longer be fully trusted to protect the German nation.[44]

Perhaps most significantly, these groups eventually challenged the monarch's right to determine Germany's foreign and defense policies. The constitutional order of the *Kaiserreich* and its constituent states rested on the monarchical principle. To suggest, as the groups increasingly did in the early twentieth century, that the monarch could not be trusted to determine what was in the best interests of the state and nation, but that instead the people's will (as revealed by the patriotic societies) must ultimately determine, was to challenge the entire existing political order. Already in 1903, Heinrich Claß, who would come to lead the Pan-Germans, had in a speech implicitly challenged monarchical control. In spring 1908, elements in the Navy League had attacked monarchism. Yet it was the *Daily Telegraph* Affair, that grossly indiscreet interview Emperor Wilhelm II gave to a British reporter, which sparked explicit attacks on Wilhelm and his personal rule, not only on the Left but from segments of the patriotic societies as well. And Claß and others began evoking a leader who (implicitly unlike the erratic and impulsive Emperor) could act successfully.[45]

The membership of these patriotic societies was generally in the hundreds of thousands, and the millions of the larger population were not embracing the attitudes toward participation and political citizenship that the societies' leaderships were expressing. Nonetheless, the groups' expansion and assertiveness reflect an evolving sense among Germans about the citizens' proper role. These people were not democrats, indeed were often explicitly antidemocratic and antiparliamentary. Yet they were challenging the narrow view of political citizenship held by conservative and even many liberal politicians and officials—and doing so from the Right.

Catholics in the *Kaiserreich*, one-third of the population, proved willing and effective in mobilizing in public protest over an issue they considered vital—defending the Catholic Church against the *Kulturkampf*. Bismarck dismissed the resistance as organized from above by the clergy, and they certainly played a role. Yet innumerable lay Catholics chose to undertake various actions to protect the clergy and the church and to protest government policies. They collected money to pay fines, cooperated to buy seized clerical property at public auction at bargain basement prices (to return it to the cleric or the church), helped hide persecuted clerics, and boycotted and harassed pro-state clerics and laity. They held monster meetings, with attendance by as many as 80 percent of adult Catholic males in small towns and rural regions and as many as 40 percent in cities. They occasionally resorted to vandalism and stone throwing. Their activist political citizenship raised enormously the cost of Bismarck's policy, undercut drastically the effectiveness of his punitive measures, and demonstrated that pursuing that policy was eliciting participation that weakened, not strengthened, Germany, contributing significantly to the policy's failure.[46]

Observers often view associational life positively, as the creation of a civil society—a realm independent of government, home, and the market in which associations, movements, and networks bring together individuals to discuss and promote action on matters of mutual concern in a civil, nonviolent, rational way, securing citizen engagement and interaction with the state for putatively shared goals. When activists and social scientists began discussing civil society in the 1970s, they were seeking to create the preconditions for democracy within undemocratic polities in Eastern Europe. Many were arguing that it could contribute to democracy in two ways. A functioning democracy arguably required a space separate from the state, preferably protected by the rule of law, in which people from all backgrounds could debate and develop alternatives to prevailing policies. Further, people had to learn values and practices appropriate to a democratic polity. Learning by doing in grassroots, democratically structured, civil society groups seemed the best way to do so.[47]

Civil society's role has, however, come to be contested, particularly in German history. While most French, British, and American scholars see civil society as a primary contributor to democracy and democratic stability, German scholars must reconcile civil society with the *Kaiserreich*'s authoritarianism and with Weimar democracy's collapse. Associational life can clearly involve antidemocratic groups, such as radical right-wing and antisemitic groups before 1918 and fascist and communist groups in the 1920s/30s. So civil society does not automatically promote democratization. Yet to the extent that civil society creates a space for nonviolent public activism and promotes attitudes conducive to democracy, Germans had begun developing arguably crucial prerequisites for democracy already in the nineteenth century under the authoritarian *Kaiserreich*. Even though Germany would experience even more repressive dictatorship in the Third Reich, those experiences of self-organization would be available among many Germans after 1918 and 1945.

So even if civil society was no panacea, Germans were able to establish a democracy with whatever advantages prior experience of civil society offered.[48]

Political parties in the *Kaiserreich* arguably developed in ways that interfered with governance and delayed democratization and parliamentarization. M. Rainer Lepsius argued that Germany had a stable party system, 1871–1928, because its parties were rooted in "milieus," in "politically motivated communities of those sharing an ethos." Those communities were emotionally powerful and mutually isolated. They held people's loyalty and interfered with both any sense of common interest and any focus on (ever-changing) policy issues. Karl Rohe pointed out that this model might work for Catholics and Social Democrats but was less convincing for liberals and conservatives, so he argued for the existence of "camps" that attracted people but were not as self-enclosed as the idea of milieus suggested. And then Jonathan Sperber's study of voting in the *Kaiserreich* showed more citizens shifting from party to party than either milieus or camps would seem to allow. The consensus now seems to be that Catholic, Social Democratic, and Protestant subcultures did exist in Germany and that they could hold many citizens' loyalty—but that they were not so all-encompassing as to prevent some Germans from shifting their party preference—e.g., as between one election where national issues were predominant (1907 and colonialism) and another where economic issues were (1912 and inflation). Yet to the extent subcultures held many people's loyalty, they introduced an element of rigidity into politics that made compromise and cooperation even more difficult.[49]

Jürgen Habermas's notion of a public sphere in which all citizens could exchange and develop their views might seem to offer a broad alternative to the narrower milieus or camps organized around minorities that historians have identified, except that Germans have often defined the public sphere so as to exclude many of their fellow citizens. Historians have argued that the public sphere has been in crucial ways a "bourgeois"—i.e., upper-middle- and upper-class project. As Dennis Sweeney has shown for the Saar region, German economic and political elites worked to set certain requirements of education and status that limited, indeed sought to preclude, access to that sphere for the working classes and, in many cases, Catholics. And elites worked to control information by limiting access to official meetings to journalists from friendly newspapers and by their ownership of most newspapers. Moreover, women were written out of the public sphere from the start by the males who controlled access to public discourse and rejected women's participation. Catholics and socialists were forced to set up parallel public spheres with their own publications and organizations. Yet even if the *Kaiserreich*'s broader public sphere could not live up to its democratic potential, it nonetheless was open enough that Catholics', socialists', and women's voices were not completely silenced.[50]

The Labor Movement and Public Political Action

Germans were most comfortable (or least uncomfortable) with extra-parliamentary political participation if it took place through formal organizations that worked through official channels; however, more aggressive forms of participation developed, most obviously in the Social Democratic and trade union movements. These groups sought a fundamental democratization of society and resorted to extra-parliamentary, public, assertive modes of action, such as strikes, public funerals, and demonstrations.

The SPD had a million members and millions of voters, and it proposed a radically democratic vision of citizenship. The party looked to Marxism as an ideological basis, but it never adopted it as its official credo. The party did look forward to a "people's state" or republic in which socialism would provide for popular (in practice, worker) democratic control—not only of politics but of economy and society as well. However, its demands for the immediate future were attainable within the existing constitutional system. And beginning in the 1890s, various SPD politicians and supporters increasingly came to accept not only the possibility of using parliamentary government (rather than revolution) to win socialism but even a continuation in Germany of a constitutional (not authoritarian) monarchy. Other SPD'ers, though, rejected "bourgeois" parliamentarism.[51]

The Social Democratic movement was quite willing to resort to certain kinds of extra-parliamentary action. It was committed to the principle that each (at least male) citizen was capable of being an independent political agent. That agency could involve voting or being a member of the SPD or allied organization or trade union. It could mean attending an indoor meeting at which public affairs were discussed. It could, for at least some movement members, also mean other forms of public political action, from public protests to, ultimately, revolution.

Since German association law was frequently implemented to block public SPD actions, the party's initial forays into the public sphere were often through public funerals for deceased leaders. Even the Prussian government was hard-pressed to deny a socialist a decent burial. Nonetheless, the authorities banned political symbols and funeral orations by non-clergy. They did in 1900 allow a funeral in Berlin for the SPD leader Wilhelm Liebknecht, which the party organized as a contrast to Kaiser Wilhelm's funeral. Because the government banned demonstrations in the central government quarter, the party had an excuse to route the funeral procession through more neighborhoods. The SPD emphasized that "anyone" could join Liebknecht's funeral procession, unlike the Kaiser's, and its publications gloried in the presence not of the social elite but of "the working people" of Berlin. Those publications also emphasized that the only decorations on the funeral route were the hundreds of thousands who voluntarily lined the streets: "this living arch, more magnificent than any wood daubed over with false gold." Notably, though, the funeral was not quite as egalitarian as the SPD suggested. One could not join the cortege as an individual but only as member of an SPD or trade union organization, who constituted "the best elements in the working class." Implicitly, the party, with a hierarchical view even of the working class, did not trust unaffiliated individual worker-citizens—but only those under SPD tutelage.[52]

In 1910 the SPD sponsored public demonstrations in favor of suffrage reform in Prussia, despite opposition from the authorities. The SPD senior leadership resisted sponsoring public demonstrations because it feared that the proletariat was not mature, not disciplined enough to be trusted to engage in them or that they could elicit police violence or that they would alienate potential bourgeois supporters. Others in the party, though, pressed increasingly for direct action, and a wave of suffrage demonstrations broke out in 1908/09. In early 1910, SPD activism for Prussian suffrage reform blossomed. The party leadership still looked to indoor meetings, and the numerous demonstrations in January and February were apparently spontaneous. In March and April the demonstrations were mostly planned by a leadership that was still ambivalent but hoped that the demonstrations would soon peter out. The SPD asserted a "right to the streets" for all citizens. Its leaders pointed out that conservatives and government had no complaints about military parades, religious processions, weddings, or carnival street celebrations, even when the latter could result in hundreds of wounded. Perhaps the most famous SPD demonstration came on March 6, 1910. The SPD planned a "Suffrage Stroll" in Berlin's Treptower Park, to evade bans on SPD demonstrations. When the Chief of Police banned even that and deployed thousands of police at Treptower Park, SPD leaders secretly told their district leaders to bring their members to the Tiergarten (5 miles away) instead—making the police chief a laughing stock.[53]

A central issue for Social Democrats in their protests was demonstrating that the mass of the population were capable as political citizens. Conservatives' and liberals' arguments against an equal suffrage and equal political citizenship rested on claims that "the masses" were inherently less capable, less intelligent, less informed, perhaps less decent than the middle and upper classes, so that those masses deserved at best a lesser political role. Workers, SPD leaders concluded, had to prove their right to political citizenship by showing that they were upstanding, orderly citizens. Discipline was a stereotypically German virtue, and Social Democrats were particularly determined to prove that workers could be just as disciplined as any other German. They touted the exemplary orderliness of the workers at demonstrations. And one SPD newspaper pointed out that at a suffrage demonstration in March 1910 marked by police violence, the workers were orderly and rational while the police were disorderly and brutal. The party appointed marshals for all its demonstrations, to enforce order. (Conservatives were outraged when the police learned to concede a central role in maintaining order at demonstrations to these representatives of a putatively revolutionary party.) Because elites said people had to be able to rule themselves before they could claim a right to rule politically, another SPD paper characterized the suffrages demonstrations as evidence of the "self-rule of the masses." The demonstrations were both a self-education in responsible joint action and a demonstration of the masses' maturity and competency. And by allowing women to join its funeral processions and, after 1908, demonstrations, the SPD implicitly ascribed such competence to them as well.[54]

Strikes are not necessarily political, but the willingness to strike has political implications, as Germans in the *Kaiserreich* realized. Even if the aims of the strike are purely economic, the strikers (usually male workers supported by women, but occasionally female workers) are asserting a right to agency. That assertion positions the workers as capable of acting in defense of their own interests, something they could and did then demand be extended to them as political as well as economic agents. It also involves putting pressure on their opponents, management, to induce or compel those opponents to do something they do not want to do.[55]

A political mass strike might compel government to act according to workers' wishes, but debate in Social Democracy about the political mass strike reveals a striking degree of ambivalence about whether and which workers could be trusted with political agency. Some SPD and trade union leaders disparaged the ability of workers to be trusted to act responsibly in the event of a mass strike. They often channeled Gustav Le Bon's dismissal of crowds as inherently irrational and uncontrollable. Some leaders though, most famously Rosa Luxemburg, were convinced that the masses would learn in the process of the mass strike how to act as efficacious political agents, as the overwhelmingly unorganized Russian workers had in their 1905 Revolution. Perhaps most common was the view that only those workers who were organized and under Social Democratic tutelage were sufficiently politically mature to be trusted as autonomous agents while the mass of unorganized workers was still too unreliable—which left the question of whether the organized and properly tutored would be able to control a mass strike. Significantly, almost all Social Democratic leaders agreed that only they, the leaders, could be trusted to make decisions. The masses were to join the SPD and a union, pay dues, vote at elections, attend SPD political assemblies that were campaign rallies or informational events, and perhaps in extremis engage in a political mass strike under party and union leadership. They were not, however, to act on their own by choosing if, how, and for what purpose to demonstrate or strike. In crucial ways, History was to happen to them.[56]

Even if one believed Social-Democratically educated workers could be trusted to act politically, one had to decide whether the mass political strike was a legitimate, democratic form of political action. Given the narrowing of the suffrage in some states and periodic threats of a *Staatsstreich* against the universal, male Reichstag suffrage, Social Democrats had to fear that the bourgeoisie might resort to force to prevent further democratization—or to eliminate the democratic suffrage. Workers might then resort to a mass strike as demonstration strike, to warn against any threatened attack on worker rights. Or they might resort to a mass strike as coercive strike, either to force the government to back down from any attempt to restrict suffrage or to force it to expand the suffrage. Yet already, Philipp Scheidemann, a party moderate, raised another issue:

> We don't want to forget that we are a party that is democratic, a party of the minority, if a very substantial one. No one will demand that the majority should pursue the policies of the minority, that we want to use the mass strike of the minority to compel the majority to pursue Social Democratic policies. That would be undemocratic. No, we demand only equal rights.

Social Democrats could contemplate coercion in the *Kaiserreich* because they did not accept the legitimacy of its constitution, but at least one of them recognized a problem with coercive demonstrations that would resurface decades later (see Chapter 5).[57]

Germans had widely varying conceptions of political citizenship under the *Kaiserreich*. The SPD and some liberals might be willing to support a system in which all adult males, and perhaps females, had equal rights as political citizens, but liberal and conservative Germans overwhelmingly preferred both to maintain limits on suffrage that denied political equality at the state and municipal level for Germans and to forgo parliamentary government. And most Germans remained convinced that political citizenship could mean voting, and perhaps belonging to formal organizations, but not broader forms of extra-parliamentary activism. Even within the SPD, those who supported broader activism generally predicated it on elite, SPD-elite, control of protest activities. Political elites needed some degree of popular engagement and even participation in politics, but few outside the labor movement, and relatively few within it, favored an autonomously active citizenry.

Wartime Mobilization and Popular Revolution

To fight the First World War successfully, Germany would need active citizen participation in public life—active and committed service by soldiers, hard work at factories and farms, willingness to pay increasing taxes, enthusiastic support from relatives for serving soldiers. German elites had to accept that, but they remained committed to preserving as much as possible of the existing distribution of political power and citizenship rights—until they stared defeat in the face.

Wilhelm II felt compelled to declare a wartime political truce, in August 1914. Germany's military had long planned to arrest Social Democratic and trade union leaders at war's outbreak, to prevent a feared, and planned, political mass strike against war. However, Chancellor Bethmann Hollweg knew two things: (1) Germany could not successfully fight the war without the participation of, let alone against, the working class; (2) Social Democratic and trade union leaders were for the most part German nationalists who would fight to defend their country, especially once he made autocratic Russia look like the aggressor. He then negotiated with those leaders, who proved willing to cooperate in return for de facto recognition as spokesmen for the workers. The Kaiser then announced, "I no longer recognize political parties, I recognize only Germans!" The German government had accepted the working class and the Social Democrats as honorable citizens of the *Kaiserreich*, and the Emperor had publicly embraced them—if perhaps only temporarily.[58]

As part of efforts to secure broad popular support as the war dragged on, various parties and politicians and the government proposed, suggested, or promised suffrage reform, but the *Kaiserreich* only delivered at war's end, in a desperate attempt to forestall revolution and placate the Americans. Many conservatives and government officials planned to use victory to consolidate, not reform, the existing system. Yet the government began the war with statements that implied but did not promise political reforms, including more egalitarian suffrage, when victory arrived. As the war remained stalemated and casualties and misery mounted, the government issued more pro-reform pronouncements, culminating in the Kaiser's April 1917 promise, in the aftermath of the Russian Revolution, of an undefined reform of the Prussian three-class suffrage. Many Germans increasingly felt that Germany could not grant the vote to war profiteers while denying it to lower-class front soldiers and even home-front victims of wartime shortages. Nonetheless, conservative politicians and officials and the military blocked the implementation of suffrage reform, in 1917/18. Only the prospect of imminent defeat and revolution finally convinced military and political elites to concede universal equal male suffrage in Prussia, though its implementation was overtaken by revolution.[59]

Wartime exigencies drove many Germans to engage in bread riots—which Belinda Davis calls extra-parliamentary democratic action. As Germany shifted resources to national defense and as the British blockade strangled imports (especially of food), resources for civilian consumption plummeted. Despite the gradual introduction of price controls and rationing, food supplies dwindled, prices continued to rise, and Germans increasingly suffered hunger, then malnutrition. By October 1915, public protests about food spread in German cities, and the protesters, usually working- or lower-middle-class women, eventually "physically threatened the shopkeepers, damaged property, and occupied shops." Protesters argued they were bolstering the war effort by fighting war profiteers whose actions were weakening Germany's home front. Contemporaries recognized the serious political implications: Citizens were taking self-conscious action on a politically charged issue, outside formal political channels. And women, previously seen as apolitical, were now the most active "political" citizens, as they forced the government to respond to popular will and accept responsibility for ensuring adequate food for the population. Crucially, facing blockade and other wartime pressures, the government simply could not secure enough food for the army *and* the civilian population. Through 1918, *c.* 700,000 Germans died of malnutrition, and millions hungered—an outcome that significantly undermined the imperial system's legitimacy and set the stage for revolution. Notably, Davis convincingly argues that the women engaged in these protests seemed indifferent to suffrage reform because their tactics were proving more democratically effective than voting.[60]

The scattered calls among food protesters for peace became a central demand amid renewed extra-parliamentary, and arguably democratic, actions: waves of strikes that swept Germany in 1917 and 1918. Already in April 1917, hundreds of thousands of workers went on strike to support shop stewards who were demanding suffrage reform and a non-annexationist peace, adding their own demands for better representation, adequate food, and redistribution of property. In January 1918 a wave of strikes involving 4 million workers swept the country, with demands including peace and workers' councils. The strikes petered out, but Germans in large numbers had asserted their right, in the midst of war, to act politically.[61]

In autumn 1918, the prospect of defeat spurred political elites to attempt revolution from above to forestall revolution from below. The German high command had realized in late September that victory was no longer attainable. They sought an armistice with the Allies and wanted the politicians to take responsibility for the military's defeat. US President Woodrow Wilson replied that the United States very much preferred to negotiate peace with a "democratic" government. The emperor appointed Prince Max of Baden as chancellor, but with representatives of left-leaning parties effectively in charge of affairs. The National Liberals and the Center had remained unwilling to push for parliamentary government earlier in the war, but the situation was getting desperate. On October 26, the parliament passed a series of constitutional amendments that theoretically established parliamentary government in Germany, though how they would have played out in practice is unclear. The Prussian legislature abolished the three-class suffrage, though the law was never implemented. Only in desperate circumstances were German political elites willing to introduce parliamentary government and broad universal equal male suffrage. But it was too late.[62]

The broadest popular participation in public life in the *Kaiserreich* came in autumn 1918—in mutiny and revolution. By October, historians believe, some one-quarter of the German Army in the West were deserters, wandering in armed groups behind the German lines. They were, as Lenin supposedly said of Russian Army deserters, voting with their feet. Their choice to give up on the war undermined government war policy. In Kiel, sailors, having mutinied against a planned suicide sortie against the British and American navies, established on November 3 sailors' councils to run their affairs. They then dispatched delegates across Germany to urge workers and soldiers to join them in overthrowing the old order. The revolution soon spread, as millions did indeed reject the orders of their military, economic, and political superiors and set up councils in military units, factories, neighborhoods, and cities. A substantial portion of the adult population of Germany had become fully active political citizens, and their actions were determining the fate of the country—however briefly.[63]

Political Distrust and the Legacy of Imperial Germany

The political culture of the *Kaiserreich* included democratic potentials, but it was by no means democratic. Most German political, economic, and social elites saw the mass of the population as insufficiently educated and mature to be trusted with political power or even any direct influence on policy. And most Germans do seem to have embraced or at least accepted an emphasis on hierarchy and order as necessary for society to function effectively. Further, given the belief in an identifiable national interest that ought to be the sole basis of political action, most Germans seem to have embraced an emphasis on the "apolitical" and a disdain for the compromises arguably necessary for representative or democratic governance.

Gerhard A. Ritter argued that already under the *Kaiserreich* the need to compromise in electoral alliances and in securing the passage of bills had begun training Germans in democracy. Yet such compromises were taking place under cover: Parties ascribed responsibility for problematic aspects of legislation to the state and its officials who drafted bills, even if the Reichstag amended those bills, in a compromise, before passage. And German parliamentarians sought to present themselves publicly as committed to ideals and sharing the widespread distaste for compromise. This mixed attitude would provide some basis for parliamentary government in the Weimar Republic, but it would fully prepare neither German politicians for making the compromises necessary for parliamentary government nor German voters for the more openly compromise-based legislation the Republic's parliament would promulgate.[64]

Germans (and non-Germans) have often seen German society as characterized by a subject mentality (*Untertanengeist*). Heinrich Mann's famous novel *Der Untertan* (literally, *The Subject*), with its stereotypical subservient protagonist, has often been seen as accurately reflecting Wilhelmine society. And Thomas Nipperdey, for example, agreed that the *Kaiserreich* was, to a notable degree, an *Untertanengesellschaft*, a society of the subservient. Rightists in the *Kaiserreich* repeatedly emphasized their commitment to monarchy and order. Roger Chickering cites the hierarchical and centralized control that leaders of the Pan-German League exercised, and Geoff Eley cites some radicals deploring the "narrow subject mentality" of some of the organization's leaders.[65]

However, this period of socioeconomic change and increased literacy and interconnection saw millions and millions of Germans join various interest groups that sought to influence public policy. Margaret Anderson acknowledges the great pressure to conform in Wilhelmine German society, but she emphasizes political activism by Social Democrats and others that was often directed against the government and elites. Even conservatives could angrily and publicly denounce a perceived betrayal at the chancellor's hands—hardly, she says, an expression of servility. And as Nipperdey, Eley, and Chickering have pointed out, the Rightists who organized masses of Germans to influence public policy also questioned aggressively the rights of existing elites to dominate the political system and the rights of government officials and eventually even the monarch to be trusted to make decisions on military and foreign policy. Those conservatives were not subservient to the state, though they clearly expected the "masses" to remain subservient to them. Meanwhile, antisemitic organizations and parties called into question the existing political order, often explicitly against elite pretensions. Radical Rightists and political antisemites insisted on the predominance of the "will of the people," as they interpreted it, to determine policy—"democratic" demands that laid a basis for a surging radical right in the Weimar Republic.[66]

Historians have disagreed sharply on whether political elites successfully manipulated mass organizations. Elites tried and occasionally succeeded, but mass organizations tried and occasionally succeeded in "manipulating" elites as well. Citizens wanted to achieve certain ends and tried various tactics to get the government to cooperate. Overall, recent research tends to emphasize that Germans were far from merely objects of elite manipulation. As Peter Steinbach summarized it, "In addition to the traditional elites there where [sic] effective representatives of modern interest groups; in addition to the willing and dumb subjects self-confident voters could be found … [who] no longer accepted just any government decree." Governing elites had certain advantages in presenting their version of reality, but Germans could and did develop their own ideas.[67]

The *Kaiserreich*'s political legacy was mixed. In some ways its parliament, organizations, and activism laid a basis for democratic governance in the Weimar Republic, but a political culture that rejected interests and compromise and the mistrust of parliament and citizens that many Germans shared would prove a heavy burden.

2

Searching for Authority

Challenges to Parliamentary Democracy in the Weimar Republic, 1918–1933

When the Gestapo interrogated Berthold von Stauffenberg, for his role in the 1944 plot to assassinate Hitler, he stoutly asserted his opposition to *this* Führer, whose incompetence was dragging Germany into an abyss—but he reiterated his support for the *Führerprinzip*, the leader principle. He also still embraced the *Volksgemeinschaft*, the (racial) community, as the alternative to pluralist democracy, partisan squabbling, and division of the German people. He is rightly lauded for his courage in resisting Hitler; but like many resisters, he was still committed to community, authority, and leadership, not popular participation or democracy.[1]

His position reflects elements of the *Kaiserreich*'s political cultures but primarily the passionate demands of many post–First World War Germans for a response to the traumas they experienced. Hyperinflation in the early 1920s and depression in the early 1930s shattered the lives of millions of Germans. Fear of the "masses," who were associated with leveling and disorder, had very deep roots, but increased political activism and instability in the Weimar Republic exacerbated those concerns. Fear of socialism was long-standing, but the Russian Revolution and the violent Leftist uprisings that plagued Germany from 1918 to 1923 made those fears immediate. The Nazis were primarily responsible for the pervasive violence of the early 1930s, but they succeeded in blaming the Communists in ways that spoke to and inflamed burgher anxieties.

Rightist irrationalism flourished between the wars (and would provoke a particularly sharp reaction in West German politics). In late-nineteenth-century Europe, positivism (applying scientific method to society and psychology) was the dominant intellectual current. By the 1890s, its rationalistic approach was under attack from both positivists who identified irrational elements in human action and those who attacked reason and celebrated irrational or a-rational ideation. By the 1920s, many thinkers on the political Right and Left were promoting feeling, will, or violence at the expense of reason. These attitudes seemed to resonate with many Germans and played a significant role in the flags, uniforms, music, slogans—and violence—that political campaigns often used in place of reasoned discourse.[2]

The Weimar Republic was a parliamentary democracy, but by 1932 most, but certainly not all, Germans rejected liberal democracy, parliaments, and individualism as they sought an effective state. They found interests-based politics and political parties divisive, paralyzing, and dangerous. They wanted community and effective leadership, which led them to struggle for a cohesive, dominant state. Many still accepted "democracy" but sought either an "authoritative (*autoritäre*) democracy" or a "leader democracy." And by 1933 many, perhaps most, desperately desired order and argued that Germans must recognize natural hierarchy, obey natural leaders, and exercise self-discipline as leaders and followers. Only then could the nation recover from its humiliation, defend itself, and reestablish its rightful position in a dangerous world.

Competing Forms of Democracy after the *Kaiserreich*'s Fall

The November Revolution of 1918 overthrew the *Kaiserreich* in the name of democracy, yet it was at least as much antiwar as pro-democracy. And Germans disagreed sharply on the meaning of democracy. Parliamentary or presidential democracies in Europe and North America were the prevailing models. Yet proposals for direct democracy were also available and could seem to have been realized in Russia's 1905 and 1917 revolutions. So no consensus ever existed on a replacement for the *Kaiserreich*—even among supporters of "democracy."

In the winter of 1918–1919, Germany had two forms of governance simultaneously. One form was the Worker and Soldier Councils that sprang up in cities as the November Revolution spread. A second form was an heir to the imperial government. Faced with growing unrest, the last Imperial Chancellor, Max of Baden, transferred power on November 9 to Friedrich Ebert, head of the largest party in the Reichstag elected in 1912, the Majority Social Democrats (MSPD, the moderate socialist wing of the SPD, which had split in 1917 over support for the war and other issues). Max's act was without constitutional justification, but it gave Ebert some legitimacy—a continuity with both the imperial government and the Reichstag elected in 1912. On the same day, with revolutionary pressures growing, Philipp Scheidemann, also MSPD, spontaneously announced from the Reichstag balcony to the crowd below the end of the monarchy and the founding of a republic, much to Ebert's annoyance. Ebert had intended to rule in coalition with the Center Party and the Progressive Party (left liberals) in the Reichstag. However, he was now pressured by council forces to establish, with the Independent Social Democrats (USPD, more radically socialist wing of the SPD), a Council of People's Commissars as the central government. Even though the revolution had effectively abrogated the imperial Reichstag, Ebert had some degree of legitimacy from "above" and "below."[3]

Supporters of council democracy sought to create a direct democracy that would grant Germany's working people effective control of government, economy, and society. All employees plus business owners who had no paid employees could vote for the councils; the latter would establish a dictatorship of the proletariat that would putatively be equivalent to a proletarian democracy because it would represent the overwhelming majority of the German people, ostensibly excluding only the tiny minority of capitalist exploiters. Supporters often envisioned two sets of councils, one dealing with political and one dealing with economic affairs. Each council delegate would be subject to immediate recall if she or he failed to act as constituents wanted, so citizens could secure accurate representation of their views. Supporters generally rejected political parties, wanting unity to arise, spontaneously, from the masses. Some Germans suggested dual parliaments, one elected by universal suffrage and one based on councils, as a compromise. However, supporters of council democracy sought to transform society radically, and they saw state bureaucracy and formal/parliamentary democracy as incapable of doing so. Moreover, some of them focused on democratizing the workplace as much or more than the larger society.[4]

However, a councils democracy seemed threatening to many Germans, whether or not they held property. Opponents asked how democratic it could be if it deliberately excluded the many who were not employed—e.g., homemakers, pensioners, disabled veterans. Property owners overwhelmingly opposed any socialism that would end private ownership of the means of production. Even small business owners with no employees, who would be allowed to vote in council elections, might worry about how long their property would survive in a councils Germany or whether they would lose political agency if they ever needed employees. Many without property were antisocialist—but especially anti-Bolshevik, appalled by Russia's Bolshevik dictatorship, attacks on religion, and civil war. Their anxieties were only exacerbated by widely reported calls from Karl Liebknecht and others for a second, radically socialist revolution and by violence in Berlin, Munich, and elsewhere. Burgher Councils (representing middle- and upper-class citizens) and Farmers Councils appeared, in an effort to create institutions that could participate in a councils system and challenge any worker councils' monopoly on political power. They, too, engaged in "strikes" and boycotts to protect their interests but failed to establish transparent and effective connections with a democratic base.[5]

Crucially, Ebert, the MSPD, and many in the USPD were committed to establishing a parliamentary democracy in Germany. Moderate and even some radical socialists vehemently opposed Bolshevism and the councils democracy associated with it. Their preference for parliamentary democracy had been building since Eduard Bernstein's 1890s argument for an evolutionary, not revolutionary, path to socialism, through democratic constitutionalism. MSPD leaders viewed the councils, a spontaneous expression of grassroots worker activism, with suspicion. As in the *Kaiserreich*, they emphasized the need for a disciplined working class under SPD tutelage to build legitimacy for socialism. Moreover, they feared that trying to introduce socialism amid the chaos of defeat and demobilization could discredit it. Their priorities were ending the war, demobilizing the soldiers, laying the basis for political democracy, and getting the economy going—and they sincerely wanted democracy, the equal political participation of *all* citizens. When a Council of Councils met in December 1918, the delegates—despite having been chosen by councils—voted 400–50 for January 19, 1919 elections for a constituent assembly that would almost certainly establish parliamentary democracy—and did so.[6]

Fearing popular activism and a rising radical (by January 1919 self-professedly Communist) movement in Germany, traditional elites sought to save what could be saved and moderate socialists sought to restore order and block further radicalization; so they crafted deals that helped to stabilize the situation in the short run but would prove a heavy mortgage on Weimar democracy. Ebert and the commander of the German Army in the West, General Wilhelm Groener, agreed that the army would help to restore order, while the new government would leave the old officer corps in positions of command. Hugo Stinnes for the industrialists and Carl Legien for the trade unions agreed that employers would accept collective bargaining, unions as representatives of the workers, and the eight-hour day; in exchange, the unions would accept employer organizations, establish a central working group for employer/employee negotiations on economic policy, and not push for immediate socialism. Moreover, Ebert was so worried about the Bolshevik threat and so convinced he needed civil service expertise for Germany's recovery that he and the MSPD made no serious efforts to democratize the military or civil bureaucracies, including the judiciary.[7]

As a result, the Weimar Republic was burdened with the continued predominance of traditional economic, military, administrative, and legal elites, who had been overwhelmingly conservative and monarchist and who were often unsympathetic to reforms and to parliamentary democracy. Hans Mommsen points to the "authoritarian climate" among career civil servants who would play crucial roles in governance and legislation in the Weimar Republic, given politicians' lack of expertise and ministers' short tenures. German judges were notoriously conservative and anti-Weimar Republic; they regularly issued rulings that undermined the republic's stability, awarding risibly light sentences to right-wing perpetrators of political violence and refusing to convict right-wing citizens of slander for telling vicious lies about left-wing politicians.[8]

In addition, Ebert and the MSPD chose to cooperate with right-wing military and paramilitary forces to block insurrectionary efforts by the radical Left—a fateful choice. The most radical socialists did not accept the MSPD's determination to focus on establishing political (parliamentary) democracy. They wanted to use the councils movement to establish a socialist democracy. Some were willing to resort to violence. The German Communist Party (established January 1, 1919) attempted a series of insurrections they believed would eventuate in successful socialist revolution. The Ebert government lacked its own military force to meet these threats. After four years of brutal war, most Germans wanted only peace. The only available military forces were the rump German Army (under authoritarian leadership) and the *Freikorps*, right-wing paramilitaries. The Ebert and subsequent parliamentary governments relied on violence and these antidemocratic forces to protect their rule against insurrectionary threats. Yet the brutality with which these forces put down worker-led insurrections alienated many anti-authoritarian Germans and eroded the Weimar Republic's legitimacy.[9]

The nationwide January 19, 1919 election transformed Germany's political landscape. With monarchy discredited, Germany needed a basis of legitimacy, which the *Volk* was now to provide—a focus on the people that influenced party names and other symbolism. Utilizing universal (male and female), equal, secret, and direct suffrage, the election produced a National Assembly that would write a constitution and serve as parliament—with a legitimacy that the councils could no longer challenge. The MSPD and USPD between them had a near majority, but the delegates were deeply divided over many questions, and many did not really favor parliamentary democracy. Not surprisingly, insurmountable problems would erode trust in the new government as well as the legitimacy of the constitution it established.[10]

Creating and Limiting a Parliamentary Democracy

The Weimar constitution established parliamentary democracy with limits. It formally established parliamentary government and gave the Reichstag substantive power over all aspects of government and of domestic and foreign policy. The chancellor and ministers were responsible to the Reichstag, not the head of state. However, its drafters, fearing parliamentary absolutism and popular disorder, sought a "counterweight" to parliament and to party rule. They hence endowed the presidency with substantial reserved powers. The citizens directly elected the president, and he could issue decrees in an "emergency" and appoint a chancellor, thereby ruling more or less independently of parliament. The mixed form of democratic governance established by the constitution had the potential, institutionally, to survive as a liberal democracy, but these presidential decree powers would contribute significantly to its demise.[11]

The constitution's expansion of suffrage and women's rights introduced dramatic change from the *Kaiserreich*. All Germans over 20 years of age, including women, now had the power to choose the president and ruling bodies and, indirectly, heads of government by equal voting in secret-ballot elections. Lowering the voting age from 25 to 20 reflected a long-standing SPD demand as well as the need to ensure that veterans, who had made such painful sacrifices for the fatherland, would have the same right to vote as war profiteers. Similarly, the SPD had long called for women's suffrage. It also recognized their many, onerous sacrifices during the war, so that other parties found it impossible to reject women's suffrage. The prewar women's suffrage movement had put the issue on the agenda, but it had been divided, weak, and unsuccessful in changing discriminatory attitudes. So it was not surprising that women in the Weimar Republic still faced massive legal restrictions and inequality: Drawing on the widely accepted belief that men and women had fundamentally different characters, the constitution stated that men and women were equal citizens only "in principle," so that in practice they could—and would—be treated differently. For example, the parliament never voted to allow German women to choose to keep their German citizenship if they married a foreigner (albeit such a policy was ubiquitous in 1920s Europe). Moreover, "prostitutes" could be deprived of the rights of citizens and placed under regulation—and any unaccompanied woman might be accused of prostitution.[12]

Proportional representation, for Weimar parliamentary elections, reflected debates on how best to represent the citizenry. The *Kaiserreich*'s governments refused to redraw parliamentary districts to reflect six decades of massive population shifts, systematically disenfranchising the SPD (based in growing cities). Hence, the SPD insisted on proportional representation, to ensure that future governments did not manipulate electoral districts at its expense. Some Germans were committed to proportional representation because they believed that it most accurately represented the will(s) of the people, even if forming stable governments would be more difficult. It created a national electorate, in place of regional electorates, because the votes of even tiny minorities that would be swamped locally could add up to secure seats nationally. MPs, though, would prove responsible to the party that ranked them on the candidate list, not to voters. Moreover, parties visibly catered to interest groups, as they scrambled to represent many groups on their candidate lists. Many Germans at the time and many historians since have deemed proportional representation disastrous, arguing that it fragmented the electorate and its representation in the Reichstag, making governance at best difficult and eventually impossible, and opening the way for the rise of the Nazi party. Recently, some scholars have pointed out that German society was deeply divided independent of the electoral system and that a first-past-the-post system (in which the candidate with the most votes wins) could have brought the Nazis to power more quickly.[13]

The Weimar Constitution gave the Reichstag power. It would initiate and pass bills: promulgating laws, levying taxes, and making appropriations. The chancellor and all ministers served only so long as they had a parliamentary majority's confidence. However, the constitution was unclear about how parliament and president were to create a government that sustained parliamentary confidence. Increasingly, in practice the president chose the chancellor, and parliament, sooner or later, would withdraw confidence. And by the late 1920s, conservatives were proposing to amend the constitution, so the government would need only the confidence of the president, not the Reichstag. The constitution did establish a second chamber, the Reichsrat, to represent the *Länder* (states), but in practice its role was primarily advisory.[14]

Many Germans feared—with some reason—that parliament responded only to economically or numerically superior groups, business and labor, at the expense of such equally valuable groups as farmers and artisans. Even as they execrated parliament as solely representing *egoistical* interests, they recognized that socioeconomic groups existed and deserved to be heard. Many Weimar Germans suggested a corporatist assembly as an alternative or addition to parliament, a body to represent not mere numbers or wealth but equally worthy "organic" groups within the body politic. Proponents sometimes cited the corporatism of Fascist Italy, but most preferred a home-grown system that would transcend class and party and "organically" represent German society as a whole. The provisional advisory Reich Economic Council reflected these goals, but it seemed only to spur conflicts and was allowed to expire.[15]

Crucially, Hugo Preuß, the constitution's chief drafter, and others resisted what they still called "parliamentary absolutism." As during the *Kaiserreich*, political elites feared the concentration of power in a body that represented the implicitly self-serving interests articulated by both parties and the masses, especially if its power were unrestrained. They wanted an effective counterbalance to parliament. Hence, the constitution created a strong presidency with independent legitimacy as an obstacle to parliamentary absolutism. The president gained legitimacy through popular, nationwide election based on universal suffrage, claiming a breadth of support that no individual MP or party could, and arguably making him more than an ersatz Kaiser. He could, theoretically, stand above parties, regions, and religious denominations as the keystone in maintaining unity. He would play some ill-defined role in forming governments, as he was responsible for appointing or dismissing the chancellor, and he could dissolve, rather than compromise with, the Reichstag, a power—a threat—he could use in any dispute.[16]

Moreover, Article 48 infamously provided that, in an emergency, the president could "take measures necessary to reestablish public security and order," including suspending such basic political rights as freedom of expression, assembly, and association. He had to secure the chancellor's signature, and the Reichstag, by majority vote, could abrogate any measure he took. The article sought to eliminate some of the worst features of the monarchy's emergency-rule powers, exercised during the war. It reflected the chaos Germany faced in early 1919, amid defeat, demobilization, continued Allied blockade, and insurrectionary unrest approaching civil war; it also reflected fundamental doubt among many Germans that a democracy or parliament could act decisively to maintain order. It could also be seen as democratic because the president was elected nationally by universal suffrage.[17]

In practice, the president and government played a much greater legislative role than the constitution suggested. The two presidents Friedrich Ebert and Paul von Hindenburg issued many crucial decrees under Article 48. Ebert was committed to democracy, but even he used his exceptional presidential powers 100 times. Moreover, to shift responsibility for hard decisions it was unwilling or unable to make, the Reichstag, in dire situations, promulgated Enabling Acts, which delegated to the government the authority to issue decrees with the force of law. Under Ebert, the Reichstag passed 700 laws, and governments issued 450 decrees with the force of law under enabling acts and Article 48. Formally, these practices could be termed democratic: they were sanctioned by constitution-amending majorities, and majority vote could revoke any presidential or enabling-act decree. Nonetheless, frequent resort to Article 48 and Enabling Acts from 1919 to 1924 set precedents for actions that superseded parliamentary rule after March 1930 and democracy after March 1933.[18]

Popular election of the president was not the constitution's only "plebiscitary" element. Citizens could petition for a referendum and the president or the Reichsrat could also demand a referendum on a law that the Reichstag had passed. The SPD had long discussed plebiscitary elements as direct empowerment of the people. They pushed for their inclusion in the Weimar constitution, on the argument that the focus of political life should be the people, not the parliament. This provision might also serve as a restraint on parliamentary absolutism. Political organizations did seek referenda, but none passed.[19]

Unlike the 1871 Imperial Constitution, the Weimar Constitution prescribed an elaborate list of civil, political, and social rights. They reflected deep-seated mistrust of parliaments and fear of parliamentary absolutism but also the desire to ensure a stable, secure role for individuals in polity and society. Many jurists asserted that the constitution's social rights were incompatible with traditional liberal rights, that the social state and the Rechtsstaat were mutually contradictory because the former involved government interventions that undercut the individual, often property-based, rights that the Rechtsstaat putatively embodied. The Republic did generally enforce its citizens' basic civil and political rights. However, after 1929, violence and the threat of violence eroded individuals' ability to exercise them, and in early 1933, presidential decrees seriously curtailed them. Nonetheless, through virtually all its existence, the Weimar Republic provided more rights for citizens than the *Kaiserreich* or, certainly, the Third Reich. Political life was fundamentally free.[20]

Judicial review could be a democratic guarantee of individual rights against executive or legislative oppression—or antidemocratic rule by unelected judges. *Kaiserreich* judges, overwhelmingly conservative monarchists, believed that their role was to adjudicate cases based solely on the statutes in force. The National Assembly discussed judicial review, but the Weimar Constitution did not mention it. Nonetheless, many Weimar jurists, antipathetic to parliamentary democracy, could see it as appropriate whenever a judge considered a law unconstitutional or otherwise legally beyond the pale. The Reichsgericht, the highest appeals court, accepted the 1924 Third Emergency Tax Decree's legitimacy but included an *obiter dictum* that it could review its constitutionality. Pleased to have its vital decree accepted, the government did not object to the broader assertion. In May 1925, Reichsgericht President Walter Simons wrote to Chancellor Hans Luther requesting legislative regulation of judicial review, to prevent confusing rulings from different courts and as a "counterweight to popular sovereignty." Unlike a monarchy, he wrote, "in a parliamentary republic ... the danger exists that without such a counterweight a transitory majority could, under the influence of fleeting opinions and political passions, introduce disorder and uncertainty into the constitution's organic development." In November 1925, the Reichsgericht reviewed and affirmed the constitutionality of the Revaluation Law, again giving the government a substantive victory on the question at hand while establishing a precedent for its right to judicial review. In 1929, it did declare a minor law unconstitutional. Most post-1929 legislation came as Article 48 decrees from the revered President Hindenburg, whom conservative judges were unlikely to challenge, and Weimar Republic courts did not exercise judicial review again. Legal scholars did engage in a bitter debate on judicial review in the later 1920s, with socialists rejecting it as ploy to limit democratic will. How judicial review would have fared if the Weimar Republic had survived is unknowable, but if a conservative judiciary had systematically deployed it as a "counterweight to popular sovereignty," it could have become a significant antidemocratic infringement on the people's rule.[21]

West Germans were convinced that the Weimar Republic had been unable to defend itself against radical opponents, but historians generally argue that Weimar's failures reflected internal political divisions, not constitutional flaws. The 1922 Law for the Protection of the Republic and others allowed Weimar governments to ban parties and associations deemed dangerous; they did so thirty-seven times in twelve years. Various laws could also punish and potentially control political violence, and Ebert used the laws in 1920 and 1923 against Communist insurrectionaries, with thousands taken into custody. Unfortunately, governments applied these laws with uneven rigor, and they were effective only against weak organizations. And conservative judges would not apply them rigorously to Rightists. They would also set a precedent for Nazi actions in 1933.[22]

Political Legitimacy and the Myth of the National Community

Who were the people, *das Volk*, from whom the constitution proclaimed, "All state authority emanates"? The citizenship law of 1913 remained the basis for formal citizenship. Anyone born to a German citizen or legally naturalized parents was a German citizen; naturalization requests were still processed by the *Länder* and reviewed by the Reichsrat. After 1918, the wartime domestic truce, the experience of those on the frontlines, and the shared home-front misery underpinned a myth of national community that transcended class or other divisions. Moreover, the wartime alliance with Austria, expansion into eastern European territories with ethnic German populations, and the Allied emphasis on self-determination for ethnically defined peoples broadened the sense of a German people and a nation that would include all ethnic Germans.[23]

In defining that community, though, the politics of exclusion persisted. Most Germans seem desperately to have wanted to overcome conflict and *Zerreißung/Zersetzung* (dismemberment/disintegration) in a fully realized unity that would transcend petty differences and secure German sovereignty. Many Germans, seeking unity and "purity"—a cohesion that would strengthen the polity to deal with a menacing world—were determined to expel from the *Volksgemeinschaft* anyone viewed as alien or disreputable, such as Jews and "Marxists." (One has to put Marxist and Marxism in quotations marks here because hostility often extended to individuals who were not Marxists but who were associated with movements seen as Marxist.) Moreover, while *Volk* simply meant people in the nineteenth century, by the mid-1920s, it had acquired a distinctly "racial" meaning, implicitly excluding those who were not perceived as German "by blood." This mix of attitudes defined the *Volk* as the ultimate source of legitimate authority, separate from, and only imperfectly represented by, the Weimar Republic. It could include ethnic Germans across central and eastern Europe but exclude German citizens who were members of disdained groups.[24]

Antisemitic attitudes were widespread and corrosive in the Weimar Republic. Influential in all the political parties except the DDP (left liberals) and SPD, they were often explicit, even virulent, in other parties (such as the DNVP (conservatives), the Nazis, and many splinter parties) and among some Catholic and many Protestant leaders. Parties on the Right had to be officially antisemitic or risk losing voters, and they could join in denouncing the Weimar Republic as a "Jewish state." Antisemitism clearly helped the Nazis grow. Yet even the Nazi Party downplayed antisemitic themes in most regions of Germany in the 1930–1933 elections because most Germans would not vote for a party just because it was antisemitic.[25]

To the extent that parliamentary democracy relies on tolerance of opposing views and those who express them, ethnic and ideological exclusions in general and antisemitism in particular reflected the absence of, and often vehement attack on, bedrock democratic values. Antidemocratic forces found them useful tools for recruitment and to isolate or exclude political opponents. And they were a harbinger of and a precondition for horrific things to come.

The influence of Marxists (i.e., anyone who fought for an autonomous voice for workers) raised deep anxieties. The non-Marxist political parties, except the Left liberals, were vociferously anti-Marxist. Many burghers had initially seen the November Revolution as a welcome end to a disastrous war and an opportunity for necessary reforms and had voted in 1919 for explicitly democratic parties. Yet waves of worker activism during and after the Revolution soon terrified most of them. Periodic Communist uprisings and some workers' attempt to extend the general strike against the 1920 Rightist Kapp Putsch to attain socialist goals proved particularly threatening. Even conservative Germans recognized that workers must be integrated into the *Volksgemeinschaft*—but workers should know their place and not threaten the traditional social order. Burgher antipathy to worker activism, especially strikes, increasingly extended to the Weimar Republic, which allowed workers a substantive political role—indeed, it allowed an SPD president and SPD chancellors! Middle- and upper-class Germans could not agree on any consensus partisan position, but most ceased voting for democratic parties and frequently united in local "citizens' blocs" against the perceived socialist/Bolshevik threat.[26]

The anxieties about a socialist threat were only exacerbated when the unions and the SPD began talking about "economic democracy." Socialists had long argued that political democracy was incomplete without economic democracy to secure for the masses the wherewithal to exercise an equal political role. The failure to secure socialism through the November Revolution left many on the Left deeply disappointed. In hyperinflation's aftermath, as business owners reasserted power within their enterprises, the unions sponsored proposals for economic democracy in the form of councils with equal worker/management membership which would supervise economic developments. Such proposals became an official goal for left- and right-wing labor movement supporters from 1928. Many supporters saw it not only as a way to ride herd on business leaders but as a step toward socialism. Many opponents did, too, and business leaders were terrified at the prospect. These fears contributed substantively to the business community's increasing conviction that it must destroy Weimar democracy to save itself.[27]

Having imagined a coherent national community by excluding the disdained, most Germans continued, as in the *Kaiserreich*, to repudiate "interests" as a divisive threat to that community. They believed that interests were inherently corrupt, materialistic, and egotistical. Even when they supported a special-interest party (e.g., for landlords or creditors or farmers), they explained it as a temporary expedient to defend against other corrupt interests or, more frequently, in moralistic, not materialist, terms. For example, creditors who had seen hyperinflation destroy the value of their assets wanted material recompense; they justified that demand in terms not of their interests, but of protecting the sanctity of contracts and the rule of law. Farmers' parties argued for not any egotistical group interests, but the *nation's* need to feed itself. As Peter Fritzsche argues, "Speaking a morally drenched language of corruption, betrayal, and virtue, they came to identify their own interests and needs with national political renewal."[28]

Having dismissed competing egotistical interests as illegitimate, many, perhaps most, Germans believed the country needed—and could have—a political system that would represent the interests of Germans and Germany as a whole. They believed that individual interests—if permissible at all—must be subordinate to the single *Gesamtinteresse*, an all-encompassing national interest. They viewed society as a body in which each citizen functioned as a vital, but subordinate, part of the organism. The *Gesamtinteresse* was essential to overcoming the bitter class interests dividing the republic and to building a harmonious, conflict-free, unified society to embody the *Volksgemeinschaft*. Democracy must reflect both the *Gesamtinteresse* and a putative collective will of all the people, not the interest-based opinions of contentious group and class representatives. Many Germans implicitly (and a few Weimar-era political theorists explicitly) called for a state based on Rousseau's idea of a general will that embodied the *Gesamtinteresse*, existed prior to political action, and needed only to be recognized and implemented to establish "true democracy." Support for this notion extended from the far right to some SPD members.[29]

Given their commitment to *Gesamtinteresse* and *Volksgemeinschaft*, most Germans rejected pluralism and compromise. Pluralism assumes that societies contain varying interests entitled to expression and representation. *Gesamtinteresse* and *Volksgemeinschaft* considered particular interests illegitimate and their expression or representation an assault on the community's good and Germany's future. The acceptance of compromise assumes that varying interests exist, that no single answer to the problems facing a society can be satisfactory, and that a community without conflict is impossible. Believers in a single interest/community might in practice compromise, but they still saw compromise as a betrayal of unity and principle.[30]

Having rejected interests, pluralism, and compromise, many Weimar-era Germans rejected political parties as well. Those who did not support the SPD or KPD often vociferously supported notionally nonpartisan lists in municipal elections, and the Nazis insisted that they were a movement, not a party (though Weimar legislation required that they register as a party to run in elections). Such Germans saw parties as representing particular interests, hence inherently corrupt. They believed parties promoted divisive conflict by promoting those special interests over the common good and that partisan strife inherently paralyzed Germany, weakening it against its many enemies. Many Germans, including some on the Left, wanted to eliminate political parties in favor of an apolitical public life that they were convinced was possible—even as they promoted their own interests and views.[31]

Parliamentarism was also the target of abuse. Party leaders determined election to parliament and its votes, so many Germans saw MPs as just party hacks, inevitably co-opted by economic interests for egotistical ends. Parliamentary actions then were always tawdry business deals among corrupt individuals, a view strengthened by periodic press reports of (relatively minor) corruption scandals. These attacks on parliamentarism seem to attack democracy, yet many were launched in the name of democracy, insisting that parliament could *only* represent private interests and never the will of the people as a whole. Only overthrowing Weimar parliamentary democracy could, many believed, create a "true democracy."[32]

Moreover, many Germans never fully accepted the Weimar Republic as a legitimate "state." Only a dwindling minority upheld monarchism though the 1920s. Nonetheless, the monarchical principle—separating the state, embodied in the monarch, from the constitution that the monarch voluntarily granted—was entrenched. And that state, even absent a monarch, was assumed to embody the good of the whole as against society's mere interests. Many then saw the state as prior and superior to the post-revolutionary regime the Weimar Constitution established. The state had legitimacy beyond the constitution, and for many Germans the Weimar Republic, however democratic in origin and intent, did not embody the state or the "popular will."[33]

A series of specific threats also eroded the Weimar Republic's legitimacy, starting with its origins in defeat. Origin in defeat was never going to be glorious. However, army and conservatives quickly concocted the "stab-in-the-back legend," that Germany had never been defeated in the field but that only a nefarious attack on the home front by treacherous revolutionaries (explicitly or implicitly Jews and Marxists) had led to defeat. This gross misrepresentation gained wide credence. For those who believed it, the revolutionaries who had overthrown the *Kaiserreich* had betrayed the German Army and the German people; such traitors, the "November criminals," should be purged from the body politic, and their corrupt offspring—the Republic—should be destroyed.[34]

The Versailles Treaty struck a severe blow to the republic's legitimacy. Many Germans supported democracy, 1918/19, in hopes of a better deal in peace negotiations, as US President Woodrow Wilson seemingly promised. Whatever Wilson's 1918 intentions, the 1919 Treaty was, from the perspective of virtually all Germans, a crying injustice; they rejected its relatively draconian provisions and, especially, its ascription to Germany alone of responsibility for the war's outbreak. When the new republic could not block the draconian conditions but had to vote to accept them, it became identified with defeat, national humiliation, and enormous hardship.[35]

Most Germans apparently had not supported democracy from conviction but in hopes of a better pay-off than the discredited monarchy had delivered—a better deal from the peace negotiations or an effective barrier to Bolshevism. Their support hinged on their approval of the outcomes it generated. In practice, all a democracy can promise is a fair procedure allowing popular input into decision-making. No system can guarantee desirable outcomes, overall or for specific groups or individuals. Too many variables are in play. Nonetheless, most Germans in the interwar period—perhaps most people everywhere—focused on outcomes. The Weimar Republic resulted from defeat, signed the crushing Versailles Treaty, presided over a 100 trillion percent inflation and a brutal stabilization, and fell into the worst depression in German history with unemployment among the worst in the world. Its outcomes were horrific. The four or five "good" years from the mid-to late 1920s were insufficient to develop any broad commitment to democracy or the republic.[36]

Many scholars have noted that initial lack of legitimacy did not inevitably doom the Weimar Republic. The obvious counterexample is France's Third Republic, also founded in defeat. Monarchists dominated its early parliaments but divided into three groups that could not cooperate. Gradually, public opinion shifted, a growing majority voted for pro-Republic parties, and the Third Republic secured legitimacy. Conceivably, the Weimar Republic, with more favorable outcomes, might also have gradually secured legitimacy.[37]

Yet in the event Germans increasingly moved away from a parliamentary-democratic political culture. Their expectations of solely positive outcomes, disdain for "egotistical" interests and divisive parties, insistence on a harmonious *Gesamtinteresse*, rejection of pluralism and compromise, and fear of Marxism did arguably become the predominant political culture in the Weimar Republic, given what Germans increasingly said and what the organizations and parties they supported had to say. The elements of this political culture had roots in the *Kaiserreich*, but they were not reflections of some timeless German national character. They were never universally shared and after 1918 rested primarily in the contrast between an imagined wartime unity and the divisiveness and problems of the 1920s/30s. And many people who shared them would exercise the rights of democratic citizenship. However, they increasingly made Weimar's liberal democracy unacceptable, even for those who still argued for some form of democracy.

Seeking Stability through *autoritäre Demokratie*

A striking and fateful development in the Weimar Republic was the increasing emphasis on leadership and the "leader principle." Nineteenth-century leadership models included monarchs, military officers, and, especially, Otto von Bismarck, the unifier of Germany. The 1925 election of First World War Field Marshall Paul Hindenburg as president both reflected and strengthened the (military) leadership model. Right, Center, and occasionally Left-leaning Germans contrasted the "party hacks" who dominated Weimar parties with the "personalities"—men of character and conviction—that they thought were needed in leadership positions; parliaments, they said, were incapable of selecting authentic, efficacious "personalities." Many spoke of leaders in the plural and seemed to seek not a dictatorship but a system in which citizens would choose among benevolent leadership elites.[38]

However, increasingly setting the tone were those seeking a single great man who would embody the people's will and act with the necessary authority and determination to solve Germany's pressing problems and restore it to its proper greatness. The Nazis are most infamous, but many other parties and organizations anointed someone as "the leader." Notably, dictator in the early twentieth century did not necessarily denote a brutal thug but something like the *temporary* absolute ruler whom the ancient Roman Republic elected to master a crisis. Moreover, in the *Kaiserreich*, Germans had experienced an authoritarian system that secured rights for most, if not all, citizens. Few could imagine before 1933 how thoroughly the Nazis would sweep away the Rechtsstaat or how brutally they would act.[39]

This focus on—for many, an obsession with—leadership could represent an authoritarian attack on the Weimar Republic and democracy, but it also elicited calls for an "*autoritäre Demokratie*," where *autoritär* means not "authoritarian" but "in command," capable of making and implementing decisions. Given the Weimar political system's apparent dysfunctionality in the face of devastating problems, Germans were rightly concerned about efficacy. After 1919, only a minority voted for the pro-parliamentary-democracy parties, the Center, SPD, and DDP. Crucially, implicit and explicit support for authoritative democracy spanned the political spectrum. In 1930, the DDP replaced "Democratic" in its name with "State," and even in the SPD, the only party still committed to the Weimar constitution, some activists pushed for "*autoritäre* democracy."[40]

Parallel to calls for authoritative democracy were increasing calls for "leader democracy." Max Weber and other early-twentieth-century commentators did not trust the masses to make political decisions but saw a need to engage them politically, not least in the event of war. And even conservatives under Weimar saw the need for a loyal mass base for authoritarian rule. The failure of Weimar parliamentary politics to throw up any charismatic leaders strengthened the search for a modern means of

Führerauslese, evaluation and selection of the most suitable leaders. Individuals across the political spectrum called for reforms to create a system that would generate not just competent but statesmanlike leaders, those "personalities" who would also express, perhaps embody, the authentic will of the people. They were defining democracy as a system assuring popular participation in selecting a leader or leaders but not in forming policy or the political will.[41]

Given these attitudes toward leadership, Weimar policymakers resisted popular participation in policy formation. Both senior civil servants and politicians tended to think of themselves as experts who should be allowed to get on with the important business of governance without untutored citizens muddying the waters. They were willing to accept information and even proposals from powerful economic interests but ignored demands for input by other interests or groups. When offering an audience to citizens seemed politically expedient, it was an empty gesture. For example, President Hindenburg's state secretary wrote to a colleague that the President, Chancellor, and Justice Minister would receive the representatives of creditors impoverished by inflation and explain, not discuss, proposed legislation, but "then the president" would decide for "the execution and promulgation of the bill." Government officials in this democracy had no interest in *listening* to citizens to whom they deigned to grant an audience, and citizens saw and resented it. It strengthened their sense that the existing democratic system could not represent them or the popular will.[42]

Popular Demonstrations and the Rise of the Antidemocratic Right

Despite politicians' preference for a passive citizenry and many citizens' preference for authoritative leadership, Weimar-era citizens organized and acted to influence the political system—and to a remarkable degree. *Kaiserreich* citizens had not been all passive subjects, but Weimar citizens outdid them.

The political camps often remained structured around nineteenth-century conflicts that had characterized the *Kaiserreich*. The camps were neither homogeneous nor immutable, organized more along ideological or religious than class lines. About a third of SPD votes came from nonworkers and about a third of DNVP (conservative) votes came from workers. The Marxist camp was split between the MSPD and USPD in the late 1910s/early 1920s and between SPD and KPD in the mid-twenties through early thirties. The Center Party and Bavarian People's Party drew perhaps 50 percent of Catholic voters up to 1933. The Protestant liberal-conservative camp included many workers, usually from smaller cities or villages and smaller workshops. Always less cohesive than the other two camps, it splintered in the twenties. From 1924–1930, its many splinter parties complicated electioneering and coalition formation and contributed to a sense of fragmentation and instability (with never fewer than fourteen parties in 1920s Reichstags). And its fragments mostly coalesced within the Nazi Party in the early 1930s. The combination of deep ideological differences and proportional representation made parties focus narrowly on congenial voters. They were relatively indifferent to their broad appeal, to the detriment of compromise and governance.[43]

Social and citizen participation was vibrant in Weimar Germany. The number of organizations increased 50 percent from 1914 to 1919 and by another third by 1930, with membership apparently increasing at similar rates. A major impetus was defensive, a bourgeois response to the increasing role of unions and the Social Democrats during the war and revolution. As vehemently as burghers denounced interests and insisted on the preeminence of ideals, they still felt compelled to develop powerful organizations to defend their own interests until a better day, constitutionally and politically. Organizations and clubs remained divided along class and denominational lines, but the prewar predominance of notables gave way to a leadership drawn from various social strata, reflecting a new assertiveness by ordinary citizens.[44]

"Civil society" did not create a democratic system in the *Kaiserreich* and could not defend democracy in the Weimar Republic. With social and political organizations blossoming, a diverse realm of social and political activism opened between the political system and family/business/self. Yet it did not reconcile many Germans to the Weimar Republic and its institutions. Many organizations were antidemocratic, and the Nazis sought to use various organizations for political influence or to recruit. Suggesting that civil society somehow made dictatorship more likely, as political scientist Sheri Berman does, goes too far, but civil society was no automatic guarantor of democracy.[45]

While German women attained the vote and equal citizenship in 1918–1919 "in principle," their political role remained constrained by men's and their own expectations. Women increased their participation in many organizations, created organizations of their own, and joined women's auxiliaries created by male-dominated organizations. After 1919, their political activism and voting declined somewhat, even while their activism in welfare and social policy increased; after 1929, their voting increased; yet some were always politically active. Women across the political spectrum participated actively in electioneering, as even the conservatives in the DNVP recognized the need to recruit women voters, who were a majority of voters after wartime male deaths. Women did tend to avoid the KPD through 1932 and the Nazis at least until 1932. The New Woman of the 1920s, like the flapper in Britain and the United States, embodied a new degree of social activism and wider opportunities. Opportunities, though, began narrowing before the Nazis seized power, under the pressure of the Great Depression. Weimar-era German women generally assumed that they were equal to men but more maternal, caring, and emotional. That made it easier for both sexes to see women's role as restricted to the domestic sphere or to political questions bearing on nurturance, even as it cast them as too emotional, without the cool rationality necessary for leadership. The widely embraced pseudo-science of crowd psychology dismissed crowds as, among other things, feminine—and hence, irrational, suggestible, and not to be taken seriously.[46]

At the same time, Germans were experiencing a masculinity crisis. They had invested enormously in the (masculine) glories of their soldiers' victories; defeat and the Versailles Treaty now humiliated those men. Germans often dismissed negotiation and democracy as weak and therefore unmanly. Political participation did become a major venue for masculine assertion, most notably in paramilitary organizations, such as the Nazi Storm Troopers (SA). Such participation tended to marginalize women, leaving them at best as binders of wounds. Paramilitaries drove the violence that characterized German politics in the immediate postwar years and early 1930s. That violence terrified many voters, undercut the Weimar Republic's legitimacy, and bolstered the Nazis, who claimed to be fighting the waves of violence they were themselves driving.[47]

In the Weimar Republic, both democratic and antidemocratic political citizenship meant activism—for a significantly higher proportion of the population than at any time before the 1970s. In the *Kaiserreich*, primarily workers took their political grievances to the streets, as strikers or SPD demonstrators. The 1918 revolution taught Germans that if they wanted political impact, they had to march and (at least threaten to) strike or boycott. From 1918 to 1933, across the political spectrum, millions engaged in public political activity. In the early 1930s alone, citizens engaged in tens of thousands of assemblies and thousands of demonstrations, to express their political views and to pressure the political system. Contempt for "the masses" accompanied demands for, and acts of, mass participation; democratic rights were exercised by those who fought to deny those rights to others. Some Germans did reject extra-parliamentary action because they did not trust the masses to act autonomously and believed that citizens should act politically only by voting or through parties and parliament. Yet this view was obscured, as more groups were taking to the streets, carrying banners, and shouting slogans—for or against the republic.[48]

Germans took advantage of the right of petition, a form of political citizenship almost universally accepted in principle. Even in the Middle Ages, Germans could petition the ruler for redress of grievances, and Article 126 of the Weimar Constitution guaranteed every German the right to petition authorities or elected representatives. Petitioning in the Weimar Republic was primarily individual, not collective. Authorities and representatives know that petitions are a relatively low-commitment form of political action, so while petitioning was not unusual, the evidence suggests it was not particularly efficacious.[49]

The most common form of extra-parliamentary action in Weimar Germany was the traditional indoor meeting. Under the Empire, Germans occasionally attended meetings of various sizes, as group members or to listen to campaign speeches. Building on nineteenth-century liberal ideas of politics as reasoned dialogue, the meetings often included an opportunity for opposing speakers to contribute to the discussion, though this practice became problematic late in the Weimar Republic, as violence at campaign events spread. Weimar Germans, across the political spectrum, embraced public meetings as a form of citizen action, and their number seems to have increased substantially after 1918 and again after 1929, when the Nazis began holding myriad events in German cities, towns, and villages, which other parties sought to copy. These flurries of political activity gave citizens a role to play between and during elections, albeit relatively passively, as most simply sat and listened. Dieter Ohr argues that such assemblies were better attended when they included a "non-political" component, often entertainment.[50]

Some Germans also worried about the effect of popular suffrage on reason in politics. Weimar Germans continued to emphasize the importance of reason and prudence in politics in general, but especially in public demonstrations. Some also emphasized the inappropriateness of emotion in public protest, which was associated with the crowd as mob but could also be used to negatively characterize the newly enfranchised female citizen. However, the Nazis vigorously appealed to emotion—e.g., with symbols, flags, and torchlight parades. Even the moderate Left was drawn to (at best a-rational) symbolism in the face of Nazi appeals to emotion, for example, flags, singing, the symbol of three arrows (to paint across the Nazi swastika). Reasoned discourse was not yet the central trope for democratic citizenship it would become following the Third Reich, but it was an aspiration.[51]

Many on the radical Left were unwilling to rely on reasoned discourse. The Weimar Republic came into existence as the result of insurrection against the *Kaiserreich*, but as its moderate Leftist leaders sought to secure stable democratic order, they alienated those who wanted socialism now. Even before the republic was formally established, a series of Left-wing insurrections sought to overthrow all vestiges of the power of old elites and establish a new socialist order. The Leftist insurrectionaries sought to create a dictatorship of the proletariat that would lead to a comprehensive political, economic, and social democracy. They saw the parliamentary democracy that the MSPD was negotiating with elites as a mask for continued capitalist rule, and they could see their uprisings as extra-parliamentary democratic actions. Governments turned to the *Freikorps* and the Reichswehr (the army), which crushed Communist uprisings, 1919–1923. Violence at a Leftist demonstration also led the government to ban demonstrations in the area in Berlin around the Reichstag and government offices.[52]

In 1923, France and Belgium occupied the Ruhr, sparking a mix of peaceful and violent protest. By seizing control of Germany's industrial heartland, the French and Belgians hoped to coerce Germans into fulfilling reparation obligations. The German government ordered that no coal be delivered from the Ruhr, and the occupation sparked a wave of passive resistance by the citizenry. Workers, the SPD, and the unions played a key role. (Businesses generally sought ways to cooperate with the French, to reduce their costs.) Government and SPD sponsored demonstrations against Franco-Belgian policy which attracted hundreds of thousands of protesters. Some individuals went over to active resistance, with campaigns of sabotage. Eventually, hyperinflation and severe economic misery undercut support for passive resistance, leading to its collapse.[53]

Right-wing extremists also resorted to violence, rather than reason, in attempts to overthrow the Weimar Republic. They were willing to challenge the state's monopoly on the use of force, a key characteristic of the modern state and most certainly of the *Kaiserreich*. The most striking example was the Kapp Putsch in March 1920. Wolfgang Kapp was a mid-level civil servant. During the First World War, he co-founded the Fatherland Party to mobilize public opinion—under elite control—to demand an unconditional German victory, an annexationist peace, and continued authoritarian government. On March 13, 1920, he and General Walther von Lüttwitz tried to seize power in Berlin, hoping to overthrow the Weimar Republic and establish a new authoritarian order. The Reichswehr proved unwilling to defend democracy, as its commander refused to order his soldiers to fire on insurrectionary fellow soldiers. So government and union leaders called for a general strike to break the putsch. Millions of workers across Germany supported the strike and the republic, and many Berlin civil servants also refused to cooperate with the putschists. The attempted coup prompted two kinds of political activism. Its supporters asserted a right to act not only outside but against the constitutional, democratic order, in favor of an ill-defined authoritarian alternative. Its opponents asserted a right and a duty to go beyond voting, to engage actively, at some risk, in defending the existing democratic political order. Their strike constituted the broadest, but certainly not the only, public activism in defense of the Weimar Republic.[54]

Another aspect of right-wing violence in the early republic was murder. The Freikorps helped to put down both worker insurrections and peaceful strikes. They defended Germans in areas of the East outside Germany (e.g., the Baltic states) and in territories that the Versailles Treaty assigned to other nations. As self-proclaimed defenders of Germandom, the groups identified "traitors" and executed them. That included assassinating Weimar politicians, most famously Matthias Erzberger of the Center party, who helped to negotiate the 1918 Armistice, and Foreign Minister Walther Rathenau, who worked to strengthen Germany's international position in desperate circumstances but who was Jewish and a symbol to the radical Right of the hated Weimar system. These assassinations were intended to provoke a communist uprising that could be used as an excuse to overthrow the republic. Instead, they spurred two rounds of legislation that allowed the government to ban calls for violence and anti-Republic organizations.[55]

The Beer-Hall Putsch of November 9, 1923 was a watershed. Led by Adolf Hitler and retired General Erich Ludendorff, it sought to seize power in Munich as the base for a march on Berlin to seize national power. It failed miserably. It marked the end of attempts to violently overthrow the Weimar Republic but also the Nazis' grudging acceptance that they could only come to power "legally." (It did not end all resort to violence.) Its "martyrs," as well as Hitler's dramatic performance at his trial, brought him charismatic leadership of the Nazi Party, the radical Right, and, ultimately, the Reich.[56]

Pro-Weimar groups and individuals demonstrated frequently. The republic organized Constitution Day celebrations that attracted some popular support. Tellingly, though, the Reichstag never mustered a majority to make it a national holiday, so it was more divisive than unifying. Election campaigns were lively, with party-sponsored meetings and parades. Unlike Nazi SA marches, which were to be observed not joined, most parties' parades were open to any who chose to join. Most spectators, though, remained passive, even if their presence could be interpreted as support for the marchers. Marchers felt best about their project and sought the best impression through an orderly, self-controlled, "disciplined," display. Pro- (and anti-) Weimar parades tended to have an acclamatory thrust. They usually did not protest or push any specific policy, so political citizenship generally meant not the exercise of individual judgment and active efforts to advance a personal view. Instead one expressed a political identity—Catholic, worker, veteran—or supported a movement, party, or paramilitary organization.[57]

After 1924, the Reichsbanner (a paramilitary group created by the SPD, left liberals, and Center to defend the Weimar Republic against the Communists and the Nazis) organized thousands of popular demonstrations. While committed to the Weimar Republic, its leadership and members were not completely committed to parliamentary democracy. Its activists looked more to street politics, especially when, amid the political conflicts of the early 1930s, they created the Iron Front of activists willing to go to the streets against communist and Nazi paramilitary groups. They looked to persuade not through rational interest politics but through symbolic expression. So they adopted uniforms, flags, and slogans, a la Right-wing paramilitaries; and Reichsbanner units were all-male, to emphasize their ability to engage in combat for democracy. At the same time, its parades and demonstrations often included women, children, disabled veterans, and the unemployed, acknowledging a political role for all citizens.[58]

During the Weimar Republic, members of the middle classes—usually right-of-center—swept into the streets in enormous numbers. The signing of the Versailles Treaty brought out crowds to denounce the cruel and unjust "dictate" of the Allies, and students demonstrated annually against the Treaty. Even civil servants protested in the streets when inflation eroded their salaries badly enough. French occupation of the Ruhr spurred outraged protests, and Hindenburg's election as president and his birthdays brought out perhaps bigger, joyful crowds. Right-of-center groups such as the Stahlhelm would hold national festivals to which other (politically acceptable) groups were invited. The waves of protest in agrarian communities were particularly striking, especially in 1928, which witnessed over 150 protest actions; in one, approximately 140,000 participated in towns across Schleswig-Holstein. The demonstrators often disdained the parliament and argued for the overthrow of the Weimar "system" and its replacement by a fairer political and economic order. Usually, as in the Hindenburg demonstrations, they were affirming an identity and a political ideology rather than seeking to influence specific policy outcomes. The repeated waves of demonstrations constituted a dramatic expansion of political citizenship and of often self-consciously "democratic" action, often by individuals opposed to Weimar democracy. However, different demonstrations implied different degrees and concepts of popular activism.[59]

Significantly, burgher activism, even when anti-Weimar, was usually defensive. Given ideological and partisan divisions, burgher found it easier to unite against something than for something. Fear of Bolshevism and workers was a driving force. The November Revolution and subsequent Communist insurrections, 1919–1923, terrified many. Nazi Storm Troopers drove the street violence that swept Germany after 1929, but the Nazis successfully pinned the blame on the Communists. As putative bulwarks against a Communist threat, groups such as the Stahlhelm and the SA easily secured support and recruits. Moreover, individual Germans who felt threatened by the 1919 worker strikes or 1928+ mortgage foreclosures resorted to various tactics in defense of their interests, couched as moral claims.[60]

Despite their own defensive activism, Rightist Germans often expressed disdain for, or fear of, other citizens "taking politics to the streets." Right-of-center citizens did not oppose protests against the Versailles Treaty or Stahlhelm parades or celebrations of Hindenburg's birthday. Their targets were proletarian strikes, Reichsbanner parades, and Social Democratic or Communist demonstrations. In the latter contexts, as Peter Fritzsche writes, they rejected "bowing to the 'voice of the streets.'" These middle-class protests did not embrace the autonomous, activist democratic citizen—yet they relied on democratic forms of political activity.[61]

Conservative defensive activism took a range of forms. Calls for strikes, boycotts, or other direct actions outnumbered actual protests in the Republic's first years. Such calls originated in the November Revolution's immediate aftermath as an adaptation of worker tactics. Farmers, doctors, and civil servants all proposed to go "on strike," to refuse to deliver goods or services, in pursuit of their goals. Some, though, did act on those calls. For example, some proposed a "general strike" by all burghers to oppose worker radicalism and to achieve other political ends, and one broke out in Bremen in 1919. As inflation soared, food riots, like those during the war, were a common tactic. Most such rhetoric and actions disappeared with the end of the inflation (though food riots recurred occasionally during the Depression). In the late 1920s, some farmers resorted to aggressive direct action, especially in Schleswig-Holstein. Bankrupt farmers commonly threatened tax strikes and attempted to block foreclosures by intimidating would-be buyers at auctions. In a few cases, bombs destroyed property. These extra-parliamentary political actions did not represent farmers' opinions generally. They reflected a determination by desperate minorities to draw attention, through direct action, to just demands they thought the parliamentary-democratic system was not adequately addressing. They were, though, more a repudiation of the system, if not necessarily of democracy, than an attempt to hold it to its own principles.[62]

Throughout the Weimar period, paramilitary groups were on the rise. The most famous was the Nazi SA, but the Right-wing nationalist Stahlhelm, the pro-Weimar Reichsbanner, and the communist Rote Frontkämpferbund and successor organizations were influential. The Stahlhelm began as a veterans' organization but expanded to include nonveterans who embraced its "spirit of the front." It claimed to stand above parties and to exclude partisanship from German politics. The other groups were founded to prevent opponents from disrupting a party's political meetings. Each soon became the public face of its political movement and often clashed with opposing paramilitaries. They all emphasized masculinity, uniforms and flags, obedience and hierarchy, strong leadership, youth, and action. Putatively, hierarchy and obedience transformed threatening masses into disciplined troops. They claimed to act solely in self-defense.[63]

In fact, the groups, especially the SA, promoted a culture of violence. After 1929, their clashes, especially those between Nazis and Communists, deprived the Weimar Republic of the monopoly on the use of force that scholars cite as a key characteristic of the modern state and that Weimar Germans clearly expected it to wield. The brutal violence of the First World War played a role in the rise of political violence, but most Germans (and most veterans) were not violent, and most members of paramilitaries in the early 1930s were too young to have fought in the First World War. Fear of civil war was widespread, as Nazis and Communists clashed repeatedly, and the Reichsbanner and even the Stahlhelm were occasionally drawn into public brawling. The Nazis were most responsible; the SA deliberately engaged in provocation of or outright attacks on political opponents. The party sought not to seize power directly, but to discredit the Weimar Republic by revealing its inability to maintain order. It knew it could not win a civil war on the streets and was careful to retreat whenever the state pushed back. Unfortunately, the authorities—and the burghers—saw the Nazis as a valuable bulwark against a perceived Communist threat and were generally willing to let them get away with violence, even murder. Ultimately, as Bernd Weisbrod argues, many in the bourgeoisie were willing to accept violence as the price for changing the Weimar system.[64]

The End of Weimar Democracy

Despite the relative stability of the later 1920s, support for the Weimar constitution had eroded considerably before the Depression hit. Elected in 1925, President Paul von Hindenburg was committed to strong governance that would unify the nation, not to democracy. Because he swore to uphold the constitution when taking office, he would not subvert it directly, but he was inclined to push, within its wording, toward more commanding presidential governance, especially as his attempts to overcome partisan bickering failed. By 1928, important segments of German industry were determined to replace the constitution with a more commanding, indeed, authoritarian political order. That year, heavy industry defied the state by refusing to accept a mandatory arbitration ruling on wages and by locking its workers out of the plants to break their strike. Big agriculture had long been politically conservative and never accepted the republic, but by the later 1920s, even small farmers were often alienated by a political system that could not respond effectively to the world agricultural depression that began in 1927. The urban small-business sector, long unhappy with free-market competition, felt it was being crushed by big business, big agriculture, and big labor. In 1928, the Center Party, originally a key supporter of the Weimar constitution and parliamentary government, elected a new party chairman, Monsignor Ludwig Kaas, who began moving the party toward the Right. In 1930, the German Democratic Party, another once stalwart supporter of the constitution, became the German State Party, committed to overcoming partisan bickering and creating a force that claimed to be, as Larry Jones wrote, "capable of freeing the state from the tyranny of outside interests." Arch-conservative Alfred Hugenberg, who would have no truck with Weimar parliamentarism, became head of the conservative DNVP.[65]

A dispute over unemployment insurance marked the beginning of the end. Many in the business community increasingly resented the Weimar social state, especially its interventions in their practices and profits. When increasing unemployment exhausted funding for benefits in 1929, some change was necessary. The right-liberal DVP responded to demands from business supporters who were determined to push the SPD out of government and overthrow Weimar parliamentary governance; it refused to support a fiscal package the SPD-led government negotiated with its coalition partners. The SPD Reichstag delegation withdrew confidence from its own chancellor, precipitating the government's downfall on March 27, 1930.[66]

President Hindenburg chose Heinrich Brüning (Center Party) as the new chancellor because both favored a presidential government—one independent of the Reichstag and "not bound to the parties." Hindenburg was committed to a unified Germany that would reassert its greatness. By 1930, he was convinced that parliament could represent only divisive interests and never establish a commanding government; so the parliament and political parties had to be superseded. Historians still debate Brüning's intentions, but he shared Hindenburg's desire for a more commanding government that did not depend on the Reichstag. Brüning did not want to rule *against* the Reichstag; whether, if he had managed to solve Germany's immediate problems, he would have then established a more effective "democratic" alternative, as he subsequently claimed, is less clear. Hindenburg and Brüning established a ministerial government responsible to the president and ruling through Article 48 decrees, if necessary over the head of the Reichstag. When the Reichstag overturned a presidential decree, Hindenburg dissolved it, and Brüning reissued the decree, substantively ending parliamentary governance. Brüning issued more decrees, leaving the parties the choice of letting the decrees stand without their input or risking new elections. He and Hindenburg ruled under Article 48 for two years because, after September 1930, the SPD feared that any other course would either prompt the Center to withdraw its support from the democratic Prussian Land government, or lead to a Hitler dictatorship to replace Brüning, or require new elections that would only help the KPD and the Nazis. The president and chancellor had fundamentally crippled the constitutional basis of the Reichstag's role.[67]

The Brüning government substantively ended *parliamentary democracy* in Weimar Germany, though whether it ended democracy is a more complicated question. While Brüning and Hindenburg did not actually rule against the Reichstag, they effectively sidelined it, while opening the way for those like Papen, Schleicher, and Hitler, who wanted to eliminate it entirely as a political force. On the other hand, Hindenburg was democratically elected, careful to rule in accord with the letter of the constitution, and would be re-elected in 1932 in a fair, democratic election. His disdain for the Reichstag and the parties, which Brüning at least partially shared, was almost certainly shared by most Germans, especially given the platforms of the parties for which they chose to vote. The system he dominated could be characterized as a presidential or elected dictatorship, but many Germans would have seen the governments after March 1930 as closer to "true democracy" than the parliamentary governments that preceded them.

The Reichstag elections of September 1930, with the enormous increase in the Nazi vote, were a second major blow to parliamentary democracy and eventually any democracy in Germany. After decades of research, the consensus holds that Nazism was not a revolt of the lower-middle class or any other specific group in German society. Rather, the Nazis were Germany's first *Volkspartei*, the first party to appeal to voters across the social spectrum, although they did appeal to some groups more than others. Catholics were not well represented in the Nazi vote nor were women, at least until 1933. Many blue-collar workers, usually from smaller towns and enterprises, voted for the Nazis, but workers were still underrepresented. White-collar workers and civil servants were slightly underrepresented, but self-employed individuals were overrepresented. Strikingly, Richard Hamilton has shown that the Nazi vote in demographically upper-middle-class precincts was substantially higher than the national average.[68]

This spread reflected Hitler's ability to convince many Weimar Germans that his was the party of the *Volksgemeinschaft*. He posited a racially determined German *Volk* that was superior to all other peoples in the world and the basis of a German nation. Even if most early 1930s Nazi supporters did not fully buy into this racialized view, they did buy into the broader project of creating a community of all true Germans. The Nazis developed narrowly focused campaign literature for each significant social group in the electorate. It promised to protect that group's interests—not as interests but as morally justified claims. Particularly compelling was the promise to integrate into the fold workers who had been "seduced" by Marxism. The overarching message was Nazi representation of the *Gesamtinteresse*, but how they could reconcile *all* these various interests was never clear. Nonetheless, their clamor for community and *Gesamtinteresse* seems to have resonated with millions of Germans disillusioned with party squabbling and parliamentary democracy.[69]

Recognizing the longing for *Volksgemeinschaft* is crucial to understanding the Nazis' success, which, while unimaginable without the Depression, began earlier. Hitler had built an effective organization with an appealing message. It began paying off in autumn 1929, when the Nazi vote began to double and triple in local and *Land* elections. Once the Depression hit, millions of Germans faced unemployment and economic misery, and the presidential governments, committed to counterproductive economic doctrines, proved incapable of dealing with the Depression. Parliamentary democracy had been weakened, perhaps fatally, but Germans still had options. Eventually, millions chose the Nazis, who had a positive message appealing to a plurality, if not yet a majority, of German voters.[70]

Brüning's rule by presidential decree had eroded support for parliamentary democracy, but Hindenburg eventually replaced him with Franz von Papen, who sought a return to the governing style of the *Kaiserreich*. Whatever "democratic" role for parliament Brüning might have envisaged, Papen wanted a permanent constitutional change to reestablish governments that were above the parties and independent of the Reichstag. He saw parliamentary compromise as weakness. He resigned from the Center Party before taking the office of Chancellor and ruled with nonparty "experts," widely dismissed as the "cabinet of barons." He used a presidential decree to suspend the pro-parliamentary-democracy government of Prussia, by far the biggest *Land*; his commissioner ruled in its stead. Mass unemployment and economic misery and the bitter split between Social Democrats and Communists had so weakened the labor movement that it could not mount against Papen's Prussian coup a general strike like the one that blocked the Kapp Putsch. Yet Papen could not effectively rule Germany. In July 31, 1932 Reichstag elections, parties supporting him got only 6 percent of the vote. Whatever attitudes toward or conceptions of democracy voters had, they did not want a return to the authoritarian *Kaiserreich*, to rule by "barons." Meanwhile, elites wanted parliamentary democracy to end, but they needed a government that had some solid footing in the people.[71]

As the next chancellor, Hindenburg chose General Kurt von Schleicher, who had been the army's "political" agent for years. The First World War's outcome had confirmed for soldiers like Schleicher that Germany could not win a European war without political stability and popular support, so the army needed an authoritative government with a mass base. He convinced himself that he could build an extra-party, extra-parliamentary mass base by co-opting the trade unions, the Stahlhelm, and some Nazi supporters. He promised the unions a job-creation program. He hoped to wean the "valuable elements" among the Nazis away from unproductive opposition and into government, securing them for Germany's future; so he enlisted Nazi leader

Gregor Strasser either to pressure Hitler to cooperate or to detach enough supporters from Hitler to build his own mass base. Schleicher failed. The unions were not willing to cooperate; the Stahlhelm did not trust him; and Strasser, failing to get Hitler's cooperation, resigned.[72]

With Papen and Schleicher having failed and the first signs of economic recovery suggesting that the Weimar constitution might survive, political and economic elites were willing to gamble on Hitler's mass base. The Nazis never topped, in a free election, the 37.3 percent of the vote they garnered in July 1932; they secured only 33.1 percent in the November elections. Even in the semi-free election of March 1933, they got only 43.9 percent. They verged on collapse in December 1932, with membership and donations falling, but no other right-of-center mass base replaced them. They came to power because German big business, big agriculture, the military, and conservatives were determined to definitively destroy Weimar parliamentary democracy and saw a cabinet including the Nazis as their last opportunity. Behind the scenes, Papen, Hugenberg, military leaders, and various government officials put sufficient pressure on the elderly, ailing, and exhausted President Hindenburg that he appointed Hitler chancellor on January 30, 1933. These elites thought they could "tame" Hitler—instead, he would tame them.[73]

Weimar parliamentary democracy failed, though not because Germans were inherently authoritarian or antidemocratic. Devastating economic and political events significantly undermined support for it, in its early years and even more so in the early 1930s. Some Germans were clearly nostalgic for the *Kaiserreich*. Yet political culture mattered. Many Germans saw parliamentary democracy as undemocratic, a rule of egotistical, materialistic elites at the expense of ideals, the *Gesamtinteresse*, and the will of the people. They also deplored the divisiveness and ineffectuality of the existing system. Some did want an authoritarian solution, but some sought an *autoritäre* or leader democracy that they hoped would give democratic voice to the real Germany, even perhaps at the expense of the liberal rights that political theorists generally argue are crucial for democracy. They sought a government of and for the people through strong, cohesive leadership. Hitler took advantage of this by emphasizing community and authority, wrapped in a-rational but compelling symbolism. Having secured a mass base, he came to power because conservative elites, including the army, wanted to destroy parliamentary democracy but needed some mass base for a stable replacement.

3

Agency in a Total State

Compliance and Non-Compliance in the Third Reich, 1933–1945

May 1 had been the workers' holiday in Germany since 1890, and the Nazis were determined to take the day away from the "Marxists"—to use it as a symbol not of class conflict but of national unity. They declared May 1, 1933, for the first time, a national holiday, the Holiday of National Work. This renaming repudiated the German labor movement's internationalism and allowed the Nazis to include workers, managers, and owners in the festivities. In the past, workers had *chosen* to come together to celebrate as workers and to challenge their employers. The Nazis *commanded* employers to bring their workers to the festive sites and workers to attend. They emphasized community, order, and discipline.[1]

The Nazis' restructuring of May 1 reflected their need to create political stability and the basis for future war by engaging (almost) every German politically—but on Nazi terms, under Nazi control. They believed that Germany had lost the First World War only because of a "stab in the back" by insufficiently committed home-front citizens. Publicly, they blamed Jews and "Marxists," but they knew that exhausted citizens and soldiers had also given up. Hence, to win a future war, thereby reversing the Versailles Treaty and gaining "living space" in Eastern Europe, they first had to secure voluntary popular engagement. Yet they abhorred representative democracy. They wanted citizen participation, but as acclamation of the regime, its policies, and its putative *Volksgemeinschaft* (racial community). So they must somehow maintain control while channeling the autonomous political activism that flourished after 1918.

The Nazis hence promoted their leader principle, which "solved" the problem of the masses by insisting that Hitler embodied the popular will, "true democracy," and the *Volksgemeinschaft*, so that each citizen must actively support him and the regime unquestioningly. The regime blocked formal political channels for most citizens, while defining as political many actions that would be simple human interactions in most societies. It then sought to promote various forms of pro-regime popular political activity. And once in power the Nazis did manage to silence virtually all open protest, enforce publicly a single acceptable political culture, and secure sufficient popular engagement to fight the Second World War to the bitter end.

Germans reacted in varying ways to the compulsions and demands they faced. Many embraced pro-regime action, whether voluntary or compelled, as democratic because they accepted the regime's assertion that Hitler embodied the people's will. They supported the regime in the ways that it preferred, such as donating to Nazi charities, cheering the *Führer's* speeches, backing the war effort, and, all too often, shunning or persecuting those excluded from the *Volksgemeinschaft*. Nonetheless, numerous Germans challenged the regime's political culture and submissive political citizenship by acting in ways—e.g., non-conformity, refusal, opposition, resistance—that the regime considered politically unacceptable. In the Third Reich, saying *Guten Tag* instead of *Heil Hitler*, speaking to a neighbor the regime defined as Jewish, or giving a sermon calling for love of one's neighbor could challenge the regime. Moreover, as in all societies, people took actions that lacked political intent but had political consequences—e.g., seeking higher wages in an economy stressed by rearmament costs, staying home rather than getting a job in a munitions factory, or giving food to a starving slave laborer.

In retrospect, most Germans came to agree that actions in support of brutal dictatorship could scarcely be considered democratic, while opposition to the regime might be considered democratic. Nonetheless, in the 1930s and 1940s Germans who acted in ways we might find deplorable, indeed criminal, could see themselves acting democratically, for the people and the will of the "people."

Dismantling Constitutional Governance and the Rechtsstaat

The Nazi regime never issued a formal constitution, nor did it repeal the Weimar Republic's constitution. Although legalistically it derived its powers from the Weimar constitution, the Third Reich was a substantively different state, and various decrees and enabling acts, and Hitler's pronouncements, were constitutive of its functioning. The shift to a new political order began with decrees issued by President Paul Hindenburg under Article 48, Weimar Constitution. On February 4, 1933, a decree "for the protection of the German people" suspended fundamental constitutional rights of expression, press, and assembly. The law was nominally to protect against political unrest and street violence but actually to limit other parties' campaigning in snap parliamentary elections set for March 5. After a fire (allegedly set by a Dutch communist) burned the Reichstag building on February 27, the Nazis convinced Hindenburg to issue a new Article 48 decree "in defense against Communistic violence endangering the state." It further restricted political rights, suspended indefinitely constitutional protections for personal liberty (so that the authorities could detain any individual for any reason, in practice indefinitely), and enabled the central government to intervene in state governance.[2]

After winning a bare electoral majority with their coalition partners, the Nazis bullied through the Reichstag on March 24, 1933, an Enabling Act allowing Hitler to rule by decree, an act that provided the regime a constitutional basis and appearance of legitimacy but that eliminated checks and balances. Two-thirds of votes had gone to antidemocratic parties; Communist deputies were already arrested or in hiding; and the Catholic parties were leaning toward authoritarianism. Catholic and German State Party deputies surrendered to a combination of intimidation and resignation. So Hitler's coalition assembled the two-thirds of deputies present necessary to pass the March 24 act as a constitutional amendment to the Weimar constitution. The act was, though, unconstitutional because of the arrests of Reichstag deputies and the intimidation but also because the government had arbitrarily altered the composition of the Reichsrat, which also had to vote yes with a two-thirds majority. Nazi constitutional scholar (and SS officer) Ernst Rudolf Huber saw it as constitutionally different from earlier Weimar enabling acts because they had been temporary, while it set up a new Reich. Hitler could now rule by decree for at least four years, and, crucially, he could do so independently of Hindenburg. With Hindenburg's 1934 death, the last potential constitutional check on Hitler disappeared, and the Enabling Act was extended and renewed, eventually indefinitely.[3]

The Nazi regime denied the existence of individual rights as against the community or the state. Nazi jurists argued that in the liberal state the individual only needed rights as a defense against the state because the state and the society were separate. In the Third Reich, they declared, state and community were identical, so individual rights were unnecessary. In any event, the common, democratic, good must take precedence over individual interests. So, as Huber declared, there were no individual freedoms the state must respect. Indeed, as the regime began dismantling individual rights, virtually no German jurist protested because they generally agreed that in an organic state individual rights were inherently anti-community. And while individuals could expect the community and the state to offer protections, citizens had primarily duties.[4]

The Nazi attack on rights was part of an attack on the Rechtsstaat. Opponents and conservative supporters of Nazism had in early 1933 counted on the Rechtsstaat to preserve a realm of personal freedom within which they could survive politically. The Nazis, though, dismantled the Rechtsstaat—with the assistance of much of the judiciary. The basic principle of Nazi jurisprudence was that every legal provision must be interpreted in terms of the *Volksgemeinschaft*'s needs and of the "healthy sentiments of the people" (as defined by the Nazis)—not in any narrowly legalistic way. Rights and due process, to the extent they existed, applied only to loyal "Aryans" (the putatively racially pure Germans) and not to the "racially" or otherwise alien, and the authorities could intervene arbitrarily on behalf of the community wherever they thought necessary. For example, the courts would not enforce contracts to which a Jew and an Aryan were parties and police would not protect Jews against SA violence, while even Aryans could have their property seized by the state for communal ends—without compensation. Moreover, if they were deemed socially or politically "alien to the community," Germans could face arbitrary arrest and indefinite, brutal, perhaps fatal incarceration, with no recourse. Yet most Germans seem not to have mourned the demise of the Rechtsstaat because they expected that as loyal members of the *Volksgemeinschaft* they had nothing to fear.[5]

Elections in the Third Reich were plebiscites, up or down votes on Hitler and his policies which were designed to legitimate his rule. They were not to enable voters to make decisions democratically but to demonstrate that the people approved Hitler's rule and decisions he had already made. Even Reichstag elections were in effect plebiscites, with all the candidates committed to Hitler and his policies. Citizens thus had no role in policy formation—only an opportunity to acclaim their leader and certain of his more popular policies. The regime, though, touted such acclamation as across-the-board support for Hitler and all his policies.[6]

Nazi jurists asserted that Hitler could impose any policy he chose and that his absolute power was the constitution (cf. jurist Dr. Hans Frank: "Our constitution is the will of the *Führer*"). Nonetheless, in practice, historians agree, the regime was a polycracy—a system in which multiple power centers competed for authority under Hitler's overarching, but not-always-exercised, rule. Although Hitler could get his way on any issue he chose, he lacked the will and perhaps the ability to undertake the systematic work necessary to be aware of, let alone control, the multiplicity of issues facing the government of a complex modern society. So he left most issues to be hashed out among his subordinates, generally signing off on any consensus position, ordering his subordinates to keep talking to one another if they had no consensus, and only intervening if absolutely necessary. He also frequently created special offices for specific issues, adding to the congeries of authorities pursuing their own policies. Hitler may have deliberately created this competition, perhaps seeing a Social Darwinist advantage or opportunities to divide and conquer, though both possibilities remain debated. The result was clearly a massive degree of inefficiency, with very negative consequences. For example, Albert Speer, the Armaments Minister, was never able to secure effective control over labor in the war economy, as Labor Plenipotentiary Fritz Sauckel, various Gauleiter (regional leaders), and Josef Goebbels as Plenipotentiary for Total War diverted workers according to their priorities, leading to gross inefficiencies in war production. Crucially, it did not prevent Hitler from establishing policy on issues he most cared about—rearmament, the Holocaust, foreign policy, military affairs.[7]

Defining the *Volksgemeinschaft*

On February 3, 1933, Hitler assured military leaders that he would carry through the "strictest leadership, elimination of the cancer of democracy." Nonetheless, for all Hitler's private contempt for democracy, his regime and its supporters implicitly embraced "democracy" by presenting him as a true representative of the popular will. Parliamentary democracy, they argued, could represent only a multiplicity of interests and never the people. Adolf Hitler, they asserted, embodied and expressed the interests and will of the people as a whole (implicitly excluding Jews, Gypsies, unreconstructed Marxists, and other "enemies of the people"). Hitler characterized himself as representing "true democracy," "German democracy." And appealing to successful plebiscites, he declared, "My pride is that I know no statesman in the whole world who with greater right than I can say that he is the representative of his people." Such apologia for an arbitrary and brutal dictatorship reflect the need in the twentieth century to legitimate rule through an appeal to the people. They also reflected the widely shared repudiation of parliamentary democracy by interwar Germans.[8]

Before they seized power, the Nazis had promoted racial community in general; in power they emphasized the specific term *Volksgemeinschaft*. For the Nazis, only race could serve as the basis of a community and a *demos*, and for Germany it must be the Aryan race. Race also served as the basis of morality. Nazism rejected the existence of universal moral laws—morality was whatever helped the race.[9]

In the infamous Nuremberg Laws of 1935, the Nazis aligned the formal legal structures of citizenship, and the substance of the *demos*, with their conceptions of the "race." They prescribed that a *Reichsbürger* (German citizen) could only be someone of Aryan or related blood; people of other "races," most notably Jewish but also African, Asian, et al., could not be citizens and did not enjoy the "rights" of citizens. The laws also forbade marriage or sexual intercourse outside marriage between a German (or individuals of related blood) and Jews et al. Aryans were those who were ethnically German, though the Nazis had problems determining who exactly that meant. Similarly, the laws did not define "Jews" because the regime could not agree quickly enough on the appropriate criteria. Only after months of sharp debates among the Interior Ministry, SS, Party, and Hitler could Hitler issue decrees that established complex definitions of Jews of various "degrees"—and because the Nazis' racist assumptions were so divorced from reality, those definitions depended ultimately on religious, *not* racial, heritage. Notably, the Nuremberg laws also reserved citizenship for those whose *Verhalten* (behavior, attitude) showed that they were willing and able to be loyal to the German people (or, rather, to Nazi conceptions thereof). The regime defined various individuals as *gemeinschaftsfremd* (alien to the community) on racial, political, and social grounds, including "asocial" behavior, and denied them the protections loyal citizens could expect. Needing women's support for the regime and its policies, the Nazis did accord German women citizenship, including the suffrage. That did not mean equality as citizens for women, whose role was to be child bearers and homemakers.[10]

Michael Wildt argues that "the *Volksgemeinschaft* was produced above all by sharply and violently drawing boundaries—that is, by exclusion." And the Nazis did work diligently to exclude the *gemeinschaftsfremd* (Jews especially) with various forms of discrimination. Wildt sees the vitriol the Nazis aimed at outsiders as more important for creating a sense of community than the positive attributes the Nazis ascribed to the *Volksgemeinschaft*. That seems too strong an argument, as the Nazis worked assiduously to build on existing German notions of ethnic, cultural, and racial inclusiveness. And most Germans did develop enormous pride in their identity as members of a pure and powerful *Volksgemeinschaft*, especially as the victories flowed in from 1938 to 1941. And they did so even in areas with no Jewish presence. Both exclusion (racial and social) and inclusion played significant roles in establishing the *Volksgemeinschaft*.[11]

Creating Consent within the *Volksgemeinschaft*

The Nazi *Volksgemeinschaft* offered a mix of unity and hierarchy that many Germans found attractive or at least acceptable. Many Germans had long deplored the social divisiveness that parliaments revealed or, many thought, fostered. Germans repeatedly touted, into the 1940s, the "Spirit of 1914," the extraordinary sense of national unity that the First World War's outbreak elicited among many Germans and that they believed had prevailed during the war. Moreover, many Germans expected and some even wanted another war and desperately hoped for a social unity that would guarantee German victory next time. The *Volksgemeinschaft* promised that desired unity and an end to social divisiveness, not least by freeing German workers from Marxism and allowing their re-incorporation into the community. Crucially, the Nazi *Volksgemeinschaft* would guarantee both equality of all Germans qua Germans and a social hierarchy based on individual Germans' varying merits. The Nazis saw Germans as superior to non-Germans but some Germans as inherently superior to other Germans. Yet they emphasized the "honor" of all working Germans and presented the community as an organic whole in which members had different functions of varying importance but in which each had a meaningful role. The successful could then expect their success to be rewarded, while the relatively unsuccessful could still feel that they would be honored for whatever contribution they made to the community—and would be superior to any alien Other.[12]

Similarly, because many Germans in the Weimar Republic had vehemently objected to parliamentarianism's putative promotion of "egoistical" private interests above the common good, they could embrace the *Volksgemeinschaft*'s central principle that the common good must outweigh self-benefiting. The Nazis presented service to the *Volk* as the highest ethical command. This meant that duties had precedence over rights, for example, private property rights might have to give way to one's duty to sacrifice for the Fatherland. Moreover, the Nazis promoted performance for the community as honorable and deserving of reward, and individual Germans often perceived their own interests as serving the higher good of the community. So they could see such a "performance community" as a better guarantor of their position than a parliamentary "democracy" in which economic leverage and mere numbers would predominate.[13]

Historians have presented considerable evidence that many Germans accepted the Nazi claim that the regime had created a *Volksgemeinschaft*—or that it would do so in future. Certain aspects of the Third Reich could contribute to a perception that the Nazis were delivering on their promise. The Nazis' emphasis on hierarchy alongside the value and honor of all honest work for the community led, Norbert Frei has argued, to a certain "uncoupling of income and social status." Many working and lower-middle-class Germans appreciated the respect that the regime showed them for their contributions to the community, greater respect than the society had shown before 1933. The Nazis offered some individuals opportunities for social mobility, either through piecework rates that rewarded the efficient or through new career paths or voluntary leadership positions in Nazi organizations for individuals from modest backgrounds. The regime also sought to bind citizens to the movement through less tangible offerings, such as an aestheticization of politics (e.g., the Nuremberg party rallies, torchlight parades) and the new leisure opportunities in "Strength through Joy" programs. Moreover, as John Connelly and others have pointed out, individual Germans instrumentalized the *Volksgemeinschaft* to help them secure personal advantages from the regime—e.g., better housing.[14]

Some scholars have insisted that the Nazis had neither created a *Volksgemeinschaft* nor convinced Germans that one existed. Detlef Peukert dismissed it as "primarily a façade." Tim Mason saw evidence of workers' dissatisfaction and their rejection of the Nazis' claims for community, such as ballot spoiling in elections for works councils and systematic efforts to circumvent Nazi constraints on their workplace bargaining rights. Ian Kershaw sees evidence of various forms of "disillusionment and discontent" in Nazi and SPD reports on popular opinion as revealing the "propaganda varnish of the 'National Community.'" These scholars point to evidence from many Germans of often intense antipathy to the Third Reich that could reflect a repudiation of the notion of any organic community or of the Nazi claim to have created one.[15]

Three points need to be made to understand these conflicting interpretations. First, individual Germans could embrace some aspects of Nazi rule and dislike or deplore others (e.g., welcoming the elimination of a Jewish competitor while complaining about wartime shortages). Second, attitudes could change over time. Economic recovery and early victories made some Germans more receptive to Nazism; war's burdens and looming defeat raised serious doubts for some Germans; direct experience of Nazi terror, for oneself or a relative or friend, embittered some. Third, clearly many Germans accepted the Nazis' claim to have created or to be creating a *Volksgemeinschaft*, even if others did not. The Nazis did *not* create a true community. Nonetheless, and crucially, they did convince enough Germans that they had or that they would once victory had been won that they secured sufficient popular support to maintain power for a dozen years without any significant challenge and to fight a major war for nearly six painful years.[16]

The Third Reich's political culture was not purely collectivistic but included individualistic elements. The Nazis, as Social Darwinists, embraced individual initiative and achievement—so long as it benefited the *Volksgemeinschaft*. They believed that some Germans were better than others and that individuals should be recognized and rewarded according to how well they did their job and what they contributed to the community. They hoped to use competition within the community to maximize efficiency and effectiveness. So they often emphasized piecework and other incentives in ways that allowed individuals to pursue their self-interest. As Moritz Föllmer has argued, the Nazi regime was also willing to allow "legitimate" self-expression and self-development, that is, so long as they accorded with the *Volksgemeinschaft*'s interests. Significantly, individual Germans often embraced the possibilities that the new regime offered, seeking to bend its policies, institutions, and preferences to serve their individual desires. Individual Germans' political culture was often much more individualistic and self-interested than the official one. Nazi Germany was certainly not a realm of "do your own thing," but its citizens were not all cogs in a machine.[17]

Although many Germans accepted or embraced various aspects of Nazi rule, violence was indispensable to its seizure and maintenance of power. After January 1933, thousands of Communists and other Leftists were incarcerated, Communist Reichstag deputies were arrested or driven underground or into exile, and other deputies were intimidated in the run-up to the passage of the Enabling Act. And violence played a continuing role as the regime consolidated its power in spring 1933. SA and party members forced their way into government offices, seizing control and expelling unwanted officials. Crucially, as Hermann Beck has shown, once the Enabling Act empowered Hitler, the Nazis turned on their conservative allies, with hundreds joining Communists, Social Democrats, liberals, and Catholics in facing Nazi repression. The SA set up dozens of concentration camps, arbitrarily seized and incarcerated opponents, and brutalized them. Some were murdered; most were released. Admonished not to reveal details of their treatment, they revealed enough to make clear to Germans that challenging the regime could bring down horrific punishment. And the concentration camps and arbitrary jurisprudence remained until the regime's collapse.[18]

A powerful force for cementing Nazi rule was *Gleichschaltung*, that is, forcing all organizations in Germany either to dissolve or to come under Nazi control. Most important was the elimination of non-Nazi political parties. All the other parties were banned or dissolved themselves by mid-1933, and a July 14, 1933, law then banned the formation of any but the Nazi Party. The trade unions were abolished in May and June 1933 and replaced by the German Labor Front, a Nazi creation and tool. The destruction of working-class clubs destroyed much of the basis for connections among workers. Many other organizations engaged in self-*Gleichschaltung*. In some cases, the organizations already or soon had Nazi majorities; in others they avoided take-over or dissolution by electing Nazis to key leadership positions; in still others key leaders joined the Nazi Party. In other cases, the Nazis dissolved organizations, forcibly amalgamated them to Nazi organizations, or imposed Nazi leaders. However, the Nazi effort to take over the Lutheran churches in Germany failed, so that by summer 1933 the only remaining openly non- (though not usually anti-!) Nazi organizations in Germany were religious. At least some organizations were, however, only nominally *gleichgeschaltet*, as members sought to preserve a group's existence while outwardly conforming to Nazi expectations. Nonetheless, by mid-1933, Germany lacked a civil society of autonomous organizations in which and through which individuals could develop and express political views.[19]

The Third Reich's economic, foreign-policy, and military successes were indispensable to its survival. The party began its rise in 1929 in rural areas suffering from agricultural depression. It expanded in the early 1930s because of its (vague) promises to deal with the depression and to reverse the Versailles Treaty. Germans, including powerful groups such as industry and the military, accepted Nazi rule because they expected it to deliver. And it did deliver, in the medium term. The regime implemented reflationary monetary and fiscal policies that the business and financial communities had blocked under democratic governance, so that by 1936 Germany had secured full employment. Weekly real wages had also recovered by 1937/38. For workers, Norbert Frei wrote, "the regaining of secure existence soon weighed more heavily than the preceding loss of political rights." Most Germans enthusiastically welcomed Hitler's peaceful foreign-policy successes, from 1936 to March 1939. Germans were apprehensive about war in 1939, but stunning military successes, from 1939 to 1941, generated solid support. Moreover, Hitler feared home-front support could collapse if German civilians suffered as they had in the First World War, so he insisted on maintaining consumer goods production into 1942 and beyond, to secure the popular engagement necessary for victory. Growing apprehensions after 1942 would drive a new dynamic (see below), but a decade of substantive successes provided a solid base for support for the regime, successes the Weimar Republic had never enjoyed.[20]

Despite the psychological and material developments promoting support for the regime, citizens frequently held political views that departed from Nazi ideology. For instance, the Nazi regime embraced a mixture of Social Darwinism, violence, and eugenics. Hitler and the Nazis insisted that life was a struggle in which only the fittest would survive; hence, conflict and violence were what Nature demanded. They were also convinced that modern society prevented the proper operation of "natural" selection. That made eugenics necessary, including incentives for "racially fit" families to reproduce, forced sterilization for the "unfit," and eugenic murder to eliminate the unproductive or dangerous from the community. Most Germans, however, seem to have rejected open violence within German society (albeit perhaps primarily because of the destruction of property and the disorderliness it involved) and even the hidden violence of eugenic murder.[21]

Nazi antisemitism met a very mixed reaction among Germans—but one in which a deadly quiescence ultimately prevailed. Most Germans initially found the repeated SA boycotts of Jewish businesses, let alone their violence against Jews, repugnant; by the late 1930s years of Nazi propaganda had convinced most Germans that excluding Jews from German society was the proper policy (especially Germans who could benefit by eliminating Jewish competitors or securing Jewish property at bargain-basement prices). Germans still found destructive and disorderly violence repugnant, and some Germans continued to criticize persecution into the war years. Most, though, chose to look away, even during the war years when most Germans knew that mass violence against civilians was rife and that "horrible things" were happening in the East. Soldiers on leave reported on mass shootings of Jews and vicious reprisals against Soviet citizens, and at least some Germans knew, through rumors, of mass murder by poison gas. Still, even the Confessing Churches, which opposed the Nazis, failed to speak out on the fate of the Jews. Hitler knew he had to keep the Holocaust secret, at least officially, since so long as Germans did not have to confront it openly, they would allow it to happen. Quiescence was all Hitler needed.[22]

If most Germans generally never fully bought the Nazis' vicious antisemitism, broad segments of the population remained vehemently anti-Marxist. The Nazis got enormous credit for having apparently "solved" the problem of Marxism so quickly in early 1933, by crushing the Communist Party, SPD, and trade unions. Members of the peasantry and the urban lower-middle classes were often dissatisfied with specific Third Reich policies (e.g., increasing regulations, wartime shortages), but most continued to support the regime as a bulwark against any Marxist revival. The Christian Churches would face a degree of Nazi persecution, but they, too, supported the Third Reich as a bulwark against Bolshevism. Once Hitler had invaded the Soviet Union, most Germans would enthusiastically support the regime to "protect Europe from Bolshevism."[23]

A desire for order and authority remained a powerful factor in many Germans' political attitudes. The Nazis had been responsible for much of the street violence that created an aura of disorder in the late Weimar Republic, but they had successfully blamed most of it on the Communists. And once in power, they eliminated public brawling by crushing the Communists and other opposition. They also reduced many other instances of "disorder," such as non-conformity and indiscipline. They made it clear that firm, indeed "harsh," measures were being used to restore order, but kept violence and harsh measures mostly out of sight in concentration camps and prisons. Hence, Germans could very often welcome Nazi terror when it was directed against "aliens" such as homosexuals or "asocials" or Jews—and they did not have to look at it. Crucially, as Robert Gellately points out, "'Good citizens' were unlikely to be faced by the prospect of a stay in a concentration camp." Furthermore, the Nazis claimed, falsely, to have more or less ended crime. Indeed, older Germans often continued into the 1970s to remember, approvingly, the Third Reich as a state that at least maintained order.[24]

Conscience is a fraught subject for the Third Reich. Claudia Koonz chose a provocative book title, *The Nazi Conscience*, as she elucidated how so many Germans could have cooperated in the horrific policies the Third Reich implemented. "In order to function efficiently," she writes, "perpetrators need to maintain a moral self in the face of staggering crime." So, she argues, the regime claimed to establish a new, a true, moral order, one rooted in race, eugenics, and Social Darwinism. The regime devoted massive resources to teaching Germans, explicitly or implicitly, that conscience required obedience to one's *Führer*, the predominance of community over individual interests, and a commitment to a Social Darwinistic struggle on behalf of the racial purity and predominance of one's race. Eugenic murder, aggressive war, and the Holocaust could then seem not just acceptable but "right." Yet those not seduced by the Nazis' pretense found it difficult to act according to their consciences. As Michael Geyer and John Boyer point out, for Germans in the Third Reich, "the difficulties of thinking politics in the first place were and remained major obstacles." Some Germans did act according to conscience, to protect Jews and to attempt to overthrow Hitler, but most would find it impossible to think outside the box that their culture and their *Führer* had constructed—at least not enough to risk potentially dangerous action.[25]

What Ian Kershaw calls the "Hitler Myth" was crucial for the regime's functioning and survival. Germans often ascribed to Hitler all the good things that happened in the Third Reich, while they ascribed the bad things to the party hacks below him. Propaganda Minister Josef Goebbels devoted enormous effort to promoting the myth of the good Hitler, as the greatest leader in human history, who devoted himself wholly, at the sacrifice of personal pleasure, to the prosperity and greatness of the German people. Goebbels did not devote similar efforts to promoting the Nazi Party and its officials, and Kershaw suggests that Hitler benefited from the disdain most Germans felt toward his subordinates. Hence, Germans often reassured themselves that the *Führer* would protect Germany and them and that when anything went wrong, "if the *Führer* only knew," he would fix it. Hitler also functioned as the symbol of unity of the German people, despite the egoistical interests that Germans often encountered among individual Nazis. Evidence of widespread doubts about his leadership only began to appear in the second half of the war (see below), but even in early 1945 many Germans still reassured themselves that the *Führer* would somehow win through. Such unquestioning support for Hitler meant that most Germans could support the Third Reich even if they had serious reservations about specific policies.[26]

No opinion surveys are available for the Third Reich, but scholars studying a range of sources are in broad agreement that most Germans supported the regime, from 1933 until nearly the bitter end. To some degree this reflected fear, with terror and consent inextricably intermixed. Germans knew that the Gestapo could and would incarcerate, brutalize, and perhaps kill open dissidents. Yet most Germans seem not to have feared that they would experience such a fate. Rather, most Germans seem to have approved of some or all of the regime's results, whether crushing the labor movement, securing full employment, promoting a *Volksgemeinschaft*, overthrowing the Versailles Treaty, or winning unprecedented victories. And many perceived concrete advantages for themselves.[27]

Germans' reactions in 1944/45 were mixed, but most Germans, especially soldiers, remained sufficiently committed to the regime to enable Germany to fight until total defeat. While ideological support for the regime and Nazism remained the crucial force among some Germans, increasing disaffection from the party and even from Hitler developed after the defeat at Stalingrad. Despite occasional resurgences, as when the regime promised secret weapons or in reaction to the assassination attempt against Hitler, popular support for the regime was increasingly fragile. One reflection of this was the enormous rise after 1942 in terror as a tool for maintaining control. Yet terror alone does not explain the level of commitment. Germans did remain nationalistic and committed to a *Volksgemeinschaft*, and they did have trouble envisioning an alternative to the Third Reich (and very few could imagine returning to the Weimar Republic). The primary motive for fighting on, though, seems to have been absolute terror at the prospect of defeat. Desperate fears of Bolshevism had been a major reason for Nazi electoral successes and regime popularity. Crucially, Germans, and soldiers above all, knew that Germany had engaged in an unprecedentedly brutal, criminal war against other peoples, especially Jews. Many remained convinced by the Nazi claim that the Jews controlled the Soviet Union and the United States and would dictate postwar policy. Soldiers and civilians feared that they and fellow Germans would be subject to the same terror and devastation that they had inflicted on others. That fear kept them fighting long past any reasonable prospect of avoiding defeat.[28]

Political Engagement and Disengagement

Germans acted as political citizens during the Third Reich. They mostly did so in support of the regime—or at least in compliance with it. Yet most of them sooner or later acted against its prescriptions.

Citizens engaged with the regime by voting in referenda, to approve or reject certain proposals or candidate slates proposed by Hitler. The referenda (even the internationally supervised and free 1935 plebiscite in the Saar on reunion with Germany) produced more than 80 and 90 percent votes for Hitler's position and implicitly for him. It took courage and conviction to vote against Hitler in the context of massive regime propaganda, carefully crafted questions about popular policy outcomes (such as the merger with Austria), and doubts about how secret the elections were. Yet those massive reported numbers still showed substantial, almost certainly much greater than 50 percent, support for Hitler and his regime, giving him significant legitimacy as Germany's ruler.[29]

The Third Reich is famous for its aestheticization and careful orchestration (*Inszenierung*) of politics, to maximize Nazi control; citizen participation was crucial to the processes. Most famous was the carefully staged annual party rally in Nuremberg. The Nazis created an elaborate physical infrastructure, but at the base of each rally were the crowds of enthusiastic Germans, demonstrating their support for Adolf Hitler and the regime. Those crowds were all more or less volunteers. Other public demonstrations that the regime staged over its twelve-year rule could include enthusiastic supporters, but many citizens were more or less dragooned into participation. For example, employees and employers, the "working folk," were all expected to attend the Nazis' May Day, whether they wanted to or not; they were generally marched from their workplace to the demonstration site (albeit some ducked out at the first opportunity).[30]

Beyond that were innumerable other larger or smaller public events that Germans were pressured to attend—from Hitler's birthday parades to party rallies before elections and plebiscites to Nazi staging of traditional celebrations to wartime marches asserting German determination versus its enemies. In every fest, popular participation was a central element and an implicit statement of support for Hitler, the Third Reich, and Nazi values and policies. The fests did become more orchestrated and centrally directed and less attractive. And Jean-Christoph Caron has emphasized that the compulsion to attend, to fly the Nazi flag, to honor Nazi speakers could all be felt as *Gewalt*, as an exercise of force against the citizen. Some participated unwillingly, but for many the fests were, as Joan L. Clinefelter points out, "experienced as proof that the *Volksgemeinschaft* had been realized." The fests were, though, about the inclusion of all good Germans and the exclusion of "aliens." They constituted political citizenship, but merely as acclamation. Participants were not to express personal views about specific issues, and certainly not to dissent, but simply to affirm publicly their support for Hitler, the regime, and its policies—whatever they may have thought privately.[31]

For the Nazi leaders, popular participation meant male and female participation—though on different terms. Hitler and Nazi leaders were committed to ideas of male superiority and male bonding. Hitler insisted, for example, that women's primary task was the bearing and rearing of children and that they must not participate in "politics" in any form because it was "unworthy" of them. Yet because the Nazis blamed Germany's First World War defeat on the home front, which had been disproportionately female, they were convinced that they must mobilize women to the same degree as men, if in different tasks. Women did not necessarily welcome this mobilization. For example, religious women retreated from initial support for the regime; during the war, many women refused urgings to take up war work and those who did were often less productive than female slave laborers.[32]

That emphasis on mobilizing women meant opportunities for women, as well as the constraints that Nazi male chauvinism entailed. The Nazis did introduce policies that limited women's options, such as firing female civil servants married to employed males and barring women from various occupations. Nonetheless, the regime provided women with innumerable opportunities for paid work and volunteer social and, in practice, political action. Germany had long had a higher female participation rate in paid work than either Britain or the United States. The Nazi rearmament boom meant a labor shortage that offered employment opportunities for women and a degree of upward mobility, as many could move to more highly paid blue-collar or to white-collar jobs. Some women used the ability to denounce others to the Gestapo to try to change power relationships within the family and the community. Nazi women's and social welfare organizations offered many leadership roles, and during the war women often had to take on formerly male tasks because the men were off at the front. Women gained prestige and often considerable self-confidence as a result. In some cases—e.g., women who helped settle Germans in traditionally Polish areas (by expelling the Catholic and Jewish Poles)—they became complicit in Nazi atrocities. Women were acting as agents, often on their own behalf, as in employment decisions and even in volunteering for Nazi projects. Yet much of their autonomous activity was predicated on their acting in accord with male leaders' Nazi policy goals.[33]

The Nazis demanded full engagement from all Aryans, but many Germans withdrew into private life, to a greater or lesser degree. The Nazis demanded a very high intensity of commitment, of fulfilling "duties." Some Germans found these demands abhorrent, but for many others they were simply overwhelming. So scholars frequently point to a withdrawal into the private sphere or into niches separate from the officially exalted community and communal culture. None seek to quantify the phenomenon, reflecting the impossibility of doing so. Yet evidence is available, for example, avoidance of official ceremonials, preference for non-political films. This kind of retreat challenged the Nazi's preferred political culture of mass citizen mobilization and engagement. Yet it was seldom a form of resistance but rather an accommodation that proved system-stabilizing because it generally ended in a defensive self-absorption.[34]

A characteristic form of political citizenship in Nazi Germany was the denunciation. The regime considered it a duty for citizens to report crimes, including thought crimes, to the authorities, usually to the Gestapo but also to other party and state agencies. The regime never made this a legal requirement, because the Gestapo was flooded with (often false) denunciations (though only a small minority ever denounced anyone) and because of fears of damage to social cohesion from compulsory denunciation. Some Nazi laws, for example, against sexual intercourse between Aryan and non-Aryan, against friendly relations between Jews and non-Jews, or against listening to foreign radio, could only be enforced with the aid of denunciations. The Gestapo had some informants, but to keep track of the society they never needed to *compel* large numbers of citizens to become informants—unlike the DDR's Stasi (see Chapter 6). Scholars who have studied denunciations agree that perhaps only a quarter were motivated by political or ideological commitment. Instead, most denouncers instrumentalized the denunciation to aid them in pursuing private goals such as divorce, eliminating a competitor, or gaining revenge for a personal slight. Instrumentalization reflected both a degree of agency and self-assertion and an attempt to use the political system to gain personal ends.[35]

Denunciation in the Third Reich was morally fraught. It usually involved betraying a personal relationship (as denunciations by strangers were very infrequent). It could involve spouses and in-laws (though seldom, if ever, child and parent). The *c.* 75 percent of denunciations that seem to have been for private reasons (except perhaps to get the authorities to take seriously a case of sexual assault) seem unequivocally morally deplorable, a recruitment of state power to crush another human being. The regime saw denunciations for political reasons as admirable political citizenship because they advanced the needs of the *Volksgemeinschaft*, which predominated over any individual need, right, or relationship. Yet they were also instances of individual agency and individual political participation. Moreover, in any state, citizens are expected to assist the authorities by identifying lawbreakers. One could argue, as Gisela Diewald-Kerkmann suggests, that denunciation in a Rechtsstaat is not inherently inhuman because the denounced person should secure due process and because the laws are putatively just and legitimate. In Nazi Germany, however, denouncers delivered an individual up to an arbitrary, barbarous regime—and knew they were doing so. Even if denouncers thought they were acting in accord with the popular will and in the interests of the *Volksgemeinschaft*, absent legal protections for the accused, the denouncers scarcely seem to be acting democratically.[36]

Most civilians in the Third Reich acted in ways of which the regime disapproved—but that did not mean all were resisters. By 1944/45 only black market activities could keep a "normal consumer" nourished, and most Germans on the home front did what they needed to do to stave off malnutrition for themselves and their families. Many listened to foreign radio stations. Relatives of German POWs held by the Soviets shared Soviet leaflets with, and listened to Soviet radio broadcasts announcing, the names of POWs. Some criticized the regime, even publicly. Strikingly, some took real risks to help hide Jews (with a network of perhaps twenty people needed to hide one Jew) and to provide food and other aid to foreign workers. Historians generally agree on limiting "*Widerstand* (resistance)" to actions that aimed at the regime's overthrow and entailed risk to one's life or freedom. They debate sharply about exactly how to characterize less perilous activities. They generally agree in seeing a range of activities from non-compliance to refusal to dissent/opposition to resistance. Some do not see actions driven by private interests or single-issue criticisms as opposition to the regime, while others see as meaningful only actions that were in some sense successful or effective. However, in any regime individuals often use the political system for private ends; they often have mixed motives and mixed attitudes toward politics; and they may or may not be successful. So to capture the range of political agency, political action under Nazism seems best seen as both actions intended to have political effects and those that, independent of intent, supported or challenged the regime's political goals or norms.[37]

Faced with a new social and moral order, Germans worked to come to terms with it, to adjust their attitudes and behavior to new circumstances, completely or partially. They could, however, pick and choose. Nazism could not in practice control every one of every Germans' activities. Individual Germans could try to swallow the system whole, or they could, and more usually did, embrace some aspects and ignore or even reject others. Teachers, for example, found that if they kept a low profile, they could emphasize some and de-emphasize other aspects of the curriculum. Farmers, craftsmen, and shopkeepers could embrace nationalism, economic recovery, and the idea of a *Volksgemeinschaft* even while bitterly attacking—and perhaps disobeying—specific Nazi economic regulations. Most Christians could tell themselves Christianity and Nazism were broadly compatible, especially given the perceived Nazi role as necessary bulwark against Bolshevism. However, increased attendance at Catholic religious processions could constitute "demonstration Catholicism" and the Confessing Church rejected Nazi pretensions; both were assertions of Christian faith against Nazi interventions in religious life. Individuals could be visibly compliant in some ways to divert attention from their non-compliance, or even rejection, in other areas. The norm, then, was neither submission nor resistance but a mix of approval, indifference, and rejection.[38]

Petitions were commonplace in the Third Reich and were in some senses political. Usually, individuals wrote to powerful figures seeking assistance for personal problems—e.g., getting better housing. And John Connelly notes that if a local leader denied their petition, citizens could feel sufficient impunity as members of the *Volksgemeinschaft* to appeal to the leader's superior. Notably, Nazi efforts to remove crucifixes from classrooms and to remove an insufficiently cooperative Protestant bishop generated floods of telegrams, letters, and (unusually, sometimes collective) petitions, with political intent and consequences. They helped compel the regime to change its policy, as it restored the crucifixes and the bishop. An individual petition could also have political consequences. Hitler's private chancellery had received petitions from parents of children with congenital birth defects, asking permission to have the child killed. In August 1939 he responded to such an appeal from the Knauer parents by ordering the initiation of a program of eugenic murder that would claim over 200,000 victims. While some would hesitate to characterize requests for individual housing assistance as "politics," others would see them as such. And petitions are certainly political if they seek broader policy changes—or initiate them.[39]

Non-conformity was everywhere in the Third Reich, but it could be political and without substantive consequences. The Nazis' determination to create a total state and completely unified *Volksgemeinschaft* failed. Germans undertook an enormous range of actions that the regime criminalized, anathematized, or at least disdained. For example, the number of Germans offering the Hitler greeting and their rigor in doing so did fluctuate, both over time and in reaction to specific issues, such as the removal of crucifixes. The regime saw it as a crucial sign of support for the Third Reich and of national unity, so to refuse to give it vigorously was a political statement. Yet the growing refusals did not have substantive effects. Listening to foreign broadcasts and telling anti-Nazi jokes were both illegal and ubiquitous—and they could get you incarcerated in a concentration camp or even executed. Yet most Germans, if caught telling such jokes, got away with a warning. And telling jokes might be system-stabilizing, as they could act as a safety valve for frustrations and were usually focused, fatalistically, on human weaknesses. The Nazis expected the Hitler Youth to dominate youth free time and fully socialize them in National Socialism. Yet youth increasingly evaded membership or at least attendance. Moreover, the appearance of youth groups who clearly rejected Nazi values and controls showed the limits to Nazi socialization and was perhaps dangerous for the future, albeit its immediate consequences were few.[40]

Other forms of non-compliance by citizens were more consequential and arguably political. In elections to workplace consultative councils, about one-third of workers refused to approve the Nazis' proposed list of representatives, a rebuke to the regime. To manage the economic pressures arising from forced-pace rearmament, the Nazis imposed controls on workers and their compensation. The workers sought to evade these restrictions, sometimes with the connivance of their employers (who needed to attract and keep good and skilled workers and did not want to attract Gestapo attention). Such efforts occasionally involved collective action, including some minor strikes, but usually involved changing jobs or other individual actions. Instances of malingering also increased significantly during the war. The regime never compelled women to enter the factories, though it urged them to do so. Many women, especially soldiers' wives and middle- and upper-class women, refused. German women were also less productive than female foreign slave laborers who were dying on starvation rations (though that may partially reflect higher absenteeism among German women who had to attend to their families amid desperate wartime difficulties). German male workers, especially youths, were also accused of unjustified absenteeism and indiscipline. These behaviors were arguably not consciously political, but rather attempts to advance private interests. Yet they had political consequences in that they cut against the regime's efforts to hold down rearmament costs and maximize output.[41]

The Nazis had criminalized criticism of the regime or the party, yet criticism flourished. Crucially, much of it was arguably "grumbling"—expressions of dissatisfaction that can be made against any institution by those subject to its vagaries, without necessarily constituting any fundamental threat to the institution. Germans, even fanatical Nazis, certainly were willing to gripe, usually privately but occasionally publicly. In principle, the regime could find much of such grumbling "political" and subject to prosecution. In practice, it was not a fundamental threat and may have served as a safety valve. Other forms of criticism were more clearly political in that they were aimed at the system and its functioning. For example, Wolf Gruner has identified in police records numerous instances of non-Jewish Germans criticizing persecution of the Jews, as well as of Jewish Germans defying Nazi measures and openly criticizing the regime, its policies, and even Hitler.[42]

Crucially, most such political criticism was aimed at the party or party officials, their luxury, corruption, and inefficiency—but not at Adolf Hitler. Individuals could express real bitterness toward the party hacks, the "little Hitlers," while continuing to support the regime and its goals out of a deep commitment to Adolf Hitler and his leadership. Only toward the end of the war did criticism of Hitler begin to surface, and he retained substantial support, especially in the military, until the end. Criticism could have substantive consequences. For example, the regime introduced draconian regulations on workers in early September 1939, to support the war economy, but popular unrest led it to withdraw many of them. Such criticism could not constitute a fundamental threat because it focused on specific elements of regime policy and never offered a coherent moral and political alternative.[43]

Public Protest

Historians often talk of "refusal" or "opposition" to refer to actions that moved beyond verbal criticism to open activism versus Nazi policy—e.g., demonstrations and strikes. The Nazis had banned demonstrations in early 1933. So public protests were unusual but not unknown in the Third Reich. For example, a few demonstrated publicly in sympathy with eugenic murder victims. A small demonstration protested an antisemitic Swedish film shown in 1935. Wives of men conscripted to be sent off to help build the defensive Siegfried Line along the French border demonstrated at the train station. Occasionally, strikes broke out as well, with Tim Mason citing a list of 192 strikes from February 1936 to July 1937. Such open efforts at affecting opinion, though, quickly drew massive repression.[44]

Among the most successful instances of open opposition were campaigns of petitions, street demonstrations, and school strikes by Protestants and Catholics against Nazi attacks on the churches' social position. Hitler and some Nazi leaders were deeply committed to replacing Christianity with Nazism as Germans' dominant ideology. Hitler, though, sought to postpone open conflicts with the churches because his wars needed religious believers' support. Nonetheless, local Nazis in Oldenburg and Bavaria sought to remove crucifixes from school classrooms, replacing them with pictures of Hitler, and to remove a Protestant bishop who had resisted certain Nazi measures on religious grounds (even while supporting the regime). The open opposition by committed Christians moved to open protests; it led Hitler to restore the bishop to office and to have the crucifixes rehung. Some Christians, notably Archbishop Galen, openly attacked the Nazis' eugenic murder campaign. Needing Christians' support for the war effort, Hitler suspended the official eugenic murder campaign—but eugenic murders continued sub rosa, and in greater numbers, until *after* the regime's demise. Scholars have emphasized that Christians openly opposed the regime only when churches' institutional interests were directly affected, for example, in controlling property and some aspects of education or in being co-opted into morally fraught eugenic policies (as administrators of old-age homes or hospitals). Individual priests and ministers often came into conflict with the regime, and perhaps one-third of Catholic priests were incarcerated for shorter or longer periods by the Gestapo. Some Catholic and Protestant bishops did send letters of protest to Hitler about the Holocaust, and Catholic bishops had a letter read from pulpits in 1943 rejecting the killing of innocents (which could mean German victims of Allied bombing rather than Jewish or other victims of Nazism). However, the churches followed the Biblical prescription, "Obey the magistrates; they are ordained by God." They did not protest the continued unofficial eugenic murders nor did they protest publicly the extermination of the Jews. And the churches, deeply fearful of Bolshevism, remained generally strongly supportive of the regime and its foreign policy. Open opposition in Nazi Germany usually required a strong institutional base (the churches) and a sense that one's own crucial interests were being directly affected, and it seldom involved direct attack on the regime or its main priorities.[45]

On Rosenstraße in mid-Berlin, in early 1943, a six-day protest took place over the deportation of Jewish spouses of Aryan Germans. Goebbels was determined to make Berlin "free of Jews" as a birthday present for the *Führer*. He ordered a round-up of remaining Jews in Berlin, several thousand skilled workers and *c.* two thousand Jewish spouses of Aryans. The wives and husbands learned that the spouses were being held at the Rosenstraße Jewish Community Center. Aryan spouses, apparently mostly the wives (with some children), began assembling outside the Jewish center. Periodically cries would arise from the crowd, "We want our husbands back." Women returned each day. Periodically, the security forces would threaten to machine-gun them, and they would scatter, some crying, "You murderers! To shoot at women!" "You cowards!"— but soon reassemble. Goebbels was fearful about the state of public opinion so soon after the German defeat at Stalingrad; the first massive air raid on Berlin, on March 1, amid the Rosenstraße protests, added to his concern. And the Nazis had always hesitated to deal aggressively with the Jewish spouses for fear of setting off debate among their Aryan relatives about government policies, a concern all the greater now that the Holocaust was in full swing. He hence agreed to release the spouses, and most (though not all!) survived the war. This protest, among the longest and largest in the Third Reich, was successful in its goal, securing the spouses' release.[46]

The Rosenstraße protests are widely admired, but their political status has been debated. As Nathan Stoltzfus points out, if you define resistance as opposition to the regime, as historians often do, the Rosenstraße protests were not resistance because the spouses did not seek fundamental political change or, indeed, an end to the Holocaust. They simply wanted *their* spouses released. One could, he argues, still see single-issue protest such as this as resistance because the demonstrators were acting collectively to attain an end the Nazis saw as political. Moreover, they were implicitly rejecting the Nazi regime as incompatible with the existence of their own families, and they had a broader impact, helping block proposals to introduce mandatory divorce intended for Aryan couples who were infertile. Some have wondered if the Holocaust might have been stopped if Germans had protested against it—and in particular if the Rosenstraße women had done so. Yet fighting for their spouses was dangerous enough in the Third Reich. Moreover, unlike the armed resisters seeking to overthrow the regime, the unarmed women achieved their policy goal.[47] Notably, though, the same concerns arise with political citizenship more generally. Individuals often attempt to change a specific policy for private benefit through the political system. In democratic polities we generally take individuals' efforts to secure economic or other advantages for themselves as political, even if we deplore such private efforts, in principle or in specific cases. So dismissing these women's self-endangerment as non-political because not ambitious enough does seem unreasonable.

Germans did prove capable of significant opposition to one Nazi policy, at risk of their lives. As a convinced Social Darwinist, Hitler apparently really believed that only one master race existed and that all others did not deserve to live. He said in 1942 and 1944/45 that a defeated German people did not deserve to live. He then issued orders in September 1944 and March 1945 for retreating German troops to engage in scorched-earth tactics on German soil that would deprive Germans of the means for future existence. Munitions Minister Albert Speer worked diligently to modify and then sabotage the orders. Some SS and other troops obeyed orders to devastate, but most did not. And German civilians also resisted these orders in their own factories and towns. Moreover, Germans in 1945 often sought to surrender their village, town, or city to the Allies, at the risk of their own lives. So many Germans under Nazism proved capable of standing up to the regime—when their ox was getting gored.[48]

The broadest resistance (organized effort to overthrow the Nazi regime) was in the Communist milieu. Expecting repression, the Communists had in the early 1930s prepared underground cells to defend the workers against any repressive regime. They were convinced that a fascist revolution in Germany would only reveal to Germans the truth of Communism. Conversely, the Nazis, as well as the conservatives in Germany, had long seen the Communists as their most dangerous enemy and were prepared and determined to take them down. Organized Communist resistance involved many Germans and continued into 1935. Much of it consisted of clandestine meetings but also of various propaganda efforts, often at great cost to those caught. The regime, though, went after the Communists systematically and persistently, incarcerating and sometimes killing the activists. Eventually the Nazis succeeded in crushing organized Communist resistance. Nonetheless, scattered Communist resistance, with some broader leadership, did continue until 1945.[49]

Germans have devoted considerable attention to the White Rose, a brave but ultimately futile attempt to challenge the regime and change public opinion. The groups' members were motivated primarily by religious concerns about the regime's brutal policies in the East, against Jews and other peoples. They sought not the regime's violent overthrow but a change in public opinion through the leaflets they wrote, reproduced, and sought to distribute, through the mails and by scattering them from a high floor into the courtyard of the University at Munich. They found little resonance among the populace. The Gestapo soon caught them, and several were executed after closed trials. They had virtually no chance of successfully challenging the regime, given widespread support for Hitler, near universal terror at the prospect of Soviet occupation, and Gestapo ruthlessness. They may have hoped only to make a statement of conscience, and they have served, especially since the 1980s, as a model for Germans and others of courage, decency, and activism in the face of inhumanity.[50]

The resistance with the greatest possibility of success was organized within the military. They had access to weapons—and to Hitler. In 1938, some senior military officers discussed the possibility of a coup against Hitler, but Chamberlain's capitulation at Munich undercut those efforts. Remarkable and resounding German successes, 1939–1941, further solidified Hitler's position. With the tide turning against Germany in 1942, efforts within the military to overthrow the regime, which seemed to mean assassinating Hitler, developed. Those efforts crystalized in "Operation Valkyrie," an effort to assassinate Hitler and establish a military dictatorship. The conspirators' reactionary perspective is remarkable. They imagined that they could negotiate a separate peace with the UK and United States, retain Germany's central and eastern European conquests, and continue the war against the SU. The Weimar Republic and its institutions had been thoroughly discredited, and they had no intention of restoring constitutional democracy. They sought an authoritarian state in which traditional elites would dominate, though they recognized (as they had in 1933 when they supported Hitler) that they would have to secure some sort of (limited!) popular participation in governance. Even if they had succeeded in assassinating Hitler, it is not clear they could have secured the popular support to control the country.[51]

Horizons of Democratic Action

Nazi policies and tactics were not exactly the "democratic tenets" von Hardenberg had had in mind in 1807, but they were related. Like von Hardenberg, the Nazis believed they had to engage the citizens, give them some feeling of participation, and secure their at least nominal approval to ensure political stability and active support when (not if) war broke out. Nazi choices were strongly influenced by that belief, most obviously in Hitler's insistence on maintaining consumer goods production and access for Germans well into the Second World War.

Assessing citizen action in the Third Reich raises difficult questions about what constitutes democratic political action. For example, it was pressure from grassroots activists that forced the Nazi regime to accept a one-day boycott of Jewish businesses on April 1, 1933. In March 1933, groups of SA men were seeking to promote boycotts of Jewish businesses and other steps to isolate Jews, and engaging in violence against them, but Hitler and most of the higher party leadership opposed such measures, since at that time securing power and reviving the economy were their immediate goals. Yet scattered boycotts continued, spurred by grassroots activists. Further grassroots pressure would contribute to the regime's decision to promulgate the Nuremberg Laws in 1935 and would be part of the run-up to the vicious pogrom of November 9, 1938.[52]

If antisemitic activism from below was a form of political citizenship, was it *democratic* political citizenship? To speak of democratic citizenship is to highlight the agency of individual citizens in seeking and securing substantive political changes (as, for example, Belinda Davis does when she characterizes First World War–era food riots as "extra-parliamentary democratic action"). The SA and Nazi Party activists who pressed for discriminatory, often violent, measures against Jews acted on their own initiative to seek, and did ultimately secure, substantive policy changes. So it might seem that they were engaged in extra-parliamentary democratic action. However, one of the central elements in most definitions of democracy is the protection of minority rights and the possibility for a member of a minority to become in future, politically, a member of a majority. The Nazis generally rejected the project of rights, limited what rights they were willing to concede even to members of their racial community, and sought to write many German citizens out of the *demos*, the people. So Nazis' actions arguably could not be democratic, even if grassroots or autonomous.

After 1945 most Germans and non-Germans would argue that the Third Reich was no democracy at all because in practice no individual or party can ever embody the will of the people and because its actions were dictatorial. Hence, the only action under its rule that could be said to be democratic is action that was directed against it or its policies. Nonetheless, people disagree about what constitutes democracy. Many Germans had voted Nazi in the expectation that their regime would be a "true democracy" because they believed Adolf Hitler embodied the will of the people and because he had secured massive yes votes in plebiscites. So from their perspective, if you were acting in accord with Hitler's ideals, on your own initiative, you were acting "democratically."

Germans have participated politically in all manner of ways across the decades—sometimes under compulsion but more often voluntarily. Exploring participation in the Third Reich reveals just how complex citizen reaction to political events could be and how varied modes of participation become when formal avenues of political access are closed. Germans were to a considerable degree supportive of the Nazi regime. The regime did deploy its power to prevent much open political opposition. But it also offered an efficacious alternative (at least in the medium term) to the discredited Weimar Republic. Moreover, its approach to politics resonated with widely shared values (e.g., community, order, race-thinking, conquest). Yet even in those circumstances, many Germans did not abandon efforts at agency. The Nazis' brutal regime drastically limited their options, but many of them took what opportunities they could find to act.

Upon the Third Reich's collapse, Germans had been practicing various forms of political action, both explicit and implicit, for decades. Most were still committed to the ideal of a *Volksgemeinschaft*, opposed to Marxism, contemptuous of parliamentarism and political parties, and uncomfortable with conflict and interests. How, then, would post-1945 West Germans prove able to build and come to support a parliamentary democracy?

4

Re-Imagining Democracy

Creating a Federal Republic in Postwar West Germany

West Germany initially became a stable representative democracy by creating a kind of leaders democracy. The new republic benefited from far better economic and political outcomes than the Weimar Republic. The first chancellor, Konrad Adenauer, was a powerful but democratically elected figure who did help Germans transition from a single dictatorial leader to a more democratic representation. However, instead of a single leader, the system ultimately privileged the political parties and their leaders, along with some powerful interest groups and their leaders, as the people's representatives in addressing the society's problems. Like antidemocratic elites, West Germany's democratic elites needed popular participation for stability and legitimacy but viewed popular participation beyond voting with deep suspicion. Postwar Germans were initially skeptical of parties and parliaments, but by the mid-1960s, most West Germans came to accept pluralism, conflict, and compromise—and parties and parliamentary democracy. Yet increasing dissatisfaction with Adenauer's assertive style and a generational shift (away from people dominated by memories of Weimar and often by complicity in the Third Reich) contributed to increasingly critical attitudes.

Democracy Imposed?

The Allied powers occupying the defeated Germany declared on July 5, 1945, that they were assuming the "supreme governing power" in Germany, effectively suspending Germany's existence as a sovereign state. All political authority lay with the occupiers. The different occupation zones, though, very quickly went their own ways. On institutional and political issues, the Allies took steps that precluded some options for Germans in their zones. The occupiers initially imposed bans on political activity in general. Because they did not yet trust Germans, all four also suppressed the Antifascist Committees that had popped up spontaneously to address democratically the problems of Germany's devastated cities. They moved aggressively to block Nazi and right-wing-authoritarian individuals and groups from gaining access to the public sphere. And they allowed only those they considered reliably "democratic" to gain the necessary licenses for newspapers, magazines, and political parties and positions (with Communists initially acceptable in every zone).[1]

American political scientist Richard L. Merritt wrote *Democracy Imposed*, emphasizing non-democratic elements in (West) German political culture and asserting an indispensable American and Allied role in compelling defeated Germans to accept democracy. After the disaster that Hitler and his party had brought on Germany, those who had chosen to reject Weimar parliamentary democracy and support the Nazis in the early 1930s had to justify that choice. They and those younger had also heard twelve years of Nazi propaganda continuing earlier denunciations of parties and parliamentarianism. Even after 1945, many if not most Germans retained serious doubts about political parties and parliamentary government. Many held political values similar to those that had prevailed in the late Weimar Republic. In August 1947, 55 percent of Germans polled thought Nazism was a good idea badly implemented, while only 35 percent characterized it as a bad idea, suggesting that many Germans were at best ambivalent about parliamentary democracy. Parties remained anathema for many, and suspicion of parliaments, including of the threat of "parliamentary absolutism," remained. Indeed, when polled, most respondents replied that if Germany had to have parties, they wanted there to be only one, presumably embodying the *Gesamtinteresse*. Those attitudes were never universal and would change, but they seemed predominant in the late 1940s.[2]

Despite Merritt's characterization, the Western Allies could not simply impose the broad changes that they sought. Having generally bought the misguided stereotype of authoritarian Germans, the Western Allies sought to impose a fundamental transformation in German culture and values, to ensure that Germany would not unleash yet another aggressive war; they pursued "democratization" to do so. The Americans, for example, sought fundamental changes in education and the civil service, to create democratic German models based on American practice. Yet Germans resisted those efforts and succeeded in blocking many of them. The occupiers soon realized that they had to give Germans some voice in their own affairs through local and then *Land* governments, and the Western Allies looked to substantively "democratic" institutions in their Cold War competition with the Soviets.[3]

In the event, the occupiers' efforts and need for local support enabled occupied-Germany's pro-democratic forces to structure a West German democracy by building on German precedents. In 1945, the least compromised individuals who entered public life had usually been members of democratic Weimar-era parties. They generally accepted parties as good or at least necessary, while seeking an improved parliamentary system. Moreover, Karlheinz Niclauß argues, once political parties and a party system had constituted themselves in 1945/46 under Allied sponsorship, their leaders took for granted the reestablishment of parliaments in which they would compete for power (though, he acknowledges, it was unclear how the populace would react). And when the Allies began establishing representative bodies to give Germans some role in their own governance, the representatives began remaking those bodies like parliaments, with more than merely advisory roles. When the various *Länder* in the west and Bizonal authorities then began acting like parliamentary party states (including adapting the Weimar Reichstag's Standing Rules, creating coalitions, dividing into "government" and opposition), they foreclosed other options. And by 1948, after multiple *Land* elections, *Landtag* deputies, organized in political parties, and *Land* officials, usually party members, were no longer agents of the Allies but were legitimated through electoral and parliamentary majorities.[4]

Reconceiving Parliamentary Democracy

Prompted by the Western Allies, in summer 1948, to create a West German state, the Germans did so in the Parliamentary Council, which was primed to create a parliamentary democracy. The Minister Presidents of the *Länder* in the western zones, still hoping for German unity, insisted that the new state must be provisional: (1) It would rest on a "Basic Law" and not a "constitution"—implying that a "real" constitution would be promulgated once Germany was unified, and (2) it would be approved not by a popular referendum but by the *Land* legislatures (*Landtage*). Some Minister Presidents opposed parliamentary democracy and sought a political system that would operate through consensus (though what that might mean in practice was unclear). The *Land* parliaments elected Parliamentary Council members proportional to each party's success in the most recent *Land* election. The delegates were theoretically representatives of the (West) German people, but they were by occupation committed to parliamentarianism and party government. Moreover, two-thirds of the Parliamentary Council members had been politically active during the Weimar Republic. These Germans were almost certainly going to create a parliamentary party democracy—and they did.[5]

However, they were determined to learn from Weimar-era mistakes. Generally, the CDU/CSU (right-of-center) and FDP (European liberals) blamed the collapse of democracy and the rise of Nazism on the perceived inadequacies of the Weimar Republic's constitution, though the SPD (social democrats) recognized other inadequacies as well. They all sought to correct that document's perceived weaknesses, so that the Basic Law is often seen as an "anti-Weimar constitution." (Albeit Germans were arguably often reacting not to the Weimar Republic's problems but to the Third Reich.)[6]

The Basic Law (*Grundgesetz*, hereafter GG) established a federal state, with significant powers reserved to the *Länder*. While Americans preferred a federal Germany based on American constitutional traditions, Germans had their own reasons for preferring federalism. By 1948 the *Länder* had established their political legitimacy based on German regionalist traditions going back a century and a third or more, and recent democratic elections further affirmed their legitimacy. Moreover, the Third Reich had eliminated the *Länder* as part of creating a centralized dictatorship, so the Parliamentary Council and Germans looked to federalism as a bulwark against an excessive centralization that could be a threat to freedom and a precursor of dictatorship. And Catholics in the CDU/CSU embraced the principles of subsidiarity and opposed "Prussian" centralization.[7]

The Federal Republic successfully developed by drawing on Germans' own traditions. Key terminologies, such as chancellor for the head of government, reflected centuries-old German tradition, and key institutions such as the Bundesrat (discussed below) were clear analogs to earlier institutions. Friedrich Kießling asserts, "The foundation of the Bonn democracy succeeded just because one could connect substantively to accustomed concepts."[8]

Although some Germans still feared "parliamentary absolutism," the Council's members reacted against the president's role in Weimar's collapse by strengthening parliament. A strong lower house of parliament (the Bundestag) would have the power to form a government and, together with the upper house (the Bundesrat), promulgate laws and therefore would not be easily outmaneuvered or overrun, by the president or otherwise. The Americans and Britons had effectively blocked proposals for a corporatist upper chamber. The Council ultimately rejected proposals for a Senate, whose members would be elected by citizens from each *Land* or by *Landtage*. The *Land* governments would choose the Bundesrat representatives, so it represented the interests of the *Länder* and of the parties in *Land* governments and only indirectly a *Land*'s people. The Bundesrat's powers were primarily suspensive, but its approval was necessary for measures that would directly affect *Land* competencies—e.g., in taxation or administration. This requirement became a powerful lever, as a substantial share of legislation proved to involve taxation or administration by the *Länder*.[9]

The Parliamentary Council did recognize the need for checks and balances that would prevent any parliamentary absolutism by the Bundestag. Federalism was one such element, by reserving certain powers to the *Länder* and limiting central government jurisdiction. The drafters saw selection of Bundesrat delegates by the *Land* governments, not the people, as a counterweight to popular passions and party maneuvering and hence as providing a more rational and objective (*sachlich*) element. Another check on parliamentary power was the Constitutional Court (*Bundesverfassungsgericht*), which would exercise judicial review of legislative and executive actions. In the aftermath of the Nazi seizure of power, CDU'ers and CSU'ers could support it to defend federalism, and SPD'ers could support it to control a judiciary still dominated by Third Reich–era judges. It was not explicitly an equal branch of government with parliament. However, it successfully battled the first Federal Minister of Justice to secure its autonomy and that of its budget, and it then gradually secured across the 1950s a monopoly on interpretating the GG, at the expense of the Bundesgerichtshof (the highest appeals court) and the professors of state law. It has no direct enforcement powers, but it has managed to secure broad and deep legitimacy, so that, despite periodic criticism and occasional challenges, its ruling are accepted and implemented as law. Parliament could amend the constitution with two-thirds votes in both chambers, but certain constitutional provisions, those seen as most vital to preserving the new Federal Republic's democratic character—Art. 1 (inviolability of the value of each human being, human rights) and Art. 20 (Federal Republic of Germany (FRG) as democratic and social federal state with popular sovereignty and the Rechtsstaat)—were protected from any constitutional amendment.[10]

To avoid the Weimar Republic's revolving door cabinets, the Parliamentary Council made the FRG chancellor stronger than the Weimar chancellor had been. The only member of the government directly accountable to the Bundestag would be the chancellor; he or she would name all other ministers, could fire any minister, and would establish the guidelines for government policy. The first chancellor, Konrad Adenauer, further strengthened the office by establishing the Federal Chancellor's Bureau, which provides chancellors with independent knowledge and coordinates ministers' activities. To strengthen the government, the GG established the principle of constructive no-confidence. Weimar Republic governments had fallen when they lost a no-confidence vote to a coalition of parties that had no ability to form a replacement government, contributing substantively to the aura of instability and incapability that plagued that republic. Under the GG, a no-confidence vote would only succeed if a majority could form a government to replace the one being challenged. While the stability of FRG governments may reflect more the absence (until recently) of significant anti-GG parties in the Bundestag, observers often identify the constructive no-confidence provision as a major element in the FRG's stability. It also increased the chancellor's power because dissatisfied coalition partners could less easily threaten his/her continuance in office. Notably, some supported it because they thought it would force parliament to act more responsibly, instead of throwing out governments on a whim.[11]

Postwar–West German political elites were committed to a representative democracy and opposed to any direct democratic elements. Several postwar *Land* constitutions had provided for referenda or initiatives. The Parliamentary Council, though, sharply limited any plebiscitary elements in the GG. The experience of the Weimar Republic had convinced many Germans that direct democracy was dangerous, even though none of the Weimar Republic plebiscites had secured a majority. A powerful element here was a fear that the masses were too vulnerable to demagogy, given the support Hitler had secured before 1933 and his success with carefully crafted plebiscites in the 1930s. Some also feared that the Communists would prove too effective in disrupting the new state with demagogic referenda. And indeed, referenda and plebiscites in mid-twentieth-century Europe were generally associated with dictatorial states. The GG hence only allowed plebiscites in relation to territorial changes among the *Länder*. Germans have generally continued to insist that the FRG is a representative democracy, so that direct democratic elements such as plebiscites were unacceptable.[12]

The experience of the Weimar Republic convinced members of the Parliamentary Council that they wanted a relatively weak president. The Weimar Republic president had possessed considerable powers, in forming a government and in ruling by decree under Art. 48. And he had had an alternative and arguably superior basis of legitimacy, vis-à-vis the Reichstag, through his popular election nationwide. The FRG president would be elected not by the citizenry but by a special assembly representing the Bundestag and the *Länder*, depriving him or her of plebiscitary legitimacy. He would not have decree powers and would play a very circumscribed role in the formation and dissolution of governments. His role would be primarily symbolic.[13]

For Bundestag elections, all West German citizens would have an equal, secret ballot, and they would vote under a system of proportional representation. However, parties would need a minimum share of the vote, set in 1953 at 5 percent, to be able to claim seats in the parliament's lower house, the Bundestag, a limit that has kept many smaller parties out of the parliament. As in the Weimar Republic, no significant voices were raised questioning universal equal suffrage. The GG had set the voting age at 21 (but all parties agreed on reducing it to 18, in time for the 1972 Bundestag election).[14]

The Parliamentary Council was determined, after the brutal experience of Nazi dictatorship, to ensure the rights of German citizens. The GG begins with a catalog of fundamental rights, ones that are implicitly human and not civil rights because they precede the organizational sections that founded the Federal Republic. Those basic rights "bind the legislature, the executive, and the judiciary as directly enforceable law." They reflected an acceptance by the Catholic Church and by Protestants, after experience of fascism and Communism, of human rights as a defense against the totalitarianism and statism that threatened the churches and freedom of conscience. Fundamental rights include the basic rights to due process of law and to political participation. Unlike the Weimar constitution, the GG states simply, "Men and women shall have equal rights." Notably, only a vigorous campaign, including waves of petitions, secured this provision; moreover, it would take decades for the Bundestag to revise statutes that discriminated against women. The GG indirectly characterizes the Federal Republic as a Rechtsstaat by requiring the *Länder* to have constitutions corresponding to "the principles of the republican, democratic, and social Rechtsstaat in the sense of this Basic Law." Especially after the Third Reich's lawlessness, the promise of due process and of legal certainty which a Rechtsstaat offered was enormously reassuring. The GG does not include the Weimar constitution's elaborate set of social rights because the SPD did not want to give courts still dominated by Nazi-era judges too much scope to use judicial review to limit social legislation.[15]

Crucially, the Constitutional Court ruled that the rights in the GG constituted an "objective order of values" which dominated "all areas of law." The GG refers repeatedly to the "free-democratic basic order"; the court has characterized the latter as a complex of values in itself, independent of natural law or any external source of values and fundamental to the FRG's functioning as a democratic republic. And they argued that because it (or rather the court's conceptualization of it) ruled all the law, it—and the Constitutional Court—would determine the constitutionality of all legislation and governmental action. The court has ruled that any limitation on fundamental rights could only come where rights were in conflict with one another and only to the degree necessary to maintain more important rights as against less important, in specific situations. That interpretation had broad implications for politics and life in the FRG, and it would prove crucial in defining the scope—and limits—of political citizenship.[16]

Yet if the GG established broad rights for citizens, it also established the FRG as a "militant democracy" or "democracy capable of defending itself"—by limiting the rights of its opponents. Germans almost uniformly, though inaccurately, thought that the Weimar Republic had failed because it had been unable to defend itself. Also, recent developments in Eastern Europe spurred fears of Communist subversion. So West Germans set out systematically, in *Land* constitutions and especially in the GG, to ensure that the Federal Republic would be capable of defending itself. The GG provided that its Articles 1 and 20, protecting the inviolable value of each human being and establishing the republic as a democratic and social federal state, could not be amended. A fundamental principle, which the Constitutional Court affirmed, was that fundamental rights would be secured, but only for those who supported those democratic values and not for those who opposed the "free-democratic basic order." If, to combat the free-democratic basic order, one abused fundamental rights, then one forfeited those rights. Already in 1950 the government ruled that civil servants could not be members of Communist or neo-Nazi parties but must be supporters of the free-democratic basic order, and a 1953 law passed with government and SPD support affirmed that every civil servant must be fully committed to West Germany's democratic order. (Albeit ex-Nazis and -Communists were not banned, and ex-Nazis often enforced the rules to protect democracy.) The GG also permitted the banning of organizations and parties that threatened that order. Only the Constitutional Court could ban parties, and it banned a neo-Nazi party in 1952 and the Communist Party in 1956. Subsequently, German governments have banned various extremist organizations, usually for promoting Nazi ideas. Until recently, the FRG has not been threatened by the kinds of broadly based antidemocratic parties that plagued the Weimar Republic, so its stability has rested more on the political legitimacy it developed over the decades. However, its character as a "democracy that can defend itself" has proven a significant element in its identity.[17]

The GG provided, in effect, that (West) German citizenship would be based on ethnicity. Given long-standing nationalism, Nazi ideology, and (initially) minimal non-German minorities, West Germans thought of citizenship in ethnic terms. Moreover, various Eastern European countries had expelled millions, as Germans, from their territories, only reaffirming the ethnic basis of identity and citizenship; most ended up in Germany. To deal with these expellees, the GG defined as German any who had German citizenship or who entered Germany's December 31, 1937, borders as a person of German stock or their spouse or descendant. The Allies, by repealing the 1935 Nazi citizenship law, had restored the 1913 law and citizenship by descent, and the Constitutional Court affirmed its validity. The *Länder* ruled on naturalization requests, supposedly according to common guidelines; however, they varied in their openness to granting citizenship to those not of German ethnicity. Under the GG, any whom the Third Reich had deprived of citizenship could apply for its restoration. This allowed some exiles, including some Jewish Germans, to regain citizenship. The GG also asserted that no one of any ethnicity could be deprived of their German citizenship if it would make them stateless. The Federal Republic promulgated legislation that provided that German women who married foreigners did not lose their citizenship, albeit this was typical by then of European citizenship rules. And only after 1990 would it pass legislation beginning to ease naturalization for non-ethnic Germans and asylum seekers (see Chapter 7).[18]

The Bundestag amended the GG in various ways, notably, to allow West German rearmament in the mid-1950s. Given the Imperial Army's and Reichswehr's opposition to democracy and support for authoritarian governance, guaranteeing an army that would support democracy seemed crucial. Sharp debates resulted in parliamentary establishment of the Bundeswehr under firm democratic control. Traditional "corpselike obedience" was rejected as authoritarian and too inflexible for modern combat. And the "citizen soldiers" were guaranteed many constitutional rights. Individual soldiers and officers have supported radical right groups, but overall the Bundeswehr has proved a reliable institution for a democratic polity.[19]

The most controversial amendment allowed the government to declare a State of Emergency and to circumvent various constitutional restrictions. The Parliamentary Council had discussed including some such powers but had not done so. Many opposed such measures because they feared a repeat of the 1930s slide to Nazism. The SPD resisted allowing decrees or enabling acts because it wanted to force parliament to take responsibility for government decisions. In 1959, Federal Interior Minister Gerhard

Schroeder (CDU) introduced a bill for broad emergency powers for the chancellor. The bill reflected lingering CDU/CSU suspicions of parliament and preference for strong leadership. Massive opposition quickly blossomed to the bill's provisions, during a "state of exception," for limiting fundamental rights (including the right to strike) and for conscripting civilians, and to granting such powers with only a bare parliamentary majority. Some proponents did seem motivated by lingering authoritarian conceptions, but some preferred a carefully calibrated constitutional basis for emergency action as the best protection of democracy. The SPD supported the legislation in principle, in part to prove its reliability as a party capable of governing. Over the next eight years massive pressure from the unions, from the SPD, and from extra-parliamentary groups forced significant changes that sharply limited the rights that could be suspended, required a two-thirds Bundestag majority to declare a state of emergency, and established a Bundestag/Bundesrat committee to supervise any exercise of emergency powers. The final bill still evoked massive and fervent opposition from those who feared it was a slippery slope to a neo-fascist dictatorship. Given developments such as the *Spiegel* Affair (see below) and the presence in powerful positions of judges and other officials with Nazi pasts, such fears were not unreasonable, and their assertive expression contributed to putting substantially more constraints on arbitrary power than originally intended. The powers the law grants have never been exercised, sparing Germans any risks it might entail but leaving unclear what if any dangers might obtain if it is ever invoked.[20]

In return for supporting the 1968 state-of-emergency amendment to the GG, the SPD secured two constitutional amendments. One established a right for individual citizens to appeal to the Constitutional Court if their rights were infringed. The other established for every German a right to resist any "person or persons seeking to abolish this [constitutional] order." The 1959 "state of exception" bill had sought to limit the right to strike. The unions, though, argued vehemently that only the general strike provided proven protection for democracy in Germany, as the 1920 Kapp Putsch had shown. CDU'ers insisted that this right to resist could never be used against a law passed by a democratically elected representative body. In fact, though, innumerable Germans would appeal to this right to resist in protests and civil disobedience, for example, against nuclear power plants and nuclear missiles (see Chapter 5).[21]

Changing Views of Political Parties and Pluralism

The GG recognized the political parties and specified that they would work on the "formation of the political will." Given Germans' long history of antipathy toward parties, that recognition granted the parties an unprecedented degree of constitutional legitimacy. The provision proposed to channel popular participation in political life through structured organizations, organizations that would assume a tutelary role in mediating popular passions and interests. Democratic politicians continued to prefer this form of democracy: as selection of leaders who would temper popular input. And the Constitutional Court generally supported the major parties and this preeminent mediating function. Challenges to this preeminence would develop slowly in the 1950s and early 1960s but would become increasingly aggressive by the late 1960s.²²

GG drafters sought to counter any recurrence of Weimar's "splintering" of the vote among multiple parties. Some favored majority, or first-past-the-post, electoral districts. Some, especially in the CDU/CSU, wanted single-member electoral districts so that people would have a specific person (a "personality") representing them. Yet the SPD insisted on proportional representation as the best reflection of society's range of opinion. Moreover, the Allies had licensed multiple parties, and smaller parties in the Parliamentary Council demanded proportional representation, as the only way they could survive. As a compromise, each voter has two votes: one to be cast for one candidate in a single-member district from which half of the deputies would be elected; the other to be cast for party lists from which the other half of the deputies would be chosen, proportional to the overall vote for each party. However, in practice the system established proportional representation, and the voters chose party, not personality. To limit splintering, electoral law required a party to win at least three districts or to get at least 5 percent of the vote, initially in any *Land* but from 1953 in the whole Federal Republic, to get any seats under proportional representation. The system contributed to the sharp reduction in Bundestag parties, from ten in 1949 to three, 1961–1983. It also meant that deputies were creatures of the party that selected them—not the independent delegates Art. 38 GG said they should be. Moreover, excluding parties with fewer than 5 percent of the electorate contradicted the presumption that the party system and the Bundestag represented *all* West Germans.²³

Although the GG legitimized and implicitly privileged the parties, Germans' long-standing disapproval, often disdain, for political parties remained a powerful force in the early Federal Republic. Even committed democrats could be uncomfortable with parties—as obstacles to democratic discussion and decision-making. Many Germans remained committed to the idea that a single, unified common good existed that rational people could recognize and support. Parties, by contrast, could only represent discrete, "egoistical," and often implicitly corrupt, interests. As late as 1967/68, 63 percent of those polled thought interest groups endangered the common good—albeit this was a mostly over-50-years-of-age sample. And in December 1952, 44 percent of those polled favored "a single strong national party which really represented the interests of all classes of our people." The success of the CDU/CSU and SPD rested in no small part on their professed character as "people's parties" (*Volksparteien*) not interest-based parties, ones that proposed to join Germans of all classes in support of the common good. While overall, postwar Germans seem to have been more likely to acknowledge that interests would inevitably play some role in politics, they emphasized the need to channel such interests through the political parties (which were to be catch-all parties committed to the common good) or perhaps broad interest groups such as business groups, unions, and churches.²⁴

By the 1960s, West Germans seemed comfortable accepting the existence of multiple interests that could legitimately participate in political life. Both Klein and Niclauß argue that the Parliamentary Council created in effect a pluralist polity by the choices it made. Faced with persecutions in anti-pluralist fascist and communist states, the Catholic Church accepted pluralism. In a July 1966 poll of higher education students, 81 percent agreed that interest groups belonged in a democracy. The SPD tacitly accepted the existence of competing social interests, and its crucial Bad Godesberg program (1959) was predicated on pluralism. Kaspar Maase argues that even *Heimatfilme* (homeland films), supposedly a traditionalist genre, combined nostalgia for a comforting past with a realization that the present was pluralist.[25]

Similarly, the polity slowly moved toward acceptance of compromise. Many Germans had long seen compromise as despicable, a sign of indecision, betrayal of principle, and weakness of will. Closely studying democratization in Schleswig-Holstein after 1945, Allan Borup was struck by the shift from aversion to compromise in the Weimar Republic to "a more strongly marked utilitarianism" in the Federal Republic, which encouraged compromise. By 1968, 51 percent of youth rejected the notion that compromise with political opponents is dangerous and usually a betrayal of one's own cause. The GG was predicated on political compromise, and policymakers and citizens in practice engaged in compromise under the Federal Republic. The CDU and SPD cooperated in the Bundestag—e.g., over contested issues such as compensation for war-damaged—to produce compromises that would legitimate the new Federal Republic. Indeed, most bills were compromises, worked out in effective committee work, for which government *and* opposition then voted.[26]

Nevertheless, an aversion to conflict, as Ralf Dahrendorf put it, remained predominant into the 1960s and 1970s. Polling around 1970 showed only one-third of respondents rejecting an assertion that the political opposition exists to support, not criticize the government (though over two-thirds of students rejected it). And only one-fourth rejected the assertion that clashes among different interests harm the society (though two-thirds of students rejected it). Nonetheless, political and social theorists and journalists increasingly promoted the idea that conflict and its peaceful resolution were central to democratic politics (and students were picking up on it). Adenauer and Schumacher, key political leaders of the late 1940s and early 1950s, sought to draw sharp lines between government and opposition, accustoming West Germans to the existence in a parliamentary democracy of a self-confident opposition. In practice, interest-group leaders and even members could recognize that they must commit to a political struggle if they wanted to secure their interests. Most crucially, West Germans did not choose to vote for parties that proclaimed they would eliminate conflict, as they had in the Weimar Republic.[27]

The growing, if slow, acceptance of pluralism, conflict, and compromise contributed to a growing acceptance of political parties as necessary elements in a democratic polity. Political theorists have long argued that parties are inevitable, the only viable means to organize, mobilize, and mediate among the multiple, often competing, interests that exist in any complex society. Both Adenauer and Schumacher believed parties were necessary and worked to promote their roles, in the Parliamentary Council and afterwards. The Constitutional Court helped legitimate parties by ruling that they bridged the traditional society/state gap by representing society and helping to shape policy. By March 1956 the share of West Germans who preferred a single party to represent all classes had dropped to 25 percent. And since the late 1950s, a consistent three-quarters of those polled have accepted the need for multiple parties. Further, by 1971, 89 percent of Germans accepted that a political opposition is necessary for democracy, and 86 percent accepted that every democratic party should in principle have an opportunity to participate in government. Nonetheless, even while recognizing the need for parties at the national level, West Germans often still preferred de facto non-partisanship at the local level, through multi-party or supra-partisan lists. And acceptance of parties could often mean focusing the formation of the political will in the parties, as the GG suggested, so that their mediating role predominated over citizens' actions. The FRG was then arguably a leaders or party democracy. As Ilona Klein suggests, the GG had established not "rule of the people" but "rule for the people."[28]

Order, Authority, and Evolving Democratic Culture

Even after 1945, authoritarian traditions retained influence among significant numbers of citizens in West Germany. In March 1946, two-fifths of Germans polled agreed one should always obey orders from the state without question. In August 1946 only a third gave answers "in a democratic direction" in response to a series of questions on social and political attitudes, albeit only 18 percent agreed that "only a government with a dictator is able to create a strong nation." And into the 1960s around half of Germans (depending on the year) saw Nazism as a good idea badly implemented; 1950s polls showed majority or near-majority support for the idea that if the war had not occurred Hitler would be one of the greatest statesmen, suggesting broad acquiescence in authoritarian leadership. In a 1970 poll, only 51 percent rejected the assertion that allowing all to talk is not good because "only when some are in command can we keep our state in order."[29]

To exercise authority in the new state, Germans initially tended to favor strong leaders, either in the sense of a leadership elite or of a strong man (albeit not a "leader," as Hitler had discredited that word). Karl Bracher has pointed to the way calls for a strong chancellor had an anti-parliamentary, antidemocratic thrust. Germans have often seen democracy as a system for enabling citizens to select legitimate leaders from a leadership elite, who would make decisions until the next election. Discussions of leadership and authority in the early West Germany reflected this attitude, as did the way annual party conventions were generally not spaces for discourse leading to decision but occasions for legitimating leaders and their policy proposals.[30]

Given this widespread political culture of order and authority, Konrad Adenauer, as first chancellor, arguably played a key role in West Germany's development of a stable democracy. The GG gave the chancellor more power than had the Weimar Constitution, and Adenauer further strengthened the office. His chancellorship was so strong that West Germany in the 1950s has often been described as a chancellor democracy. That strength reconciled to the new republic many Germans who looked to strong leadership, to rulership with authority, and who were suspicious of parliaments. Adenauer showed Germans that authority and democracy could go together. Yet as assertive and even authoritarian as Adenauer's attitudes could be, he had democratic legitimacy through parliament, recognized the need to bring powerful interest groups on board, and accepted the rule of law. And polling showed in the early 1950s a strong correlation between support for Adenauer and support for the Federal Republic, albeit that correlation was no longer determinative by the late 1950s.[31]

Fear of massification was widespread in postwar Germany, influencing political choices. Many Germans believed that ignorant, demagogued masses had brought the Nazis to power (ignoring the key role Conservative elites had played in the Nazi seizure of power). Such fears had influenced GG drafters' choices to reject plebiscitary elements and establish a strong Constitutional Court. Fears of "mass society" as culturally demeaning and debilitating went back into the nineteenth century and were frequently repeated amid postwar fears of both Communism and consumerism as agents of massification. Many Europeans, and Germans, feared the mass society would be leveled, uniform, manipulated. "Mass democracy" was a pejorative for many, who clearly longed to continue the political predominance of notables. And many commentators expressed serious reservations as to whether the average citizen was informed enough to be trusted with determinative political power. Many Germans also doubted the political maturity of the German people. Even worker movement leaders had anxieties about uncontrollable actions "from below." In 1947, a majority of those polled expressed doubts Germans were capable of democracy, and in later polls substantial minorities still did so. Such fears gradually declined, but they remained a powerful force for many Germans into the 1970s.[32]

Ludwig Erhard based his 1965 call for a *formierte* (shaped, structured) society on the need for a strong state and a strong sense of the common good as against powerful interests and untutored masses. Erhard wanted to be a people's chancellor with an immediate relationship with the voters, implicitly bypassing the GG-established parliament and parties (and echoing 1920s debates). He feared that, in parliament, an overdeveloped pluralism of private interests would generate government interventions that would paralyze the economy. Rüdiger Altmann originally proposed the *formierte* society with Adenauer in mind, and its statist bent seems more appropriate to Adenauer than to the free-market Erhard, who never explained how it would work in practice. Moreover, this "formed society" was easily attacked as a "uniformed society." Such a militarized, conformist, and potentially authoritarian conceptualization sank without a trace—after Nazism and in a decade of growing individualism, growing acceptance of pluralism, and fears that the debate over state-of-emergency legislation was a harbinger of renewed authoritarianism.[33]

How the early Federal Republic should have come to terms with its Nazi past remains a contested question. Concentration camp survivor Eugen Kogon argued that so many Germans had belonged to Nazi organizations (8 million to the party alone) that Germans faced a choice: either kill them all or reconcile them to the new democracy; the former, he wrote, was not an option for a Christian or a democratic country. The FRG could scarcely have secured democratic stability if it denied the millions who had supported the Nazi regime any prosperous and honorable position in the new society—a conclusion the Americans, amid the Cold War, also came to accept. West Germans, many of whom had supported a horrifically brutal regime, agreed that Germany must punish "war criminals" but integrate the rest. Allied trials of Nazi leaders legitimated West Germans' choice to acknowledge Nazi crimes while blaming them on a tiny group of evil Nazis. That the German Army had committed atrocities on a massive scale was simply denied. Mostly, West Germans chose silence about Nazi crimes and about their own and their neighbors' actions during the Third Reich, while filling the silence with "war stories" about their own victimization by the regime and the Allies. And masking historical reality probably was, as Norbert Frei said, necessary to secure "mass allegiance to the democratic parties." The government soon passed amnesties for Germans penalized in the de-Nazification process. Hence, into the 1960s men who had been active during the Nazi period dominated the civil service, judiciary, medical profession, and press. They reconciled themselves to the new, successful, anti-Communist (and, as it happened, democratic) republic. However, their presence delayed the development of democratic values, and the failure to come to terms with the past was a weighty moral burden for the FRG and a potentially serious challenge to democracy, with political consequences into the 1970s.[34]

A defense of Western culture (*das Abendland*) was a powerful force to help re-legitimate all manner of institutions compromised through collaboration with Nazism. As Maria Mitchell has shown, conservative and moderate Germans could appeal to a deeply rooted and highly respected traditional, Christian culture against a secularist and materialist Nazi regime, secularist and materialist Communism, and materialist/consumerist Western "civilizations." Elites could then reassert their role as leaders and Germany's role as an honorable member of the community of nations. This commitment to Western culture also provided a bridge between Catholics and Protestants within the CDU, which had been founded after 1945 to overcome the previous confessional divide.[35]

Anti-Communism, often presented as anti-totalitarianism, was a particularly powerful force in West German politics. The Third Reich had been vehemently anti-Communist; for many Germans, casting the FRG as an anti-Communist bulwark gave it considerable legitimacy—without necessarily committing one to democracy. And characterizing anti-Communism as anti-totalitarianism allowed one to distance oneself from not only the current regimes in East Germany/Eastern Europe but also the defeated and internationally discredited Nazi regime. Anti-Communism was also effectively deployed against any challenges to the 1950s/60s right-of-center governments in Bonn, as left-of-center criticism was generally stamped as Communist or under Communist control. Given persistent CDU/CSU efforts to tar the SPD as fellow travelers of the Communists, SPD'ers felt constrained in policies and tactics by the need to distinguish their party sharply from any taint of association with Communists. Moreover, into the 1960s and even 1980s, public protests were regularly denounced as guided by Communists or their fellow travelers and so inherently illegitimate.[36]

Yet for all its deployment against democratic freedom of expression in the 1950s, anti-Communism played a key role in legitimating democracy as a political system in the eyes of many initially skeptical 1950s West Germans, primarily, though not entirely, in non-democratic terms. Fear of Communism made the FRG and even parliament look good in comparison. Conservatives might still oppose liberal-pluralist democracy and fear the masses, but they had to preserve the FRG as a bulwark against the Communist East. And earlier fears of massification increasingly were deployed not against democracy but against totalitarianism. The result, as Kaspar Maase argues, was that attacking democracy became unacceptable, while praising it and freedom as bulwarks against the Communist East became desirable. Meanwhile, the SPD was to some degree protected into the 1960s because it could dismiss any politicking to its left as Communism and hence illegitimate. Notably, though, in the 1962 *Spiegel* Affair, government attempts to appeal to anti-Communism to legitimate its prosecution of the magazine failed to generate significant popular support. Anti-Communism was powerful in the 1950s, but in the 1960s its influence began waning.[37]

The *Spiegel* Affair burst over Germany in October 1962. The proudly muckraking periodical had become a thorn in the side of the powerful, including the Adenauer government and, especially, the right-wing Franz-Josef Strauß (CSU). It had also been sharply anti-Catholic. When it published a scathing article on weaknesses in West Germany's defenses, the government (prodded by Strauß) arrested the publisher and a journalist on charges of treason for revealing classified information (which apparently had all already been published elsewhere). They also interfered with publication of its next issue and spent over a week searching the editorial offices, further interfering with publication. The government soon had to admit that it had not followed due process in arranging for the arrest of Conrad Ahlers, a *Spiegel* reporter, in Spain. The revelation that Strauß, who despised and feared *Der Spiegel*, had played a significant role in going after the magazine—and had lied about it—only aggravated concerns with the methods used. Even more worrying for many, Adenauer twice asserted flatly in the Bundestag that the accused were guilty of "treason for money," even though their cases were before the courts. The upshot was that Strauß lost his ministry, Adenauer (who was already under pressure to step down) had to agree to resign within months, and none of the accused was convicted of treason.[38]

The *Spiegel* Affair was significant in West Germany's transition toward a more critical and participatory democracy, as it both reflected changing attitudes and bolstered a growing rejection of authoritarian elements in political culture and governance. Protests against the arrests began almost immediately, initially in small student demonstrations. Intellectuals quickly followed. Professors then began to weigh in, with open letters with more and more signatures. The press was increasingly critical, fearful, not unreasonably, that a government that had tried repeatedly in the 1950s to constrain the media now seemed set to use vague accusations of treason to muzzle its critics. Strauß's lies about his role only increased widespread fears of authoritarian tendencies. And many saw Adenauer's outbursts, effectively trying West German citizens without benefit of due process, as a threat to the Rechtsstaat. The government had not helped its case by choosing the Gestapo method of nighttime raids on offices and homes and by dragging out the search of *Spiegel*'s premises for a week. All this was happening against vivid memories of the Third Reich. Popular reaction was more unfavorable than favorable: 47 percent of those polled thought either that the whole case was simply a means to muzzle *Der Spiegel* or at least that the methods used were impermissible in a Rechtsstaat, while only 27 percent completely approved. When the Constitutional Court finally ruled on *Spiegel*'s suits against the government, it split evenly, so *Spiegel* did not win. Nonetheless, even those justices who voted against the magazine on the legal merits of its specific claims agreed that freedom of the press was a primary value that could only be limited under very special circumstances. Long term, the affair decisively strengthened democratic forces of freedom of expression and of protest and weakened traditional anti-Communist and statist assumptions.[39]

Cultivating a Democratic Political Culture

West Germany could not develop a democratic political culture instantaneously, but it arguably needed one. Postwar Germans, while criticizing various aspects of the Weimar Republic's constitution and institutions, often believed that its fate showed that one needed the appropriate attitudes to make the new republic a "living" rather than a merely formal democracy.

The Western Allies, especially the United States, worked to change (West) German culture in a democratic direction. As victors and aid providers to Germans and as protectors against the threat of Soviet expansion, they had power, and their constitutional and social systems held considerable respect. US postwar re-education efforts included (mostly failed) school reforms to cultivate democratic values. In German cities, the United States set up "America Houses," to expose Germans to American literature and films and to programs to inculcate American democratic values, especially around democratic discussion. The US government and American groups such as trade unions sponsored exchange programs that brought thousands of Germans to the United States, and they seem to have produced generally very positive views of American culture and politics among the participants. Observers have often seen the relaxed and open behavior of Americans, especially US troops stationed in Germany, as offering an alternative and more democratic habitus than Germans had had (albeit many Germans were aware of racial problems in the US military, even after segregation as a policy ended).[40]

American movies were also used to introduce "democratic" ideas. These efforts suffered, however, from the lack of a clear program that defined what sort of films Americans should make or bring to Germany to change minds. German (and American) youth in the 1950s and 1960s did use American popular culture to begin separating themselves from their parents' traditional views and to secure a degree of self-assertion and openness that challenged many of the more authoritarian elements in political culture. Moreover, French and some other Western European films also offered models of less hierarchical and authoritarian, more individualistic and autonomous ways of living.[41]

Perhaps just as crucially, West Germans felt threatened by Soviet and East German pressures even after occupation ended. Individualism and freedom of action and expression were key markers separating West Germany from the threatening East. And West Germans had to take seriously Western political preferences (parliaments, pluralism, public debate) as they sought to ensure American and NATO protection and acceptance in the new European Economic Community. They were now ineluctably part of a Western conversation.[42]

Discussion of cultural democratization is ultimately enormously frustrating: One can easily identify correspondences between cultural initiatives and changing cultural attitudes, and even find individual assertions of causal connections (perhaps most strikingly in discussions of exchange programs, especially with the United States). However, one cannot prove causality. Nina Verheyen does see the Americans as successful in the late 1940s in laying the basis for a more interactive, potentially critical and democratic, style of discourse in Germany. Hermann-Josef Rupieper examined various American efforts at democratization, but he sees the exchange programs that brought thousands of West Germans to the United States in the late 1940s and 1950s as most successful in promoting a democratic political culture, among the visitors and, indirectly, in Germany. Ultimately, exposure to American and Western European models clearly offered an attractive, in key ways compelling, alternative that does seem to have influenced somewhat the gradual opening of West German political culture to democratic ideas and values.

Engaged Citizenry in a Nascent Democracy

West German media was in flux in the 1950s. The Allies had sought to license only reliably democratic individuals to publish periodicals or to work in radio. However, the de facto end of de-Nazification brought with it the return, especially in the print media and often in leading editorial positions, of many individuals who had worked in the media during the Third Reich. The media in 1950s West Germany then generally bought into Adenauer's conservative political and economic consensus. Yet journalists had a professional self-interest in securing their autonomy. So already in the 1950s the media were sponsoring public discussion and dialog as key elements in democratic life, and they resisted efforts at censorship and government supervision of the press. And 1950s youth radio sought to develop a critical capacity among its listeners and to inform youth about democracy and the FRG's institutions.[43]

By the 1960s a critical media was opening up the political culture. By the late 1950s, those who had come of age during and after the war increasingly staffed the media. They had often been disillusioned by their experience of the Third Reich's 1945 defeat and now by Adenauer's conservative, stagnant administration, and they had often visited the United States. They began taking seriously West Germany's character as a democracy and the need for an informed citizenry. Adenauer's effort to dominate public opinion by creating a federal government–controlled TV channel exacerbated these concerns, even after the Constitutional Court ruled that only the *Länder* could set up broadcast channels. And West Germany's public TV channels sought to develop their own critical and pro-democratization journalism, so that programs such as *Panorama*, *Report*, and *Monitor* often outraged politicians but offered millions of viewers alternative perspectives in the 1960s and 1970s. Crucially, the public was ready for a more critical media, as circulation of left-of-center publications soared in the 1960s.[44]

Dialogue and discussion would become central elements in West Germany's democratic political culture by the 1960s. While the United States had actively promoted discussion and dialogue, Germans developed and embraced it for their own reasons. Nazism had been based on the primacy of will and on violence in imposing political solutions on willing or unwilling German citizens. After the devastation that strategy had brought to Germany, many Germans sought an alternative. They increasingly found it in dialogue. The goal was to convince fellow citizens, not to ram something down their throats. And this emphasis on dialog has long outlasted the occupation, remaining a central element in German political culture. It is not uncontested, as some conservatives continue to attack deliberative democracy as undermining all authority, and some Germans have rejected convincing fellow citizens in favor of "struggle," pressure, and even compulsion (see Chapter 5).[45]

Closely related to dialog was a pervasive commitment to reason and objectivity (*Sachlichkeit*) and a repudiation of emotion in politics. Nazis had rejected reason and objectivity in favor of will, passion, and violence. In the face of the Holocaust and nuclear weapons, re-establishing politics on a rational, objective basis—to ensure reasonable solutions and undercut the risk of any new totalitarianism—could seem the only way. Rational argumentation must replace violence as the basis of political decision-making. Even conservative Germans could then see democracy as the best alternative. Nonetheless, Germans often still feared that the loudest protests could trump reason, or that emotion could again sweep citizens away, so they were hypersensitive to any sign that politics was drifting away from reason or toward emotion. Attacking the masses as inherently less rational, more emotional, and susceptible to demagogy did justify elite claims to priority in forming the political will, but many Germans do seem to have sincerely, if inaccurately, blamed Hitler's rise entirely on emotional masses. These views would play a crucial role in Germans' reactions to efforts to broaden political participation beyond party and formal interest-group membership.[46]

Contemporaries and historians have often seen the 1950s and early 1960s as a period, in reaction to Nazism, of widespread popular political apathy, contrasting the quietism of those years with the growing popular activism from 1967 on. Late-1940s polls consistently showed over 60 percent of Germans preferring to leave politics to others. And in the 1950s German sociologist Helmut Schelsky postulated a "skeptical generation" that, disillusioned by the "politics" in the Third Reich, had retreated from the political sphere (though some scholars dismiss his view as overstated). West Germans did have a high voter turnout in elections, but scholars have seen here more a sense of duty than a commitment to democracy. And public opinion polls showed that while majorities of Germans were politically informed (more so than in many other countries) and accepted people's right to political participation, only small minorities regularly engaged politically beyond voting. And that was just fine with many scholars and politicians; even Almond and Verba and Ralf Dahrdendorf of political culture fame, while urging the importance of participation for democracy, did not envision everyone participating, or participating to an equal degree—indeed they rejected universal political participation.[47]

Yet values and actions were changing. A lively debate developed on the need for a less authoritarian fatherhood and child-rearing. Surveys of Germans' assessment of the appropriate values to teach children showed increasing support for "self-reliance," a decline in "love of order," and a precipitous decline in "obedience." Many Germans embraced political participation as central to citizenship and to long-term political stability, often applauding the shift from a subject to a citizen political culture. From 1952 to 1968, the number of West Germans rejecting the assertion that voting was the *only* way to influence public policy increased steadily. And political engagement did increase during the 1960s. Many Germans may have reacted to their experience of the Third Reich by stepping back politically, but the idea of political participation (on which democratic governance is based) was alive in the early Federal Republic, laying the basis for a politically engaged citizenship.[48]

The GG had granted the parties an implicitly privileged role in the "formation of the political will," and most Germans in the early Federal Republic were quite willing to grant the parties—along with certain large, formal interest groups—that privileged role. The SPD, for example, was only willing to support extra-parliamentary political actions in exceptional circumstances, such as the debate over securing nuclear weapons for the West German armed forces. And internally, the SPD, as did the CDU/CSU, expected members to provide information but primarily to provide support for party leaders, not to promote policy options from below. That perspective was widely shared. Indeed, legislation on state secrets implied that citizens who discovered unconstitutional actions that were secret were to inform their parliamentary deputy, not the public. And significant numbers of 1950s/early 1960s West Germans did participate in party life, c. 3 percent as party members and 10 to 13 percent (perhaps 20 percent of male voters and 7 percent of female voters in 1961) by attending election rallies.[49]

Petitions were another, long-standing, though relatively modest, form of political participation. The GG guaranteed everyone the right, singly or as a group, to petition government offices and the parliament. Letters to officials could be acclamatory (in the tradition of homage to monarchical rulers), pleading (for individual assistance or policy changes), or critical. Michaela Fenske has examined petitions by individuals in Lower Saxony. The petitioners tended to be older, socialized in the *Kaiserreich* or the Weimar Republic, very respectful of authority, and likely to use model petitions dating back to the early modern period. They also tended to emphasize a restoration or maintenance of order. Yet by the 1960s she sees a growing political content in the letters. Increasingly, they reacted to the growing wave of demonstrations—either to embrace demonstrators' demands or demand a restoration of order and decency. She also emphasizes that politicians and officials responded to every petition—even if not always positively. Although petitions fit easily into a model of governance that minimized popular participation, Fenske rightly argues that they exceeded the party-focused model of forming the political will by acknowledging the citizen's right to express an opinion. Yet officials could reach out to individual petitioners without committing themselves to substantive steps. And even petition campaigns, though public and usually oppositional, were often organized by large interest groups—without the crowds in the streets and visible pressure that political elites found unacceptable. And the SPD even complained about a public petition sent to the unions to recruit them to act against proposed state-of-emergency legislation, saying petitions should only go to the parliament.[50]

Although West German policymakers scarcely embraced citizen participation, they proved much more responsive to the citizenry than their predecessors—already by 1950. Minister Presidents answered citizen petitions assiduously. Adenauer recognized the need to tie big official interest groups (e.g., business, agriculture, unions, expellees, churches) to his policies. And conservative Finance Minister Fritz Schäffer (CSU), for example, agreed, acknowledging that in a democracy it was better to "consult with the political forces in good time" so that bills "would go into the legislative bodies with some prospect of success and acceptance."[51]

Political elites were not only dismissive of popular protests but also often denounced them as "pressure from the streets" or "Nazi and Communist tactics" and hence as illegitimate. Already in February 1950 August-Martin Euler (FDP) insisted that the Bundestag must never be seen as submitting to "pressure from the streets." Citizens were to offer advice and express concerns, but parties and government were to form the political will, in response to reasoned arguments. The repudiation of "pressure from the streets" would also prove a recurring objection to the student demonstrations of the later 1960s, and not just by political and social elites. The leadership of the Berlin branch of the German Civil Service Youth, for example, asserted that "in a democratic Rechtsstaat political differences of opinion are not to be conducted in the streets." And politicians who took demonstrations seriously were often denounced as cravenly "capitulating to the streets." These attitudes reflected a mix of disdain for the "masses," fears of a repetition of 1930s street politics, and elitist presumption. It also echoed nineteenth-century elite hopes for keeping popular "participation" to an unavoidable minimum.[52]

Public protest was constitutionally protected, with guarantees of the right to assemble and to express one's opinion, but 1950s/60s West Germans generally found protest at best distasteful, as it challenged their sense of order—in physical public space and in the hierarchy of political authority. Many remained fearful of the "masses" and dubious about their fellow citizens' maturity. And political elites regularly accused protesters of being Communist or under the control of Communists. So even citizens who were pro-democratic could be anti-demonstration. Polling of opinion on demonstrations only began in the context of the student unrest after 1966. When polled about student demonstrations in July 1967, 53 percent agreed students should not demonstrate because they lacked the necessary judgment and insight, while only 31 percent agreed that it was good for them to demonstrate because it is good for people to go into the streets to express concern over political deficiencies. When the question was asked again in November 1970, 58 percent agreed students should not demonstrate and 31 percent again agreed it was good if they did. In May 1969 of those polled 39 percent agreed student unrest had gone too far and that one should limit freedoms, for example, to demonstrate, if it was a matter of calm and order; 53 percent agreed that one might not limit basic freedoms because of such unrest. Many West Germans would protest publicly in the 1950s and 1960s, but most West Germans clearly looked with deep suspicion on such exercises of democratic, constitutionally guaranteed rights—at least by those with whom they did not agree politically.[53]

The West German labor movement (DGB) was ambivalent about demonstrations and political uses of the strike, as it long had been. Its leaders knew that a general strike had contributed significantly, perhaps decisively, to defeating the Kapp Putsch against the Weimar Republic. They were quite willing to contemplate a general strike in defense of democracy again. They did hold a one-day general strike in November 1948 to protest rising food prices and frozen wages—but only under considerable pressure from union members. Some workers and unions also engaged in warning strikes and protests on highly contested issues such as factory councils' powers, co-determination, rearmament, nuclear weapons, and the state-of-emergency legislation, but the DGB was hesitant to take the political risks that demonstrating involved. A key concern for union leaders was discipline—making sure the leadership retained control of the workers and reassuring the larger society that the workers were not a loose cannon.

Union leaders faced numerous issues, many more important to them than protesters' concerns. Moreover, the DGB's reaction makes perfect sense in terms of the prevailing political culture's emphasis on the parties' privileged role in the formation of the political will, especially since that political culture had accepted special influence for large formal organizations such as the Federal Association of German Industry, the Association of Expellees—and the DGB. The unions were on board in the prevailing political system, and union leaders usually saw no advantage to rocking that boat by supporting citizen activism.[54]

West Germans did protest in the 1950s over socioeconomic concerns. The first big demonstration in the new capital of Bonn (on February 10, 1950) was by truckers outraged over fuel price rises. Workers demonstrated in support of co-determination in factories, and miners protested job cuts, with calm and extraordinary discipline. Various categories of war victims protested. The expellees, initially seeking assistance through burden-sharing legislation and later seeking improved burden-sharing, held major demonstrations from 1951 on, in Bonn and across the Federal Republic. After the 1957 pension reform increased payments to retired social insurance recipients, the war-injured organized a wave of demonstrations across the Federal Republic, to secure improved benefits for themselves. Some policymakers, convinced that citizens should work only through the parties and large interest groups, proposed cutting government assistance to groups that protested publicly, though they apparently thought better of it.[55]

In postwar Germany, the Christian churches were occasionally active publicly, and members of both did get involve in protests. The Catholic Church mobilized a letter and petition campaign aimed at the Parliamentary Council, in support of confessional schools, the rights of the churches, and Church views on family and parental law. In 1951, the Catholic Church, its hierarchy, and its members promoted an active boycott campaign against a film, *Die Sünderin*, seen as a dire threat to "the last vital forces of morality." Screenings were interrupted by white mice, tear gas, and stink bombs (the same tactics the Nazis had used against *All Quiet on the Western Front*); public demonstrations of various sizes occurred in many towns, and counter-protests also erupted. Catholics also demonstrated vigorously against Rolf Hochhuth's 1963 play, *The Deputy*, which criticized Pope Pius XII's silence about the Holocaust. Most notable for the Protestant churches were the debates about nuclear weapons; those debates divided official Lutheran organizations, as some Lutherans demanded that the church oppose nuclear weapons and the concept of nuclear deterrence as un-Christian. Some Protestant clergy and laity then cooperated in organizing public indoor assemblies against nuclear weapons. In the larger context of 1950s/60s West German politics and society, such protests were relatively unimportant, but they illuminate the potential for citizen activism and helped legitimate protest for the future.[56]

Into the 1960s the issue that drew the most West Germans into citizen activism was defense—rearmament and nuclear weapons. The victorious Allies had disarmed Germany in 1945, but the Cold War pushed each side to seek to rearm its German friends. Many West Germans vigorously opposed rearmament so soon after a second crushing defeat. The SPD, lacking the Bundestag votes to block Adenauer's rearmament plans, sought extra-parliamentary support to stop rearmament. So it overcame its reservations about citizen activism and its commitment to parties and parliament as the locus of the formation of the political will; it worked with unions and others outside parliament to promote an *ohne Mich* (count me out) movement against rearmament and conscription. Once rearmament and conscription became reality, it abandoned support for extra-parliamentary action. Yet when Adenauer and Strauß began working to secure nuclear weapons for West German forces, the SPD joined again with extra-parliamentary forces—e.g., from the unions and the Lutheran churches—to protest vigorously against any German nukes. The party even pushed for plebiscites at the *Land* level on the issue, despite its general emphasis on parliamentary governance. Once the Adenauer/Strauß proposal was effectively scotched by Allied opposition, the SPD again withdrew its support from protest groups.[57]

The 1950s/60s SPD rejected an activist citizenry. It had long emphasized the need for solidarity behind the party's program, educating the (not yet fully politically mature) masses, and mobilizing its supporters. And after the Weimar Republic's failures, it was committed to strong parliamentary governance to preclude another slide into dictatorship. All these concerns militated for party predominance in forming the political will and against extra-parliamentary citizen activism. The SPD might be tempted to turn to citizen activism on vital issues, but it always reverted to a restrained conception of the citizen's role.

The Easter Marches in 1960s West Germany were a tiny but significant expansion of citizen activism. Inspired by the British Campaign for Nuclear Disarmament, the marches grew out of dissatisfaction among a tiny minority with the SPD's and DGB's abandonment of the movement against American nuclear weapons on German soil. The movement involved marches, mostly at Easter, and other activities to demand no nuclear weapons and disarmament. It permitted only individuals, not organizations, to participate; it allowed only one speaker at each march. Both choices reflected its need to counter accusations that it was under Communist control or influence—reflecting just how powerful anti-Communism was in West Germany, even in the 1960s. It also reflected the inherent tension between individual citizen action and a movement's need for sufficient discipline to focus on clear aims and to preclude actions that could discredit the movement. The movement grew slowly in the early 1960s, with relatively few press reports on its activities and frequent accusations of Communist ties. It did not succeed in creating a nuclear-free zone in Central Europe or securing disarmament. However, it contributed to the decision not to build a West German atomic bomb; it succeeded in reaffirming the constitutional right of Germans to protest publicly; and it encouraged a broader range of attitudes toward foreign affairs.[58]

Another early example of citizen activism in the Federal Republic elicited a crucial Constitutional Court decision that bolstered citizen rights, especially public protest. Veit Harlan made films under the Nazis, most notoriously the viciously antisemitic *Jud Süß*, which Joseph Goebbels developed to justify the Nazis' murderous policies toward Jews. In 1950, Harlan's new film *Unsterbliche Geliebte* was being touted in West Germany. Erich Lüth (SPD head of the Hamburg Press Office) thought that honoring so notorious a director threatened West Germany's international reputation, so he called for a boycott of the film. The film's distributor asked the courts, under a Civil Code tort provision, to levy damages and enjoin Lüth from promoting a boycott. A lower court convicted Lüth and issued the injunction, but he appealed to the

Constitutional Court, arguing that his right of free expression under the GG entitled him to urge fellow citizens to boycott the film. The Constitutional Court issued a sweeping ruling unequivocally reasserting that the GG embodied an "objective order of values," a "free-democratic basic order," that influenced all law and that the Civil Code could not contradict. Specifically, it emphasized that the freedom of expression to which Lüth appealed was a central value necessary to a democratic order, one that trumped the distributor's claims under the Civil Code. It also established a principle of "proportionality" that limited the scope of decisions when constitutional provisions conflicted. The court had powerfully extended the reach of the GG (and its own power). It had also powerfully underwritten the rights of citizens to participate actively in public affairs, including by public protest and activism.[59]

The "*Halbstarken* (punks/hooligans)" engaged in public actions that reflected cultural democratization and a gradual loosening of social constraints but that adults generally met with a mixture of horror and disdain. Some West German youths, primarily from working-class backgrounds, clashed with police in the mid-1950s, occasionally around showings of American movies (e.g., *Blackboard Jungle*, *Rock around the Clock*). Often, the clashes developed not from criminal activities but from police efforts to enforce traditional notions of orderliness and deference and from their suspicion of groups of (lower-class) young people hanging around in public places. The *Halbstarken* were not expressing political opinions or asserting political citizenship; their actions reflected social alienation and a youthful, often working-class, self-assertion that challenged social repressiveness and implicitly demanded increased citizen freedom of action. And they were democratically asserting a right to utilize public spaces and to determine for themselves what constituted culture. Moreover, their fashion choices and hairstyles constituted what Sabine von Dirke calls a "symbolic articulation of dissent." Most striking is how vehemently adults reacted, amid and long after the events. A majority of those polled thought press reporting on *Halbstarken* was "greatly exaggerated" (and it was), and letters to the editor were divided. Nonetheless, for many adults, including many politicians, the *Halbstarken*, both by rejecting traditional notions of authority and respectful behavior and by embracing a foreign (American) culture, threatened established norms and the social order. They saw the *Halbstarken* phenomenon, as educator Adolf Busemann put it, as an "abuse of democratic freedom." And historian Uta Poiger notes how adults could dismiss such spontaneous gatherings as running "counter to proper political involvement, which all mainstream parties defined as voting, organized involvement in political parties, and service to the state." Notably, although such clashes were only common c. 1955–57, the slur *Halbstarken* was regularly deployed into the late 1960s to delegitimize any public protest by young people.[60]

Defining Democracy in Mid-1960s West Germany

That the Federal Republic's economic and political successes played a significant role in its stability and in German democratization is almost universally accepted. The obvious counterexample is the Weimar Republic, whose economic and political difficulties eroded support for its democratic and parliamentary state forms and left Germans associating democracy with unemployment and weak foreign policy. Polling data for the early 1950s suggest that a majority of Germans was more concerned with economic security than democratic rights, so that the Federal Republic risked the same fate if it failed to deliver economically. And it did deliver, in unprecedented security of employment and of income (through a job or through social programs), rising living standards, and international security and respect. Its economic successes clearly did help reconcile to democracy such disparate groups as civil servants, businessmen, the generation that had matured under Nazi indoctrination, and supporters of the Weimar-era Conservative Revolution and their students. Furthermore, Germany's rapid recovery from the 1966/67 recession, its first, was widely credited to Economics Minister Karl Schiller (SPD), so the SPD could now count as economically reliable. And, as David Conradt argues, such successes over time built up a reservoir of goodwill for the political system that could survive economic shocks such as recessions. Observers vary, seeing economic prosperity and political stability as indispensable, significant, or merely useful for the Federal Republic's survival. We cannot know exactly what would have happened to the Federal Republic absent positive economic and political outcomes, but the argument for their significance, and perhaps indispensability, does seem indisputable.[61]

Not all West Germans supported parliamentary democracy, however. When asked in 1967 if it was better to have multiple politicians in charge or give all governing power to the one best politician, 61 percent were for multiple politicians and 27 percent favored giving all power to one man. Moreover, 32 percent still thought Hitler would be one of Germany's greatest statesmen had it not been for the Second World War. Perceiving a tension between democracy and freedom, many Germans considered the Rechtsstaat more important than broad democratic participation. A significant minority held views that suggested at best grudging support for parliamentary democracy. Whether the alternative would be a leaders democracy or a dictator is unclear.[62]

Nevertheless, by the mid-1960s, West Germans had generally come to accept the Federal Republic, its constitution, and its democracy. There was high voter turnout, and from the later 1950s into the twenty-first century, voters gave pro-democratic parties, the CDU/CSU, SPD, FDP, and Greens, more than 90 percent of the vote in Bundestag elections, a sharp contrast with the Weimar Republic's political trajectory. Despite brief surges of support in *Land* elections, radical right parties never secured more than a tiny minority of Bundestag votes before 2017. When asked when things had gone best in Germany, those saying during the *Kaiserreich* or 1933–39 dropped from 87 percent in 1950 to 26 percent in 1963, while those saying the present rose to 62 percent. Substantial majorities agreed that democracy was the best form of government (74 percent overall, 90 percent of those with an *Abitur*, the high school degree allowing matriculation at a university). The number who wished there were only one party had dropped from a quarter in the 1950s to 9 percent in 1967. At least among students in higher education, 81 percent agreed that interest groups had a role to play in a democracy. And in 1962 69 percent agreed that a parliament was necessary. In the 1960s, asked what they thought of the Bundestag as their people's representation, over half said good or very good, a quarter to a third said moderate, and 4 to 7 percent said bad. Germans had never all been pro-authoritarian, but available evidence suggests that by the mid-1960s most had become pro-democratic.[63]

Acceptance of democracy did not mean agreement on what democracy looks like. Even supporters of the Federal Republic and of parliamentary democracy often favored a relatively minor role for citizens. Comments in the 1950s and 1960s on the nature of democracy tended strongly to emphasize democracy as the selection of leaders, with decision-making concentrated in an elected leader or in parliament. Fear of the masses persisted in West German political culture into the 1960s, and beyond. And even to the extent that participation was accepted, the predominant ethos, certainly among political elites but among many other Germans as well, was that such participation must be exercised through the political parties and the parliament, not through popular activism and certainly not through "pressure from the streets." And while 74 percent could in 1968 accept that citizens had a right to demonstrate in the streets, support for that dwindled to 30 percent if a demonstration might impair public order.[64] Indeed, even those such as Dahrendorf who insisted on the need for citizen engagement as part of a democratic political culture could still oppose *too much* citizen activism. West German policymakers did recognize a need to respond to popular opinion, but they clearly wanted that opinion mediated and controlled through parties and a few large, cooperative interest groups.

Yet a more participatory conception of democracy was available in the early Federal Republic. Some political theorists, most famously Jürgen Habermas, were beginning to develop theories of participatory, deliberative democracy. More strikingly, like many Germans in the *Kaiserreich* and Weimar Republic, millions of West Germans took to the streets in the 1950s/60s in various forms of protest. Truckers, expellees, trade unionists, war-injured, ex-POWs, Protestants upset at rearmament and nuclear weapons, Catholics upset at particular movies, et al.: people from all sorts of backgrounds concerned about all sorts of issues chose to act as citizens in ways that went beyond mere voting. Political and social elites and indeed most Germans viewed such activities with suspicion—at least when someone with opposing views engaged in them. They were very much minority activities. Yet they happened, and they were harbingers of things to come.

5

Daring More Democracy

The Rise of Extra-Parliamentary Political Action in West Germany, 1968–1980s

In 1969, Willy Brandt, as first SPD chancellor since the Weimar Republic, told West Germans that his new government wanted to "dare more democracy." He would "give every citizen the opportunity to participate in reforming the state and society, and not only through hearings in the Bundestag, but also through our constant contact with representative groups within the population and by offering transparency about government policies." Yet he considered self-evident the "strict regard for the forms of parliamentary democracy." Brandt's vision had striking similarities to that of early nineteenth-century Prussian reformers: He was a democrat whose citizens would elect their leaders, and he was not hostile to demonstrators. However, he seemed to expect citizens simply to provide information to policymakers and government to communicate more effectively to the people.[1]

West Germans, though, more than took him at his word about daring more democracy. They did not act only through traditional parliamentary forms and "representative groups" (by which he meant the parties and traditional formal organizations). Rather, after 1970 they replaced the early Federal Republic's party-dominated leaders democracy with a participatory democracy in which many citizens participated much more actively—in Citizens Initiatives (*Bürgerinitiativen*), demonstrations, direct actions, civil disobedience, and more. They exercised much more influence over policymaking and implementation than German citizens ever had. Under the newly prevailing conception of political culture, political citizenship no longer meant following political affairs somewhat and voting every few years. It now could mean active attempts by citizens to influence, pressure, or indeed coerce policymakers and officials.

Brandt and the SPD's 1969 electoral victory reflected a mix of social change and citizen fatigue with CDU/CSU domination of the government. Educational attainments had been steadily growing, as had white-collar employment, both of which correlate with increased political activity. Millions of voters had come of age since the FRG's founding, and they were less concerned with the issues of the past and more open to criticism of the existing order. The CDU/CSU had headed the government for twenty years. The Grand Coalition of CDU/CSU and SPD that ruled at the federal level from 1966 to 1969 implicitly granted the SPD a CDU/CSU seal of approval as a trustworthy member of the FRG's political culture. Adenauer had won one election with the campaign slogan, "No experiments!" Enough voters wanted to move beyond such a cautious mindset that Brandt got the chance to create a new coalition with the FDP, whose voters had moved beyond nationalism and markets to embrace more social openness.[2]

Political Stability Amid Economic and Cultural Change

By the 1970s West Germans' support for democracy proved deep enough to withstand economic difficulties. West Germany's economy hit a rough patch in the mid-1970s and unemployment remained a problem through the 1980s—but economic shortcomings have not threatened the Federal Republic's democracy in the way the Weimar Republic's economic difficulties had contributed to its demise. Support for democracy and positive system outcomes still had some correlation, and far Right parties did have brief periods of minor success during 1970s/80s downturns. Nonetheless, West Germans were sufficiently prosperous and the social safety net strong enough to reassure them.[3]

Meanwhile, West Germans, like people elsewhere, were becoming increasingly "post-material" in their values. Growing prosperity in the 1950s/60s led to a greater sense of security and an openness or ability to turn from material concerns to other values and issues. Increased educational attainments seem also to have turned people's attention from immediate material concerns to values-based issues. And people who had grown up with that new sense of security and education proved likely to remain post-material even after the economy soured in the 1970s. Post-materialists were less interested in consumer culture but also less focused on duty, order, and obedience. They proved willing to invest time and resources in self-development and self-expression, to be attained through new lifestyles or new activities. Politically, this meant a focus on different issues than the traditional economic and class-based ones, ranging from local quality of life to ecological concerns to global human rights. And it correlated with a much greater desire for influence over policy and a much greater openness to political protest than was common among those with more materialist values.[4]

"Mastering the past" (coming to terms with and taking responsibility for Nazi crimes) was a perennial issue in West Germany, but a broad movement to do so developed only slowly. Into the 1970s, most Germans chose to ignore the broad complicity of many Germans in wartime atrocities and crimes. However, West Germany's allies (often victims of Nazi criminality) blocked outright denial, and the GDR regularly "outed" war criminals and ex-Nazis in FRG positions of power. The late 1960s student movement attacked West German elites for their frequent complicity, in their younger years, in the Third Reich and its crimes (though Christina von Hodenberg points to evidence that young people seldom confronted their own parents). Yet only the gradual retirement and dying out of the perpetrator generation opened space for a more sincere coming to terms with the past. Then in 1979, the broadcast of a Hollywood "soap opera," *Holocaust*, drew 30 million West Germans to discuss seriously the country's brutal past—by personalizing the issues and offering some characters whose values viewers could embrace. Since the 1980s, grassroots pressure from survivors and their supporters has kept the issue in the public eye, while teachers across Germany systematically ensured that the Holocaust and other war crimes would be covered in school. The media reported regularly on newly revealed Nazi crimes and prosecutions for those crimes. Grassroots pressure for memorializing that past spurred the creation of admonitory monuments across the country, into the twenty-first century.[5]

West Germany had established a democracy without addressing Germany's brutal past, but coming to terms with that past was arguably a crucial contributor to securing democratization. Doing so helped inculcate values necessary for a democracy, such as toleration, and challenged values dangerous to democracy, such as hatred, discrimination, violence. It also sought to warn Germans against political choices that might result in any recurrence of Nazi crimes. And the grassroots nature of much memorialization contributed to an inner democratization of individuals and the society. Yet only in the 1990s did Germans begin addressing the fact that their citizenship remained ethnically based even after the horrific, ethnically based crimes of the Nazis.[6]

Although by 1969 the student movement did not enjoy the popular attention it had in 1967–1968, its embrace of citizen activism had directly challenged the political elite's control and would have lasting effects on West German political culture. The student movement had grown influential as many young people, with support from some older Germans, became concerned about the lack of any significant opposition in parliament, about proposals to amend the GG to allow imposition of a state of emergency, and about the need to transform a rigid German university system being crushed under a growing flood of students. Strongly influenced by Marxism and by American protest techniques and seeking to reject the authoritarianism they saw in German politics and daily life, student activists embraced changes in dress, deportment, and culture and sought to reveal the repressiveness of West German society through provocative and occasionally violent tactics. Because, in their view, oligarchically organized political parties and a deceitful media landscape made parliament an inadequate means for democratic expression, they created alternative media and cultural venues—the beginning of a counterpublic. However, when in 1968 the movement failed to block GG amendment to allow government imposition of a state of emergency, it began to splinter and to decline.[7]

The student movement of 1967/68 drew so much popular attention because it involved an elite segment of the population and played out in a media world that now included television, but its role was complex. As significant as the '68ers proved, West German culture was becoming more liberal, more democratic, and more participatory from the late 1950s, which the student movement built on (see Chapter 4). And change continued over the years after the student movement fell apart. Meanwhile, the developments associated with the West German student movement had analogs in countries across the globe. And the '68ers politicized not only people on the Left but people on the Right, as center and right-of-center students engaged politically and adopted some of the Left's tactics. Notably, as von Hodenberg points out, the student movement's major substantive influence was in spurring a women's movement that would lead to dramatic social changes. However, the student rebels, significantly, did pioneer many protest tactics and drew attention to the possibility of protest.[8]

The new forms of citizen participation that developed after 1970 were not uncontested—and some were hotly contested. Citizens Initiatives could be rejected as threats to representative democracy. Increased citizen participation fed into anxieties that post-industrial societies, swamped with demands, were becoming ungovernable. Civil disobedience could seem a direct attack on the Rechtsstaat and democratic majorities. Critics' worst fears were not realized, as West Germans came to accept much higher levels of citizen participation than in the past while remaining prosperous, politically stable, and democratic. But disagreements flourished—and remain today.

Expanding Protest in an Activist Democracy

West Germany's constitutional framework remained mostly unchanged after 1968. However, policy changes created a new context that influenced the development of political culture and political citizenship.

Brandt's new SPD/FDP coalition did amend the criminal code to make participation in political demonstrations and other protests less risky. Previously, if some participants in a demonstration acted criminally, others present could be arrested if they did not *immediately* disburse at police orders. And thousands of citizens had been arrested at demonstrations in the later 1960s. Yet at a large demonstration, participants could often convincingly argue that they had not *heard* any order to disburse, so indictments and convictions were relatively infrequent. And police had difficulty identifying the violent (and perhaps a certain incentive to arrest nonviolent, and hence less dangerous, individuals, rather than risk injury trying to seize the violent), so peaceable demonstrators and innocent bystanders were the usual arrestees. The new government passed an amnesty law for most of those convicted, to integrate overwhelmingly peaceful protesters into West German democracy. Crucially, the coalition also amended the criminal code so that mere presence at a demonstration that turned violent was no longer grounds for arrest. Conservatives would argue vehemently into the 1980s that only a reversion to the original language would prevent violence at demonstrations.[9]

Into the 1970s, West German judges adjudicating demonstration law tended to be conservative, sharing long-standing suspicions of mass political action in general and especially of politics from the street. By the late 1960s, younger judges began issuing rulings more favorable to demonstrators, but through the 1970s appeals courts (especially the highest, the Bundesgerichtshof) often overruled them, as in its 1969 Laepple decision defining blockades as criminal coercion. It also ruled in 1972 that each individual demonstrator was potentially liable for any damages that any other demonstrator caused during a demonstration—albeit by 1984 it ruled that only those actively participating in acts of violence would be liable. And even in the mid- and late 1970s courts tended to support harsh police measures against demonstrators. The Constitutional Court, in the 1959 Lüth decision (see Chapter 4), had begun emphasizing the primacy of democratic values and rights, and especially freedom of opinion and expression, within the GG and in West German political life. However, the violence that the Communist splinter parties, Spontis, and Autonomous unleashed, especially at anti-reactor demonstrations and in connection with squatting, produced widespread anxiety, as did increasing use of civil disobedience at demonstrations. It was unclear how courts would rule on demonstration rights in the 1980s.[10]

However, the Constitutional Court's unanimous 1985 Brokdorf decision (overturning a blanket ban on demonstrations in the vicinity of a nuclear reactor construction site near Brokdorf) affirmed the centrality of public protest to a democratic formation of the political will, with significant consequences. The court built on the Lüth decision's assertion of the centrality of freedom of opinion and expression for democratic governance. Yet it did not have to make public protest a central, indeed "indispensable," element in citizen expression. Citizens did have other means of expression, for example, voting, petitions, appeals to politicians and formal and informal organizations. Mass demonstrations would always have costs (e.g., policing, traffic disturbances), but West Germany had recently experienced repeated violence by extremists at otherwise peaceful demonstrations, with many injured among police as well as demonstrators. Fear of such violence had justified the blanket ban on demonstrations near Brokdorf. Nonetheless, the court ruled that protest was so central to a democratic formation of the political will that the possibility of a violent minority was insufficient to deprive the peaceful majority of its right to demonstrate. Limits on demonstrations must be extremely narrow and imposed only where clear evidence, not mere supposition, was available that violence or other pressing grounds for a ban or limitation would obtain. The court noted that demonstrating's larger purpose was as means of intellectual debate and of influencing the formation of the political will, but it affirmed that the right to demonstrate includes the right simply to express an opinion, as an immediate unfolding of one's personality, even if it is unlikely to change others' opinions. Had the Constitutional Court handed down its decision in 1981, after four years of often violent anti-reactor and squatter demonstrations, its ruling might have been much less favorable to demonstration rights. However, it handed down its ruling in 1985, after four years of overwhelmingly peaceful anti-missile demonstrations that were much more widely supported, including by many in the judiciary. This decision undercut conservative efforts to sharply restrict rights to public protest, and it established firmly a right to public protest and to activist citizenship in the Federal Republic.[11]

The FRG remained a militant democracy. "Antidemocratic" organizations continued to face bans. Concerns with potential threats to democracy—or at least to the existing state—increased in the early 1970s. Student leader Rudi Dutschke had proposed that student radicals plan not only for revolution but for a "long march through the institutions," in attempting to transform (West) German society, economy, and politics. Conservatives especially began to worry that Marxist radicals were infiltrating the civil service and would subvert the existing order. Meanwhile, Willy Brandt's reforms, and especially his *Ostpolitik* of détente with the East, had antagonized many and opened him and the SPD to accusations of being soft on, or even catspaws for, Communism. Hence, his government met with the *Land* Interior Ministers to reaffirm the policy of blocking antidemocratic individuals from the civil service—while ensuring Rechtsstaat principles prevailed. The resulting 1972 Radicals Decree systematized reviews of current and would-be civil servants suspected of antidemocratic attitudes. Individuals could be barred from the civil service not only for membership in antidemocratic organizations but for participation in actions organized by such groups or for protesting the decree. Around 2000 civil servants were investigated for antidemocratic acts, and a few hundred lost their jobs. All civil service applicants were liable to investigation for antidemocratic acts or opinions, thousands were investigated, and hundreds or thousands (depending on the source) were denied positions. Many more West Germans, apprehensive of such charges, feared to join organizations that might conceivably be deemed "antidemocratic"—by current or future governments. Opponents referred to the decree as a *Berufsverbot*, a ban on exercising one's profession, because governments effectively monopolized many professional positions in West Germany.[12]

Meanwhile, in the 1970s, foreign and domestic terrorists (virtually all far Left) killed dozens of people in West Germany, producing a moral panic among many West Germans. The political Right responded with insistent demands to strengthen the state and weaken popular participation. The CDU/CSU did fear Leftist subversion of the FRG. However, it used these events to challenge the social-liberal government and attack as "sympathizers" anyone they viewed as insufficiently vehement in denouncing terrorism or who criticized their proposed anti-terrorist measures as too extreme. These attacks led to fears for the Rechtsstaat and democracy. The SPD and FDP did resist the more draconian proposals, though some measures did lead to increased harassment of left-of-center groups and individuals. Then, when terrorists seized hostages and flew them to Mogadishu, Somalia, West German security forces successfully freed the hostages, restoring the government's credibility and discrediting the terrorists.[13]

A backlash developed, on the Left and among the broader citizenry, against repressive measures and the risks of a "surveillance state." By the 1980s, most West Germans feared less an extremist subversion of the FRG a la the Weimar Republic and more an insidious dictatorship a la Orwell's *1984*. With the 1972 Radicals Decree, Brandt had sought consistency and Rechtsstaat principles, but in practice neither obtained. Different *Länder* implemented the decree differently, depending on which party dominated the *Land* government. Moreover, West Germans increasingly insisted only *membership* in an antidemocratic organization should be grounds for exclusion from the civil service. They vigorously opposed *Gesinnungsschnüffelei* (snooping around to winkle out a person's inner thoughts) or attempts to block employment for participation in a demonstration, which they saw as unconstitutional criminalization of thought or of political expression; yet in practice that is what investigators in some *Länder* often did. Citizen activists and, increasingly, SPD'ers came to see the Radicals Decree as unconstitutional. SPD-dominated *Länder* and the SPD/FDP coalition federal government were increasingly unwilling to pursue cases, and by the 1980s it fell into disuse, as even the CDU/CSU moved on to other issues.[14]

West German democracy faced potentially serious legal challenges in the 1970s but came out of them more secure and lively. Reforms to the penal code and judicial decisions expanded the scope of legally approved political protest. The *Berufsverbot* and anti-terrorism legislation were deployed to persecute hundreds of individual Germans, with some broader chilling effect on dissent. However, their scope was limited by SPD and FDP resistance, and they fell into desuetude from the 1980s. Overall, the Rechtsstaat survived to create a secure framework for democratic activism.

Security, Order, and Rational Debate in the Rechtsstaat

Post-1945 West Germans (citizens and the state) embraced an increasing emphasis on security. Germans had experienced enormous insecurity in the twentieth century's first half. Beyond the usual insecurities of human life and of market economies (e.g., unemployment, disability), West Germans had had to cope with the consequences of two world wars, two inflations, and a brutal dictatorship. The social state, whose roots reach into the 1880s, was perhaps the most crucial reflection of the search for security. Debates about foreign policy and especially defense policy revolved around often sharply differing conceptions of security and how to attain it. Concern for security spilled over into political culture. It was a frequent theme in elections, particularly for the CDU/CSU. Moreover, anxiety about the perceived disorderliness of various protests, and especially about the occasional violence at them, was for many Germans a matter of security. So where Germans had often responded to 1960s demonstrations with calls for "*Ruhe und Ordnung* [calm and order]," typical responses to late 1970s/80s demonstrations were calls for "*Sicherheit und Ordnung* [security and order]."[15]

Concern for order and security could elicit an emphasis on authority and state power. Conservatives have often argued that order through state authority is a prerequisite for individual freedom and democracy; for many, perceptions of disorder in the 1970s and 1980s exacerbated fears of inadequate citizen (self-)discipline and authority. Citizens and courts in the 1970s and early 1980s often supported harsh police measures against demonstrators, amid terrorism and occasionally violent demonstrations, to reassert authority and reestablish order. Indeed, the CDU/CSU argued that only a political culture of duties, legality, order, and service—and a commitment to the state—could ensure stability. And in a 1979 survey, 46 percent reported that they could not agree with the "modern conception" that "all is criticized, authority is no longer recognized." Notably, concerns with authority might also include a reference to the need for leadership, but not to a leader. Hitler apparently did poison that well for most Germans—at least for public consumption.[16]

Concern with authority contributed to the fear, widespread in the mid- to late-1970s Western world, that democracies were becoming ungovernable because democratic citizens were developing unrealistic expectations as to what or how much government could effectively do. A cohort of commentators came to deplore (as wildly utopian) insistent demands for government intervention to address various problems and the resulting "interventionist state." The sheer number of issues government was expected simultaneously to address seemed inevitably to overload the political system. And increased citizen activism seemed a fundamental element in this burgeoning problem, as citizens did not simply elect competent leaders but sought to intervene themselves in governance. References to ungovernability would dwindle and nearly disappear in the 1980s, as no Western democracy imploded from issue overload, but the concern has been echoed in varying terms in subsequent decades.[17]

Anti-Communism, often as anti-totalitarianism, had been a powerful force in 1950s and 1960s West Germany; it weakened but did not disappear in the 1970s and 1980s. After the construction of the Berlin Wall, Germans had to come to terms with the existence of a divided Germany and world. And after decades of Cold War, the prospect of hot war or successful subversion seemed to many less likely and hence less threatening. Moreover, West Germany's *Ostpolitik* of détente with the Communist bloc proved stable and beneficial to East Germans. Yet the political Right in the 1970s and 1980s still tried to deploy anti-Communism, most notably in the context of the *Berufsverbot* and the debate about stationing new nuclear missiles in West Germany. Protesters debated their relationship to Communists who sought to join their protests, and they often felt compelled to distance themselves from the Communists. And when the Institut für Demoskopie polled people on their opinion of demonstrations against the missile-stationing, the share opposing such demonstrations more than doubled when the question included "even if communist groups are among the participants"—but only from 16 percent to 38 percent.[18]

West Germans tended to emphasize the necessity of the Rechtsstaat—but in different ways. The Rechtsstaat could be seen (cf., the *Kaiserreich*) as a substitute for democracy, a guarantor of theoretically equal rights and protection from arbitrariness for all citizens, even if most had no political voice. After the experience of Nazi dictatorship, it gained new legitimacy as a necessary bulwark against governmental arbitrariness or violence. Many Germans now saw the Rechtsstaat as an indispensable complement to democracy: The Rechtsstaat's laws had to have some legitimate base, and only democracy, many West Germans now argued, could provide that; however, the laws a democratic legislature promulgated could only be effectuated if a functioning Rechtsstaat existed to enforce them and to prevent their being undercut by powerful economic and social forces. It would also provide the legal-political framework within which citizens, including minorities, could exercise their democratic rights. Yet for many other Germans the Rechtsstaat stood primarily for the maintenance of legal security, respect for law, and the state's monopoly on the legitimate exercise of force. Terrorism, occasional violence at demonstrations, and civil disobedience exacerbated anxieties in this regard. All these concerns could be closely tied to an overweening concern with the maintenance of order, so that for many West Germans the Rechtsstaat became not about enforcing democratic will or individual rights but securing authority. It also served for some to justify a narrow conception of democracy in which citizen activism was at best unnecessary and at worst a disorderly threat to the Rechtsstaat.[19]

A recurring aspect of German political culture has been an emphasis on reason and objectivity as central values for political activity. The Third Reich had repudiated both in favor of will—with devastating consequences. Postwar Germans hence frequently emphasized that only a fundamental rejection of Nazi values—and their replacement by reason and objectivity—could protect Germans from a new disaster. Politics had to be a matter of rational argumentation and rational discourse.[20]

Technocracy reflected rationalism. Since the 1930s, many people, and not just in Germany, had sought to conduct politics through "expert" advice. The assumption was that a neutral elite, (social and natural) scientists, could identify the rational solution to pressing social problems. Such claims tended to dismiss, implicitly or explicitly, citizen input. By the 1970s, many were challenging technocracy as antidemocratic and as fundamentally flawed because supposedly neutral expert advice was often politicized and not all issues could be addressed simply with rationalistic analysis.[21]

Some West Germans challenged the emphasis on reason with an embrace of emotion. Some emphasized joy and empathy as central to any meaningful political action; others extolled a liberation of the sensuous or the power of imagination. An increased emphasis on the individual and individual development, often called the "new subjectivity," included a new respect for emotion as an expression of authentic individual identity. Some focused on *Betroffenheit*, that one was directly touched by an issue or a value and must express the feelings and concerns thereby elicited. For others, what counted as rationalism in West Germany was actually capitalist or patriarchal oppression; hence, only by attacking "rationalism" could one hope to overthrow those brutal ideologies and move on to a better future.[22]

In the mid-1970s the Autonomous and the Spontis (spontaneous ones) set the tone at many universities. They appealed to people's subjectivity and personal feelings—not to abstract theorizing—to revolutionize everyday life and transform society. Often influenced by anarchism but also by the Alternative Movement (discussed below), they rejected any rulership or hierarchy, as well as a capitalist economy and the existing polity. Having given up on the workers as a mass base, they looked to the new social movements, especially the anti-reactor, squatter, and peace movements, for their base. Members often made significant sacrifices and were deeply committed to their perception of West German society and of how to transform it, but their deliberate avoidance of any concrete ideology led to repeated splits and withdrawals. And the Autonomous rejected the state's monopoly on violence, leading politicians and right-of center media to characterize them as "chaotics (*Chaoten*)" interested only in brutal disruption.[23]

While some critiqued the emotionalism of protesters as a reflection of absurdly utopian hopes, the emphasis on emotion could also be utilitarian. Protesters often concluded that rational analysis was never going to win over the voters—but only more or less emotional appeals. And while a formal speech might work with critical analysis, a mass demonstration could only make an impact by relying on powerful symbols—especially if one wanted to get on TV. Albeit some protesters did worry that the emphasis on emotion and joy could go too far, and by the mid-1980s this emphasis was waning, although it never completely disappeared.[24]

Still, West Germans continued to prefer rational argumentation, and many were horrified at what they perceived as repudiations of reason and objectivity by the student movement and later by various new social movements. When Jürgen Habermas deplored the "left fascism" he saw in the student movement, he was reacting against the emotion and voluntarism of some student leaders, which he saw as dangerously similar to Nazi values; and his deliberative democracy has a rationalistic basis. Other left-liberal and social democratic intellectuals and commentators would also denounce protest movements whenever they detected signs of anything less than full commitment to reason and objectivity. And commentators warned that television, by its nature, privileged symbolism, emotion, and violence, even as broadcasters promoted discussion programs for rational analysis. Thus, for all the paeans to symbolism and imagination, calls for reason and objectivity continued to predominate in discussions of public protest.[25]

Parliamentary Politics and the Flourishing of Pluralism

Although in the late 1970s some Germans were complaining that the parties were bureaucratic, oligarchic institutions that represented only themselves, West Germany's parties never faced the widespread vitriol that earlier German parties had suffered. The parties apparently were generally accepted, if occasionally grudgingly, as necessary, if imperfect, mechanisms for organizing the political will. When West Germans were asked if they were disappointed with the parliamentary parties, only 25 percent in 1978 and 30 percent in 1982 said yes.[26]

West Germans also seem to have become more accepting of conflict as inevitable in a society. Some West Germans rejected conflict in the name of a common good and social cohesion, but such attitudes were far less commonly or vociferously expressed than in the past. And more Germans explicitly acknowledged that conflict within a society—albeit peaceful conflict—was inevitable. Indeed, some Germans could welcome conflict as productive, as promoting creativity within the society. And by 1972 95 percent of those interested in politics and two-thirds of those with no interest in politics accepted that political competition was important in the West German political system.[27]

In the 1970s and 1980s some commentators expressed concerns about West Germans' willingness to compromise, but its general acceptance proved to be a stabilizing element in political culture. Compromise had clearly come to be widely recognized as a key element in a democratic society. However, the rise of the new social movements (NSMs, large single-issue movements with broad support and activist agendas) and the citizens initiatives raised fears that their members were so committed to a specific issue or a particular interest that they would be unwilling to compromise. In the event, citizens initiatives proved willing to negotiate with the political system, at the local and higher levels, about their issues. And the NSMs, often working through the Greens, also proved willing to compromise. Not all West Germans proved comfortable with compromise, but it did become the predominant ethos.[28]

Democracy is the rule of the majority, but West Germans had to join other democracies in establishing how minorities fit in. Two principles that seemed to attract widespread agreement were that a democracy must protect minority rights (of both dissenting and ethnic/religious minorities) and that minorities had to have some hope of becoming (part of) the majority at some point. Some commentators also argued that the democratic system had to be structured so that minorities could feel that they had a substantive opportunity to contribute to ongoing policymaking processes. Notably, some Germans argued that when a decision would have irreversible consequences, for example, a nuclear reactor producing long-lived radioactive waste or a missile stationing that might make war more likely, minorities were entitled to demand more than a formally or minimally majority decision. Other Germans, though, insisted vehemently on majority rule and rejected any minority right to veto or to impose their own preference (see below).[29]

A particularly striking development was the general, albeit not complete, acceptance of political pluralism. Already by the 1960s, increasing numbers of West Germans seemed willing to accept that modern societies are divided into numerous different interests and that individuals and groups have a right to promote their interests within a competitive political system. Observers generally agreed that most West Germans had by the 1970s fully accepted both the reality of a plurality of interests and the necessity of giving them voice. Yet scholars recognized that pluralism could only work if citizens shared a basic acceptance of the legitimacy of the political system and its values. And some commentators remained sufficiently uncomfortable with the influence of private interests that they could question pluralism. Overall, West Germans do seem to have come to terms with pluralism, but lingering doubts about it influenced some attitudes toward NSMs as interest groups.[30]

Support for "democracy" in West Germany had become substantial. In 1967, 74 percent agreed that democracy was the best state form for Germany, a level that would have been unthinkable in the 1920s and 1930s, or even in the 1950s. And confidence that one could master any serious problems facing West Germany with a multiparty democracy increased from 66 percent in 1975 to 80 percent in 1982, while those preferring a one-party system with a strong government fell from 17 to 6 percent. West Germans, overwhelmingly, seemed comfortable with "democracy." The mean for satisfaction with the Federal Republic's democracy, 1976–1991, was 77 percent. And in 1989 95.9 percent favored democracy in principle and 82.2 percent characterized it as the best form of government. Notably, 85 percent of those satisfied with their own economic situation were satisfied with democracy, but only 32 percent of those dissatisfied with their own economic situation. So while these numbers were substantial, not every West German was happy with democracy. However, what kind of democracy remained an open question.[31]

Despite Brandt's 1969 call to "dare more democracy," the SPD remained deeply ambivalent about what that would mean. The party had always been committed to "democracy" as the only legitimate political system, yet it had been concerned that the masses, especially those not under SPD tutelage, were not yet politically mature enough for autonomous action. The rise of the Nazis had only strengthened SPD suspicion of extra-parliamentary activity. And SPD leaders, not surprisingly, thought that they were quite capable of processing popular opinion and needs and realizing them politically. The postwar SPD hence tended to perceive democracy as parliamentary democracy and to insist that political action must occur within the framework the GG had established. That could mean working vigorously through the GG and the Rechtsstaat to address terrorism—but also insisting popular will must be channeled through parties and parliament. The party resisted plebiscitary proposals, with only a couple of exceptions. Its officials recognized a role for active citizens, but generally through traditional organizations, not through citizens initiatives or direct action. And they opposed appeals to the "right to resistance" that the party and the unions had gotten inserted into the GG—except when the GG itself was directly threatened.[32]

The CDU/CSU was even more inclined to emphasize the purely parliamentary element in West German democracy. The CDU's first leader, Konrad Adenauer, practiced a somewhat authoritarian leadership style. For example, he strictly organized party conventions to preclude discussion by party members, a practice that would continue, albeit less rigorously, after his retirement. It could not ignore post-1968 pressures for increased participation by members, but it limited participation. The party also resisted extra-parliamentary influences on the formation of the political will. For example, in 1982 the West Berlin CDU asserted that acting outside parliament meant ignoring democracy's rules in favor of violence and protest. The CDU/CSU fought to reverse the 1970 demonstration reform, insisting that the police must again have the right to arrest any demonstrator who failed to disperse *immediately* when the police so ordered.[33]

The FDP remained committed to liberal ideals of individual freedom and proved a bulwark against CDU/CSU attempts to limit West Germans' rights in the name of security. While in coalition with the SPD, 1969–1982, the FDP joined the SPD in imposing legislation against terrorism that did limit individual rights in some ways. However, the coalition partners never went as far as the CDU/CSU demanded. And while in coalition with the CDU/CSU in the 1980s, the FDP sought to counter the CSU hardliners in the Interior Ministry. At their 1983 party convention, the FDP emphasized that "a limitation of the right to demonstrate is the false path" and that "a legal sharpening of the penal aspects of the right to demonstrate is not necessary." The party did agree to sharpened rules against masking oneself at a demonstration and against bringing "defensive weapons" to a demonstration; but it rejected CDU/CSU efforts to increase the state's power to limit public demonstrations by reversing the 1970 reform of demonstration rights.[34]

The Greens developed from the participatory politics of the 1970s and struggled, ultimately unsuccessfully, to implement a new "grassroots democratic" politics. Two concerns drove this effort. First, representative democracy, even with increased citizen participation, seemed to many incapable of accurately representing the will of the people on the enormous range of issues a government and legislature would face. Parties took election results as a mandate to implement the party's platform in all regards, even if a substantial majority of voters opposed the party position on a specific issue (most notably, in the 1980s nuclear missile stationing). Parliamentary elections, then, seemed capable only of selecting leaders who would rule more or less independently of the citizens until the next election. Instead, some Greens proposed moving as many decisions as possible to local levels, with, presumably, more citizen input. Others proposed some version of an imperative mandate, in which parliamentary delegates had to vote on each issue as their party members or their electors instructed them, or of a direct or councils democracy, in which delegates could be recalled and replaced if they failed to follow the popular will. Second, majority rule required imposing policies on minorities. So proponents of direct democracy often sought some sort of consensus decision-making, in which issues would be thoroughly discussed until some overwhelming consensus developed. Most commentators rejected such proposals as impractical, especially as they would have required a degree of engagement that most citizens do not seem to have been willing to provide.[35]

Although some activists always resisted party formation, many concluded in the later 1970s that citizens initiatives alone would not give them sufficient influence on policy, so Alternative lists, to challenge the main parties, were necessary. These lists echoed the non-partisan lists center and right-of-center Germans had long promoted, especially on the municipal level, against partisan politics. The membership of the lists was heterogeneous. When these local lists joined together to form the Greens, they did seek to move beyond the highly structured, often hierarchical organization of the main parties to create a more democratic structure. They sought to block the creation of insiders and outsiders within the party and to guarantee the broadest input. They hence tried such policies as choosing conference speakers by lot, preventing individuals from becoming "professional" politicians, banning the holding of multiple offices for the party, insisting on an imperative mandate from voters to Bundestag deputies on each issue, and requiring each Bundestag deputy to give up his/her seat to another Green half-way through a term. Members of the women's movement had played a key role in the party's formation, and they convinced the party to institutionalize equal roles for men and women in the party. The equal role for women has survived, and has influenced other parties, but most of the grassroots democratic efforts have been chipped away. Once individual party members began serving as legislators, they faced pressures to accommodate to parliamentary practice. The "realists" in the party soon prevailed, with their insistence that effective representation of Green concerns required structure, experience, and consistency. The Greens have provided a way for various movements, most notably the ecological, peace, and women's movements, to influence public policy, but they have not fundamentally altered the Federal Republic's parliamentary democracy.[36]

In the 1970s, political elites sought to defend but citizens increasingly challenged the privileged position in the "formation of the political will" that the GG had granted the parties. Throughout the 1970s and 1980s politicians and political commentators would remind the citizenry that the GG assumed that democracy would function through the mediation of parties in representing the people's will or interests, assisted by certain formal, established organizations (such as trade unions and chambers of commerce). They viewed any other forms of citizen input with suspicion. Indeed, some Germans declared that any extra-parliamentary opposition (outside the parties) was extra-constitutional. Yet Germans have since the *Kaiserreich* insisted on participating in politics, on expressing directly their own opinions. And by the 1970s increasing numbers of West Germans were demanding broader citizen input into decisions that affected their lives.[37]

Expanding Horizons of Political Participation

After the 1960s, the numbers of those engaging in political activity fluctuated, but they increased compared with the Republic's early decades. Increasingly, commentators across much of the political spectrum (though not all in the CSU) would identify political participation beyond voting as an important or vital characteristic of democratic or "mature" citizens. West Germans certainly still disagreed about appropriate *forms* of political activism, but they generally accepted its appropriateness in the abstract.[38]

Between 1959/60 and 1974, the percentage of West Germans thinking they could act politically to help change local policy increased from 62 to 67 percent, to change national policy from 38 to 56 percent. The percentage saying they had participated in some form of political activity beyond voting went from 16 percent in 1959 to 34 percent in 1974, 48 percent in 1981, and 57 percent in 1990. And the percentage reporting they had taken part in two or more grassroots activities increased from 9 percent in 1974 to 13 percent in 1981 and 20 percent in 1990. Significant numbers of West Germans were embracing a participatory citizenship.[39]

Participation was not equally distributed across German society. Studies of protesters across recent decades revealed a very strong correlation between increasing education and increasing political participation beyond voting, as well as increased support for democracy in the abstract. Scholars often interpret this in terms of socialization; that is, the values and skills people learned, in formal education or elsewhere, played a significant role in their interest in and ability to engage in political participation. Others identified middle-class social status (independent of education) as contributing to the skills and connections needed to participate effectively in organizations and to interact successfully with the media, administrators, and politicians. And greater work flexibility and leisure in many middle- and upper-middle-class occupations also contributed to the ability to participate. (N.B.: For decades, working-class individuals, often with limited formal education and without middle-class socialization, skills, and flexibility, successfully created a pro-democratic labor movement and helped it to flourish under hostile conditions, so we need a study of how to reconcile these similar but contrasting developments.)[40]

Positive assessments of participation characterized it as democratic but also useful. The consensus into the 1960s seemed to be that the burgher's first duty was calm—but thereafter participation became increasingly central. Numerous commentators insisted that broad citizen participation was essential for a democratic state. Others, though, could emphasize a more pragmatic approach, that citizen participation was not so much essential for democracy as expedient for keeping policymakers informed and on their toes. Obviously, the concepts here are related, but the tone in each is very different.[41]

Some opposition to participation did continue in the 1970s and 1980s, though it was minimal compared to past decades. Even among proponents of participation, some did still conceptualize it in terms of participation in an organization. Organization leaders were always tempted to limit participation. For example, Frank Bösch describes how Adenauer and his colleagues structured CDU party conferences to limit discussion time drastically, how a young Helmut Kohl pushed successfully to open up discussion—and how an older Kohl sought to limit it. Yet even within the CDU, member participation increased. Popular support for broad participation grew in the early 1970s, declined in the later 1970s in the face of occasional violence at demonstrations, and increased again in the early 1980s as massive peace demonstrations remained nonviolent.[42] Lingering doubts remained for some Germans, but most debated the nature and scope of participation, not the right to protest.

Women's roles as citizens changed in the 1970s and 1980s—but slowly. Traditionally, males had dominated the "public sphere" of politics. Women's participation was dramatically lower and mostly confined to "women's issues" (e.g., motherhood, social welfare, education); their leadership roles were nearly non-existent. A broad women's movement developed, spurred initially when male leaders at a SDS (socialist student) conference, in September 1968, refused to live their rhetoric by treating women and women's issues fairly. It developed in multiple directions but, still facing dismissive male attitudes, women's participation in political activism only slowly increased. For example, even in the 1980s, party membership in West Germany was 70 percent male and 30 percent female. Yet between 1965 and 1976, the proportion of West Germans who would be "pleased" if a woman participated in politics rose from 27 to 62 percent among men and from 32 to 66 percent among women. One 1970s women's movement organized around abortion law reform, but thereafter women's activism focused on numerous projects (e.g., women's shelters, day care, book stores) that reflected women's life experiences and social positions. Women deployed a range of protest forms (including, for a few groups, violence). With the anti–nuclear reactor movement and especially with the peace movement, women broadened their political roles to include traditionally "male" issues such as the economy and international affairs. And they did so as participants and in leadership positions—though sexism continued to be a constraint. And the Greens in the 1980s contributed to increasing the number of women who could make careers as politicians, especially by establishing quotas for women among party leaders and representatives. By the 1980s, cultural change and the women's movement had established in principle that women as equal citizens had an equal role and right of participation in public life, though in practice male norms and expectations still predominated.[43]

West Germany's increasingly participatory politics is often ascribed to generational changes, which may have played a role. Opinion polling across decades generally shows more support for activist forms such as demonstrations among younger than older respondents. Sometimes this is ascribed to the young being more liberal or activist and the older being more conservative. Sometimes increased participation is ascribed to the life experiences of a specific generation, with the '68ers seen as particularly open to political activism because of their youthful experiences in the 1960s. Any simple ascriptions seem problematic. For example, while youth were more likely to appear at demonstrations, that may have more to do with the time flexibility that lack of family and other burdens give the young than with a generational level of openness to political activity. Unfortunately, data on Citizens Initiative membership by age are not available—but might show more participation by the middle-aged or elderly than by youth. Moreover, Klaus Allerbeck argues that differences in activism apply more to those from the middle and upper strata than to those from the lower and lower-middle strata and that the old/young difference increases with educational level. And education levels were higher among younger cohorts. A generational shift *c.* 1970 did contribute to the development of a more participatory culture, but age alone was not the determining factor in political choices. And by the 1980s a new norm developed of political participation for citizens of all ages.[44]

West German citizens continued to use petitions to express their opinions and influence public policy. The most famous petition in the 1970s and 1980s was the Krefelder Appeal, calling for West Germany to refuse to allow the stationing of new medium-range, American, nuclear-tipped missiles on its territory; it collected millions of signatures and helped make opposition to the missiles a central political issue—even though the German Communist Party initiated it. Other issues, such as reform of abortion legislation, also drew millions of signatures. In the late 1970s, 82 percent of West Germans approved of signing a petition as a means of expressing a political opinion. West Germans ranked relatively high internationally in having signed a petition, with 42 percent of German youth having done so, compared with 48, 27, 24, and 21 percent of American, British, Dutch, and Austrian youths respectively. And in broader surveys the numbers of West Germans saying they had signed a petition was 31 percent in 1974, 47 percent in 1981, and 57 percent in 1990. Yet policymakers, of course, did not respond to every petition, leaving citizens to look to further means to influence policy.[45]

The flourishing of tens of thousands of citizens initiatives has been a striking and important development in West German political culture. They began appearing in the 1960s but really took off in the 1970s. They developed independently of the student movement, though they drew on some of its liberalizing and participatory imperatives. Soon, substantially more Germans belonged to citizens initiatives than to political parties. The basis of membership was not class but ideological goals or collective goods. Usually focused on specific issues, they could be politically and ideologically heterogeneous. Having post-materialist values was the best predictor of membership, albeit not a determinant one. Initiatives initially sought to influence administrative decisions about policy implementation, for example, on road noise or provision of public parks. They soon began working to influence legislation. They could serve as an early warning system for problems that the parties or formal organizations were unaware of or had proved unwilling to address (anything from a neighborhood playground to improved mass transit to fears of nuclear power plants); some wished to confine them to that role. Initiatives, though, wanted substantive influence. Even observers with reservations could admit that their rapid growth showed that something beyond parties and formal organizations was necessary to give citizens an adequate sense of participation in the political system. Some supporters envisioned the initiatives as the basis of a grassroots-democratic alternative to parliamentary democracy, but most members emphasized them as a supplement to liberal democratic institutions and as mobilizing citizens for democracy.[46]

Citizens initiatives were, nonetheless, hotly contested. They began as single-issue organizations, and some commentators protested that they promoted only "egotistical" interests and were indifferent to the common good. Past concerns about "interests" had not disappeared, even if they had weakened. The political parties were deeply ambivalent about the initiatives. Some politicians welcomed them, at least publicly, as appropriate forms of democratic participation, but the initiatives did compete with the parties for public favor. And when the initiatives began promoting legislative proposals, they began putting often unwelcome pressure on parties and formal organizations. So the initiatives came to be criticized as increasing ungovernability with their demands and as unrepresentative (how could one know which and how many members/ supporters they really had?). In the later 1970s, citizens initiatives became associated with the anti-reactor movement and with the violence that usually far-Leftist political activists engaged in, and popular willingness to join citizens initiatives dropped from 51 percent in 1976 to 36 percent in 1981 (though it later rose again). Overall, citizens initiatives became an accepted part of West German political culture, but they were never completely uncontroversial.[47]

The *Alternativen* (Alternatives), in the 1970s and early 1980s, both retreated from and broadened the "political." The student movement's dissolution, long-standing frustrations with capitalism and consumerism, aversion to the Marxist Left's rigid ideologizing, a proliferation of opportunities and niches in a newly affluent society, and the spread of post-materialist values created spaces in which hundreds of thousands of mostly young West Germans sought to imagine and realize alternative modes of living. They were committed to personal development, experience, and "authenticity"; they rejected "cold" rationality and consumerism. Albeit as Alexander Sedlmaier points out, this anti-consumerism was mostly not about consuming less but consuming differently. In various West German cities, especially West Berlin, certain neighborhoods became "alternative," homes for countercultures that challenged the existing order. Various businesses commercialized aspects of these countercultures, spreading them to (segments of) the larger society but also undermining the Alternatives' anti-consumerist and anti-materialist goals. Moreover, by 1984, 60 percent of Alternative social assistance groups were getting government subsidies. Just how coherent the Alternatives were as a movement was always debatable, even though a substantial number of West Germans had a sense of shared values and goals. Elements of their countercultures survive into the twenty-first century, but it did decline as a project across the 1980s.[48]

One key strain within the Alternatives rejected the formally political and sought instead personal, cultural, or social transformations as means for revolutionary change. After 1960s radical projects failed, and not only in West Germany, political change seemed unlikely or too far in the future. Radically changing individuals might change society, but in practice individual transformations seemed to require exchange and cooperation with one's fellows. Hence, creating alternative modes of life, that would then spread to the larger society, could seem the only way to achieve meaningful change, to overcome capitalism, consumerism, et al. A notable example of this was the women's movement's effort to create anti-authoritarian child care and preschool institutions that would transform the society by transforming/emancipating the children—and hence tomorrow's adults and culture. One could see these as counsels of despair after the failures of the student and anti-State-of-Emergency-Law movements, but they were also ways of achieving significant changes in the here and now (and, for example, German child-rearing practices have changed dramatically since the 1960s). They did, however, mean an indeterminate number of West Germans were consciously withdrawing from politics as traditionally understood.[49]

The Alternatives contributed significantly to widening the definition of the political, blurring the political/private boundary, and democratizing values. The women's movement emphasized the ways matters usually considered private were political and the necessity of dramatically expanding the definition of the political to include the multitude of ways in which the society oppressed women—and others. That movement was much broader than the Alternatives, but many feminist activists worked within the Alternative movement, in childcare, feminist book stores, women's centers, et al. And this expansion was not confined to feminists: Others emphasized the need to address the quotidian, people's day-to-day lives and the problems they often faced in a changing society. Citizens initiatives could align with the Alternatives in putting on the political agenda issues such as urban noise and traffic that were not traditionally seen as political. Since the 1950s, dress, hairstyle, music choices, et al. could all be political statements. And the Alternatives' emphasis on grassroots democracy and rejection of hierarchy and authority contributed to an increasing acceptance of individual autonomy in West German society. Moreover, the Alternatives' emphasis on the personal and the emotive fed into new protest forms, for example, die-ins.[50]

The squatting movements that periodically arose in West German cities from the late 1960s provoked mixed reactions. Many German cities suffered from housing shortages. Yet many dwellings sat idle, as speculators sought to run buildings down enough to justify, legally, razing them and replacing them with profitable alternatives. The squatters got considerable popular support, for example, 53 percent of those polled in 1981 thought the squatters were right in their criticism of urban development and clear-cut urban renewal (perhaps not surprising, given widely perceived corruption and profiteering by property speculators). Some squatters just wanted a roof over their heads, but often they came out of the Alternatives and sought to secure spaces in which they could develop an authentic identity or broadly democratic mode of living. Squatters generally ran their squats with direct democratic meetings and consensus. City governments occasionally reacted sympathetically but usually negatively, and conservatives denounced squatting as an assault on property rights and the Rechtsstaat. The squatters often split, as some sought negotiations leading to their occupation's legalization, while others rejected any truck with the (capitalist) system. About two-thirds of squats negotiated some long-term right to occupy, and the rest were cleared by police. The violence often involved (sometimes initiated by police, sometimes by squatters) did not help the squatters' public reputation. Some long-term settlements did provide meeting spaces for Alternatives.[51]

The far Left and the Alternatives agreed that the public sphere in West Germany had become corrupted by powerful status-quo forces, so that creating new publics or a "counterpublic" was necessary. The student movement had vehemently attacked Axel Springer's publishing empire; they thought he bore significant responsibility, with his nationalist, authoritarian, and deeply deceptive reporting, for deluding West Germans about late capitalism's realities. The far Left continued this line of argument. The Alternatives saw consumer society as deeply inauthentic, so that the only means to real change was to fundamentally redefine the culture, to create counterpublics that would enable individuals to build and spread authentic ways of living. The creation of emancipated spaces, as communes or neighborhoods, was a starting place. And attempts to create an alternative media of hundreds of periodicals, culminating in the founding of the newspaper *taz*, were another.[52]

The determination to create counterpublics reflected deep concerns with the role of media: their framing, criteria, preferences, effects. A social movement does not exist if it is not present to the citizenry. A protest was only public if the public knew it had occurred. And only media, of some description, could make a movement or protest known beyond its participants and a narrow circle of onlookers. Protesters often saw the media as indifferent or compromised, and media outlets did often take sides (implicitly or explicitly) on issues of public concern. The media, and especially television, were (in)famous for favoring sheer numbers, pictures, sensationalism, and violence as criteria in judging whether an event was worthy of exposure. And their desire to focus on identifiable leaders would often lead to tensions within movements. Nonetheless, despite attempts to create alternative media, protesters had to appeal to mass media to get broad publicity. They all struggled to structure their protests in ways that would get media attention—to their issues and not simply to the spectacle of direct action. Meanwhile, those uncomfortable with public protests deplored the media's willingness to give a platform to (implicitly misguided) activists, and a literature grew that agonized over mass-media emotionalism and the threat that seemed to pose to rational discourse. Almost no one was happy with the role of the media in channeling protest—but for wildly different reasons.[53]

Public Protests

The GG guaranteed rights of expression, assembly, and demonstration for West German citizens, but the right to protest remained contested. Those seeking political change looked to public protests to inform and influence public opinion about policy concerns. The goal could be convincing interlocutors and fellow citizens, but it could also be pressuring or even compelling the government to act in desired ways. The range of types of protest was enormous, and many forms, from happenings to civil disobedience, remained widely unacceptable. Those participating in public protests were likely to be younger and middle class, but protests drew people from all age cohorts except the very youngest and oldest and from all social strata. Setting up a table in the market square on a Saturday was a frequent, low-key, personal form of activism. In opposition to the introduction of NATO medium-range missiles into the Federal Republic, millions attended early-1980s demonstrations and thousands risked arrest in blockades and other acts of civil disobedience—highlighting the broad willingness among West Germans for direct action to express political opinions and to influence, perhaps pressure, policymakers. West Germans continued to debate public protest's effectiveness, though proponents could point to examples of success, for example, in pushing the United States to negotiate with the SU over intermediate-range missiles or in blocking specific nuclear facilities at Wyhl and Gorleben.[54]

Some West Germans continued to insist that protests were inappropriate. Some argued, occasionally pointing to the Weimar Republic's fate, that street activism undercut the representative institutions the GG had established. More common were explicit or implicit appeals to the need for order and structure, which public protests were thought inevitably to challenge. Such concerns sometimes drew on decades of fears of the masses. Franz-Josef Strauß went so far as to characterize demonstrators as "animals," and "animals" could scarcely be taken seriously as citizens with rights of participation in public discourse. Federal Interior Minister Friedrich Zimmermann (CSU) said demonstrators were not "normal" if they did not disperse when the police ordered them to do so. The CDU/CSU hence fought throughout the 1970s and early 1980s to repeal the 1970 amendments to the demonstration legislation, so that police could once again order any demonstrators to disperse by asserting that violence was occurring or might occur and then arresting anyone who did not disappear forthwith. In 1969, when asked about student "*Unruhen* (unrest, disturbances, riots)," 53 percent said demonstration freedom in GG must not be curtailed, while 39 percent said it should in the case of the students. After violence from hard left groups at several late-1970s anti-reactor demonstrations, a March 1981 poll showed 42 percent opposed demonstrations and only 29 percent favored them. Yet after peaceful demonstrations against missile stationing became predominant, in June 1982 51 percent approved of such demonstrations and only 24 percent disapproved. Those who could contemplate the government passing a law to forbid all public protest demonstrations fell from 53 percent in 1974 to 39 percent in 1989. A core of West Germans clearly remained who were uncomfortable with the right to protest publicly, at least if presented with evidence of disorder.[55]

Those statistics reflect a general though not universal acceptance among West Germans by the 1980s of public protest as part of democratic life and democratic citizenship. Even political elites, often grudgingly, came to see that public opinion could not be channeled solely through formal interest groups, parties, and parliament. And more and more West Germans proved willing to participate, so that West Germany had comparable rates with other democracies. When West Germans were asked if they had participated in a lawful demonstration, 9 percent said yes in 1974, 15 percent yes in 1981, and 21 percent yes in 1990. About 62 percent of those polled in the late 1970s approved of lawful demonstrations. Albeit in a 1989 poll, 35.7 percent said they would under no circumstances take part in a demonstration. Notably, whereas 1920s/30s activism had generally been directed toward a specific political party or leader, 1970s/80s activism was generally directed toward a specific issue/policy (e.g., against reactors, for abortion law reform).[56]

Citizens still faced hard tactical choices as to which forms of protest would be most efficacious. They drew on foreign, particularly US, models of activism, while developing their own techniques (e.g., "die-ins," where protesters lay motionless in a pedestrian zone to admonish passers-by as to the risks of nuclear energy and nuclear missiles). A broad palette of unconventional, often playful techniques soon complemented the conventional techniques of petitions, speeches, and demonstrations. As Max Kaase emphasizes, conventional and unconventional techniques were not substitutes but complements—citizens who resorted to unconventional techniques seldom abandoned conventional ones. Moreover, techniques long considered "unconventional" could become so common as to be conventional. A continuing issue was how to maximize a protest's positive impact on public opinion and policymakers. Protesters generally emphasized eclecticism and "imagination" but often disagreed on how unusual one could be without alienating the average citizen (e.g., happenings as too frivolous) and whether violence (against things or people) was counterproductive. And different protest techniques could imply vastly differing conceptions of political citizenship.[57]

In West Germany's post-Nazi political culture, a widespread presumption prevailed that the point, indeed for many the only legitimate consequence, of any act of political citizenship, including demonstrations, should be to convince an opponent or policymaker through rational and objective argumentation. Conflict could break out within a movement over whether it should confine itself to seeking to convince others, but the consensus view clearly was that a demonstration was to provide enlightenment to the masses or to policymakers. It was to stimulate discussion—objective, well-reasoned debate—on central political issues. In a repeated phrase dismissing violence at demonstrations, West Germans insisted that "*Steine sind keine Argumente*"—(throwing) stones does not constitute (rational) argumentation. The attempt by many demonstrators, from the 1960s on, to bring an element of imagination to political action would often be dismissed by observers as reducing a demonstration to "*ein Happening*"—a frivolous (because not objective and rational) waste of time, one that demeaned the serious project of forming the political will. This presumption was perhaps unsurprising, after Nazism's emotionalism, irrationality, and violence. However, it was also deployed to delegitimize more assertive forms of political activism, and it could resonate with otherwise sympathetic observers who remained committed to rational and objective politics.[58]

Provocation was a central element in political protest for many West Germans, but a problematic one. In the 1960s, the German artists' group Subversive Action, influenced by the Dutch Provos, had introduced provocation as a tactic to attract attention. Kommune I in West Berlin had, from 1967, taken up the practice, with a vengeance. Provocation was soon ubiquitous on the student Left. Many saw it, some into the 1980s, as the only way to pierce the citizenry's narrow-mindedness and the media's corruption, forcing them to pay attention and securing a wider public's attention to one's views. As Rudi Dutschke asserted, "With provocations we can create a public space for ourselves in which we can spread our ideas, our wishes, and our needs. Without provocation we will not be noticed at all." For some it was legitimate only as a way to draw otherwise inattentive or deceived voters into a rational discussion of the issues, but for others it could seem an end in itself. It hence risked alienating potential supporters and was always controversial.[59]

West German protesters were quite willing in the 1970s and 1980s to assert that the purpose of demonstrations was to put "pressure (*Druck*)" on policymakers, and fewer commentators objected. In a model of democracy purely as reasoned discourse among all citizens, pressure on policymakers would have no place, indeed would be illegitimate. When student protesters first began seeking to "pressure" policymakers in 1967/68, numerous commentators vehemently denounced (often as Nazi and Communist tactics) any "pressure from the streets" by self-selected minorities—as incompatible with democracy in general and representative democracy and the GG in particular. Johannes Agnoli responded that policymakers were subject to pressure from various interests all the time. Indeed, he argued, if average citizens petitioned, they would be ignored, while a letter from the Association of German Industrialists would constitute far more pressure than any student demonstration. Subsequently, supporters of demonstrations took it for granted that public protests might inform and spark dialog, but that they could also be a means of exercising pressure on policymakers. They often cast them, implicitly or explicitly, as ways to raise the costs to policymakers of persisting in a given policy or of failing to respond to citizen demands. Some West Germans continued to reject "pressure from the streets." However, having accepted the pluralist nature of (West) German society, most seem also to have accepted that the varying interests within that pluralist society would seek to pressure, and that broad-based citizen efforts were no less acceptable than narrowly self-interested ones.[60]

More problematic were proposals to deploy protest actions as means of compulsion (*Zwang*). Some protesters were willing to be quite blunt that when an issue was crucial enough (e.g., nuclear power or nuclear waste, nuclear war), a degree of compulsion by the citizenry was necessary if the political system was unresponsive to popular protests. Others could allude to elements of compulsion as means to provoke a necessary public debate on a vital issue. West German protesters seemed readier to reject compulsion than to reject pressure in popular protest. Implicitly, they were echoing Philipp Scheidemann's 1913 objection to the political mass strike, that as democrats they could not expect to impose a minority view on the majority. Opposition to compulsion was closely tied to concern with coercion (*Nötigung*), which was a crime under German law, but only if it was reprehensible (*verwerflich*). Considerable debate would develop, in the context of civil disobedience and blockades, as to what constituted coercion and when it was reprehensible.[61]

The 1970s saw the widespread introduction of civil disobedience as a protest tactic. In the 1960s Michael Vesper, returning from a year as an exchange student in the United States, had sought to introduce US-style protest tactics, including civil disobedience, to the West German student movement. Civil disobedience took off in West Germany with the anti-reactor movement. In 1975, citizens of the area around Wyhl, accompanied by students and others from the region, established an ongoing occupation of the proposed site of a nuclear reactor, eventually compelling the *Land* government to abandon plans for that reactor. The anti-reactor movement would continue to use site occupation, blockades, and other forms of civil disobedience. One analysis suggests that 18.5 percent of anti-reactor actions, 1970–92, involved some civil disobedience. The squatting movement in West German cities often couched its efforts as civil disobedience. The early 1980s movement against the stationing of medium-range US nuclear missiles also engaged extensively in civil disobedience, and even some judges participated in illegal blockades—much to the outrage of conservatives. Indeed, one survey showed 40 percent of jurists in the mid-1980s expressing a positive view of civil disobedience. Two surveys, 1974 and 1980, did show a drop in willingness "in an unusual situation" to participate in civil disobedience from 30.8 percent to 26.4 percent. And in a 1976 survey, only 12 percent would participate in a demonstration that blocked traffic and only 7 percent would occupy factories or office buildings. Civil disobedience nonetheless played an increasing role in West German politics, with blockades and occupations per year rising from less than 100 in *c.* 1970 to over 200 in the late 1970s and still in the hundreds in the 1980s.[62]

Supporters of civil disobedience presented it as a necessary step by mature political citizens in the face of failures within the political system. They argued that the government frequently failed to listen to its citizens when they confined themselves to petitioning or even to public demonstrations, and that the parties were not necessarily responsive either. If an issue was pressing enough, citizens were then entitled to resort to civil disobedience. An action could be illegal but still legitimate because a higher principle was at stake. German *theorists* of civil disobedience generally followed American precedents. They emphasized that civil disobedience in a democracy was predicated on accepting in principle majority rule and the constitutional order, even as one challenged their inadequacies; one must be prepared to accept the legally mandated punishments if one chose to act illegally, to demonstrate one's sincerity and commitment to the constitutional order; and they emphasized that civil disobedience had to be completely nonviolent.[63]

In practice, German proponents of civil disobedience disagreed on key issues. While supporters often identified civil disobedience as a means, in extremis, to compel dialog and rational discussion, others said bluntly that the goal was to pressure or even to compel policymakers to act in specific ways that protesters wanted. Some even said that if the issue were vital enough (e.g., if nuclear waste threatened citizens' constitutionally guaranteed right to bodily integrity), then they were entitled to prevent the actions that posed that threat, no matter what the majority of their fellow citizens and of the Bundestag thought. Even though theorists, following David Thoreau and Dr. Martin Luther King, Jr., emphasized the need to be willing to go to jail, virtually no Germans who engaged in civil disobedience expressed any willingness at all to go to jail. Indeed, they denounced any attempt to arrest citizens for acts of civil disobedience as "criminalization of dissent." Proponents of "civil disobedience" emphasized repeatedly that it must be completely nonviolent. However, small but committed groups from the splinter communist parties, Autonomous, and Spontis engaged in violence, against things and sometimes persons, during demonstrations and pushed for violence at site occupations and other events. Civil disobedience remains part of German activists' protest repertory, though its use has declined. Yet these disagreements remain lively topics of debate.[64]

Civil disobedience elicited vehement opposition from some politicians and scholars. For some, concerns with order were predominant. They saw any toleration of deliberate law-breaking as a threat to the Rechtsstaat and to lawfulness. They warned, often graphically, of the chaos that could result if citizens got the idea that obedience to the law was voluntary, so long as one could say one's conscience or some higher principle legitimated lawlessness. Others worried that civil disobedience was a threat to democratic governance. If any significant minority disagreed with a majority decision, they could, in the name of civil disobedience, take steps to block the implementation of that decision. That seemed all the more likely because civil disobedience proponents so universally denied they should have to suffer any punishment for their law-breaking, turning civil disobedience, these opponents complained, into a no-cost tool for a minority to dictate policy to the majority. Moreover, once established as a legitimate tool, civil disobedience could be used by anyone in the society, from far Left to far Right.[65]

In justifying civil disobedience, protesters often appealed to a "right to resistance." To secure the 1968 constitutional amendments allowing State-of-Emergency Legislation, the government had to include in Art. 20 GG a "right of every German to resist any who undertakes to overthrow this [constitutional] order, when no other remedy is available." In the 1960s many Germans saw the Federal Republic as fundamentally flawed because of its failure to purge ex-Nazis from positions of power and influence or because of the predominance of capitalist economic elites within it. This suspicion survived into the 1980s and beyond and was strengthened by the perceived failure of constitutional institutions to allow any meaningful citizen input on life-and-death issues such as nuclear power and nuclear weapons. So for at least some protesters the Federal Republic, despite three decades of increasing democracy, was not fully legitimate. In addition, many Germans had come to deplore the failure of 1940s Germans to seek to overthrow the criminal Nazi regime; they were hence primed to value "resistance" and to fear that they, too, might be found wanting if they did not resist immoral policies. For the anti-reactor movement, then, the phrase "Where injustice becomes law, resistance becomes a duty" became a mantra. And it seemed to provide German constitutional sanction for actions to protect, in this case, the constitutionally guaranteed right to bodily integrity for each citizen—using illegal means.[66]

Most commentators rejected this argument as patently groundless. The wording of the GG made clear that the right to resistance pertained only when the constitutional order was under threat, not when some specific policy might seem problematic or even unconstitutional. It would only apply when the GG's normal legal and political procedures no longer functioned—and certainly not against policy decisions the Bundestag and Bundesrat had democratically legitimated. Moreover, some commentators pointed out that for protesters in the democratic Federal Republic to compare themselves, implicitly or explicitly, to those who had risked life and torture resisting Hitler was the height of arrogant self-aggrandizement.[67]

Resistance was an attractive concept for West German protesters. It did put them in the company of those who had resisted Hitler, even for protesters who did not explicitly draw the comparison. And it legitimated civil disobedience by giving it a putative constitutional sanction. Moreover, it helped convince protesters that any suggestion they should be punished for breaking the law while engaging in civil disobedience was an illegitimate "criminalization of dissent" rather than a logical consequence of breaking democratically promulgated laws.

Nonviolence was a central issue for many West Germans—and especially for supporters of civil disobedience. Pacifist strains in Germany went back into the nineteenth century, and the experience of two brutal world wars ensured their continued influence. The American civil rights movement, an important touchstone for many in West Germany's social movements, had emphasized nonviolence on moral and pragmatic grounds. West German theorists of civil disobedience, usually rooted in West Germany's Lutheran churches, emphasized the sanctity of human lives and a principled opposition to violence. Moreover, proponents of nonviolence often argued that means and ends were inextricably intertwined, so that violent means could not produce the nonviolent society that any rational person must seek. Many supporters of social movements, though, were unwilling to reject in principle any use of violence.

They almost universally could agree that using violence in a democratic state such as West Germany was hard to justify and would probably prove counterproductive to securing mass support for one's goals. Yet they could also argue that in extremis (e.g., tyrannicide, a new Nazism) violence might be necessary. Overall, West German protest movements, except for some squatter groups, remained committed to nonviolence.[68]

Despite a broad commitment to nonviolence among West German protesters, the late 1960s through early 1980s were marked by violence at some West German protests and by sharp debates over what constituted *Gewalt* (which can mean force or power as well as violence). In the 1960s, a subset of West Germans argued that modern societies rested on "structural *Gewalt*": that the threat of unemployment, the power of advertising, the imposition of social mores, the state's monopoly on force, and a range of other factors constituted exercises of force by the state and other powerful actors that prevented individuals from being really free. Moreover, the police tended to treat any challenge to prevailing norms as criminal. So citizens protesting publicly often faced police brutality (*Gewalt*), which conservatives often lauded and *never* condemned—despite its frequent viciousness, gratuitousness, and illegality. (Notably, a substantial minority in polls approved of police "beating demonstrators" if a demonstration turned violent; that minority dwindled, but only from 44 percent in 1982 to 30 percent in 1989.) The late-1960s student movement debated whether violence against things or against persons could be legitimate in a society characterized by structural *Gewalt*. To spark a rebellion to overthrow the FRG's liberal capitalist order, a tiny minority would move to terrorism, an extreme form of violence, including against persons. Others on the Left, among Communist groups, Autonomous, and Spontis, also embraced violence, against things and people (against police), as part of a "repertory" of tactics to counter official *Gewalt*, keep the police off balance, reveal the current order's brutality, and lay the groundwork for revolution.[69]

The waves of violence that broke out at anti-reactor demonstrations and in connection with squatting in the late 1970s probably contributed to the temporary decline in support for public protest and the reassertion of nonviolence. The press often presented a sensationalistic narrative of squatting as a criminal/terroristic attack on Western Civilization and democracy. Moreover, conservatives insisted that even psychological pressure or any illegality at demonstrations constituted *Gewalt* (violence) and that its perpetrators should be punished and their cause dismissed. Hence, many in the NSMs came to see violence as disastrously counterproductive. The peace movement then insisted categorically that no one who resorted to violence could be a supporter of peace or a peace movement member. Violence against people (police) by demonstrators mostly, though not entirely, disappeared in the 1980s. However, violence against things remained an element in protests—and violence against people, aimed primarily at immigrants, resurfaced after 1989 on the far Right (see Chapter 7). One key goal of democracy is to provide processes for the peaceful resolution of differences and the peaceful transfer of power. The appeal to *Gewalt* was then problematic, and the overwhelming majority of postwar Germans (70 to 74 percent in one set of polls, 94.4 to 96.9 percent in another set) repudiated it completely, and a dwindling minority could accept it against persons (from 7 percent in 1978 to 3 percent by 1989). And Federal Interior Ministry statistics showed a steady decline in violence at demonstrations, from

36 percent of demonstrations "unpeaceful" in 1969 to 7.5 percent in the 1970s and 3.6 percent in the 1980s, even as criteria for an "unpeaceful" demonstration expanded to include late registration, noise, and photographing security personnel.[70]

A Participatory Democracy

West Germans created in the 1970s and 1980s a more participatory democracy. That development was contested, but it has proved substantive and (at least relatively) long-lasting. Substantial majorities in polls embraced democracy—but attitudes toward what democracy should mean were varied and in some ways contradictory: some emphasized a strong institutional framework with a minimum consensus of values that could constructively channel and contain popular input. Others sought a broad democratization of West Germany and its life through the inculcation of more democratic social attitudes. Some wanted a more "democratic," often in practice less hierarchical or authoritarian, social structure for its own sake. By the 1970s there are remarkably few references to democracy as the periodic selection of leaders; often a commentator mentioned it simply as a model that still had support from some unnamed others, suggesting that this definition of democracy was no longer a politically viable option.[71]

West German political elites remained strongly attracted to a conceptualization of democracy that emphasized the institutional framework the GG had established and the role of formal organizations, while implicitly downplaying the participation of average citizens. They grumbled that citizens initiatives were self-selected minorities with no formal legitimacy, even when (as with nuclear missiles) they were clearly expressing an opinion shared by many and perhaps most citizens; they saw them as a potential threat, as Sebastian Haffner put it, to the "ordered determination and implementation of the majority will." They could reject government by opinion poll because the representative system the GG had established was designed to allow the rational discussion of complex issues and the careful compromises that would lead to the best policy outcomes. They still could see parties and formal organizations as the only serious actors deserving of a place at the table, even when citizens initiatives were reflecting the views of more people than traditional organizations (albeit a few commentators saw even formal organizations as problematic because they represented individual interests, not the common good). They could above all point to the GG itself as the constitutional basis for governance in Germany. That document did allow for citizen expression of opinion, but its drafters had envisioned a limited citizen role and had offered citizens no formal role in policymaking beyond party membership.[72]

Nevertheless, by the mid-1980s, in a dramatic shift from 1950s/60s attitudes, most political elites and most citizens seem to have accepted, often to have embraced, a model of democracy and democratic citizenship in which citizens had a right and perhaps an obligation to participate directly in political-will formation. Numerous commentators stated that the rise of the citizens initiatives reflected the inadequacy of the older, party- and parliament-based, model. The initiatives' rise, they argued, showed that West Germany had suffered from a democracy deficit. Effective governance then required the ability of citizens to participate actively in political life—not merely as an "early warning system" but as agents in the process of political decision-making. Habermas's deliberative democracy is a sophisticated version of an attitude toward politics that many Germans (a fair number of whom may never have heard of him) had embraced. Over half of Germans, 1977/78, thought that Bundestag delegates should base their votes on a bill, if they knew what the majority of citizens thought, on the citizenry's opinion, not their own. Albeit 30 to 40 percent thought the delegates should vote according to what they thought was right, as the GG framers had intended. This pressure for a more active citizenry spilled over into demands by some for a broader democratization of German society and broader citizen participation rights within non-governmental institutions and organizations (e.g., schools, interest groups) and contributed to a less hierarchical, more open society. This new model faced substantial resistance in some quarters; for example, a not-insignificant minority could envision police "beating" demonstrators. Nonetheless, after the Constitutional Court's Lüth and Brokdorf decisions, which declared broad freedom of expression to be an indispensable element in the FRG's free-democratic basic order, any attempt to rein in the new citizen activism might well be declared unconstitutional. By no means did all West Germans embrace the new model, but it clearly became the predominant one from the mid-1980s. And despite fears that increased citizen participation could undermine representative democracy, that increase has so far seemed a system-stabilizing element.[73]

Although a core of West Germans continued to oppose public protest, much of what counted as unconventional protest behavior in the 1960s had by 1990 become, as Peter Gundelach argues, "part of the regular repertory of political activity."[74] The breadth of protest, in numbers and in methods, helps explain the assertively pro-protest tenor of the Constitutional Court's Brokdorf decision. It probably would not have been as liberal in interpreting the GG if it had handed down its decision immediately after the wave of anti-reactor demonstrations marred by far-Left violence, instead of after four years of peaceful protest against nuclear missiles by broad segments of the society, including judges. Moreover, that Constitutional Court decision took the wind out of the sails of conservative efforts to move the Federal Republic back toward a mid-1960s party/parliamentary democracy. By 1989, West Germans across the political spectrum were embracing public protest in their own efforts to achieve political goals. East Germans would join them.

6

Political Citizenship in a Dictatorship

Negotiating Agency in East Germany, 1945–1989

In 1978, while doing research in the German Democratic Republic (GDR), I happened to share a restaurant table with five men who were recuperating at a rehabilitation center that the communist regime had set up for those injured on the job. They were quite surprised to be sitting with an American. After we had chatted for fifteen minutes or so, one of the workers said, "So, what do you think of the GDR?" The waitress, who was passing by, must have known from my accent and earlier visits to the restaurant that I was American; she whirled around and said peremptorily, "No! You are *not* going to talk about politics in here!" As she continued toward the kitchen, I looked at my interlocutors; they were clearly waiting for me to respond to the question. I decided to say something positive and then something mildly critical—and see how things developed. I had no sooner expressed the positive when one of the other workers broke in, said, "Good!" and changed the subject, to the visible relief of a couple of the others.

This exchange echoes comments that scholars have made about the GDR. The regime strove to control completely the public sphere and the content of politics, and even a waitress felt compelled to act (ultimately successfully) as enforcer of a de facto ban on potentially critical public "political" discussion. My GDR interlocutors resented the *Bevormundung*, the political infantilization, that her intervention involved, and they asserted *some* degree of agency. Nonetheless, they knew that sharp limits existed, ones they best not push—not in public and especially with new acquaintances whom they did not really know and hence could not trust.

The GDR was an authoritarian, but not totalitarian, state. Claiming that its Communist party, the Socialist Unity Party (SED), embodied the will of the working people, the regime lauded itself as "democratic"—but it was a party dictatorship. Like the Third Reich, it needed popular engagement and legitimacy. It hence sought to create an appearance of democratic citizenship, with elections and innumerable meetings that were ostensibly dialogs. However, it used the meetings to promote its views, prevented any substantive citizen role in political decision-making, and persecuted any attempts at freedom of expression or public action that challenged regime policy. A participatory dictatorship, the regime secured frequent acts of "participation" from its citizens—as formalistic legitimation of its rule and active or nominal support of its policies. Yet the regime failed to secure total control. Instead, citizens sometimes participated in ways that secured agency, pursued personal agendas that undercut regime policy, or even asserted their own conceptions of political citizenship. Moreover, citizen activism eventually led to the regime's overthrow.

One-Party Rule

At the beginning of the GDR was the Soviet Union. When the Soviets entered Germany in 1945, they installed German Communists in key positions of power in their zone's administration. They pursued land reform and nationalizations that radically transformed the economy. They helped push through the April 1946 forced merger of the German Communist Party and the SPD into the Communist-controlled SED. Reacting to the Western Allies' sponsorship of the FRG, they sponsored the GDR's 1949 creation as a communist state. Unlike the FRG, the GDR never escaped the shadow of this foreign sponsorship.[1]

The GDR did promulgate constitutions (ultimately three of them)—but their provisions bore almost no relationship to political reality. For example, none of the democratic elements and protections of individual rights the constitutions guaranteed was effectively implemented. The regime prepared the 1949 and 1968 constitutions with the nominal input of tens of thousands of citizens in innumerable meetings, but any substantive effect was nugatory. It was the SED, not any of the constitutions, that was the country's institutional basis. The party claimed for itself a "leading role" as the representative of the people as a whole, equipped by its Marxist-Leninist ideology to understand (better than the people themselves) their true interests. Membership in it (and hence being subject to its control) was a de facto requirement for *any* significant leadership position. The 1968 and 1974 constitutions affirmed its "leading role," as did the nominally independent "bloc parties" it permitted as eyewash. The nominally democratic political institutions that the constitutions promised were only implemented to the extent that they furthered SED policies and power.[2]

The SED could nonetheless see the GDR as "democratic" because it defined democracy as the rule of the people *through* the SED. The SED followed democratic centralism from the start and officially established it in the GDR's 1968 and 1974 Constitutions as the "constitutive principle of the structure of the state." Developed by Vladimir Lenin, democratic centralism posited that the masses were too oppressed to understand their own best interests and that only a party of professional revolutionaries, fully knowledgeable of Marxist principles (as clarified by Lenin), could identify the best policies. Moreover, because existing elites would fight to the death any threat to their rule, the party must operate with iron discipline to realize those policies. In theory, fully democratic discussion would precede decision-making, after which the party decision would be absolutely binding. In practice, power was centralized but democratic discussion ceased, as the party leadership controlled the agenda and punished any dissent. Convinced that it had a monopoly on Truth, the SED embraced a Rousseauian assumption that a single true interest for all working Germans (i.e., the ones who counted) existed, which the SED embodied; this embodiment created an identity between the SED/GDR regime and the will of the people. Hence, no legitimate interest separate from it, and no justifiable opposition to it, could exist. Moreover, it must monopolize power, and any challenge to SED rule or even criticism of SED policies was unacceptable. It guaranteed that monopoly by nominating chosen candidates for all offices, with no alternatives.[3]

Suffrage in the GDR was in theory democratic but in practice not. The constitutions provided for "free, universal, equal, and secret" voting for citizens, with citizenship granted to anyone of German descent, from Eastern Europe or Germany. (Albeit only in 1967 did the state legally define a separate GDR citizenship, because unification under Communist auspices was looking improbable and West German economic success was making unification under West German auspices increasingly attractive to East Germans.) However, government officials handed voters preprinted ballots for the "National Front" that they were expected to drop unchanged into the urns. They could in principle enter a voting booth and make changes, but officials would know that they had done so, leaving such voters vulnerable to harsh repressive measures. Moreover, the vote counting was fraudulent, so the regime in every election declared greater than 98 percent turnout and more than 99 percent support for government candidates.[4]

The regime permitted four "anti-fascist" bloc parties—but as obedient tools of SED rule. The East German CDU and the Liberal Democratic Party had organized spontaneously in 1945/46; the Soviets created the German Farmers Party and the National Democratic Party in 1948 to divide the bourgeois electorate. Allowing the bloc parties to continue to participate in political life gave the GDR a veneer of democratic legitimacy. To ensure SED control, it purged by the early 1950s every independent leader, leaving the bloc parties as tools of the regime, little more than transmission belts for SED policies. After 1933, many Germans saw divisions among the anti-fascist forces as responsible for Hitler's rise to power. Support for "anti-fascist" unity was thus widespread, not least as the basis for the forced merger of the Communist and Social Democratic parties into the SED. Hence, the SED could also insist that all the bloc parties had to join the SED in a National Front and a unity list for elections (though such a list was almost certainly unconstitutional, given the constitution's provision for election on the basis of proportional representation). Moreover, the SED added to the unity list candidates from SED-controlled mass organizations (the unions, youth movement, and women's movement). The result was nominally democratic elections with no substantive choices.[5]

The GDR claimed to be democratic in part by establishing on paper the parliamentary absolutism many Germans had feared. The constitution reposed *all* power in the hands of the "democratically" elected parliament. Indeed, the regime rejected any checks and balances against parliamentary action. Communists had long dismissed *Rechtsstaat* as "legal formalism" that merely let conservative judges protect powerful private interests by blocking democratic policymaking. So the SED dismissed the need for independent judges to act as a check on the parliament, and the regime effectively controlled judges. The constitution included no mechanisms for judicial review, and the regime dismantled the administrative court system in 1953. The SED controlled parliamentary deputies, and the *only* instance of a less-than-unanimous vote in the parliament was fourteen no-votes by Christian Democrats on the 1973 bill liberalizing abortion law (albeit Honecker approved this anomaly, for the optics). So no institutional obstacle to SED power existed.⁶

The regime touted its commitment to its citizens' rights and sought to enforce the equal rights for women that the constitutions guaranteed, but it disparaged and certainly did not protect "bourgeois" individual rights. Competing with other parties after Nazi dictatorship, it did include bourgeois rights (e.g., freedom of expression, association, and assembly) in its constitutions. Yet they were, it insisted, unnecessary because the citizen's and the state's interests were identical, so the citizen no longer needed protection from the state through individual rights or an independent court system (something the Nazis had also asserted). And those rights became effectively meaningless, as the regime criminalized them if they "threatened the social order" (as the regime defined it). Instead, it emphasized social and socialist rights—e.g., to employment. Indeed, it asserted, rights could only be realized through socialist revolution and democratic centralism.⁷

Because the SED, in its view, represented the true interests of all East Germans, any opposition to or even criticism of the party, its policies, or the GDR must be maleficent. To "protect" the public from such iniquity, the SED established a repressive system, based in the Ministry for State Security, or Stasi. Initially, the regime relied on violence and incarceration for repression, and between 1945 and 1953, thousands died and tens of thousands were arrested. After Stalin's death, the regime reserved the possibility of incarceration, but it relied primarily on (the threat of) non-physical sanctions against the non-compliant. Those sanctions almost always sufficed because one's job, housing, education, vacations, and almost everything else—as well as that of one's family members!—depended on retaining the regime's goodwill. The regime also established a rigorous pre-publication censorship system to block critical voices. It attacked openly oppositional or even critical activities, though it targeted some groups over others; for example, it suppressed more vigorously peace movement activists (who might have contacts with foreign opponents of the arms race) than environmental activists. Unlike in the Third Reich, GDR citizens generally proved unwilling to denounce others. Hence the regime had to recruit, usually with threats, increasing numbers of "IMs" (unofficial collaborators, informants) to spy on friends, co-workers, and even family members. In the 1980s the Stasi also deployed IMs systematically to sabotage any opposition, for example, through fomenting conflicts within oppositional circles. And potential violence always loomed in the background, as in the police brutality in 1989 demonstrations.⁸

The Berlin Wall's 1961 construction solidified SED rule and the GDR as a state. In the 1950s, some 3 million citizens, voting with their feet, fled the GDR—an embarrassment and a drain on economy and society. Closing the last escape for East Germans fundamentally restructured relationships within the society. The state, no longer fearful of debilitating flight, could experiment, to a degree, with new and sometimes more draconian policies. The populace, no longer able to flee if things got too bad, had to come to terms with the existing regime and try to make a life for themselves and their families within it. And after the initial shock, most East Germans apparently did accept their new situation.⁹

Legitimacy and the Erosion of Popular Support

Even though the regime had incarcerated its populace with the Wall, it still needed some degree of positive support. It could not secure stability with repression alone.

Like earlier German regimes, the GDR secured a degree of legitimacy and stability when it delivered for its citizens in material terms—especially given its competition, and its citizens' ongoing comparisons, with the FRG. SED and GDR leader Walter Ulbricht sought to do so in the 1950s/60s through investment, economic reform, and growth. And living standards did rise for most East Germans. When Erich Honecker came to power in 1971, he offered the citizens an implicit agreement (often called a social contract): they were to work diligently at their jobs (and forgo criticism of the regime); in return, the state would provide growing living standards and a seamless social safety net. Scholars generally agree that economic growth and social benefits secured a substantial degree of support for the regime into the 1980s.[10]

The regime also promoted policies to ensure women's equality of economic opportunity and proposed a more egalitarian distribution of household chores between spouses. Women made up 50 percent of university and 70 percent of advanced students by the mid-1980s, and women perceived GDR society as more open to women than the FRG. However, a glass ceiling did prevail at work. Women's net wages averaged 12 percent less than men's, and women continued to bear a disproportionate share of domestic labor, thus keeping them from the extra "political" work required to secure career advancement.[11]

To a significant degree, anti-fascism was the GDR's moral basis. The SED touted the GDR as the "better Germany" because it had thoroughly repudiated Nazism and had, it claimed, systematically de-Nazified politics, the economy, law, and culture by purging "all" Nazis and eliminating capitalism. It denounced the FRG as a scarcely disguised continuation of the Third Reich, revealing the Nazi pasts of major political, business, and other players in West Germany. Moreover, SED leaders claimed legitimacy because they had often suffered persecution in the Weimar Republic or Third Reich for their youthful anti-fascism. East German intellectuals cited official anti-fascism to justify their support for the regime and SED predominance. The regime also explained away various problems, such as the June 17, 1953, uprising (discussed below), as the result of subversion by "fascist" West Germany. By the 1980s, though, four decades after Hitler, younger citizens found anti-fascism unconvincing as legitimation for the SED.[12]

East Germans, like earlier Germans, have faced accusations of being unusually subservient to authority, from fellow East Germans (e.g., Stefan Wolle, characterizing them as all too often taking "a joy in submission") and some Western observers. Proponents of that view saw East Germans as rooted in traditional German culture and the Third Reich, each of which emphasized the individual's subordination to authoritarian superiors: father, monarch, government officials, *Führer*. A combination in the GDR of continued acceptance (even by non-believers) of the traditional Lutheran emphasis on the authority of the magistrate and Communist insistence on obedience to the party line purportedly inculcated in East Germans a mentality as subjects, not citizens. Such generalizations, though, are problematized because East Germans did exercise agency and ultimately rebelled.[13]

Similarly, East Germans are often characterized as deeply committed to security (in having basic needs met and in having confidence in law and order). The SED emphasized that it offered its citizens economic security (no unemployment!) that no capitalist society could match. And amid 1989/90 revolutionary disorder, East Germans were often motivated by concerns with where future security was likely to lie. The SED emphasized order as a key aspect of the society they had created, and scholars have perceived East Germans as susceptible to appeals to order against "rowdies" of various sorts. Moreover, in the 1990s, 51 percent of East Germans in the unified Germany gave *Ruhe und Ordnung* (calm and order) as the highest political value. East Germans could also deplore the disorderliness in practice of the GDR's "planned" economy (e.g., repeated shortages of even vital goods). On the other hand, in the early 1990s, after unification, East Germans were more likely than West Germans to reject aggressive policing methods or bans on various protest tactics. East Germans may by the 1980s have been more appreciative of order than West Germans, but they were not committed to it above all.[14]

The GDR shared the traditional German emphasis on community. The regime insisted on the community's priority over the individual and each individual's obligation to the collective—to the GDR as whole and various subsidiary collectivities (e.g., work brigade, neighborhood). And the regime asserted the existence of a single social interest that it embodied, to which all private and individual interests must be subordinate. Scholars have generally argued that the citizenry shared these views. East Germans did seem uncomfortable with conflict and suspicious of egotistical interests or attitudes. For example, opposition groups in the 1980s often dismissed those seeking exit visas from the GDR as a selfish interest and refused any cooperation with them. East Germans in the opposition generally preferred consensus-based, direct democratic forms of governance and were uncomfortable with parties and parliamentarism. Scholars occasionally allude to German Romanticism and the Third Reich as bases for embraces of the communal. We have no historical studies confirming this, and Detlef Pollock rejects it because its proponents do not show any connections between early nineteenth-century thought and GDR citizens.[15]

The regime wanted enthusiastic support from its citizens, but it had to settle for manufacturing acclamation. Membership in the SED or a mass organization was near-mandatory to avoid harassment; it did constitute participation—but was pro forma for most. Voting, too, was an acclamatory undertaking, as everyone understood that no real choice was available. Public holidays featured elaborate parades. For those working, participation was often mandatory. People must report to their workplaces and were marched to the parade site, to be participants or spectators. People sought stratagems for begging off or ducking out, but citizens had to, and mostly did, attend. This could feel like a "mass public humiliation" to the citizenry. Similarly, meetings at the workplace or for organizations were often mandatory. Groups then engaged in "decision-making" processes, but the result was never an independent decision but always an acclamation of prescribed regime policy. At shop-floor meetings, for example, workers might criticize specifics, but officials ultimately secured acclamation of the SED's preordained position. Such events were about acclamation of the regime, not the participants' interests or well-being.[16]

The SED's repeated calls for "participation" and for the citizens to "work along with" (*mitwirken, mitgestalten*) public-policy formation thus did not mean any substantive citizen role in decision-making. As Sigrid Meuschel points out, "working with" is not self-determination. The SED assumed the citizenry still needed tutelage (especially because 1930s Germans had helped put Hitler in power and had supported him in plebiscites). However, it needed information from citizens and active support to secure its goals. Citizen "participation" was, in this context, a transmission belt between regime and people, where the regime would provide the direction and the people would respond with information, enthusiastic support, and active implementation of SED policy. Like its predecessors, the nineteenth-century authoritarian monarchies, the SED sought popular engagement with the state without any significant popular control over it.[17]

Margarete Mommsen-Reindl comments that East Bloc citizens participated far more than those in the West but that the forms of participation only strengthened the citizens' sense of impotence. Most citizens responded with apathy, participating publicly only to the extent absolutely unavoidable. Immediately post-1945, this reflected for many disillusionment and exhaustion after Nazi dictatorship and crushing defeat. It soon reflected a sense that individual political conduct was a pointless exercise, given political infantilization and SED control. As Christiane Lemke puts it, political activism seemed "burdensome, formalistic, and unfruitful." Even though most East Germans seem to have withdrawn from "politics," the regime's demands still meant they had to position themselves in relation to it and had to adapt (*anpassen, arrangieren*), and almost all East Germans did. Most conformed outwardly to SED expectations ("ritual" acceptance) but sought to advance their own interests and values. This conformity, as Detlef Pollock argues, reflected not some German mentality as subjects (not citizens) but bitter experience with repression.[18]

Scholars generally agree on the acquiescence and (outward) conformity but disagree on East Germans' inner life. Some treat adaptation as producing a more or less unified person who accepted a particular set of terms and just got on with it. Others see East Germans living two lives, with an external mask and a very different internal persona. Still others emphasize a process of continuing adaptation, as individuals maneuvered self-consciously to maximize autonomy and self-realization amid varying regime demands. We can expect 16 million people to have differing ways of coping with a fraught situation, so these multiple perspectives presumably reflect different solutions by different individuals to a difficult problem. Knowing just how many adapted in any given way is probably impossible. Crucially, though, most East Germans almost certainly did come to terms with the existing order while neither actively supporting nor actively opposing it—at least until the later 1980s.[19]

Adaptation included self-censorship. People knew that limits existed and generally what they were. They hence responded publicly in ways acceptable to the regime. That could mean reiterating officially sanctioned formulas in public and leaving sincerity for the private realm. For example, the regime had an approved explanation of the June 17, 1953, uprising (as a West German–sponsored fascist putsch attempt), and East Germans—recognizing that expressing an alternative opinion could lead to persecution—accepted that public discussion of alternative explanations was taboo;

albeit most apparently avoided that sensitive topic in private as well. Self-censorship could also mean self-consciously deploying approved tropes to secure space for pursuing one's own goals or to recruit state resources to pursue such goals. It included state officials editing out negative information as they reported up the chain of command, to avoid angering their superiors. So self-censorship could reflect passivity or agency.[20]

Given the narrow possibilities for citizen participation and democracy, one of East Germans' bitterest and apparently most widely shared complaints was about the *Bevormundung* (infantilization) that characterized life under the SED. Many of them resented the regime's constant indoctrination and control; they struggled to secure self-respect as mature and responsible adults—not children—as against a regime that never considered its own citizens fully capable of autonomy. And the 1980s rise of post-materialist values among at least some East Germans brought increased desires for self-realization—in terms incompatible with the regime's priorities. The regime's repressive apparatus proved sufficient to forestall politically effective expressions of the anger at infantilization. That anger did simmer, as the *Stasi* reported, and citizens increasingly demanded the right to be *mündige* (mature, self-responsible) citizens. And Detlef Pollack and Ilko-Sascha Kowalczuk both identify this anger as a key motivation for those who protested in 1989.[21]

One striking reaction to infantilization, the controlled public sphere, and *Stasi* repression was withdrawal on a massive scale, leading to a putative "niche society." Most East Germans did not find meaning or comfort or connection in official culture or official collectivities. They sought these things instead in various non-official, non-public spaces and contexts. Family or a circle of friends could provide such contexts, but so could a sports club, church, or other collectivity. They were the center of most East Germans' energy, commitment, and loyalty. For example, 64 percent of a sample of East Germans interviewed in the 1990s agreed that they had lived their lives in and through their niches. The niches were both a private alternative to an alienating public sphere and realms of sociability. The "niches" only very infrequently constituted resistance or opposition, and for many people they were a retreat from the (SED-dominated) "political."[22]

East Germans could retreat into what has been described as an alternative scene or scenes, but that characterization raises questions. In East Germany, as elsewhere, some individuals consciously and more or less openly separated themselves from the prevailing culture or politics. Efforts at networking developed, but such alternatives were scarcely a unified phenomenon, having widely varying views on what was wrong with the society and where it should go. And they lacked the alternative media that in West Germany and elsewhere created some commonality amid heterogeneity. Some participants were self-consciously political; some were driven into politics by occasional Stasi efforts to criminalize non-conforming behaviors. For example, you could squat in an abandoned apartment and face no consequences; if you and others squatted in an entire building, the authorities could come down on you like a ton of bricks. Most in these scenes, though, were apolitical, often consciously so, rebelling more against philistinism than the SED state. They simply wanted to drop out. Some evidence suggests that many East German citizens deeply resented these scenes for their explicit and implicit criticisms of "normal" life. Some scholars see these scenes as eroding SED power by visibly eroding the SED claim to total control. Others emphasize the minimal political role the apolitical groups played in 1989/90. Overall, they may be more significant as signs of simmering dissatisfaction than as political agents, but more research is necessary.[23]

Starting already in the 1960s, youth increasingly found little resonance in antifascism, took the East German consumer society for granted, and were alienated by regime attempts to control them through official youth organizations. The most widespread form of youth nonconformity was listening to Western rock music. East German officials were even more frightened by youth culture than West Germans and were convinced that *Beat* (rock music et al.) represented a carefully planned Western strategy of infecting East German youth to seduce them away from communism. Not just the music, but the hair and clothing styles that accompanied it were part of the plot. The regime hence sought to block access to the music (particularly in army and police barracks) and harassed or punished those caught sporting inappropriate hair and clothing styles. A 1965 crackdown in Leipzig on East German bands that played Western music led to an open protest that was crushed. Ultimately the regime succeeded only in alienating substantial numbers of young people. By the early 1970s, though, so many youths were listening, and so openly, that Honecker conceded that youth could listen to *Beat* and even sport jeans and long hair; he was acknowledging failure and accepting a role for a Western-influenced youth culture.[24]

East German officials particularly sought to break up groups of youth, usually working-class men, who were hanging out, often with provocative intent. Some scholars associate the groups with the *Halbstarke* in 1950s West Germany. These young men were asserting themselves, often in ways designed to provoke their elders, but their goals were not political. For the most part, only government repression could elicit from them political assertions. For example, when East German youth got too close to the Berlin Wall while attempting to hear a rock concert in West Berlin, police efforts to force them back led to political slogans from the embittered crowd. However, East German youth, unlike West German, were never a significant political force.[25]

The presence or absence of a public in the GDR is debated. The SED sought, successfully, to create an official public sphere that it could totally dominate; it worked diligently, not least with repression and censorship, to block the creation of any autonomous public sphere(s). And the opposition in 1989 placed building such an autonomous public sphere at the top of its demands. Yet some scholars have insisted that East Germans created public spheres beyond the official one. They often use terms such as "limited public sphere" or "counter public" to characterize these spheres. They point to various subcultures as loci for such spheres, to a *samizdat* body of illegal or unofficial publications, or to petitions as an "ersatz public sphere."[26]

Western German media brought the West and its culture—and the occasional East German dissident—into virtually every East German living room, and observers argue that it functioned as a kind of public sphere, at least for some East Germans. Initially, the regime sought to ban Western media; after 1971 it recognized that attempts to block access were provoking widespread disobedience and could provoke more, so it stopped trying. Some 80 percent of East Germans then regularly watched West German TV. East

Germans had more confidence in West German than in East German news programs, describing fellow East Germans who for topographical reasons could not receive West German TV signals as living in "the valley of the clueless." Yet the correlation between watching Western TV and demonstrating in 1989 was apparently modest. East German activist Ehrhart Neubert suggested watching may have de-politicized East Germans, as you could not protest if you were glued to your TV, while Stefan Wolle characterizes escaping to the West through your TV as system-stabilizing.[27]

Overall, "counter publics" scarcely existed. The Western media reported only on what *some* East Germans were saying; each non-official public that existed in the GDR was limited in size and could communicate with others only in limited ways. The SED did fail to monopolize public discourse, but space for a broad discussion of public issues open to every East German did not exist.

Scholars occasionally refer to "civil society elements" appearing in the GDR (as at least some East Germans sought to promote such group formation); however, the SED forestalled any realm of autonomous social groups. East Germany lacked a civil society in which various groups and associations worked to represent citizen interests and views and to enliven discussion of public issues. Moreover, to the extent civil society elements existed in the GDR, they were—unlike, for example, in Poland—confined to an intelligentsia that did not reach out to working people. And some note that the putative niche society tended to undercut civil society by focusing people's attention on small, closely knit groups, not broader, political activities.[28]

Nevertheless, East Germans developed alternative political cultures within their niches, and they were capable of criticizing the regime and its policies, even while recognizing limits to open criticism. Meanwhile, younger East Germans were becoming increasingly committed to self-realization and self-determination. These popular attitudes played out in the 1980s in various forms of political engagement—and eventually in revolution.

Citizen Activism and Agency

Scholars have shown that East German citizens had their own interests and sense of self-will, and that they acted with a degree of self-assertion, despite their repressive environment. The regime presented working people (in practice virtually every adult East German) as politically active citizens, and people often took this as license to publicly criticize obvious problems and shortcomings. Already in the 1960s, when asked if young workers should speak up if they saw a problem, a substantial majority of East Germans polled said yes. And meetings in factories could be lively. Petitions were a central element in GDR political culture, and scholars report a strikingly assertive tone, and often no signs of a submissive tone, in the petitions. And the education system was trying both to inculcate loyalty and submission to the regime and to teach sufficient self-confidence and self-assertion to provide effective workers. East Germany was a dictatorship, and East Germans understood the limits—but within those limits they criticized broadly.[29]

One strategy East Germans deployed was to use the regime's own rhetoric to their advantage. As Jonathan Zatlin notes, "Petitioners demonstrated an admirable virtuosity in exploiting socialist argumentation to express their desires and improve their material situation." The regime made promises to its citizens about the benefits its rule would bestow, cast in morally charged ideological terms. Citizens repeatedly demanded that the regime's promises be fulfilled and that its moral claims be realized. In some contexts, groups could also appeal to regime rhetoric to protect certain traditional rights or to secure resources, notionally for regime purposes but in fact for their own.[30]

Notably, those toward the bottom of the social hierarchy apparently had greater freedom to criticize than those higher up. With labor inefficiently deployed, East Germany had a labor shortage; workers were generally so valuable that supervisors hesitated to denounce workers to the Stasi. However, individuals who were ambitious needed SED approval for promotion and could not afford to do anything but follow the party line, so they generally avoided overt criticism. However, willingness to express non-conformist opinions was rising from the mid-1980s.[31]

While we lack sources to know what most East Germans thought democracy meant, the self-consciously oppositional forces favored grassroots or councils democracy, not representative democracy. In line with their support for socialism, opposition figures tended to be suspicious of bourgeois parliamentary democracy and party democracy. Yet they fully understood that SED "democracy" did not provide the effective citizen role in decision-making that democracy promises. So they called for free elections and eventually began pushing for substantive political rights (freedom of speech, of association, of assembly, of the press, etc.) to provide for substantive citizen input. When they organized their own groups, they emphasized grassroots, direct democratic governance. And when the SED system began dissolving in November 1989, they sought not parliamentary democracy but some form of consensus-based direct democracy for the GDR. They feared that embracing parliamentary democracy a la West Germany would mean abandoning socialism—and a separate GDR state.[32]

Almost all East Germans sought a more democratic version of socialism. East German oppositionists, outside observers, and scholars agree that the East German opposition sought to reform the GDR into a truly democratic socialism. Some argue that demanding an alternative would have been impossible, either because the regime would have come down even harder than it did or because it equaled calling for the GDR's disappearance (who needed a capitalist East Germany next to a capitalist West Germany?). Others emphasize that East German intellectuals sincerely embraced anti-fascism and socialist values. Among the populace, identification with the GDR and socialist values and confidence in socialism's future had been strong in the 1970s; in the 1980s, it was declining significantly among working youth, though university students rarely vocalized such views. East Germans were clearly painfully aware by autumn 1989 of the system's serious problems. Nonetheless, Laurence McFalls's 1990/91 interviews and Robert Rohrschneider's 1992 and 1995 surveys lead both to see continuing approval of socialist values combined with disillusionment with GDR reality by 1989. And East Germans polled in late 1989 expressed real reservations about the immediate introduction of a market economy because they valued "socialist" successes such as guaranteed jobs. At least one late November 1989 poll showed 86 percent support for reformed socialism and only 5 percent for a capitalist way, though that dropped to 56 percent for reformed socialism by February 1990. In 1980s East German opinion was moving against socialism, and the March 1990 election was clearly a vote for the FRG's social market economy, but support for "socialist" values remained.[33]

East Germans spoke only infrequently of human rights, checks and balances, pluralism, and parties—elements that scholars generally see as key to securing effective democratic influence for the citizenry. East Germans certainly wanted the *Rechtsstaat* and were concerned with political rights, and oppositional forces did discuss rights. Detlef Pollack sees gradually growing use of rights talk from the mid-1980s. Indeed, some opposition figures founded the Initiative for Peace and Rights in 1986. Yet only in autumn 1989 did rights become central discussion topics for East German opposition groups, a striking delay relative to earlier vibrant human rights movements in other East European Communist states. East Germans were to some degree influenced by Communist ideology here, with its emphasis on social rights. Similarly, oppositionists only infrequently mentioned checks and balances, which the SED had systematically attacked as a limit on the people's democratic decision-making. Pluralism did find occasional support, but it clashed with the traditional and SED emphasis on a single social interest to which all private interests must give way. Indeed, those most distancing themselves from the SED system sought to avoid conflict and viewed pluralism as chaos. Consensus on the "right" policy, not concessions leading to compromise among competing interests, was the mantra. Moreover, opposition groups resisted proposals to create political parties.[34]

The SED's political culture blocked reform from above. The party always had reformists (individuals and occasionally small groups). The party leadership around Ulbricht pushed the reformist New Economic System in the mid-1960s, but the radical 1968 reformism in Czechoslovakia frightened the regime into backing off. Open reformers within the party were by 1970 marginalized and persecuted if they failed to fall into line. In 1989, looming crisis generated both efforts at the center to push Honecker aside and efforts by regional leaders to push reform. Indeed, evidence from later 1989 shows considerable sentiment among rank-and-file SED'ers for dramatic change. Nonetheless, the SED was absolutely committed to its monopoly on power and hence opposed to anything, including reformism, which might threaten that monopoly. This meant, inter alia, that party reformers could not be seen connecting with oppositional figures. And even when party leaders seemed to embrace reforms, as in late 1989/early 1990, the goal was to maintain SED power.[35]

The most common form of citizen activism in the GDR was the petition (estimates of 500,000 to one million per year in the 1980s), with women being more likely to submit them. Every GDR constitution guaranteed the right to petition. The SED regime welcomed petitions and established rules to ensure they all received a (eventually a rapid) response. They provided a welcome source of information on citizens' concerns—and after the June 17, 1953, uprising, the government wanted to know what citizens might be angry about. Ulbricht also hoped to use petitions to control the bureaucracy, by informing officials of subordinates' inadequacies (though it is unclear that the regime used petitions in this regard). Petitioning could be system-stabilizing:

One had to recognize the regime as a potentially legitimate and cooperative social arbiter, and one usually resorted to the regime's own rhetoric, which strengthened one's case but implicitly bought into the regime's ideology. And petitions generally individualized complaints, hindering collective action. Most petitions sought relief for private concerns (e.g., housing, travel), though some complained about broader concerns (e.g., workplace inequities, shortages of goods, unequal access to goods). Some petitioners even included threats (e.g., to absent oneself from acclamatory events, resign from an organization). Some scholars see petitions as an ersatz public sphere, though most scholars would object that they were not actually public. The petitions met with varying degrees of success, though some scholars see substantial regime responsiveness—not least just before elections. Notably, scholars have seen a sharp change in petitioners' tone: supplicatory in the 1950s and 1960s, increasingly a self-confident assertion of equal rights as a citizen by the 1980s, and increasingly sharp and critical from the mid-1980s.[36]

Collective petitions did exist. At least some East Germans believed they were forbidden, and one scholar reports a petition-signing campaign that led to arrests. Yet sources occasionally discuss collective petitions, with up to 1000 signatures. One scholar refers to a collective petition that got SED attention and resulted in agreement with the workers' demand. And Paul Betts sees an increase in collective petitions in the 1980s as evidence citizen dissatisfaction was "beginning to take on broader political overtones"—just the sort of development that made collective petitions seem dangerous to the regime. Notably, in October 1989 over 200,000 people signed an appeal by the New Forum (a newly created opposition group) for substantive political reform.[37]

The innumerable meetings the regime prescribed were scripted, but people challenged the scripts. Often, citizens used meetings to raise difficult questions, for example, dismissing scripted efforts to "discuss" foreign policy in favor of asking about shortages. Strikingly, the regime held thousands of meetings in 1948 and 1968 to discuss drafts of the constitution. It sought legitimacy for a product it was going to dictate anyway. In 1968, citizens used these occasions not so much to discuss constitutional provisions as to raise questions about the Wall and reunification and to provoke lively debate on the meaning of the constitutional guarantee of "personal freedom." Ultimately, though, everyone knew that the official meetings were ritual occasions for creating the illusion of popular participation and that the Stasi would persecute anyone who pushed too hard. That the regime felt compelled to secure the appearance of popular participation reflects the realities of modern political life; that the regime ensured that such participation was substantively meaningless reflects its determination to maintain dictatorial control.[38]

Every strike in the GDR was a political act because the SED asserted that workers could not strike against factories "they" owned—but strikes occurred despite SED repression. The 1949 constitution included a right to strike, but the concept disappeared from the labor law in 1950 and from subsequent constitutions. After the massive strikes of June 17, 1953, and subsequent harsh repression, most strikes were small and brief. Outraged workers, usually a small group from a single work unit, downed tools to get management to address localized, primarily bread-and-butter, concerns—work hours, food quality in the canteen, wage inequities. Strikes almost always involved blue-collar workers (from unskilled up to skilled), though white-collar workers might express sympathy. Strikers did not want the Stasi to get involved, and management did not want higher officials to know labor unrest had broken out in their shop. So both sides had an incentive for a rapid resolution that might include some concessions from management and that usually avoided punishment for the workers. Sources generally speak of *Arbeitsniederlegungen*, work stoppages, rather than strikes. And most strikes were never reported or recorded, so we can never know how many occurred. Strikes were more expressions of worker anger than substantive means of improvement. Strikes with explicitly political goals did occasionally break out, for example, after the Berlin Wall was built, but especially in 1989/90.[39]

Working people had no influence on broader policy, but shop-floor workers secured substantial power over shop-floor economics—which, amazingly and crucially, contributed significantly to the regime's collapse. Three major factors explain this development. Given the system's inefficiency, the GDR suffered from a major labor shortage, so managers *needed* cooperative workers. After June 17, 1953, the regime wanted no major conflicts with working people and put enormous pressure on managers to avoid any (open) shop-floor conflict. And management shared with its labor force a need for easily attainable quotas—for workers to maximize their incomes, for management to meet plan targets and stave off anger from above. Workers hence had substantial bargaining power—through malingering, absenteeism, quitting, work stoppages, et al. They pressed to limit quotas, maintain or increase incomes, and address income inequities and other problems, while managers sought to avoid conflict that might come to the attention of superiors or might prevent attainment of plan quotas. The five-day work week was a notable example. Worker pressure in the early 1960s brought it to workplaces across the GDR as de facto standard practice, so that the regime's proposed introduction of a legal five-day week *every other* week would have been a worsening of what most workers already had and not the generous gift SED leaders had thought when they announced it. Crucially, across the 1970s and 1980s worker incomes consistently rose more than productivity, leading to increased demand for (often imported) consumer goods, inflationary pressures—and ultimately to damagingly inadequate investment. The GDR's post-1973 economic stagnation had multiple causes, but worker agency was a significant contributor. The workers were simply pursuing better wages and working conditions, not, by all accounts, any political goal. Yet their agency had significant political consequences—undermining the regime's very viability.[40]

A more open, assertive form of political activity was to resign—from the SED, the union, or other official group. Waves of such resignations occurred in 1953 after the worker uprising, in 1961 after the regime built the Berlin Wall, in 1980 when the Solidarnosc trade union rose in Poland, and from the mid-1980s, especially as the regime rejected Soviet-style reformist policies. An especially large wave of resignations (e.g., 11 percent of trade-union, 22 percent of SED members) hit in autumn 1989, as public protest was growing. And citizen petitions could include a threat to resign from one or another organization absent some redress. Resignation was not an act of public protest. In most societies it would not be an act of political citizenship. Yet the SED demanded that citizens join and be active in official organizations of various sorts. To resign from such organizations, or even to fail to keep up one's activities, was a political statement. We do not have research on the scope of resignations across time or on the degree of persecution one could suffer if one did resign. Nonetheless, resigning was a political act that clearly took some courage.[41]

While most East Germans avoided public action that questioned regime policies, some did undertake various forms of public protest. When the regime sought the collectivization of agriculture, for example, it faced substantial protests. The regime put enormous pressure on farmers to join the collective farms, but meetings to urge farmers to join were often marked by vigorous protests and flat refusals. The regime backed off in the early 1950s but renewed pressure toward the decade's end. Flight to West Germany by farmers who faced collectivization was a brake on the process. When the regime pressed ahead, it could face vandalism and other forms of protest. Only the Berlin Wall and the end of flight as an option forced the last farmers into the collectives, though reports of public protests continued.[42]

The June 17, 1953, uprising was the most notable public protest in pre-1989 East Germany. To increase investment, the regime introduced measures to squeeze consumption. Soviet leaders knew from their East German sources how wildly unpopular these measures were. Under Soviet pressure, East German leaders reversed most of the measures—except increased production quotas for workers, nominally the regime's base. Angered at this exception, East Berlin construction workers struck and protested on June 16, 1953, with other workers joining. The American RIAS radio station in West Berlin broadcast news of the protests and strikes, and protests spread across East Berlin and East Germany on June 17, 1953. Most strikers were workers, but broad segments of the population, including many SED'ers, joined the protests. The SED, lacking confidence in its own security forces, called in Soviet troops, who put down the uprising brutally. Strikes continued sporadically into July, but brutal repression ended the protests. The original goals of the strikes and protests were economic (primarily work quotas and food prices), but protesters added political demands (e.g., freedom for political prisoners, freedom of expression, free elections), so that scholars generally see it becoming a political uprising. The SED, convinced of its own rightful monopoly on political expression, viewed any strikes or protests as treasonous, but workers' burgeoning political demands here terrified it. The uprising brought a massive expansion of the repressive apparatus. Crucially it also contributed to significant worker influence on shop-floor and hence national economics: As Jonathan Zatlin points out, in the 1980s the regime feared to lower worker living standards to pay off Western loans because "the uprising of June 17, 1953 had seared the correlation between austerity measures and political discontent into their memory."[43]

The Soviet bloc's invasion of Czechoslovakia and crushing of the Prague Spring in 1968 sparked a wave of protest in the GDR. The Czechs' effort to create a democratic "socialism with a human face" seems to have resonated for many East Germans. And its crushing was deeply disillusioning. Graffiti and leaflets opposing the invasion appeared in various East German cities. Spontaneous protests broke out in at least some places. And many East Germans refused to sign the resolutions the SED vehemently promoted, which approved the invasion as a defense of socialism against counterrevolution. The protests were intense and relatively numerous—but unorganized. The regime reacted harshly, and such protests soon died out. They were apparently the most widespread protests between 1953 and 1989.⁴⁴

More localized protest was commonplace. Reports of workplace protests on various issues, within the workplace and beyond, were frequent. Specific regime policies could elicit protests, for example, replacing "parental authority" with "parental care" in the Civil Code, a proposal to raze the war-damaged University Church in Leipzig, expelling the popular protest singer Wolf Biermann. Waves of graffiti, sabotage, and flyers could materialize spontaneously in different places. Individuals could refuse to vote in various elections or to pay dues, or they could resign from various groups. East Germany was most certainly not a protest culture or a democratic one. Nonetheless, East Germans were never completely quiescent.⁴⁵

East Germans resisted efforts at rearmament (as did West Germans). Memories of the world wars, fears for oneself or one's relatives or friends in the event of war, concern that rearmament would come at the expense of consumption, and opposition to shooting at fellow Germans in the West all played a role. The protest was mostly passive, a refusal to volunteer for the military. Yet opposition was widespread enough that the regime only dared introduce conscription once the Berlin Wall had gone up, precluding flight to avoid it. And when a whole high school class showed up in black to protest conscription's introduction, they were expelled from school, denied the *Abitur* (high school degree necessary for higher education), and sent to work, while the "ringleaders" were imprisoned. The introduction of paramilitary training in the schools in 1982 also sparked protests.⁴⁶

In the 1980s, GDR's human rights, peace, and environmental groups found protection within certain Protestant parishes. Church officials were largely quietist after the Honecker regime in 1978 agreed to allow the churches internal autonomy in return for support for socialism. Nonetheless, the Protestant-Church leadership proved unable to control all the voices within it. Individual Protestant pastors answered to their congregations; perhaps 10 percent of them (taking advantage of the regime's concession of internal autonomy to the churches) were willing to provide de facto sanctuary for dissident groups on church property. The groups had to at least nominally pursue religious ends. They could and did publish material "for internal church use only"—while circulating it to some outside the church. And the churches provided a perhaps indispensable framework for networking among groups in different cities, while also promoting nonviolent tactics. The groups and the churches would be catalysts in 1989 for increasingly activist movements, culminating in revolution.⁴⁷

Public activism resumed in the early 1980s around nuclear weapons and peace. A massive peace movement had sprung up in West Germany opposing NATO's decision to station new intermediate-range nuclear-armed missiles in Europe. The SED praised that movement because it could weaken NATO, but that gave East Germans license to push for peace as well. GDR peace movements were rooted among conscientious objectors, who could do their required military service in non-combat construction units (though with lifelong discrimination thereafter). The Protestant, and to a lesser extent Catholic, Church provided a base for peace efforts, offering peace prayers, peace discussion sessions, and meeting space. Peace groups appeared across the GDR. They did not formally cooperate, but they did network. The churches supported efforts to wear "Swords into plowshares" badges that included a sculpture of that name the Soviets had given the UN. The SED saw this as unacceptable political speech, banned the symbol, and persecuted any who dared wear it. The regime's fear of independent political action trumped its self-proclaimed devotion to peace, so the peace movement did reveal regime hypocrisy. The movement declined sharply when West Germany stationed new missiles in 1983, but it served as a basis for human rights and environment movements and continued peace efforts in the later 1980s.[48]

The GDR did have a small environmental movement in the 1980s, with some activism. Environmental problems in the GDR were calamitous, with serious consequences for health and well-being, especially in the south. East Germans looked to West Germany's burgeoning environmental movement for a model and for occasional support, particularly from the Greens. The Soviet Union's Chernobyl reactor disaster heightened concerns and criticism. The movement's most visible expression was the Environmental Library, which had a degree of protection because it was based in East Berlin's Zion Church. However, when the Stasi arrested several members, only massive publicity in Western media led to their release without penalty and to the group's continued activity. Environmental groups sprang up spontaneously in many localities, though they did also network. They attempted, sometimes successfully, to influence policy, primarily with petitions, though occasionally with small protests (e.g., flyers). Some observers complained that the groups were easily co-opted by the state because they usually focused on "private" problems (i.e., local issues) and could be bought off with concessions. The SED still considered them a threat because they reflected citizen activism and a potential for greater activism.[49]

The GDR, along with the Soviet Union and other East European states, had signed the 1977 Helsinki Accords, which included a commitment to a list of individual rights. In Poland, Hungary, and Czechoslovakia, human rights movements sprang up to pressure their governments to live up to those promises; in the GDR activists initially focused on peace or chose to adopt SED rhetoric, in hopes of a reformed socialism. The peace movement's failure did lead in 1985 to the founding of the Initiative for Peace and Human Rights (*IFM*), and other groups followed. However, the groups did not have the same weight as Polish, Hungarian, and Czechoslovak groups. And the *IFM* split in 1986: Some activists favored social rights and social revolution and rejected a focus on individual rights. Others, in the *IFM* and other groups, had come to see establishing human rights, particularly effective rights of political participation and activism, as prerequisite for achieving peace, environmental, and other goals. The groups' activities consisted primarily of discussions, though the *IFM* did publish a periodical, *Grenzfall*. The regime sought to suppress human rights efforts as a dire threat to its monopoly on political power, primarily by infiltrating the groups with unofficial collaborators to sabotage them—e.g., by fomenting conflict. Various groups, on October 4, 1989, jointly demanded enforcement of the Helsinki Accords and UN human rights declaration and free elections.[50]

Revolution

In the 1980s, the GDR's economy was slowly collapsing—and with it the regime's legitimacy. After 1973, that economy proved unable to cope with increased energy prices, technological change, global economic competitiveness, and soaring wages. Only increasing indebtedness to the West (especially West Germany), increased dependence on subsidies from West Germany, and a collapse in maintenance and investment spending kept the East German economy afloat. By 1989, the indebtedness was unmanageable, and the economy's productive capital was falling into ruin. The regime estimated, internally, that only a 25 to 33 percent cut in living standards would suffice to stabilize the economy. Individual East Germans knew the situation was catastrophic. They could see in their own workplaces the erosion of productive capital and the input shortages; they could see in retail shops the growing shortages, or outright absence, of goods. In a 1988 survey, 74 percent of respondents identified inadequate consumer goods as an "extremely urgent" problem, and only 23 percent expected significant improvement by 2000. And continued SED propaganda on the GDR economy's wonderfulness only outraged citizens, who were demanding economic rebuilding.[51]

Economic desolation created severe problems, but East Germans did have other concerns that contributed to the erosion of regime legitimacy and appearance of protest. A 1988 survey showed more (84 percent) citing environmental than economic (74 percent) problems as "extremely urgent." The early centers of protest in the south were more economically impacted than Berlin—but also much more affected by gross pollution. And people did complain about pollution. Moreover, citizens usually perceived economic issues as moral problems—e.g., promotion of the unqualified but "loyal" at work, inability to do "quality work" in run-down factories, grossly unequal access to consumer goods based on arbitrary grounds (such as having a generous West German relative or living in the right city). The effective end of social mobility was also a concern, symbolized not least by an aging and rigid leadership.[52]

As problems grew across the 1980s in East Germany, the SED regime's obvious inability to address those problems, to reform society, further eroded its legitimacy. As shortages of goods and inputs and the productive infrastructure's slow-motion collapse became obvious, East Germans increasingly knew that the current situation was simply unsustainable, that drastic change was unavoidable. Identification with the GDR and socialism among youth began its steep decline from the mid-1980s. Yet the regime proved ever more incapable of making changes—as its flat refusal to emulate Soviet leader Mikhail Gorbachev's restructuring effort demonstrated. The SED had spent four decades proclaiming, "Learning from the Soviet Union means learning victory!" Suddenly, the leadership not only rejected demands it imitate the reformist efforts of its fraternal socialist country, it even banned a German-language version of a Soviet magazine, *Sputnik*, that contained an article touting the restructuring effort. That ban spurred a wave of petitions from citizens demanding access to the magazine, a significant decline in morale within (and even resignations from) the SED, and protests at workplaces, and it accelerated the erosion of the regime's legitimacy. Moreover, by mid-1989 East Germans knew that dramatic changes were taking place in Poland and Hungary. The SED's rejection of restructuring made clear that drastic *political* reform was a prerequisite to addressing the GDR's potentially fatal economic problems.[53]

Protests did occur in pre-September 1989 East Germany, but they were few, small, and usually unreported. The centers of protest activity were some of the Protestant parishes. Sympathetic ministers were allowing dissident groups to meet at the church. Crucially, when a political issue arose, they might well sponsor vigils and intercessory services, where participants were unlikely to get arrested, making people aware of concerns around those issues. For example, a small group of individuals appeared with their own placards (often just quoting Rosa Luxembourg that "Freedom is freedom for those who think differently") at the SED's annual parade in honor of its murdered martyrs, Luxemburg and Karl Liebknecht; the regime arrested them, with considerable brutality. These events were reported on West German television, which East Germans watched, and were the occasion for vigils and intercessory services. Would-be émigrés would occasionally protest publicly, in hopes that they would be arrested and expelled or bought out by West Germany (which had a policy of in effect ransoming "political" prisoners from the GDR). At the Leipzig Trade Fair (with its many international guests), 650 East Germans (soon surrounded by 850 security personnel) demonstrated in March 1989. The crushing of Chinese democracy demonstrators in June 1989 elicited numerous protests. Such protests show that at least some East Germans saw political citizenship as more than just participation in SED approved—or required— activities; they were a tiny minority through the summer of 1989, but they set the stage for more.[54]

East Germans had long known that GDR election returns were fraudulent, but in 1989 opposition groups managed to provide solid evidence that that was the case—another blow to SED and regime legitimacy. Protests had occurred at every GDR election from 1950 on. In 1986 poll watchers had observed at a few precincts. Opposition groups were by 1989 organized enough that they managed to secure volunteer poll watchers for the May 7 municipal elections at precincts across East Germany, for example, at 83 of 84 in Leipzig-Mitte. The watchers observed the precinct-level vote counts and recorded the results. When the regime published "official" results for each precinct with the usual greater than 98 percent turnout, and more than 99 percent yes to National Front candidates, the watchers were able to demonstrate massive fraud by the regime. The actual results in the observed precincts were generally under 90 percent turnout, with *c.* 10 percent no votes over all. West German media broadcast the news to most East Germans. Tellingly, the regime destroyed the May elections documents in June 1989. Measuring the impact of these revelations is impossible, but most observers are convinced that it did delegitimize the regime, including among SED'ers who would be making decisions in autumn 1989 on how to respond to protests. The opposition organized (small) protests on the 7th of subsequent months to protest election fraud. The Stasi quickly crushed the protests, but with a brutality that further discredited the regime.[55]

Emigration had always been a political act in the GDR, but a renewed and burgeoning wave of flight in the later 1980s played a significant role in spurring revolution. To apply to leave the GDR was to "vote with one's feet," and to declare that the GDR was a fundamentally flawed society that was irreparable. The regime hence viewed flight with contempt and fear, and it made life miserable for any who applied to emigrate—even as it let substantial numbers go, to release pressure. Opposition groups often resented would-be émigrés as "selfish" individuals whose departure weakened opposition forces—and the economy. Many East Germans, though, including in the opposition, sympathized with exiters (would-be émigrés). The exiters contributed to revolution in two key ways. First, already under enormous repressive pressure, they were willing to risk public protest in hopes of getting deported; so they were among the first to take to the streets. Second, most were relatively well-trained and productive younger working people. Their flight left visible gaps in workplaces, production, and the provision of medical care and education, increasing the pressure on the East German economy and state; those who wanted to stay then felt compelled to push harder, and publicly, for reform, before growing flight bled the economy to death. This concern increased exponentially in summer 1989 when Hungary (which East Germans could visit) opened its border with Austria, and the steady trickle of émigrés became a flood.[56]

The GDR had the means for repression. It had a far larger and more pervasive repressive apparatus in 1989 than in earlier decades, with an expressed willingness by higher officials to use violence to suppress dissent. The Stasi in 1989 had over 91,000 full-time employees and around 175,000 unofficial collaborators (in a country of 16.6 million). It could call on army units and on militias, the *Kampfgruppen*, in all larger workplaces. The regime had praised the Chinese Communist regime's bloody June 1989 repression of a democracy movement and had discussed internally resorting to such measures in the GDR if necessary. And the regime did resort to brutal violence in suppressing demonstrations in January, June, July, September, and early October 1989.[57]

Yet by autumn, SED-leadership indecision and a decreasing willingness among lower-level leaders and security forces to implement violence weakened the regime. The regime's dependence on foreign loans and subsidies made brutal repression problematic. Gorbachev had made clear that the Red Army would not intervene, as it had in 1953, to prop up the SED regime. The growing size of protesting crowds and their nonviolence undercut SED claims that protesters were either "rowdies" or a few dupes of West German provocateurs. Lower-level SED leaders were increasingly aware of the parlous state of the GDR economy and the pressing need for reform; they proved unwilling to take responsibility for brutal violence in defense of a system collapsing in slow motion. They apparently also perceived plummeting morale and growing unwillingness to act repressively within the security forces, especially the army and the *Kampfgruppen* (though how serious a risk this was needs to be researched). Moreover, the regime was torn with indecision from the top-down. The senior-most leadership was in October 1989 caught up in a struggle over replacing Erich Honecker; they also knew they were dependent on Western economic aid and hence on Western-media driven perceptions of the regime. At key moments, such as October 9, they proved unwilling to give clear instructions to hesitant lower-level leaders. A comprehensive policy of brutal repression by a unified leadership might have crushed the protest movement—but the regime proved unable to muster such a policy in autumn 1989.[58]

Key to the 1989 protests' success was their overwhelmingly nonviolent character. Violence characterized demonstrations in Dresden and Plauen in early October 1989, as exiters resorted to stone- and even Molotov-cocktail-throwing. And the security forces repeatedly engaged violently against demonstrators up to early October. However, East German demonstrators were overwhelmingly peaceful. Some ascribe this to the churches, which preached nonviolence at the peace prayers in churches that were the usual starting point for demonstrations. Yet relatively few East Germans by 1989 identified as Christians, and only a tiny minority of demonstrators could fit inside the churches before demonstrations. Opposition groups embraced nonviolence for pragmatic reasons: Violence would legitimate SED claims that demonstrators were just rowdies, and any demonstrator violence would have provoked counterviolence from security forces, under standing orders. In some places the opposition distributed flyers urging demonstrators to nonviolence, and they apparently organized small groups to isolate any individuals who seemed prone to provoking violence (and who might have been Stasi provocateurs). Some scholars ascribe the prevailing nonviolence to the demonstrators themselves, arguing that demonstrators knew they could only lose if demonstrator violence provoked a violent response from well-armed security forces. And Matthias Damm and Mark Thompson assert that a crucial basis was "a certain understanding of the logic of nonviolent resistance that was also widespread in the GDR"—perhaps drawn from West German TV reports on nonviolence in demonstrations there. And arguably one of the major constraints on Stasi violence in October 1989 was that demonstrators' nonviolence completely undercut SED claims that these were only violent rowdies.[59]

The most famous and consequential acts of democratic citizenship in autumn 1989 were the massive demonstrations that started at St. Nicholas Church in central Leipzig and, crucially, spread across the Republic. The church sponsored a peace prayer every Monday evening. Exiters had started meeting outside the church and demanding publicly after the prayer that they be allowed to leave the GDR (often hoping to get arrested and deported). When Hungary opened its border with Austria in mid-1989 and flight from the GDR via Hungary snowballed, East Germans had to act to prevent the country from bleeding to death demographically and economically. When the peace prayers resumed after a summer hiatus, on September 4, 1989, tensions and participation rose. The exiters would shout "We want out!" but now faced the countercry of "We're staying here!" from the "Here-stayers." As increasing numbers appeared on subsequent Mondays, the Stasi searched desperately for "ringleaders"—but there were none to be found. Rather, more and more Here-stayers were simply showing up outside the church, desperate to speak up to spark reforms that would staunch the flow of exiters and save the economy. On October 2, when a security forces' loudspeaker blared, "Here speaks the People's Police," the crowd responded with "*We are the people!*"—a slogan with deeper and increasingly obvious political ramifications. As late as October 9, according to post-1989 surveys, demonstrators expected violence from the Stasi. Yet as the number of demonstrators grew, the chance the Stasi would injure or arrest a given individual fell, so more and more dared to protest. And local officials in Leipzig, urged on by respected local personalities like conductor Kurt Masur, were unwilling to order violence. Lacking clear orders, the Stasi and police did not act to break up the October 9 Leipzig prayer meeting/demonstration of at least 70,000 people. West German TV broadcast to East Germany smuggled footage of the demonstration—emboldening people in Leipzig and across East Germany. The number of demonstrations and participants soared, for example, in Leipzig from 70,000 on October 9 to 500,000 on November 6. Nationwide, perhaps 260 protests with 4 million participants occurred, October 9 to November 9. And between August 1989 and April 1990 over 3,100 political protests occurred in 522 GDR municipalities.[60]

The development of political citizenship in autumn 1989 was complex. Scholars generally agree that the opposition did not cause the revolution—they were simply too few and isolated and lacking in any plan for or intention of overthrowing the regime. And available data suggests opposition members were no more likely to demonstrate in 1989 than non-members. Yet the opposition served as a vital crystallization point. Most citizens had hesitated to risk open protest, but the opposition showed the way. The Monday evening prayer meetings in Leipzig and elsewhere, which the opposition sponsored under the aegis of sympathetic pastors, provided a known location where people could appear "innocently," supposedly pursuing normal activities like shopping; the presence of numerous like-minded people in the area then gave confidence to risk participating in a demonstration. The opposition lacked the numbers to organize the growing demonstrations. It pushed for nonviolence and sought to isolate the violence-prone, but given its tiny numbers, only the active inclination of the mass of the crowd to discipline and isolate the violent could prevail—usually without benefit of marshals. And without leaders, the demonstrators chose the slogans by which ones they were willing to join in shouting—an ongoing plebiscite. "*We* are the people" started as a challenge to the People's Police, but it quickly became a democratic challenge to SED pretensions. Notably, only a minority demonstrated, perhaps 5 to 7 percent in many places, c. 14 or 15 percent unusually—though that's still large percentages compared to demonstrations in democracies. "Intellectuals" in the streets were too few: the enormous crowds were only possible because significant numbers of blue- and white-collar workers joined the demonstrations, and most of those arrested at a October 6 protest were worker youths. Moreover, the protests swept across the entire GDR, in large cities and small communities. Notably, the SED challenged the demonstrators with the same argument as earlier Germans, including many 1950s/60s West Germans—that one could not make politics in the streets or succumb to coercion from the streets. Yet that is just what the citizens were demanding against an undemocratic and unresponsive polity.[61]

The growing demonstrations across the GDR placed the new SED government under irresistible pressures. Erich Honecker's removal in mid-October, shortly after the large October 9 Leipzig demonstration, convinced many that demonstrations were the way to achieve change. And Honecker's replacement, Egon Krenz, had no popular legitimacy, not least because he had administered the fraudulent May 1989 elections and had publicly praised the Chinese Communist government's bloody June 1989 crackdown on democracy demonstrators. The number of émigrés only increased in autumn 1989, spurring further demonstrations to get reforms. The regime scrambled to offer concessions in late October, to buy time, but protest continued. And by October

31 officials knew the GDR faced imminent bankruptcy, leading to dependence on a West German government demanding free elections and independent parties. In desperation, the Politburo decided on November 9, 1989, to allow direct travel to West Germany, though with some restrictions. Politburo spokesman Günter Schabowski botched the report on the new regulations at a live press conference, and floods of East Berliners appeared at border crossings on the night of November 9. Their numbers and determination forced the border guards to open the gates. The Berlin Wall "fell." This unmistakable mass popular exercise of agency and political citizenship by East Germans fatally undercut regime power.[62]

The erosion of SED power in autumn 1989 allowed increased press activity that generated devastating revelations about economic decay and corruption in the SED regime. East German journalists began publishing reports that accurately reflected the developing situation. West German journalists had increased ability to move around the country and improved sources from newly emboldened citizens. Among the discoveries was concrete evidence of the lives of relative luxury that SED elites were enjoying—while their fellow citizens had increasing difficulty finding basic necessities. TV reports on the SED elite's villa quarter, Wandlitz, shocked East Germans, as did film of a traffic stop of a high-ranking official whose trunk proved to be full of luxury items. Inequality in this supposedly egalitarian society was minor by world standards but far beyond what people had suspected of the GDR. Moreover, Martin Sabrow has argued, these revelations provided a convenient justification for repudiating earlier support for the regime, as one could now know that it had been betraying its own values. And these revelations undercut any lingering hopes that the GDR could be reformed.[63]

After November 9, reunification was increasingly *a* and eventually *the* option. Before November 1989, reunification seemed absurd. Not only was the SED in near-complete control and totally committed to a separate GDR, but the great powers (which could veto significant changes in Central-European borders) seemed certain to oppose it. Opposition groups had favored reform within the GDR, a democratic socialism, and into 1990 many if not most opposition group members opposed unification. In October 1989, demonstrators still seemed to favor "*We* are the people" over "We are *one* people." The East Germans whom Laurence McFalls interviewed, December 1990 to May 1991, remembered feeling German only *after* post–November 9 visits to the FRG. Surveys taken in East Germany show a gradual shift toward support for unification, from 48 percent in late November 1989 to 85 percent in late April 1990 (albeit only 13 percent thought the GDR should merge with the FRG immediately and without conditions). East Germans had no reason to trust the SED or still pro-socialist opposition leaders to impose the drastic reform citizens wanted, but East Germans could only engage for unification once it seemed feasible. Crucially, the GDR's political and economic dissolution by early 1990 and the cavalier promises of "flourishing landscapes" by West German Chancellor Helmut Kohl and other West German politicians created the context in which most East Germans could conclude that unification under West German control was the best option. The GDR was doomed.[64]

The events of 1989/90 in the GDR did constitute a revolution. Some observers have resisted that term: because no one intended a revolution, because no violence was involved, because no counter-elite took power, because it was rather the implosion of a bankrupt system. Some call it a "peaceful revolution" to qualify it. Yet most scholars now think of it as a revolution. Many revolutions have happened without people intending it, including the 1789 French Revolution and the 1917 February Revolution in Russia. East Germans' action from below did rapidly overturn the existing social, economic, and political order without using elections, which fits most definitions of revolution. West German government and parties did significantly influence early 1990 developments, but the March 1990 elections do seem to have reflected popular will in East Germany: for unification and the social market economy. And they did lead to a new elite in East Germany. Nonetheless, as Konrad Jarausch wrote, the failure to hold an up or down vote on the negotiated unification, after a revolution devoted to greater popular participation, did leave a "bitter aftertaste." And East and West Germans would face numerous challenges, as they sought to construct a new, democratic political future.[65]

The GDR was a dictatorship, often a brutal one—but with a complex mix of political cultures. Like other twentieth-century regimes, the GDR had to secure "democratic" legitimacy—through its own self-justifying definition of democracy and through the (pseudo-)democratic methods of (fraudulent) elections and (manufactured) popular acclamation. And the regime encouraged, for its own reasons, traditional emphases on community over individual and on a single common interest and against pluralism. East Germans did seek agency. Though some have deplored the passivity of GDR citizens as a reflection of a putative traditional German authoritarianism, East German citizens were reacting within the potentially brutal constraints they faced—and they were acting. They used the regime's rhetoric of popular participation to secure concessions, through petitions and otherwise. They criticized and protested and maneuvered as they thought they could. Their self-assertion in the workplace contributed to the system's ultimately fatal economic problems. When the regime could no longer deliver economically and otherwise, its legitimacy collapsed, as strikingly large numbers of citizens took to the streets and overthrew a powerful dictatorial regime. East Germans went into a unified Germany desiring a more democratic future, but with their own mix of experiences.

7

Coming to Fruition?

Unification and Democracy in the Berlin Republic

In 1992, a wave of often violent, radical right-wing protests against foreigners swept the newly unified Germany; that wave both reflected popular, if intolerant, citizen activism and elicited a wave of pro-democratic counterdemonstrations. During the late 1980s and early 1990s, hundreds of thousands of asylum seekers and nominally ethnic Germans from Eastern Europe sought refuge in the FRG. Amid the substantial disruptions of unification, many Germans perceived them as an inundation swamping their culture. Many of the protests were taking place in the "new *Länder*" (those once part of the former East Germany), where very, very few of these immigrants had settled. In reaction to the violence against immigrants (and occasionally against the disabled), a CDU politician called for a mass demonstration against hatred of foreigners, to be held in Berlin on November 8, 1992 (a day before the anniversary of the 1938 Nazi pogrom against Jews). Leaders of all parliamentary parties (except the CSU) and 350,000 citizens attended. That demonstration helped spark a wave of grassroots-organized demonstrations against violence and hatred of foreigners across (mostly western) Germany; individual demonstrations could attract up to hundreds of thousands of citizens. The demonstrations usually involved silent, candle-lit, marches. TV, with its preference for the visually striking and emotionally engaging, frequently covered such protests.[1]

These conflicting protests make manifest how most Germans have accepted a participatory democracy—even as some questioned fundamental democratic values such as tolerance and non-violent problem resolution. The new Berlin Republic (as reunified Germany came to be called), like earlier German states, included citizens with multiple, widely varying political attitudes and practices. Most Germans embraced a commitment to democracy and to key democratic values and broadly similar conceptions of participation and political citizenship. And from 2000 Germany did have a new citizenship law that expanded the *demos*, the people who could count as citizens, to more easily include non-ethnically German individuals who had been born and socialized in Germany. Hence a predominant democratic culture seems to prevail in the reunified Germany, certainly as democratic as in Germany's European neighbors. Yet the German debate over a *Leitkultur* (a defining culture to which immigrants must assimilate) and the rise of a new radical right show continuing conflict over what might constitute Germanness and hence citizenship. Moreover, Germans still do not completely agree on what democracy means, and some Germans hold views that are scarcely democratic (as do some people in other democracies). Post-reunification Germany is a stable democratic state—but German history does not end with a simple triumph of "democracy."

The Creation of the Berlin Republic

The GG provided two methods for unification: a new constitution for a newly reunited Germany (Art. 146) or the accession of the former GDR *Länder* to the FRG (Art. 23); however, the latter was arguably inevitable in 1990, as all the bargaining power lay with the prosperous, stable FRG. Most East Germans would have preferred a slower unification process in which they could bargain to preserve some of the social protections the GDR had offered its citizens. Given the GDR's economic and political collapse, however, they could not wait. And West Germans, often triumphalist about East Germans' obvious desire to adapt West German institutions, were in no mood for concessions, let alone a brand-new, untested constitution. Even the Greens' motion for at least a referendum on unification failed. The State Treaty of May 18, 1990, that established a currency and economic union constituted a de facto annulment of GDR sovereignty, and the Unification Treaty of August 31, 1990, effectively committed the GDR to Article 23: reunification by the two countries' parliaments through East German acceptance of the GG. The Bundestag did establish a constitutional commission to examine possible constitutional amendments.[2]

The institutional framework of the Berlin Republic was fundamentally that of the Bonn Republic (as the old West Germany came to be called): the FRG was and is a representative democracy, and post-unification Germans generally seem to support that. Citizens vote for representatives, who then select a government. Institutionally, the citizenry can influence policy primarily by their choice of candidates and their ability to replace at the next election representatives who are not responsive to citizen desires, though they also have rights of expression and protest to influence policy. The citizenry's (indirect) decisions are then implemented through the Rechtsstaat. This conception of democracy had in 1949 reflected, and to some extent still did in the 1990s, doubts about the degree of citizen rationality. Indeed, in the early FRG support had been strongest for a leadership model in which citizens simply chose leaders periodically, and some 1990s Germans (e.g., in the CDU/CSU) still favored this conception. East Germans' March 1990 vote in support of parties calling for accession to the FRG was de facto a vote for representative government, not any direct democracy of the sort East German dissidents propounded. Support for representative democracy does remain higher in the old *Länder* than the new *Länder*.[3]

Germans introduced a few changes to the reunified republic's institutional framework. German policymakers rewrote GG Article 23 (once reunification was accomplished) to reassure their neighbors. Fears that a reunified Germany might emulate its Second and Third Reich predecessors in aggressiveness were widespread in many European countries in 1990. Eliminating the old Art. 23 was part of reassuring Germany's eastern neighbors that it would not seek to reverse the Second World War's outcome by demanding the accession to the FRG of territories Germany had in 1945 lost to Czechoslovakia, Poland, Russia, or Lithuania. The new Art. 23 instead focused on situating a peaceful Germany in a new Europe. It stipulated that the FRG would work to create a democratic, rule-of-law, social, and federal European Union (EU) and could (with Bundestag and Bundesrat consent) transfer sovereign rights to make that possible. The provisions did imply limits on the sovereign powers of the German *demos* under EU constraints. Unfortunately, the EU arguably suffers from a democracy deficit, as EU citizens have limited influence on EU policy.[4]

Germans expanded citizenship significantly. West and East Germany had presumed German ethnicity as the basis of citizenship, putatively to assimilate German expellees from Eastern Europe after the Second World War and to preserve the possibility of reunification. No question existed in 1990 that 16 million East Germans, who had never lived in West Germany, would become FRG citizens upon unification—while millions of descendants of immigrants, who had been born and socialized in the FRG, could not easily become so. In making naturalization easier in 1990 (to deal with asylum seekers from Eastern Europe) and 1999 (with a new center-left government), Germany did redefine citizenship—albeit grudgingly. By the twenty-first century, nearly one-fifth of Germany's population has a (non-ethnically German) "migration background," though only about half of those are German citizens. German governments and politicians have insisted that (West) Germany was not to be a "land of immigration" or a multicultural society, and much of the population seemingly agrees. Fearing that immigrants or their children might "islamize" Germany, many demanded a *Leitkultur*, a (*German*) defining culture that all must adopt. Hence, applicants must "accept the basic ethical, legal, and cultural principles that govern public life in Germany" to get citizenship. The 1990 Aliens Law eliminated bureaucratic discretion in rejecting naturalization applications. The 1999 citizenship law shifted from *jus sanguinas* (blood, descent) to *jus soli* (birthplace) as the basis for German citizenship. Children born before 2000 on German soil of two non-German parents must, between 18 and 23, officially opt for German citizenship and, with narrow exceptions, renounce any other citizenship. With some limitations, children born on German soil to non-German parents after 1999 automatically acquire citizenship. Moreover, the law only partially eased naturalization for immigrants. The introduction of German language, culture, and citizenship examinations as prerequisites to naturalization (comparable to a number of other countries) has proved an obstacle for some. De jure, Germany has recognized citizenship as independent of ethnicity; de facto, many if not most Germans still seem to see Germanness as ethnic.[5]

Since 1991, any citizen of an EU member country has automatically acquired (derivative and secondary) European citizenship. To promote labor mobility, that citizenship guaranteed freedom of movement across the EU. It also guaranteed common diplomatic and consular protections for all EU citizens abroad, the right to petition the European Parliament and a new European Ombudsman, and voting rights for local elections when resident in another EU state (see below). European citizenship does not guarantee other rights, which are only protected through the home nation. Some policymakers emphasized a common European cultural, and perhaps ethnic, identity in promoting this citizenship. In practice, governments have not eliminated all discriminations against non-national citizens. European citizenship has not significantly changed the citizenship of Germans, though some had hoped it might prove the basis of a fundamentally new political identity.[6]

The Berlin Republic had the Bonn Republic's suffrage—though also a debate on suffrage for resident aliens. The GG provisions and FRG legislation on suffrage were extended to all in the reunified Germany. One issue that had percolated since the 1980s, in Germany and elsewhere, was whether resident aliens should be allowed to vote, and if so, only in municipal elections or also in state and national elections. Proponents argued that resident aliens had an interest in the society's governance, because its decisions affected them, as well as rights to participation as human beings. They argued that the GG provision allowing transfer of sovereign power to transnational institutions implied an open conception of citizenship, especially if one limited alien suffrage to EU citizens. Opponents argued that resident aliens lacked a long-term commitment to the society, were not subject to the same obligations as citizens, might come under pressure from home-country politicians as to how to vote, and might have divided loyalties in the event of conflict. When the Constitutional Court ruled on two cases, it rejected any right of municipalities to grant voting rights to aliens on the grounds that the GG had reserved power to the *Volk* and that the *Volk* were German nationals and naturalized Germans. The court reaffirmed that the *demos* in Germany consisted only of German citizens. Exceptionally, it allowed EU citizens to vote in local and European Parliament elections.[7]

The FRG remained a "democracy that could defend itself," against perceived extremist threats. The government retained the ability to ban extremist organizations with antidemocratic goals, as well as to petition the Constitutional Court to ban similarly extremist parties. It has used that power to ban numerous organizations as antidemocratic. The government's effort to ban the far-right Nationaldemokratische Partei Deutschland did fail, but only when it came out that half the party's board of directors were paid informants of the federal security authorities. West and East Germans generally support such limits to tolerance, presumably given Germans' historical experience with extremists. Their effectiveness is debated because radicals form new organizations and recode symbols, while their withdrawal into ghettoes and secrecy may make them harder to monitor and reach.[8]

A Unified Political Culture?

A central focus for those studying German politics since 1990 has been the linked questions of whether post-unification East Germans developed a democratic political culture and whether East and West Germans now share the same (democratic) political culture. Researchers almost universally agreed that a democratic state could only survive if the citizens had a democratic political culture appropriate to the state's democratic institutions. And many observers feared that East Germans socialized under an authoritarian (perhaps "totalitarian") system could not have entered the FRG with, or easily learn, democratic values. Exact assessments have varied considerably, but the results overall suggest relatively strong support for democracy and democratic attitudes in old and new *Länder*. So a modest optimism prevailed.[9]

To the extent that support for democracy depends on outcomes, the picture as between East and West should be mixed—and it is. West German politicians promised East Germans a flourishing future in a unified Germany. Yet all too many East Germans did not get one. And even West German attitudes toward FRG institutions fluctuated in the 1990s in the face of economic and other difficulties. Surveys of East German attitudes showed some correlation between poor economic conditions, generally and for individual respondents, and relatively low approval of the existing (democratic) system. Approval of democracy in the abstract, though, has remained high and does not correlate in any simple fashion with economic (dis)satisfaction, for West or East Germans. As East Germans have suffered severe economic dislocation, the fact that they remain overall supporters of democracy has been some reassurance for most but not all scholars and commentators.[10]

Scholars and commentators assume that how individuals are socialized affects their political culture, but the impact on East Germans of SED indoctrination proved complex. Despite some early alarmism that forty years of Communism, atop German traditions of authoritarianism, had left the FRG with 16 million new antidemocratic citizens, scholars quickly concluded that the SED official political culture had not been all-pervasive in the GDR; unofficial political cultures had been influential. Although some surveys suggested that more East than West Germans leaned toward authoritarian views and values, East Germans overall favored democracy, and in the 1990s only 10 percent favored an alternative to democracy, as did 6 percent of West Germans. East Germans did have a more favorable view of socialism than West Germans and a more egalitarian view of politics and economy, so the experience of SED socialism did have some impact—just more on their conception of democracy than their support for it in principle.[11]

Scholars had known since the early 1980s that many East Germans appeared to have turned their backs on the SED, and presumably on its socialization efforts, by withdrawing into niches, which offered alternative elements of socialization. Increasing knowledge of the agency and participation discussed in Chapter 6 also made clear that East Germans had not been the mere obedient subjects that many had feared. Moreover, the SED could not monopolize East Germans' socialization. Over 80 percent of East Germans watched West German television, so East Germans could be well-informed on Western values and political parties, and many were. Western media presentations had convinced many East Germans of the West's superiority over the GDR and its institutions and culture. Personal contacts were also crucial. Many West Germans in the 1970s/80s visited relatives in East Germany, bringing gifts and a different (political) culture. And an easing of travel restrictions in the 1980s meant that more East Germans visited West Germany, bringing back their own experiences of and reports on West German prosperity and freedom. (Albeit other East Europeans without access to personal contacts or West German media also escaped the pervasive socialization their Communist regimes sought.) Proving the exact degree and nature of influence is, however, difficult.[12]

Some scholars have argued that understanding East Germans' political culture requires going beyond early socialization to look at situational influences. So the experience of the autumn 1989 revolution might explain why East Germans have proved more likely than West Germans to approve of political demonstrations. East Germans may have had a socialization in socialism, but they also experienced more immediately and painfully than most West Germans the uncertainty that a market economy can impose, as their economy imploded in the 1990s and did not fully recover in the twenty-first century.[13]

Whether because of GDR socialization or 1990s experience of market-driven economic disruption, East Germans were much more committed to social provision and security than West Germans. East Germans had broadly rejected SED-style socialism by 1990. However, by the mid-1990s, over half of East Germans surveyed characterized socialism as a good idea badly implemented or blamed poor leadership, not socialism per se, for the GDR's collapse. The East Germans supported a market economy, but they very much wanted it to be a *social* market economy, one in which the government ensured an adequate social safety net, including perhaps a right to a job. And many of them saw the FRG social state as inferior to the GDR's provisions. Thus, East Germans were more likely to express approval of socialism or to prefer a stronger state role in the economy (52.6 percent in a 1993 poll), though there were West German supporters of socialism as well (24.2 percent).[14]

By the 1990s, a shift toward post-materialist values seemed to have played a possibly significant role in the democratization of many, more often younger, Germans. Reflecting broad changes in economy and society toward affluence and the tertiary economy, survey results showed Germans increasingly likely to hold post-materialist values (though West Germans more so than East Germans). Surveys also showed positive correlations between post-materialist values and both willingness to engage in a range of protest actions and support for various democratic values. And post-materialist values correlated strongly negatively with support for violence or for Right-extremist parties and antidemocratic attitudes.[15]

Scholars see a central role for education in promoting democratization. Surveys show a strong positive correlation between more education and both greater support for democratic values and greater willingness to participate through conventional or unconventional means in political life. The argument is that more education confers more knowledge of and ability to understand political affairs, including a knowledge of democratic values. And this contributes to a greater interest in politics that is a necessary basis for support for democracy. Increased education also correlates with decreased support for authoritarian values, while less education correlates with hatred of foreigners. Increased education, as more pupils follow a white-collar track in secondary school and as more youth attend university, is hence arguably a key factor in the democratization of Germany and in the shift toward a more participatory democracy. (Albeit lesser-educated working-class voters were more likely to vote for pro-democratic parties in the *Kaiserreich* and the Weimar Republic than were the better educated, and voters in upper-middle class precincts, presumably better educated, gave the Nazis the highest votes in the 1932 elections.)[16]

Many Germans favored more direct democratic elements in FRG democracy, but their goals varied. Both West and East Germans desired increased opportunities for plebiscites, in the 80 percent range. The constitutions in the new *Länder* included more opportunities for plebiscitary input than the federal or most old *Länder* constitutions. Nonetheless, political elites resisted plebiscites, both in the Unification Treaty discussions and in the Constitutional Commission, reflecting doubts about citizens' rationality and knowledge. East Germans were more likely than West Germans to favor direct democracy elements, for example, one-quarter of East Germans but only 2 percent of West Germans in one survey. Calls for more direct democracy often lack specificity, beyond a more participatory decision-making role for the citizenry. Supporters of direct democracy in the old *Länder* often came out of the 1970s and 1980s new social movements, which had sought a dialogic, consensus democracy. Support for more direct democracy was apparently strongest among Greens supporters. Because the desires expressed are so general and held by a minority, they have not seemed a serious challenge to the FRG's representative-democratic constitution.[17]

New Norms of Political Participation

The Bonn Republic became a more participatory democracy from the late 1960s (see Chapter 5), and support for such a democracy is strong in the Berlin Republic. When surveyed in the 1990s, substantial majorities of West and East Germans, usually more than 80 or even 90 percent, supported democracy, in principle, as the best form of government, and scholars generally saw support for key democratic values as very high as well. Germans no longer debated publicly whether broad citizen activism was acceptable or potentially dangerous. A notable marker of the widespread acceptance of a more participatory democracy is the 1990 *Deutschlands Politische Kultur* by Kurt Sontheimer (the influential historian and political scientist): From the late 1960s into the 1980s he had expressed fears that the participatory thrust of post-1968 FRG politics threatened to unleash another wave of political irrationalism, undermining democracy in ways his 1962 work on the Weimar Republic had documented; but in 1990 he acknowledged that broad citizen participation and protest did not have to be system de-stabilizing and could be a positive factor. And surveys and other sources showed a widespread (albeit not universal) acceptance among Germans of citizen activism as a key element in a truly democratic polity. Support for activism was generally higher in the old *Länder* than the new *Länder*, though East Germans were more supportive of the right to demonstrate than West Germans.[18]

Germany's voter turnout has remained high and is generally in the middle range among European democracies. The "cost" of voting is relatively low and democratic societies generally have a "voting norm" that one is expected to do one's civic duty and vote, to preserve the people's democratic rights or to stand up for one's beliefs. Voting in most societies rises with education (as individuals become more knowledgeable and self-confident), with group membership (as individuals become more socially connected and minded), and with age (up to the 60s, as individuals have more responsibilities and connections). The slight fall in voting in the old *Länder* since the 1970s led to concerns about a crisis of democracy, though it arguably reflects an unproblematic decline after an unusually highly politicized era. The lower voter turnout in the new *Länder* than in the old *Länder* in the 1990s raised some concerns. Notably, women's voting participation, slightly lower than men's in the 1950s/60s, has been on a par with men's since the 1990s, and women as a percentage of Bundestag delegates has gone from 9.8 percent in 1983 to 31.2 percent in 2017. Overall, voting patterns suggest an ongoing commitment to democratic governance among most Germans.[19]

Germans not only accepted various forms of participation and protest as elements in democracy, they often expressed a willingness to engage in them and sometimes actually did. Support for citizens initiatives was notably high, as some Germans saw them as a necessary supplement to political parties. Depending on the survey, up to 80 percent expressed willingness to sign a petition and *c.* 60 percent said they had done so; 50 to 60 percent expressed a willingness to participate in an authorized demonstration and *c.* 35 percent said they had done so; *c.* 20 percent expressed a willingness to participate in an unauthorized demonstration while 7 to 11 percent said they had done so. East Germans were less likely than West Germans to participate in political actions, but East Germans were more likely to approve of demonstrations. Citizen participation partially substituted for traditional activities such as party membership but overall proved a supplement, not a threat, to traditional political activity. While self-reporting (on willingness or on participation) is not indubitable, available data suggest that most Germans have accepted in principle a more participatory form of democracy than prevailed before the 1970s.[20]

Scholars identified various correlates that might explain openness to engaging in political participation. Among the most consistently important were (higher) interest in the political, higher educational attainments, higher socioeconomic status, belief in democracy, and social organization membership. Increased education contributes to an increased sense of efficacy in the world, which apparently contributes to a willingness to attempt to influence the world through individual or collective protest actions. Less education does also correlate with less support for democracy and less willingness to participate in political affairs—with one exception: less education does correlate with willingness to engage in *violent* political action. Bettina Westle has identified factors such as distance from nationalism, friendliness toward foreigners, acceptance of both democracy and socialism, and seeing a need to draw consequences from the crimes of the Third Reich as correlated with increased support for conventional but especially non-institutionalized participation forms. And Karl-Dieter Opp and Steven E. Finkel have identified post-materialism, critical friends, and Alternative group memberships as strong correlates of political activism.[21]

Confidence that one's actions can influence policy would seem to be a prerequisite for choosing to act politically, but scholars have not found consistent correlations. Self-confidence and confidence in system responsiveness do seem to play a role, but how they interact is not clear. East Germans expressed less confidence in the system but seemed in the early 1990s to have some confidence in their own ability to influence policy (perhaps reflecting the recent citizen role in overthrowing the SED regime).

Moreover, citizens may demonstrate not because they think they can change policy but because they feel morally compelled to take a stand. Parsing people's beliefs and motives here is difficult.[22]

If citizen participation was widely accepted, so was an increased range of protest forms. Much of this development had already happened in the old *Länder* by the 1980s (see Chapter 5), but it spread to the new *Länder* in the 1990s. Willingness to participate in various legal protest forms was roughly similar in both. By the 1980s, most citizens came to see many formerly unconventional and illegitimate forms as conventional and legitimate—e.g., demonstrations and boycotts. And in some surveys majorities could express a willingness to join in most legal forms of protest, even if only minorities ever actually did so. Not surprisingly, Germans (and others) were much more likely to sign a petition than to participate in a demonstration. In international comparisons, Germany ranked 17th of 21 countries in having signed a petition (51 percent), but 10th in having participated in a challenging action (a lawful demonstration, boycott, unofficial strike, or building occupation, 30 percent as of 1999). Fear had been widespread in 1970s/80s West Germany that the increasing acceptance of "unconventional" protest forms would lead to instability, indeed "ungovernability," by undermining the carefully structured formal representative and party-dominated model of governance that had prevailed in the 1950s (see Chapters 4 and 5). By the 1990s most scholars agreed that such fears proved misplaced, as the FRG remained a stable democratic polity.[23]

Illegal protest was common in the late 1970s/early 1980s, when blockades and other forms of civil disobedience were a central element in the anti-nuclear power and anti-missile protests, but support for them seems to have slipped. Although they continued to be used—e.g., in the protests against the transport of nuclear waste—those protests were unusual in their persistence and in the use of civil disobedience. Overall, both West and East Germans were less supportive of public protest if disorder or violence was involved. Fears in the 1980s that rising civil disobedience threatened political stability have also ebbed, as Germans have generally not engaged in civil disobedience.[24]

The Resurgence of the Extreme Right and Democratic Robustness

Although Germans overwhelmingly rejected violence, right-wing violence exploded in the immediate aftermath of reunification and has recurred. Left-wing violence did not completely disappear, but after the spike in asylum seekers and other immigrants after 1989, Right-extremist attacks on "foreigners" (Jews, immigrants, and German citizens/legal residents of African or Asian descent), and even occasionally on disabled Germans, soared in 1992/93. Support for Right-extremism has fluctuated in the FRG's history. Hostility to immigrants, and occasional violence, had become a significant factor in Right-extremism since the 1980s—in both West and East Germany. The appearance of violent Right-extremism in the old *Länder* in the late 1980s/early 1990s and its surge in new *Länder* in the 1990s led to headlines and debates about its causes and implications. Its supporters tended to be populist, that is, to believe that democracy meant a system in which the interests and will of the (ethnically defined) people (as opposed to the egotistical interests of a corrupt minority and of non-ethnic Germans) could be realized, perhaps by a strong leader. Right-wing activists adopted a broad range of protest methods: petitions, rallies, site occupations, sabotage, and violence. Even though violent attacks occurred in both the old and the new *Länder*, the near absence of immigrants in the new *Länder* and doubts about East Germans' support for democracy meant that attention tended to focus on attacks in the East.[25]

Most of the assailants were young males with less education who faced or feared economic or social marginalization, were anti-immigrant, and were drawn to (ethnically charged) nationalism; yet resort to violence did not correlate at all clearly with actual economic deprivation. Scholars hence turn to social psychological explanations, such as anomie, for moving from extreme-right views to physical violence. Whereas violent Left-extremists tended to reject state power, violent Right-extremists tended to demand the strong hand of the state even as they resorted to extra-state activism, which they justified as necessary because the courts were not maintaining order effectively. Those with Right-extremist sympathies tended to oppose democratic values (e.g., tolerance, freedom of expression, minority rights) and often the FRG constitutional order, even as they made populist claims to speak for the true *demos*. In the old *Länder*, twentieth-century Right-extremism was historically associated with political parties and organizations, while in the new *Länder* it was more spontaneous and more violent. Yet willingness to engage in political violence was never expressed by more than 10 percent of respondents, with generally 1 to 4 percent having done so; overall rates of Right-extremism have been low and did not seem to vary much as between the old and the new *Länder*.[26]

Confidence in the FRG's democratic institutions declined somewhat across the 1990s, particularly among East Germans. The position of political parties in the Berlin Republic is weaker than in the Bonn Republic, though nowhere near as weak as in the Weimar Republic. Trust in the political parties and belief that they represent the citizens' interests fluctuated after 1990, yet seldom did more than a plurality in West or East express confidence in the parties, and the trend was downward. Confidence in parties was less in the East than in the West. Membership in the parties also declined, and only a minority of members participated in party affairs. Scholars have attributed these declines variously to the parties being rooted in nineteenth-century cleavages (e.g., religious sects, capitalist/worker); to more participatory, and self-assertive conceptions of democracy; and to the perception that the parties are bureaucratized and self-interested agglomerations. Nonetheless, post-unification German voters still voted predominantly for pro-democratic parties, and the anti-party conceptions of politics that were so influential in the 1870s to 1940s did not revive strongly.[27]

Membership in social and political organizations has fluctuated in German history, but it has grown substantially since the 1950s in the old *Länder* and since 1990, though not as much, in the new *Länder*. Women were generally less likely to belong to social organizations, which may have contributed to their lesser participation in political activities. Trust in organizations suffered somewhat in the 1990s, but it was still relatively high, and generally higher than for the political parties. The growth of organizational life among immigrants was potentially an encouraging sign for their integration into the FRG's political culture.[28]

Noted sociologist and political commentator Ralf Dahrendorf promoted in the 1960s, and most West German political scholars have come to embrace, a liberal model of democracy as a society that accepted pluralism, opposition, conflict, and compromise. In the 1980s such a model seemed to have triumphed (see Chapter 5), but by the 1990s its triumph was not so clear. While Germans generally supported the existence of an opposition—scholars have asked if an opposition was necessary for a democracy and have gotten substantial majorities, indeed often over 90 percent saying yes—they did not necessarily want it to oppose the government. Up to 39 percent in the old *Länder* and up to 53 percent in the new *Länder* have agreed the opposition's task is not to criticize but to support the government. Political and social elites were more accepting of the open conflict a liberal democracy entails, but near majorities of the population across Germany were still uncomfortable with such a conflict of interests. For example, although 94.9 percent of East German political elites and 87.4 percent of West German political elites rejected the assertion that interest-group clashes hurt the FRG, in a general survey, only 46 percent of East Germans and 49 percent of West Germans rejected such an assertion. Asked in another survey whether group and association interests must always be subordinate to the common good, 50 percent in the East and 55 percent in the West said yes. In addition, surveys showed a persistence of potentially authoritarian views and values, particularly among East Germans, with many continuing to place a high value on order, diligence, and discipline as well as strong leadership. These survey results seemed to some observers to substantiate the concern expressed by Dahrendorf and others that Germans were too inclined to shy away from conflict and to prefer to believe in a single shared national interest.[29]

Germans could be and were proud about the outcome of Germany's fraught twentieth-century history. They had overcome a painful and morally problematic history and created a unified, prosperous, respected and democratic Germany.

Forward to the Past?

While the FRG remains a stable democracy in the twenty-first century, it is not in stasis. Recent developments, some echoing the past, illustrate how democracy remains a work in progress.

For some Germans, the 1999 citizenship law did not settle the question of who was entitled to German citizenship. Some on the Right have embraced the term "Bio-German" as a positive self-description for an ethnically German FRG citizen; they contrast this with "Passport-German"—an individual who has a German passport and (officially) German citizenship but who, as one with a "migration background," they do not see as fully or really German. Notions of citizenship and the *demos* have long rested on equality, at least before the state, but this ethnic distinction refuses to recognize that equality and posits a differentiated citizenship that seems incompatible with democracy as rule of all the people.[30]

Anxieties about immigrants have become a central issue in German politics, with implications for democracy. Two notable movements are the Patriotic Europeans Against the Islamization of the Occident (PEGIDA) and the Alternative for Germany

(AfD). Founded in 2014, PEGIDA sees Muslim immigrants as conspiring to subvert Western civilization and sponsors occasionally violent protests drawing on popular anger at cosmopolitan elites and demanding strict limits on immigrants. The AfD began as a political movement against Germany's response to the Eurozone crisis, but since 2015 it has moved to the Right. Some of its leaders have ties to Neo-Nazis, break with various anti-Nazi taboos, or have demanded reassertion of (ethnic) German identity and pride. Official AfD documents avoid terminology from the past, but leading AfD figures have called for a *Volksgemeinschaft*, referred to the "lying press," and characterized the current system as "degenerate," echoing Nazi terminology. It also emphasizes law and order, authority, family values, and a *Gesamtinteresse* over individual interests. It does present itself as the paladin of democracy against a corrupt professional-political elite and the "old parties"; it echoes here Weimar-era criticisms of parliamentary governance (though criticism of perceived corruption in parliamentary governance are not confined to Germany). It calls for plebiscites on the federal level, direct election of the Federal President, and other "direct democratic" measures. In the twenty-first century, the AfD must support "democracy" if it is to have legitimacy, but it is offering a "populist" challenge to the GG's representative democracy, with authoritarian and anti-system rhetoric.[31]

The AfD vote is broad-based. An AfD vote does not correlate with personal economic difficulties but with being anti-gay marriage, anti-immigration, dissatisfied with how democracy is working in the FRG, and (in the new *Länder*) inclined to think socialism was a good idea badly implemented. And like populists elsewhere, the AfD has attracted considerable working-class support by claiming to defend welfare-state gains against threats from immigrants. Germans in the new *Länder* are significantly more likely to vote AfD than those in the old *Länder*, especially in areas that could not receive West German TV under the GDR—but two-thirds of AfD voters live in the old *Länder*. Germany has had spikes of right-wing extremism before, as have other countries, but never as large as the AfD. And its rise is part of a broader challenge in many democracies to the existing order as not effectively representative of popular will. So it is a potentially significant development.[32]

The AfD's rise reflects the erosion of the postwar party landscape, with echoes of the Weimar Republic. The erosion of the pro-Weimar Republic parties across the 1920s arguably partly reflected a party system rooted in nineteenth-century cleavages that no longer resonated in the same ways, for example, over religion and class. And by 1932 a majority of Reichstag seats were held by parties, the Nazis and Communists, determined to destroy the Weimar Republic, so no pro-Republic democratic government was possible. From the late 1950s into the 1990s, the pro-democratic CDU/CSU, SPD, and FDP were getting around 90 percent of the votes. Erosion began with the rise of the Greens and accelerated with the Left's appearance to the SPD's left. Both, at least initially, questioned the GG's representative democracy but have accepted its structure while seeking to increase citizen participation within it. Both have participated in governing coalitions, at least at the state level, and they are not fundamentally opposed to GG democracy. They represent different elements of a new social class of educated, often post-materialist, tertiary-sector, voters. Meanwhile, the decline of the working class as a share of the German population was eroding the SPD's base, while the decline in religious self-identification was eroding the CDU/CSU's base. The flood of immigrants in 2015 contributed to the AfD's success in state elections and eventually in the 2017 Bundestag elections, when it was the first right-wing party to secure seats in the Bundestag, with 12.6 percent of the vote. The AfD currently has only 9.7 percent of Bundestag seats, so the Berlin Republic does not yet face the existential threat from popular votes for anti-system parties that the Weimar Republic did. Albeit the mainstream parties' unwillingness to enter coalitions with the anti-system AfD does make governing more difficult by narrowing the options for coalitions.[33]

Even before the COVID-19 pandemic, Germany's economy faced headwinds, which might undermine the existing political order. It was not as stressed as some other developed economies, as it remained highly competitive internationally in various fields such as autos and machine tools. However, recovery from the 2008 financial and Euro crises was slow, and some regions faced high unemployment from restructuring. Broad areas in the new *Länder* have never recovered from the GDR economy's collapse. And the rise of China and potentially dramatic shifts to electric and self-driving cars threatened key sectors in the German economy. Moreover, the long-term consequences of the pandemic-induced economic difficulties are likely to be substantial but are impossible to predict. Failure to deliver for the citizens fatally compromised the authoritarian *Kaiserreich*, the democratic Weimar Republic, and the Communist-dictatorial GDR. The need to deliver remains an issue for any regime. And among Germans polled in 2019, 28 percent of those who thought the economic situation was good were dissatisfied with democracy, but 63 percent of those who thought it was bad were dissatisfied.[34]

Popular protest remains a central element in the Berlin Republic's political culture. Various forms and focuses of protest have predominated in different periods. Some have challenged representative democracy, such as the massive protests against a new railway station in Stuttgart that reject repeated majority decisions in the state parliament. For some, most notable has been the populist Right's embrace of central elements of the protest culture developed, usually by the Left, in the 1970s and 1980s. Particularly striking has been PEGIDA's adoption of strategies from the 1970s *Autonomen* and of the central motifs of the East German 1989 revolution (weekly Monday evening protests and the slogan "We are the people"). Elements on the Right continue to resort to violence as protest, as did elements on the Left in the 1970s and 1980s. At least equally striking, though, have been the often grassroots-organized counterdemonstrations that have sprung up to counter PEGIDA and AfD demonstrations, counterdemonstrations that often drew more, indeed many more, protesters than the Right. And despite Germany's relatively successful response to the COVID-19 pandemic, lockdowns have elicited protests, often spurred by the Right, which have in turn elicited counterdemonstrations. So far the protest culture seems to favor the pro-democratic forces, but as the Weimar Republic showed, protest can cut in different directions.[35]

A major 2019 study of democratic attitudes in various countries, by the Pew Research Center, offers grounds for optimism and concern. Germany tends to rank toward the middle, among the thirty-four countries surveyed, on most of the measures of support for democracy or democratic values that the study documents. About 68 percent of

Germans polled are satisfied with democracy, 36 percent are not, tied for fifth among the thirty-four countries, and the dissatisfied are 6 percent fewer in 2019 than in 2018. However, those polled in Germany who think the state is run for the benefit of all fell from 86 percent in 2002 to 48 percent in 2019. In 2019 86 percent were for fair judiciary and free speech, but only 60 percent for free opposition parties. Around 70 percent thought it important to have honest elections with at least two parties regularly. About 62 percent thought voting gave people like them some say, but 36 percent disagreed.[36] So about two-thirds of those surveyed give consistently pro-democratic responses—probably enough for stability, but less than similar polls in the 1990s and not a ringing endorsement.

Germany is a stable democracy, quite possibly more stable than most. Yet factors that worked for and against democratic stability in the past have not disappeared. Germany will quite probably remain a stable democracy for the foreseeable future—but one cannot simply take that for granted.

Conclusions

Participation and its limits are a thread through German (and others') history. German political elites since the Napoleonic Wars, of all stripes, have recognized that popular engagement and legitimacy were indispensable, yet they have always sought to limit popular influence. Authoritarian monarchs and twentieth-century dictators felt compelled to include "democratic" elements or to create the appearance of democracy, even as they sought to maximize control. But even sincere democrats, like Willy Brandt, were not looking for popular activism. They looked to the people for selection of leaders, information, and legitimacy, but they have tended to see policymaking as a matter for elites or experts, not untutored masses. And if voicing doubts about citizens' "maturity" came to seem unwise, concerns about "ungovernability" remained.

Regimes, democratic or otherwise, must deliver. The *Kaiserreich*, the Weimar Republic, and the GDR all collapsed when their citizens concluded that they were not providing the desperately desired—material goods or victory or peace. Regimes can survive short-term difficulties if they have enough political capital with their citizens, but political capital is not enough to guarantee survival.

Varying ideas about the nature of society and state influenced Germans' choices about the forms the state and participation should take. Many Germans have assumed that a single set of ideals and a single communal interest exist. The state's purpose was to protect and realize those ideals and that interest. Individual and group interests were hence egoistic and materialistic. And parliaments and parties were suspect because they inherently privileged individual and group interests. Most Germans, since the 1950s, seem gradually to have come to accept pluralism: that a modern society is inherently multifarious, that identifying a single communal interest is perhaps impossible but certainly problematic in practice, and that individual and groups interests hence are entitled to representation. Yet not all Germans agree, and some can still find individual and group interests, partisanship, and parliamentary divisiveness reprehensible. Whether that will become again a politically significant factor remains to be seen, but the recent rise of populist movements (and not just in Germany) suggests that significant numbers of people have doubts about pluralism and parliamentarism.

Germans have had competing conceptions of democracy. Fears of "parliamentary absolutism" influenced both the Weimar constitution's and the GG's drafters. The drafters created democratic republics—but with limits. Weimar's plebiscitary president and the Bonn and Berlin Republics' Constitutional Court have been means to constrain unlimited parliamentary power, reflecting disdain for and fear of egotism, materialism, divisiveness, and the people's voice, even mediated through parliamentarians. Democracy was hence often about *Führerauslesung*, assessing, choosing, and legitimating leaders who could advance the people's interest(s). After that, the people need, and should, say no more. With the Weimar Republic's serial crises, many Germans not surprisingly looked for a democracy that could exercise authority, a leader democracy with a single ruling leader, or if necessary an authoritarian state. Even when the GG drafters, chastened by Nazi brutality and defeat, turned against an authoritarian solution, they still thought in terms of *Führerauslesung*, choosing to privilege the political parties and their leaders in forming the political will. Yet since the nineteenth century some Germans have always wanted democracy as substantive citizen voice in policy formation. Whether that could be achieved within a parliamentary system or only through some direct democracy has remained a matter of debate. And the rise of populism, in Germany and elsewhere, suggests that suspicion of parties and parliament and a belief in a "real" people who constitute a shared interest/will that can be embodied in strong and efficacious leadership have not disappeared.

Across twelve decades and six regimes, some Germans were always activist. Even supporters of authoritarian governance and opponents of democratic values could take to the streets—in the Empire, in the Weimar Republic, and in the Bonn and Berlin Republics. Protesters might favor draconian controls on others, but they asserted their own right to protest vigorously. And even in dictatorial regimes, some Germans protested. Occasionally they did so openly; more usually, given the risks, they did so privately, or quietly, or indirectly. And people's "private" actions could have political meaning and political consequences. Surveys show Germans becoming more open to public political activism after the 1960s. Yet political action was always part of some Germans' political culture—and political activism can be pro- or antidemocratic.

The goals of political activism have varied. Political elites often recruited citizens for acclamatory public demonstrations. Kaiser Wilhelm I's funeral, the Nürnberg party rallies, GDR Mayday parades were all tools to secure citizen engagement and support. Democratic elites also sponsored acclamatory public demonstrations, for example, the 1968 West Berlin demonstration in support of US policy in Vietnam, the 1992 Berlin demonstration against hatred of foreigners. Public assemblies and demonstrations have often been in support of a political party, a leader, or a movement. Recently, though, public protests have increasingly addressed a policy issue or problem, for example, anti-reactor demonstrations at Wyhl or grassroots-organized demonstrations against hatred of foreigners. This new focus marks a decisive shift in and a substantive broadening of citizen input into political decision-making.

Germans have held an enormous range of beliefs about what forms of political activism constituted legitimate political citizenship. Legal provisions have mattered. Legal barriers to demonstrations under the Empire led SPD'ers to turn political funerals into "splendid demonstrations," though opponents could still deplore this instrumentalization of a solemn occasion. Germans under the Third Reich and the GDR instrumentalized petitions and factory meetings to raise problems. Hungry women during the First World War, desperate farmers in the late Weimar Republic, and anti-reactor and anti–nuclear weapon protesters in the 1970s and 1980s all proved willing to break the law in pursuit of their goals, though only since the 1960s have Germans formalized such law-breaking as "civil disobedience." More broadly, legal forms of political activism that were seen as at best unconventional and at worst demagogic have since the 1960s come to be widely accepted as legitimate and conventional. Notably, populist movements in the Berlin Republic have adopted some of the same tactics as earlier political movements (e.g., PEGIDA Mondays). Some Germans have always accepted such activism and some still oppose it, but the prevailing political culture in Germany since the 1970s accepts a vibrant and varied citizen activism as a central element in democracy, a position affirmed by the Constitutional Court.

If citizen activism is central to democracy, to what end should it be deployed? The prevailing opinion in Germany seems to be that rationally convincing fellow citizens of the rightness of one's position should be the point of activism. That attitude developed in reaction to the irrationalism, and disastrous consequences, of Nazism. It has survived despite a greater emphasis on emotion and imagination since the 1960s. With the increasing acceptance of pluralism and interests in German politics, Germans have become increasingly willing to see pressure (such as economic elites have long exercised on government officials) as a legitimate goal of political activism. Compulsion has proved more problematic. Some Germans have been willing to present civil disobedience as a means to compel governments to change policy on morally charged issues (e.g., stationing nuclear weapons), even if majorities support the government. Most Germans have disagreed, and civil disobedience has a marginal role in German politics. Public protest has included violence, but except during the Weimar Republic it has generally been a distinctly minority tactic.

Given the range of attitudes among Germans, Germany's democratization could only be complicated. No simple transition from authoritarianism to democratic stability took place. After the Empire's foundation, some Germans always favored democracy, even if the prevailing political cultures, official or popular, favored authoritarian rule. Even supporters of authoritarianism could use democratic tactics against what they saw as inadequacies. Even in dictatorships, Germans retained and exercised a degree of agency. And the establishment of democracy did not produce instant democrats. Already in 1920 over half of Germans were voting for non-democratic parties, and millions in the 1920s/early 1930s participated in antidemocratic assemblies and paramilitaries. And 1950s and 1960s Germans generally had a narrow view of democracy, with little role for citizens beyond voting. Even the triumph of a more participatory model among most Germans by the 1980s and 1990s did not mean all Germans favored it. Moreover, the rise of radical right and populist movements in the last few years reflects continuing doubts among at least some Germans that parliamentary systems can adequately represent the "people's" interests and about values (e.g., tolerance, pluralism) that have seemed central to stable and effective democratic governance. Such doubts suggest that democratic means might be deployed in attempts to secure the people's will in ways that arguably threaten democracy—especially if the government fails to deliver for a significant share of the citizenry.

Germans have built a stable democracy. Nonetheless, democratization has not been and could not be a story of virtue triumphant, with a happy ending, or any ending at all—it can only be a work in progress.

Notes

Introduction

1. Cf., for example, Michael McFaul, "Democracy Promotion as a World Value," *Washington Quarterly* 28:1 (December 2004), 148–52; Drew DeSilver, "Despite Global Concerns about Democracy, More Than Half of Countries Are Democratic," Pew Research Center, FactTank (https://www.pewresearch.org/fact-tank/2019/05/14/more-than-half-of-countries-are-democratic/, accessed April 5, 2020).
2. Cf. here Hedwig Richter, *Moderne Wahlen* (Hamburg: Hamburger Edition, 2017), 14.
3. James J. Sheehan, *German History 1770–1866* (Oxford: Oxford University Press, 1989), 304–5, passim; quotations: Karl August Freiherr von Hardenberg, "Über die Reorganisation des Preußischen Staats" (September 12, 1807), GHI-DC, *Deutsche Geschichte in Dokumenten und Bildern*; Thomas Rohkrämer, *A Single Communal Faith? The German Right from Conservatism to National Socialism* (New York: Berghahn Books, 2007), 47, 58; Richter, *Moderne Wahlen*, 8–9.
4. Tim B. Müller/Hedwig Richter, "Einführung: Demokratiegeschichten. Deutschland (1800–1933) in transnationaler Perspektive," *Geschichte und Gesellschaft* 44:3 (2018), 326.
5. Hayden White, "Interpretation in History," in idem (ed.), *Tropics of Discourse* (Baltimore, MD: Johns Hopkins University Press, 1986), 58–62, 70; Tim B. Müller, "Von der 'Whig Interpretation' zur Fragilität der Demokratie. Weimar als geschichtstheoretisches Problem," *Geschichte und Gesellschaft* 44:3 (2018), 432–3, 436.
6. Hans Ulrich Wehler, *Deutsche Gesellschaftsgeschichte*, 4. durchgesehene Aufl. der broschierten Studienausgabe (München: C.H. Beck, 2008), Vol. 1, 209; Matthew Levinger, "The Prussian Reform Movement and the Rise of Enlightened Nationalism," in Philip G. Dwyer (ed.), *The Rise of Prussia: 1700–1830* (Harlow, UK: Longman, 2000), 260–1, 266, passim.
7. Levinger, "Reform Movement," 270–1; Dirk Götschmann, *Bayerischer Parlamentarismus im Vormärz. Die Ständeversammlung des Königreichs Bayern 1819–1848* (Düsseldorf: Droste Verlag, 2002), 40, 46, 48–50; Paul Nolte, *Staatsbildung als Gesellschaftsreform in Preußen und den süddeutschen Staaten, 1800–1820* (Frankfurt/M: Campus Verlag, 1990), 23, 30, 33, 37, 58, 86, 94, 98, 104, 173, 176–8, 191, 196.
8. Götschmann, *Parlamentarismus*, 36, 59–60, 64; Hans Gangl, "Der deutsche Weg zum Verfassungsstaat im 19. Jahrhundert," in Ernst-Wolfgang Böckenförde (ed.), *Probleme des Konstitutionalismus im 19. Jahrhundert* (Berlin: Duncker & Humblot, 1975), 52; Hartwig Brandt, *Landständische Repräsentation im deutschen Vormärz. Politisches Denken im Einflußfeld des monarchischen Prinzips* (Neuwied: Luchterhand, 1968), 35–7, passim.

9   Wehler, *Gesellschaftsgeschichte*, I, 451–2; Brandt, *Repräsentation*, 6, 43; Götschmann, *Parlamentarismus*, 41–3.
10 Götschmann, *Parlamentarismus*, 52; Wolfgang Durner, *Antiparlamentarismus in Deutschland* (Würzburg: Königshausen & Neumann, 1997), 20–35; Levinger, "Reform Movement," 53–4, 83, 273; Nolte, *Staatsbildung*, 90; Wehler, *Gesellschaftsgeschichte*, I, 446–7, 451.
11 Götschmann, *Parlamentarismus*, 50–1, 58–61, 64, 881, 890–92; Levinger, "Reform Movement," 94; Nolte, *Staatsbildung*, 104.
12 Wolfram Siemann, *The German Revolution of 1848*, trans. Christiane Banerji (New York: St. Martin's Press, 1998), 35–9, 44, 70–1, 95–109, 126, 167, 171–7, 185; Mike Rapport, *1848. Year of Revolution* (New York: Basic Books, 2009), 21–2, 29, 219–21, 264, 266, 291, 341; Richter, *Moderne Wahlen*, 148–54, passim.

Chapter 1

1   Quotation: Ludwig Rexhäuser in *Partei und Gewerkschaften*. Wörtlicher Abdruck des Punktes: "Partei und Gewerkschaften" aus dem Protokoll der Konferenz der Gewerkschaftsvorstände vom 19.-23. February 1906 in *Economics Pamphlets*, # 31 (Duke University Library), 24; Karl Kautsky, "Die Aktion der Masse," [*Neue Zeit* 30:1], in Antonia Grunenberg (ed.), *Die Massenstreikdebatte* (Frankfurt: Europäische Verlagsanstalt, 1970), 261.
2   Dieter Grimm, *Deutsche Verfassungsgeschichte 1776-1866* (Frankfurt/M: Suhrkamp, 1988), 113; Lothar Gall, *Bismarck. The White Revolutionary. Vol. I. 1815–1871*, trans. J. A. Underwood (London: Allen & Unwin, 1986), 316, 321–2; Peter Steinbach, "Reichstag Elections in the *Kaiserreich*," in Larry E. Jones/James Retallack (eds.), *Elections, Mass Politics, and Social Change in Modern Germany. New Perspectives* (Cambridge: Cambridge University Press, 1992), 133–5; Karl Erich Pollmann, *Parlamentarismus im Norddeutschen Bund 1867-1870* (Düsseldorf: Droste Verlag, 1985), 68–71.
3   "Reich Constitution of 1871," passim; Ernst-Wolfgang Böckenförde, "Der Zusammenbruch der Monarchie und die Entstehung der Weimarer Republik," *Recht, Staat, Freiheit* (Frankfurt/M: Suhrkamp, 1991), 309; James Sheehan, *German Liberalism in the Nineteenth Century* (Chicago: University of Chicago Press, 1978), 131–4; Hans-Ulrich Wehler, *Deutsche Gesellschaftsgeschichte 1849-1918*, 2nd ed. (München: C.H. Beck Verlag, 2006), 854–7.
4   Fritz Hartung, *Deutsche Verfassungsgeschichte. Vom 15. Jahrhundert bis zur Gegenwart*, 8th ed. (Stuttgart: K. F. Koehler Verlag, 1950), 268–9, 270–2; Wilfried Loth, *Das Kaiserreich. Obrigkeitsstaat und politische Mobilisierung* (München: Deutscher Taschenbuch Verlag, 1997), 25.
5   "The Reich Constitution of 1871," in Elmar M. Hucko, *The Democratic Tradition: Four German Constitutions* (Oxford: Berg Publishers, 1987) (for quotation, Art. 29); Gordon Craig, *Germany 1866-1945* (New York: Oxford University Press, 1980), 38–55; Wehler, *Deutsche Gesellschaftsgeschichte*, 864–5; David Blackbourn, "New Legislatures: Germany, 1871–1914," *Historical Research* 65 (1992), 202–8.
6   David Blackbourn, *History of Germany 1780-1918. The Long Nineteenth Century*, 2nd ed. (Oxford: Blackwell Publishing, 2003), 292; Ronald J. Ross, *The Failure of Bismarck's Kulturkampf. Catholicism and State Power in Imperial Germany*,

1871–1887 (Washington, DC: The Catholic University of American Press, 1998), 11–14, 7, 95–101, 158–79, 186, passim.
7 Manfred Rauh, *Die Parlamentarisierung des Deutschen Reiches* (Düsseldorf: Droste Verlag, 1977), 162–4, 169–71, 182–201; H. Pogge von Strandmann, "Staatsstreichpläne, Alldeutsche, und Bethmann Hollweg," in idem (ed.), *Die Erforderlichkeit des Unmöglichen. Deutschland am Vorabend des ersten Weltkrieges* (Frankfurt/M: Europäische Verlagsanstalt, 1965), 29; Christoph Schönberger, "'Die überholte Parlamentarisierung' Einflußgewinn und fehlende Herrschaftsfähigkeit des Reichstags im sich demokratisierenden *Kaiserreich*," *Historische Zeitschrift* 272:3 (June 2001), 624, 637–8.
8 Walter Euchner, "Sozialdemokratie und Demokratie. Zum Demokratieverständnis der SPD in der Weimarer Republik," *Archiv für Sozialgeschichte* 26 (1986), 129; Schönberger, "Parlamentarisierung," 643, 648, 657, 665; Geoff Eley, *Reshaping the German Right. Radical Nationalism and Political Change after Bismarck* (New Haven, CT: Yale University Press, 1980), 304, 314, 349; Dieter Grosser, *Vom monarchischen Konstitutionalismus zur parlamentarischen Demokratie* (Den Haag: Martinus Nijhoff, 1970), esp. 3, 14, 207–8, 213–14.
9 Thomas Kühne, *Dreiklassenwahlrecht und Wahlkultur im Preußen 1867–1918. Landtagswahlen zwischen korporativer Tradition und politischer Massenmarkt* (Düsseldorf: Droste Verlag, 1994), 402–4, 458; Pogge von Strandmann, "Staatsstreichpläne," 7–45; Margaret Lavinia Anderson, *Practicing Democracy. Elections and Political Culture in Imperial Germany* (Princeton: Princeton University Press, 2000), 244–50, 422–4.
10 Ann Goldberg, *Honor, Politics, and the Law in Imperial Germany, 1871–1914* (Cambridge: Cambridge University Press, 2010), 74, 81–5, 101, 104; Blackbourn, *History of Germany,* 309–10.
11 Hans Fenske, *Deutsche Verfassungsgeschichte. Vom Norddeutschen Bund bis heute*, 2nd ed. (Berlin: Colloquium Verlag, 1984), 16; Blackbourn, *History of Germany*, 309–10; Alex Hall, *Scandal, Sensation and Social Democracy. The SPD Press and Wilhelmine Germany, 1890–1914* (Cambridge: Cambridge University Press, 1977), 14, 41–2, 64–72; Gary D. Stark, *Banned in Berlin. Literary Censorship in Imperial Germany, 1871–1918* (New York: Berghahn Books), 2009, 87–91, 248–50; Ross, *Kulturkampf,* 1–7, 55–6, 58, passim; Vernon Lidtke, *The Outlawed Party. Social Democracy in Germany, 1878–1890* (Princeton: Princeton University Press, 1966), 73–4, 77–8, 160–1, 241–54, passim.
12 Eli Nathans, *The Politics of Citizenship in Germany. Ethnicity, Utility and Nationalism* (Oxford: Berg, 2004), 91–2; Andreas Fahrmeir, *Citizenship. The Rise and Fall of a Modern Concept* (New Haven, CT: Yale University Press, 2007), 66, 68, 71.
13 Nathans, *Politics of Citizenship*, 111–59; M. Rainer Lepsius, "Parteiensystem und Sozialstruktur: zum Problem der Demokratisierung der deutschen Gesellschaft," in Gerhard A. Ritter (ed.), *Deutsche Parteien vor 1918* (Köln: Kiepenheuer & Witsch, 1973), 73; Matthew Fitzpatrick, *Purging the Empire. Mass Expulsions in Germany, 1871–1914* (Oxford: Oxford University Press, 2015), 39–89.
14 Peter Walkenhorst, *Nation—Volk—Rasse. Radikaler Nationalismus im Deutschen Kaiserreich 1890–1914* (Göttingen: Vandenhoeck & Ruprecht, 2007), 149–58, 160–5; Nathans, *Politics of Citizenship*, 63, 169–90; Fahrmeir, *Citizenship*, 91; Fitzpatrick, *Purging*, 93–176.
15 Cf. Geoff Eley, "Making a Place in the Nation. Meanings of 'Citizenship' in Wilhelmine Germany," in idem/James Retallack (eds.), *Wilhelminism and It Legacies. German Modernities, Imperialism, and the Meanings of Reform, 1890–1933* (New York: Berghahn Books, 2003), esp. 23–6; Loth, *Kaiserreich,* 83, 89.

16 Pollmann, *Parlamentarismus*, 343; Thomas Rohkrämer, *A Single Communal Faith? The German Right from Conservatism to National Socialism* (New York: Berghahn Books, 2007), 19, 35, passim; Hans-Ulrich Wehler, *The German Empire 1871-1918*, trans. Kim Traynor (Leamington Spa: Berg Publishers, 1985), 130-1; Manfred Hettling, *Politische Bürgerlichkeit. Der Bürger zwischen Individualität und Vergesellschaftung in Deutschland und der Schweiz von 1860 bis 1918* (Göttingen: Vandenhoeck & Ruprecht, 1999), 234-9; Schönberger, "Parlamentarisierung," 659; Sheehan, *Liberalism*, 14.
17 For quotation, cited in Nancy R. Reagin, *A German Women's Movement. Class and Gender in Hannover, 1880-1933* (Chapel Hill: University of North Carolina Press, 1995), 7; Grosser, *Konstitutionalismus*, 4, 17; Hettling, *Politische Bürgerlichkeit*, 179, 182-3, 234-7; Fritz Stern, "The Political Consequences of the Unpolitical German," in idem (ed.), *The Failure of Illiberalism. Essays on the Political Culture of Modern Germany* (New York: Alfred A. Knopf, 1972), 1-22; Rudy Koshar, *Social Life, Local Politics, and Nazism. Marburg, 1880-1935* (Chapel Hill: University of North Carolina Press, 1986), xiii-xiv, 6, passim; Dennis Sweeney, *Work, Race, and the Emergence of Radical Right Corporatism in Imperial Germany* (Ann Arbor: Univ. of Michigan Press, 2009), 69-71, 113-16; Sheehan, *Liberalism*, 233-6; Marie-Luise Recker/Andreas Schulz, "Parlamentarismuskritik und Antiparlamentarismus in Europa," in idem (eds.), *Parlamentarismuskritik und Antiparlamentarismus in Europa* (Düsseldorf: Droste Verlag, 2018), 9, 18-19; Kevin Repp, *Reformers, Critics, and the Paths of German Modernity. Anti-Politics and the Search for Alternatives, 1890-1914* (Cambridge: Harvard University Press, 2000), esp. 212-30.
18 Karl Heinrich Pohl, "Kommunen, kommunale Wahlen und kommunale Wahlrechtpolitik. Zur Bedeutung der Wahlrechtsfrage für die Kommunen und den deutschen Liberalismus," in Simone Lässig et al. (eds.), *Modernisierung und Region in wilhelminischen Deutschland. Wahlen, Wahlrecht und Politische Kultur* (Bielefeld: Verlag für Regionalgeschichte, 1995), 107, 115-20; Sheehan, *Liberalismus*, 237.
19 Dieter Langewiesche, *Liberalism in Germany*, trans. Christiane Banerji (Princeton, NJ: Princeton University Press, 2000), 3-4; Stern, "Political Consequences," 10.
20 Sheehan, *Liberalism*, 14-15, 17-18, 152, Langewiesche, *Liberalism*, 180-1.
21 Pohl, "kommunale Wahlen," 133-5; Sheehan, *Liberalism*, 229; Anderson, *Practicing Democracy*, 137-8; Richard J. Evans, "'Red Wednesday' in Hamburg: Social Democrats, Police and Lumpenproletariat in the Suffrage Disturbances of 17 January 1906," *Social History* 4:1 (January 1979), 1-31; James Retallack, *Red Saxony. Electoral Battles and the Spectre of Democracy in Germany, 1860-1918* (Oxford: Oxford University Press, 2017), 8-10, 273-4, 286-303, 412-13, 430-5, passim.
22 James Retallack, *The German Right, 1860-1920* (Toronto: University of Toronto Press, 2006), 193-6, 206-7, 209; Kühne, *Dreiklassenwahlrecht*, 384-5, 498; Walter Gagel, *Die Wahlrechtsfrage in der Geschichte der deutschen liberalen Parteien 1848*-1918 (Düsseldorf: Droste Verlag, 1958), 63, 67.
23 Kühne, *Dreiklassenwahlrecht*, 469, 477, 502-5; James Retallack, *Notables of the Right. The Conservative Party and Political Mobilization in Germany, 1876-1918* (Boston: Unwin Hyman, 1988), 162; Dennis Sweeney, "Liberalism, the Worker and the Limits of Bourgeois *Öffentlichkeit* in Wilhelmine Germany," *German History* 22:1 (2004), quotation on 54.
24 Ute Frevert, *A Nation in Barracks. Modern Germany, Military Conscription and Civil Society* (Oxford: Berg Publishers, 2004), 113-21, passim; Pollmann, *Parlamentarismus*, 203; Pogge von Strandmann, "Staatsstreichpläne," 16; Retallack, *German Right*, 197.

25 Richard J. Evans, *The Feminist Movement in Germany 1894–1933* (London: Sage Publications, 1976), 71–108; Volker Berghahn, *Imperial Germany, 1871–1914. Economy, Society, Culture and Politics* (Providence: Berghahn Books, 1994), 237–9; Ute Rosenbusch, *Der Weg zum Frauenwahlrecht in Deutschland* (Baden-Baden: Nomos Verlag, 1998), 291, 303, 334–40, passim; Ute Planert, "Women's Suffrage and Antifeminism as a Litmus Test of Modernizing Societies. A Western European Comparison," in Sven Oliver Müller/Cornelius Torp (eds.), *Imperial Germany Revisited. Continuing Debates and New Perspectives* (New York: Berghahn Books, 2013), 107–21; Gisela Bock, "Frauenwahlrecht—Deutschland um 1900 in vergleichendere Perspektive," in Michael Grüttner et al. (eds.), *Geschichte und Emanzipation: Festschrift für Reinhard Rürup* (Frankfurt: Campus Verlag, 1999), 96–123.

26 Kühne, *Dreiklassenwahlrecht*, 471; Simone Lässig, "Wahlrechtsreformen in den deutschen Einzelstaaten," in idem et al. (eds.), *Modernisierung und Regionen in wilhelminischen Deutschland* (Bielefeld: Verlag für Regionalgeschichte), 145–6, 159; Hedwig Richter, *Moderne Wahlen. Eine Geschichte der Demokratie in Preußen und den USA im 19. Jahrhundert* (Hamburg: Hamburger Edition, 2017), 357–9, passim; Pogge von Strandmann, "Staatsstreichpläne," 19, 25.

27 Kühne, *Dreiklassenwahlrecht*, 384–5; Grosser, *Konstitutionalismus*, 209, 214; Retallack, *The German Right*, 202; Gagel, *Wahlrechtsfrage*, 67–69; Hettling, *Politische Bürgerlichkeit*, 179; Alastair Thompson, *Left Liberals, the State and Popular Politics in Wilhelmine Germany* (Oxford: Oxford University Press, 2000), 86, 129–31.

28 Retallack, *Notables*, 103 (quotation), 211; Gagel, *Wahlrechtsfrage*, 151–2, 154.

29 Jonathan Sperber, *The Kaiser's Voters. Electors and Elections in Imperial Germany* (Cambridge: Cambridge Univ. Press, 1997), 3–5, 288–9; Stanley Suvall, *Electoral Politics in Wilhelmine Germany* (Chapel Hill: University of North Carolina Press, 1985), 5–8, 59–60, 244; Siegfried Weichlein, "Wahlkämpfe, Milieukultur und politische Mobilisierung im Deutschen *Kaiserreich*," Lässig et al. *Modernisierung*, 69–75.

30 Berghahn, *Imperial Germany*, 335–6; Anderson, *Practicing Democracy*, 102, 104–5, 213, 416; Blackbourn, "Legislatures," 208–9; Thomas Kühne, ‚Die Jahrhundertwende, die „lange" Bismarckzeit und die Demokratisierung der politischen Kultur," in *Otto von Bismarck und Wilhelm II: Repräsentanten eines Epochenwechsels?* edited by Lothar Gall (Paderborn: Schöningh, 2001): 85–118, 89.

31 Michael L. Hughes, "Splendid Demonstrations: The Political Funerals of Kaiser Wilhelm I and Wilhelm Liebknecht," *Central European History* 41 (2008), 231–2, 236–7, 241, passim.

32 Hughes, "Splendid Demonstrations," 232–3, 235–7, 241, passim; Werner Blessing, "The Cult of the Monarchy, Political Loyalty and the Workers' Movement in Imperial Germany," *Journal of Contemporary History* 13 (1978), 357–73.

33 Peter Steinbach, "Legacies of the German Empire," in Dirk Berg-Schlosser and Ralf Rytlewski (eds.), *Political Culture in Germany* (New York: St. Martin's Press, 1993), 32, 36, 40–1; Eley, *Reshaping*, 41–4, passim; Roger Chickering, *We Men Who Feel Most German. A Cultural Study of the Pan-German League, 1886–1914* (Boston: Allen & Unwin, 1984), 24–5, passim; Marilynn Coetzee, *The German Army League. Popular Nationalism in Wilhelmine Germany* (New York: Oxford University Press, 1990), passim; Dan S. White, *The Splintered Party. National Liberalism in Hessen and the Reich, 1967–1918* (Cambridge: Harvard University Press, 1976), 142–3; Shulamit Volkov, *The Rise of Popular Antimodernism in Germany. The Urban Master Artisans, 1873–1896* (Princeton, NJ: Princeton University Press, 1978), 237–66, passim; Ross, *Kulturkampf*, 129–32, passim.

34 Sitzung des Kgl. Staatsministeriums, May 10, 1907, Geheimes Staatsarchiv Preußischer Kulturbesitz, Berlin, Rep 84a, 5374, Bl. 300–11; Evans, *Feminist Movement*, 10–11, 25, 72–3; Paul Adolph, *Vereinsgesetz vom 19. April 1908*, 2nd ed. (Leipzig: Roßberg'sche Verlagsbuchhandlung, 1914), III–V, 1–3, 7–14; Vernon L. Lidtke, *The Alternative Culture* (New York: Oxford University Press, 1985), 31; Eleanor L. Turk, "German Liberals and the Genesis of the Association Law of 1908," in Konrad H. Jarausch/Larry E. Jones (eds.), *In Search of a Liberal Germany. Studies in the History of German Liberalism from 1789 to the Present* (New York: Berg Publishers, 1990), 237–60; Anderson, *Practicing Democracy*, 295–8; Kirsten Heinsohn, "Im Dienste der deutschen Volksgemeinschaft: Die 'Frauenfrage' und konservativen Parteien vor und nach dem Ersten Weltkrieg," in Ute Planert (ed.), *Nation, Politik und Geschlecht. Frauenbewegungen und Nationalismus in der Moderne* (Frankfurt: Campus Verlag, 2000), 215–16.

35 Klaus Tenfelde, "Civil Society and the Middle Classes in Nineteenth-Century Germany," in Nancy Bermeo/Philip Nord (eds.), *Civil Society before Democracy. Lessons from Nineteenth-Century Europe* (Lanham: Rowman & Littlefield Publishers, 2000), 85–6, 91–2, 94–5, 97; Dieter Gosewinkel/Jürgen Kocka, "Editor's Preface," in John Keane (ed.), *Civil Society. Berlin Perspectives* (New York: Berghahn Books, 2007), ix–xi; Jürgen Kocka, "Zivilgesellschaft in historischer Perspektive," *Forschungsjournal neue soziale Bewegungen* 16:2 (June 2003), 29–31; Volker Heims, *Das Andere der Zivilgesellschaft. Zur Archäologie eines Begriffs* (Bielefeld: transcript Verlag, 2002), 27–30, 42–3, 52, 57; Eley, *Reshaping*, 192–3; Chickering, *We Men*, 183–4; Kühne, "Jahrhundertwende," 115–17.

36 Peter Pulzer, *The Rise of Political Anti-Semitism in Germany and Austria*, Rev. ed. (Cambridge: Harvard University Press, 1988), 47–55, 88–9, 99–109, 111–15; Stefan Breuer, *Die Völkischen in Deutschland. Kaiserreich und Weimarer Republik* (Darmstadt: Wissenschaftliche Buchgesellschaft, 2010), 25–32, 49–55, 62–3, 68–70, passim; Geoff Eley, "Anti-Semitism, Agrarian Mobilization, and the Conservative Party: Radicalism and Containment in the Founding of the Agrarian League, 1890–93," in Jones/Retallack (eds.), *Between Reform*, 196–227; Wehler, *Deutsche Gesellschaftsgeschichte*, Vol. 3, 924–34, 1063–6.

37 Arnd Bauerkämpfer, "Einleitung: Die Praxis der Zivilgesellschaft," in idem (ed.), *Die Praxis der Zivilgesellschaft. Akteure, Handeln und Strukturen im internationalen Vergleich* (Frankfurt/M: Campus Verlag, 2003), 16–19; Hettling, *Politische Bürgerlichkeit*, 6–7, 156–7, 231; Berghahn, *Imperial Germany*, 221–40; Thompson, *Left Liberals*, 93; Eley, *Reshaping*, 50–1, 67, 75–6, 78–80, passim; Suvall, *Electoral Politics*, 32–6.

38 Lidtke, *Alternative Culture*, 21–101; Adina Lieske, "Bildung und öffentliche Partizipation. Sozialdemokratische Bildungsaktivitäten in Leipzig und Pilsen vor 1914," Bauerkämpfer, *Zivilgesellschaft*, 106–12, 115–19, 124–5; Geoff Eley, *Forging Democracy. The History of the Left in Europe, 1850-2000* (Oxford: Oxford University Press, 2002), 81–2, 95, 110.

39 Thomas Adams, *Philanthropy, Civil Society, and the State in German History, 1815-1989* (Rochester: Camden House, 2016), 131–3; Ute Frevert, *Women in German History. From Bourgeois Emancipation to Sexual Liberation* (New York: Berg, 1989), 113–15, 138–47, passim; Ute Planert, "Vater Staat und Mutter Germania: Zur Politisierung des weiblichen Geschlechts im 19. und 20. Jahrhundert," in idem (ed.), *Nation*, 17–50; Andrea Süchting-Hänger, "'Gleichgroße mut'ge Helferinnen' in der weiblichen Gegenwelt. Der Vaterländische Frauenverein und die Politisierung

konservativer Frauen 1890–1914," in Ute Planert (ed.), *Nation*, 131–41; Michael B. Gross, "Kulturkampf und Geschlechterkampf. Anti-Catholicism, Catholic Women, and the Public," in Frank Biess et al. (eds.), *Conflict, Catastrophe and Continuity. Essays on Modern German History* (New York: Berghahn Books, 2007), 30–2, 35–7; Mary Jo Maines, "'Genossen und Genosseninnen' Depictions of Gender, Militancy, and Organizing in the German Socialist Press, 1890–1914," in David E. Barclay/Eric D. Weitz (eds.), *Between Reform and Revolution. German Socialism and Communism from 1840–1990* (New York: Berghahn Books, 2009), 146–60; Eva Rosenhaft, "Women, Gender, and the Limits of Political History in the Age of 'Mass' Politics," in Jones/Retallack (eds.), *Elections*, 152–5; Reagin, *Women's Movement*, 23–4, 42, 45, 71, 73, passim; Evans, *Feminist Movement*, 26, 29, 36–7; Gisela Brinker-Gabler, "Die Frauenbewegung im Deutschen Kaiserreich—Die Revolution entläßt ihre Kinder," in Ingeborg Drewitz (ed.), *Die deutsche Frauenbewegung* (Bonn: Hohwacht, 1983), 60–1, 64–9; Sweeney, *Work*, 64–5, 88–9; Gisela Mettele, "The City and the *Citoyenne*. Associational Culture and Female Civic Virtues in 19th-century Germany," in Karen Hagemann et al. (eds.), *Civil Society and Gender Justice. Historical and Comparative Perspectives* (New York: Berghahn Books, 2008), 82–90; Gunilla Budde, "The Family—A Core Institution of Civil Society: A Perspective on the Middle Classes in Imperial Germany," in Karen Hagemann et al. (eds.), *Civil Society and Gender Justice*, 121–30.

40 David Blackbourn, "The Politics of Demagogy in Imperial Germany," in idem (ed.), *Populists and Patricians: Essays in Modern German History* (London: Allen & Unwin, 1987), 217, 229–30, 233; Eley, *Reshaping*, 73–4, 81–2, 213–14, passim; Chickering, *We Men*, 57; Dirk Stegmann, "Between Interest and Radical Nationalism. Attempts to Found a New Right-Wing Party in Imperial Germany, 1887–94," in Larry E. Jones/James Retallack (eds.), *Between Reform, Reaction, and Resistance. Studies in the History of German Conservatism from 1789 to 1945* (Providence: Berg Publishers, 1983), 169–70.

41 Ibid., 225 (quotation), 234–6; Volkov, *Antimodernism*, 273–90; Jorg-Detlef Kühne, "Demokratisches Denken in der Weimarer Verfassungsdiskussion—Hugo Preuß und die Nationalversammlung," in *Demokratisches Denken in der Weimarer Republik*, edited by Christoph Gusy (Baden-Baden: Nomos Verlagsgesellschaft, 2000): 115–33, 303.

42 The standard works in English on such groups are Eley, *Reshaping*; Chickering, *We Men*; and Coetzee, *German Army League*.

43 Eley, *Reshaping*, 188, 193, 195–6, 279, 326–7; Chickering, *We Men*, 47–8, 62, 286.

44 Retallack, *Notables*, 100, 212 (quotation); Eley, *Reshaping*, 195–6, 248–9, 268–9, 342; Chickering, *We Men*, 67–8, 197, 216–17, 272.

45 Eley, *Reshaping*, 196, 280, 284–7; Chickering, *We Men*, 215–17, 222–3, 266; Michael Wildt, "Volksgemeinschaft und Führererwartung in der Weimarer Republik," in Ute Daniel et al. (eds.), *Politische Kultur und Medienwirklickeit in der 1920er Jahren* (München: R. Oldenbourg Verlag, 2010), 184.

46 Ross, *Kulturkampf*, 56–7, 102–5, 129–56; David Blackbourn, *Marpingen. Apparitions of the Virgin in Nineteenth-Century Germany* (New York: Knopf, 1994), 238–47.

47 Michael Edwards, "Introduction: Civil Society and the Geometry of Human Relations," in idem (ed.), *The Oxford Handbook of Civil Society* (Oxford: Oxford University Press, 2011), 4–10, John Ehrenberg, "The History of Civil Society Ideas," in idem (ed.), *The Oxford Handbook of Civil Society*, 23–5; Philip Nord, *The Republican Moment. Struggles for Democracy in Nineteenth-Century France* (Cambridge: Harvard University Press, 1995), 7–14, passim.

48 Tenfelde, "Civil Society," 100–3; Simone Chambers/Jeffrey Kopstein, "Bad Civil Society," *Political Theory* 29:6 (December 2001), 837–60; Adams, *Philanthropy*, 7, passim; Sheri Berman, "Civil Society and the Collapse of the Weimar Republic," *World Politics* 49:3 (April 1997), 401–29.
49 Lepsius, "Parteiensystem," 62, 73, 75, passim; Karl Rohe, *Wahlen und Wählertraditionen in Deutschland: Kulturelle Grundlagen deutscher Parteien und Parteiensysteme im 19. und 20. Jahrhundert* (Frankfurt/M: Suhrkamp, 1992), 9, 19–22, 92, 116, passim; Sperber, *Kaiser's Voters*, 3–7, 282–6, 288.
50 Sweeney, *Work*, 13–14, 53–4, 64–5, 123, 137–40; Kathleen Canning, *Gender History in Practice. Historical Perspectives on Bodies, Class & Citizenship* (Ithaca, NY: Cornell University Press, 2006), 15, 18–19, 165–6.
51 Lidtke, *Outlawed Party*, 43–4, 236–40, 317–18, 323–4; Detlef Lehnert, "Sozialdemokratie und Parlamentarismus. Von der Reichsgründungszeit zur neuen deutschen Einheit," in idem (ed.), *SPD und Parlamentarismus. Eintwicklungen und Problemfelder 1871–1990* (Köln: Böhlau Verlag, 2016), 9–12, 18–19; Rauh, *Parlamentarisierung*, 159–60; Schönberger, "Parlamentarisierung," 648, 657.
52 Hughes, "Splendid Demonstrations," 246–8.
53 Bernd Jürgen Warneken et al., *Als die Deutschen demonstrieren lernten. Das Kulturmuster "friedliche Straßendemonstration" im preußischen Wahlrechtskampf 1908–1910* (Tübingen: Tübinger Vereinigung für Volkskunde, 1986), 7–9, 15, 17, 21, 24, 27, 421–44, passim; cf. also Evans, "Red Wedensday," 4–31.
54 Hughes, "Splendid Demonstrations," 251; Warneken et al., *demonstrieren*, 85–104.
55 Cf. David Crew, *Town in the Ruhr. A Social History of Bochum, 1860–1914* (New York: Columbia University Press, 1979), 136.
56 Michael L. Hughes, "'The Knife in the Hands of the Children'? Debating the Political Mass Strike and Political Citizenship in Imperial Germany," *Labor History* 50:2 (May 2009), 117–19, passim; Detlef Lehnert, *Sozialdemokratie zwischen Protestbewegung und Regierungspartei 1848–1983* (Frankfurt/M: Suhrkamp, 1983), 101–4, 106.
57 Ibid., 121–7; Scheidemann quote in *Protokoll über die Verhandlungen des Parteitages der Sozialdemokratischen Partei Deutschlands. Abgehalten in Jena vom 14. bis 20. September 1913* (Berlin: Verlag Buchhandlung Vorwärts, 1913), 308.
58 For quote, Craig, *Germany*, 340; Volker Berghahn, *Modern Germany. Society, Economy and Politics in the Twentieth Century* (Cambridge: Cambridge University Press, 1988), 41–2; Loth, *Kaiserreich*, 143; Gunter Mai, "'Verteidigungskrieg' und 'Volksgemeinschaft.' Staatliche Selbstbehauptung, national Solidarität und soziale Befreiung in Deutschland in der Zeit des Ersten Weltkrieges (1900–1925)," in Wolfgang Michalka (ed.), *Der Erste Weltkrieg: Wirkung, Wahrnehmung, Analyse* (München: Piper, 1994), 585, 588.
59 Gagel, *Wahlrechtsfrage*, 167–9; Reinhard Pateman, *Der Kampf um die preußischen Wahlreform im ersten Weltkrieg* (Düsseldorf: Droste Verlag, 1964), 242–61; Jörn Retterath, *"Was ist das Volk?" Volk- und Gemeinschaftskonzepte der politischen Mitte in Deutschland 1917–1924* (Oldenbourg: deGruyter, 2016), 102–8; Euchner, "Sozialdemokratie," 129; Belinda Davis, *Home Fires Burning. Food, Politics, and Everyday Life in World War I Berlin* (Chapel Hill: University of North Carolina Press, 2000), 92, 121, 198.
60 Davis, *Home Fires*, 95–105; Friedhelm Boll, *Massenbewegungen in Niedersachsen 1906–1920, Eine sozialgeschichtliche Untersuchung zu den unterschiedlichen Entwicklungstypen Braunschweig und Hanover* (Bonn: Verlag Neue Gesellschaft, 1981), 11–13, 147–50, 193–4, 201, 205–6, passim; Jürgen Kocka, *Facing Total War:*

German Society 1914–1918, trans. Barbara Weinberger (Cambridge University Press, 1984), 48–9, 59; cf. Peter Fritzsche, *Germans into Nazis* (Cambridge: Cambridge University Press, 1998), 59–60, 66–74.
61 Davis, *Home Fires*, 200–3, 220–8, 213, passim; Boll, *Massenbewegungen*, 207–8, 216–17, 235–9, passim; Kocka, *Total War*, 49, 57–9; A. J. Ryder, *The German Revolution of 1918. A Study of German Socialism in War and Revolt* (Cambridge: Cambridge University Press, 1967), 116–17.
62 Retterath, *Volk*, 110–23; Loth, *Kaiserreich*, 163–6; Ryder, *Revolution*, 119–27.
63 Ralf Hoffrogge, *Working Politics in the German Revolution. Richard Müller, the Revolutionary Shop Stewards and the Origins of the Council Movement*, trans. Joseph B. Keady (Leiden: Brill, 2014), 61–4; Mark Jones, "The Crowd in the November Revolution, 1918," in Klaus Weinhauser (ed.), *Germany 1916–1923. A Revolution in Context* (Bielefeld: Transcript Verlag, 2015), 37–8, 44–7, 50–6; Davis, *Home Fires*, 233–7; Fritzsche, *Germans into Nazis*, 90.
64 Eley, *Reshaping*, 44–5, 57; Gerhard A. Ritter, 'Die Reichstagwahlen und die Wurzeln der deutschen Demokratie im Kaiserreich'. *Historische Zeitschrift* 275, no. 2 (October 2002): 623–66, 389–90, 402; Steinbach, "Legacies," 37, 41; Martin Greiffenhagen, *Kulturen des Kompromisses* (Opladen: Leske & Budrich, 1999), 19–20, passim; cf. Chapters 2 and 4.
65 Thomas Nipperdey, "War die Wilhelminische Gesellschaft eine Untertanengesellschaft?" in idem (ed.), *Nachdenken über die deutsche Geschichte: Essays* (München: Deutscher Taschenbuch Verlag, 1991), 173–5 and passim; Chickering, *We Men*, 158–9, 197; Eley, *Reshaping*, 190, passim.
66 Steinbach, "Legacies," 29, 41; Anderson, *Practicing Democracy*, 10, 253–4; Ritter, "Reichstagwahlen," 391; and cf. Peter Blickle, *Obedient Germans? A Rebuttal. A New View of German History*, trans. Thomas Brady (Charlottesville: University of Virginia Press, 1997), 64–72, passim.
67 Steinbach, "Legacies," 40–1.

Chapter 2

1 Michael Wildt, "Volksgemeinschaft und Führererwartung in der Weimarer Republik," in Ute Daniel (ed.), *Politische Kultur und Medienwirklichkeit in den 1920er Jahren* (München: Oldenbourg, 2010), 200–1.
2 For pre-1914, see, still, H. Stuart Hughes, *Consciousness and Society. The Reorientation of European Social Thought 1890–1930* (New York: Vintage Books, 1958); Kurt Sontheimer, *Antidemokratisches Denken in der Weimarer Republik. Die politischen Ideen des deutschen Nationalismus zwischen 1918 und 1933*, 2nd ed. (München: Nymphenburger Verlagshandlung, 1964), 45–6, 51–2, 61–8, 72, 326–7; Kurt Sontheimer, "Die politische Kultur der Weimarer Republik," in Karl Dietrich Bracher et al. (eds.), *Die Weimarer Republik 1918–1933. Politik Wirtschaft Gesellschaft* (Düsseldorf: Droste Verlag, 1987), 463–4; Hans Mommsen, *The Rise and Fall of Weimar Democracy*, trans. Elborg Forster and Larry Eugene Jones (Chapel Hill: University of North Carolina Press, 1989), 305, 457; Jerry Z. Muller, *The Other God That Failed. Hans Freyer and the Deradicalization of German Conservatism* (Princeton, NJ: Princeton University Press, 1987), 14–16, 42–3, 167–8.

3   Christoph Gusy, *Die Weimarer Reichsverfassung* (Tübingen: Mohr Siebeck, 1997), 11–14; Ernst-Wolfgang Böckenförde, "Der Zusammenbruch der Monarchie und die Entstehung der Weimarer Republik," in *Recht, Staat, Freiheit*, edited by idem, 306–43 (Frankfurt/M: Suhrkamp, 1991), 319–21; Sabine Roß, *Politische Partizipation und Nationaler Räteparlamentarismus: Determinanten des politischen Handelns der Delegierten zu den Reichsrätekongressen 1918/1919* (Köln: Zentrum für historische Sozialforschung, 1999), 13–16, passim; Hans-Joachim Bieber, *Bürgertum in der Revolution. Bürgerrate und Bürgerstreiks in Deutschland 1918–1920* (Hamburg: Christians, 1992), 52–8.
4   Peter von Oertzen, *Betriebsräte in der November Revolution* (Düsseldorf: Droste Verlag, 1963), 89–97, 197, 297–9; Wolfgang Durner, *Antiparlamentarismus in Deutschland* (Würzburg: Königshausen & Neumann, 1997), 44–55, 72–91; Kathleen Canning, "War, Citizenship, and Rhetorics of Sexual Crisis: Reflections on States of Exception in Germany, 1914–1920," in Geoff Eley et al. (eds.), *German Modernities from Wilhelm to Weimar. A Contest of Futures* (London: Bloomsbury, 2016), 251; Ricardo Bavaj, *Von links gegen Weimar. Linkes antiparlamentarisches Denken in der Weimarer Republik* (Bonn: JHW Dietz Verlag, 2005), 27, 30, 37, 39, 48–52, 487–8.
5   Mark Jones, *Founding Weimar. Violence and the German Revolution of 1918–1919* (Cambridge: Cambridge University Press, 2016), 5, 12, 86–8, 99, 145–7; Bieber, *Bürgertum*, 9–10, 50–1, 53–8, passim; Jonathan Osmond, *Rural Protest in the Weimar Republic* (New York: St. Martin's Press, 1993), 31.
6   A. J. Ryder, *The German Revolution of 1918. A Study of Socialism in War and Revolt* (Cambridge: Cambridge University Press, 1967), 134–5, 180–1; Richard Breitman, *German Socialism and Weimar Democracy* (Chapel Hill: University of North Carolina Press, 1981), 11–12, 16, 20, 22; Roß, *Partizipation*, 190, 214–15, 336, 342; Böckenförde, "Zusammenbruch," 324.
7   F. L. Carsten, *The Reichswehr and Politics 1918 to 1933* (Oxford: Clarendon Press, 1966), 11–12, 15; Mommsen, *Weimar Democracy*, 87; Gerald D. Feldman, "German Business between War and Revolution: The Origins of the Stinnes-Legien Agreement," in Gerhard A. Ritter (ed.), *Entstehung und Wandel der modernen Gesellschaft. Festschrift für Hans Rosenberg zum 65. Geburtstag* (Berlin: Walter de Gruyter, 1970), 312–13; Breitman, *German Socialism*, 18–19, 26–7; Gregg O. Kvistad, *The Rise and Demise of German Statism. Loyalty and Political Membership* (Providence: Berghahn Books, 1999), 56–9.
8   Karl Dietrich Bracher, *Die Auflösung der Weimarer Republik. Eine Studie zum Problem des Machtverfalls in der Demokratie*, 5th ed. (Villingen: Ring-Verlag, 1971), 174–5, passim; Mommsen, *Weimar Democracy*, 29–30; Bernd Weisbrod, "The Crisis of Bourgeois Society in Interwar Germany," in Richard Bessel (ed.), *Fascist Italy and Nazi Germany. Comparisons and Contrasts* (Cambridge: Cambridge University Press, 1996), 35; Andrew McElligott, *Rethinking the Weimar Republic. Authority vs. Authoritarianism 1916–1936* (London: Bloomsbury, 2014), 101–4, 111–13.
9   Robert Waite, *Vanguard of Nazism. The Free Corps Movement in Postwar German 1918–1923* (New York: W. W. Norton & Co., 1952), 10–16, 29–93, passim; Carsten, *Reichswehr*, 21–3; Jones, *Founding Weimar*, 83–4, 171–2, 186–7, 194–5, 224–5, 244–6, 249–50.
10 Jörn Retterath, "Der Volksbegriff in der Zäsur des Jahres 1918/19. Pluralistisches und holistisches Denken im katholischen, liberalen und sozialdemokratischen Milieu," in Heidrun Kämper et al. (eds.), *Demokratiegeschichte als Zäsurgeschichte. Diskurse der frühen Weimarer Republik* (Berlin: de Gruyter, 2014), 106–7; Jorg-Detlef Kühne,

"Demokratisches Denken in der Weimarer Verfassungsdiskussion—Hugo Preuß und die Nationalversammlung," in Christoph Gusy (ed.), *Demokratisches Denken in der Weimarer Republik* (Baden-Baden: Nomos Verlagsgesellschaft, 2000), 122–3; Böckenförde, "Zusammenbruch," 334–5.

11 "Weimar Constitution of 1919," in Elmar Hucko (ed.), *The Democratic Tradition. Four German Constitutions* (Oxford: Berg Publishers, 1987); Hans-Ulrich Wehler, *Deutsche Gesellschaftsgeschichte*, Vol. 4 (München: C.H. Beck, 2003), 350–3; Marcus Llanque, "Mehr Demokratie wagen: Weimar und die direkte Demokratie," in Friedrich Ebert Stiftung (ed.), *Die Weimarer Verfassung. Wert und Wirkung für die Demokratie* (Berlin: Wagemann Medien, 2009), 147–55; Benjamin Carter Hett, *The Death of Democracy. Hitler's Rise to Power and the Downfall of the Weimar Republic* (New York: Henry Holt and Company, 2018), 24–7.

12 "Weimar Constitution of 1919," Art. 17, 109; Bernd Weisbrod, "Die Politik der Repräsentation. Das Erbe des ersten Weltkrieges und der Formwandel der Politik in Europa," in Hans Mommsen (ed.), *Der Erste Weltkrieg und die europäische Neuordnung* (Köln: Böhlau Verlag, 2000), 17–18; Geoff Eley, "General Thoughts," in idem/J. Palmowski (eds.), *Citizenship and National Identity in Twentieth-Century Germany* (Stanford: Stanford University Press, 2008), 243; Kathleen Canning, "Claiming Citizenship, Suffrage and Subjectivity in Germany after the First World War," in idem (ed.), *Gender History in Practice. Historical Perspectives on Bodies, Class, and Citizenship* (Ithaca, NY: Cornell University Press, 2006), 218, 228–9; Raffael Scheck, *Mothers of the Nation. Right-Wing Women in the Weimar Republic* (Oxford: Berg, 2004), 66–7; Julia Roos, *Weimar through the Lens of Gender. Prostitution Reform, Women's Emancipation, and German Democracy, 1919-1933* (Ann Arbor: University of Michigan Press, 2010), 16–25, 91–2.

13 Richard Bessel, "The Formation and Dissolution of a German National Electorate from *Kaiserreich* to 3rd Reich," in Larry Jones/James Retallack (eds.), *Elections, Mass Politics, and Social Change in Modern Germany* (Cambridge: Cambridge University Press, 1992), 407–8; Thomas Mergel, *Parlamentarische Kultur in der Weimarer Republik. Politische Kommunikation, symbolische Politik und öffentliche Meinung im Reichstag* (Düsseldorf: Droste Verlag, 2002), 404–6; Mommsen, *Weimar Democracy*, 478.

14 "Weimar Constitution of 1919," Art. 54; Bernd Hoppe, *Von der parlamentarischen Demokratie zum Präsidialstaat. Verfassungsentwicklung am Beispiel der Kabinettsbildung in der Weimarer Republik* (Berlin: Duncker & Humblot, 1998), 14–15, 202, passim; Gusy, *Reichsverfassung*, 131–3; Mommsen, *Weimar Democracy*, 253–4; Richard J. Evans, *The Coming of the Third Reich* (New York: The Penguin Press, 2004), 83, 85.

15 Bieber, *Bürgertum*, 225–6; Peter C. Caldwell, "The Citizen and the Republic in Germany, 1918-1935," in Eley/Palmowski (eds.), *Citizenship*, 48–9; Heinrich August Winkler, *Mittelstand, Demokratie und Nationalsozialismus. Die politische Entwicklung von Handwerk und Kleinhandel in der Weimarer Republik* (Köln: Kiepenheuer & Witsch, 1972), 111–16; Muller, *God that Failed*, 176–7; Martin Broszat, „Soziale Motivation und Führerbindung des Nationalsozialismus,' *Vierteljahrshefte für Zeitgeschichte* 18, no. 4 (1970), 395; Wolfgang Pyta, *Dorfgemeinschaft und Parteipolitik, 1918-1933* (Düsseldorf: Droste Verlag, 1996), 189–90, 202; Jürgen Bergmann, "Politische Anschauungen und politische Kultur des Handwerks in der Weimarer Republik," in Lehnert/Megerle (eds.), *Pluralismus*, 175–6, 181, 185–6; Gerhard Stoltenburg, *Politische Strömungen im Schleswig-*

Holstein Landvolk 1918-1933 (Düsseldorf: Droste Verlag, 1962), 195-6; Wehler, *Gesellschaftsgeschichte*, Vol. 4, 345; cf. also Otto Kirchheimer/Richard Bavaj, "Otto Kirchheimers Parlamentarismuskritik in der Weimarer Republik," *Vierteljahrshefte für Zeitgeschichte* 55:1 (2007), 41-2; Osmond, *Rural Protest*, 46-7.

16 Thomas Mergel, "Dictatorship and Democracy, 1918-1939," in Helmut Walser Smith (ed.), *The Oxford Handbook of Modern German History* (Oxford: Oxford University Press, 2011), 427; Kühne, "Demokratisches Denken," 124-5; Christoph Möllers, "Das parlamentarische Gesetz als demokratische Entscheidungsform—Ein Beitrag zur Institutionenwahrnehmung in der Weimarer Republik," in Gusy (ed.), *Denken*, 434; Horst Möller, "Zwei Wege des deutschen Parlamentarismus: Preußen und Reich," in Adolf Birke/Kurt Kluxen (eds.), *Deutscher und Britischer Parlamentarismus* (München: K.G. Saur, 1985), 136-8; McElligott, *Rethinking*, 184-5.

17 Achim Kurz, *Demokratische Diktatur? Auslegung und Handhabung der Weimarer Verfassung 1919-1925* (Berlin: Duncker & Humblot, 1992), 22-4, 27-30, 44-6; Michael Stürmer, "Der unvollendete Parteienstaat. Zur Vorgeschichte des Präsidialregimes am Ende der Weimarer Republik," *Vierteljahrshefte für Zeitgeschichte* 21: 2 (April 1971), 122-6.

18 Kurz, *Demokratische Diktatur?*, 13, 25, 47, 108-9, 146, 157, 188, passim; Wilhelm Mößle, "Die Verordnungsermächtigung in der Weimarer Republik," in Horst Möller/Manfred Kittel (eds.), *Demokratie in Deutschland und Frankreich 1918-1933/40. Beiträge zu einem historischen Vergleich* (Munich: R. Oldenbourg Verlag, 2002), 269-80; Gusy, *Reichsverfassung*, 110-11; Ludwig Richter, "Das präsidiale Notverordnungen in den ersten Jahren der Weimarer Republik. Friedrich Ebert und die Anwendung des Aritkels 48 der Weimarer Reichsverfassung," in Eberhard Kolb (ed.), *Friedrich Ebert als Reichspräsident: Amtsführung und Amtsverständnis* (München: R. Oldenbourg, 1997), 209, 248-9, 252, passim.

19 Möllers, "Das parlamentarische Gesetz," 434-5; Walter Euchner, "Sozialdemokratie und Demokratie. Zum Demokratieverständnis der SPD in der Weimarer Republik," *AfS* 26 (1986), 126, 144.

20 Peter C. Caldwell/William E. Scheuermann (eds.), *From Liberal Democracy to Fascism* (Boston: Humanities Press, 2000), 137-8; Hedrun Kämper, "Demokratisches Wissen in der frühen Weimarer Republik. Historizität—Agonalität—Institutionalisierung," in idem et al. (eds.), *Demokratiegeschichte als Zäsurgeschichte. Diskurse der frühen Weimarer Republik* (Berlin: de Gruyter, 2014), 55-71; Sontheimer, *Denken*, 110.

21 Michael L. Hughes, *Paying for the German Inflation* (Chapel Hill: University of North Carolina Press, 1988), 56-7, 66-7, 159-62 (quotation: 160); Gertrude Lübbe-Wolff, "Safeguards of Civil and Constitutional Rights—The Debate on the Role of the *Reichsgericht*," in Hermann Wellenreuther (ed.), *German and American Constitutional Thought: Contexts, Interaction, and Historical Realities* (New York: Berg Publishers, 1990), 353-72; Noah Benezra Strote, *Lions and Lambs. Conflict in Weimar and the Creation of Post-Nazi Germany* (New Haven, CT: Yale University Press, 2017), 25-7, 33, 39.

22 Sontheimer, *Denken*, 230; Michael Dreyer, "Weimar als wehrhafte Demokratie—ein unterschätztes Vorbild," in Sebatian Lasch (ed.), *Die Weimarer Verfassung—Wert und Wirkung für die Demokratie* (Erfurt: n.p., 2009), 163-7; Christoph Gusy, *Die Lehre vom Parteienstaat in der Weimarer Republik* (Baden-Baden: Nomos Verlagsgesellschaft, 1993), 38-41, 45; Jane Caplan, "Political Detentions and the Origins of the Concentration Camps in Nazi Germany, 1933-1935/36," in Neil Gregor (ed.), *Nazism, War and Genocide* (Exeter: University of Exeter Press, 2005), 27-8.

23 Andreas Fahrmeir, *Citizenship: The Rise and Fall of a Modern Concept* (New Haven, CT: Yale University Press, 2007), 119, 133; Sontheimer, *Denken*, 317–18.
24 Jörn Retterath, "*Was is das Volk?*" *Volks- und Gemeinschaftkonzepte der politischen Mittel in Deutschland 1917-1924* (Oldenbourg: de Gruyter, 2016), 3–5, 60, 64, 68–9, 276–7, 296, 318–28; Gusy, *Lehre*, 87, 94; Mergel, "Dictatorship," 424–5, 433, 447; David Imhoof, *Becoming a Nazi Town. Culture and Politics in Göttingen between the World Wars* (Ann Arbor: University of Michigan Press, 2013), 5–6, 15, 43–4, 47–8; Sontheimer, *Denken*, 121–2, 308, 315–16, passim; Roger Woods, *The Conservative Revolution in the Weimar Republic* (New York: St. Martin's Press, 1999), 1–2, 12–13, 64, 77, 111; Michael Wildt, "*Volksgemeinschaft*. A Modern Perspective on National Socialist Society," in Martina Steber/Bernhard Gotto (eds.), *Visions of Community in Nazi Germany. Social Engineering and Private Lives* (Oxford: Oxford University Press, 2014), 44–7; Stefan Vogt, *Nationaler Sozialismus und Soziale Demokratie. Die sozialdemokratische Junge Rechte 1918-1945* (Bonn: Dietz Verlag, 2006), 82, 84, 184; Gerhard Hirschfeld, "Die Attraktion des Ersten Weltkrieges für die Nazi-Bewegung," in Brockhaus (ed.), *Attraktion*, 77; Moritz Föllmer, "The Problem of National Solidarity in Interwar Germany," *German History* 23 (May 2005), 203–4, 206–7, 211, 215, 219–21.
25 Sontheimer, *Denken*, 165–6, 313–14; Rudy Koshar, *Social Life, Local Politics, and Nazism. Marburg, 1880-1935* (Chapel Hill: University of North Carolina Press, 1986), 63–70, 182–3; Wehler, *Gesellschaftsgeschichte*, Bd. 4, 501–11, passim; Larry Eugene Jones, "Conservative Antisemitism in the Weimar Republic. A Case Study of the German National Peoples Party," in idem (ed.), *The German Right in the Weimar Republic. Studies in the History of German Conservatism, Nationalism, and Antisemitism* (New York: Berghahn Books, 2014), 79–107; Brian E. Crim, "Weimar's 'Burning Question.' Situational Antisemitism and the German Combat Leagues, 1918-33," in Jones (ed.), *The German Right in the Weimar Republic*, 194–219.
26 Bieber, *Bürgertum*, 242–3, 259, 287–8, 364; Heinrich August Winkler, *Von der Revolution zur Stabilisierung. Arbeiter und Arbeiterbewegung in der Weimarer Republik 1918-1924* (Berlin: J.H.W. Dietz Nachf., 1984), 322, 309–10, 322–35; Peter Fritzsche, *Rehearsals for Fascism. Populism and Political Mobilization in Weimar Germany* (New York: Oxford University Press, 1990), 26–7, 55–6, 69–70, 75–9; Woods, *Conservative Revolution*, 63, 80–1; Oded Heilbronner, *Catholicism, Political Culture, and the Countryside. A Social History of the Nazi Party in South Germany* (Ann Arbor: University of Michigan Press, 1998), 146–8, 178, 181, 193, 224–5, 236.
27 Euchner, "Sozialdemokratie und Demokratie," 152–8; H.A. Winkler, "Unternehmer und Wirtschaftsdemokratie in der Weimarer Republik," *Probleme der Demokratie heute: Tagung der Deutschen Vereinigung für Politische Wissenschaft in Berlin, Herbst 1969* (Opladen: Westdeutscher Verl, 1971), 310–13; Michael Schneider, *Unternehmer und Demokratie. Die freien Gewerkschaften in der unternehmerischen Ideologie der Jahre 1918 bis 1933* (Bonn-Bad Godesberg: Neue Gesellschaft GmbH, 1975), 80–91, 157, 165–6; Günter Könke, *Organisierter Kaptialismus, Sozialdemokratie und Staat. Eine Studie zur Ideologie der sozialdemokratischen Arbeiterbewegung in der Weimarer Republik* (Stuttgart: Franz Steiner Verlag, 1987), 99–113, 121, 126, 154–6, 173–7.
28 Peter Fritzsche, *Germans into Nazis* (Cambridge: Cambridge University Press, 1998), 119, 181–2, 198 (quotation); Jürgen Bergmann, "Politische Anschauungen und politische Kultur des Handwerks in der Weimarer Republik im Spannungsverhältnis vom Tradition, Ideologie und materiellen Interessen," in Detlef Lehnert/Klaus Megerle (eds.), *Pluralismus als Verfassungs- und Gesellschaftsmodell.*

Zur politischen Kultur in der Weimarer Republik (Opladen: Westdeutscher Verlag, 1993), 173, 193–5; Sontheimer, *Denken*, 150, 152–3, 182, 224, 342, 350; Schneider, *Unternehmer*, 22, 54.

29 Caldwell, "Citizen," 50–3; Christoph Gusy, "Fragen an das 'demokratische Denken' in der Weimarer Republik," in idem (ed.), *Denken*, 648–53; Hoppe, *Demokratie*, 233, 257; Stefan Jonsson, *Crowds and Democracy. The Idea and Image of the Masses from Revolution to Fascism* (New York: Columbia University Press, 2013), 215, 251; Muller, *God that Failed*, 10–11, 59–60, 63–4, 203–4; Michael Wildt, "Die Ungleichheit des Volkes," in Frank Bajohr/idem (eds.), *Volksgemeinschaft. Neue Forschung zur Gesellschaft des Nationalsozialismus* (Frankfurt/M: Fischer Taschenbuchverlag, 2009), 27; Vogt, *Nationaler Sozialismus*, 212, 216, passim.

30 Bieber, *Bürgertum*, 363; Christoph Schöneberger, "Demokratisches Denken in der Weimarer Republik," in Gusy (ed.), *Denken*, 664–6; Thomas Mergel, "Führer, Volksgemeinschaft und Maschine. Politische Erwartungsstrukturen in der Weimarer Republik und dem Nationalsozialismus," in Wolfgang Hardtwig (ed.), *Politische Kulturgeschichte der Zwischenkriegszeit 1918–1939* (Göttingen: Vandenhoeck & Ruprecht, 2005), 97, 105; Schneider, *Unternehmer*, 22, 92; Jürgen Bergmann, "'Das Land steht rechts!' Das 'agrarische Milieu,'" in Detlef Lehnert/Klaus Megerle (eds.), *Politische Identität und nationale Gedenktage. Zur politischen Kultur in der Weimarer Republik* (Opladen: Westdeutsche Verlag, 1989), 192, 205.

31 James Diehl, *Paramilitary Politics in Weimar Germany* (Bloomington: Indiana University Press, 1977), 225, 265; Fritzsche, *Rehearsals*, 83, 111; Robert G. Moeller, *German Peasants and Agrarian Politics, 1914–1924. The Rhineland and Westphalia* (Chapel Hill: University of North Carolina Press, 1986), 121–2, 131–2; Imhoof, *Nazi Town*, 1, 14, 48, 54; Gusy, *Lehre*, 66, 75, 87; Frank Bösch, "Militante Geselligkeit. Formierungsformen der bürgerlichen Vereinswelt zwischen Revolution und Nationalsozialismus," in Hardtwig (ed.), *Kulturgeschichte*, 155–8; Ernst Müller-Meiningen, *Parlamentarismus. Betrachtungen, Lehren und Erinnerungen aus deutschen Parlamenten* (Berlin/Leipzig: Verlag Walter de Gruyter, 1926), 3, 33, 52–4, 59–61; Curt Hotzel, "Die großen Frontsoldatentage," in Franz Seldte (ed.), *Der Stahlhelm*, Bd. 1 (Berlin: Stahlhelm Verlag, 1932–33), 124, 126.

32 Martin Vogt, "Das 'Versagen' der politischen Parteien in der Weimarer Republik," in Wolfgang Michalka (ed.), *Die nationalsozialistsiche Machtergreifung* (Paderborn: Schöningh, 1984), 60–1, 63, 65, 70; Heinrich Hildebrandt/Walter Kettner (eds.), *Stahlhelm-Handbuch* (Berlin: Stahlhelm Verlag, 1931), 24, 50, 58; William L. Patch, Jr., *Heinrich Brüning and the Dissolution of the Weimar Republic* (Cambridge: Cambridge University Press, 1998), 19; Mergel, *Kultur*, 370, 375–9; Winkler, *Mittelstand*, 77–8, 115–16; Sontheimer, *Denken*, 109, 188–9, 226–8; John McCormick, "Feudalism, Fascism, and Fordism: Weimar Theories of Representation and Their Legacy in the Bonn Republic," in Caldwell/Scheuerman (eds.), *Liberal Democracy*, 58–62; Caldwell, "Citizen," 40–1.

33 Gusy, *Lehre*, 60–1, 68–70, 77–8; Michael Wildt, *Hitler's Volksgemeinschaft and the Dynamics of Racial Exclusion* (New York: Berghahn Books, 2012), 266; Sontheimer, *Denken*, 33, 266.

34 Dietmar Schirmer, "Politisch-kulturelle Deutungsmuster: Vorstellungen von der Welt der Politik in der Weimarer Republik," in Lehnert/Megerle (eds.), *Gedenktage*, 40–3; Waite, *Vanguard*, 55, 134, 136; Gerhard Hoch, *Das Scheitern der Demokratie im ländlichen Raum. Das Beispiel der Region* Kaltenkirchen/Henstedt-Ulzburg *1870–1933* (Kiel: Neuer Malik Verlag, 1988), 173–4.

35 Mommsen, *Weimar Democracy*, 75, 87; McElligott, *Rethinking*, 37, 40–3; Jürgen Bergmann/Klaus Megerle, "Gesellschaftliche Mobilisierung und negative Partizipation," in Peter Steinbach (ed.), *Probleme politischer Partizipation in der Weimarer Republik* (Stuttgart: Klett Cotta, 1982), 413.
36 Bieber, *Bürgertum*, 271; Bessel, "Formation and Dissolution," 416–18; Pyta, *Dorfgemeinschaft*, 232; Stoltenburg, *Strömungen*, 95, 120–1, 168–69.
37 Mergel, "Führer," 91–2; Bergmann, "Land steht rechts!," 205–6; Hans Mommsen, "Ist die Weimarer Republik an Fehlkonstruktionen der Reichsverfassung gescheitert? Chancen und Scheitern der ersten deutschen Republik," in Michael Schultheiß/Julia Roßberg (eds.), *Weimar und die Republik. Geburtsstunde eines demokratischen Deutschlands* (Weimar: Weimar Verlagsgesellschaft Ltd., 2009), 105–23.
38 Wolfgang Hardtwig, "Der Bismarck Mythos. Gestalt und Funktion zwischen politischer Öffentlichkeit und Wissenschaft," in idem (ed.), *Kulturgeschichte*, 74–8, 88; Mergel, "Führer," 105–6, 108–10; Kristin McGuire, "Feminist Politics beyond the Reichstag. Helen Stöcker and Visions of Reform," in Kathleen Canning et al. (eds.), *Weimar Politics/Weimar Subjects. Rethinking the Political Culture of Germany in the 1920s* (New York: Berghahn Books, 2013), 140–1, 148; Vogt, *Nationaler Sozialismus*, 225, 227, 331–4; Hoch, *Scheitern*, 173–4; Marcus Llanque, "Massendemokratie zwischen *Kaiserreich* und westlicher Demokratie," in Gusy (ed.), *Denken*, 56–8, 64–6; Wolfgang Mommsen, *Max Weber and German Politics 1890-1920*, trans. Michael L. Steinberg (Chicago: University of Chicago Press, 1984), 394–6, 402.
39 Sontheimer, *Denken*, 267–5, passim; Ernst Nolte, "Diktatur," in Otto Brunner et al. (eds.), *Geschichtliche Grundbegriffe*, Vol. I (Stuttgart: Klett-Cotta, 1972), 900–24; Woods, *Conservative Revolution*, 106; Rudolf Heberle, *From Democracy to Nazism. A Regional Case Study on Political Parties in Germany* (New York: Grosset & Dunlap, 1970), 51, 86, 123; Gotthard Jaspar, *Die gescheiterte Zähmung* (Frankfurt/M: Suhrkamp, 1986), 177.
40 Vogt, *Nationaler Sozialismus*, 213, 218, 306–7, 334; Joris Gijsenbergh, "The Semantics of 'Democracy' in Social Democratic Parties. Netherlands, Germany and Sweden, 1917–1939," *Archiv für Sozialgeschichte* 53 (2013), 168; Gusy, *Reichsverfassung*, 451–3, 457–8; Hans Klueting, "'Vernunftrepublikanismus' und 'Vertrauensdiktatur': Friedrich Meinecke in der Weimarer Republik," *Historische Zeitschrift* 242:1 (February 1986), 81, 85–9, 98; Udi Greenberg, *The Weimar Century. German Émigrés and the Ideological Foundations of the Cold War* (Princeton, NJ: Princeton University Press, 2014), 133.
41 Llanque, "Massendemokratie," 64–7; Gusy, *Lehre*, 86, 88, 98–100, 106; Vogt, *Nationaler Sozialismus*, 225–30, 331–4; Thomas Rohkrämer, *A Single Communal Faith? The German Right from Conservatism to National Socialism* (New York: Berghahn Books, 2007), 47, 58, 154–5; Mergel, *Parlamentarische Kultur*, 70, 339, 368–71; Wolfgang Mommsen, "Zum Begriff der 'Plebiszitären Führerdemokratie' bei Max Weber," *Kölner Zeitschrift f Soziologie und Sozialpsychologie* 15 (1963), 295–303; Klueting, "Vernunftrepublikanismus," 86, 88, 91, 95; Mommsen, *Weber*, 394–6, 402.
42 Michael L. Hughes, "Restitution and Democracy in Germany after Two World Wars," *Contemporary European History* 4:1 (1994), 2–5; Büro des Reichspräsidenten to Kempner, July 11, 1925, BAK, R 43 I/2456.
43 Jürgen Falter, "Social Bases of Cleavages in the Weimar Republic, 1919–1933," in Jones/Retallack (eds.), *Elections*, 372–3, 393; Detlef Lehnert, "Von der politisch-kulturellen Fragmentierung zur demokratischen Sammlung?" in idem/Megerle (eds.), *Pluralismus*, 77–9, 94–5, 112–13; Wehler, *Gesellschaftsgeschichte*, 358–9.

44 Fritzsche, *Germans*, 132–3; Osmond, *Rural Protest*, 37; Imhoof, *Nazi Town*, 25–39, 77; Bieber, *Bürgertum*, 38–41, 82–4, 144, 272; Fritzsche, *Rehearsals*, 42–3, 75, 168–9.
45 Sheri Berman, "Civil Society and the Collapse of the Weimar Republic," *World Politics* 49:3 (April 1997), 401–29; Heilbronner, *Catholicism*, 190–1.
46 Julia Sneeringer, *Winning Women's Votes. Propaganda and Politics in Weimar Germany* (Chapel Hill: University of North Carolina Press, 2002), 2, 9, 43–4, 68, 78–9, 81–4, 274; Canning, "Claiming Citizenship," 221, 223, 236–7; Kirsten Heinsohn, "Im Dienste der deutschen Volksgemeinschaft: Die 'Frauenfrage' und konservative Parteien vor und nach dem Ersten Weltkrieg," in Ute Planert (ed.), *Nation, Politik und Geschlecht. Frauenbewegungen und Nationalismus in der Moderne* (Frankfurt: Campus Verlag, 2000), 224–8; Bösch, "Militante Geselligkeit," 167–70; Elizabeth Harvey, "Serving the Volk, Saving the Nation: Women in the Youth Movement and the Public Sphere in Weimar Germany," in Jones/Retallack (eds.), *Elections*, 201, 209–13; Jonsson, *Crowds*, 9, 11, 22–3, 62–6, 179–81.
47 Martina Kessel, "Demokratie als *Grenzverletzung*. Geschlecht als symbolisches System in der Weimarer Republik," in Metzler/Schumann (eds.), *Geschlechter(un)ordnung*, 90, 95–6; Dirk Schumann, "Political Violence, Contested Public Space, and Reasserted Masculinity in Weimar Germany," in Canning et al. (eds.), *Weimar Publics/Weimar Subjects*, 236–49; Sven Reichert, "Gewalt, Körper, Politik. Paradoxien in der deutschen Kulturgeschichte der Zwischenkriegszeit," in Hardtwig (ed.), *Kulturgeschichte*, 220–2, 225–7; McElligott, *Rethinking*, 203–4; Klaus Theweleit, *Male Fantasies*, Vol. I–II, trans. Chris Turner. (Minneapolis: Univ. of Minnesota Pr., 1987), Vol. I–II, passim; Moritz Föllmer, *Individuality and Modernity in Berlin. Self and Society from Weimar to the Wall* (Cambridge: Cambridge University Press, 2013), 92, 95.
48 Bieber, *Bürgertum*, 49–51, 175–89, 205–6, 220–4, 282–4, 381–2, 393; Hotzel, "Frontsoldatentage," 104, 109; Klaus Große Kracht, "Campaigning against Bolshevism: Catholic Action in Late Weimar Germany," *Journal of Contemporary History* 53:3 (2018), 564–5; Fritzsche, *Rehearsals*, 14–15, 32–3, 39, 42–4, 62–3, 171–2, 189, 210–11, 216–18, 341–2; Mommsen, *Weber*, 395.
49 "Weimar Constitution," Art. 126; Stoltenberg, *Strömungen*, 121, 131, 174; Bieber, *Bürgertum*, 283.
50 Bieber, *Bürgertum*, 334–7, 369, 380–2, 393; Fritzsche, *Rehearsals*, 12, 32–3, 91–2, 156, 171, 210–15; Pyta, *Dorfgemeinschaft*, 194–5; Dieter Ohr, *Nationalsozialistische Propaganda und Weimarer Wahlen. Empirische Analyse zur Wirkung von NSDAP Versammlungen* (Opladen: Westdeutscher Verlag, 1997), 142–52, 224–33.
51 Diehl, *Paramilitary*, 190–1, 197; Llanque, "Massendemokratie," 42, 46–7; Stoltenburg, *Strömungen*, 126; Sneeringer, *Women's Votes*, 68, 75, 78, 282; Karl Rohe, *Das Reichsbanner Schwarz Rot Gold. Ein Beitrag zur Geschichte und Struktur der politischen Kampfverbände zur Zeit der Weimarer Republik* (Düsseldorf: Droste Verlag, 1966), 98, 404–5, 409; Thomas Mergel, *Propaganda nach Hitler. Eine Kulturgeschichte des Wahlkampfs in der Bundesrepublik 1949–1990* (Göttingen: Wallstein Verlag, 2010), 45, 49, 54–7; Molly Loberg, *The Struggle for the Streets of Berlin: Politics, Consumption, and Urban Space, 1914–1945* (Cambridge: Cambridge University Press, 2018), 113–14.
52 Waite, *Vanguard*, 58–93; Detlev Peukert, *The Weimar Republic. The Crisis of Classical Modernity*, trans. Richard Deveson (New York: Hill and Wang, 1989), 32–3; Marie-Luise Ehls, *Protest und Propaganda: Demonstrationen in Berlin zur Zeit der Weimarer Republik* (Berlin: de Gruyter, 1997), 48, 62.

53 Conan Fisher, *The Ruhr Crisis, 1923-1924* (Oxford: Oxford University Press, 2003), 72-4, 96, 101, 107, 179-82, 184-5, 189, 192-8, 290; Ehls, *Protest*, 90-1.
54 Stefan Breuer, *Die Völkischen in Deutschland. Kaiserreich und Weimarer Republik* (Darmstadt: Wissenschaftliche Buchgesellschaft, 2010), 196; Breitman, *German Socialism*, 51-6; Gotthard Jasper, *Der Schutz der Republik. Studien zur staatlichen Sicherung der Demokratie in der Weimarer Republik 1922-1930* (Tübingen: J.C.B. Mohr, 1963), 26-9; Johannes Erger, *Der Kapp-Lüttwitz Putsch. Ein Beitrag zur deutschen Innenpolitik 1919/1920* (Düsseldorf: Droste Verlag, 1967), passim; Winkler, *Von der Revolution*, 300-11, passim.
55 Waite, *Vanguard*, 212-7; Jasper, *Schutz*, 34-91; Shulamit Volkov, "On the Primacy of Political Violence—The Case of the Weimar Republic," in José Brunner et al. (eds.), *Gewalt*, 61-2.
56 Joachim Fest, *Hitler*, trans. Richard Winston/Clara Winston (New York: Vintage Books, 1974), 182-96; Ian Kershaw, *Hitler. 1889-1936: Hubris* (New York: W. W. Norton & Co., 1999), 205-12, 214-19.
57 Bieber, *Bürgertum*, 283-4, 382; Diehl, *Paramilitary*, 40-1, 194; Hotzel, "Frontsoldatentage," 104, 111, passim; Ehls, *Protest*, 115, 123, 165, 173, 231.
58 Manuela Achilles, "With a Passion for Reason: Celebrating the Constitution in Weimar Germany," *Central European History* 43:4 (December 2010), 672-89; Ralf Poscher, "Einführung," in idem (ed.), *Der Verfassungstag* (Baden-Baden: Nomos Verlagsgesellschaft, 1999), 13-22; Nadine Rossol, "Performing the Nation: Sports, Spectacles, and Aesthetics in Germany, 1926-1936," *Central European History* 43:4 (December 2010), 617, 619-20, passim; Rohe, *Reichsbanner*, 96, 98, 104-7, 224-6, 260-3, 365, 392-3, 405-7, 417-19; Donna Harsch, *German Social Democracy and the Rise of Nazism* (Chapel Hill: University of North Carolina Press, 1993), 104-5, 171-3, 176; Donna Harsch, "The Iron Front. Weimar Social Democracy between Tradition and Modernity," in Barclay/Weitz (eds.), *Reform and Revolution*, 251-7, 260-1.
59 Bieber, *Bürgertum*, 49-50, 282-4; Diehl, *Paramilitary*, 119, 192; Ehls, *Protest*, 62, 82, 114, 198, 361; Fritzsche, *Rehearsals*, 12, 62-8, 114-18, 156-8; Pyta, *Dorfgemeinschaft*, 196-7, 200-17; Frank Bösch, *Das konservative Milieu: Vereinskultur und lokale Sammlungen in ost- und westdeutschen Regionen (1900-1960)* (Göttingen: Allstein Verlag, 2002), 67-8, 71, 73-5; Osmond, *Rural Protest*, 77, 132-6, 149; Eva Rosenhaft, *Beating the Fascists? The German Communists and Political Violence 1929-1933* (Cambridge: Cambridge University Press, 1983), 50, 58, 118; Stoltenberg, *Strömungen*, 111-14, passim.
60 Bieber, *Bürgertum*, 175-6, 360, 364; Stoltenberg, *Strömungen*, 51-2, 124, 128-30; Diehl, *Paramilitary*, 21, 109, 137; Hildebrand/Kettner, *Handbuch*, 10, 49.
61 Fritzsche, *Rehearsals*, 67, 83-4; Hoppe, *Demokratie*, 258; Ehls, *Protest*, 351-2; Bergmann/Megerle, "Mobilisierung," 392, 394, 406-9.
62 Bieber, *Bürgertum*, 175-6, 182-7, 205-8, 220-4, 293-4, 33-4, 391-2; Pyta, *Dorfgemeinschaft*, 200-17; Osmond, *Rural Protest*, 31-2, 65-70, 74, 76-7; Schumann, "Einheitssuche," 95; Rosenhaft, *Beating the Fascists?* 53-4; Bergmann/Megerle, "Mobilisierung," 402, 411; Heberle, *Democracy*, 78; Hoch, *Scheitern*, 171-2; Stoltenberg, *Strömungen*, 49, 124-5, 128-30, 132-4, 172-8.
63 Richard Bessel, *Political Violence and the Rise of Nazism* (New Haven: Yale University Press, 1984), 45, 47-8, 153-4; Diehl, *Paramilitary*, 137, passim; Reichert, "Gewalt," 219-22, 225-7; Hotzel, "Frontsoldatentage," 105, 108, 111; Volker Berghahn, *Der Stahlhelm. Bund der Frontsoldaten 1918-1935* (Düsseldorf: Droste Verlag, 1966), 113, 169, passim; Rohe, *Reichsbanner*, 49-54, 98-9, 104-8, passim.

64 Bessel, *Political Violence*, 1–2, 75, 81–2, 90–2, 96, passim; Volkov, "Primacy," 58, 65; Diehl, *Paramilitary*, 196–7, passim; Rosenhaft, *Beating the Fascists?* ix, 1–2, 18–19, 81–4; Dirk Schumann, "Einheitssucht und Gewaltakzeptanz. Politische Grundpositionen des deutschen Bürgertums nach 1918," in Mommsen (ed.), *Weltkrieg*, 83–105; Theweleit, *Male Fantasies*, Vol. II, 3–4; Reichert, "Gewalt," 393, 396–9; Bernd Weisbrod, "Gewalt in der Politik. Zur politischen Kultur in Deutschland zwischen den beiden Weltkriegen," *Geschichte in Wissenschaft und Unterricht* 43 (1992), 392, 395, 399–400, 403.

65 For industry, see Wehler, *Gesellschaftsgeschichte*, 380, Peukert, *Weimar Republic*, 125–6, Fritz Blaich, "Staatsverständnis und politische Haltung der deutschen Unternehmer 1918-1930," in Bracher et al. (eds.), *Weimarer Republik*, 162–5, 173–5; for agriculture and urban small business see Stoltenberg, *Strömungen*, passim, Winkler, *Mittelstand*, passim, and Bergmann/Megerle, "Mobilisierung," passim; for parties, see Peukert, *Weimar Republic*, 219, Larry E. Jones, *German Liberalism and the Dissolution of the Weimar Party System, 1918–1933* (Chapel Hill: University of North Carolina Press, 1988), 317, 370–3 (quotation: 372), passim, and John A. Leopold, *Alfred Hugenberg. The Radical Nationalist Campaign against the Weimar Republic* (New Haven, CT: Yale University Press, 1977), 27–31, 45–54; Harsch, *Social Democracy*, 51–9.

66 Jones, *German Liberalism*, 354–8; Mommsen, *Weimar Democracy*, 287–91; Breitman, *German Socialism*, 152–60; Manfred Funke, "Republik im Untergang. Die Zerstörung des Parlamentarismus als Vorbereitung der Diktatur," in Bracher et al. (eds.), *Weimarer Republik*, 506–7; Reinhard Neebe, "Die Großindustrie und die Machtergreifung," in Michalka (ed.), *Machtergreifung*, 111–12.

67 Pyta, "Hindenburg," 34–43; Wolfgang Pyta, *Gegen Hitler und für die Republik. Die Auseinandersetzung der deutschen Sozialdemokratie mit der NSDAP in der Weimarer Republik* (Düsseldorf: Droste Verlag, 1989), 209–16; Neebe, "Großindustrie," 113–16; Mommsen, *Weimar Democracy*, 391 (quotation cited), 394; Funke, "Republik," 511; Peukert, *Weimar Republic*, 258, 359, 362–2, 401; Patch, *Brüning*, 1–10, 72–3, 324–5; Hans Boldt, "Der Artikel 48 der Weimarer Reichsverfassung - Sein historischer Hintergrund und seine politische Funktion," in Michael Stürmer: *Die Weimarer Repubik* (Königstein: Verlagsgruppe Athenäum, 1980), 299–301; Bracher, *Auflösung der Weimarer Republik*, 271–6; Jasper, *gescheiterte Zähmung*, 55–60; Harsch, *Social Democracy*, 89–90, 95–9.

68 Jürgen W. Falter, "Die Wähler der NSDAP 1928–1933: Sozialstruktur und parteipolitische Herkunft," in Wolfgang Michalka (ed.), *Die nationalsozialistische Machtergreifung* (Paderborn: Schöningh, 1984), 49–50, 52–6; idem, "Social Bases," 383–94; Thomas Childers, *The Nazi Voter. The Social Foundations of Fascism in Germany, 1919–1933* (Chapel Hill: University of North Carolina Press, 1983), 155–9, 164–6, 169–72, 185–90, 221–4, 227–8, 240–3, 253–7; Richard J. Hamilton, *Who Voted for Hitler?* (Princeton, NJ: Princeton University Press, 1982), 81–6, 121, passim.

69 Alexander Meschnig, "Die Sendung der Nation: Vom Grabenkrieg zur NS-Bewegung," in Gudrun Brockhaus (ed.), *Die Attraktion der NS-Bewegung* (Essen: Klartext Verlag, 2014), 33, 40; Roger Griffin, "Die größten Verführer aller Zeiten? Die Anziehungskraft des Nazismus," *Die Attraktion der NS-Bewegung*, 218–20; Peter Fritzsche, "Die Idee des Volkes und der Aufstieg der Nazis," *Die Attraktion der NS-Bewegung*, 161, 165, 172; Thomas Rohkrämer, "Die fatale Attraktion der Nationalsozialismus in der Weimarer Republik," *Die Attraktion der NS-Bewegung*, 83.

70 Michael H. Kater, *The Nazi Party. A Social Profile of Members and Leaders 1919-1945* (Cambridge: Harvard University Press, 1983), 49; Dietrich Orlow, *The History of the Nazi Party: 1919-1933* (Pittsburgh, PA: University of Pittsburgh Press, 1969), 176-9, passim; Kershaw, *Hitler*, Vol. I, 318-19.
71 Joachim Petzold, *Franz von Papen. Ein deutsches Verhängnis* (München: Buchverlag Union, 1995), 61, 68-9, 102-3; Funke, "Republik," 511-14; Mommsen, *Weimar Democracy*, 435, 437, 454, 475; Carsten, *Reichswehr*, 376-7; Breitman, *German Socialism*, 181-8; Harsch, *Social Democracy*, 193-202; Christopher Clark, *Iron Kingdom. The Rise and Downfall of Prussia, 1600-1947* (Cambridge: Belknap Press, 2008), 644-8; McElligott, *Rethinking*, 193-5.
72 Irene Strenge, *Kurt von Schleicher. Politik im Reichswehrministerium am Ende der Weimarer Republik* (Berlin: Duncker & Humblot, 2006), 16-19, 172-80, 204-8; Hett, *Death of Democracy*, 82-5, 93; Funke, "Republik," 516-17; Harsch, *Social Democracy*, 220-1; Peter Hayes, "'A Question Mark with Epaulettes'? Kurt von Schleicher and Weimar Politics," *Journal of Modern History* 52 (1980), 35-65; Rohkrämer, *Single Faith?* 47, 58, 154, 194; Mommsen, *Weimar Democracy*, 453, 487-9, 499; Petzold, *Papen*, 158; Carsten, *Reichswehr*, 371, 384, 386-90.
73 Dietmar Petzina et al. (eds.) *Sozialgeschichtliches Arbeitsbuch*, Vol. III (München: Verlag C.H. Beck, 1978), 174; Larry Eugene Jones, "Nazis, Conservatives, and the Establishment of the Third Reich, 1932-1934," *Tel Aviver Jahrbuch für deutsche Geschichte* XXIII (1994), 41-53; Petzold, *Papen*, 130-1, 134-5, 147-50; Neebe, "Großindustrie," 118; Leopold, *Hugenberg*, 121-38; Carsten, *Reichswehr*, 390-7; Mommsen, *Weimar Democracy*, 512, 515.

Chapter 3

1 "Ein starkes, wehrhaftes Deutschland," *Deutsche Zeitung* 38:101a (April 30, 1933); "Zum 1. Mai," *Frankfurter Zeitung* 77:319-20 (April 30, 1933); "Die Kundgebung auf dem Römerberg," *Frankfurter Zeitung* 77:323 (May 2, 1933); Dr. F.K., "Volksverbundenheit," *Deutsche Allgemeine Zeitung* 72:202 (May 2, 1933); "In diesem Geiste," *Kölnische Zeitung* #236 (May 2, 1933); "Der Sinn der Feier," *Kölnische Zeitung* #236 (May 2, 1933); "Mustergültige Ordnung am Tag der deutschen Arbeit," *Deutsche Allgemeine Zeitung* 72:202 Beiblatt (May 2, 1933); Alf Lüdtke, "Wo blieb die 'rote Gefahr'? Arbeitererfahrungen und deutscher Faschismus," in idem (ed.), *Alltagsgeschichte. Zur Rekonstruktion historischer Erfahrungen und Lebensweisen* (Frankfurt/M: Campus Verlag, 1989), 235-6.
2 Hermann Beck, *The Fateful Alliance. German Conservatives and Nazis in 1933: The Machtergreifung in a New Light* (New York: Berghahn Books, 2008), 96-7, 107-12; Martin Broszat, *Der Staat Hitlers* (München: Deutscher Taschenbuch Verlag, 1979), 88, 90, 93, 100-5; Norbert Frei, *National Socialist Rule in Germany. The Führer State, 1933-1945*, trans. Simon Steyne (Oxford: Oxford University Press, 1993), 36-7, 46; Ernst Rudolf Huber, *Verfassungsrecht des Großdeutschen Reiches* (Hamburg: Hanseatische Verlagsanstalt, 1939), 37-8.
3 Gotthard Jaspar, *Die gescheiterte Zähmung* (Frankfurt/M: Suhrkamp Verlag, 1986), 127, 133-8; Huber, *Verfassungsrecht*, 42; Broszat, *Staat Hitlers*, 108; Frei, *Rule*, 44-5; Hans Boldt, *Deutsche Verfassungsgeschichte: Politische Strukturen und ihr Wandel*, Vol. 2 (München: Deutscher Taschenbuch Verlag, 1990), 261, 263, 269; Karl Dietrich

Bracher, *The German Dictatorship: The Origins, Structure, and Effects of National Socialism*, trans. Jean Steinberg (New York: Praeger Publishers, 1974), 195–7, 202, 210–11.

4   Arthur Kaufmann, "Rechtsphilophie und Nationalsozialismus," Hubert Rottleuthner (ed.), *Recht, Rechtsphilosophie und Nationalsozialismus* (Wiesbaden: Franz Steiner Verlag, 1983), 6–8; Diemut Majer, "Rechtstheoretische Funktionsbestimmungen der Justiz im Nationalsozialismus am Beispiel der völkischen Ungleichheit," *Recht, Rechtsphilosophie und Nationalsozialismus*, 166–70; Nicole Kramer/Armin Nolzen, "Einleitung," in idem (eds.), *Ungleichheiten im "Dritten Reich." Semantiken, Praktiken, Erfahrungen* (Göttingen: Wallstein Verlag, 2012), 9; Huber, *Verfassungsrecht*, 25–6, 361.

5   Boldt, *Verfassungsgeschichte*, 275; Broszat, *Staat Hitlers*, 403–9, 413–14; Richard J. Evans, *The Third Reich in Power* (New York: Penguin Press, 2005), 44–6, 71–5; Jaspar, *Zähmung*, 177, 179–82; Rolf Pohl, "Das Konstrukt 'Volksgemeinschaft' als Mittel zur Erzeugung von Massenloyalität im Nationalsozialismus," in *"Volksgemeinschaft": Mythos,wirkungsmächtige sociale Verheißung oder soziale Realität im "Dritten Reich?" Zwischenbilanz einer kontroversen Debatte* (Paderborn: Schöningh, 2012), 69–70; Michael Wildt, *Hitler's Volksgemeinschaft and the Dynamics of Racial Exclusion. Violence against Jews in Provincial Germany, 1919–1939*, trans. Bernard Heise (New York: Berghahn Books, 2012), 105–9, 141; Richard J. Evans, "Coercion and Consent in Nazi Germany," *Proceedings of the British Academy* 151 (2006), 54.

6   Frei, *Rule*, 66–8, 71–4; Broszat, *Staat Hitlers*, 127–8; Janosch Steuwer, *"Ein Drittes Reich, wie ich es auffasse": Politik, Gesellschaft und privates Leben in Tagebüchern 1933–1939* (Göttingen: Wallstein Verlag, 2017), 369–74, 380–1, 387–8, 462–5, 477–81; Bernd Stöver, *Volksgemeinschaft im Dritten Reich. Die Konsensbereitschaft aus der Sicht sozialistischer Exilberichte* (Düsseldorf: Droste Verlag, 1993), 308; Boldt, *Verfassungsgeschichte*, 271; Huber, *Verfassungsrecht*, 45, 53, 199–203; Ian Kershaw, *The "Hitler Myth." Image and Reality in the Third Reich* (Oxford: Oxford University Press, 1989), 1, 62–3, 71, 78, 258, 261.

7   Huber, *Verfassungsrecht*, 42, 44, 46, 49, 53, 55; quote cited in Alan Bullock, *Hitler. A Study in Tyranny*, Rev. ed. (New York: Harper Colophon Books, 1964), 403; Peter Hüttenberger, "Nationalsozialistische Polykratie," *Geschichte und Gesellschaft* 2:5 (1976), 417–42; Boldt, *Verfassungsgeschichte*, 280–3; Frank Bajohr, "Die Zustimmungsdiktatur. Grundzüge nationalsozialistischer Herrschaft in Hamburg," in Forschungsstelle für Zeitgeschichte in Hamburg (ed.), *Hamburg im "Dritten Reich"* (Göttingen: Vandenhoeck & Ruprecht, 2005), 73–4; Hans Mommsen, "Hitlers Stellung im nationalsozialistischen Herrschaftssystem," in Hirschfeld/Kettenacker (eds.), *Führerstaat*, 50–4, 56–60; Broszat, *Staat Hitlers*, 355–9, 379–85; Hans-Ulrich Thamer, *Verführung und Gewalt. Deutschland 1933–1945* (Berlin: Siedler Verlag, 1986), 342–7; Alan Milward, *The German Economy at War* (London: Athlone Press, 1965), 81, 87, 112–15, 134, 178–9.

8   First quote cited in Jaspar, *Zähmung*, 153; Huber, *Verfassungsrecht*, 154–5, 161–3, 194–7, 199–202, 209–11; Kaufmann, *Rechtsphilosophie*, 10; second quote cited in Allan Borup, *Demokratisierung in der Nachkriegszeit* (Bielefeld: Verlag für Regionalgeschichte, 2010), 84; third quote cited in Bullock, *Hitler*, 404; Sven Reichardt, "Beteiligungsdiktaturen in Italien und Deutschland," in Detlef Schmiechen-Ackermann et al. (eds.) *Das Ort der "Volksgemeinschaft" in der Gesellschaft* (Paderborn: Schöningh, 2018), 136–9.

9   Thomas Kühne, *Belonging and Genocide. Hitler's Community, 1918-1945* (New Haven, CT: Yale University Press, 2010), 1, 4-5, 14, 23, 37, 42-3; Wolfgang Bialis, *Moralische Ordnungen des Nationalsozialismus* (Göttingen: Vandenhoeck & Ruprecht, 2014), 10-12, 28-30, 36, 39, 49-50, 54-5.
10 Cornelia Essner, *Die "Nürnberger Gesetze" oder Die Verwaltung des Rassenwahns 1933-1945* (Paderborn: Schöningh, 2002), 55-61, 78, 154, 171-2, passim; Huber, *Verfassungsrecht*, 151, 153, 361, 364-5; Nicole Kramer, *Volksgenossinnen an der Heimatfront. Mobilisierung, Verhalten, Erinnerung* (Göttingen: Vandenhoeck & Ruprecht, 2011), 40-2; James Q. Whitman, *Hitler's American Model. The United States and the Making of Nazi Race Law* (Princeton, NJ: Princeton University Press, 2017), 127-31; Peter Schwerdtner, "Personen- und, Persönlichkeitsschutz und Rechtsfähigkeit im Nationalsozialismus," in Rottleuthner (ed.), *Recht*, 87-9.
11 Wildt, *Hitler's Volksgemeinschaft*, 36-7, 96-7, 125-6, 267 (quote), 272; Marion A. Kaplan, *Between Dignity and Despair. Jewish Life in Nazi Germany* (New York: Oxford University Press, 1998), 5, 9, 21, 43-6; Kühne, *Belonging and Genocide*, 1, 4-5, 14, 23, 37, 42-6; Bialis, *Ordnungen*, 28-30, 54-7; Robert Gellately/Nathan Stoltzfus, "Social Outsiders and the Construction of the Community of the People," in idem (eds.), *Social Outsiders in Nazi Germany* (Princeton, NJ: Princeton University Press, 2001), 4, passim; Jill Stephenson, "The Volksgemeinschaft and the Problems of Permeability: The Persistence of Traditional Attitudes in Württemberg Villages," *German History* 34:1 (2016), 49-69; Ian Kershaw, "Persecution of the Jews/Popular Opinion," *Yearbook of the Leo Baeck Institute* XXVI (1981), 288.
12 Bialis, *Ordnungen*, 37; Gellately/Stoltzfus, "Social Outsiders," 4; Timothy W. Mason, *Sozialpolitik im Dritten Reich. Arbeiterklasse und Volksgemeinschaft* (Opladen: Westdeutscher Verlag, 1977), 23-4, 26-7; Alexander Meschnig, "Die Sendung der Nation: Vom Grabenkrieg zur NS-Bewegung," in Gudrun Brockhaus (ed.), *Attraktion der NS-Bewegung* (Essen: Klartext Verlag, 2014), 33, 40; Peter Fritzsche, "Die Idee des Volkes und der Aufstieg der Nazis," *Attraktion der NS-Bewegung*, 161, 164; Rüdiger Hachtmann, "'Volksgemeinschaftliche Dienstleiter?' Anmerkungen zu Selbstverständnis und Funktion der Deutschen Arbeitsfront und der NS-Gemeinschaft 'Kraft durch Freude,'" in Detlef Schmiechen-Ackermann (ed.), *"Volksgemeinschaft": Mythos, wirkungsmächtige soziale Verheißung oder soziale Realität im "Dritten Reich?" Zwischenbilanz einer kontroversen Debatte* (Paderborn: Schöningh, 2012), 113.
13 Bialis, *Ordnungen*, 13, 24, 34, 36, 48, 55; Moritz Föllmer, *Individuality and Modernity in Berlin. Self and Society from Weimar to the Wall* (Cambridge: Cambridge University Press, 2013), 111; Bajohr, "Zustimmungsdiktatur," 76-7; Kramer/Nolzen, "Einleitung," 9; Hachtmann, "Dienstleiter?" 122.
14 Quotation: Norbert Frei, "People's Community and War: Hitler's Popular Support," in Hans Mommsen (ed.), *The Third Reich between Vision and Reality: New Perspectives on German History 1918-1945* (Oxford: Berg Publishers, 2001), 64; Detlef Peukert, *Inside Nazi Germany: Conformism, Opposition, and Racism in Everyday Life*, trans. Richard Deveson (New Haven, CT: Yale University Press, 1987), 72, 91; Martin Broszat, "Soziale Motivation und Führerbindung des Nationalsozialismus," *Vierteljahrshefte für Zeitgeschichte* 18:4 (1970), 396; Norbert Frei, "'Volksgemeinschaft.' Erfahrungsgeschichte und Lebenswirklichkeit der Hitler-Zeit," in idem (ed.), *1945 und wir: Das dritte Reich* (München: Beck Verlag, 2005), 110-16; Alf Lüdtke, "'The Honor of Labor.' Industrial Workers and the Power of Symbols under National Socialism," in David Crew (ed.), *Nazism and German*

Society 1933-1945 (London: Routledge, 1994), 74-5, 92-8; Hans-Josef Steinberg, "Die Haltung der Arbeiterschaft zum NS-Regime," in Jürgen Schmädeke/Peter Steinbach (eds.), *Der Widerstand gegen den Nationalsozialismus. Die deutsche Gesellschaft und der Widerstand gegen Hitler* (München: Piper Verlag, 1985), 870-2; Detlef Schmiechen-Ackermann, "Einführung," in idem (ed.), *"Volksgemeinschaft": Mythos, wirkungsmächtige soziale Versheißung oder soziale Realität im "Dritten Reich?"* (Paderborn: Schöningh, 2012), 17-36; Pohl, "Konstrukt," 69-73; Hans-Ulrich Thamer, "Die Widersprüche der 'Volksgemeinschaft' in den späten Kriegsjahren," *"Volksgemeinschaft": Mythos, wirkungsmächtige soziale Versheißung oder soziale Realität im "Dritten Reich?,"* 292-4; Martina Steber/Bernhard Gotto, "Volksgemeinschaft. Writing the Social History of the Nazi Regime," in idem (eds.), *Visions*, 4-7, 20-3; Peter Fritzsche, *Life and Death in the Third Reich* (Cambridge: Belknap Press of Harvard University Press, 2008), 37, 51-3, 106-7.

15 Peukert, *Inside*, 187; Mason, *Sozialpolitik*, 114, 130, 173-4, passim; Ian Kershaw, *Popular Opinion and Political Dissent in the Third Reich. Bavaria 1933-1945* (Oxford: Clarendon Press, 1983), 75-6, 108, 291, 373.

16 Frei, "Volksgemeinschaft," 110, 114; David Welch, *The Third Reich. Politics and Propaganda* (London: Routledge, 1993), 52-61; Hans-Ulrich Wehler, *Deutsche Gesellschaftsgeschichte 1914-1949*, Vol. 4 (München: C.H. Beck, 2008), 681, 684-9, 716-19, passim; Reichardt, "Beteiligungsdiktatur," 146-52; David Welch, "Nazi Propaganda and the *Volksgemeinschaft*: Constructing a People's Community," *Journal of Contemporary History* 39:2 (April 2004), 214, 236-8, passim.

17 Bialis, *Ordnungen*, 38; Föllmer, *Individuality*, 101, 103, 107-8, 111, 114, 120, 124-6, 158-62; Moritz Föllmer, "Was Nazism Collectivistic?" *Journal of Modern History* 82 (2010), 62, 64, 67, 72-4, 76, 78, 82-3, 88-9; Frei, "Volksgemeinschaft," 122-4; Michelle Mouton, *From Nurturing the Nation to Purifying the Volk. Weimar and Nazi Family Policy, 1918-1945* (Cambridge: Cambridge University Press, 2007), 99, 104, 275, 279-81.

18 Wolfgang Sauer, *Die Mobilmachung der Gewalt* (Frankfurt/M: Ullstein Verlag, 1974), 237-55; Beck, *Fateful Alliance*, 103-4, 115-17, 129-38, 157-8, 230-3, 236-42; Robert Gellately, *Backing Hitler. Consent and Coercion in Nazi Germany* (Oxford: Oxford University Press, 2001), 17, 19, 22-3, 51-2, 58-60; William Sheridan Allen, *The Nazi Seizure of Power. The Experience of a Single German Town 1922-1945*, Rev. ed. (New York: Franklin Watts, 1984), 184-90, 195; Jane Caplan, "Political Detentions and the Origins of the Concentration Camps in Nazi Germany, 1933-1935/36," in Neil Gregor (ed.), *Nazism, War and Genocide* (Exeter: University of Exeter Press, 2005), 23-35.

19 Bracher, *Dictatorship*, 214, 216-19, 225; Broszat, *Staat Hitlers*, 117-26, Beatrix Herlemann, "Communist Resistance between Comintern Directives and Nazi Terror," in Barclay/Weitz (eds.), Reform and Revolution, 359; Beck, *Fateful Alliance*, 253-94; Frei, *Führer State*, 66-7; Reinhard Mann, *Protest und Kontrolle im Dritten Reich. Nationalsozialistische Herrschaft im Alltag einer rheinischen Großstadt* (Frankfurt/M: Campus Verlag, 1987), 124-5, 131-5, 180-4; Ulrich Herbert, "Arbeiter im 'Dritten Reich,'" *Geschichte und Gesellschaft* 15 (1989), 328; Jill Stephenson, *Nazi Organisation of Women* (London: Croom Helm, 1981), 98, 135-6.

20 Frei, *Rule*, 1, 78 (quotation); Kershaw, *Hitler Myth*, 253-4, 258; Hans Dieter Schäfer, *Das gespaltene Bewußtsein. Über deutsche Kultur und Lebenswirklichkeit 1933-1945* (München: Carl Hansler Verlag, 1981), 116-17; Stöver, *Volksgemeinschaft*, 120-3; Ulrich Herbert, "Echoes of the *Volksgemeinschaft*," in Steber/Gotto (eds.), *Visions*,

61–2; Kristin Semmens, "A Holiday from the Nazis? Everyday Tourism in the Third Reich," in Lisa Pine (ed.), *Life and Times in Nazi Germany* (London: Bloomsbury, 2016), 135, 141, 144.

21 David Bankier, *Germans and the Final Solution. Public Opinion under Nazism* (Oxford: Blackwell Publishers, 1996), 38–41, 68–71, 83–7; Bialis, *Ordnungen*, 10–12, 27, 30, 43–4; Claudia Koonz, *The Nazi Conscience* (Cambridge: Belknap Press of Harvard University Press, 2003), 104–5, 146; Henry Friedlander, *The Origins of the Nazi Genocide. From Euthanasia to the Final Solution* (Chapel Hill: University of North Carolina Press, 1995), 9–20, 23, 67–8, passim.

22 Wildt, *Hitler's Volksgemeinschaft*, 1–5, 119–20, passim; Marlis Steinert, *Hitler's War and the Germans* (Athens: Ohio University Press, 1977), 135–47; Ian Kershaw, "Alltägliches und Außeralltägliches: ihre Bedeutung fur die Volksmeinung 1933–1939," in *Reihen fast geschlossen*, edited by Detlef Peukert and Jürgen Reulecke (Wuppertal: Hammer, 1981), 286; Peter Longerich, "*Davon haben wir wir nichts gewusst!" Die Deutschen und die Judenverfolgung* (München: Siedler, 2006), 11–12, 52–3, 91, 96–100, 115–21, passim; Bankier, *Germans*, 68–71, 90–4, 104–15; Wolf Gruner, "Indifference? Participation and Protest as Individual Responses to the Persecution of the Jews as Revealed in Berlin Police Logs and Trial Records 1933–45," in Susanna Schrafstetter/Alan E. Steinweis (eds.), *The Germans and the Holocaust: Popular Responses to the Persecution and Murder of the Jews* (New York: Berghahn Books, 2015), 62, 65–8, 71; Heidi Gerstenberger, "Acquiescence?" in David Bankier (ed.), *Probing the Depths of German Antisemitism: German Society and the Persecution of the Jews, 1933–1941* (New York: Berghahn Books, 2000), 31–5; Victoria Barnett, *For the Soul of the People: Protestant Protest against Hitler* (New York: Oxford University Press, 1992), 128–39, 152–3.

23 Lothar Kettenacker, "Sozialpsychologische Aspekte der Führer-Herrschaft," in Gerhard Hirschfeld/idem (eds.), *Der "Führerstaat": Mythos und Realität. Studien zur Struktur und Politik des Dritten Reiches* (Stuttgart: Klett-Cotta, 1981), 116; Kershaw, *Popular Opinion*, 36, 64, 111–12, 117–18, 131, 356; Steinert, *Hitler's War*, 129–30; Peukert, *Inside*, 43.

24 Brockhaus, *Attraktion*, 18–19; Jasper, *Zähmung*, 175; Peukert, *Inside*, 71, 197–9, 215; Gellately, *Backing Hitler*, 19, 33–5, 60 (quotation), 82, 88–9, 120.

25 Koonz, *Conscience*, 60, 68 (quotation), 99, 189, 254, 259, 273; cf. also Bialis, *Ordnungen*, passim; Klemens von Klemperer, "'What Is the Law that Lies behind These Words?' Antigone's Question and the German Resistance against Hitler," in Michael Geyer/John Boyer (eds.), *Resistance against the Third Reich 1933–1990* (Chicago: University of Chicago Press, 1994), 144; Michael Geyer/John Boyer, "Introduction: Resistance against the Third Reich as Intercultural Knowledge," *Resistance against the Third Reich 1933–1990*, 10 (quotation); Gerhard Paul/Klaus-Michael Mallmann, *Milieus und Widerstand. Eine Verhaltensgeschichte der Gesellschaft im Nationalsozialismus* (Bonn: Verlag J.H.W. Dietz Nachfolger, 1995), 135, 235–6.

26 Frei, "Volksgemeinschaft," 112–13, 115, 125; Kershaw, *Popular Opinion*, 149, 356; Kershaw, *Hitler Myth*, 83, 94–5, 98, 104, 128, 138, 152, 199, 257; Nathan Stoltzfus, *Hitler's Compromises: Coercion and Consensus in Nazi Germany* (New Haven, CT: Yale University Press, 2016), 97–8, 194–5, 202; Hans Mommsen, "Der Widerstand gegen Hitler und die deutschen Gesellschaft," in Schmädeke/Steinbach (eds.), *Widerstand*, 7–8; Bajohr, "Zustimmungsdiktatur," 89, 101, 106, 108; Steinert, *Hitler's War*, 7, 39, 60–1, 129–30.

27 Gellately, *Backing Hitler*, 170–2, 179–80, 224–5, 245–6, 250, 253; Evans, "Coercion," 80; Nathan Stoltzfus, *Resistance of the Heart: Intermarriage and the Rosenstrasse Protest in Nazi Germany* (New York: W. W. Norton & Co., 1996), 3, 6, 133; Detlev Schmiechen-Ackermann, "Social Control and the Making of the Volksgemeinschaft," in Steber/Gotto (eds.), *Visions*, 243–51; Eric Johnson, *Nazi Terror: The Gestapo, Jews, and Ordinary Germans* (New York: Basic Books, 1999), 14–15, 254, 354.

28 Nicholas Stargardt, *The German War. A Nation under Arms. Citizens and Soldiers* (New York: Basic Books, 2015), 3–8, 244–7, 302, 377–81, 461–4, 470–2; Ian Kershaw, *The End: The Defiance and Destruction of Hitler's Germany, 1944–45* (New York: Penguin Press, 2011), 8–10, 12–15, 97–101, 117–22, 270–1; Fritzsche, *Life*, 267, 269, 284–5; Frank Bajohr, "Uber die Entwicklung eines schlechten Gewissens. Die deutsche Bevölkerung und die Deportationen 1941–1945," Birthe Kundrus/Beate Meyer *Die Deportation der Juden aus Deutschland: Pläne-Praxis-Reaktionen 1938–1949* (Göttingen: Wallenstein, 2004), 186–7, 190–4; Frei, *Rule*, 150; Kershaw, *Popular Opinion*, 329, 364–5, 369–70; Peukert, *Inside*, 144; Kühne, *Belonging and Genocide*, 131–6.

29 Kershaw, *Hitler Myth*, 1, 62–3, 71, 77–9; Otmar Jung, "Wahlen und Abstimmung im Dritten Reich," in Eckhard Jesse/Konrad Löw (eds.), *Wahlen in Deutschland* (Berlin: Duncker & Humblot, 1998), 69–92; Steuwer, *Drittes Reich*, 359, 362–3, 392–3.

30 Peter Reichel, *Der schöne Schein des Dritten Reiches. Faszination und Gewalt des Faschismus* (Frankfurt/M: Fischer Taschenbuch Verlag, 1993), passim; George L. Mosse, *The Nationalization of the Masses: Political Symbolism and Mass Movements in Germany from the Napoleonic Wars through the Third Reich* (New York: Howard Fertig, 1975), 79–81, 182, 200; Werner Freitag, "Der Führermythos im Fest. Festfeuerwerk, NS-Liturgie, Dissens und '100% KDF-Stimmung,'" in idem. (ed.), *Das Dritte Reich im Fest. Führermythos, Feierlaune und Verweigerung in Westfalen 1933–1945* (Bielefeld: Verlag für Regionalgeschichte, 1997), 11, 13–19, 24–30, 33, 35, 57, 59.

31 Freitag, "Führermythos," 33, 35, 37–9; Jean-Christoph Caron, "Gewalt im Fest. Die Maifeiern in Hagen und Hohenlimburg," in Freitag (ed.), *Dritte Reich*, 109–15; Steuwer, *Drittes Reich*, 432–5; Longerich, *Davon haben wir*, 24–5; Joan L. Clinefelter, "Representing the *Volksgemeinschaft*: Art in the Third Reich," in Pine (ed.), *Life in Third Reich*, 188–9 (quotation); Stoltzfus, *Resistance*, 65–7.

32 Franka Maubach, "'Volksgemeinschaft' als Geschlechtergemeinschaft. Zur Genese einer nationalsozialistischen Beziehungsform," in Brockhaus (ed.), *Attraktion*, 252–68; Stephenson, *Women*, 12–13, 145–6, 182; Koonz, *Conscience*, 2, 67, 222–3, 255; Ulrich Herbert, *Hitler's Foreign Workers: Enforced Foreign Labor in Germany under the Third Reich*, trans. William Templer (Cambridge: Cambridge University Press, 1997), 333–4, 389.

33 Wehler, *Gesellschaftsgeschichte*, Vol. 4, 753–60; Vandana Joshi, *Gender and Power in the Third Reich: Female Denouncers and the Gestapo* (New York: Palgrave Macmillan, 2003), 44–7, 118–19, 195–6; Kershaw, *Popular Opinion*, 307; Kramer, *Volksgenossinnen*, 37–41, 49–51, 57, 95–102, 147, 161–5, 341–8; Adelheid v. Saldern, "Victims or Perpetrators? Controversies about the Role of Women in the Nazi State," in Crew (ed.), *Nazism*, 146–58; Matthew Stibbe, *Women in the Third Reich* (London: Arnold, 2003), 133–6, 141, passim; Stephenson, *Women*, 19, 33–7, 56–7, 115–16, 122; Claudia Koonz, "Ethical Dilemmas and Nazi Eugenics: Single-Issue Dissent in Religious Contexts," in Geyer/Boyer (eds.), *Resistance*, 16–17, passim; Elizabeth Harvey, *Women and the Nazi East: Agents and Witnesses of Germanization* (New Haven, CT: Yale University Press, 2003), 1–18, 294, 297–300.

34 Peukert, *Inside*, 77–9, 84, 239; Föllmer, *Individuality*, 158–9, 164–5; Steinberg, "Haltung der Arbeiterschaft," 869–70; Martin Broszat, "A Social and Historical Typology of the German Resistance to Hitler," in David Clay Large (ed.), *Contending with Hitler: Varieties of German Resistance in the Third Reich* (Cambridge: Cambridge University Press, 1991), 27–8, 45; Kershaw, *Hitler Myth*, 207.

35 Gellately, *Backing Hitler*, 25, 73, 114, 122, 133–40, 158, 162–3, 188, 192–3, 201–3; Gisela Diewald-Kerkmann, *Politische Denunziation im NS-Regime oder Die kleine Macht der "Volksgenossen"* (Bonn: J.H.W. Dietz Nachfolger, 1995), 9, 20–1, 72, 82, 100, 136–51; Gruner, "Indifference?" 67–72; Christel Wickert, "Popular Attitudes to National Socialist Antisemitism: Denunciations for 'Insidious Offenses' and 'Racial Ignominy,'" in Bankier (ed.), *Probing*, 282–7; Johnson, *Terror*, 20–1, 109, 153–5, 282–3, 331, 363–4, 367–9; Joshi, *Gender*, xi–xvi, 16, 49, 119, 171, 192–6; Mann, *Protest*, 293, 295, 299.

36 Sheila Fitzpatrick/Robert Gellately, "Introduction to the Practices of Denunciation in Modern European History," in idem (eds.), *Accusatory Practices: Denunciation in Modern European History* (Chicago: University of Chicago Press, 1997), 17–20; Robert Gellately, "Denunciations in Twentieth-Century Germany: Aspects of Self-Policing in the Third Reich and the German Democratic Republic," *Accusatory Practices: Denunciation in Modern European History*, 205–6; Diewald-Kerkmann, *Denunziation*, 22–3, passim.

37 Klaus Tenfelde, "'Workers' Opposition in Nazi Germany': Recent West German Research," in Maier (ed.), *Rise*, 107–11; Martin Broszat, "Resistenz und Widerstand: Eine Zwischenbilanz des Forschungsprojekts 'Widerstand und Verfolgung in Bayern 1933–1945,'" in idem, *Nach Hitler. Der schwierige Umgang mit unserer Geschichte* (München: R. Oldenbourg Verlag, 1987), 69–90; Allan Merson, *Communist Resistance in Nazi Germany* (London: Lawrence and Wishart, 1985), 5; Ulrich Herbert, "Arbeiter im 'Dritten Reich,'" *Geschichte und Gesellschaft* 15 (1989), 352; Frank Biess, "The Search for Missing Soldiers: MIAs, POWs, and Ordinary Germans, 1943–45," in idem et al. (eds.), *Conflict, Catastrophe and Continuity. Essays on Modern German History* (New York: Berghahn Books, 2007), 121–2; Wolf Gruner, *Widerstand in der Rosenstraße. Die Fabrik-Aktion und die Verfolgung der "Mischehen" 1943* (Frankfurt/M: Fischer Taschenbuch Verlag, 2005), 77–83; Kershaw, *Popular Opinion*, 2–5, 176; Ian Kershaw, "Widerstand ohne Volk? Dissens und Widerstand im Dritten Reich," in Schmädeke/Steinbach (eds.), *Widerstand*, 780–95; Stolzfus, "Widerstand," 220–1, 234–41.

38 Koonz, *Conscience*, 141, 159–60, 178; Alf Lüdtke, "The Appeal of Exterminating 'Others': German Workers and the Limits of Resistance," in Geyer/Boyer (eds.), *Resistance*, 56; Werner K. Blessing, "'Deutschland in Not, wir im Glauben'. Kirche und Kirchenvolk in einer katholischen Region," in *Von Stalingrad zur Währungsreform. Zur Sozialgeschichte des Umbruchs in Deutschland*, edited by Martin Broszat (München: Oldenbourg Verlag, 1989), 33–5; Paul/Mallmann, *Milieus*, 14, 108, 113–14, 122, 128–9; Föllmer, *Individuality*, 166–7; Fritzsche, *Life*, 37; Kershaw, *Popular Opinion*, viii, 123–31, 143–7, 356; Kershaw, "Álltägliches," 273, 279–80, 282–5; Manfred Gailus/Armin Nolzen, "Einleitung: Vielkonkurrierende Gläubigkeiten—aber eine Volksgemeinschaft?" in idem (eds.), *Zerstrittene "Volksgemeinschaft." Glaube, Konfession und Religion im Nationalsozialismus* (Göttingen: Vandenhoeck & Ruprecht, 2011), 10–11, 22–3; Charles S. Maier, *The Rise of the Nazi Regime. Historical Reassessments* (Boulder: Westview Press, 1986), 115–17; Klaus Große Kracht, "Campaigning against Bolshevism: Catholic Action in Late Weimar Germany," *Journal of Contemporary History* 53, no. 3 (2018), 555–63.

39 John Connelly, "The Uses of *Volksgemeinschaft*: Letters to the NSDAP Kreisleitung Eisenach, 1939-1940," *Journal of Modern History* 68:4 (1996), 901-2, 905, 913-14, 930; Blessing, "Deutschland in Not," 31, 46; Kershaw, *Popular Opinion*, 169-71, 203-4, 210-11, 349-57; Jeremy Noakes, "The Oldenburg Crucifix Struggle of November 1936: A Case Study of Opposition in the Third Reich," in Peter Stachura (ed.), *The Shaping of the Nazi State* (London: Croom Helm, 1978), 218-21; Christiane Kuller, "The Demonstrations in Support of the Protestant Provincial Bishop Hans Meisner. A Successful Protest against the Nazi Regime?" in Stoltzfus/Maier-Katkin (eds.), *Protest*, 38-54; Friedlander, *Genocide*, 39-40.

40 Blessing, "Deutschland in Not," 37, 42; Mann, *Protest*, 7-9, 261-3; Broszat, "Typology," 29-30; Kershaw, *Popular Opinion*, 50, 84, 221; Dieter Rebentisch, "Die 'politische Beurteilung' als Herrschaftsinstrument der NSDAP," in Peukert/Jürgen (eds.), *Reihen fast geschlossen*, 117-18; Steinert, *Hitler's War*, 207-8, 213-15; Peukert, *Inside*, 144-74; Johnson, *Terror*, 325-31; Rudolf Herzog, *Heil Hitler, das Schwein ist Tot! Lachen unter Hitler—Komik und Humor im Dritten Reich* (Berlin: Eichborn, 2006), 11-12, 77-8, 182, 190-1; Stargardt, *German War*, 79; Arno Klönne, "Jugendprotest und Jugendopposition. Von der HJ-Erziehung zum Cliquenwesen der Kriegszeit," in Martin Broszat et al. (eds.), *Bayern in der NS-Zeit*, Vol. 4 (München: Oldenbourg, 1981), 532, 550-2, 589-92, 594, 599-620.

41 Wolfgang Zollitsch, "Die Vertrauensratswahlen von 1934 und 1935. Zum Stellenwert von Abstimmungen im 'Dritten Reich' am Beispiel Krupp," *Geschichte und Gesellschaft* 15:3 (1989), 361-81; Mason, *Sozialpolitik*, 161-3, 126-9, 285, 289, 314; Günther Morsch, "Streik im 'Dritten Reich,'" *Vierteljahrshefte für Zeitgeschichte* 36:4 (1988), 673-5, 682-3, passim; Herbert, "Arbeiterschaft," 341-2; Kershaw, *Popular Opinion*, 55-60, 82-91, 95-105; Peukert, *Inside*, 110-12, 214; Wehler, *Gesellschaftsgeschichte*, Vol. 4, 738-9; Herbert, *Workers*, 329-31, 389; Kramer, *Volksgenossinen*, 61-3, 175-9; Kershaw, "Alltägliches," 283; Stephenson, *Women*, 10-84.

42 Gruner, "Indifference?" 65-74; Wolf Gruner, "Defiance and Protest. A Comparative Microhistorical Reevaluation of Individual Jewish Reponses to Nazi Persecution," in Claire Zalc/Tal Bruttmann (eds.), *Microhistories of the Holocaust* (New York: Berghahn Books, 2017), 209-26; Kershaw, *Popular Opinion*, 127-30; Peukert, *Inside*, 63-5; Longerich, *Davon haben wir*, 25-6, 63, 251, 291, 320.

43 Kershaw, *Hitler Myth*, 97, 161-6, 170, 187, 192-3, 217-18, 220-1; Kershaw, *Popular Opinion*, 46-7, 64, 82-3, 104-5; Peukert, *Inside*, 68-75; Bankier, *Germans*, 27, 51-2; Frei, "Volksgemeinschaft," 125.

44 Kershaw, *Hitler Myth*, Vol. 2, 426; Koonz, *Conscience*, 180; Mason, *Sozialpolitik*, 123-23, 130; Stoltzfus, *Resistance*, xxii.

45 Stoltzfus, *Compromises*, 53-78, 86-100, 107, 124-39, 204; Noakes, " Oldenburg Struggle," 211-29; Kershaw, *Popular Opinion*, 163-223, 246-55, 335-60; Kershaw, "Persecution," 280; Longerich, *Davon haben wir*, 227; Günther v. Norden, "Zwischen Teilkooperation und Widerstand. Rolle der Kirche und Konfessionen," in Schmädeke/Steinbach (eds.), *Widerstand*, 228-37; Paul/Mallmann, *Milieus*, 113-19, 128-35; Stargardt, *German War*, 144-51, 249, 260-1; Antonia Leugers, "Der Protest in der Rosenstraße und die Kirchen," in idem (ed.), *Berlin, Rosenstraße 2-4: Protest in der NS-Diktatur* (Annweiler: Plöger, 2005), 57-74; Gellately, *Backing Hitler*, 102-5.

46 Stoltzfus, *Resistance,* xvii-xxiv, 215-63; Stoltzfus, "Widerstand," 218-41; Gernot Jochheim, *Protest in der Rosenstraße* (Stuttgart: Hoch-Verlag, 1990), 130, 134-5; Leugers (ed.), *Rosenstraße*, passim; Johnson, *Terror*, 422-4; Wolf Gruner, *Widerstand*,

139–42, 148–56 (albeit he doubts Goebbels ever intended to deport the spouses, 157–66, passim).

47 Cf. Stoltzfus, *Resistance*, 266–70, 273–5; Johnson, *Terror*, 422–3.
48 Ronald Hansen, *Disobeying Hitler: German Resistance after Valkyrie* (Oxford: Oxford University Press, 2014), 162–204; Frei, *Rule*, 146; Wolfgang Zollitsch, "Modernisierung im Betrieb. Arbeiter zwischen Weltwirtschaftskrise und Nationalsozialismus," in Schmiechen-Ackermann (ed.), *Anpassung*, 101; Jill Stephenson, "'Resistance' to 'No Surrender': Popular Disobedience in Württemberg in 1945," in Francis R. Nicosia/Lawrence D. Stokes (eds.), *Germans against Nazism: Nonconformity, Opposition, and Resistance in the Third Reich* (New York: Berg Publishers, 1990), 355; Stargardt, *German War*, 227.
49 Peukert, *Inside*, 104–5, 122–5; Merson, *Communist*, 96–121, 141–6, 182, 231–2, 26, 248, 256–7, 286, 309, passim; Michael Zimmermann, "'Ein schwer zur bearbeitende Pflaster': der Bergarbeiterort Hochlaumark unter dem Nationalsozialismus," in Peukert/Reulecke (eds.), *Reihen*, 73–4; Beatrix Herlemann, "Communist Resistance," 357–69; Broszat, "Typology," 27–8.
50 Christiane Moll, "Acts of Resistance: The White Rose in the Light of New Archival Evidence," in Geyer/Boyer (eds.), *Resistance*, 172–200; Kershaw, *Hitler Myth*, 194–5; Paul/Mallmann, *Milieus*, 137–41; Johnson, *Terror*, 305, 561–2.
51 Mommsen, "Widerstand gegen Hitler," 7–17; Hans Mommsen, "Verfassungs- und Verwaltungsreformpläne der Widerstandsgruppen des 20. Juli 1944," in Jürgen Schmädeke and Peter Steinbach (eds.), *Der Widerstand gegen den Nationalsozialismus. Die deutsche Gesellschaft und der Widerstand gegen Hitler* (München: Piper Verlag, 1985), 570–97; Peter Steinbach, "Wiederherstellung des Rechtsstaats als zentrale Zielsetzung des Widerstands," in Schmädeke/Steinbach (eds.), *Widerstand*, 625–36; Ian Kershaw, "Widerstand ohne Volk? Dissens und Widerstand im Dritten Reich," in Schmädeke/Steinbach (eds.), *Widerstand*, 794–5; Christoph Klessmann, "Das Problem der 'Volksbewegung' im deutschen Widerstand," in Schmädeke/Steinbach (eds.), *Widerstand*, 822–9; Peter Hoffmann, *The History of the German Resistance, 1933–1945*, trans. Richard Barry (Cambridge: MIT Press, 1979), 69–98, 301–506.
52 Wildt, *Volksgemeinschaft*, 1–2, 85–6, 92–4, 105–9, 126–7, passim; Steuwer, *Drittes Reich*, 168–9; Kershaw, "Persecution," 264–70, 274, 280; Gruner, "Indifference?" 62–3, 65; Bankier, *Germans*, 34–8, 80–5; Longerich, *Davon haben wir*, 58–7, 72–3, 112–15, 119–21.

Chapter 4

1 Wolfgang Benz, *Von der Besatzungsherrschaft zur Bundesrepublik. Stationen einer Staatsgründung 1946–1949* (Frankfurt/M: Fischer Verlag, 1985), 11–40; Rebecca L. Boehling, *A Question of Priorities. Democratic Reform and Economic Recovery in Postwar Germany* (Providence: Berghahn Books, 1996), 156–8, 162–7, 171–7; Sean Forner, *German Intellectuals and the Challenge of Democratic Renewal: Culture and Politics after 1945* (Cambridge: Cambridge University Press, 2014), 149–50; Friedrich Karl Fromme, *Von der Weimarer Verfassung zum Bonner Grundgesetz: die verfassungspolitische Folgerungen des Parlamentarischen Rates und nationalsozialistischer Diktatur* (Berlin: Duncker & Humblot, 1999 [1958]), 16–17.

2   Richard L. Merritt, *Democracy Imposed: US Occupation Policy and the German Public, 1945-1949* (New Haven, CT: Yale University Press, 1995); Greenberg, *The Weimar Century*, 7-9, passim; Ullrich, *Weimar Komplex*, 190-6, 217, 241-5, 248-52; Anna J. Merritt/Richard L. Merritt (eds.), *Public Opinion in Occupied Germany: The OMGUS Surveys, 1945-1949* (Urbana: University of Illinois Press, 1970), 1; Hans Mommsen, "Von Weimar nach Bonn: Zum Demokratieverständnis der Deutschen," in Axel Schildt/Arnold Sywottek (eds.), *Modernisierung im Wiederaufbau. Die westdeutsche Gesellschaft der 50er Jahre* (Bonn: Verlag J. H. W. Dietz Nachf., 1993), 745-6; Peter Brandt, "Germany after 1945. Revolution by Defeat?" in Reinhard Rürup (ed.), *The Problem of Revolution in Germany, 1789-1989* (Oxford: Berg Publishing, 2000), 130-3, 141.
3   Arnd Bauerkämper et al., "Einleitung: Transatlantische Mittler und die Demokratisierung Westdeutschlands 1945-1970," in idem (eds.), *Demokratiewunder. Transatlantische Mittler und die kulturelle Öffnung Westdeutschlands 1945-1970* (Göttingen: Vandenhoeck & Ruprecht, 2005), 28-9; Manfred Wüstemeyer, "Re-education—die Verlierer lernen Demokratie," in Holger Afflerbach/Christoph Cornelißen (eds.), *Sieger und Besiegte. Materielle und ideelle Neuorientierungen nach 1945* (Tübingen: Francke Verlag, 1997), 220-34; James F. Tent, *Mission on the Rhine. Reeducation and Denazification in American-Occupied Germany* (Chicago: University of Chicago Press, 1982), 313-15, passim; Nina Verheyen, *Diskussionslust: eine Kulturgeschichte des "besseren Arguments" in Westdeutschland* (Göttingen: Vandenhoeck & Ruprecht, 2010), 65-9, 76-9, 87-8, 118, 148-9; Hermann-Josef Rupieper, *Die Wurzeln der westdeutschen Nachkriegsdemokratie. Der amerikanische Beitrag 1945-1952* (Opladen: Westdeutscher Verlag, 1993), 243-6, 426-7, passim; Konrad Jarausch, *After Hitler. Recivilizing Germans, 1945-1995* (Oxford: Oxford University Press, 2006), 20, 44, 62, 64, 97.
4   Karlheinz Niclauß, *Der Weg zum Grundgesetz. Demokratiegründung in Westdeutschland 1945-1949* (Paderborn: Schöningh, 1998), 17, 176-7; Ilona K. Klein, *Die Bundesrepublik als Parteienstaat: zur Mitwirkung der Parteien an der Willensbildung des Volkes 1945-1949* (Frankfurt/ M: Peter Lang, 1990), 88, 132-3, 201-2, 211, 217-18; Alf Mintzel, "Der akzeptierte Parteienstaat," in Martin Broszat (ed.), *Zäsuren nach 1945: Essays zur Periodisierung der deutschen Nachkriegsgeschichte* (München: Oldenbourg Verlag, 1990), esp. 75, 78-9, 81, 83; Ullrich, *Weimar Komplex*, 292; Udo Wengst, *Staatsaufbau und Regierungspraxis 1948-1953. Zur Geschichte der Verfassungsorgane in der Bundesrepublik Deutschland* (Düsseldorf: Droste Verlag, 1984), 23-5, 29, 31-6.
5   Fromme, *Weimarer*, 17; Ullrich, *Weimar Komplex*, 270-1; Benz, *Besatzungsherrschaft*, 185-6, 194-7; Hans Mommsen, "The Origins of Chancellor Democracy and the Transformation of the German Democratic Paradigm," *German Politics & Society* 25:2 (2007), 7-10.
6   Fromme, *Weimarer*, 21-6, 30-1, 48-9, 135-6, 162-4, 176-7, passim; Maria, Mitchell, *The Origins of Christian Democracy: Politics and Confession in Modern Germany* (Ann Arbor: University of Michigan Press, 2012), 164; the articles in Christoph Gusy (ed.), *Weimars lange Schatten—"Weimar" als Argumente nach 1945* (Baden-Baden: Nomos Verlag, 2003); Niclauß, *Grundgesetz*, 27-31, 41.
7   Hans Boldt, *Deutsche Verfassungsgeschichte*, Vol. 2 (München: dtv, 1984), 316; Fromme, *Weimarer*, 30-1; Niclauß, *Weg*, 112, 185; Ullrich, *Weimar Komplex*, 211-12, 292; Wengst, *Staatsaufbau*, 21; Mitchell, *Origins of Christian*, 164-5.

8 Friedrich Kießling, *Die undeutschen Deutschen. Eine ideengeschichtliche Archäologie der alten Bundesrepublik 1945-1972* (Paderborn: Schöningh, 2012),8, 15–16, 18 (quotation), 81; Wehler, *Gesellschaftsgeschichte*, Vol. 5, 246; Konrad Jarausch, "Amerikanische Einflüsse und deutsche Einsichten. Kulturelle Aspekte der Demokratisierung Westdeutschlands," in Bauerkämper et al. (eds.), *Demokratiewunder. Transatlantische Mittler und die kulturelle Öffnung Westdeutschlands 1945-1970* (Göttingen: Vandenhoeck & Ruprecht, 2005), 69, 79; Anselm Doering-Manteuffel, *Wie westlich sind die Deutschen? Amerikanisierung und Westernisierung im 20. Jahrhundert* (Göttingen: Vandenhoeck & Ruprecht, 1999), 55; Martin Greschat/Jochen-Christoph Kaiser (eds.), *Christentum und Demokratie im 20. Jahrhundert* (Stuttgart: W. Kohlhammer, 1992), 1, 5, 8; Rupieper, *Wurzeln*, 63, 171–2.
9 Boldt, *Verfassungsgeschichte*, 318–19; Benz, *Besatzungsherrschaft*, 212–13; Niclauß, *Weg*, 213–15, 219–21, 231–2; Wengst, *Staatsaufbau*, 315.
10 Wengst, *Staatsaufbau*, 78, 325; Niclauß, *Weg*, 215; Fromme, *Weimarer*, 189, 191; Justin Collings, *Democracy's Guardians. A History of the German Federal Constitutional Court 1951-2001* (Oxford: Oxford University Press, 2015), xxv–xxvi, 3–4, 9–14, 34–7, 60, 73, 79, passim; Strote, *Lions and Lambs*, 152–3; Karlheinz Niclauß, "Der Parlamentarische Rat und das Bundesverfassungsgericht," in Robert Chr. van Ooyen/Maring H.W. Möllers (eds.), *Das Bundesverfassungsgericht im politischen System* (Wiesbaden: Verlag für Sozialwissenschaften, 2006), 121–2; Frieder Günther, *Denken vom Staat her. Die bundesdeutsche Staatsrechtslehre zwischen Dezisionismus und Integration 1949-1970* (München: Oldenbourg, 2004), 93–4, 102–3, 109; Donald Kommers, "Building Democracy: Judicial Review and the German Rechtsstaat," in John S. Brady et al. (eds.), *The Postwar Transformation of Germany. Democracy, Prosperity, and Nationhood* (Ann Arbor: University of Michigan Press, 1999), 96–7; Manfred Baldus, "Frühe Machtkämpfe. Ein Versuch über die historischen Gründe der Autorität des Bundesverfassungsgerichts," in Thomas Henne and Arne Riedlinger (eds.), *Das Lüth Urteil* (Berlin: Berliner Wissenschafts-Verlag, 2005), 237–47.
11 Anselm Doering-Manteuffel, "Strukturmerkmale der Kanzlerdemokratie," *Der Staat* 30 (1991), 4–5, 8; Fromme, *Weimarer*, 119–21, 170; Karlheinz Niclauß, *Kanzlerdemokratie. Regierungsführung von Konrad Adenauer bis Angela Merkel*, 3rd ed. (Wiesbaden: Springer, 2015), 42, 67–9; Niclauß, *Weg*, 60; Wengst, *Staatsaufbau*, 70–1; Karl Bracher, "Die Kanzlerdemokratie," in Richard Löwenthal and Hans-Peter Schwarz (eds.), *Die zweite Republik* (Stuttgart: Seewald Verlag, 1974), 184.
12 Raimund Lammersdorf, "'Das Volk ist streng demokratisch.' Amerikanische Sorgen über das autoritäre Bewusstsein der Deutschen in der Besatzungszeit und frühen Bundesrepublik," in Bauerkämper et al. (eds.), *Demokratiewunder*, 93–4; Fromme, *Weimar*, 159–62; Andreas Wirsching, "Konstruktion und Erosion: Weimar Argumente gegen Volksbegehren und Volksentscheid," in Christoph Gusy (ed.), *Weimars lange Schatten—'Weimar' als Argumente nach 1945* (Baden-Baden: Nomos Verlag, 2003), 335, 340–1, passim; Matt Qvortup, "Referendums in Western Europe," in idem (ed.), *Referendums around the World* (Cham, Switzerland: Palgrave Macmillan, 2018), 43–4; Niclauß, *Weg*, 192–3, 197–9.
13 Wengst, *Staatsaufbau*, 71–2; Fromme, *Weimarer*, 45–60, 89–92.
14 Benz, *Besatzungsherrschaft*, 249–51; Elizabeth Noelle/Erich Peter Neumann, *Jahrbuch der öffentlichen Meinung 1947-1955* (Allensbach: Verlag für Demoskopie, 1967), Vol. IV, 363; Ullrich, *Weimar Komplex*, 281–4, 401–10, 438–43; Rolf Poscher, "Das Weimar Wahlrechtsgespenst," in Gusy (ed.), *Schatten*, 258–77; Eckard Jesse,

Wahlrecht zwischen Kontinuität und Reform. Eine Analyse der Wahlsystemdiskussion und der Wahlrechtsänderungen in der Bundesrepublik Deutschland 1949-1983 (Düsseldorf: Droste Verlag, 1985), 91-7, 221-34, 325-32.

15 Elmar M. Hucko, *The Democratic Tradition. Four German Constitutions* (Oxford: Berg Publishers, 1989), 193-265; Martin und Sylvia Greiffenhagen, *Ein schwieriges Vaterland. Zur politischen Kultur Deutschlands* (München: List Verlag, 1979), 87; Samuel Moyn, *Christian Human Rights* (Philadelphia: University of Pennsylvania, 2015), 10-11, 59-60, 63, 75, 87, 96, 107-10, 123; Boldt, *Verfassungsgeschichte*, 324-5; Collings, *Guardians*, xxvi, 54, 60, 106; Fromme, *Weimar*, 24-5, 207-13; Robert G. Moeller, *Protecting Motherhood. Women and the Family in Postwar West Germany* (Berkeley: University of California Press, 1993), 38-56; Mitchell, *Origins*, 175-6.

16 Collings, *Guardians*, xxiv, 1-2, 39-40, 49-51, 58; Günther, *Denken*, 194-5; Arne Riedlinger, "Vom Boykott zur Verfassungsbeschwerde. Erich Lüth und die Kontroverse um Harlans Nachkriegsfilme," in idem/Henne (eds.), *Lüth*, 184; Henne, "Von 0 auf," 208-9, 282-4.

17 Hucko, *Tradition*, 196, 201; Gregg O. Kvistad, "Building Democracy and Changing Institutions: The Professional Civil Service and Political Parties in the Federal Republic of Germany," in John S. Brady et al. (des.), *The Postwar Transformation of Germany. Democracy, Prosperity, and Nationhood* (Ann Arbor: Univ. of Michigan Pr., 1999), 70-4; Dominick Rigoll, *Staatsschutz in Westdeutschland. Von der Entnazifizierung zur Extremistenabwehr* (Göttingen: Wallstein Verlag, 2013), 9-10, 14, 43-50, 84, 88, 109, 111, 121-2; Collings *Guardians*, 39-44; Rüdiger Thomas, "Zur Auseinandersetzung mit dem deutschen Kommunismus in der Bundeszentrale für Heimatdienst," in Stefan Creuzberger/Dierk Hoffmann (eds.), *"Geistige Gefahr" und Immunisierung der Gesellschaft. Antikommunismus und politische Kultur in der frühen Bundesrepublik* (München: Oldenbourg, 2014), 131-3; Fromme, *Weimarer*, 30, 181-93; Katharin Groh, "Zwischen Skylla und Charybdis. Die streitbare Demokratie," in Gusy (ed.), *Schatten*, 432-7, 443-9, 452-3.

18 Andreas Fahrmeir, *Citizenship. The Rise and Fall of a Modern Concept* (New Haven, CT: Yale University Press, 2007), 173-6; Kommers, "Building," 111-13; Christiane Lehmke, "Crossing Borders and Building Barriers: Migration, Citizenship and State Building in Germany," in Jytte Klausen/Loise Tillly (eds.), *European Integration in Social and Historical Perspective, 1850 to the Present* (Lantham: Rowman & Littlefield, 1997), 88, 91, 94-5; Eli Nathans, *The Politics of German Citizenship. Ethnicity, Utility and Nationalism* (Oxford: Berg Publishers, 2004), 235, 237-8.

19 David Clay Large, *Germans to the Front. West German Rearmament in the Adenauer Era* (Chapel Hill: University of North Carolina Press, 1996), 8-9, 194-5, 248, 269; Jarausch, *After Hitler*, 38-9.

20 Michael Schneider, *Demokratie in Gefahr? Der Konflikt um die Notstandsgesetze* (Bonn: Verlag Neue Gesellschaft, 1986), passim; Heinrich Oberreuter, *Notstand und Demokratie. Vom monarchischen Obrigkeits- zum demokratischen Rechtsstaat* (München: Verlag Ernst Vögel, 1978), passim; Ullrich, *Komplex*, 449-52; Wolfgang Kraushaar, "Die Furcht vor einem 'neuen 33.' Protest gegen die Notstandsgesetzgebung," in Dominick Geppert/Jens Hacke (eds.), *Streit um den Staat. Intellektuelle Debatten in der Bundesrepublik 1960-1980* (Göttingen: Vandenhoeck & Ruprecht, 2008), 144-7; Boris Spernol, *Notstand der Demokratie. Protest gegen die Notstandsgesetzgebung und die Frage der NS-Vergangenheit* (Essen: Klartext, 2008), 7-9, 17, 20, 23-4, 32, 77-8, 87, 89-91; Karin Hanshew, *Terror and Democracy in West Germany* (Cambridge: Cambridge University Press, 2012), 45-67.

21 Hucko, *Tradition*, 202; Jutta Limbach, *Die Demokratie und ihre Bürger. Aufbruch zu einer neuen politischen Kultur* (München: C.H. Beck, 2003), 33; Schneider, *Gefahr*, 264–5; Oberreuter, *Notstand*, 214.
22 Jürgen Turek, "Demokratie und Staatsbewußtsein: Entwicklung der Politischen Kultur in der Bundesrepublik Deutschland," in Werner Weidenfeld (ed.), *Politische Kultur und deutsche Frage. Materialien zum Staats- und Nationalbewußtsein in der Bundesrepublik Deutschland* (Köln: Verlag Wissenschaft und Politik, 1989), 236–7; Michaela Richter, "From State Culture to Citizen Culture: Political Parties and the Postwar Transformation of Political Culture in Germany," in Brady et al. (eds.), *Transformation*, 131–3; Klein, *Parteienstaat*, 32, 53, 227, 232–3; Wolfgang Kraushaar, *Die Protest-Chronik 1949-1959. Eine illustrierte Geschichte von Bewegung, Widerstand und Utopie, Vol. I: 1949-1952* (Hamburg: Rogner & Bernhard, 1996), 10; Niclauß, *Weg*, 176, 192–3.
23 Benz, *Besatzungsherrschaft*, 249–51; Ullrich, *Weimar Komplex*, 281–4, 401–10, 438–43; Poscher, "Das Weimar Wahlrechtsgespenst," 258–77; Jesse, *Wahlrecht zwischen Kontinuität und Reform*, 91–7, 221–34, 325–32; Jürgen Dittberner, *Parteienstaat ade? Zur Geschichte und Kultur der politischen Parteien in Deutschland* (Berlin: Logos Verlag, 2015), 11.
24 Borup, *Demokratisierungsprozesse*, 106; Strote, *Lions and Lambs*, 230; Greifenhagen, *Vaterland*, 81; Klein, *Parteienstaat*, 235–8, 262; Forner, *Intellectuals*, 112; Julia Angster, *Konsenskapitalismus und Sozialdemokratie. Die Westernisierung von SPD und DGB* (München: Oldenbourg Verlag, 2003), 355–60, 438, 447; Günther, *Denken*, 201–2;
25 Klein, *Parteienstaat*, 62, 134, 262; Niclauß, *Weg*, 345; Angster, *Konsenskapitalismus*, 11–12, 17, 49, 218–19, 363, 411, 418–20, 438; Günther, *Denken*, 13, 198, 235–9, 276, 291, 298; Mark Edward Ruff, *The Battle for the Catholic Past in Germany, 1945-1980* (New York: Cambridge University Press, 2017), 102–12; James Chappel, *Catholic Modern. The Challenge of Totalitarianism and the Remaking of the Church* (Cambridge: Harvard University Press, 2018), 11, 133–6, 145, 148, 230–1; Michael L. Hughes, "Restitution and Democracy in Germany after Two World Wars," *Contemporary European History* 4:1 (1994), 12–13; Maase, *Populärkultur*, 50–77; Greenberg, *Weimar Century*, 88; Elisabeth Noelle/Erich Peter Neumann (eds.), *Jahrbuch der öffentlichen Meinung 1965-1967* (Allensbach: Verlag für Demoskopie, 1967), 364.
26 Greiffenhagens, *Vaterland*, 124–5; Martin Morlock, "Entdeckung und Theorie des Parteienstaats," in Gusy (ed.), *Schatten*, 250–2; Doering-Manteuffel, *Wie westlich*, 113; Forner, *Intellectuals*, 112; Sontheimer, *Adenauer*, 172; Borup, *Demokratisierungsprozesse*, 169–70; Michael L. Hughes, *Shouldering the Burdens of Defeat. West Germany and the Reconstruction of Social Justice* (Chapel Hill: University of North Carolina Press, 1999), 141, 149, 165, 171–7, 182–3.
27 Dahrendorf, *Society*, 139, 183–5, passim; Richter, "State Culture," 125–7; Klein, *Parteienstaat*, 62, 134; Greiffenhagens, *Vaterland*, 122–3, 125; Claudia Fröhlich/Michael Kohlstruck, "Vergangenheitspolitik in kritischer Absicht," in idem. (eds.), *Engagierte Demokraten. Vergangenheitspolitik in kritischer Absicht* (Münster: Westfälisches Dampfboot, 1999), 22; Hughes, "Restitution," 13; Hughes, *Shouldering*, 134–5.
28 Kommer, "Building Democracy," in Brady (ed.), *Transformation*, 101–3; Richter, "State Culture," 128–32, passim; Günther, *Denken*, 200–1, 272–3, 307; Benz, "Rolle," 241–5, 249; Merritt, *Imposed*, 102; Günther, *Sozialdemokratie und Demokratie*, 250; Borup, *Demokratisierungsprozesse*, 250; Greiffenhagens, *Vaterland*, 356; Klein, *Parteienstaat*, 274.

29 Merritt, *Democracy*, 92, 97–8, 100; Merritt/Merritt, *OMGUS*, 31–2, 99–100; Forner, *Intellectuals*, 186, 188–9; Günther, *Denken*, 192, 198; Gabriel Almond/Sydney Verba, *The Civic Culture. Political Attitudes and Democracy in Five Nations* (Boston: Little, Brown and Company, 1965), 112; Greiffenhagens, *Vaterland*, 106–7.
30 Bracher, "Kanzlerdemokratie," 182; Greenberg, *Weimar Century*, 36–7, 47–8; Lenk, "Konservatismus," 638, 642; Doering-Manteuffel, *Wie westlich,* 121; Kießling, *undeutschen Deutschen*, 166–9; Thomas Großbolting, "Als Laien und Genossen das Fragen lernten. Neue Formen institutioneller Öffentlichkeit im Katholizismus und in der Arbeiterbewegung der sechziger Jahre," in Matthias Frese et al. (eds.), *Demokratisierung und gesellschaftlicher Aufbruch* (Paderborn: Schöningh, 2003), 166–70; Merritt, *Democracy*, 92, 97–8, 100; Elizabeth Noelle/Erich Peter Neumann, *Jahrbuch der öffentlichen Meinung 1947–1955* (Allensbach: Verlag für Demoskopie, 1956), Vol. I, 134–6, 157.
31 Bauerkämper et al., "Einleitung," 23; Doering-Manteuffel, "Kanzlerdemokratie," 4–5, 8, 12–13; Niclauß, *Kanzlerdemokratie*, 64; Kurt Sontheimer, *Die Adenauer Ära. Grundlegung der Bundesrepublik Deutschland* (München: dtv, 1991), 171–2; Ullrich, *Komplex*, 397–8; 412–13, 594, 622; Julia Angster, "Der neue Stil. Die Amerikanisierung des Wahlkampfs und der Wandel im Politikverständnis bei CDU und SPD in den 1960er Jahren," in Frese et al. (eds.), *Demokratisierung*, 195–6.
32 Lamersdorf, "demokratisch," 92–4; Günther Ebersold, *Mündigkeit. Zur Geschichte eines Begriffs* (Frankfurt/M: Peter Lang, 1980), 110–11, 122, passim; Forner, 49, 69, 75, 94–5, 98, 188–9; Fromme, *Weimarer*, 162–4, 221; Kurt Nowak, "Protestantismus und Demokratie in Deutschland. Aspekte der politischen Moderne," in Martin Greschat/Jochen-Christoph Kaiser (eds.), *Christentum und Demokratie im 20. Jahrhundert* (Stuttgart: W. Kohlhammer, 1992), 6, 8–10; Rolf Poscher, "Das Weimarer Wahlrechtsgespenst," in Gusy (ed.), *Schatten*, 274–5; Christoph Kleßmann/Peter Friedemann, *Streik und Hungermärsche im Ruhrgebiet 1946–1948* (Frankfurt: Campus Verlag, 1977), 13, 55–6; Mitchell, *Origins*, 116–17; Heide Fehrenbach, *Cinema in Democratizing Germany. Reconstructing National Identity after Hitler* (Chapel Hill: University of North Carolina Press, 1995), 2, 4, 20; Merritt, *Democracy*, 242–3.
33 Stephen Eisel, *Minimalkonsens und freiheitliche Demokratie. Eine Studie zur Akzeptanz der Grundlagen der demokratischen Ordnung in der Bundesrepublik Deutschland* (Paderborn: Schöningh, 1986), 136–7; "Formierte Gesellschaft," Konrad Adenauer Stiftung, *Geschichte der CDU*, URL: http://www.kas.de/wf/de/71.8787/, accessed April 12, 2016; Niko Switek, "Ludwig Erhard: Formierte Gesellschaft," in Karl-Rudolf Korte (ed.), *"Das Wort hat der Herr Bundeskanzler": Eine Analyse der grossen Regierungserklärungen von Adenauer bis Schröder* (Wiesbaden: VS Verlag für Sozialwissenschaften, 2002), 130–2; Gerd Hardach, "Krisen und Reform der Sozialen Marktwirtschaft. Grundzüge der wirtschaftlichen Entwicklung in der Bundesrepublik der 50er und 60er Jahren," in Axel Schildt et al. (eds.), *Dynamische Zeiten. Die 60er Jahre in den beiden deutschen Gesellschaften* (Hamburg: Hans Christians Verlag, 2000), 211; Volker Hentschel, *Ludwig Erhard. Ein Politikerleben* (München: Olzog, 1996), 561–2; Moses, *Intellectuals*, 177–8; Schneider, *Gefahr*, 156–7, 175.
34 Eugen Kogon, "Das Recht auf den politischen Irrtum," *Frankfurter Hefte* 2:6 (1947), 655; Norbert Frei, *Adenauer's Germany: The Politics of Amnesty and Integration*, trans. Joel Golb (New York: Columbia University Press, 2002), 30, 303–12; Jeffrey Herf, *Divided Memory. The Nazi Past in the Two Germanies* (Cambridge: Harvard University Press, 1997), 6–7, 202–3, 206–8, 220–6, 232–4, 267–8; Steven M.

Schroeder, *To Forget It All and Begin Anew. Reconciliation in Occupied Germany, 1944-1954* (Toronto: University of Toronto Press, 2013), 3-5, 16-18, 44-5, 59-60, 161; Günther, *Denken*, 67-73; Moses, *Intellectuals*, 45-6, 69, 186-7; Clemens Vollnhals, "Einleitung," in idem (ed.), *Entnazifizierung. Politische Säuberung und Rehabilitierung in den vier Besatzungszonen 1945-1949* (München: dtv dokumente, 1991), 55-6, 59-64; Maria Daldrup, "Vergangenheitsbewältigung und Demokratisierungsansätze im Deutschen Journalisten Verband," in Franz-Werner Kersting et al. (eds.), *Die Zweite Gründung der Bundesrepublik. Generationswechsel und intellektuelle Wortergreifungen 1955-1975* (Frankfurt: Steiner Verlag, 2010), 243-68; Fröhlich/Michael Kohlstruck, "Vergangenheitspolitik," 7-22; Ralph Giordano, *Der zweite Schuld. oder Von der Last Deutscher zu sein* (Köln: Kiepenheuer & Witsch, 2000), 16-17, 22, 32, 36-40, passim.

35 Mitchell, *Origins*, 93-6, 101-3, 183-4, 198-200, passim; Anson Rabinbach, "Restoring the German Spirit: Humanism and Guilt in Post-War Germany," 34; Günther, *Denken*, 192; Lenk, "Konservatismus," 638; Fehrenbach, *Cinema*, 7, 102, 119.

36 Mitchell, *Origins*, 5-7, 126-39; Angster, *Konsenskapitalismus*, 15-17, 69; Creuzberger/Hoffmann, "Antikommunismus und politische Kultur in der Bundesrepublik," in idem. (eds.), *Gefahr*, 2, 5-6; Till Kössler, "Die Grenze der Demokratie. Antikommunismus als politische und gesellschaftliche Praxis in der frühen Bundesrepublik," in Creuzberger and Hoffmann (eds.), „*Geistige Gefahr,"* 229-49; Klaus Günther, *Sozialdemokratie und Demokratie 1946-1966. Die SPD und das Problem der Verschränkung innerparteilicher und bundesrepublikanischer Demokratie* (Bonn: Verlag Neue Gesellschaft, 1979), 239-40, 247-8; Erich D. Weitz, "The Ever-Present Other. Communism in the Making of West Germany," in Hanna Schissler (ed.), *The Miracle Years. A Cultural History of West Germany, 1949-1968* (Princeton, NJ: Princeton University Press, 2001), 222-3, 225, passim; Hans Karl Rupp, *APO in der Ära Adenauer. Der Kampf gegen die Atombewaffnung in den fünfziger Jahren* (Köln: Paul Rugenstein, 1980 [1970]), 81, 135-8, 174-5, 187-8, 217-18, 236-7; Doering-Manteuffel, *Wie westlich*, 42.

37 Ullrich, *Komplex*, 382, 394; Marcus Payk, "Antikommunistische Mobilisierung und konservative Revolte. William S. Schlamm, Winfried Martini und der 'kalte Bürgerkrieg' in der westdeutschen Publizistik der späten 1950er Jahre," in Thomas Lindenberger (ed.), *Massenmedien im Kalten Krieg. Akteure, Bilder, Resonanzen* (Köln: Böhlau Verlag, 2006), 136, passim; Edward Ross Dickinson, *The Politics of German Child Welfare from the Empire to the Federal Republic* (Cambridge: Harvard University Press, 1996), 297; Kaspar Maase, *Was macht Populärkultur politisch?* (Wiesbaden: VS-Verlag, 2010), 104-7; Diane Parness, *The SPD and the Challenge of Mass Politics. The Dilemma of the German Volkspartei* (Boulder, CO: Westview Press, 1991), 5-6, 27; Frank Bösch, "Die *Spiegel* Affäre und das Ende der Adenauer Ära," in Martin Doerry/Hauke Janssen (eds.), *Die Spiegel Affäre. Ein Skandal und seine Folgen* (München: Deutsche Verlags-Anstalt, 2013), 223.

38 Schoenbaum, *Spiegel*, 27-149; Ronald F. Bunn, *German Politics and the Spiegel Affair. A Case Study of the Bonn System* (Baton Rouge: Louisiana State University Press, 1968), 37-58, 92-141.

39 Schoenbaum, *Spiegel*, 151-228 and passim; Dorothee Liehr, *Von der Aktion gegen den SPIEGEL zur SPIEGEL Affäre. Zur gesellschaftspolitischen Rolle der Intellektuellen* (Frankfurt: Peter Lang, 2002), 20, 23-4, 29, 63, 65-8, 73-5, 127, 131-7, 186; Günther, *Denken*, 240-2; Bösch, "Protest," 98-104; Bunn, *Politics*, 58-60, 66-79, 130-2, 154-7; Norbert Frei, "*Der Spiegel*, die Freiheit der Presse und die Obrigkeit in der

Bundesrepublik," in Martin Doerry/Hauke Janssen (eds.), *Spiegel Affäre. Ein Skandal und seine Folgen*. (München: Deutsche Verlags-Anstalt, 2013), 39–42; Axel Schildt, "'Augstein raus—Strauß rein.' Öffentliche Reaktionen auf die *Spiegel* Affäre," in Doerry and Jansse (eds.), *Spiegel Affäre*, 179, 188–201; Moses, *Intellectuals*, 172–3; Kießling, *undeutschen Deutschen*, 258–61; Noelle/Neumann, *Jahrbuch*, Vol. 3, 97; Collings, *Guardians*, 79–89; Wolfgang Hoffmann-Riem, "Die Spiegel Affäre—ein Versagen der Justiz?" in Doerry/Janssen (eds.), *Spiegel*, 136–48.

40   Eberhard Pikart, "Auf dem Weg zum Grundgesetz," in Richard Löwenthal/Hans-Peter Schwarz (eds.), *Die zweite Republik. 25 Jahre Bundesrepublik Deutschland— eine Bilanz* (Stuttgart: Seewald Verlag, 1974), 154; Doering-Manteuffel, *Wie westlich*, 36–41, 60–75; Rupieper, *Wurzeln*, 8–9, 171–2, 427; Nina Verheyen, "Eifrige Diskutanten. Die Stilisierung des 'freien' Meinungsaustausches zu einer demokratischen Kulturtechnik in der westdeutschen Gesellschaft der fünfziger Jahren," in Fulda et al. (eds.), *Demokratie im Schatten der Gewalt. Geschichtliche Privaten im deutschen Nachkrieg* (Göttingen: Wallenstein Verlag, 2010), 112–21; Axel Schildt, "Die USA als 'Kulturnation.' Zur Bedetung der Amerikhäuser in den 1950er Jahre," in Alf Lüdtke et al. (eds.), *Amerikanisierung. Traum und Alptraum in Deutschland des 20. Jahrhunderts* (Stuttgart: Franz Steiner Verlag, 1996), 257–69; Kaspar Maase, "Amerikanisierung von unten. Demonstrative Vulgarität und kulturelle Hegemonie in der Bundesrepublik der 50er Jahren," in Lüdtke et al. (eds.), *Amerikanisierung*, 291–313; Manfred Wüstemeyer, "Re-education—die Verlierer lernen Demokratie," in Holger Afflerbach/Christoph Cornelißen (eds.), *Sieger und Besiegte. Materielle und ideelle Neuorientierungen nach 1945* (Tübingen: Francke Verlag, 1997), 224–7.

41   Jennifer Fay, *Theaters of Occupation. Hollywood and the Reeducation of Postwar Germany* (Minneapolis: University of Minnesota Press, 2008), ix–xv, 36–7, 102–6, passim; Doering-Manteuffel, *Wie westlich*, 62–3.

42   Herbert, "Liberalisierung," 32–3; Kießling, *undeutschen Deutschen*, 310, 375, 380–1.

43   Merritt, *Imposed*, 296–7; Christoph Hilgert, "'… den freien, kritischen Geist unter der Jugend zu fördern.' Der Beitrag des Jugendfunks zur zeitgeschichtlichen und politischen Aufklärung von Jugendlichen in den 1950er Jahren," in Franz-Werner Kersting et al. (eds.), *Die zweite Gründung der Bundesrepublik. Generationswechsel und intellektuelle Wortergreifungen 1955–1975* (Stuttgart: Franz Steiner Verlag, 2010), 21–33; Verheyen, "Diskutanten," 100, 103–4, passim; Marcus M. Payk, "'die Herrn fügen sich nicht; sie sind schwierig.' Gemeinschaftsdenken, Generationenkonflikte und die Dynamisierung des Politischen in der konservativen Presse der 1950er und 1960er Jahre," in Franz-Werner Kersting et al. (eds.), *Die zweite Gründung der Bundesrepublik. Generationswechsel und intellektuelle Wortergreifungen 1955–1975* (Stuttgart: Franz Steiner Verlag, 2010), 45, 63.

44   Hodenberg, "Journalisten," 293, 295, 297–304; Christina von Hodenberg, *Konsens und Krise. Eine Geschichte der westdeutschen Medienöffentlichkeit 1945–1973* (Göttingen: Wallstein Verlag, 2006), 441–9, passim; Frank Bösch, "Später Protest. Die Intellektuellen und die Pressefreiheit in der frühen Bundesrepublik," in Dominick Geppert/Jens Hacke (eds.), *Streit um den Staat. Intellektuelle Debatten in der Bundesrepublik 1960–1980* (Göttingen: Vandenhoeck & Ruprecht, 2008), 92–8, 105–8; Gerhard Lampe, *Panorama, Report und Monitor. Geschichte der politischen Fernsehmagazine 1957–1990* (Konstanz: UVK Medien, 2000), 25–7, 56–7, 81–3, 88, 118, 261, 271, 346–7, passim; Wehler, *Gesellschaftsgeschichte*, Vol. 5, 267–75; Lindner, *Jugendprotest*, 232–4; Collings, *Guardians*, 72, 75–8.

45 Kießling, *undeutschen Deutschen*, 304–11; Klein, *Parteienstaat*, 62; Moses, *Intellectuals*, 49–50, 96, 203–5, 212–15; Verheyen, *Diskussionslust*, 11–12, 14–15, 21–2, 148–9, passim; Thomas Küster, "Das Erlernen des Dialogs. Veränderungen des gesellschaftlichen Klimas nach 1968 am Beispiel eines Gütersloher Gymnasiums," in Frese et al. (eds.), *Demokratisierung*, 701–2.

46 Ebersold, *Mündigkeit*, 161, 165, 181; Verheyen, *Diskussionslust*, 11, 43–5; Moses, *Intellectuals*, 127; Christina von Hodenberg, "Konkurrierende Konzepte von 'Öffentlichkeit' in der Ordnungskrise der 60er Jahre," in Frese et al. (eds.), *Demokratisierung*, 212, 214; Franz-Werner Kersting, "'Unruhediskurs.' Zeitgenössische Deutungen der 68er Bewegung," in Frese et al. (eds.), *Demokratisierung*, 723, 735–6; Oberreuter, *Notstand*, 231–3; Lindner, *Jugendprotest*, 53–4, 150, 158; Anselm Doering-Manteuffel, "Politische Kulktur im Wandel," in Andreas Dornheim/Sylvia Greiffenhagen (eds.), *Identität und politische Kultur* (Stuttgart: Verlag W. Kohlhammer, 2003), 148–50.

47 Merritt, *Imposed*, 329–30; Merritt/Merritt, *Opinion*, 191, 195, 211, 314–16; Dahrendorf, *Society*, 65, 295, 315, 319; Ebersold, *Mündigkeit*, 170, 172–3; Arnold Sywottek, "Politik und Verwaltung," in Axel Schildt and Arnold Sywottek (eds.), *Modernisierung im Wiederaufbau. Die westdeutsche Gesellschaft der 50er Jahre* (Bonn: Verlag JHW Dietz Nachf, 1993), 735.

48 Till van Rahden, "Wie Vati Demokratie lernte. Religion, Familie und die Frage der Autorität in der frühen Bundesrepublik Deutschland," in Daniel Fulda et al. (eds.), *Demokratie im Schatten der Gewalt. Geschichte der Privaten im deutschen Nachkrieg* (Göttingen: Wallstein Verlag, 2010), 128–9, 132–3, 142–4, passim; Forner, *Intellectuals*, 3–4, 13–15, 75, 77, 190–1; Stephan Schlak, *Wilhelm Hennis. Szenen einer Ideengeschichte der Bundesrepublik* (München: Beck, 2008), 55–6, 152–6, 161; Greiffenhagens, *Vaterland*, 78; Klaus Allerbeck, *Demokratisierung und sozialer Wandel in der Bundesrepublik Deutschland. Sekundäranalyse von Umfragedaten 1953-1974* (Opladen: Westdeutscher Verlag, 1976), 22; Noelle/Neumann, *Jahrbuch*, Vol. I, 251.

49 Hucko, *Tradition*, 202; Günther, *Sozialdemokratie*, 48–50, 129, 175, 178–83, 224; Parness, *SPD*, 3, 24–5, 58, 84–5; Wehler, *Gesellschaftsgeschichte* Vol. 5, 9–11, 240; Schoenbaum, *Spiegel*, 186; Anders Widfeldt, "Party Membership and Party Representativeness," in Hans-Dieter Klingemann/Dieter Fuchs (eds.), *Citizens and the State* (Oxford: Oxford University Press, 1995), 139; Thomas Mergel, *Propaganda nach Hitler. Eine Kulturgeschichte des Wahlkampfs in der Bundesrepublik 1949–1990* (Göttingen: Wallstein Verlag, 2010), 131–2, 145.

50 Fenske, *Demokratie*, 10, 27–31, 49, 64, 88, 115–16, 148–50, 223–4, 288–95, 360–72, 392–8; Rupp, *APO*, 61, 128, 135, 231–3; Schneider, *Gefahr*, 129, 221.

51 Fenske, *Demokratie*, 115–16; Niclauß, *Kanzlerdemokratie*, 55, 71; Rohe, "State Tradition," 226; Michael L. Hughes, "Restitution," 9–10 and sources cited there; for quotation, Pressekonferenz, December 8, 1950, BAK, B145/I/9.

52 Deutscher Bundestag, *Stenographische Berichte*, 1. Wahlperiode, 1228; Rupp, *APO*, 127, 213–14; Wolfgang Kraushaar, "Ordnung und Protest in der Ära Adenauers," in Frieder Günther (ed.), *Denken vom Staat her. Die bundesdeutsche Staatsrechtslehre zwischen Dezisionismus und Integration 1949-1970* (München: Oldenbourg, 2004), 21, 25; Günther, *Denken*, 241–2; Schneider, *Gefahr*, 133, 144; Greiffenhagen, *Vaterland*, 108; Michael L. Hughes, "Reason, Emotion, Pressure, Violence: Modes of Demonstration as Conceptions of Political Citizenship in 1960s West Germany," *German History* 30:2 (2012), 222–46 (quotation: 241).

53 Horst-Pierre Bothien, *Auf zur Demo! Straßenprotest in der ehemaligen Bundeshauptstadt Bonn 1949-1999. Eine Dokumentation* (Essen: Klartext, 2009),8, 15; Kössler, "Grenzen," in Creuzberger/Hoffmann (eds.), *Geistige*, 236–8; Nick Thomas, *Protest Movements in 1960s West Germany. A Social History of Dissent and Democracy* (Oxford: Berg Publishers, 2003), 116–17; Schneider, *Gefahr*, 246; Ullrich, *Komplex*, 366; Noelle/Neumann, *Jahrbuch*, Vol. 4, 365; idem., *Jahrbuch*, Vol. 5, 230, 464.

54 Gerhard Beier, *Der Demonstrations- und Generalstreik vom 12. November 1948 im Zusammenhang mit der parlamentarischen Entwicklung Westdeutschlands* (Frankfurt/M: Europäische Verlagsanstalt, 1975), 20, 30–2, 37–40, 63–4; Dick Geary, "Social Protest in Western Germany after 1945," *Contemporary German Studies* 1 (1985), 5–15; Kleßmann/Friedemann, *Streiks*, 13, 42–56, 58, 67, 75–6; Kraushaar, "Ordnung," 15–16; Rupp, *APO*, 55–6, 72, 83–4, 91, 139–42, 155–7, 162, 164–73, 190–1, 221–2, 230–1; Schneider, *Gefahr*, 42, 44, 71–4, 76–7, 129–31, 164–5, 183–5, 211–14, 247, 250–1, 256–7.

55 Bothien, *Auf zur Demo!* 14–16, 20–2, 33–4, 44; Hughes, *Shouldering*, 145–8; Hosemann, "Kriegsopferversorgung," 62, 66–7.

56 Mitchell, *Origins of Christian*, 166–8; Fehrenbach, *Cinema*, 92–3, 131–4; Ruff, *Battle*, 5–6, 52–3, 67–71, 176–7, 184, 187; Rupp, *APO*, 91–3, 143–8, 175–6.

57 Bothien, *Auf zur Demo!* 23, 41; Kraushaar, "Ordnung," 21–5; Rupp, *APO*, 54–60, 66–77, 82–3, 89, 98–104, 124–9, 159, 173–89, 196–7, 201, 213–16, 236–7; Thomas, *Protest*, 32, 35–6; Michael Geyer, "Cold War Angst. The Case of West German Opposition to Rearmament and Nuclear Weapons," in Hanna Schissler (ed.), *The Miracle Years. A Cultural History of West Germany, 1949-1968* (Princeton: Princeton University Press, 2001), 388–9, 399, passim.

58 Karl A. Otto, *Vom Ostermarsch zur APO. Geschichte der außerparlamentarischen Opposition in der Bundesrepublik 1960-1970* (Frankfurt: Campus Verlag, 1977), 44–5, 48, 67–8, 72–3, 80–1, 92, 98, 104, 127, 132–3, 178, passim; Holger Nehring, *Politics of Security. British and West German Protest Movements and the Early Cold War, 1945-1970* (Oxford: Oxford University Press, 2013), 142–5, 198–211, passim; Rupp, *APO*, 236–40.

59 Henne/Riedlinger, "Zur Historisierung der Rechtssprechung des Bundesverfassungsgerichts—ein Programm und ihre Folgen," in idem (eds.), *Lüth*, 1–4, 13; Riedlinger, "Boykott," 176–9, 184–5; Henne, "Vom 0," 220–1; Rainer Wahl, "Lüth und die Folgen. Ein Urteil als Weichenstellung für die Rechtsentwicklung," ibid., 371–94; Collings, *Guardians*, 57–62.

60 Thomas Grotum, *Die Halbstarken. Zur Geschichte einer Jugendkultur der 50er Jahre* (Frankfurt: Campus Verlag, 1994), 77–9, 84–5, 140, 146–50, 186–9; Lindner, *Jugendprotest*, 25–31, 44–5, 84–5; Kalb, *Coming of Age*, 87–132; Sabine von Dirke, *"All Power to the Imagination!" West German Counterculture from the Student Movement to the Greens* (Lincoln: University of Nebraska Press, 1997), 20–7 (quotation: 22); Kaspar Maase, "Establishing Cultural Democracy. Youth, 'Americanization,' and the Irresistible Rise of Popular Culture," in Schissler (ed.), *Miracle*, 435, 437, 443; Poiger, *Jazz*, 80–3, 97–100 (quotations: 97–8 and 99).

61 Jarausch, "Amerikanische Einflüsse," 74–5; Bernhard Diestelkamp, "Kontinuität und Wandel in der Rechtsordnung 1945 bis 1955," in Ludolf Herbst (ed.), *Westdeutschland 1945-1955. Unterwerfung, Kontrolle, Integration* (München: Oldenbourg, 1986), 96; Gusy, "Einleitung," 16–19; Anna J. Merritt/Richard L. Merritt (eds.), *Public Opinion in Semisovereign Germany. The HICOG Surveys, 1949-1955*

(Urbana: University of Illinois Press, 1980), 65; Conradt, "German Political Culture," 222–3, 229, 262–3; Ullrich, *Komplex*, 395–7, 412–16; Greiffenhagens, *Vaterland*, 104–5; Herbert, "Liberalisierung," 32, 44.

62 Noelle/Neumann, *Jahrbuch*, Vol. 5, 204, 224.

63 Gerhard A. Ritter/Merith Niehuss, *Wahlen in der Bundesrepublik Deutschland. Bundestag und Landtagswahlen 1946–1987* (München: C.H. Beck, 1987), 74–5; Noelle/Neumann, *Jahrbuch*, Vol. 4, 181, 364; ibid., Vol. 5, 209, 222–3.

64 Noelle/Neumann, *Jahrbuch*, Vol. 3, 255; Noelle/Neumann, *Jahrbuch*, Vol. 5, 223–4, 459; Mitchell, *Origins*, 91–2; Moses, *Intellectuals*, 78, 93, 99–100; Poiger, *Jazz*, 99; Rupp, *APO*, 27–8; Schneider, *Demokratie*, 129–31; Turek, "Demokratie und Staatsbewußtsein," 234; Christina von Hodenberg, "Die Journalisten und der Aufbruch zur kritischen Öffentlichkeit," in Ulrich Herbert (ed.), *Wandlungsprozesse in Westdeutschland. Belastung, Integration, Liberalisierung 1945–1980* (Göttingen: Wallstein Verlag, 2002), 295.

Chapter 5

1 "Daring More Democracy" (October 28, 1969), GHDI, *Two Germanies* (URL: http://germanhistorydocs.ghi-dc.org/sub_document.cfm?document_id=901, accessed 18 August 2016).

2 Frederick C. Engelmann, "Perceptions of the Great Coalition in West Germany, 1966–1969," *Canadian Journal of Political Science* 5:1 (March 1, 1972), 47; Peter Pulzer, *German Politics 1945–1995* (Oxford: Oxford University Press, 1995), 76, 79–81.

3 Oscar W. Gabriel, "Demokratiezufriedenheit und demokratische Einstellungen in der Bundesrepublik Deutschland," *Aus Politik und Zeitgeschichte* B22 (1987), 37.

4 Ronald Inglehart, *The Silent Revolution. Changing Values and Political Styles Among Western Publics* (Princeton, NJ: Princeton University Press, 1977), 7, 9, 15, 21, 23, 33, 51, 58, 60–1, 72, 97, 233; Frankland/Schoonmaker, *Protest*, 54–5, 73; Hans D. Klingemann, "Ideological Conceptualization and Political Action," in Samuel Barnes/Max Kaase (eds.), *Political Action. Mass Participation in Five Western Democracies* (Beverly Hills: Sage Publications, 1979), 345–8, 355–67; Karl-Werner Brand et al., *Aufbruch in eine andere Gesellschaft. Neue soziale Bewegungen in der Bundesrepublik*, 2nd ed. (Frankfurt: Campus Verlag, 1984), 33–5, 58, 154–7; Kurt Sontheimer, *Zeitwende? Die Bundesrepublik Deutschland zwischen alter und alternativer Politik* (Hamburg: Hoffmann und Campe, 1983), 33–41; Heiner Meulemann. "Wertwandel in der Bundesrepublik zwischen 1950 und 1980: Versuch einer zusammenfassenden Deutung vorliegender Zeitreihen," in Dieter Oberndörfer et al. (eds.), *Wirtschaftlicher Wandel, religiöser Wandel und Wertwandel: Folgen für das politische Verhalten in der Bundesrepublik Deutschland*, 391–411.

5 Jeffrey Herf. *Divided Memory. The Nazi Past in the Two Germanies* (Cambridge: Harvard University Press, 1997), 244–5, 249–52, 261, 283–5, 301–12, 333, 349–50; Hermann Lübbe, "Der Nationalsozialismus im deutschen Nachkriegsbewußtsein," *Historische Zeitschrift* 236 (1983), 581–2, 591–3, 596–9; Michael L. Hughes, "'Through No Fault of Our Own.' West Germans Remember Their War Losses," *German History* 18:2 (2000), 193–213; Robert G. Moeller, *War Stories. The Search for a Usable Past in the Federal Republic of Germany* (Berkeley: University of California Press, 2001), 1–21, passim; Christina von Hodenberg, *Das andere Achtundsechzig. Gesellschaftsgeschichte*

einer Revolte (München: C.H. Beck, 2018), 55–61, 65, 67–70; Ralph Giordano, *Die zweite Schuld. oder Von der Last Deutscher zu sein* (Köln: Kiepenheuer & Witsch, 2000), 126–7; Jenny Wüstenberg, *Civil Society and Memory in Postwar Germany* (Cambridge: Cambridge University Press, 2017), 5–9, 32–3, 35–8, 53, 58–60, 63, 93, 162, 228, 235–6, 263; Peter Reichel, *Vergangenheitsbewältigung in Deutschland. Die Auseinandersetzung mit der NS-Diktatur in Politik und Justiz* (München: C.H. Beck, 2007), 67–8, 145–8, 158–76, 181–98, 201, 210–11, 215; Erich Langenbacher, "The Mastered Past? Collective Memory Trends in Germany since Unification," in Jeffrey J. Anderson/Erich Langenbacher (eds.), *From the Bonn to the Berlin Republic. Germany at the Twentieth Anniversary of Unification* (New York: Berghahn Books, 2010), 64–83.

6   Cf. Wüstenberg, *Civil Society*, passim; Herf, *Memory*, 346–47.

7   Nick Thomas, *Protest Movements in 1960s West Germany. A Social History of Dissent and Democracy* (Oxford: Berg, 2003), 49–182; Timothy Scott Brown, *West Germans and the Global Sixties. The Anti-authoritarian Revolt, 1962–1978* (Cambridge: Cambridge University Press, 2013), 85–91, 238, 334–40; Gerhard A. Ritter, "Der Anti-parlamentarismus und Antipluralismus der Rechts- und Linksradikalen," in Kurt Sontheimer et al. (eds.), *Der Überdruß an der Demokratie. Neue Lnke und alte Rechte—Unterschieden und Gemeinsamkeiten* (Köln: Markus Verlag, 1970), 62–9; Eley, *Forging Democracy*, 417–19; Meike Vogel, *Unruhen im Fernsehen. Protestbewegung und öffentlich-rechtliche Berichterstattung in der 1960er Jahren* (Göttingen: Wallstein Verlag, 2010), 85–8; Martin Klimke, *The Other Alliance. Student Protest in West Germany and the United States in the Global Sixties* (Princeton, NJ: Princeton University Press, 2010), 35, 52–4, 58–9, 73–4, passim.

8   See, for example, Christina von Hodenberg/Detlef Siegfried (eds.), *Wo "1968" liegt. Reform und Revolte in der Geschichte der Bundesrepublik* (Göttingen: Vandenhoeck & Ruprecht, 2006), passim; Anna von der Goltz, "A Polarized Generation? Conservative Students and West Germany's '1968,'" in idem (ed.), *"Talkin' 'bout My Generation?" Conflicts of Generation Building and Europe's "1968"* (Göttingen: Wallstein Verlag, 2011), 195–215; Manfred Görtemaker, *Kleine Geschichte der Bundesrepublik Deutschland* (München: C.H. Beck, 2002), 192; Hodenberg, *Achtundsechzig*, 107–10, 148.

9   Hans-Christian Ströbele, "Vorwort," in Martin Kuscha (ed.), *Demonstrationsfreiheit. Kampf um ein Bürgerrecht* (Köln: presseverlagsanstalt, 1986), 7; Janine Gaumer, *Wackersdorf. Atomkraft und Demokratie in der Bundesrepublik 1980–1989* (München: oekom, 2018), 227–8; Dieter S. Lutz, "Amnestie—Eine Einführung," *Sicherheit und Frieden (S+F)/Security and Peace* 11:4 (1993), 188–9; Heiko Drescher, *Genese und Hintergründe der Demonstrationsstrafrechtsreform von 1970* (Düsseldorf, 2005), 176–81, 227–8, 245–8, 270–1, passim.

10 Anselm Doering-Manteuffel, "Fortschrittsglaube und sozialer Wandel. Die Entstehung der anti-AKW Bewegung," in Anselm Doering-Manteuffel et al. (eds.), *Der Brokdorf-Beschluss* (Tübingen: Mohr Siebeck, 2015), 101–2; Lepsius, "Versammlungsrecht," in Doering-Manteuffel, Anselm et al. (eds.), *Brokdorf-Beschluss*, 114–15; Helmut Schwörer-Roßnagel, "Sitzblockade als Nötigung—Eine kurze Bestandsaufnahme," in Narr et al. (eds.), *Ziviler Ungehorsam*, 320–3; Arndt Sinn, "Das Nötigungsstrafbarkeit von Protesthandlungen," in Martin Löhnig et al. (eds.), *Ordnung und Protest. Eine gesamtdeutsche Protestgeschichte von 1949 bis heute* (Tübingen: Mohr Siebeck, 2015), 120–1; Alexander Sedlmaier, *Consumption and Violence. Radical Protest in Cold War West Germany* (Ann Arbor: University of Michigan Press, 2014), 148, 186–9.

11 Doering-Manteuffel et al., "Einführung," in idem. et al. (eds.), *Brokdorf*, 3–4; Oliver Lepsius/Anselm Doering-Manteuffel, "Die Richterpersönlichkeit und ihre protestantische Sozialisation," in Doering-Manteuffel et al. (eds.), *Brokdorf-Beschluss*, 167; Auszug, BVerfG 69, 315, ibid., 17–55; Martin Kutscha, "Der Kampf um ein Bürgerrecht. Demonstrationsfreiheit in Vergangenheit und Gegenwart," in idem. (ed.) *Demonstrationsfreiheit*, 24–5, 46–7; Klaus Dammann, "Rache des Rechtsstaates—oder Aufbegehren der Akteure," in Doering-Manteuffel et al. (eds.), *Brokdorf-Beschluss*, 167–9; Lepsius, "Versammlungsrecht," 113–14, 117–18, 135–8, 142, 149, 153; Limbach, *Demokratie*, 94–5; Karl-Heinz Meyer, *Das neue Demonstrations- und Versammlungsrecht*, 2nd ed. (München: C.H. Beck, 1986), 1–3.

12 Gordon Botsch, *Die extreme Rechte in der Bundesrepublik Deutschland 1949 bis heute* (Darmstadt: WBG, 2012), 27–30, 39–40, 83–4; Dominick Rigoll, *Staatsschutz in Westdeutschland. Von der Entnazifizierung zur Extremistenabwehr* (Göttingen: Wallstein Verlag, 2013), 9, 60–1, 84, 95–7, 255–8, 281, 295, 305–6, 322–4, 337–46, 372–4, 415, 424; Gregg Kvistad, *Statism*, 102, 104–7, 120, 126, 130–2, 208; Karin Hanshew, *Terror and Democracy in West Germany* (Cambridge: Cambridge University Press, 2012), 132–3; Michael März, *Linker Protest nach dem Deutschen Herbst. Eine Geschichte des linken Spektrums im Schatten des "starken Staates," 1977–1979* (Bielefeld: transcript Verlag, 2012), 310, passim.

13 Karin Hanshew, *Terror*, passim; Christian Schletter, *Grabgesang der Demokratie. Die Debatten über das Scheitern der bundesdeutschen Demokratie* (Göttingen: Vandenhoeck & Ruprecht, 2015), 127–9; Ruud Koopmans, *Democracy from Below. New Social Movements and the Political System in West Germany* (Boulder, CO: Westview Press, 1995), 67–8, 70, 74; März, *Protest*, 98–9, 124–5; Hanno Balz, "Kampf um die Grenzen. 'Terrorismus' und die Krise öffentlichen Engagements in der Bundesrepublik der siebziger Jahre," in Knoch (ed.), *Bürgersinn*, 294–310; Jörg Requate "Gefährliche Intellektuelle? Staat und Gewalt in der Debatte über die RAF," in Dominick Geppert/Jens Hacke (eds.), *Streit um den Staat. Intellektuelle Debatten in der Bundesrepublik Deutschland 1960–1980* (Göttingen: Vandenhoeck & Ruprecht, 2008), 251–4, 266–7; Brown, *West Germany*, 352–3; Nicolas Büchse, "Von Staatsbürgern und Protestbürgern. Der Deutsche Herbst und die Veränderung der politischen Kultur in der Bundesrepublik," Knoch, *Bürgersinn*, 311–20.

14 Koopmans, *Democracy*, 65–6; Schletter, *Grabgesang*, 314–37; Rob Burns/Wilfried van der Will, *Protest and Democracy in West Germany. Extra-Parliamentary Opposition and the Democratic Agenda* (New York: St. Martin's Press, 1988), 180–1; Sabine von Dirke, *All Power to the Imagination! The West German Counterculture from the Student Movement to the Greens* (Lincoln: University of Nebraska Press, 1997), 71–2; von Beyme, "Neo-Korporatismus," 236, 260–1; Eva Kolinsky, *Parties, Opposition and Society in West Germany* (New York: St. Martin's Press, 1984), 240–42; März, *Protest*, 81–2, 110–14, 121–2, 124–5, 130–1; Rigoll, *Staatsschutz*, 347, 353–4, 356–60, 365–6, 441, 444, 446–8, 454–6, 472–3; Hanshew, *Terror*, 145–7, passim; Brown, *Global Sixties*, 350–1.

15 Mergel, *Propaganda*, 18, 271–7; Holger Nehring, *The Politics of Security. British and West German Protest Movements and the Early Cold War, 1945–1970* (Oxford: Oxford University Press, 2013), 2–3, 31–6, 84–5, 257–8, 276–7, 287; Schletter, *Grabgesang*, 11; Thomas Rudner/Heinz Stapf, "Das Private ist politisch—Zur Entwicklung eines neuen Politikverständnisses," in Ralf Zoll (ed.), *Vom Obrigkeitsstaat zur entgrenzten Politik. Politische Einstellungen und politisches Verhalten in der Bundesrepublik seit den 60er Jahren* (Opladen: Westdeutscher Verlag, 1999), 115–17; cf. Ulrich Beck, *Risikogesellschaft. Auf dem Weg in eine andere Moderne* (Frankfurt: Suhrkamp Verlag, 1986).

16 Oskar Negt, "Gesellschaftliche Krise und Demonstrationsfreiheit," in Sebastian Cobler et al. (eds.), *Das Demonstrationsrecht* (Reinbek bei Hamburg: Rowohlt, 1983), 18–21; Anselm Doering-Manteuffel, in idem et al. (eds.) *Brokdorf*, 100–3; Büchse, "Von Staatsbürgern," 317–18; Noelle-Neumann/Piel (eds.), *Jahrbuch, 1978–1983*, 113; Kolinsky, *Parties*, 189–93.

17 Claus Offe, "Ungovernability: On the Renaissance of Conservative Theories of Crisis," Jürgen Habermas, *Observations on "The Spiritual Situation of the Age,"* trans. Andrew Buchwalter (Cambridge: MIT Press, 1985), 67–88; Jens Hacke, "Der Staat in Gefahr. Die Bundesrepublik der 1970er Jahre zwischen Legitimitätskrise und Unregierbarkeit," in Dominick Geppert/idem (eds.), *Streit*, 188–206; Gabriele Metzler, "Staatsversagen und Unregierbarkeit," in Konrad Jarausch (ed.), *Das Ende der Zuversicht? Die 70er Jahre als Geschichte* (Göttingen: Vandenhoeck & Ruprecht, 2008), 243–60; Schletter, *Grabgesang*, 151.

18 Joachim Scholtyseck, "Mauerbau und Deutsche Frage. Westdeutsche Intellektuelle und der Kalte Krieg," in Geppert/Hacke (eds.), *Streit*, 74–5; Koopsman, *Democracy*, 43; Steve Breymann, *Why Movements Matter. The West German Peace Movement and U.S. Arms Control Policy* (Albany: State University of New York Press, 2001), 56, 66–7, 94, 96, 118, 28; Noelle-Neumann/Piel, *Allensbacher Jahrbuch*, 320.

19 Jarausch, *After Hitler*, 169; Matthew G. Specter, *Habermas. An Intellectual Biography* (Cambridge: Cambridge University Press, 2010), 8, 22, 134, 175; "Auszug der Entscheidung BVerfGE 69, 315," Anselm Doering-Manteuffel et al. (eds.), *Brokdorf*, 53; Rupert Scholz, "Demokratie und freiheitlicher Rechtsstaat," in Sarcinelli (ed.), *Streitkultur*, 304; Walter Schmitt-Glaeser, *Private Gewalt im politischen Meinungskampf. Zugleich ein Beitrag zur Legitimität des Staates* (Berlin: Duncker & Humblot 1992), 76–7, 93, 100; Isensee, Josef. "Widerstand und demokratische Normalität," in Peter Eisenmann et al. (eds.), *Jurist und Staatsbewußtsein* (Heidelberg: V. Decker und Müller, 1987), 42–4, 46–7; Hasenöhrl, "Zivilgesellschaft," 95, 98; cf. also Michael L. Hughes, "Rechtsstaat and *Recht* in West Germany's Nuclear Power Debate, 1975–1983," *Law and History Review* 33:2 (2015), 411–34.

20 Jarausch, *After Hitler*, 156–7; Mergel, *Propaganda*, 45, 49, 55–7, 60, 82, 194–5, 230, 296–7; Reinhard Mußgnug, "Bürgerinitiativen und die Mitwirkung des Bürgers an der Verwaltung," in Kurt H. Biedenkopf/Rüdiger v. Voss (eds.), *Staatsführung, Verbandsmacht und innere Souveränität. Von der Rolle der Verbände, Gewerkschaften und Bürgerinitiativen in der Politik* (Stuttgart: Verlag Bonn Aktuell, 1977), 159; Riccardo Bavaj, "Verunsicherte Demokratisierer. 'Liberal-kritische' Hochschullehrer und die Studentenrevolte von 1967/68," in Geppert/Hacke (eds.), *Streit*, 151–3, 162; Sontheimer, *Zeitwende?* 44, 62–3, 130, 200–1, 257; Specter, *Habermas*, 103, 112–14, 118–22, 142; Vogel, *Unruhen*, 48–50, 205–10.

21 Dolore L. Augustine, *Taking on Technocracy. Nuclear Power in Germany, 1945 to the Present* (New York: Berghahn Books, 2018), 1–6, 40–2, 51, 78–82, 119; Specter, *Habermas*, 91, 99, 107, 123, 125, 206.

22 Tim Warneke, "Aktionsformen und Politikverständnis der Friedensbewegung. Radikaler Humanismus und die Pathosformel des Menschlichen," in Reichert (ed.), *Alternative*, 455, 461–5; Friederike Bruhöfener, "'Angst vor dem Atom.' Emotionalität und Politik im Spiegel bundesdeutscher Zeitungen," in Patrick Bernhard/Holger Nehring (eds.), *Den Kalten Krieg denken. Beiträge zur sozialen Ideengeschichte seit 1945* (Essen: Klartext, 2014), 285, 287, 292–4, 299–306; von Dirke, *All Power to the Imagination!* 40–1, 97; Nehring, *Security*, 244, 270–1, 298, 301, 303; Susanne Schregel, "Konjunktur der Angst. 'Politik der Subjektivität' und

'neue Friedensbewegung,' 1978-1983," in Bernd Greiner et al. (eds.), *Angst im Kalten Krieg* (Hamburg: Hamburger Edition, 2009), 500-3, passim; Balstier, *Straßenprotest*, 12, 17, 40-1, 51, 54, 108, 179-80, 224, 228, 238; Kathrina Fahlenbrach, "Protest in Television. Visual Protest on Screen," in idem. (ed.), *Media*, 241-2.

23 Brown, *West Germany*, 174-5, 186, 211, 214-15, 303-4, 326; Katharina Karcher, *Sisters in Arms. Militant Feminisms in the Federal Republic of Germany since 1968* (New York: Berghahn Books, 2017), 7-8; Stamm, *Alternative*, 56-64, 101-3, passim; März, *Protest*, 224-31; Claus Richter, *Die überflüssige Generation. Jugend zwischen Apathie und Aggression* (Bodenheim: Athenäum Verlag, 1979), 133-5, 143-4; Görtemaker, *Bundesrepublik*, 283-4; von Dirke, *All Power*, 85-8, 92; Thomas Schutze/Almut Gross, *Die Autonomen. Ursprünge, Entwicklung und Profil der Autonomen* (Hamburg: Konkret Literatur Verlag, 1997), 7, 20-4, 26-9, 36-7, 56-7, 64-6, 148-9, 160-2, passim; Wolfgang Kraushaar, "'Good Vibrations.' Ein Gespräch mit Wolfgang Kraushaar über Popkultur und Protestbewegung," *Mittelweg 36* (2016), 59-60.

24 von Dirke, *All Power to the Imagination!* 40-1, 97; Brown, *West Germans*, 142, 194-5; Nehring, *Security*, 244, 270-1; Schregel, "Konjunktur der Angst," 500-2, passim; Bruhöfener, "'Angst vor dem Atom,' 285, 292-4; Balstier, *Straßenprotest*, 12, 17, 40-1, 51, 54, 108, 179-80, 224, 228, 238; Kathrina Fahlenbrach, "Protest in Television. Visual Protest on Screen," in idem. (ed.), *Media*, 241-2; Vogel *Unruhen*, 205-10, 276, 282-3; Warneke, "Aktionsformen," 455, 461, 463-4.

25 Gerd Langguth, *Protestbewegung—Entwicklung, Niedergang, Renaissance. Die Neue Linke seit 1968* (Köln: Verlag Wissenschaft und Politik, 1983), 40, 237-41; Sontheimer, *Zeitwende?* 27, 130, 189, 197-8, 200-1, 250-1, 256; Bruhöfener, "'Angst vor dem Atom,' 287; Ingo Juchler, *Die Studentenbewegungen in den Vereinigten Staaten und der Bundesrepublik Deutschland der sechziger Jahre* (Berlin: Duncker & Humblot, 1996), 231-2, 244, 253-5; Hughes, "Reason," 232-3.

26 Leggewie, Claus. "Bloß kein Streit! Über die Sehnsucht nach Harmonie und die anhaltenden Schwierigkeiten demokratischer Streitkultur," in Ulrich Sarcinelli (ed.), *Demokratische Streitkultur. Theoretische Grundpositionen und Handlungsalternativen in Politikfeldern* (Bonn: Bundeszentrale für politische Bildung, 1990), 55-7; Joachim Raschke, "Einleitung," in idem (eds.), *Bürger und Parteien. Ansichten und Analysen einer schwierigen Beziehung* (Opladen: Westdeutscher Verlag, 1982), 9, 14-15, 20-2; Bernd Guggenberger, "Bürgerinitiativen: Krisensymptom oder Ergänzung des Parteiensystems?" in Raschke (ed.), *Bürger und Parteien*, 191, 194, 197-8; Peter Haungs, "Bürgerinitiativen und Probleme der parlamentarischen Demokratie in der Bundesrepublik Deutschland," in Guggenberger/Kempf (eds.), *Bürgerinitiativen*, 165; Jutta Limbach, *Die Demokratie und ihre Bürger. Aufbruch zu einer neuen politischen Kultur* (München: C.H. Beck, 2003), 54-5; Eckhard Jesse, *Die Demokratie der Bundesrepublik Deutschland. Eine Einführung in das politische System* (Berlin: Colloquium Verlag, 1978), 103; E. Gene Frankland/ Donald Schoonmaker, *Between Protest and Power. The Green Party in Germany* (Boulder, CO: Westview Press, 1992), 30-1, 59, 103; Noelle-Neumann/Piel (eds.), *Allensbacher Jahrbuch, 1979-1983*, 267.

27 Raschke, "Einleitung," 21-2; Jan-Werner Müller, "Introduction," in idem. (ed.), *German Ideologies since 1945: Studies in the Political Thought and Culture of the Bonn Republic* (New York: Palgrave Macmillan, 2003), 14;Vogel, *Unruhen*, 192-4, 296; Gabrielle Metzler, "Der lange Weg zur sozial-liberalen Politik," in Knoch (ed.), *Bürgersinn*, 165; Breymann, *Movements*, 73-4; Conradt, "Changing German Political Culture," 240.

28 Kurt Sontheimer, *Zeitwende?* 243, 255; Richard Stöss, "Parteien und soziale Bewegungen. Begriffliche Abgrenzung," in Roth/Rucht (eds.), *Neue Bewegungen*, 293–4; Steffani, "Mehrheitsentscheidung," in Roth/Ruchт (eds.), *Neue Bewegungen*, 346; Joachim Raschke, *Soziale Bewegungen. Ein historisch-systematischer Grundriß* (Frankfurt: Campus Verlag, 1985), 278; Guggenberger, "Bürgerinitiativen," 194; Josef Isensee, "Staatshoheit und Bürgerinitiativen," in Biedenkopf/v. Voss (eds.), *Staatsführung*, 140.

29 Brun-Otto Bryde, "Der Beitrag des Bundesverfassungsgerichts zur Demokratisierung der Bundesrepublik," in Robert Christian van Ooyen/Martin H.W. Möller (eds.), *Das Bundesverfassungsgericht im politischen System* (Wiesbaden: Verlag für Sozialwissenschaft, 2006), 322, 325–7; Schmitt-Glaeser, *Gewalt*, 86–7, 163, 215–16, 219–20; Sontheimer, *Zeitwende?* 253–6; Cobler, "Der demonstrative Kampf um die Versammlungsfreiheit. Zur Einführung," in idem et al. (eds.) *Demonstrationsrecht*, 8; Oliver Lepsius, "Versammlungsrecht und gesellschaftliche Integration," in Doering-Manteuffel et al. (eds.), *Brokdorf*, 119–23; Bernd Guggenberger, "Krise der repräsentativen Demokratie. Die Legitimität der Bürgerinitiativen und das Prinzip der Mehrheitsentscheidung," in idem/Kempf (eds.), *Bürgerinitiativen*, 33, 35–6, 42, 48–9; Schletter, *Grabgesang*, 153, 164; Isensee, "Widerstand," 45–6; Steffani, "Mehrheitsentscheidung," 344–53, 358–61.

30 Leggewie, "Bloß kein Streit!" 55; Rudolf Wassermann, "Ist der Rechtsstaat noch zu retten? Zur Krise des Rechtsbewußtseins in unserer Zeit," in Manfred Schleker (ed.), *Widerstand—Protest—Ziviler Ungehorsam* (Sankt Augustin: COMDOK Verlagsabteilung, 1988), 48; Schmitt-Glaeser, *Private Gewalt*, 151–2, 161–2; Zoll, "Einleitung," in idem (ed.), *Vom Obrigkeitsstaat*, 9; Philipp Herder-Dornreich, "Verbände und ihre ordnungspolitische Einordnung," in Biedenkopf/v. Voss (eds.), *Staatsführung*, 53, 69; Dominick Geppert/Jens Hacke, "Einleitung," in idem (eds.), *Streit*, 12, 14.

31 Noelle/Neumann, *Jahrbuch*, 223; Noelle-Neumann/Piel, *Jahrbuch*, 223; Manfred Küchler, "Staats-, Parteien-oder Politikverdrossenheit," in Raschke (ed.), *Bürger*, 41–3; Hans-Dieter Klingemann/Dieter Fuchs (eds.), *Citizenship and the State* (Oxford: Oxford University Press, 1995); Dieter Fuchs et al., "Support for the Democratic System," 338, 341, 348.

32 Brand et al., *Aufbruch*, 231; Gabriele Metzler, *Konzeptionen Politischen Handelns von Adenauer bis Brandt. Politische Planung in der pluralistischen Gesellschaft* (Paderborn: Schöningh, 2005), 358–62, 417–18; Hanshew, *Terror*, 63–6, 80, 113–14, 132, 143–5; Nehring, *Security*, 295; Raschke, *Bewegungen*, 65–6; Breyman, *Movements*, 186; Sedlmaier, *Consumption*, 154–6.

33 Frank Bösch, *Macht und Machtverlust. Die Geschichte der CDU* (Stuttgart: Deutsche Verlags-Anstalt, 2002), 7, 30, 59, 77, 95–6, 135, 143; Mergel, *Propaganda*, 150; Büchse, "Staatsbürgern," 315–18, 323; Hanshew, *Terror*, 35–6, 50–1, 59–62, 136–7, 143–5, 211; Sedlmaier, *Consumption*, 36–7; Sebastian Cobler, "Der demonstrative Kampf um die Versammlungsfreiheit. Zur Einführung," in idem et al. (eds.), *Demonstrationsrecht*, 9–11; Burns/van der Wille, *Protest*, 240; Lepsius, "Versammlungsrecht," 149.

34 Hanshew, *Terror*, 143–5, 192–3, 207–14; Bundesparteitag Karlsruhe, 18./19. 11. 1983, in Hans-Jürgen Beerfeltz et al. (eds.), *Das Programm der Liberalen. Zehn Jahre Programmarbeit der F.D.P. 1980–1990* (Baden-Baden: Nomos Verlagsgesellschaft, 1990), 224; Peter Lösche/Franz Walter, *Die FDP Richtungsstreit und Zukunftszweifel* (Darmstadt: Wissenschaftliche Buchgesellschaft, 1996), 117; Jürgen Dittberner, *Die*

       FDP. Geschichte, Personen, Organisation, Perspektiven. Eine Einführung (Wiesbaden: Verlag für Sozialwissenschaften, 2005), 74.
35 Frankland/Schoonmaker, *Protest*, 36, 59, 105, 108–12, 114, 170; Markus Klein/Jürgen W. Falter, *Der lange Weg der Grünen. Eine Partei zwischen Protest und Regierung* (Munich: Verlag C.H. Beck, 2003), 87–8.
36 Frankland/Schoonmaker, *Protest*, 8–9, 32, 36, 59, 70, 105, 108–12, 117, 153; Klein/Falter, *lange Weg*, 20–6, 52, 56–7, 74–5, 78, 87–97; Herbert Kitschelt, "New Social Movements and the Decline of Party Organization," in Dalton/Kuechler (eds.), *Challenging*, 180, 197; Lutz Metz, "Von den Bürgerinitiativen zu den Grünen. Entstehungsgeschichte der 'Wahlalternativen' in der Bundesrepublik Deutschland," in Roth/Rucht (eds.), *Neue Bewegungen*, 264, 268–76; Brand et al., *Aufbruch*, 107–8; von Dirke, *"All Power,"* 185–6; Alexander, "Alternative Liste," 28, 43–5, 47; Burns/van der Wille, *Protest*, 230–3, 242–7, 264–7; Kristina Schulz, *Der lange Atem der Provokation. Die Frauenbewegung in der Bundesrepublik und Frankreich 1968–1976* (Frankfurt: Campus Verlag, 2002), 234–5.
37 Vogel, *Unruhen*, 252, 256–8, 261–7, 297; Sontheimer, *Zeitwende?* 12; März, *Protest*, 74–5, 84–5; Limbach, *Demokratie*, 54–5; Cobler, *Demonstrationsrecht*, 8; Doering-Manteuffel et al., *Brokdorf-Beschluss*, passim; Volkmar Götz, "Versammlungsfreiheit und Versammlungsrecht im Brokdorf-Beschluß des Bundesverfassungsgerichts," *Deutsches Verwaltungsblatt* 100 (1985), 1347.
38 Karl Werner Brand, "The Political Culture of the New Social Movements," in Dirk Berg-Schlosser/Ralf Rytlewski (eds.), *Political Culture in Germany* (New York: St. Martin's Press, 1993), 116, 124–5; Udo Kempf, "Bürgerinitiativen—Der empirische Befund," in Guggenberger/idem (eds.) *Bürgerinitiativen*, 310–11; Habbo Knoch, "'Mündige Bürger,' oder: Der kurze Frühling einer partizipatorischen Vision. Einleitung," in idem (ed.), *Bürgersinn*, 14–15, 37–8, 46–8; Peter Häberle, "Verfassungsgerichtsbarkeit in der offenen Gesellschaft," in van Ooyen/Möllers (eds.), *Bundesverfassungsgericht*, 37; Koopmans, *Democracy*, 52, 78–9, 107.
39 Max Kaase/Alan Marsh, "Political Action Repertory. Changes over Time and a new Typology," in Barnes/Kaase (eds.), *Political Action*, 140–1; Max Kaase/Kenneth Newton, *Beliefs in Government* (Oxford: Oxford University Press, 1995), 51; Roland Roth/Dieter Rucht, "Soziale Bewegungen und Protest—eine theoretische Zwischenbilanz," in Roth/Rucht (eds.), *soziale Bewegungen*, 646–53.
40 Bettina Westle, "Politische Legitimität und politische Partizipation in der Bundesrepublik Deutschland der achtziger Jahren," in G. Meyer/F. Ryxzka (eds.), *Political Participation and Democracy in Poland and West Germany* (Warsaw: Ośrodek Badań Społecznych, 1991), 87, 99–100, 112; Inglehart, *Revolution*, 15, 294, 298; Armbruster/Leisner, *Bürgerbeteiligung*, 11–12, 18–19, 106–7, 120–3; Kaase/Marsh, "Action Repertory," 146–8, 173, 176–7, 186, 188; Hans Joas/Frank Adloff, "Transformations of German Civil Society: Milieu change and Community Spirit," in John Keane (ed.), *Civil Society. Berlin Perspectives* (New York: Berghahn Books, 2007), 109–10; Matthew Namiroff Lyons, *The Grassroots Network. Radical Nonviolence in the Federal Republic of Germany, 1972–1985*, Western Societies Program. Occasional Paper #20. Center for International Studies, Cornell University, 1988, 4–5; Karl-Heinz Stamm, *Alternative Öffentlichkeit. Die Erfahrungsproduktion neuer sozialen Bewegungen* (Frankfurt: Campus Verlag, 1988), 172–3.
41 Armbruster/Leisner, *Bürgerbeteiligung*, 1, 95, 189, 196–7; Balstier, *Straßenprotest*, 289–91; Burns/van der Will, *Protest*, 34; Hacke, "Staat in Gefahr," 195–6; Haungs, "Bürgerinitiativen," 164; Knoch, "Mündige Bürger," 14–15, 17–18, 33, 37–8; Vogel, *Unruhen*, 61–2.

42 Armbruster/Leisner, *Bürgerbeteiligung*, 114–27, 167–8; Mergel, *Propaganda*, 149–50; Bösch, *Macht*, 7, 30, 59, 96, 100, 135, 143; Schmitt-Glaeser, *Gewalt*, 88; Sontheimer, *Zeitwende?* 132; Max Kaase, "Politische Beteiligung in den 80er Jahren: Strukturen und Idiosynkrasien," in Jürgen Falter et al. (eds.), *Politische Willensbildung und Interessenvermittlung* (Opladen: Westdeutscher Verlag, 1984), 342, 348.

43 Schulz, *Atem*, 81–90, passim; Karcher, *Sisters*, 23, 30, 34–5, 57–8, 62, 73–4; Birgit Meyer, "Die 'unpolitische' Frau. Politische Partizipation von Frauen oder: Habe Frauen ein anderes Verständnis von Politik?" *APZ* 1992 B25-26, 8–13; Thomas, *Protest Movements*, 229–30; Anders Widfeldt, "Party Membership and Party Representativeness," in Klingemann/Fuchs (eds.) *Citizenship*, 148; Conradt, "Changing German Political Culture," 260–1; Langguth, *Protestbewegung*, 233, 251; Görtemaker, *Kleine Geschichte*, 280–1; Breyman, *Movements*, 237; Nehring, *Politics*, 8, 70, 122–5, 212, 222; Frankland/Schoonmaker, *Greens*, 108, 112.

44 Noelle/Neumann, *Jahrbuch, 1968–1973*, 230; Noelle-Neumann/Piel, *Jahrbuch, 1978–1983*, 315; Klaus Allerbeck et al., "Generations and Families. Political Action," in Barnes/Kaase (eds.), *Political Action*, 514–17; Klaus Allerbeck, *Demokratisierung und sozialer Wandel in der Bundesrepublik Deutschland. Sekundäranalyse von Umfragedaten 1953–1974* (Opladen: Westdeutscher Verlag, 1976), 42, 46, 53–9; Inglehart, *Revolution*, 33, 67, 87, 96, 107; Kaase, "Beteiligung," 345; Linda Apel, "Die Opposition der Opposition: Politische Mobilisierung an Oberschulen jenseits der Protestgeneration," in Massimiliano Livi et al. (eds.), *Die 1970er Jahre als schwarzes Jahrzehnt. Politisierung und Mobilisierung zwischen christlichen Demokraten und extremen Rechten* (Frankfurt: Campus Verlag, 2010), 57–8, 65–7, 71–2; Kendall L. Baker et al., *Germany Transformed. Political Culture and the New Politics* (Cambridge: Harvard University Press, 1981), 44, 49, 54–5.

45 Udo Kempf, "Bürgerinitiativen—Der empirische Befund," in Guggenberger/Kempf (eds.), *Bürgerinitiativen*, 305; Breyman, *Movements*, 67, 163, 240; Schulz, *Atem*, 162; Klaus R. Allerbeck et al., "Generations and Families: Political Action," in Barnes/Kaase (eds.), *Political Action*, 505; Table TA. 2, in Barnes/Kaase (eds.), *Political Action*, 545; Wolfgang Beer, "Die Motive des Widerstandes gegen Atomkraftwerke und der Prozeß der Mobilisierung breiter Bevölkerungsschichten," in Hans-Christoph Buchholtz et al. (eds.), *Widerstand gegen Atomkraftwerke. Informationen für Atomkraftgegener und solche, die es werden wollen* (Wuppertal: Peter Hammer Verlag, 1978), 107; Richard Topf, "Beyond Electoral Participation," in Klingemann/Fuchs (eds.), *Citizens*, 88.

46 Guggenberger/Kempe, "Vorbemerkung," in idem (eds.), *Bürgerinitiativen*, 14–17; Guggenberger, "Krise," 30, in Güggenerger/Kempe (eds.), *Bürgerinitiativen*; Russel Dalton/Manfred Kuechler/Wilhelm Bürklin, "The Challenge of new Movements," in Dalton/Kuechler (eds.), *Challenging the Political Order. New Social Movements in Western Democracies* (Oxford: Oxford University Press, 1990), 11–12; Ronald Inglehart, "Values Ideology and Cognitive Mobilization in New Social Movements," in Dalton/Kuechler (eds.), *Challenging*, 53, 58, 60, 64–5; Armbruster/Leisner, *Bürgerbeteiligung*, 136–7, 145, 180, 189–90, 193; Brand et al., *Aufbruch*, 86–7, 89–98; Metz, "Bürgerinitiativen," 263–6; quotation: Helga Grebing, "Demokratie ohne Demokraten? Politisches Denken, Einstellungen und Mentalitäten in der Nachkriegszeit," in Everhard Holtmann (eds.), *Wie neu war der Neubeginn?: Zum deutschen Kontinuitätsproblem nach 1945* (Erlangen: Universitätsbund, 1989), 9; Stephen Milder, *Greening Democracy. The Anti-Nuclear Movement and Political Environmentalism in West Germany and Beyond, 1968–1983* (Cambridge: Cambridge University Press, 2017), 90–1, 105–6, 126–7, 186–8, 237, 245.

47 Steffani, "Bürgerinitiativen," in Guggenberger/Kempe (eds.), *Bürgerinitiativen*, 57–8, 61–2, 72–6; Sebastian Haffner, "Die neue Sensibilität des Bürgers," in Güggenberger/Kempe (eds.), *Bürgerinitiativen*, 86–9; Uwe Thayer, "Bürgerinitiativen—Grüne/Alternativen—Parlament und Parteien in der Bundesrepublik," in Güggenberger/Kempe (eds.), *Bürgerinitiativen*, 124, 129, 135–7, 143; Udo Kempf, "Bürgerinitiativen—Der empirische Befund," in Güggenberger/Kempe (eds.), *Bürgerinitiativen*, 312–14; Armbruster/Leisner, *Bürgerbeteiligung*, 178–81, 187; cf. the articles and discussion in Biedenkopf/v. Voss (eds.), *Staatsführung*, passim; Brand et al., *Aufbruch*, 97, 113–14; Metz, "Bürgerinitiativen," 263.

48 Michael Warner, *Publics and Counterpublics* (New York: Zone Books, 2002), 56–7, 119, 121, 124, 154; Reichert, *Authentizität*, 37–8, 55, 116, 186–99; von Dirke, *Power*, 7, 67–8, 108–9, 116, 178–9, 215–17, passim; Thomas/Gross, *Autonomen*, 33–4; Josef Huber, *Wer soll das alles ändern. Die Alternativen und die Alternativenbewegung*, 7, 26–7, 65; Sven Reichardt/Detlef Siegfried, "Das Alternative Milieu," in idem (eds.), *Das Alternative Milieu. Antibürgerliche Lebensstil und linke Politik in der Bundesrepublik Deutschland und Europa, 1968-1983* (Göttingen: Wallstein Verlag, 2010), 9–13, 16; Dieter Rucht, "Das alternative Milieu in der Bundesrepublik. Ursprünge, Infrastruktur und Nachwirkung," in Reichardt/Siegfried (eds.), *Alternative*, 61–86; Sedlmaier, *Consumption*, 15, 30, 104, 282; Siegfried, "Klingt gut," 10, 15, 21–3, 26–34; Sontheimer, *Zeitwende?* 13–16, 30, 38–40, 62–3; Kraushaar, "Vibrations," 63–6, 77; Stamm, *Alternative Öffentlichkeit*, passim; März, *Protest*, 210–11, 216–22, 225, 227, 387.

49 Thomas Schmid, "Die Wirklichkeit eines Traumes. Versuch über die Grenzen des autopoetischen Vermögens," in Lothar Baier et al. (eds.), *Die Früchte der Revolte. Über die Veränderungen der politischen Kultur durch die Studentenbewegung* (Berlin: Verlag Klaus Wagenbach, 1988), 24–5; Reichert, *Authentizität*, 55, 134–6, 873; Sebastian Haumann/Susanne Schregel, "Andere Räume, andere Städte und die Transformation der Gesellschaft. Hausbesetzungen und Atomwaffenfreie Zone als alternative Raumpraktiken," in Hanno Balz/ Jan-Henrik Friedrichs (eds.), *"All We Ever Wanted ..." Eine Kulturgeschichte europäischer Protestbewegungen der 1980er Jahre* (Berlin: Karl Dietz Verlag, 2012), 53, 55, 57–60, 62–3; Warner, *Publics*, 62, 77; Stamm, *Alternative Öffentlichkeit*, 51–2, 99, 105–7; Brown, *Global*, 329, 354; Pascal Eitler, "'Alternative' Religion. Subjektivierungspraktiken und Politisierungsstrategien im 'New Age' (Westdeutschland 1979-1990)," in Reichert/Siegfried (eds.), *Alternative*, 337, 341–43; Schulz, *Atem*, 65–6, 71, 91–2, 171.

50 Schulz, *Atem*, 14–15, 48, 74–5, 83, 91–2; Brown, *Global*, 280, 296–7; Rudner/Stapf, "Das Private ist politisch," 118, 128–30, passim; Huber, *Wer soll*, 65; Balz/Friedrichs, "Individualität und Revolte," in idem (eds.), *"All We Ever Wanted,"* 18, 28; Reichert, *Authentizität*, 18, 20, 35, 50, 162, 181–2, 219–21.

51 Freia Anders, "Wohnraum, Freiraum, Widerstand. Die Formierung der Autonomen in dn Konflikten um Hausbesetzungen Anfang der achtziger Jahre," in Reichert/Siegfried (eds.), *Alternative*, 473–4, 477, 480, 482, 488 491–2, 494–6; Barbara Sichtermann/Kai Sichtermann, *Das ist unser Haus. Eine Geschichte der Hausbesetzung* (Berlin: Aufbau Verlag, 2017), 12, 14–15, 20–7, 41; Georg Katsiaficas, "Preface," in Bart van der Steen et al. (eds.), *The City Is Ours. Squatting and Autonomous Movements in Europe from the 1970s to the Present* (Oakland, CA: PM Press, 2017), ix–xi; Alex Vasudevan, "Autonomous Urbanisms and the Right to the City: The Spatial Politics of Squatting n Berlin, 1968–2012," in van der Steen et al. (eds.), *City Is Ours*, 132, 136–9; idem, *The Autonomous City. A History of Urban Squatting* (London: Verso, 2007), 102, 110–14, 130, 133; Schmitt-Glaeser, *Private Gewalt*, 52–60, 122–3, 128.

52 Brown, *Global*, 122; Juchler, *Studentenbewegungen*, 270; Vogel, *Unruhen*, 79–86, 261–2; Stamm, *Alternative Öffentlichkeit*, passim; Dirke, *All Power*, 97–8; Ilse Lenz, "Das Private ist politisch? Zum Verhältnis von Frauenbewegung und alternativem Milieu," in Reichardt/Siegfried (eds.), *Alternative*, 375; Hanshew, *Terror*, 244–5; Kathrin Fahlenbrach/Laura Stapane, "Visual and Media Strategies of the Peace Movement," in Christoph Becker-Schaum et al. (eds.), *The Nuclear Crisis. The Arms Race, Cold War Anxiety, and the German Peace Movement of the 1980s* (New York: Berghahn Books, 2016), 222–4.

53 Sven Reichardt, "Große und Sozialliberale Koalition (1966–1974)," in Roland Roth/Dieter Rucht (eds.), *Die soziale Bewegungen in Deutschland seit 1945* (Frankfurt: Campus Verlag, 2008), 78; Vogel, *Unruhen*, passim; Kathrin Fahlenbrach, *Protest-Inszenierungen. Visuelle Kommunikation und kollektive Identitäten in Protestbewegungen* (Wiesbaden: Westdeutscher Verlag, 2002), 32, 117; idem, "Introduction. Media and Protest Movements," in idem (ed.), *Media and Revolt. Strategies and Performances from the 1960s to the Present* (New York: Berghahn Books, 2016), 4–5; Todd Michael Goehle, "Challenging Television's Revolution. Media Representations of 1968 Protests in Television and Tabloids," in Fahlenbrach et al. (eds.), *Media*, 217–18, 223–4; Fahlenbrach, "Protest in Television. Visual Protest on Screen," in Fahlenbrach et al. (eds.), *Media*, 236–46; Peter Hocke, "Auswahlkriterien von Massenmedien bei der Berichterstattung über lokalen Protest. Eine Prüfung der Nachrichtenwert-Theorie anhand medienunabhängiger Demonstrationsdaten," in Heribert Schatz et al. (eds.), *Politische Akteure in der Mediendemokratie. Politiker in den Fesseln der Medien?* (Opladen: Westdeutscher Verlag, 1998), 203–22; Bernd Weisbrod, "Öffentlichkeit als politischer Prozeß," in idem (ed.), *Die Politik der Öffentlichkeit—Die Öffentlichkeit der Politik. Politische Medialisierung in der Bundesrepublik* (Göttingen: Wallstein Verlag, 2003), 16–20; Frank Bösch/Manuel Borutta, "Medien und Emotionen in der Moderne. Historische Perspektiven," in idem (eds.), *Die Massen bewegen: Medien und Emotionen in der Moderne* (Frankfurt: Campus Verlag, 2006), 13–15, 27–30, passim.

54 Peter Gundelach, "Grass-Roots Activity," in Jan v. Deth/Elinor Scarbrough (eds.), *The Impact of Values* (Oxford: Oxford University Press, 1995), 421–2; Max Kaase/Kenneth Newton, *Beliefs in Government* (Oxford: Oxford University Press, 1995), 51, 145; Schulz, *Atem*, 54, 65; Erich Küchenhoff, "Ziviler Ungehorsam als aktiver Verfassungsschutz," in Schleker (ed.), *Widerstand*, 79–80; Roth/Rucht, "Einleitung," in idem (eds.), *Bewegungen seit 1945*, 26–7; Balstier, *Straßenprotest*, 27–8; Brand et al., *Aufbruch*, 130; Breyman, *Movements*, 105, 107, 208, 238; Frank Uekötter, *The Greenest Nation? A New History of German Environmentalism* (Cambridge: MIT Press, 2014), 98.

55 Mußgnug, "Bürgerinitiativen," 159; Elmar Wiesendahl, "Neue soziale Bewegungen und moderne Demokratie," in Roth/Rucht (eds.), *Neue Bewegungen*, 370–1; Schletter, *Grabgesang*, 182, 227; Balstier, *Straßenprotest*, 63–5; Isensee, "Widerstand," 51; Langguth, *Protestbewegung*, 23, 26, 235–6; Negt, "Krise," 17–21; Thomas Blanke/Dieter Sterzel, "Die Entwicklung des Demonstrationsrechts von der Studentenbewegung bis heute," in Cobler (ed.), *Demonstrationsrecht*, 80–1; Noelle/Neumann, *Jahrbuch, 1968–1972*, 230; Noelle-Neumann/Piel, *Jahrbuch, 1978–1983*, 530, 613.

56 Balstier, *Straßenprotest*, 9, 118–26, 129–30, 141–4, 253–4, 289, passim; Alan Marsh/Max Kaase, "Measuring Political Action," in Barnes/Kaase (eds.), *Action*, 70, 81–4; Blanke/Sterzel, "Entwicklung," 58–61; Kolinsky, *Parties*, 190–4; Friedhelm Neidhardt/

Dieter Rucht, "Protestgeschichte der Bundesrepublik Deutschland 1950–1994: Ereignisse, Themen, Akteure," in Rucht (ed.), *Protest*, 35–8, 54–5: Er; Table TA. 2, Barnes/Kaase (eds.), *Political Action*, 545; Noelle-Neumann/Piel, *Jahrbuch, 1978–1983*, 315, 530; Hans-Dieter Schwind et al. (eds.), *Ursachen, Prävention und Kontrolle von Gewalt. Analysen und Vorschläge der Unabhängigen Regierungskommssion zur Verhinderung und Bekämpfung von Gewalt*, Vol. IV. *Politische Gewalt und Repression* (Berlin: Duncker & Humblot, 1990), 17; Gundelach, "Grass-Roots Activity," 424; Bettina Westle, "Zur Akzeptanz der politischen Parteien und der Demokratie in der Bundesrepublik Deutschland," in Max Kaase/Hans-Dieter Klingemann (eds.), *Wahlen und Wähler. Analysen aus Anlass der Bundesgagswahl 1987* (Opladen: Westdeutscher Verlag, 1990), 258, 274–7, 281–2.

57 Klimke, *Other Alliance*, 52–6, 58–9, 70–4; Jarausch, *After Hitler*, 168–9; Dieter Rucht/ Jochen Roose, "Von der Platzbesetzung zum Verhandlungstisch? Zum Wandel von Aktionen und Struktur der Ökologiebewegung," in Rucht (ed.), *Protest*, 199–200; Kaase, "Beteiligung," 340; Roger Karapin, *Protest Politics in Germany. Movements on the Left and Right since the 1960s* (University Park: Pennsylvania State University Press, 2007), 31–2, 46–7; Koopmans, *Democracy*, 82; Warneke, "Aktionsformen," 452–6; Breyman, *Movements*, 124, 156, 177, 184, 193; Balstier, *Straßenpolitik*, 251.

58 Balstier, *Straßenprotest*, 141, 175, 224–5, 242, 245, 250; Burns/van der Wille, *Protest*, 12, 18–19; Lyons, *Grassroots*, 23, 41–2; Meyer, *Demonstrationsrecht*, 3; Gaumer, *Wackersdorf*, 17; Thomas Ellwein, "Politische Verhaltenslehre heute," in Raschke (ed.), *Bürger*, 210; Warneke, "Aktionsformen," 455, 461; Schmitt-Glaeser, *Gewalt*, 19, 25, 44, 108, 224–5.

59 Quotation cited in Jarausch, *After Hitler*, 170; Werner Lindner, *Jugendprotest seit den fünfziger Jahren: Dissens und kultureller Eigensinn* (Opladen: Leske + Budrich, 1996), 173–78; Stamm, *Alternative*, 27, 168; Brown, *Global*, 46, 55–6, 168–9, 238.

60 Balstier, *Straßenprotest*, 61, 115, 127, 178, 225–6, 242; Michael L. Hughes, "Reason, Emotion, Pressure, Violence: Modes of Demonstration as Conceptions of Political Citizenship in 1960s West Germany," *German History* 30 (2012), 241; Wolfganga Rudzio, *Die organisierte Demokratie—Parteien und Verbände in der Bundesrepublik* (Stuttgart: J.B. Metzler, 1977), 17, 34–6, 48, 50; Lyons, *Grassroots*, iv; Küchenhoff, "Ungehorsam," 60–1; Stamm, *Alternative*, 154, 192; Neidhardt/Rucht, "Protestgeschichte," 28, 35; Isensee, "Staatshoheit," 141–2, 148.

61 Lyons, *Grassroots*, 23, 41–2; Balstier, *Straßenprotest*, 61, 225, 307; Sinn, "Nötigungsstrafbarkeit," 117–23, 129–30; Karapin, *Protest*, 47; Raschke, *Bewegungen*, 279–80; Isensee, "Widerstand," 45; Blanke/Sterzel, "Entwicklung," 60, 75–6; Schmitt-Glaeser, *Gewalt*, 19, 23, 25, 75–9, 102, 107–10, 222–3, 227.

62 Klimke, *Other Alliance*, 37, 41, 52–4; Stephen Milder, "Between Grassroots Activism and Transnational Aspirations: Anti-Nuclear Protest from the Rhine Valley to the Bundestag, 1974–1983," *Historical Social Research/Historische Sozialforschung* 39:1 (2014), 191–6; Wassermann, "Rechtsstaat," 45–6; Balstier, *Straßenprotest*, 248–9; Hasenöhrl, "Zivilgesellschaft," 86, 95–6; Dieter Fuchs, "Die Aktionsformen der neuen sozialen Bewegungen," in Falter et al. (eds.), *Willensbildung*, 623–26; Neidhardt/ Rucht, *Protestgeschichte*, 55; Conradt, "Changing German Political Culture," 250.

63 Susanne Schregel, "'Dann sage ich, brich das Gesetz.' Recht und Protest im Streit um den NATO-Doppelbeschluss," in Löhnig et al. (eds.), *Ordnung*, 136–7; Wolf-Dieter Narr et al., "Den eigenen Menschenrechten, nicht dem Staat gehorchen? Von der Freiheit derjenigen, die zivilen Ungehorsam leisten," in idem (eds.), *Ziviler Ungehorsam*, 35, 38; Armin Kuhn, "Zwischen gesellschaftliche Intervention und

radikaler Nischenpolitik. Häuserkämpfe in Berlin und Barcelona am Übergang zur neoliberalen Staat," in Balz/Friedrichs (eds.), *All We Ever Wanted*, 39–40; Wolf-Dieter Narr, "Gewaltfreier Widerstand um der Demokratie und des Friedens willen," in Cobler et al. (eds.), *Demonstrationsrecht*, 142, 152, 156, 160; Dieter Rucht, "Die konstruktive Funktion von Protesten in und für die Zivilgesellschaft," in Ralph Jessen et al. (eds.), *Zivilgesellschaft als Geschichte. Studien zum 19. und 20. Jahrhundert* (Wiesbaden: Verlag für Sozialwissenschaft, 2004), 146–7.

64 Balstier, *Straßenprotest*, 32–3, 145–6, 241–2; Bernd Guggenberger, "Die Grenzen des Gehorsams—Widerstandsrecht und atomares Zäsurbewußtsein," in Roth/Rucht (eds.), *Neue Bewegungen*, 328–33, 340–1; Lyons, *Grassroots*, iv, 23; Michael L. Hughes, "Civil Disobedience in Transnational Perspective: American and West German Anti-Nuclear-Power Protesters, 1975–1982," *Historical Social Research* 39:1 (2014), 242–6.

65 Isensee, "Staatshoheit," in Biedenkopf/v. Voss (eds.), *Staatsführung*, 148, 151; Steffani, "Bürgerinitiativen," in Guggenberger/Kempf (eds.), *Bürgerinitiativen*, 75; Wassermann, "Rechtsstaat," 48, 51; Hasenöhrl, "Zivilgesellschaft," 95–6; Isensee, "Widerstand," 43, 45–8; Scholz, "Demokratie," 309–10; Arnold Köpcke-Duttler, "Ziviler Ungehorsam. Einige verfassungsrechtliche Versuche seiner Behinderung und ihre Kritiker," in Narr et al. (eds.), *Ziviler Ungehorsam*, 309–10; Raschke, *Bewegungen*, 322–3, 327–8.

66 Narr, "Widerstand," 139–40, 143–6, 149–53, 160–7; Hanshew, *Terror*, 66–7, 70–4, 153.

67 Hasenöhrl, "Zivilgesellschaft," 96–7; Isensee, "Widerstand," 41, 50–2; Martin Borowski, "Protest unter Berufung auf die Gewissensfreiheit," in Löhnig et al. (eds.), *Ordnung*, 166–8; Bernd Guggenberger, "Die Grenzen des Gehorsams—Widerstandsrecht und atomares Zäsurbewußtsein," in Roth/Rucht (eds.), *Neue Bewegungen*, 327–8; Scholz, "Demokratie," 309–10; Klaus Arndt, "Widerstand und ziviler Ungehorsam in der Demokratie," in Schleker (ed.), *Widerstand*, 16, 18.

68 Lyons, *Grassroots*, 4, 17, 25–7, 36, 43, 46–7; Theodor Ebert, "Direkte Aktion in Formaldemokratien," in Julius Hans Schoeps and Christopher Dannmann (eds.), *Die rebellischen Studenten. Elite der Demokratie oder Vorhut eines linken Faschismus?* (München: Bechtle Verlag, 1968), 126–36; Theodor Ebert, *Gewaltfreier Aufstand. Alternative zum Bürgerkrieg*, 3rd ed. (Waldkirch: Waldkircher Verlagsgesellschaft, 1983), passim; Wolfgang Sternstein, *Überall ist Wyhl. Bürgerinitiativen gegen Atomanlagen aus der Arbeit eines Aktionsforschers* (Frankfurt: Haag+Herchen Verlag, 1978), 112, 253; Narr et al., "Menschenrechte," 35, 42–3; Sven Reichardt, "Civility, Violence, and Civil Society," Keane, *Civil Society*, 142–4, 159; Hasenöhrl, "Zivilgesellschaft," 84–5, 89–91; Hanshew, *Terror*, 179–84, 248–50, 257.

69 Andrew S. Tomkins, *Better Active than Radioactive! Anti-Nuclear Protest in 1970s France and West Germany* (Oxford: Oxford University Press, 2016), 57–8, 150–1, 165–6; Hanshew, *Terror*, 82–8, 92–3, 95, 103–4, 106, 174; Lindner, *Jugendprotest*, 188–91, 205–10, 222–8.

70 Balstier, *Straßenprotest*, 65, 107, 113, 253–6; Hasenöhrl, "Zivilgesellschaft," 91–2, 94; Narr et al., "Menschenrechte," 31, 36; Jake Smith, "Apathy, Subversion, and the Network Sublime: Envisioning Youth Unrest in West Germany, 1980–1987," in Knud Andresen and Bart van der Steen (eds.), *A European Youth Revolt? Youth Movements, Revolt, and Transgression in the 1980s* (Basingstoke: Palgrave, 2016), 236–8; Breyman, *Movements*, 167, 189; Raschke, *Bewegungen*, 282–5; Frankland/Schoonmaker, *Protest*, 59, 91; Kaase, "Beteiligung," 348; Noelle-Neumann/Köcher, *Jahrbuch*, 606, 608.

71 Rolf Zoll, "Partizipatorische Demokratievorstellung. Eine Alternative zum obrigkeitsstaatlichen Demokratieverständnis," in Zoll (ed.), *Obrigkeitsstaat*, 19-21; Metzler, "Staatsversagen," 246-9; Specter, *Habermas*, 197-200; Sarcinelli, "Weg," 35; v. Hodenberg/Siegfried, *"1968,"* 115-20, 126; Roland Roth/Dieter Rucht, "Soziale Bewegungen und Protest—eine theoretische und empirische Bilanz," 659, 664-5; Brown, *Global*, 147-8; Jan Hansen, "Der Protest und die Mächtigen: Zu den Auswirkungen von Friedensbewegung, Nuclear Weapons Freeze Campaign und Solidarnosc auf das Bonner 'Establishment,'" in Balz/Friedrichs (eds.), *"All We Ever Wanted,"* 234; Armbruster/Leisner, *Bürgerbeteiligung*, 1, 93, 95.

72 Narr, "Widerstand," 146; Sontheimer, *Zeitwende*, 130-3, 242-4, 255-6, 270; Guggenberger, "Krise," 24-6, 32-3; Horst Zilleßen, "Bürgerinitiativen und repräsentative Demokratie." In Guggenberger/Kempf (eds.), *Bürgerinitiativen*, 104-5, 111-12; for quotation, Sebastian Haffner, "Bürgerinitiativen: Sinn und Unsinn," in Guggenberger/Kempf (eds.), *Bürgerinitiativen*, 12; Hoeres, "Aneignung und Abwehr der Demoskopie im intellektuellen Diskurs der frühen Bundesrepublik," In Kersting et al. (eds.), *zweite Gründung*, 71-2, 77-8, 80; Knoch, "Mündige Bürger," 31-2; Limbach, *Demokratie*, 50; Raschke, *Bewegungen*, 65.

73 Armbruster/Leisner, *Bürgerbeteiligung*, 1, 95; Balstier, *Straßenprotest*, 290-1, passim; Lepsius, "Versammlungsrecht," 117-18, 142; Narr et al., "Menschenrechte," 26-33; Roth/Rucht, "sozialen Bewegungen," 659, 664-6; Specter, *Habermas*, 65, 101, 134, 181, passim; Noelle-Neumann/Piel, *Jahrbuch*, Vol. 8, 236; Jarausch, *After Hitler*, 180; Frankland/Schoonmaker, *Protest*, 2, 24, 90, 99; Torsten Gass-Bolm, "Revolution im Klassenzimmer? Die Schülerbewegung 1967-1970 und der Wandel der deutschen Schule," in von Hodenberg/Siegfried (eds.), *1968*, 130, passim; BVerfGE 69, 315, Brokdorf (URL: http://www.servat.unibe.ch/dfr/bv069315.html, accessed October 14, 2016); Kaase, *Development*, iii.

74 Gundelach, "Grass-Roots Activity," 436.

Chapter 6

1 Christoph Kleßmann, *Die doppelte Staatsgründung. Deutsche Geschichte 1945-1955* (Göttingen: Vandenhoeck & Ruprecht, 1989), 67-78, 135-42, 202-8, 261-9, passim; Lothar Kettenacker, *Germany since 1945* (Oxford: Oxford University Press, 1997), 18-20, 25-6, 46-8; Gareth Pritchard, *The Making of the GDR, 1945-1953. From Antifascism to Stalinism* (Manchester: Manchester University Press, 2000), 56-75, 110-15, 124-32, 142-3; Martin Sabrow, "Dictatorship as Discourse. Cultural Perspectives on SED Legitimacy," in Konrad H. Jarausch (ed.), *Dictatorship as Experience. Towards a Socio-Cultural History of the GDR* (New York: Berghahn Books, 1999), 196, passim.

2 Mark Allinson, *Politics and Popular Opinion in East Germany, 1945-1968* (Manchester: Manchester University Press, 2000), 140-1; Thomas Friedrich, "Aspekte der Verfassungsentwicklung und der individuellen (Grund)Rechtsposition in der DDR," in Helmut Kaelble et al. (eds.), *Sozialgeschichte der DDR* (Stuttgart: Klett-Cotta, 1994), 487, 490-2; Heike Amos, *Die Entstehung der Verfassung in der Sowjetische Besatzungszone/DDR 1946-1949. Diktatur und Widerstand* (Münster: Lit Verlag, 2006), 322-6; André Steiner, *The Plans that Failed. An Economic History of the GDR*, trans. Ewald Osers (New York: Berghahn Books, 2010), 1, 4; Peter C. Caldwell,

Dictatorship, State Planning, and Social Theory in the German Democratic Republic (Cambridge: Cambridge University Press, 2003), 3; Roger Woods, *Opposition in the GDR under Honecker 1971-1985. An Introduction and Documentation* (New York: St. Martin's Press, 1986), 4.

3   Albert S. Lindemann, *A History of European Socialism* (New Haven, CT: Yale University Press, 1983), 176-7; Caldwell, *Dictatorship*, 9-10, 54, 183; Winfried Thaa, "Das Demokratiekonzept der DDR im Umbruch?" in Ilse Spittmann-Rüle/Gisela Helwig (eds.), *Die DDR im vierzigsten Jahr. Geschichte, Situation, Perspektiven* (Köln: Deutschland Archiv, 1989), 159; Woods, *Opposition*, 3, 5, 17; Stefan Wolle, *Die heile Welt der Diktatur: Alltag und Herrschaft in der DDR 1971-1989* (Berlin: C.H. Links Verlag, 1998), 99; Patrick von zur Mühlen, *Aufbruch und Umbruch in der DDR: Bürgerbewegungen, kritische Öffentlichkeit und Niedergang der SED Herrschaft* (Bonn: Verlag JHW Dietz Nachf., 2000), 41, 82; Barbara Koelges, *Der Demokratische Frauenbund. Von der DDR-Massenorganisation zum modernen politischen Frauenverband* (Wiesbaden: Westdeutscher Verlag, 2001), 58; Andreas Glaeser, *Political Epistemics. The Secret Police, the Opposition, and the End of East German Socialism* (Chicago: University of Chicago Press, 2011), 121-4; Verfassung der Deutschen Demokratischen Republik vom 6. April 1968, Art. 47, http://www.documentarchiv.de/ddr/verfddr.html#KAPITEL%204-2 (accessed June 22, 2018).

4   Verfassung der Deutschen Demokratischen Republik vom 6. April 1968, Art. 54, http://www.documentarchiv.de/ddr/verfddr.html#KAPITEL%204-2 (accessed June 1, 2017); Amos, *Entstehung*, 328-9; Wolle, *Welt*, 84, 120; Bernd Lindner, *Die demokratische Revolution in der DDR 1989/90* (Bonn: Bundeszentrale für politische Bildung, 2010), 40; Laurence H. McFalls, *Communism's Collapse, Democracy's Demise? The Cultural Content and Consequences of the East German Revolution* (New York: New York University Press, 1995), 34-35, Woods, *Opposition*, 9; Mary Fulbrook, "Germany for the Germans? Citizenship and Nationality in a Divided Nation," in David Casarani/idem (eds.), *Citizenship, Nationality and Migration in Europe* (London: Routledge, 1996), 95-97.

5   Allinson, *Politics*, 23-4, 27-31, 34-5, 37-3, 151-3; Amos, *Entstehung*, 311-17, 324-7; Gary Bruce, *Resistance with the People. Repression and Resistance in Eastern Germany 1945-1955* (London: Rowman & Littlefield, 2003), 76-81, 86-92, 102-3, 127-32, 163-4, passim; Sigrid Meuschel, *Legitimation und Parteiherrschaft. Zum Paradox von Stabilität und Revolution in der DDR 1945-1989* (Frankfurt: Suhrkamp, 1992), 39, 46, 51-2; Armin Mitter/Stefan Wolle, *Untergang auf Raten. Unbekannte Kapitel der DDR Geschichte* (München: Bertelsmann, 1993), 37, 40, 143-53.

6   Meuschel, *Legitimation*, 87, 89-93, 173-3; Friedrich, "Aspekte," 485; Felix Mühlberg, *Bürger, Bitten und Behörden. Geschichte der Eingabe in der DDR* (Berlin: Karl Dietz Verlag, 2004), 13, 53-5, 166; Ilko-Sascha Kowalczuk, *Endspiel. Die Revolution von 1989 in der DDR* (Munich: C.H. Beck, 2009), 44-5.

7   Paul Betts, *Within the Walls. Private Life in the German Democratic Republic* (Oxford: Oxford University Press, 2010), 26; Ned Richardson-Little, "Dictatorship and Dissent: Human Rights in East Germany in the 1970s," in Jan Eckel/Samuel Moyn (eds.), *The Breakthrough: Human Rights in the 1970s* (Philadelphia: University of Pennsylvania Press, 2013), 49-52, 58-66; Peter E. Quint, *The Imperfect Union. Constitutional Structures of German Unification* (Princeton, NJ: Princeton University Press, 1997), 38-40; Meuschel, *Legitimation*, 85-6, 91-4, 148, 172-3; Mühlberg, *Bürger*, 156-7.

8   Bruce, *Resistance*, 84–7, 100–3, 122–3, 125–6, 128–32, 161–2; Mary Fulbrook, *Anatomy of a Dictatorship. Inside the GDR 1949–1989* (Oxford: Oxford University Press, 1995), 46–55, 98–9; Woods, *Opposition*, 3, 17–18; Mühlen, *Aufbruch*, 83; von zur Mühlen, *Aufbruch*, 17–19; Wolle, *Welt*, 143–50; Sylvia Klötzer/Siegfried Lokatis, "Criticism and Censorship Negotiating Cabaret Performance and Book Production," in Jarausch (ed.), *Dictatorship*, 252–3, 255, 258–9; Wayne C. Bartee, *A Time to Speak Out. The Leipzig Citizen Protests and the Fall of East Germany* (Westport: Praeger, 2000), 7–8, 108–9; Betts, *Walls*, 31–41, 45–6; Gisela Diewald-Kerkamnn, "Vertrauensleute, Denunzianten, Geheime und Inoffizielle Mitarbeiter in diktatorischen Regimen," in Arnd Bauerkämper et al. (eds.), *Doppelte Zeitgeschichte. Deutsch-deutsche Beziehungen 1945–1990* (Bonn: J.H.W. Dietz Nachf., 1998), 288–92.

9   Steiner, *Plans*, 105–6, 108–9, 115; Detlef Pollack, "Modernization and Modernization Blockages in GDR Society," in Jarausch (ed.), *Dictatorship*, 33; Jonathan R. Zatlin, *The Currency of Socialism. Money and Political Culture in East Germany* (Cambridge: Cambridge University Press, 2009), 47.

10 Gareth Dale, *Popular Protest in East Germany, 1945–1989* (London: Routledge, 2005), 62–4; Meuschel, *Legitimation*, 127, 228, 234, 307; Iris Häuser, *Gegenidentitäten. Zur Vorbereitung des politischen Umbruchs in der DDR* (Münster: Lit, 1996), 83–4; Jonathan Grax, *The Role of the Masses in the Collapse of the GDR* (New York: St. Martin's Press, 2000), 21, 150.

11 Wolle, *Welt*, 173–7; Ute Gerhard, "Die staatlich institutionalisierte 'Lösung' der Frauenfrage. Zur Geschichte der Geschlechterverhältnisse in der DDR," in Hartmut Kaelble et al. (eds.), *Sozialgeschichte der DDR* (Stuttgart: Klett-Cotta, 1994), 383–403; Christiane Lemke, *Die Ursachen des Umbruchs. Politische Sozialisation in der ehemaligen DDR* (Opladen: Westdeutscher Verlag, 1991), 228–51; Andrew I. Port, *Conflict and Stability in the German Democratic Republic* (Cambridge: Cambridge University Press, 2007), 206–13, 253–7; Jeanette Z. Madarász, *Conflict and Compromise in East Germany, 1971–1989. A Precarious Stability* (Basingstoke: Palgrave Macmillan, 2003), 68–75, 97–9, 132–4.

12 Meuschel, *Legitimation*, 28–9, 42–3, 70–1, 101, 153–4; Richard Millington, *State, Society and Memories of the Uprising of 17 June 1953 in the GDR* (Basingstoke: Palgrave Macmillan, 2014), 27–8, 34–5; Christiane Olivo, *Creating a Democratic Civil Society in East Germany* (Basingstoke: Palgrave Macmillan, 2001), 63; Christian Joppke, *East German Dissidents and the Revolution of 1989. Social Movements in a Leninist Regime* (New York: NYU Pr., 1995), ix, 31–3, 58–9, 195–6; Clara M. Oberle, "Antifascist Heroes and Nazi Victims. Mythmaking and Political Reorientation in Berlin, 1945–47," in Konrad Jarausch et al. (eds.), *Different Germans, Many Germanies. New Transatlantic Perspectives* (New York: Berghahn Books, 2017), 108–19; John Torpey, *Intellectuals, Socialism, and Dissent* (Minneapolis: University of Minnesota Press, 1995), 14–15, 31, 79, 135–7.

13 Wolle, *Welt*, 121 (quote), 268–9; Pritchard, *Making*, 17; Ralf Rytlewski, "Ein neues Deutschland? Merkmale, Differenzierungen und Wandlungen in der politischen Kultur der DDR," in Hans Georg Wehling (ed.), *Politische Kultur in der DDR* (Stuttgart: Verlag W. Kohlhammer, 1989), 18–19, 24; Manfred Opp de Hipt, "Deutsche Lust am Staat? Marxist-leninistisches Staatsverständnis und realsozialistische Wirklichkeit in der DDR," Wehling, *Politische Kultur*, 54, 63; Heinz Niemann, *Hinterm Zaun: politische Kultur und Meinungsforschung in der DDR* (Berlin: Edition ost, 1995), 64; Greg Eghigian, "Homo Munitus. The East

German Observed," in Katherine Pence and Paul Betts (eds.), *Socialist Modern. East German Everyday Culture and Politics* (Ann Arbor: University of Michigan Press, 2008), 38–42; Rudolf Woderich, "Mentalitäten zwischen Anpassung und Eigensinn," *Deutschland Archiv* 25:1 (1992), 23–5.

14 Wolle, *Welt*, 126, 227; Christoph Geisel, *Auf der Suche nach einem dritten Weg. Das politische Selbstverständnis der DDR-Opposition in den achtziger Jahren* (Berlin: C.H. Links Verlag, 2005), 174–5; Gerd Meyer, "Deutschland: Ein Staat—zwei politische Kulturen," in Hans-Georg Wehling (ed.), *Länderprofile. Politische Kulturen im In- und Ausland* (Stuttgart: W. Kohlhammer Verlag, 1993), 30; Elisabeth Noelle-Neumann/Renate Köcher (eds.), *Allensbacher Jahrbuch der Demoskopie 1984–1992* (München: K.G. Saur, 1993), 607, 610.

15 Lemke, *Ursachen*, 72, 78, 115–18; Martin Jander, "Formierung und Krise der Opposition in der DDR. Die 'Initiative für unabhängige Gewerkschaften,'" in Ulrike Poppe et al. (eds.), *Zwischen Selbstbehauptung und Anpassung. Formen des Widerstandes und der Opposition in der DDR* (Berlin: CH Links Verlag, 1995), 299; Meuschel, *Legitimation*, 18, 62, 73, 91, 98–9, 115, 148, 209–10; Simone Tippach-Schneider, "Blumen für die Hausgemeinschaft. Kollektivformen in der DDR—ein Überblick," in Andreas Ludwig (ed.), *Fortschritt, Norm und Eigensinn. Erkundungen im Alltag der DDR* (Berlin: C.H. Links Verlag, 1999), 243–52; Joppke, *Dissidents*, 36, 104, 180, 207.

16 Peter Voss, "Citizens against the State: Political Protest in the GDR," in Klaus-Dieter Opp et al. (eds.), *Origins of a Spontaneous Revolution: East Germany, 1989* (Ann Arbor: University of Michigan Press, 1995), 18; Esther von Richthofen, *Bringing Culture to the Masses. Control, Compromise and Participation in the GDR* (New York: Berghahn Books, 2009), 114; Fulbrook, *Anatomy*, 139–40 (quote); Peter Förster/Günther Roski, *DDR zwischen Wende und Wahl. Meinungsforscher analysieren den Umbruch* (Berlin: Links Druck Verlag, 1990), 43; Jan Palmowski, *Inventing a Socialist Nation. Heimat and the Politics of Everyday Life in the GDR, 1945–1990* (Cambridge: Cambridge University Press, 2009), 75–8; Port, *Conflict*, 140–2; Jeffrey Kopstein, *The Politics of Economic Decline in East Germany, 1945–1989* (Chapel Hill: University of North Carolina Press, 1997), 165.

17 Meuschel, *Legitimation*, 86–7, 98–9, 176–7, 206, 210; Lemke, *Ursachen*, 13, 78–80, 137; Thaa, "Demokratiekonzept," 152, 156, 158; Ellen Bos, *Leserbriefe in Tageszeitungen der DDR: zur "Massenverbundenheit" der Presse, 1949–1989* (Opladen: Westdeutscher Verlag, 1993), 5, 59, 61, 65–6, 89, 118–21, 140–1, 226; Mary Fulbrook, *The People's State. East Germany Society from Hitler to Honecker* (New Haven: Yale University Press, 2005), 191–2, 235–8, 257; Niemann, *Zaun*, 35; Koelges, *Demokratische Frauenbund*, 54, 56–7, 59, 64–5, 71; Olaf Klenke, *Kampfauftrag Mikrochip Rationalisierung und sozialer Konflikt in der DDR* (Hamburg: VSA-Verlag, 2008), 128–31.

18 Margarete Mommsen-Reindl, "Partizipation—Osteuropäische Länder," in Dieter Nohlen (ed.), *Wörterbuch Staat und Politik* (München: Piper, 1998), 471–2; Ilko-Sascha Kowalczuk,"Von der Freiheit, Ich zu sagen. Widerständiges Verhalten in der DDR," in Poppe et al. (eds.), *Selbstbehauptungen*, 96–7; Mark Allinson, "Public Opinion," in Patrick Major and Jonathan Osmond (eds.), *The Workers' and Peasants' State. Communism and Society in East Germany under Ulbricht 1945-1971* (Manchester: Manchester Univ. Pr., 2002) 100; Linda Fuller, *Where Was the Working Class? Revolution in East Germany* (Urbana: University of Illinois Press, 1999), 35–6, 56; Lemke, *Ursachen*, 215–16 (quotation).

19 Allinson, *Politics*, 36-7, 95, 123-4, 128, 154-5, 161-3, 166; Meyer, "Deutschland," 17; Mary Fulbrook, "'Normalisation' in the GDR in Retrospect: East German Perspectives on Their Own Lives," in idem (ed.), *Power*, 279, 304; McFalls, *Collapse*, 87-8; Dale, *Protest*, 72-3; Pollock, *Protest*, 205-7; Konrad H. Jarausch, "Care and Coercion. The GDR as Welfare Dictatorship," in Jarausch (ed.), *Dictatorship*, 62; Alf Lüdtke, "Practices of Survival—Ways of Appropriating 'The Rules': Reconsidering Approaches to the History of the GDR," in Mary Fulbrook (ed.), *Power and Society in the GDR, 1961-1979. The "Normalisation of Rule?"* (New York: Berghahn Books, 2013), 184-5; Palmowski, *Inventing*, 14, 304, 311-13; Wolle, *Welt*, 227, 265, 336; Thomas Gensicke, *Mentalitätswandlungen im Osten Deutschlands seit den 70er Jahren* (Speyer: Forschungsinstitut für Öffentliche Verwaltung, 1992), 27, 31, 38, 41.

20 Lemke, *Ursachen*, 110-12, 119; Wolle, *Welt*, 145; Josef Schmid, *Kirchen, Staat und Politik in Dresden zwischen 1975 und 1989* (Koln: Bohlau Verlag, 1998), 270; Millington, *State*, 123-4, 181; Palmoski, *Inventing*, 12-13, 138-44; Patrick Major, *Behind the Berlin Wall. East Germany and the Frontiers of Power* (Oxford: Oxford University Press, 2010), 13-14.

21 Gerd Meyer, "Der versorgte Mensch. Sozialistischer Paternalismus: bürokratische Bevormundung und soziale Sicherheit," in Wehling (ed.), *Kultur*, 29-53; Häuser, *Gegenidentitäten*, 55, 96-7, 168, 177; Detlef Pollack, "Kulturelle, soziale und politische Bedingungen der Möglichkeit widerständigen Verhaltens in der DDR," in Ehrhardt Neubert/Bernd Eisenfeld (eds.), *Macht—Ohmacht—Gegenmacht. Grundfragen zur politische Gegnerschaft in der DDR* (Bremen: Edition Temmon, 2001), 356; Madarász, *Conflict*, 142-4, 154, 170-1; Harry Müller, "Lebenswerte und nationale Identität," in Walter Friedrich/Helmut Griese (eds.), *Jugend und Jugendforschung in der DDR* (Opladen: Leske + Budrich, 1991), 125-6; Dale, *Protest*, 90, 144; Lothar Probst, *Ostdeutsche Bürgerbewegung und Perspektiven der Demokratie. Entstehung, Bedeutung und Zukunft* (Köln: Bund Verlag, 1993), 88; Detlef Pollack, *Politische Protest. Politisch alternative Gruppen in der DDR* (Opladen: Leske + Budrich, 2000), 143, 245; Kowalczuk, *Endspiel*, 78-9.

22 Woods, *Opposition*, 30; Lemke, *Ursachen*, 164-5, 208-10, 224-6; Woderich, "Mentalitäten," 26, 28; Palmowski, *Inventing*, 14, 115-16; Ralf Rytlewski, "Soziale Kultur als politische Kultur: die DDR," in Dirk Berg-Schlosser/Jakob Schissler (eds.), *Politische Kultur in Deutschland* Sonderheft 18 (1987), *Politische Vierteljahresschrift*, 241; Betts, *Walls*, 142-5; McFall, *Collapse*, 85-90; Martin Sabrow, "Der Wille zur Ohnmacht und die Macht des Unwillens," in Neubert/Eisenfeld (eds.), *Macht*, 339.

23 Häuser, *Gegenidentitäten*, passim; Mühlen, *Aufbruch*, 141, 156-9, 164-71, 176-7; Rüddenklau, *Störenfried*, 24-5, 182; Stefan Wolle, "'Es geht seinen sozialistischen Gang,'" in Neubert/Eisenfeld (eds.), *Macht*, 307-15; Detlef Pollack, *Politischer Protest*, 68-76; Geisel, *Suche*, 175, 199, 203-4; Poppe et al., "Opposition," 22; Klaus Michael, "Zweite Kultur oder Gegenkultur? Die Subkulturen und künstlerische Szenen der DDR und ihr Verhältnis zur politischen Opposition," in Detlef Pollack/Dieter Rink (eds.), *Zwischen Verweigerung und Opposition. Politischer Protest in der DDR 1970-1989* (Frankfurt: Campus Verlag, 1997), 122-5.

24 Neubert, *Opposition*, 128-30; Mark Fenemore, *Sex, Thugs and Rock 'n' Roll. Teenage Rebels in East Germany* (New York: Berghahn Books, 2009), 22-3, 31-2, 70-81, passim; Toby Thacker, "The fifth column. Dance music in the early German Democratic Republic," in Patrick Major/Jonathan Osmond (eds.), *The Workers' and Peasants' State. Communism and Society in East Germany under Ulbricht 1945-1971* (Manchester: Manchester University Press, 2002), 227-40; Dorothee Wierling,

"Der Staat, die Jugend und der Westen. Texte zu Konflikten der 1960er Jahre," in Alf Lüdtke/Peter Becker (eds.), *Akten. Eingaben. Schaufenster. Erkundungen zu Herrschaft und Alltag* (Berlin: Akademie Verlag, 1997), 225–30; Gabrielle Stiller, "Pädagogismus versus Unterhaltung. Zur Entwicklung der Unterhaltungskultur in der DDR," in Wehling (ed.), *Kultur*, 147–52.

25 Dorothee Wierling, "Youth as an Internal Enemy. Conflicts in the Education Dictatorship of the 1960s," in Pence/Betts (eds.), *Socialist Modern*, 162–72; Neubert, *Opposition*, 128–31, 205–7; Wolle, *Welt*, 43–4, 51, 73–4.

26 von zur Mühlen, *Aufbruch*, 16, 21, 25, 43–6, 70, 103, 113, 157; Ulrike Poppe, "'Der Weg ist das Ziel.' Zum Selbstverständnis und der politischen Rolle oppositioneller Gruppen in der 80er Jahren," in Poppe et al. (eds.), *Selbstbehauptung*, 254–5; Olivo, *Creating*, 71–2, 78–82; Hubertus Knabe, "Samisdat—Gegenöffentlichkeit in den 80er Jahren," in Eberhard Kuhrt et al. (eds.), *Opposition in der DDR von den 70er Jahren zum Zusammenbruch der SED-Herrschaft* (Opladen: Leske + Budrich, 1999), 299–314; Judd Stitziel, "Shopping, Sewing, Networking, Complaining. Consumer Culture and the Relationship between State and Society in the GDR," in Pence/Betts (eds.), *Socialist Modern*, 272.

27 Major, *Behind the Wall*, 191–3; Lemke, *Ursachen*, 187–92, 276–7; Torpey, *Intellectuals*, 126; Wolle, *Welt*, 70–1, 135–6; McFalls, *Collapse*, 52; Neubert, *Opposition*, 143–4; Klaus Dieter Opp, "The Dynamics of the Revolution," in Klaus-Dieter Opp et al. (eds.), *Origins of a Spontaneous Revolution: East Germany, 1989* (Ann Arbor: University of Michigan Press, 1995), 195.

28 McFalls, *Collapse*, 9, 62–4; Fuller, *Where*, 78–9; Probst, *Bürgerbewegung*, 75–6; Olivo, *Creating*, 2–3, 9, 84–5; Joppke, *Dissidents*, 18–21, 104, 106; Steven Pfaff, *Exit-Voice Dynamics and the Collapse of East Germany* (Durham, NC: Duke University Press, 2006), 61–2.

29 von Richthofen, *Bringing Culture*, 10–12; Peter Hübner, *Konsens, Konflikt und Kompromiß. Soziale Arbeiterinteressen und Sozialpolitik in der SBZ/DDR 1945–1970* (Berlin: Akademie Verlag, 1995), 95, 212, 241, passim; Ina Merkel/Felix Mühlberg, "Eingaben," in Ina Merkel (ed.), *Wir sind nicht die Meckerecke der Nation. Briefe an das Fernsehen der DDR* (Berlin: Schwarzkopf und Schwarzkopf, 2000), 36; Niemann, *Zaun*, 77, 89–90; Meyer, "versorgte Mensch," 36; Jonathan Zatlin, "Ausgaben und Eingaben. Das Petitionsrecht und der Untergang der DDR," *Zeitschrift für Zeitgeschichte* 10 (1997), 902–17; Lemke, *Ursachen*, 126; Mühlberg, *Bürger*, 245.

30 Zatlin, *Currency*, 236 (quotation), 319; Betts, *Walls*, 186–7; Esther von Richthofen, "Communication and Compromise: The Prerequisites for Cultural Participation," in Fulbrook (ed.), *Power*, 131, 144; Stitziel, "Shopping," 272; Merkel/Mühlberg, "Eingaben," 37; Palmowski, *Inventing*, 110, 138–44, 183–4, 226–34, 302–4; Port, *Conflict*, 146–7.

31 Stitziel, "Shopping," 271, 274; Allinson, "Public Opinion," 99, 102–7; Mitter/Wolle, *Untergang*, 111–12, 130; Port, *Conflict*, 76–78, 115–17, 140–2; Fuller, *Working Class*, 147–8, 150; Bernd Gehrke, "Demokratiebewegung und Betriebe in der 'Wende,'" in idem/Renate Hürtgen (eds.), *Der betriebliche Aufbruch im Herbst 1989: Die unbekannte Seite der DDR-Revolte* (Berlin: Bildungswerk Berlin, 2001), 225, 228; Müller, "Lebenswerte," 128, 141; Rytlewski, "Soziale Kultur," 244; Dale, *Protest*, 90, 176.

32 Jarausch, *Different Germans*, 170–2; Richardson-Little, "Dictatorship," 58–60, 62.

33 Grax, *Masses*, 136–7; Madardsz, *Conflict*, 125; Major, *Behind the Wall*, 177–8, 255–6; Uwe Thaysen, "Die ausgelieferte Opposition," in Neubert and Eisenfeld (eds.), *Macht*, 39–47.

34 Ehrhart Neubert, "Was waren Opposition, Widerstand und Dissidenz in der DDR? Zur Kategorisierung politischer Gegnerschaft," in Kuhrt et al. (eds.), *Opposition*, 24–5; Pollack, *Protest*, 98–102, 124–6; Uwe Thaysen, *Der Runde Tisch. Oder: Wo blieb das Volk? Der Weg der DDR in die Demokratie* (Opladen: Westdeutscher Verlag, 1990), 52, 175–6; Rüddenklau, *Störenfried*, 76–7; Pollack, *Protest*, 72, 223–5; Lindner, *Revolution*, 68–9; Martin Jander et al., "DDR-Opposition in den 70er und 80er Jahren. Ein Beitrag zu Geschichte und Forschungszustand," in Klaus Schroeder (ed.), *Geschichte und Transformation des SED-Staates: Beiträge und Analyse* (Berlin: Akademie Verlag, 1994), 242–3; Thaa, "Demokratiekonzept," 158; Irene Kukutz, "'Nicht Rädchen, sondern Sand im Getriebe, den Kreis der Gewalt zu durchbrechen.' Frauenwiderstand in der DDR in den 80er Jahren," in Poppe (ed.), *Selbstbehauptungen*, 298; Richardson-Little, "Human Rights," 170–2; Olivo, *Creating*, 94, 123, 128–33.

35 Pfaff, *Exit-Voice*, 48–9, 60; Neubert, *Opposition*, 234–9; Meuschel, *Legitimation*, 161–3, 183–9, 208; von zur Mühlen, *Aufbruch*, 33–5, 198–200; Poppe, "Opposition," 18; Pollack, *Protest*, 124–5; Kowalczuk, "Freiheit," 110–11; Fulbrook, *Anatomy*, 256–62.

36 Mühlberg, *Bürger*, 7, 14, 27, 57, 61, 70–1, 92, 122, 129, 133, 181; Zatlin, *Currency*, 235–6, 238, 289, 293, 295–9, 310; Betts, *Walls*, 173–90; Katherine Pence, "Women on the Verge. Consumers between Private Desires and Public Crisis," in Pence/Betts (eds.), *Socialist Modern*, 295–8; Merkel/ Mühlberg, "Eingaben," 15–43; Siegfried Suckut et al., "Einleitung," in idem (eds.), *Volksstimmen. "Ehrlich aber deutlich"—Privatbriefen an die DDR-Regierung* (Munich: dtv Verlag, 2016), 50–67; Major, *Berlin Wall*, 202, 210–12; Madarász, *Conflict*, 149–53; Thomas Lindenberger, "Die Diktatur der Grenzen. Zur Einleitung," in idem (ed.), *Herrschaft und Eigen-Sinn in der Diktatur. Studien zur Gesellschaftsgeschichte der DDR* (Köln: Bohlau Verlag, 1999), 32; Klenke, *Kampfauftrag*, 161–2, 168, 170, 181, 208–9, 226, 228, 231, 233; Dale, *Protest*, 69, 176.

37 Renate Hürtgen, "'Keiner hatte Ahnung von Demokratie, im Betrieb sowieso nicht.' Vom kollektiven Widerstand zur Eingabe oder Warum die Belegschaften 1989 an Anfang eines Neubeginn standen," in Gehrke/idem (eds.), *Aufbruch*, 200; Mühlen *Aufbruch*, 54; Rüddenklau, *Störenfried*, 62–3; Klenke, *Kampfauftrag*, 214–16, 231, 233; Betts, *Walls*, 190 (quotation).

38 Gerd Meyer, "Der versorgte Mensch. Sozialistischer Paternalismus: bürokratische Bevormundung und soziale Sicherheit," 38–9; Port, "Grumble Gesellschaft," 802–4; Amos, *Entstehung*, 261–4, 351; Major, *Berlin Wall*, 53–4; Allinson, "Public Opinion," 105–6; Richardson-Little, "Dictatorship," 56.

39 Port, *Conflict*, 195–6; Kowlaczuk, "Freiheit," 106–8; Torsten Diedrich, *Waffen gegen das Volk. Der 17. Juni 1953 in der DDR* (München: Oldenbourg, 2003), 45, 83, 127–8, 133, 163; Peter Hübner, "Arbeitskonflikte in Industriebetrieben in der DDR nach 1953," Diedrich, *Waffen*, 178–91; idem, *Konsens*, 179–80, 187–97; Major, *Berlin Wall*, 138–40; Klenke, *Kampfauftrag*, 15, 217–19, 249, 256; Lindner, *Revolution*, 119; Thaysen, *Runde Tisch*, 65.

40 Kopstein, *Politics*, 24, 28, 31, 37–8, 157, 160, 184; Zatlin, *Currency*, 161; Dale, *Protest*, 67–9; Hübner, *Konsens*, 124–5, 128–9, 185–7, 196–9, 202, 209, 221; idem, "Arbeitskonflikte," 179, 184, 187–91; Klenke, *Kampfauftrag*, 186–9, 197, 201, 204–5, 214; Port, *Conflict*, 42, 154–5, 164–81; idem, "Grumble Gesellschaft," 798–9.

41 Gareth Pritchard, "Workers and the Socialist Unity Party of Germany in the Summer of 1953," in Major/Osmond (eds.), *Workers' and Peasants' State*, 117–22; Major, *Berlin Wall*, 168; Mitter/Wolle, *Untergang*, 116–17, 466, 510–11; Dieter Rink,

"Ausreiser, Kirchengruppen, Kulturopposition und Reformer. Zu Differenzen und Gemeinsamkeiten in Opposition und Widerstand in der DDR in den 70er und 80er Jahren," in Pollock/idem (eds.), *Verweigerung*, 65; Torpey, *Intellectuals*, 121; Klenke, *Kampfauftrag*, 181, 228, 231, 240; Fuller, *Where?* 148–50.

42 Jonathan Osmond, "Kontinuität und Konflikt in der Landwirtschaft der SBZ/DDR zur Zeit der Bodenreform und der Vergenossenschaftlichung, 1945–1961," in Bessel/Jessen (eds.), *Grenzen*, 151–63; Bruce, *Resistance*, 167–9; Neubert, *Opposition*, 32, 131–3; Port, *Conflict*, 28–33; Arnd Bauerkämper, "Abweichendes Verhalten in der Diktatur. Probleme einer kategorialen Einordnung am Beispiel der Kollektivierung der Landwirtschaft in der DDR," in Bauerkämper et al. (eds.), *Doppelte*, 297–311.

43 Dale, *Protest*, 16–32, 50–5; Allinson, *Politics*, 54–61; Bruce, *Resistance*, 176–255; Mitter/Wolle, *Untergang*, 92–137; Diedrich, *Waffen*, passim; Christoph Klessmann/Bernd Stöver, "Einleitung: Das Krisenjahr 1953 und der 17. Juni in der DDR in der historischen Forschung," in idem (eds.), *1953—Krisenjahr des Kalten Krieges in Europa* (Köln: Bohlau Verlag, 1999), 20–5; Ulrich Mählert (ed.), *Der 17. Juni 1953. Ein Aufstand für Einheit, Recht und Freiheit* (Bonn: Verlag J.H.W. Dietz Nachf, 2003), 8, 19, 30, passim; Zatlin, *Currency*, 72.

44 Woods, *Opposition*, 30; Torpey, *Intellectuals*, 60–4; Mitter/Wolle, *Untergang*, 451–4; Hubertus Knabe, "Kirche, Intellektuelle, unorganisierter Protest. Unabhängige politische Bestrebungen in der DDR in den 60er und 70er Jahren," in Bernd Lindner et al. (eds.), *Zum Hebst '89. Demokratische Bewegung in der DDR* (Leipzig: Forum Verlag, 1994), 33–4; Fulbrook, *Anatomy*, 194–9; Neubert, *Opposition*, 163–7; Allinson, *Politics*, 149–55.

45 Betts, *Walls*, 57; Andrew Demshuk, *Demolition on Karl Marx Square. Cultural Barbarism and the People's State in 1968* (New York: Oxford University Press, 2017), passim; Klenke, *Kampfauftrag*, 13, 161–2, 210–11; Dale, *Protest*, 68–72; Neubert, *Opposition*, 32, 64–7, 131–2, 177–80; Port, "Grumble Gesellschaft," 788–90; Bernd und Peter Eisenfeld, "Widerständiges Verhalten in der DDR 1979–1982," in Kuhrt et al. (eds.), *Opposition*, 83–90; Torpey, *Intellectuals*, 67; Pritchard, *Making*, 190–202.

46 Port, *Conflict*, 128–31; Diedrich, *Waffen*, 30; Bruce, *Resistance*, 164–5; Allinson, *Politics*, 67–8, 128–9; Fulbrook, *Anatomy*, 1–3.

47 Allinson, *Politics*, 87–111; Madarász, *Conflict*, 46–51, 179–83; Fulbrook *Anatomy*, 110–24; Bartee, *Time*, 63–74; Erhart Neubert, "Political Culture of Protestantism in the GDR," in Berg-Schlosser/Rytlewski (eds.), *Political Culture*, 155–66; Hubertus Knabe, "Der lange Weg zur Opposition—unabhängige politische Bestrebungen 1983 bis 1988," in Kuhrt et al. (eds.), *Opposition*, 143–6; Neubert, *Opposition*, 26, 868–9; Peter Voss, "The Role of the Church," in Opp et al. (eds.), *Origins*, 119–36; Probst, *Bürgerbewegung*, 42–3, 57–61; Schmid, *Kirchen*, 50, 55, 283–8, 401–4, passim; Lemke, *Ursachen*, 176–9, 183–5.

48 Joppke, *Dissidents*, 73–83, 87–98; Poppe, "Weg," 246–7, 249; Bernd und Peter Eisenfeld, "Verhalten," 91–104; Bartee, *Time to Speak*, 5–9, 68–70, 105, 115; Kukutz, "Nicht Rädchen," 273–83; Schmid, *Kirchen*, 38–41, 43, 186, 191, 247–50, 329–30, 379–81.

49 Rüddenklau, *Störenfried*, 44, 47, 61–4, 125–9, 198–202, 281–2; Probst, *Bürgerbewegung*, 48–50, 61–70; Lindner, *Revolution*, 15–16; Schmid, *Kirchen*, 336–47, 423–1; Dale, *Protest*, 102–3.

50 Richardson-Little, "Dictatorship," 58–5; Probst, *Bürgerbewegung*, 78–9; Torpey, *Intellectuals*, 92–9; Knabe, "Bewgungen," 556–7; Wolfgang Templin/Reinhard Weißhuhn, "Die Initiative Frieden und Menschenrechte," in Kuhrt (ed.), *Opposition*, 171–81; von zur Mühlen, *Aufbruch*, 126, 142–3, 222–3; Lindner, *Revolution*, 78–9.

51 Peter Voss, "The Goals of the Revolution," in Opp et al. (eds.), *Origins*, 49; Meuschel, *Legitimation*, 228, 234–9; Gehrke, "Demokratiebewegung," 222–4; Joppke, *Dissidents*, 123–4; Häuser, *Gegenidentitäten*, 14, 191–2, 194–6, 223; Grax, *Role*, 45–6, 51–2, 150; Gensicke, *Mentatlitätsentwicklungen*, 13–14.

52 Gensicke, *Mentalitätsentwicklungen*, 13–14; Lindner, *Revolution*, 18–19; Neubert, *Opposition*, 205; Christiane Gern, "Commonsense Explanations of the Revolution," in Opp et al. (eds.), *Origins*, 211–14; Häuser, *Gegenidentitäten*, 196, 223; Alf Lüdtke, "'…den Menschen vergessen?'—Oder: Das Jahre im Blick von MfS, SED, FDGB und staatlicher Leitung," in Lüdtke/Becker (eds.), *Akten*, 207–8; Andreas Ludwig, "Fortschritt, Norm und Eigensinn. Vorwort," in idem (ed.), *Fortschritt*, 12; Niethammer, "Structure," 14–15.

53 von zur Mühlen, *Aufbruch*, 45, 132–3; Graz, *Role*, 61, 105; Pfaff, *Exit-Voice*, 52–8; Matthias Damm/Mark R. Thompson, "Die spontane Macht der Gewaltlosen. Eine übersehene Erklärung fur den Untergang der DDR," in Michael Richter/Clemens Vollnhals (eds.), *Jahre des Umbruchs: Friedliche Revolution in der DDR und Transition in Ostmitteleuropa* (Göttingen: Vandenhoeck & Ruprecht, 2012), 213–14; Walter Süß, "Die Stimmungslage der Bevölkerung im Spiegel von MfS Berichten," in Eberhard Kuhrt et al. (eds.), *Die SED-Herrschaft und ihr Zusammenbruch* (Opladen: Leske + Budrich, 1996), 238; Klenke, *Kampfauftrag*, 232; Friedrich/Griese, *Jugend*, 137–8.

54 Pollock, *Protest*, 98, 112; Rüddenklau, *Störenfried*, 294–5, 297–8; Torpey, *Intellectuals*, 150; Wolle, *Welt*, 309.

55 Schmid, *Kirchen*, 435–6, 440–1; Major, *Berlin Wall*, 238; Rüddenklau, *Störenfried*, 292, 295; Opp, "Dynamics," 195; Neubert, *Opposition*, 810–15; Kowalczuk, *Endspiel*, 318–332; but cf. Pollack, *Protest*, 133, who discounts any impact.

56 Bernd Eisenfeld, "Die Ausreisebewegung—eine Erscheinungsform widerständigen Verhaltens," in Poppe (ed.), *Selbstbehauptung*, 192–223; Major, *Berlin Wall*, 207, 216–21, 242–3; Kowalczuk, *Endspiel*, 346–51; Müller, "Lebenswerte," in Friedrich/Griese (eds.), *Jugend*, 143; Joppke, *Dissidents*, 129–32, 134–40, 144, 150; Pollock, *Protest*, 111–18, 216, 219–20; Torpey, *Intellectuals*, 72–3, 75, 110–13, 129–30, 149; Fulbrook, *Anatomy*, 276–7.

57 Fulbrook, *People's State*, 241; Pfaff, *Exit-Voice*, 121–3, 140, 173; Sabrow, "Wille," 323–6; Andrew Port, "'There Will Be Blood.' The Violent Underside of the 'Peaceful' East German Revolution of 1989," in José Brunner et al. (eds.), *Politische Gewalt in Deutschland. Ursprünge—Ausprägungen—Konsequenzen* (Göttingen: Wallenstein Verlag, 2014), 218–27.

58 Port, "There Will Be Blood," 222, 225–5; Pfaff, *Exit-Voice*, 7, 110, 120–3, 140, 167–8, 173–4, 179, 181–6, 263; Süß, "Stimmungslage," 255; Pollack, *Protest*, 80–1, 242; Sabrow, "Wille," 317, 323–8; Charles Maier, *Dissolution. The Crisis of Communism and the End of East Germany* (Princeton, NJ: Princeton University Press, 1997), 142–4, 153; Lindner, *Revolution*, 115; Klenke, *Kampfauftrag*, 245; Klaus-Dieter Opp, "Like Hawks in a Trap: Why Wasn't the Protest Movement Crushed?" in idem et al. (eds.), *Origins*, 178–9; Gern, "Commonsense," Opp, *Origins*, 220–1; Pollock, *Protest*, 121, 217, 241–444.

59 Port, "Blood," 225, 227, 232; Lindner, *Revolution*, 89, 93–6, 100–2; Pfaff, *Exit-Voice*, 104, 127–9, 140; Peter Voss, "Why Were the Protests Peaceful?" in Opp et al. (eds.), *Origins*, 91–7; Damm/Thompson, "Macht," 203–4, 210–13, 215–16; Thaysen, *Tisch*, 159; Pollock, "Bedingungen," 317–18; Mitter/Wolle, *Untergang*, 536–8; Fulbrook, *Anatomy*, 254; Pollock, *Protest*, 242–3.

60 Pfaff, *Exit-Voice*, 103, 116, 129, 166; Lindner, *Revolution*, 85–9, 92, 96–9, 108, 113, 121; Voss, "Citizens," 19, 24; Damm/Thompson, "Macht," 210; McFalls, *Collapse*, 71–2; Detlef Pollock, "Der Zusammenbruch der DDR als Verkettung getrennter Handlungslinien," in Konrad Jarausch and Martin Sabrow (eds.), *Weg in den Untergang. Der innere Zerfall der DDR* (Göttingen: Vandenhoeck & Ruprecht, 1999), 53; Pollock, *Protest*, 216; Uwe Schwabe, "Der Herbst '89 in Zahlen—Demonstrationen und Kundgebungen vom August 1989 bis zum April 1990," in Eberhard Kuhrt et al. (eds.), *Opposition in der DDR von den 70er Jahren bis zum Zusammenbruch der SED-Herrschaft* (Opladen: Leske + Budrich, 1999), 720.

61 Voss, "Citizens," 11–12; Pollack, *Protest*, 215, 231; Mary Elise Sarotte, *The Collapse. The Accidental Opening of the Berlin Wall* (New York: Basic Books, 2014), 40; Geisel, *Suche*, 78–9; Damm/Thompson, "Macht," 208–10; Klaus-Dieter Opp and Christiane Gern. "The Social Causes of the Revolution," in Opp et al. (eds.), *Origins*; Fuller, *Where?* 33–7, 84–5, 106; Hartmut Zwahr, *Ende einer Selbstzerstörung. Leipzig und die Revolution in der DDR* (Beucha: Sax Verlag, 2014), 59, 108, passim; Pfaff, *Exit-Voice*, 115–16; Pollock, "Zusammenbruch," 63–4, 68; Klenke, *Kampfauftrag*, 246; Schwabe, "Herbst '89," 722, 731.

62 Joppke, *Dissidents*, 158–9; Pollock, "Zusammenbruch," 65–6; Major, *Berlin Wall*, 251–2; Fulbrook, *Anatomy*, 257–9; Konrad H. Jarausch, *The Rush to German Unity* (Oxford: Oxford University Press, 1994), 3–4, 59–63; Sarotte, *Collapse*, 85–124, passim.

63 Joppke, *Dissidents*, 162; Bartee, *Time*, 134–5; Gensicke, *Mentalitätsentwicklungen*, 47; Fulbrook, *Anatomy*, 259–62; Maier, *Dissolution*, 200–1; Sabrow, "Wille," 346–7; idem, "Der Konkurs der Konsensdiktatur. Überlegungen zur inneren Zerfall der DDR aus kulturgeschichtlichen Perspektive," in Jarausch/idem (eds.), *Weg*, 103–4.

64 Pollock, *Protest*, 177–8; Poppe, "Weg," 267–8; Dale, *Protest*, 165–7; Pfaff, *Exit-Voice*, 194–7; Lindner, *Revolution*, 139–45; McFalls, *Collapse*, 50–2; Förster/Roski, *DDR*, 53–5, 69, 162.

65 Konrad Jarausch, "Implosion oder Selbstbefreiung," in Jarausch/Sabrow (eds.), *Weg*, 27–8; Joppke, *Dissidents*, 134–5; Pfaff, *Exit*, 190–1; Voss, "Revolution," 156–7; Thaysen, *Tisch*, 188; Poppe et al., "Opposition," 24; Klaus-Dieter Opp, "How Could It Happen? An Explanation of the East German Revolution," in Opp et al. (eds.), *Origins*, 29; Templin/Weißhuhn, "Initiative," 184; Lindner, *Revolution*, 176–81; Jarausch, *Rush*, 115–28, 188 (quotation).

Chapter 7

1 Jeffrey Peck et al., "Natives, Strangers, and Foreigners. Constituting Germans by Constructing Others," in Konrad H. Jarausch (ed.), *After Unity. Reconfiguring German Identities* (Providence: Berghahn Books, 1997), 82–3; "Wir sind nicht nur Schönwetter-Demokraten, sondern treten auch in schwierigen Zeiten für Toleranz ein," *Frankfurter Allgemeine Zeitung* (November 8, 1992); "Der Bundespräsident kann sich kaum Gehör verschaffen," *Frankfurter Allgemeine Zeitung* (November 9, 1992); Ferdos Foroudastan, "Die schweigende Mehrheit war auf der Straße," *Frankfurter Rundschau* (November 16, 1992); "Lichterkette gegen Fremdenhaß," *Die Welt* (December 7, 1992); "Triumph des guten Willens," *taz* (December 17, 1992); *Tagesschau* 20.12.92, Ausländerfeindlichkeit Demonstrationen, Norddeutsches Rundfunk Archiv, Hamburg.

2 Hartmut Jäckel, "Die Verfassungsdebatte: Kein Abschied vom Grundgesetz," in idem (ed.), *Die neue Bundesrepublik* (Baden-Baden: Nomos Verlag, 1994), 127–31; Christiane Lemke/Helga A. Welsh, *Germany Today. Politics and Policies in a Changing World* (Lanham, MD: Rowman & Littlefield, 2018), 10–11; Manfred Kuechler, "The Road to German Unity: Mass Sentiment in East and West Germany," *Public Opinion Quarterly* 56:1 (Spring 1992), 57–8; Peter E. Quint, *The Imperfect Union. Constitutional Structures of German Unification* (Princeton, NJ: Princeton University Press, 1997), 57–61, 104, 115–18; Gert-Joachim Glaessner, *The Unification Process in Germany. From Dictatorship to Democracy* (New York: St. Martin's Press, 1992), 97–100.

3 Klaus von Beyme, *Das politische System der Bundesrepublik Deutschland. Eine Einführung*, 12th ed. (Wiesbaden: Springer VS, 2017), 48–9, 54; Oscar Gabriel, "Politische und soziale Partizipation," in idem et al. (eds.), *Handbuch Politisches System der Bundesrepublik Deutschland* (München: R. Oldenbourg, 2005), 539; Quint, *Union*, 118; Feist, "Akkulturation," Oscar Gabriel (ed.), *Politische Orientierungen und Verhaltensweisen im vereinigten Deutschland* (Opladen : Leske + Budrich, 1997), 29–32; Rüdiger Schmitt-Beck/Cornelia Weins, "Gone with the Wind (of change). Neue Soziale Bewegungen und politischen Protest im Osten Deutschlands," in Gabriel (ed.), *Orientierungen*, 329; Oscar W. Gabriel, "Wächst zusammen, was zusammen gehört?" in idem et al. (eds.), *Wächst zusammen, was zusammen gehört? Stabilität und Wandel politischer Einstellungen im wiedervereinigten Deutschland* (Baden-Baden: Nomos Verlag, 2005), 390–1.

4 Grundgesetz für die Bundesrepublik Deutschland, Art. 23; Glaessner, *Unification*, 17–26; von Beyme, *System*, 52; Quint, *Union*, 112–14; Lemke/Welsh, *Germany*, 42, 158, 168.

5 Andreas Fahrmeir, *Citizenship. The Rise and Fall of a Modern Concept* (New Haven, CT: Yale University Press, 2007), 64–6, 91–2, 174–6, 202–4, 209–12; Joyce Marie Mushaben, *The Changing Face of Citizenship. Integration and Mobilization among Ethnic Minorities in Germany* (New York: Berghahn Books, 2008), 4–5, 20; Lemke/Welsh, *Germany*, 104–5, 106, 108–12, 121; Hartwig Pautz, *Die deutsche Leitkultur: Eine Identitätsdebatte. Neue Rechte, Neorassismus und Normalisierungsbemühungen* (Stuttgart: ibidem Verlag, 2005), passim; Joyce Marie Mushaben, *From Post-War to Post-Wall Generations. Changing Attitudes Toward the National Question and NATO in the Federal Republic of Germany* (Boulder, CO: Westview Press, 1998), 315–21; Karen Schönwälder and Triadafilos Triadafilopoulos, "A Bridge or Barrier to Incorporation? Germany's 1999 Citizenship Reform in Critical Perspective," *German Politics & Society* 30:1 [102] (Spring 2012), 52–6, 58, 61; Damani J. Partridge, *Hypersexuality and Headscarfs. Race, Sex, and Citizenship in the New Germany* (Bloomington: Indiana University Press, 2012), 2, 17–18.

6 Willem Maas, *Creating European Citizens* (Lanham, MD: Rowman & Littlefield, 2007), 45–53; Peo Hansen/Sandy Brian Hager, *The Politics of European Citizenship. Deepening Contradictions in Social Rights and Migration Policy* (New York: Berghahn Books, 2010), 43–4, 60, 71, 76, 131; David O'Keeffe/Patrick M. Twomey, "Union Citizenship," in idem (eds.), *Legal Issues of the Maastricht Treaty* (London: Chancery, 1996), 87–107.

7 Gerald L. Neumann, "'We Are the People': Alien Suffrage in German and American Perspective," *Michigan Journal of International Law* 13 (1991–92), 259–89; Lemke/Welsh, *Germany*, 105, 115.

8 Robert Rohrschneider, *Learning Democracy. Democracy and Economic Values in Unified Germany* (Oxford: Oxford University Press, 1999), 110–11, 114–16, 128–30;

Michael Minkenberg, "Repressionsstrategien gegen Rechtsradikalismus und Gewalt," *Forschungsjournal Neue Soziale Bewegungen* 16:4, 31, 37–8.

9   Wolfgang C. Müller, "Politische Kultur: Konzept—Forschungsmethoden—Effekte," in Fritz Plasser/Peter A. Ulram (eds.), *Staatsbürger oder Untertanen? Politische Kultur Deutschlands, Österreichs und der Schweiz im Vergleich* (Frankfurt: Peter Lang, 1991), 12; Oskar Niedermayer, *Bürger und Politik. Politische Orientierungen und Verhaltensweisen der Deutschen*, 2nd ed. (Wiesbaden: Verlag für Sozialwissenschaften, 2001), 106–8; Dieter Fuchs, "Das Konzept der politischen Kultur: Die Fortsetzung einer Kontroverse in konstruktiver Arbeit," in idem et al. (eds.), *Bürger und Demokratie in Ost und West. Studien zur politischen Kultur und zum politischen Prozess* (Wiebaden: Westdeutscher Verlag, 2002), 27, 38; Oskar Gabriel/Katja Neller, "Einleitung," in Jürgen Falter et al. (eds.), *Wirklich ein Volk? Die politische Orientierungen von Ost- und Westdeutschen im Vergleich* (Opladen: Leske + Budrich, 2000), 15–16, 21.

10 Peter Gluchowski/Carsten Zelle, "Demokratisierung in Ostdeutschland. Aspekte der politischen Kultur in der Periode des Systemwechsels," in Peter Gerlach et al. (eds.), *Regimewechsel. Demokratisierung und politische Kultur in Ost-Mitteleuropa* (Wien: Böhlau Verlag, 1992), 252–5; Ursula Feist/Klaus Liepelt, "Auseinander oder miteinander? Zum unterschiedlichen Politikverständnis der Deutschen in Ost und West," in Max Kaase/Hans-Dieter Klingemann (eds.), *Wahlen und Wähler: Analysen aus Anlaß der Bundestagswahl 1990* (Wiesbaden: Westdeutscher Verlag, 1994), 603; Oskar W. Gabriel, "Demokratische Einstellungen in einem Land ohne demokratische Traditionen? Die Unterstützung der Demokratie in den neuen Bundesländer im Ost-West Vergleich," in Falter et al. (eds.), *Wirklich*, 52–3, 56, 59–60, 62–3.

11 Peter Gluchowski et al., "Politisch-kultureller Wandel in Deutschland. Eine Übersicht über Veränderungen und Wandlungslinien," in Plasser/Ulram (eds.), *Staatsbürger*, 197; Gabriel, "Wächst zusammen, was zusammen gehört?" 389; Anne Sa'adah, *Germany's Second Chance. Trust, Justice, and Democratization* (Cambridge: Harvard University Press, 1998), 62, 77–8; Gabriel/Neller, "Einleitung," 21–4; Feist/Liepelt, "Auseinander," 577, 582, 595; Dieter Fuchs et al., "Die Akzeptanz der Demokratie des vereinigten Deutschland. Oder: Wann ist ein Unterschied ein Unterschied?" *Aus Politik und Zeitgeschichte* (hereafter *APZ*) 51 (1997), 5–6, 8, 11; Dieter Fuchs et al., "Perspektiven der politischen Kultur im vereinigen Deutschland," *APZ* 22 (1991), 40.

12 Gluchowski/Zelle, "Demokratisierung," 244–5; Eckhard Jesse, "Zwei verschiedene politische Kulturen in Deutschland?" in Hartmut Jäckel (ed.), *Die neue Bundesrepublik* (Baden-Baden: Nomos Verlag, 1994), 103–4; Carolin Schöbel, "Sozialisation in unterschiedlichen Systemen. Zum Profil der Persönlichkeitstypen in West- und Ost-Berlin," in Hans Dieter Klingemann et al. (eds.), *Zwischen Wende und Wiedervereinigung. Analysen zur politischen Kultur in West- und Ost-Berlin* (Opladen: Leske + Budrich, 1995), 15–17, 26–7; Kurt Sontheimer, *Deutschlands politische Kultur* (München: Piper, 1990), 67–70; Fuchs et al., "Perspektiven," 36, 46; Kerstin Volkl, "Fest verankert oder ohne Halt? Die Unterstützung der Demokratie im vereinigten Deutschland," in Gabriel et al. (eds.), *Wächst*, 249–50; Henry Kreikenbom/Maxi Stapelfeld, "Steine auf dem Weg zum politischen Alltag. Vorgeprägte Orientierungen und aktuelle Erfahrungen der ehemaligen DDR-Bürger mit dem Interessenvermittlungssystem der Bundesrepublik," in Oskar Niedermayer/Klaus von Beyme (eds.), *Politische Kultur in Ost- und Westdeutschland* (Opladen: Leske + Budrich, 1996), 166–7.

13 Fuchs et al., "Akzeptanz," 6, 8; Fuchs et al., "Perspektiven," 46; Niedermayer, *Bürger*, 32.

14 Gluchowski/Zelle, "Demokratisierung," 233, 238; Fuchs et al., "Akzeptanz," 6–7; Rohrschneider, *Learning*, 4, 85–6, 95–7, 100; Feist/Liepelt, "Auseinander," 603; Ursula Hoffmann-Lange et al., "Jugend und Politik in Deutschland," in Niedermayer/von Beyme (eds.), *Kultur*, 152; Dieter Fuchs, "The Democratic Political Culture of Unified Germany," in Pippa Norris (ed.), *Critical Citizens. Global Support for Democratic Government* (Oxford: Oxford University Press, 1999), 131–3; Bettina Westle, "Politische Ordnungsvorstellungen im vereinten Deutschland zwischen Ideologie, Protest und Nostalgie," *Kölner Zeitschrift für Soziologie und Sozialpsychologie* 46 (1994), 573, 578–81, 585, 588.

15 Russell J. Dalton, *Citizen Politics. Public Opinion and Political Participation in Advanced Industrial Democracies*, 4th ed. (Washington, DC: CQ Press, 2006), 6–9, 85–95; Feist, "Akkulturation," 24, 26; Schmitt-Beck/Weins, "Gone with the Wind," 323, 344, 346, 348; Wolfgang Gaiser/Johann de Rijka, "Partizipation und politisches Engagement," in Martina Gille/Winfried Krüger (eds.), *Unzufriedene Demokraten. Politische Orientierungen der 16- bis 29-jährigen im vereinigten Deutschland* (Opladen: Leske + Budrich, 2000), 281–2; Richard Stöss, "Bestimmungen des Rechtsextremismus," in Klingemann et al. (eds.), *Wende*, 120.

16 Rohrschneider, *Learning*, 29–31; Andreas Hadjar/Rolf Becker, "Unkonventionelle politische Partizipation im Zeitverlauf. Hat die Bildungsexpansion zu einer politischen Mobilisierung beigetragen?" *Kölner Zeitschrift für Soziologie und Sozialpsychologie* 59:3 (2007), 414–20, 426, 433; Gille et al., "Orientierungen," 214–15, 226–9, 233; Ursula Hoffmann-Lange, "Das rechtliche Einstellungspotential in der deutschen Jugend," in Falter et al. (eds.), *Rechtsextremismus*, 127, 131–2; Schmitt-Beck/Weins, "Gone," 344–8.

17 Quint, *Union*, 80–1, 118, 312; Astrid Lorenz, *Demokratisierung in Ostdeutschland. Verfassungspolitische Weichenstellunen in den neue Ländern und Berlin* (Wiesbaden: Springer VS, 2013), 113–25; Oscar Gabriel, "Zwanzig Jahre nach der Vereinigung: Politische Einstellungen und politische Kultur in Deutschland," in Kurt Bohr/Arno Krause (eds.), *20 Jahre Deutsche Einheit. Bilanz und Perspektiven*, 2nd ed. (Baden-Baden: Nomos Verlag, 2011), 202; Dieter Fuchs, "Welche Demokratie wollen die Deutschen? Einstellungen zur Demokatie im vereinigten Deutschland," in Gabriel (ed.), *Orientierungen*, 97–8, 103–4; Sa'adah, *Second Chance*, 64, 66, 257–8, 266; Rohrschneider, *Learning*, 67–9, 87, 97, 232–3.

18 Dalton, *Citizen*, 258; Fuchs, "Political Culture," 131–2, 138–41; Sontheimer, *Kultur*, 31–3, 48–9; Gluchowski et al., "Wandel," in Plasser/Ulam (eds.), *Staatsbürger*, 201; Westle, "Partizipation," 136–7; Jan van Deth, "Sind Partizipierende die besseren Demokraten?" in Silke I. Keil/S. Isabell Thaidigsmann (eds.), *Zivile Bürgergesellschaft und Demokratie. Aktuelle Ergebnisse der empirischen Politikforschung* (Wiesbaden: Springer Fachmedien, 2013), 35–6; Gabriel, "Politische Partizipation," 526, 539, 572; Christian Welzel, "Modernisierung und Partizipation: Kontroversen und Befunde zur Partizipationthese," in Fuchs et al. (eds.), *Bürger*, 295.

19 Jan van Deth, "Soziale und politische Beteiligung. Alternativen, Ergänzung oder Zwillinge?" in Achim Koch et al. (eds.), *Politische Partizipation in der Bundesrepublik Deutschland. Empirische Befunde und theoretische Erklärungen* (Opladen: Leske + Budrich, 2001), 201; Dalton, *Citizen*, 39–40; Gabriel, "Partizipation," 540–2; Jesse, "Kulturen," 111; Niedermayer, *Bürger*, 195–215.

20 Gaiser/de Rijka, "Partizipation und Engagement," 275, 287, 289, 294; Iris Krimmel, "Politische Beteiligung in Deutschland—Strukturen und Erklärungsformen," in Falter (ed.), *Wirklich*, 625–6; von Beyme, *System*, 71–2; Niedermayer, *Bürger*, 12–14, 231–2.

21 Welzel, "Modernisierung," 288–93; Hadjar/Becker, "Unkonventionelle," 426, 429–33; Bettina Westle, *Kollektive Identität im vereinten Deutschland. Nation und Demokratie in der Wahrnehmung der Deutschen* (Opladen: Leske + Budrich, 1999), 314; Karl-Dieter Opp/Steven E. Finkel, "Politischer Protest, Rationalität und Lebensstile. Eine empirische Überprüfung alternativer Erklärungsmodelle," in Koch et al. (eds.), *Partizipation*, 87–8, 100.

22 Niedermayer, *Bürger*, 30–3; Opp/Finkel, "Protest," 75–6; Schöbel, "Sozialisation," 26–7; Hajar/Becker, "Unkonventionelle," 415; Silke I. Keil, "Parteiidentifikation als der 'Pudels Kern?' Zum Einfluß unterschiedlicher Formen der Parteineigung auf die Einstellungen der Bürger zu den politischen Parteien," in Gabriel (ed.), *Wächst*, 124; Jens Tenscher/Philipp Scherer, *Jugend, Politik und Medien. Politische Orientierungen und Verhaltensweisen von Jugendlichen in Rheinland-Pfalz* (Münster: LIT Verlag, 2012), 88–91, 183–4.

23 van Deth, "Beteiligung," 204–6; Dalton, *Citizen*, 65–6; Gaiser/deRijke, "Partizipation," 250–4; Hadjar/Becker, "Unkonventionelle," 412–14, 420, 429; Gabriel, "Partizipation," 559, 572–3; Martin und Sylvia Greiffenhagen, *Ein schwieriges Vaterland. Zur politischen Kultur im vereinigten Deutschland* (München: List Verlag, 1993), 112–14; Niedermayer, *Bürger*, 253–4; Welzel, "Modernisierung," 295.

24 Greiffenhagens, *Vaterland*, 172, 372; Gaiser/Rijka, "Partizipation und Engagement," 295–6; Hoffmann-Lange, "Einstellungspotential," 134; Schmitt-Beck/Weins, "Gone," 340–3; Gaiser/de Rijke, "Partizipation im Wandel," 251–3; Gluchowski et al., "Wandel," 170; Welzel, "Modernisierung," 295.

25 Niedermayer, *Bürger*, 255–8; Stöss, "Rechtsextremismus," 130–6; Partridge, *Hypersexuality*, 62–5; Norbert Frei et al., *Zur rechten Zeit. Wider die Rückkehr des Nationalismus* (Berlin: Ullstein, 2019), 161, 164–5, 171, 180, 189, passim; Ruud Koopmans/Dieter Rucht, "Rechtsradikalismus als soziale Bewegung?" in Falter et al. (eds.), *Rechtsextremismus*, 274–6; Jan-Werner Müller, "Populism (against Democracy). A Theoretical Preface and Some Episodes of a Transatlantic History," in Paul Nolte (ed.), *Transatlantic Democracy in the Twentieth Century. Transfer and Transformation* (Berlin: de Gruyter, 2016), 174, 177–80; Mushaben, *Generations*, 329–35; Fabian Virchow, "Post-Fascist Right-Wing Social Movements," in Stefan Berger/Holger Nehring (eds.), *The History of Social Movements in Global Perspective. A Survey* (London: Palgrave/Macmillan, 2017), 622, 634–6.

26 Gaiser/de Rijke, "Partizipation und Engagement," 277, 282–3, 295–7, 300, 303–8; Niedermayer, *Bürger*, 255–8; Partridge, *Hypersexuality*, 62–5; Hoffmann-Lange, "Einstellungspotential," 134–5; Koopmans/Rucht, "Rechtsradikalismus," 274–6; Volkl, "Fest verankert," 271; Mushaben, *Generations*, 81–3, 335; Westle, *Identität*, 302, 308–9, 313; Richard Stöss, "Rextsextremismus in einer geteilten politischen Kultur," in Niedermayer/von. Beyme (eds.), *Kultur*, 105–39; idem, "Bestimmungen," 102–7, 113–20, 125; Jürgen Falter, "Politischer Extremismus," 414, 420, 422; Siegfried Bühler et al., "Die Entwicklung extremrechter politischer Einstellungen West- und Ostdeutscher," in Gabriel (ed.), *Wächst*, 335–6; Lemke/Welsh, *Germany*, 83–4.

27 Gluchowski et al., "Wandel," 175–84; Lemke/Welsh, *Germany*, 49, 55; S. Isabell Thaidigmann, "Parteien und Verbände als Vertreter von Bürgerinteressen," in Falter et al. (eds.), *Wirklich*, 241–2, 245–6, 258–61, 267; Hoffmann-Lange et al., "Jugend," 147–8, 156–8; Kreikenbom/Stapelfeld, "Orientierungen," 177–80; Niedermayer, *Bürger*, 219, 230; Sa'adah, *Second Chance*, 65, 100; Sontheimer, *Kultur*, 120.

28 Boll, "Einstellungen," 50; van Deth, "Beteiligung," 201, 214; Bernhard Weßels, "Vermittlungsinstitutionen und Interessenvertretung: Zur Performanz von Mitgliederorganisationen in Deutschland," in Koch et al. (eds.), *Partizipation*, 244; Oscar Gabriel, "Partizipation," 548, 550–7; Niedermayer, *Bürger*, 88–9; Mushaben, *Changing*, 223–6.

29 Westle, *Kollektive Identität*, 304–6; von Beyme, *System*, 67–9; Oscar W. Gabriel and Hans Rattinger, "Die Struktur des Einstellungsraumes im vereinigten Deutschland," in Gabriel et al. (eds.), *Wächst*, 19; Bauer, "Orientierungen," 443; Boll, "Einstellungen," 48; Tenscher/Scherer, *Jugend, Politik*, 99–102; Jesse, "Kulturen," 109; Gille et al., "Orientierungen," 220–1; Frederick D. Weil, "The Development of Democratic Attitudes in Eastern and Western Germany in a Comparative Perspective," in idem et al. (eds.), *Research on Democracy and Society*, Vol. I. *Democratization in Eastern and Western Europe* (Greenwich, CT: JAI Pr., 1993), 210–22.

30 Karim Fereidooni, *Diskriminierungs- und Rassismuserfahrungen im Schulwesen* (Wiesbaden: Springer VS, 2016), 24–5.

31 Helga Druxes, "'Montag ist wieder Pegida-Tag!' Pegida's Community Building and Discursive Strategies," *German Politics & Society* 34:4 (2016), 17–18; Matthias Dilling, "Two of the Same Kind? The Rise of the AfD and Its Implications for the CDU/CSU," 87–9; Thomas Klikauer, "Germany's New Populist Party: The AfD," *German Politics and Society* 36:4 (December 2018), 78–83, 89–94; AfD, "Grundsatzprogramm Langversion," 15, 20, 24–6, 47–9, Available online: https://www.afd.de/grundsatzprogramm/#langversion (accessed August 25, 2020); Björn Höcke, "Auf bestem Weg zur Volkspartei," *The European*, May 21, 2015. Available online: https://www.theeuropean.de/bjoern-hoecke/10074-afd-in-der-mitte-der-gesellschaft (accessed May 18, 2020); Wilhelm Heitmeyer, "Autoritär, national, radikal," *Süddeutsche Zeitung*, April 14, 2019. Available online: https://www.sueddeutsche.de/politik/afd-populismus-extremismus-1.4407594 (accessed May 18, 2020).

32 Philipp Adorf, "A New Blue-Collar Force. The Alternative for Germany and the Working Class," *German Politics and Society* 36:4 (2018), 29–49; "Wo die AfD erfolgreich ist," *Süddeutsche Zeitung*, September 3, 2019. Available online: https://www.sueddeutsche.de/politik/afd-wahl-auswertung-bundeslaender-1.4585616 (accessed May 15, 2020); Richard Schröder, "Wer beherrscht den Osten?" *Deutschland Archiv*, July 7, 2019. Available online: https://www.bpb.de/geschichte/zeitgeschichte/deutschlandarchiv/293406/wer-beherrscht-den-osten (accessed May 15, 2020); Jonathan Olsen, "The Left Party and the AfD: Populist Competitors in Eastern Germany," *German Politics and Society* 36:1 (Spring 2018), 70–83.

33 Dilling, "Two," 93–4, 96–8; Steven Wuhs/Eric McLaughlin, "Explaining Germany's Electoral Geography," *German Politics and Society* 37:1 (Spring 2019), 1, passim; Adorf, "A New Blue-Collar Force," 29–49; Schröder, "Wer?"; Olsen, "Left Party," "Demokratie. Themenppiere der Fraktion," *Die Linke im Bundestag*. Available online: https://www.linksfraktion.de/themen/a-z/detailansicht/demokratie/ (accessed May 18, 2020).

34 Pew Research Center, "Democratic Rights Popular Globally but Commitment to Them Not Always Strong," February 27, 2020, 26. Available online: https://www.pewresearch.org/global/2020/02/27/democratic-rights-popular-globally-but-commitment-to-them-not-always-strong/ (accessed May 17, 2020).

35 Winfried Thaa, "'Stuttgart 21'—Krise oder Repolitisierung der repräsentativen Demokratie?," *Politische Vierteljahresschrift* 54:1 (2013), 1–20; Druxes, "Montag,"

18; "Berlin Far-right Supporters Outnumbered by Counter-protest," *BBC News*, May 27, 2018. Available online: https://www.bbc.com/news/world-europe-44273617 (accessed May 16, 2020); "Anti-Pegida-Demo in Dresden," *Frankfurter Allgemeine Zeitung*, October 22, 2018. Available online: https://search-proquest-com.go.libproxy.wakehealth.edu/docview/2123577788/6DA8CBDE3E1E4607PQ/27?accountid=14868 (accessed May 16, 2020); "Dresden protestiert gegen Pegida," *Deutsche Welle*, October 20, 2019. Available online: https://www.dw.com/de/dresden-protestiert-gegen-pegida/a-50908199 (accessed May 16, 2020); "Tausende gegen Corona-Maßnahmen," *Tagesschau.de*, May 5, 2020. Available online: https://www.tagesschau.de/inland/corona-demos-109.html (accessed May 17, 2020).

36 Pew Research Center, "Democratic Rights," 10, 12, 21–4.

Bibliography

Achilles, Manuela. "With a Passion for Reason: Celebrating the Constitution in Weimar Germany." *Central European History* 43, no. 4 (2010): 666–89.
Adams, Thomas. *Philanthropy, Civil Society, and the State in German History, 1815–1989*. Rochester: Camden House, 2016.
Adolph, Paul. *Vereinsgesetz vom 19. April 1908*. 2nd ed. Leipzig: Roßberg'sche Verlagsbuchhandlung, 1914.
Adorf, Philipp. "A New Blue-Collar Force. The Alternative for Germany and the Working Class." *German Politics and Society* 36, no. 4 (2018): 29–49.
AfD. "Grundsatzprogramm Langversion." Available online: https://www.afd.de/grundsatz programm/#langversion (accessed May 19, 2020).
Alexander, Keith. "The Alternative Liste Westberlin and the Evolution of the West German Left." *German Politics and Society* 34, no. 3 (2016): 26–55.
Allen, William Sheridan. *The Nazi Seizure of Power. The Experience of a Single German Town 1922-1945*. Rev. ed. New York: Franklin Watts, 1984.
Allerbeck, Klaus. *Demokratisierung und sozialer Wandel in der Bundesrepublik Deutschland. Sekundäranalyse von Umfragedaten 1953–1974*. Opladen: Westdeutscher Verlag, 1976.
Allerbeck, Klaus et al. "Generations and Families." In *Political Action*, edited by Barnes and Kaase, 487–522.
Allinson, Mark. *Politics and Popular Opinion in East Germany, 1945–1968*. Manchester: Manchester University Press, 2000.
Allinson, Mark. "Public Opinion." In *Workers*, edited by Major and Osmond, 96–111.
Almond, Gabriel and Sydney Verba. *The Civic Culture. Political Attitudes and Democracy in five Nations*. Boston: Little, Brown and Company, 1965.
Amos, Heike. *Die Entstehung der Verfassung in der Sowjetische Besatzungszone/DDR 1946-1949. Diktatur und Widerstand*. Münster: Lit Verlag, 2006.
Anders, Freia. "Wohnraum, Freiraum, Widerstand. Die Formierung der Autonomen in den Konflikten um Hausbesetzungen Anfang der achtziger Jahre." In *Alternative*, edited by Reichert and Siegfried, 473–98.
Anderson, Margaret Lavinia. *Practicing Democracy. Elections and Political Culture in Imperial Germany*. Princeton: Princeton University Press, 2000.
Angster, Julia. "Der neue Stil. Die Amerikanisierung des Wahlkampfs und der Wandel im Politikverständnis bei CDU und SPD in den 1960er Jahren." In *Demokratisierung*, edited by Frese et al., 181–204.
Angster, Julia. *Konsenskapitalismus und Sozialdemokratie. Die Westernisierung von SPD und DGB*. München: Oldenbourg Verlag, 2003.
"Anti-Pegida-Demo in Dresden." *Frankfurter Allgemeine Zeitung*, October 22, 2018. Available online: https://search-proquest-com.go.libproxy.wakehealth.edu/docview/21 23577788/6DA8CBDE3E1E4607PQ/27?accountid=14868 (accessed May 16, 2020).
Apel, Linda. "Die Opposition der Opposition: Politische Mobilisierung an Oberschulen jenseits der Protestgeneration." In *Die 1970er Jahre als schwarzes Jahrzehnt*.

Politisierung und Mobilisierung zwischen christlichen Demokraten und extremen Rechten, edited by Massimiliano Livi et al., 57–72. Frankfurt: Campus Verlag, 2010.

Armbruster, Bernd and Dr. Rainer Leisner. *Bürgerbeteiligung in der Bundesrepublik Deutschland—Zur Freizeitaktivität verschiedener Bevölkerungsgruppen in ausgewählten Beteiligungsfeldern (Kirche, Parteien, Bürgerinitiativen und Vereinen)*. Göttingen: Verlag Otto Schwarz & Co., 1975.

Arndt, Klaus. "Widerstand und ziviler Ungehorsam in der Demokratie." In *Widerstand*, edited by Schleker, 15–31.

Arzheimer, Kai. "Twenty Years After: Sozial- und wirtschaftspolitische Einstellungen und Orientierungen von Ost- und Westdeutschen im Vergleich." In *Zivile Bürgergesellschaft*, edited by Keil and Thaidigsmann, 299–336.

Arzheimer, Kai and Markus Klein. "Die friedliche und stille Revolution. Die Entwicklung der gesellschaftspolitischen Wertorientierungen in Deutschland seit dem Beitritt der fünf neuen Länder." In *Politische Orientierungen und Verhaltensweisen im vereinigten Deutschland*, edited by Oscar Gabriel, 37–59. Opladen: Leske + Budrich, 1997.

Augustine, Dolores L. *Taking on Technocracy. Nuclear Power in Germany, 1945 to the Present*. New York: Berghahn Books, 2018.

Bajohr, Frank. "Die Zustimmungsdiktatur. Grundzüge nationalsozialistischer Herrschaft in Hamburg." In *Hamburg im "Dritten Reich,"* edited by Forschungsstelle für Zeitgeschichte in Hamburg, 69–121. Göttingen: Vandenhoeck & Ruprecht, 2005.

Bajohr, Frank. "The 'Folk Community' and the Persecution of the Jews." *Holocaust and Genocide Studies* 20, no. 2 (2006): 183–206

Baker, Kendall L. et al. *Germany Transformed. Political Culture and the New Politics*. Cambridge: Harvard University Press, 1981.

Baldus, Manfred. "Frühe Machtkämpfe. Ein Versuch über die historischen Gründe der Autorität des Bundesverfassungsgerichts." In *Lüth Urteil*, edited by Henne and Riedlinger, 237–48.

Balstier, Thomas. *Straßenprotest. Formen oppositioneller Politik in der Bundesrepublik Deutschland zwischen 1979 und 1989*. Münster: Westfälisches Dampfboot, 1996.

Balz, Hanno. "Kampf um die Grenzen. 'Terrorismus' und die Krise öffentlichen Engagements in der Bundesrepublik der siebziger Jahre." In *Bürgersinn mit Weltgefühl. Politische Moral und solidarischer Protest in den sechziger und siebziger Jahren*, edited by Habbo Knoch, 294–310. Göttingen: Wallstein Verlag, 2007.

Balz, Hanno and Jan-Henrik Friedrichs. *"All We Ever Wanted ..." Eine Kulturgeschichte europäischer Protestbewegungen der 1980er Jahre*. Berlin: Karl Dietz Verlag, 2012.

Bankier, David. *Germans and the Final Solution. Public Opinion under Nazism*. Oxford: Blackwell Publishers, 1996.

Bankier, David. *Probing the Depths of German Antisemitism. German Society and the Persecution of the Jews, 1933–1941*. New York: Berghahn Books, 2000.

Barnes, Samuel and Max Kaase. *Political Action. Mass Participation in Five Western Democracies*. Beverly Hills, CA: Sage Publications, 1979.

Bartee, Wayne C. *A Time to Speak Out. The Leipzig Citizen Protests and the Fall of East Germany*. Westport: Praeger, 2000.

Bartov, Omar. "The Conduct of War: Soldiers and the Barbarization of Warfare." In *Resistance*, edited by Geyer and Boyer, 39–52.

Bauer, Petra. "Freiheit und Demokratie in der Wahrnehmung der Bürger in der Bundesrepublik und der ehemaligen DDR." In *Nation und Demokratie*, edited by Rudolf Wildenmann, 99–124. Baden-Baden: Nomos Verlag, 1991.

Bauer, Petra. "Politische Orientierungen im Übergang. Eine Analyse politischer Einstellungen der Bürger in West- und Ostdeutschland 1990/1991." *Kölner Zeitschrift für Soziologie und Sozialpsychologie* 43 (1991): 433–55.

Bauerkämper, Arnd. "Abweichendes Verhalten in der Diktatur. Probleme einer kategorialen Einordnung am Beispiel der Kollektivierung der Landwirtschaft in der DDR." In *Doppelte*, edited by Bauerkämper et al., 295-311.
Bauerkämper, Arnd et al. (eds.). *Demokratiewunder. Transatlantische Mittler und die kulturelle Öffnung Westdeutschlands 1945-1970*. Göttingen: Vandenhoeck & Ruprecht, 2005.
Bauerkämpfer, Arnd. "Einleitung: Die Praxis der Zivilgesellschaft." In *Die Praxis der Zivilgesellschaft. Akteure, Handeln und Strukturen im internationalen Vergleich*, edited by idem, 7-30. Frankfurt/M: Campus Verlag, 2003.
Bauerkämper, Arnd et al. "Einleitung: Transatlantische Mittler und die Demokratisierung Westdeutschlands 1945-1970." In *Demokratiewunder*, edited by idem, 12-37.
Bavaj, Riccardo. "Verunsicherte Demokratisierer. 'Liberal-kritische' Hochschullehrer und die Studentenrevolte von 1967/68." In *Streit*, edited by Geppert and Hacke, 151-68.
Bavaj, Riccardo. *Von links gegen Weimar. Linkes antiparlamentarisches Denken in der Weimarer Republk*. Bonn: JHW Dietz Verlag, 2005.
Bavaj, Richard. "Otto Kirchheimers Parlamentarismuskritik in der Weimarer Republik." *Vierteljahrshefte für Zeitgeschichte* 55, no. 1 (2007): 33-51.
Beck, Hermann. *The Fateful Alliance. German Conservatives and Nazis in 1933: The Machtergreifung in a New Light*. New York: Berghahn Books, 2008.
Beck, Ulrich. *Risikogesellschaft. Auf dem Weg in eine andere Moderne*. Frankfurt: Suhrkamp Verlag, 1986.
Beer, Wolfgang. "Die Motive des Widerstandes gegen Atomkraftwerke und der Prozeß der Mobilisierung breiter Bevölkerungsschichten." In *Widerstand gegen Atomkraftwerke. Informationen für Atomkraftgegner und solche, die es werden wollen*, edited by Hans-Christoph Buchholtz et al., 103-12. Wuppertal: Peter Hammer Verlag, 1978.
Beerfeltz, Hans-Jürgen et al. (eds.). *Das Programm der Liberalen. Zehn Jahre Programmarbeit der F.D.P. 1980-1990*. Baden-Baden: Nomos Verlagsgesellschaft, 1990.
Beier, Gerhard. *Der Demonstrations- und Generalstreik vom 12. November 1948 im Zusammenhang mit der parlamentarischen Entwicklung Westdeutschlands*. Frankfurt/M: Europäische Verlagsanstalt, 1975.
Benz, Wolfgang. *Von der Besatzungsherrschaft zur Bundesrepublik. Stationen einer Staatsgründung 1946-1949*. Frankfurt/M: Fischer Verlag, 1985.
Berghahn, Volker. *Der Stahlhelm. Bund der Frontsoldaten 1918-1935*. Düsseldorf: Droste Verlag, 1966.
Berghahn, Volker. *Imperial Germany, 1871-1914. Economy, Society, Culture and Politics*. Providence: Berghahn Books, 1994.
Berghahn, Volker. *Modern Germany. Society, Economy and Politics in the Twentieth Century*. Cambridge: Cambridge University Press, 1988.
Bergmann, Jürgen. "Das Land steht rechts!' Das 'agrarische Milieu." In *Politische Identität und nationale Gedenktage. Zur politischen Kultur in der Weimarer Republik*, edited by Detlef Lehnert and Klaus Megerle, 181-206. Opladen: Westdeutsche Verlag, 1989.
Bergmann, Jürgen. "Politische Anschauungen und politische Kultur des Handwerks in der Weimarer Republik im Spannungsverhältnis vom Tradition, Ideologie und materiellen Interessen." In *Pluralismus als Verfassungs- und Gesellschaftsmodell. Zur politischen Kultur in der Weimarer Republik*, edited by Detlef Lehnert and Klaus Megerle, 131-213. Opladen: Westdeutscher Verlag, 1993.
Bergmann, Jürgen and Klaus Megerle. "Gesellschaftliche Mobilisierung und negative Partizipation." In *Probleme politischer Partizipation in der Weimarer Republik*, edited by Peter Steinbach, 376-437. Stuttgart: Klett Cotta, 1982.

Berg-Schlosser, Dirk and Jakob Schissler. "Einführung. Politische Kultur in Deutschland." In *Politische Kultur in Deutschland. Bilanz und Perspektiven der Forschung*, edited by idem and idem, 11–26. Opladen: Westdeutscher Verlag, 1987.

Berg-Schlosser, Dirk and Ralf Rytlewski (eds.). *Political Culture in Germany*. New York: St. Martins Press, 1993.

"Berlin Far-right Supporters Outnumbered by Counter-protest." *BBC News*, May 27, 2018. Available online: https://www.bbc.com/news/world-europe-44273617 (accessed May 16, 2020).

Berman, Sheri. "Civil Society and the Collapse of the Weimar Republic." *World Politics* 49, no. 3 (April 1997): 401–29.

Bessel, Richard. "Political Violence and the Nazi Seizure of Power." In *Life in the Third Reich*, edited by idem, 1–15. Oxford: Oxford University Press, 1987.

Bessel, Richard. "The Formation and Dissolution of a German National Electorate from Kaiserreich to 3rd Reich." In *Elections, Mass Politics*, edited by Jones and Retallack, 399–417.

Bessel, Richard. *Political Violence and the Rise of Nazism. The Storm Troopers in Eastern Germany 1925–1934*. New Haven, CT: Yale University Press, 1984.

Bessel, Richard and Ralph Jessen. "Einleitung. Die Grenzen der Diktatur." In *Die Grenzen der Diktatur. Staat und Gesellschaft in der DDR*, edited by idem, 7–23. Göttingen: Vandenhoeck & Ruprecht, 1996.

Betts, Paul. *Within the Walls. Private Life in the German Democratic Republic*. Oxford: Oxford University Press, 2010.

Beyme, Klaus von. *Das politische System der Bundesrepublik Deutschland. Eine Einführung*. 12th ed. Wiesbaden: Springer VS, 2017.

Beyme, Klaus v. "Der Neo-Korporatismus und die Politik des begrenzten Pluralismus in der Bundesrepublik." In *Stichworte zur "Geistigen Situation der Zeit,"* edited by Jürgen Habermas, 229–62. Frankfurt: Suhrkamp Verlag, 1979.

Bialis, Wolfgang. *Moralische Ordnungen des Nationalsozialismus*. Göttingen: Vandenhoeck & Ruprecht, 2014.

Bieber, Hans-Joachim. *Bürgertum in der Revolution. Bürgerrate und Bürgerstreiks in Deutschland 1918–1920*. Hamburg: Christians, 1992.

Bieber, Ina E. "Der weibliche Blick: Verhalten sich Frauen in der Politik anders?" In *Der unbekannte Wähler? Mythen und Fakten über das Wahlverhalten der Deutschen*, edited by Evelyn Bytzek and Sigrid Roßteutscher, 253–72. Frankfurt: Campus Verlag, 2011.

Biedenkopf, Kurt H. and Rüdiger v. Voss (eds.). *Staatsführung, Verbandsmacht und innere Souveränität. Von der Rolle der Verbände, Gewerkschaften und Bürgerinitiativen in der Politik*. Stuttgart: Verlag Bonn Aktuell, 1977.

Biess, Frank. "The Search for Missing Soldiers. MIAs, POWs, and Ordinary Germans, 1943–45." In *Conflict, Catastrophe and Continuity. Essays on Modern German History*, edited by idem et al., 117–34. New York: Berghahn Books, 2007.

Blackbourn, David. *History of Germany 1780–1918. The Long Nineteenth Century*. 2nd ed. Oxford: Blackwell Publishing, 2003.

Blackbourn, David. *Marpingen. Apparitions of the Virgin in Nineteenth-Century Germany*. New York: Knopf, 1994.

Blackbourn, David. "New Legislatures: Germany, 1871–1914." *Historical Research* 65 (1992): 202–8.

Blaich, Fritz. "Staatsverständnis und politische Haltung der deutschen Unternehmer 1918–1930." In *Weimarer Republik*, edited by Bracher et al., 158–78.

Blanke, Thomas and Dieter Sterzel. "Die Entwicklung des Demonstrationsrechts von der Studentenbewegung bis heute." In *Demonstrationsrecht*, edited by Cobler, 53–87.
Blessing, Werner. "The Cult of the Monarchy, Political Loyalty and the Workers' Movement in Imperial Germany." *Journal of Contemporary History* 13 (1978): 357–73.
Blessing, Werner K. "Deutschland in Not, wir im Glauben'. Kirche und Kirchenvolk in einer katholischen Region." In *Von Stalingrad zur Währungsreform. Zur Sozialgeschichte des Umbruchs in Deutschland*, edited by Martin Broszat, 3–111. München: Oldenbourg Verlag, 1989.
Blickle, Peter. *Obedient Germans? A Rebuttal. A New View of German History*. Trsl. by Thomas Brady. Charlottesville: University of Virginia Press, 1997.
Bock, Gisela. "Frauenwahlrecht—Deutschland um 1900 in vergleichendere Perspektive." In *Geschichte und Emanzipation: Festschrift für Reinhard Rürup*, edited by Michael Grüttner et al., 96–123. Frankfurt: Campus Verlag, 1999.
Böckenförde, Ernst-Wolfgang. "Demokratie als Verfassungsprinzip." In *Demokratie und Grundgesetz. Eine Auseinandersetzung mit der verfassungsgerichtlichen Rechtssprechung*, edited by Redaktion Kritische Justiz, 8–31. Baden-Baden: Nomos Verlag, 2000.
Böckenförde, Ernst-Wolfgang. "Der Verfassungstyp der deutschen konstitutionellen Monarchie im 19. Jahrhundert." In *Modern deutsche Verfassungsgeschichte (1815–1918)*, edited by idem, 148–50, 155. Köln: Kiepenheuer & Witsch, 1972.
Böckenförde, Ernst-Wolfgang. "Der Zusammenbruch der Monarchie und die Entstehung der Weimarer Republik." In *Recht, Staat, Freiheit*, edited by idem, 306–43. Frankfurt/M: Suhrkamp, 1991.
Boehling, Rebecca L. *A Question of Priorities. Democratic Reform and Economic Recovery in Postwar Germany*. Providence: Berghahn Books, 1996.
Boldt, Hans. *Deutsche Verfassungsgeschichte: Politische Strukturen und ihr Wandel*. Vol. 2. München: Deutsche Taschenbuch Verlag, 1990.
Boll, Bernhard. "Politische Einstellungen junger Erwachsener in West- und Ostdeutschland." In *Vereintes Deutschland—geteilte Jugend: ein politisches Handbuch*, edited by Sabine Andresen, 41–52. Opladen: Leske + Budrich, 2003.
Boll, Friedhelm. *Massenbewegungen in Niedersachsen 1906–1920, Eine sozialgeschichtliche Untersuchung zu den unterschiedlichen Entwicklungstypen Braunschweig und Hanover*. Bonn: Verlag Neue Gesellschaft, 1981.
Borowski, Martin. "Protest unter Berufung auf die Gewissensfreiheit." In *Ordnung*, edited by Löhnig et al., 149–74
Borup, Allan. *Demokratisierung in der Nachkriegszeit*. Bielefeld: Verlag für Regionalgeschichte, 2010.
Bos, Ellen. *Leserbriefe in Tageszeitungen der DDR: zur "Massenverbundenheit" der Presse, 1949–1989*. Opladen: Westdeutscher Verlag, 1993.
Bösch, Frank. *Das konservative Milieu: Vereinskultur und lokale Sammlungen in ost- und westdeutschen Regionen (1900–1960)*. Göttingen: Allstein Verlag, 2002.
Bösch, Frank. "Die Krise als Chance. Die Neuformierung der Christdemokraten in den siebziger Jahren." In *Ende*, edited by Jarausch, 296–309.
Bösch, Frank. "Die *Spiegel* Affäre und das Ende der Adenauer Ära." In *Die Spiegel Affäre. Ein Skandal und seine Folgen*, edited by Martin Doerry and Hauke Janssen, 215–30. München: Deutsche Verlags-Anstalt, 2013.
Bösch, Frank. *Macht und Machtverlust. Die Geschichte der CDU*. Stuttgart: Deutsche Verlags-Anstalt, 2002.
Bösch, Frank. "Militante Geselligkeit. Formierungsformen der bürgerlichen Vereinswelt zwischen Revolution und Nationalsozialismus." In *Kulturgeschichte*, edited by Hardtwig, 151–82.

Bösch, Frank. "Später Protest. Die Intellektuellen und die Pressefreiheit in der frühen Bundesrepublik." In *Streit um den Staat. Intellektuelle Debatten in der Bundesrepublik 1960–1980*, edited by Dominick Geppert and Jens Hacke, 91–112. Göttingen: Vandenhoeck & Ruprecht, 2008.
Bösch, Frank and Manuel Borutta. "Medien und Emotionen in der Moderne. Historische Perspektiven." In *Die Massen bewegen: Medien und Emotionen in der Moderne*, edited by idem, 13–41. Frankfurt: Campus Verlag, 2006.
Bothien, Horst-Pierre. *Auf zur Demo! Straßenprotest in der ehemaligen Bundeshauptstadt Bonn 1949–1999. Eine Dokumentation*. Essen: Klartext, 2009.
Botsch, Gordon. *Die extreme Rechte in der Bundesrepublik Deutschland 1949 bis heute*. Darmstadt: WBG, 2012.
Bracher, Karl. "Die Kanzlerdemokratie." In *zweite Republik*, edited by Löwenthal and Schwarz, 179–202.
Bracher, Karl Dietrich. *Die Auflösung der Weimarer Republik. Eine Studie zum Problem des Machtverfalls in der Demokratie*. 5th ed. Villingen: Ring-Verlag, 1971.
Bracher, Karl Dietrich et al. (eds.). *Die Weimarer Republik 1918–1933. Politik Wirtschaft Gesellschaft*. Düsseldorf: Droste Verlag, 1987.
Bracher, Karl Dietrich. *The German Dictatorship. The Origins, Structure, and Effects of National Socialism*. Trsl. by Jean Steinberg. New York: Praeger Publishers, 1974.
Brand, Karl Werner. "The Political Culture of the New Social Movements." In *Political Culture*, edited by Berg-Schlosser and Rytlewski, 116–26.
Brand, Karl-Werner et al. *Aufbruch in eine andere Gesellschaft. Neue soziale Bewegungen in der Bundesrepublik*. 2nd ed. Frankfurt: Campus Verlag, 1984.
Brandt, Hartwig. *Landständische Repräsentation im deutschen Vormärz. Politisches Denken im Einflußfeld des monarchischen Prinzips*. Neuwied: Luchterhand, 1968.
Brandt, Peter. "Germany after 1945. Revolution by Defeat?" In *The Problem of Revolution in Germany, 1789–1989*, edited by Reinhard Rürup, 129–59. Oxford: Berg Publishing, 2000.
Breitman, Richard. *German Socialism and Weimar Democracy*. Chapel Hill: University of North Carolina Press, 1981.
Breuer, Stefan. *Die Völkischen in Deutschland. Kaiserreich und Weimarer Republik*. Darmstadt: Wissenschaftliche Buchgesellschaft, 2010.
Breymann, Steve. *Why Movements Matter. The West German Peace Movement and U.S. Arms Control Policy*. Albany: State University of New York Press, 2001.
Brinker-Gabler, Gisela. "Die Frauenbewegung im Deutschen Kaiserreich—Die Revolution entläßt ihre Kinder." In *Die deutsche Frauenbewegung*, edited by Ingeborg Drewitz, 53–84. Bonn: Hohwacht, 1983.
Brockhaus, Gudrun (ed.). *Die Attraktion der NS-Bewegung*. Essen: Klartext Verlag, 2014.
Brodocz, André. "Lüth und Deutungsmacht des Bundesverfassungsgerichts." In *Lüth Urteil*, edited by Henne and Riedlinger, 273–89.
Broszat, Martin. *Der Staat Hitlers*. München: Deutscher Taschenbuch Verlag, 1979.
Broszat, Martin. "Resistenz und Widerstand. Eine Zwischenbilanz des Forschungsprojekts 'Widerstand und Verfolgung in Bayern 1933–1945.'" In *Nach Hitler. Der schwierige Umgang mit unserer Geschichte*, edited by idem, 68–91. München: R. Oldenbourg Verlag, 1987.
Broszat, Martin. "Soziale Motivation und Führerbindung des Nationalsozialismus." *Vierteljahrshefte für Zeitgeschichte* 18, no. 4 (1970): 392–409.
Brown, Timothy Scott. *West Germans and the Global Sixties. The Anti-authoritarian Revolt, 1962–1978*. Cambridge: Cambridge University Press, 2013.

Bruce, Gary. *Resistance with the People. Repression and Resistance in Eastern Germany 1945–1955*. London: Rowman & Littlefield, 2003.

Brühöfener, Friederike. "'Angst vor dem Atom.' Emotionalität und Politik im Spiegel bundesdeutscher Zeitungen." In *Den Kalten Krieg denken. Beiträge zur sozialen Ideengeschichte seit 1945*, edited by Patrick Bernhard and Holger Nehring, 280–396. Essen: Klartext, 2014.

Brunner, José. *Politische Gewalt in Deutschland. Ursprünge—Ausprägungen—Konsequenzen*. Göttingen: Wallenstein Verlag, 2014.

Bryde, Brun-Otto. "Der Beitrag des Bundesverfassungsgerichts zur Demokratisierung der Bundesrepublik." In *Bundesverfassungsgericht*, edited by Ooyen and Möller, 321–31.

Buchna, Kristina. *Ein klerikales Jahrzehnt? Kirche, Konfession und Politik in der Bundesrepublik während der 1950er Jahre*. Baden-Baden: Nomos Verlag, 2014.

Büchse, Nicolas. "Von Staatsbürgern und Protestbürgern. Der Deutsche Herbst und die Veränderung der politischen Kultur in der Bundesrepublik." In *Bürgersinn*, edited by Knoch, 311–32.

Budde, Gunilla. "The Family—A Core Institution of Civil Society: A Perspective on the Middle Classes in Imperial Germany." In *Civil Society and Gender Justice. Historical and Comparative Perspectives*, edited by Karen Hagemann et al., 171–95. New York: Berghahn Books, 2008.

Bühler, Siegfried et al. "Die Entwicklung extremrechter politischer Einstellungen West- und Ostdeutscher." In *Wächst*, edited by Gabriel, 315–37.

Bullock, Alan. *Hitler. A Study in Tyranny*. Rev. Edit. New York: Harper Colophon Books, 1964.

Bundesverfassungsgericht. "Auszug der Entscheidung BVerfGE 69, 315." In *Brokdorf-Beschluss*, edited by Anselm Doering-Manteuffel et al., 17–60.

Bunn, Ronald F. *German Politics and the Spiegel Affair. A Case Study of the Bonn System*. Baton Rouge: Louisiana State University Press, 1968.

Burns, Rob and Wilfried van der Will. *Protest and Democracy in West Germany. Extra-Parliamentary Opposition and the Democratic Agenda*. New York: St. Martin's Press, 1988.

Caldwell, Peter C. "The Citizen and the Republic in Germany, 1918–1935." In *Citizenship*, edited by Eley and Palmowski, 40–56.

Caldwell, Peter C. *Dictatorship, State Planning, and Social Theory in the German Democratic Republic*. Cambridge: Cambridge University Press, 2003.

Caldwell, Peter C. and William E. Scheuermann (eds.). *From Liberal Democracy to Fascism*. Boston: Humanities Press, 2000.

Canning, Kathleen. "Claiming Citizenship. Suffrage and Subjectivity in Germany after the First World War." In *Gender History in Practice. Historical Perspectives on Bodies, Class, and Citizenship*, edited by idem, 212–37. Ithaca: Cornell University Press, 2006.

Canning, Kathleen. "The Order and Disorder of Gender in the Weimar Republic." In *Geschlechter(un)ordnung und Politik in der Weimarer Republik*, edited by Gabriele Metzler and Dirk Schumann, 59–79. Bonn: Dietz, 2016.

Canning, Kathleen. "War, Citizenship, and Rhetorics of Sexual Crisis: Reflections on States of Exception in Germany, 1914–1920." In *German Modernities from Wilhelm to Weimar. A Contest of Futures*, edited by Geoff Eley et al., 234–57. London: Bloomsbury, 2016.

Caplan, Jane. "Political Detentions and the Origins of the Concentration Camps in Nazi Germany, 1933–1935/36." In *Nazism, War and Genocide*, edited by Neil Gregor, 22–41. Exeter: University of Exeter Press, 2005.

Caron, Jean-Christoph. "Gewalt im Fest. Die Maifeiern in Hagen und Hohenlimburg." In *Fest*, edited by Freitag, 109–15.
Carsten, Francis Ludwig *The Reichswehr and Politics 1918 to 1933*. Oxford: Clarendon Press, 1966.
Chambers, Simone and Jeffrey Kopstein. "Bad Civil Society." *Political Theory* 29, no. 6 (2001): 837–860.
Chappel, James. *Catholic Modern. The Challenge of Totalitarianism and the Remaking of the Church*. Cambridge: Harvard University Press, 2018.
Chickering, Roger. *We Men Who Feel Most German. A Cultural Study of the Pan-German League, 1886–191*. Boston: Allen & Unwin, 1984.
Childers, Thomas. *The Nazi Voter. The Social Foundations of Fascism in Germany, 1919–1933*. Chapel Hill: University of North Carolina Press, 1983.
Clark, Christopher. *Iron Kingdom. The Rise and Downfall of Prussia, 1600–1947*. Cambridge: Belknap Press, 2008.
Clinefelter, Joan L. "Representing the *Volksgemeinschaft*: Art in the Third Reich." In *Life in Third Reich*, edited by Pine, 187–209.
Cobler, Sebastian. "Der demonstrative Kampf um die Versammlungsfreiheit. Zur Einführung." In *Demonstrationsrecht*, edited by idem et al., 7–16.
Coetzee, Marilynn. *The German Army League. Popular Nationalism in Wilhelmine Germany*. New York: Oxford University Press, 1990.
Collings, Justin. *Democracy's Guardians. A History of the German Federal Constitutional Court 1951–2001*. Oxford: Oxford University Press, 2015.
Confino, Alon. "The Travels of Bettina Humpel. One Stasi File and Narratives of State and Self in East Germany." In *Socialist Modern. East German Everyday Culture and Politics*, edited by Katherine Pence and Paul Betts, 133–54. Ann Arbor: University of Michigan Press, 2008.
Connelly, John. "The Uses of *Volksgemeinschaft*. Letters to the NSDAP Kreisleitung Eisenach, 1939–1940." *Journal of Modern History* 68, no. 4 (1996): 899–930.
Conradt, David P. "Changing German Political Culture." In *The Civic Culture Revisited*, edited by Gabriel Almond and Sidney Verba, 231–40. Boston: Little, Brown and Company, 1980.
Craig, Gordon. *Germany 1866–1945*. New York: Oxford University Press, 1980.
Craig, Gordon. *The Politics of the Prussian Army 1640–1945*. Oxford: Oxford University Press, 1964.
Creuzberger, Stefan and Dierk Hoffmann. "Antikommunismus und politische Kultur in der Bundesrepublik." In *"Geistige Gefahr" und Immunisierung der Gesellschaft. Antikommunismus und politische Kultur in der frühen Bundesrepublik*, edited by Stefan Creuzberger and Dierk Hoffmann, 1–13. München: Oldenbourg, 2014.
Creuzberger, Stefan and Dierk Hoffmann (eds.). *"Geistige Gefahr" und "Immunisierung der Gesellschaft." Antikommunismus und politische Kultur in der frühen Bundesrepublik*. München: Oldenbourg, 2014.
Crew, David. *Town in the Ruhr. A Social History of Bochum, 1860–1914*. New York: Columbia University Press, 1979.
Crim, Brian E. "Weimar's 'Burning Question.' Situational Antisemitism and the German Combat Leagues, 1918–33." In *The German Right in the Weimar Republic. Studies in the History of German Conservatism, Nationalism, and Antisemitism*, edited by Larry-Eugene Jones, 194–219. New York: Berghahn Books, 2014.
Dahrendorf, Ralf. *Society and Democracy in Germany*. New York: W. W. Norton & Co., 1967.

Daldrup, Maria. "Vergangenheitsbewältigung und Demokratisierungsansätze im Deutschen Journalisten Verband." In *Die Zweite Gründung der Bundesrepublik. Generationswechsel und intellektuelle Wortergreifungen 1955–1975*, edited by Franz-Werner Kersting et al., 243–68. Frankfurt: Steiner Verlag, 2010.
Dale, Gareth. *Popular Protest in East Germany, 1945–1989*. London: Routledge, 2005.
Dalton, Russel J. et al. "The Challenge of New Movements." In *Challenging the Political Order. New Social Movements in Western Democracies*, edited by Dalton and Kuechler, 3–20. Oxford: Oxford University Press, 1990.
Dalton, Russell J. *Citizen Politics. Public Opinion and Political Participation in Advanced Industrial Democracies*. 4th ed. Washington, DC: CQ Press, 2006.
Dalton, Russell J. "Communists and Democrats: Democratic Attitudes in the Two Germanies." *British Journal of Political Science* 24, no. 4 (1994): 469–93.
Dalton, Russell J. "Political Support in Advanced Industrial Democracies." In *Critical Citizens*, edited by Norris, 57–77.
Damm, Matthias and Mark R. Thompson. "Die spontane Macht der Gewaltlosen. Eine übersehene Erklärung fur den Untergang der DDR." In *Jahre des Umbruchs: Friedliche Revolution in der DDR und Transition in Ostmitteleuropa*, edited by Michael Richter and Clemens Vollnhals, 203–18. Göttingen: Vandenhoeck & Ruprecht, 2012.
Dammann, Klaus. "Rache des Rechtsstaates—oder Aufbegehren der Akteure." In *Demonstrationsfreiheit*, edited by Kutscha, 163–73.
Davis, Belinda. *Home Fires Burning. Food, Politics, and Everyday Life in World War I Berlin*. Chapel Hill: University of North Carolina Press, 2000.
"Demokratie. Themenpapiere der Fraktion." *Die Linke im Bundestag*. Available online: https://www.linksfraktion.de/themen/a-z/detailansicht/demokratie/ (accessed May 18, 2020).
Demshuk, Andrew. *Demolition on Karl Marx Square. Cultural Barbarism and the People's State in 1968*. New York: Oxford University Press, 2017.
Deth, Jan W. van. "Formen konventioneller Partizipation: Ein neues Leben alter Dinosaurier?" In *Orientierungen*, edited by Gabriel, 291–319.
Deth, Jan van. "Sind Partizipierende die besseren Demokraten?" In *Zivile Bürgergesellschaft und Demokratie. Aktuelle Ergebnisse der empirischen Politikforschung*, edited by Silke I. Keil and S. Isabell Thaidigsmann, 35–52. Wiesbaden: Springer Fachmedien, 2013.
Deth, Jan van. "Soziale und politische Beteiligung. Alternativen, Ergänzungen oder Zwillinge?" In *Politische Partizipation in der Bundesrepublik Deutschland. Empirische Befunde und theoretische Erklärungen*, edited by Achim Koch et al., 195–219. Opladen: Leske + Budrich, 2001.
Dickinson, Edward Ross. *The Politics of German Child Welfare from the Empire to the Federal Republic*. Cambridge: Harvard University Press, 1996.
Diedrich, Torsten. *Waffen gegen das Volk. Der 17. Juni 1953 in der DDR*. München: Oldenbourg, 2003.
Diehl, James. *Paramilitary Politics in Weimar Germany*. Bloomington: Indiana University Press, 1977.
Diestelkamp, Bernhard. "Kontinuität und Wandel in der Rechtsordnung 1945 bis 1955." In *Westdeutschland 1945–1955. Unterwerfung, Kontrolle, Integration*, edited by Ludolf Herbst, 85–105. München: Oldenbourg, 1986.
Diewald-Kerkmann, Gisela. *Politische Denunziation im NS-Regime oder Die kleine Macht der 'Volksgenossen.'* Bonn: J.H.W. Dietz Nachfolger, 1995.
Diewald-Kerkamnn, Gisela. "Vertrauensleute, Denunzianten, Geheime und Inoffizielle Mitarbeiter in diktatorischen Regimen." In *Doppelte Zeitgeschichte. Deutsch-deutsche*

Beziehungen 1945–1990, edited by Arnd Bauerkämper et al., 282–93. Bonn: J.H.W. Dietz Nachf., 1998.

Dilling, Matthias. "Two of the Same Kind? The Rise of the AfD and Its Implications for the CDU/CSU." *German Politics and Society* 36, no. 1 (2018): 84–104

Dirke, Sabine von. *"All Power to the Imagination!" West German Counterculture from the Student Movement to the Greens*. Lincoln: University of Nebraska Press, 1997.

Dittberner, Jürgen. *Die FDP. Geschichte, Personen, Organisation, Perspektiven. Eine Einführung*. Wiesbaden: Verlag für Sozialwissenschaften, 2005.

Dittberner, Jürgen. *Parteienstaat ade? Zur Geschichte und Kultur der politischen Parteien in Deutschland*. Berlin: Logos Verlag, 2015.

Doering-Manteuffel, Anselm et al. (eds.). *Der Brokdorf-Beschluss des Bundesverfassungsgerichts 1985*. Tübingen: Mohr Siebeck, 2015.

Doering-Manteuffel, Anselm. "Fortschrittsglaube und sozialer Wandel. Die Entstehung der anti-AKW Bewegung." In *Brokdorf Beschluß*, edited by idem et al., 83–112.

Doering-Manteuffel, Anselm. "Politische Kulktur im Wandel." In *Identität und politische Kultur*, edited by Andreas Dornheim and Sylvia Greiffenhagen, 146–58. Stuttgart: Verlag W. Kohlhammer, 2003.

Doering-Manteuffel, Anselm. "Strukturmerkmale der Kanzlerdemokratie." *Der Staat* 30 (1991): 1–18.

Doering-Manteuffel, Anselm. *Wie westlich sind die Deutschen? Amerikanisierung und Westernisierung im 20. Jahrhundert*. Göttingen: Vandenhoeck & Ruprecht, 1999.

Drescher, Heiko. *Genese und Hintergründe der Demonstrationsstrafrechtsreform von 1970*. PhD dissertation, Heinrich Heine Universität. Düsseldorf, 2005.

"Dresden protestiert gegen Pegida." Deutsche Welle, October 20, 2019. Available online: https://www.dw.com/de/dresden-protestiert-gegen-pegida/a-50908199 (accessed May 16, 2020).

Dreyer, Michael. "Weimar als wehrhafte Demokratie—ein unterschätztes Vorbild." In *Die Weimarer Verfassung—Wert und Wirkung für die Demokratie*, edited by Sebatian Lasch, 161–89. Erfurt: n.p., 2009.

Druxes, Helga. "'Montag ist Wieder Pegida-Tag!' Pegida's Community Building and Discursive Strategies." *German Politics & Society* 34, no. 4 (2016): 17–33.

Durner, Wolfgang. *Antiparlamentarismus in Deutschland*. Würzburg: Königshausen & Neumann, 1997.

Ebersold, Günther. *Mündigkeit. Zur Geschichte eines Begriffs*. Frankfurt/M: Peter Lang, 1980.

Ebert, Theodor. "Direkte Aktion in Formaldemokratien." In *Die rebellischen Studenten. Elite der Demokratie oder Vorhut eines linken Faschismus?* edited by Hans Julius Schoeps and Christopher Dannmann, 124–38. München: Bechtle Verlag, 1968.

Ebert, Theodor. *Gewaltfreier Aufstand. Alternative zum Bürgerkrieg*. 3rd. ed. Waldkirch: Waldkircher Verlagsgesellschaft, 1983.

Eckart, Rainer. "Widerstand und Opposition in der DDR." *Zeitschrift für Geschichtswissenschaft* 44 (1996): 49–67.

Edwards, Michael. "Introduction: Civil Society and the Geometry of Human Relations." In *The Oxford Handbook of Civil Society*, edited by idem, 3–14. Oxford: Oxford University Press, 2011.

Eghigian, Greg. "Homo Munitus. The East German Observed." In *Socialist Modern*, edited by Pence and Betts, 37–70.

Ehls, Marie-Luise. *Protest und Propaganda: Demonstrationen in Berlin zur Zeit der Weimarer Republik*. Berlin: de Gruyter, 1997.

Ehrenberg, John. "The History of Civil Society Ideas." In *Oxford Handbook of Civil Society*, edited by Michael Edwards, 15–28.
Eisel, Stephen. *Minimalkonsens und freiheitliche Demokratie. Eine Studie zur Akzeptanz der Grundlagen der demokratischen Ordnung in der Bundesrepublik Deutschland*. Paderborn: Schöningh, 1986.
Eisenfeld, Bernd. "Die Ausreisebewegung—eine Erscheinungsform widerständigen Verhaltens." In *Selbstbehauptung*, edited by Poppe, 192–223.
Eisenfeld, Bernd und Peter. "Widerständiges Verhalten in der DDR 1979–1982." In *Opposition*, edited by Kuhrt et al., 83–131.
Eitler, Pascal. "'Alternative' Religion. Subjektivierungspraktiken und Politisierungsstratagien im 'New Age' (Westdeutschland 1979–1990)." In *Alternative*, edited by Reichert and Siegfried, 335–52.
Eley, Geoff. "Anti-Semitism, Agrarian Mobilization, and the Conservative Party: Radicalism and Containment in the Founding of the Agrarian League, 1890–93." In *Between Reform, Reaction, and Resistance*, edited by Jones and Retallack, 187–227. Providence: Oxford, 1993.
Eley, Geoff. *Forging Democracy. The History of the Left in Europe, 1850–2000*. Oxford: Oxford University Press, 2002.
Eley, Geoff. "General Thoughts." In *Citizenship and National Identity in Twentieth-Century Germany*, edited by idem and Jan Palmowski, 233–46. Stanford: Stanford University Press, 2008.
Eley, Geoff. "Making a Place in the Nation. Meanings of 'Citizenship' in Wilhelmine Germany." In *Wilhelminism and it Legacies. German Modernities, Imperialism, and the Meanings of Reform, 1890–1933*, edited by idem and James Retallack, 16–33. New York: Berghahn Books, 2003.
Eley, Geoff. *Reshaping the German Right. Radical nationalism and Political Change after Bismarck*. New Haven, CT: Yale University Press, 1980.
Ellwein, Thomas. "Politische Verhaltenslehre heute." In *Bürger*, edited by Raschke, 204–16.
Engelmann, Frederick C. "Perceptions of the Great Coalition in West Germany, 1966–1969." *Canadian Journal of Political Science* 5, no. 1 (1972): 28–54
Engels, Jens Ivo. "Umweltschutz in der Bundesrepublik—von der Unwahrscheinlichkeit einer Alternativbewegungung." In *Alternative*, edited by Reichardt and Siegfried, 405–22.
Erger, Johannes. *Der Kapp-Lüttwitz Putsch. Ein Beitrag zur deutschen Innenpolitik 1919/1920*. Düsseldorf: Droste Verlag, 1967.
Erhardt, Klaudia. "Politisch-ideologische Einstellungsmuster und Wahlverhalten in der Umbruchphase." In *Zwischen*, edited by Klingemann et al., 63–101.
Essner, Cornelia. *Die "Nürnberger Gesetze" oder Die Verwaltung des Rassenwahns 1933–1945*. Paderborn: Schöningh, 2002.
Euchner, Walter. "Sozialdemokratie und Demokratie. Zum Demokratieverständnis der SPD in der Weimarer Republik." *Archiv für Sozialgeschichte* 26 (1986): 125–78.
Evans, Richard J. "Coercion and Consent in Nazi Germany." *Proceedings of the British Academy* 151 (2006): 53–81.
Evans, Richard J. *The Coming of the Third Reich*. New York: The Penguin Press, 2004.
Evans, Richard J. *The Feminist Movement in Germany 1894–1933*. London: Sage Publications, 1976.
Evans, Richard J. "'Red Wednesday' in Hamburg: Social Democrats, Police and Lumpenproletariat in the Suffrage Disturbances of 17 January 1906." *Social History* 4, no. 1 (1979): 1–31.

Ewald, S. "Bericht aus dem Geräte- und Reglerwerk Teltow (GRW)." In *Aufbruch*, edited by Gehrke and Hürtgen, 32–36.
Fahlenbrach, Kathrin. "Introduction. Media and Protest Movements." In *Media and Revolt*, edited by idem, 1–16.
Fahlenbrach, Kathrin. "Protest in Television. Visual Protest on Screen." In *Media and Revolt*, edited by idem et al., 235–50.
Fahlenbrach, Kathrin. *Protest-Inszenierungen. Visuelle Kommunikation und kollektive Identitäten in Protestbewegungen*. Wiesbaden: Westdeutscher Verlag, 2002.
Fahlenbrach, Kathrin and Laura Stapane. "Visual and Media Strategies of the Peace Movement." In *The Nuclear Crisis. The Arms Race, Cold War Anxiety, and the German Peace Movement of the 1980s*, edited by Christoph Becker-Schaum et al., 222–41. New York: Berghahn Books, 2016.
Fahrmeir, Andreas. *Citizenship. The Rise and Fall of a Modern Concept*. New Haven, CT: Yale University Press, 2007.
Falter, Jürgen W. "Die Wähler der NSDAP 1928–1933: Sozialstruktur und parteipolitische Herkunft." In *Machtergreifung*, edited by Michalka, 47–59.
Falter, Jürgen. "Politischer Extremismus." In *Wirklich?* edited by idem, 403–33.
Falter, Jürgen W. *Rechtsextremismus. Ergebnisse und Perspektive der Forschung*. Opladen: Westdeutschder Verlag, 1996.
Falter, Jürgen. "Social Bases of Cleavages in the Weimar Republic, 1919–1933." In *Elections*, edited by Jones and Retallack, 371–88.
Falter, Jürgen W. et al. (eds.), *Wirklich ein Volk? Die politische Orientierungen von Ost- und Westdeutschen im Vergleich*. Opladen: Leske + Budrich, 2000.
Fay, Jennifer. *Theaters of Occupation. Hollywood and the Reeducation of Postwar Germany*. Minneapolis: University of Minnesota Press, 2008.
Fehrenbach, Heide. *Cinema in Democratizing Germany. Reconstructing National Identity after Hitler*. Chapel Hill: University of North Carolina Press, 1995.
Feist, Ursula. "Zur politischen Akkulturation der vereinigten Deutschen. Eine Analyse aus Anlaß der ersten gesamtdeutschen Bundestagswahl." *APZ* B11–12 (1991): 21–32.
Feist, Ursula and Klaus Liepelt. "Auseinander oder miteinander? Zum unterschiedlichen Politikverständnis der Deutschen in Ost und West." In *Wahlen und Wähler: Analysen aus Anlaß der Bundestagswahl 1990*, edited by Max Kaase and Hans-Dieter Klingemann, 576–611. Wiesbaden: Westdeutscher Verlag, 1994.
Feldman, Gerald D. "German Business between War and Revolution: The Origins of the Stinnes-Legien Agreement." In *Entstehung und Wandel der modernen Gesellschaft. Festschrift für Hans Rosenberg zum 65. Geburtstag*, edited by Gerhard A. Ritter, 312–41. Berlin: Walter de Gruyter, 1970.
Fennemore, Mark. "The Limits of Repression and Reform: Youth Policy in the Early 1960s." In *Workers' State*, edited by Major/Osmond, 171–89.
Fennemore, Mark. *Sex, Thugs and Rock 'n' Roll. Teenage Rebels in East Germany*. New York: Berghahn Books, 2009.
Fenske, Hans. *Deutsche Verfassungsgeschichte. Vom Norddeutschen Bund bis heute*. 2nd ed. Berlin: Colloquium Verlag, 1984.
Fenske, Michaela. *Demokratie erschreiben. Bürgerbriefe und Petitionen als Medien politischer Kultur 1950–1974*. Frankfurt: Campus Verlag, 2013.
Fereidooni, Karim. *Diskriminierungs- und Rassismuserfahrungen im Schulwesen*. Wiesbaden: Springer VS, 2016.
Fest, Joachim. *Hitler*. Trsl. by Richard and Clara Winston. New York: Vintage Books, 1974.
Fischer, Conan. *The Ruhr Crisis, 1923–1924*. Oxford: Oxford University Press, 2003.

Fitzpatrick, Matthew P. *Purging the Empire. Mass Expulsions in Germany, 1871–1914*. Oxford: Oxford University Press, 2015.
Fitzpatrick, Sheila and Robert Gellately. "Introduction to the Practices of Denunciation in Modern European History." In *Accusatory Practices. Denunciation in Modern European History*, edited by idem. Chicago: University of Chicago Press, 1997.
Föllmer, Moritz. *Individuality and Modernity in Berlin. Self and Society from Weimar to the Wall*. Cambridge: Cambridge University Press, 2013.
Föllmer, Moritz. "The Problem of National Solidarity in Interwar Germany." *German History* 23 (2005): 202–31.
Föllmer, Moritz. "Was Nazism Collectivistic?" *Journal of Modern History* 82 (2010): 61–100.
Forner, Sean. *German Intellectuals and the Challenge of Democratic Renewal. Culture and Politics after 1945*. Cambridge: Cambridge University Press, 2014.
Förster, Peter and Günther Roski. *DDR zwischen Wende und Wahl. Meinungsforscher analysieren den Umbruch*. Berlin: Links Druck Verlag, 1990.
Frankland, E. Gene and Donald Schoonmaker. *Between Protest and Power. The Green Party in Germany*. Boulder: Westview Press, 1992.
Frei, Norbert. *Adenauer's Germany: The Politics of Amnesty and Integration*. Trsl. by Joel Golb. New York: Columbia University Press, 2002.
Frei, Norbert. "Der *Spiegel*, die Freiheit der Presse und die Obrigkeit in der Bundesrepublik." In *Spiegel Affäre. Ein Skandal und seine Folgen*, edited by Martin Doerry and Hauke Janssen, 37–49. München: Deutsche Verlags-Anstalt, 2013.
Frei, Norbert. *National Socialist Rule in Germany. The Führer State, 1933–1945*. Trsl. by Simon Steyne. Oxford: Oxford University Press, 1993.
Frei, Norbert. "People's Community and War: Hitler's Popular Support." In *The Third Reich between Vision and Reality. New Perspectives on German History 1918–1945*, edited by Hans Mommsen, 59–77. Oxford: Berg Publishers, 2001.
Frei, Norbert. "'Volksgemeinschaft.' Erfahrungsgeschichte und Lebenswirklichkeit der Hitler-Zeit." In *1945 und wir: Das dritte Reich*, edited by idem, 107–28. München: Beck Verlag, 2005.
Frei, Norbert et al. *Zur rechten Zeit. Wider die Rückkehr des Nationalismus*. Berlin: Ullstein, 2019.
Freitag, Werner. "Der Führermythos im Fest. Festfeuerwerk, NS-Liturgie, Dissens und 100% KDF-Stimmung." In *Das Dritte Reich im Fest. Führermythos, Feierlaune und Verweigerung in Westfalen 1933–1945*, edited by idem, 11–69. Bielefeld: Verlag für Regionalgeschichte, 1997.
Frevert, Ute. *A Nation in Barracks. Modern Germany, Military Conscription and Civil Society*. Oxford: Berg Publishers, 2004.
Frevert, Ute. *Women in German History. From Bourgeois Emancipation to Sexual Liberation*. New York: Berg, 1989.
Friedlander, Henry. *The Origins of the Nazi Genocide. From Euthanasia to the Final Solution*. Chapel Hill: University of North Carolina Press, 1995.
Friedrich, Thomas. "Aspekte der Verfassungsentwicklung und der individuellen (Grund) Rechtsposition in der DDR." In *Sozialgeschichte der DDR*, edited by Helmut Kaelble et al., 483–97. Stuttgart: Klett-Cotta, 1994.
Fritzsche, Peter "Die Idee des Volkes und der Aufstieg der Nazis." In *Attraktion*, edited by Brockhaus, 161–73.
Fritzsche, Peter. *Germans into Nazis*. Cambridge: Cambridge University Press, 1998.
Fritzsche, Peter. *Life and Death in the Third Reich*. Cambridge: Belknap Press of Harvard University, 2008.

Fritzsche, Peter. *Rehearsals for Fascism. Populism and Political Mobilization in Weimar Germany*. New York: Oxford University Press, 1990.
Fröhlich, Claudia and Michael Kohlstruck. "Vergangenheitspolitik in kritischer Absicht." In *Engagierte Demokraten. Vergangenheitspolitik in kritischer Absicht*, edited by idem, 243–68. Münster: Westfälisches Dampfboot, 1999.
Fromme, Friedrich Karl. *Von der Weimarer Verfassung zum Bonner Grundgesetz: Die verfassungspolitischen Folgerungen des Parlamentarischen Rates aus Weimarer Republik und nationalsozialistischer Diktatur*. Berlin: Duncker & Humblot, 1999 [1958].
Fuchs, Dieter. "Das Konzept der politischen Kultur: Die Fortsetzung einer Kontroverse in konstruktiver Arbeit." In *Bürger und Demokratie in Ost und West. Studien zur politischen Kultur und zum politischen Prozess*, edited by idem et al., 27–49. Wiebaden: Westdeutscher Verlag, 2002.
Fuchs, Dieter. "The Democratic Political Culture of Unified Germany." In *Critical Citizens. Global Support for Democratic Government*, edited by Pippa Norris, 123–45. Oxford: Oxford University Press, 1999.
Fuchs, Dieter. "Die Aktionsformen der neuen sozialen Bewegungen." In *Willensbildung* edited by Falter et al., 621–34.
Fuchs, Dieter et al. "Die Akzeptanz der Demokratie des vereinigten Deutschland. Oder: Wann ist ein Unterschied ein Unterschied?" *Aus Politik und Zeitgeschichte* 51 (1997): 3–12.
Fuchs, Dieter et al. "Perspektiven der politischen Kultur im vereinigen Deutschland." *APZ* 22 (1991): 35–45.
Fuchs, Dieter et al. "Support for the Democratic System." In *Citizens*, edited by Klingemann and Fuchs, 323–53.
Fuchs, Dieter. "Welche Demokratie wollen die Deutschen? Einstellungen zur Demokatie im vereinigten Deutschland." In *Orientierungen* edited by Gabriel, 81–113.
Fulbrook, Mary. *Anatomy of a Dictatorship. Inside the GDR 1949–1989*. Oxford: Oxford University Press, 1995.
Fulbrook, Mary. "Germany for the Germans? Citizenship and Nationality in a Divided Nation." In *Citizenship, Nationality and Migration in Europe*, edited by David Casarani and idem, 88–105. London: Routledge, 1996.
Fulbrook, Mary. "'Normalisation' in the GDR in Retrospect: East German Perspectives on Their Own Lives." In *Power*, edited by idem, 278–319.
Fulbrook, Mary. *The People's State. East Germany Society from Hitler to Honecker*. New Haven, CT: Yale University Press, 2005.
Fulbrook, Mary. *Power and Society in the GDR, 1961–1979. The Normalisation of Rule?* New York: Berghahn, 2013.
Fulda, Daniel et al. "Zur Einleitung." In *Demokratie im Schatten der Gewalt. Geschichtliche Privaten im deutschen Nachkrieg*, edited by idem, 7–21. Göttingen: Wallenstein Verlag, 2010.
Fuller, Linda. *Where Was the Working Class? Revolution in East Germany*. Urbana: University of Illinois Press, 1999.
Funke, Manfred. "Republik im Untergang. Die Zerstörung des Parlamentarismus als Vorbereitung der Diktatur." In *Weimarer Republik*, edited by Bracher et al., 505–31.
Gabriel, Elun T. *Assassins and Conspirators: Anarchism, Socialism, and Political Culture in Imperial Germany*. DeKalb: Northern Illinois University Press, 2014.
Gabriel, Oscar W. "Aktivisten als Träger des demokratischen Credos? Zum Zusammenhang zwischen politischer Partizipation und der Unterstützung demokraischer Prinzipien im vereinigten Deutschland." In *Demokratie*, edited by Niedermayer and Westle, 34–45.

Gabriel, Oscar W. "Demokratiezufriedenheit und demokratische Einstellungen in der Bundesrepublik Deutschland." *Aus Politik und Zeitgeschichte* B22 (1987): 34–5.
Gabriel, Oscar W. "Demokratische Einstellungen in einem Land ohne demokratische Traditionen? Die Unterstützung der Demokratie in den neuen Bundesländer im Ost-West Vergleich." In *Wirklich*, edited by Falter et al., 41–77.
Gabriel, Oscar. "Politische und soziale Partizipation." In *Handbuch Politisches System der Bundesrepublik Deutschland*, edited by idem et al., 523–74. München: R. Oldenbourg, 2005.
Gabriel, Oscar W. "Wächst zusammen, was zusammen gehört?" In *Wächst*, edited by idem et al., 385–423.
Gabriel, Oscar W. et al. (eds.). *Wächst zusammen, was zusammen gehört? Stabilität und Wandel politischer Einstellungen im wiedervereinigten Deutschland*. Baden-Baden: Nomos Verlag, 2005.
Gabriel, Oscar. "Zwanzig Jahre nach der Vereinigung: Politische Einstellungen und politische Kultur in Deutschland." In *20 Jahre Deutsche Einheit. Bilanz und Perspektiven*. 2nd ed., edited by Kurt Bohr and Arno Krause, 197–211. Baden-Baden: Nomos Verlag, 2011.
Gabriel, Oscar W. and Hans Rattinger. "Die Struktur des Einstellungsraumes im vereinigten Deutschland." In *Wächst*, edited by Gabriel et al., 9–47.
Gabriel, Oscar W. and Katja Neller. "Einleitung." In *Wirklich*, edited by Jürgen Falter et al., 9–38. Opladen: Leske + Budrich, 2000.
Gagel, Walter. *Die Wahlrechtsfrage in der Geschichte der deutschen liberalen Parteien 1848–1918*. Düsseldorf: Droste Verlag, 1958.
Gailus, Manfred and Armin Nolzen. "Einleitung: Vielkonkurrierende Gläubigkeiten—aber eine Volksgemeinschaft?" In *Zerstrittene "Volksgemeinschaft." Glaube, Konfession und Religion im Nationalsozialismus*, edited by idem, 7–33. Göttingen: Vandenhoeck & Ruprecht, 2011.
Gaiser, Wolfgang and Johann de Rijka. "Partizipation und politisches Engagement." In *Unzufriedene Demokraten*, edited by Gille and Krüger, 269–323.
Gall, Lothar. *Bismarck. The White Revolutionary. Vol. I. 1815–1871*. Trsl. by J. A. Underwood. London: Allen & Unwin, 1986.
Gangl, Hans. "Der deutsche Weg zum Verfassungsstaat im 19. Jahrhundert." In *Probleme des Konstitutionalismus im 19. Jahrhundert*, edited by Ernst-Wolfgang Böckenförde, 215–29. Berlin: Duncker & Humblot, 1975.
Gass-Bolm, Torsten. "Revolution im Klassenzimmer? Die Schülerbewegung 1967–1970 und der Wandel der deutschen Schule." In *1968*, edited by von Hodenberg and Siegfried, 113–38.
Geary, Dick. "Social Protest in Western Germany after 1945." *Contemporary German Studies* 1 (1985): 5–15.
Gehrke, Bernd. "Demokratiebewegung und Betriebe in der 'Wende.'" In *Der betriebliche Aufbruch im Herbst 1989: Die unbekannte Seite der DDR-Revolte*, edited by idem and Renate Hürtgen, 204–46. Berlin: Bildungswerk Berlin, 2001.
Gehrke, Bernd and Renate Hürtgen (eds.). *Der betriebliche Aufbruch im Herbst 1989*. Berlin: Bildungswerk, 2001.
Geisel, Christoph. *Auf der Suche nach einem dritten Weg. Das politische Selbstverständnis der DDR-Opposition in den achtziger Jahren*. Berlin: C.H. Links Verlag, 2005.
Gellately, Robert. *Backing Hitler. Consent and Coercion in Nazi Germany*. Oxford: Oxford University Press, 2001.
Gellately, Robert. "Denunciations in Twentieth-Century Germany: Aspects of Self-Policing in the Third Reich and the German Democratic Republic." In *Accusatory Practices*, edited by Fitzpatrick and Gellately, 85–120.

Gellately, Robert and Nathan Stoltzfus, "Social Outsiders and the Construction of the Community of the People." In *Social Outsiders in Nazi Germany*, edited by idem, 3–19. Princeton, NJ: Princeton University Press, 2001.
Gensicke, Thomas. *Mentalitätswandlungen im Osten Deutschlands seit den 70er Jahren*. Speyer: Forschungsinstitut für Öffentliche Verwaltung, 1992.
Gerhard, Ute. "Die staatlich institutionalisierte 'Lösung' der Frauenfrage. Zur Geschichte der Geschlechterverhältnisse in der DDR." In *Sozialgeschichte*, edited by Kaelble et al., 383–403.
Gern, Christiane. "Commonsense Explanations of the Revolution." In *Origins*, edited by Opp et al., 211–23.
Gerstenberger, Heidi. "Acquiescence?" In *Probing the Depths of German Antisemitism. German Society and the Persecution of the Jews, 1933–1941*, edited by David Bankier, 19–35. New York: Berghahn Books, 2000.
Gerth, H. Hans and Charles Wright Mills. "A Biographical View." In *From Max Weber. Essays in Sociology*, edited by idem, 3–30. New York: Oxford University Press, 1946.
Geyer, Michael. "Cold War Angst. The Case of West German Opposition to Rearmament and Nuclear Weapons." In *Miracle Years*, edited by Schissler, 376–408.
Geyer, Michael. "Traditional Elites and National Socialist Leadership." In *The Rise of the Nazi Regime. Historical Reassessments*, edited by Charles S. Maier, 57–73. Boulder, CO: Westview Press, 1986.
Geyer, Michael and John Boyer. "Introduction: Resistance against the Third Reich as Intellectual Knowledge." In *Resistance*, edited by idem, 1–11.
Gijsenbergh, Joris. "The Semantics of 'Democracy' in Social Democratic Parties. Netherlands, Germany and Sweden, 1917–1939." *Archiv für Sozialgeschichte* 53 (2013): 147–74.
Gille, Martina et al. "Politische Orientierungen." In *Unzufriedene Demokraten*, edited by Gille and Krüger, 205–65.
Gille, Martina. "Werte, Rollenbilder und soziale Ordnung." In *Unzufriedene Demokraten. Politische Orientierungen der 16- bis 29-jährigen im vereinigten Deutschland*, edited by idem and Winfried Krüger, 143–203. Opladen: Leske + Budrich, 2000.
Giordano, Ralph. *Die zweite Schuld. oder Von der Last Deutscher zu sein*. Köln: Kiepenheuer & Witsch, 2000.
Glaeser, Andreas. *Political Epistemics. The Secret Police, the Opposition, and the End of East German Socialism*. Chicago: University of Chicago Press, 2011.
Glaeser, Walter Schmitt. *Private Gewalt im politischen Meinungskampf. Zugleich ein Beitrag zur Legitimität des Staates*. Berlin: Duncker & Humblot 1992.
Glaessner, Gert-Joachim. *The Unification Process in Germany. From Dictatorship to Democracy*. New York: St. Martin's Press, 1992.
Gluchowski, Peter et al. "Politisch-kultureller Wandel in Deutschland. Eine Übersicht über Veränderungen und Wandlungslinien." In *Staatsbürger*, edited by Plasser and Ulram, 157–213.
Gluchowski, Peter and Carsten Zelle. "Demokratisierung in Ostdeutschland. Aspekte der politischen Kultur in der Periode des Systemwechsels." In *Regimewechsel. Demokratisierung und politische Kultur in Ost-Mitteleuropa*, edited by Peter Gerlach et al., 231–74. Wien: Böhlau Verlag, 1992.
Goehle, Todd Michael. "Challenging Television's Revolution. Media Representations of 1968 Protests in Television and Tabloids." In *Media and Revolt. Strategies and Performances from the 1960s to the Present*, edited by Kathrin Fahlenbrach et al., 217–33. New York: Berghahn, 2016.
Goldberg, Ann. *Honor, Politics, and the Law in Imperial Germany, 1871–1914*. Cambridge: Cambridge University Press, 2010.

Goltz, Anna von der. "A Polarized Generation? Conservative Students and West Germany's, '1968.'" In *Talkin' 'bout My Generation? Conflicts of Generation Building and Europe's '1968,'* edited by idem, 195–215. Göttingen: Wall stein Verlag, 2011.
Görtemaker, Manfred. *Kleine Geschichte der Bundesrepublik Deutschland*. München: C. H. Beck, 2002.
Gosewinkel, Dieter and Jürgen Kocka. "Editor's Preface." In *Civil Society. Berlin Perspectives*, edited by John Keane, ix–xi. New York: Berghahn Books, 2007.
Götschmann, Dirk. *Bayerischer Parlamentarismus im Vormärz. Die Ständeversammlung des Königreichs Bayern 1819–1848*. Düsseldorf: Droste Verlag, 2002.
Grax, Jonathan. *The Role of the Masses in the Collapse of the GDR*. New York: St. Martin's Press, 2000.
Grebing, Helga. "Demokratie ohne Demokraten? Politisches Denken, Einstellungen und Mentalitäten in der Nachkriegszeit." In *Wie neu war der Neubeginn?: Zum deutschen Kontinuitätsproblem nach 1945*, edited by Everhard Holtmann, 6–19. Erlangen: Universitätsbund, 1989.
Greenberg, Udi. *The Weimar Century. German Émigrés and the Ideological Foundations of the Cold War*. Princeton: Princeton University Press, 2014.
Greiffenhagen, Martin. *Kulturen des Kompromisses*. Opladen: Leske & Budrich, 1999.
Greiffenhagen, Martin und Sylvia. *Ein schwieriges Vaterland. Zur politischen Kultur Deutschlands*. München: List Verlag, 1979.
Griffin, Roger. "Die größten Verführer aller Zeiten? Die Anziehungskraft des Nazismus." In *Attraktion*, edited by Brockhaus, 213–30.
Grimm, Dieter. *Deutsche Verfassungsgeschichte 1776–1866*. Frankfurt/M: Suhrkamp, 1988.
Großbolting, Thomas. "Als Laien und Genossen das Fragen lernten. Neue Formen institutioneller Öffentlichkeit im Katholizismus und in der Arbeiterbewegung der sechziger Jahre." In *Demokratisierung und gesellschaftlicher Aufbruch*, edited by Matthias Frese et al., 147–79. Paderborn: Schöningh, 2003.
Groh, Katharin. "Zwischen Skylla und Charybdis. Die streitbare Demokratie." In *Schatten*, edited by Gusy, 423–54.
Gross, Michael B. "Kulturkampf und Geschlechterkampf. Anti-Catholicism, Catholic Women, and the Public." In *Conflict, Catastrophe and Continuity. Essays on Modern German History*, edited by Frank Biess et al., 27–43. New York: Berghahn Books, 2007.
Grosser, Dieter. *Vom monarchischen Konstitutionalismus zur parlamentarischen Demokratie*. Den Haag: Martinus Nijhoff, 1970.
Grotum, Thomas. *Die Halbstarken. Zur Geschichte einer Jugendkultur der 50er Jahre*. Frankfurt: Campus Verlag, 1994.
Gruner, Wolf. "Defiance and Protest. A Comparative Microhistorical Reevaluation of Individual Jewish Reponses to Nazi Persecution." In *Microhistories of the Holocaust*, edited by Claire Zalc and Tal Bruttmann, 209–26. New York: Berghahn Books, 2017.
Gruner, Wolf. "Indifference? Participation and Protest as Individual Responses to the Persecution of the Jews as Revealed in Berlin Police Logs and Trial Records 1933–45." In *The Germans and the Holocaust. Popular Responses to the Persecution and Murder of the Jews*, edited by Susanna Schrafstetter and Alan E. Steinweis, 59–83. New York: Berghahn, 2015.
Gruner, Wolf. *Widerstand in der Rosenstraße. Die Fabrik-Aktion und die Verfolgung der "Mischehen" 1943*. Frankfurt: Fischer Taschenbuchverlag, 2005.
Guggenberger, Bernd. "Bürgerinitiativen: Krisensymptom oder Ergänzung des Parteiensystems?" In *Bürger*, edited by Raschke, 190–203.

Guggenberger, Bernd. "Die Grenzen des Gehorsams—Widerstandsrecht und atomares Zäsurbewußtsein." In *Neue Bewegungen*, edited by Roth and Rucht, 327–43.
Guggenberger, Bernd. "Krise der repräsentativen Demokratie. Die Legitimität der Bürgerinitiativen und das Prinzip der Mehrheitsentscheidung." In *Bürgerinitiativen und repräsentatives System*. 2nd ed., edited by idem and Udo Kempf, 23–56. Opladen: Westdeutscher Verlag, 1984.
Guggenberger, Bernd and Udo Kempf (eds.). *Bürgerinitiativen und repräsentatives System*. Opladen: Westdeutscher Verlag, 1984.
Gundelach, Peter. "Grass-Roots Activity." In *The Impact of Values*, edited by Jan v. Deth and Elinor Scarbrough, 412–40. Oxford: Oxford University Press, 1995.
Günther, Frieder. *Denken vom Staat her. Die bundesdeutsche Staatsrechtslehre zwischen Dezisionismus und Integration 1949-1970*. München: Oldenbourg, 2004.
Günther, Klaus. *Sozialdemokratie und Demokratie 1946-1966. Die SPD und das Problem der Verschränkung innerparteilicher und bundesrepublikanischer Demokratie*. Bonn: Verlag Neue Gesellschaft, 1979.
Gusy, Christoph (ed.). *Demokratisches Denken in der Weimarer Republik*. Baden-Baden: Nomos Verlagsgesellschaft, 2000.
Gusy, Christoph. *Die Lehre vom Parteienstaat in der Weimarer Republik*. Baden-Baden: Nomos Verlagsgesellschaft, 1993.
Gusy, Christoph. *Die Weimarer Reichsverfassung*. Tübingen: Mohr Siebeck, 1997.
Gusy, Christoph. "Fragen an das 'demokratische Denken' in der Weimarer Republik." In *Denken*, edited by idem, 635–63.
Gusy, Christoph (ed.). *Weimars lange Schatten—"Weimar" als Argumente nach 1945*. Baden-Baden: Nomos Verlag, 2003.
Häberle, Peter. "Verfassungsgerichtsbarkeit in der offenen Gesellschaft." In *Bundesverfassungsgericht*, edited by van Ooyen and Möllers, 35–46.
Habermas, Jürgen (ed.). *Observations on "The Spiritual Situation of the Age."* Cambridge: MIT Press, 1985.
Hachtmann, Rüdiger. "'Volksgemeinschaftliche Dienstleiter'? Anmerkungen zu Selbstverständnis und Funktion der Deutschen Arbeitsfront und der NS-Gemeinschaft 'Kraft durch Freude.'" In *"Volksgemeinschaft": Mythos, wirkungsmächtige soziale Verheißung oder soziale Realität im "Dritten Reich"? Zwischenbilanz einer kontroversen Debatte*, edited by Detlef Schmiechen-Ackermann, 111–31. Paderborn: Schöningh, 2012.
Hacke, Jens. "Der Staat in Gefahr. Die Bundesrepublik der 1970er Jahre zwischen Legitimitätskrise und Unregierbarkeit." In *Streit um den Staat*, edited by Geppert and idem, 188–206.
Hadjar, Andreas and Rolf Becker. "Unkonventionelle politische Partizipation im Zeitverlauf. Hat die Bildungsexpansion zu einer politischen Mobilisierung beigetragen?" *Kölner Zeitschrift für Soziologie und Sozialpsyschologie* 59, no. 3 (2007): 410–39.
Haffner, Sebastian. "Die neue Sensibilität des Bürgers." In *Bürgerinitiativen*, edited by Guggenberger and Kempe, 83–95.
Hagenlücke, Heinz. *Deutsche Vaterlandspartei. Die nationale Rechte am Ende des Kaiserreichs*. Düsseldorf: Droste Verlag, 1997.
Hake, Sabine. *Topographies of Class. Modern Architecture and Mass Society in Weimar Berlin*. Ann Arbor: University of Michigan Press.
Hall, Alex. *Scandal, Sensation and Social Democracy. The SPD Press and Wilhemine Germany, 1890-1914*. Cambridge: Cambridge University Press, 1977.

Hamilton, Richard J. *Who Voted for Hitler?* Princeton, NJ: Princeton University Press, 1982.
Hansen, Jan. "Der Protest und die Mächtigen: Zu den Auswirkungen von Friedensbewegung, Nuclear Weapons Freeze Campaign und Solidarnosc auf das Bonner 'Establishment.'" In "*All We Ever Wanted*," edited by Balz and Friedrichs, 231–46.
Hansen, Ronald. *Disobeying Hitler. German Resistance after Valkyrie*. Oxford: Oxford University Press, 2014.
Hanshew, Karin. *Terror and Democracy in West Germany*. Cambridge: Cambridge University Press, 2012.
Hardach, Gerd. "Krisen und Reform der Sozialen Marktwirtschaft. Grundzüge der wirtschaftlichen Entwicklung in der Bundesrepublik der 50er und 60er Jahren." In *Dynamische Zeiten. Die 60er Jahre in den beiden deutschen Gesellschaften*, edited by Axel Schildt et al., 197–217. Hamburg: Hans Christians Verlag, 2000.
Hardtwig, Wolfgang. "Der Bismarck Mythos. Gestalt und Funktion zwischen politischer Öffentlichkeit und Wissenschaft." In *Kulturgeschichte*, edited by idem, 61–90.
Hardtwig, Wolfgang. "Einleitung." In *Ordnungen in der Krise. Zur politischen Kulturgeschichte Deutschlands 1900–1933*, edited by idem, 11–18. München: R. Oldenbourg Verlag, 2007.
Harsch, Donna. *German Social Democracy and the Rise of Nazism*. Chapel Hill: University of North Carolina Press, 1993.
Hartung, Fritz. *Deutsche Verfassungsgeschichte. Vom 15. Jahrhundert bis zur Gegenwart*. 8th ed. Stuttgart: K. F. Koehler Verlag, 1950.
Harvey, Elizabeth. "Serving the Volk, Saving the Nation: Women in the Youth Movement and the Public Sphere in Weimar Germany." In *Elections*, edited by Jones and Retallack, 201–22.
Harvey, Elizabeth. *Women and the Nazi East. Agents and Witnesses of Germanization*. New Haven, CT: Yale University Press, 2003.
Haumann, Sebastian and Susanne Schregel. "Andere Räume, andere Städte und die Transformation der Gesellschaft. Hausbesetzungen und Atomwaffenfreie Zone als alternative Raumpraktiken." In "*All We Ever Wanted …" Eine Kulturgeschichte europäischer Protestbewegungen der 1980er Jahre*, edited by Hanno Balz and Jan-Henrik Friedrichs, 53–72. Berlin: Karl Dietz Verlag, 2012.
Haungs, Peter. "Bürgerinitiativen und Probleme der parlamentarischen Demokratie in der Bundesrepublik Deutschland." In *Bürgerinitiativen*, edited by Guggenberger and Kempf, 156–71.
Häuser, Iris. *Gegenidentitäten. Zur Vorbereitung des politischen Umbruchs in der DDR*. Münster: Lit, 1996.
Hayes, Peter. "'A Question Mark with Epaulettes'? Kurt von Schleicher and Weimar Politics." *Journal of Modern History* 52 (1980): 35–65.
Heberle, Rudolf. *From Democracy to Nazism. A Regional Case Study on Political Parties in Germany*. New York: Grosset & Dunlap, 1970.
Heilbronner, Oded. *Catholicism, Political Culture, and the Countryside. A Social History of the Nazi Party in South Germany*. Ann Arbor: University of Michigan Press, 1998.
Heims, Volker. *Das Andere der Zivilgesellschaft. Zur Archäologie eines Begriffs*. Bielefeld: transcript Verlag, 2002.
Heinsohn, Kirsten. "Im Dienste der deutschen Volksgemeinschaft: Die 'Frauenfrage' und konservative Parteien vor und nach dem Ersten Weltkrieg." In *Nation, Politik und Geschlecht. Frauenbewegungen und Nationalismus in der Moderne*, edited by Ute Planert, 215–33. Frankfurt: Campus Verlag, 2000.

Heitmeyer, Wilhelm. "Autoritär, national, radikal." *Süddeutsche Zeitung*, April 14, 2019. Available online: https://www.sueddeutsche.de/politik/afd-populismus-extremismus-1.4407594 (accessed May 18, 2020).
Henne, Thomas. "Von 0 auf Lüth in 6½ Jahren. Zu den prägenden Faktoren der Grundrechtsentscheidung." In *Lüth Urteil*, edited by Henne and Riedlinger, 197–222.
Henne, Thomas and Arne Riedlinger (eds.). *Das Lüth Urteil aus (rechts-) historischer Sicht*. Berlin: Berliner Wissenschafts-Verlag, 2005.
Hentschel, Volker. *Ludwig Erhard. Ein Politikerleben*. München: Olzog, 1996.
Herbert, Ulrich. "Arbeiter im 'Dritten Reich.'" *Geschichte und Gesellschaft* 15 (1989): 320–60.
Herbert, Ulrich. "Echoes of the *Volksgemeinschaft*." In *Visions of Community in Nazi Germany. Social Engineering and Private Lives*, edited by Martina Steber and Bernhard Gotto, 60–9. Oxford: Oxford University Press, 2014.
Herbert, Ulrich. *Hitler's Foreign Workers. Enforced Foreign Labor in Germany under the Third Reich*. Trsl. by William Templer. Cambridge: Cambridge University Press, 1997.
Herbert, Ulrich. "Liberalisierung als Lernprozeß. Die Bundesrepublik in der deutschen Geschichte—eine Skizze." In *Wandlungsprozesse in Westdeutschland. Belastung, Integration, Liberalisierung 1945–1980*, edited by idem, 7–49. Göttingen: Wallstein Verlag, 2002.
Herf, Jeffrey. *Divided Memory. The Nazi Past in the Two Germanies*. Cambridge: Harvard University Press, 1997.
Herlemann, Beatrix. "Communist Resistance between Comintern Directives and Nazi Terror." In *Reform and Revolution*, edited by Barclay and Weitz, 357–71.
Herzog, Rudolf. *Heil Hitler, das Schwein ist Tot! Lachen unter Hitler—Komik und Humor im Dritten Reich*. Berlin: Eichborn, 2006.
Hett, Benjamin Carter. *The Death of Democracy. Hitler's Rise to Power and the Destruction of Weimar Democracy*. New York: Henry Holt and Company, 2018.
Hettling, Manfred. *Politische Bürgerlichkeit. Der Bürger zwischen Individualität und Vergesellschaftung in Deutschland und der Schweiz von 1860 bis 1918*. Göttingen: Vandenhoeck & Ruprecht, 1999.
Hildebrandt, Heinrich and Walter Kettner (eds.). *Stahlhelm-Handbuch*. Berlin: Stahlhelm Verlag, 1931.
Hilgert, Christoph. "'… den freien, kritischen Geist unter der Jugend zu fördern.' Der Beitrag des Jugendfunks zur zeitgeschichtlichen und politischen Aufklärung von Jugendlichen in den 1950er Jahren." In *Die zweite Gründung der Bundesrepublik. Generationswechsel und intellektuelle Wortergreifungen 1955–1975*, edited by Franz-Werner Kersting et al., 21–41. Stuttgart: Franz Steiner Verlag, 2010.
Hirschfeld, Gerhard. "Die Attraktion des Ersten Weltkrieges für die Nazi-Bewegung." In *Attraktion*, edited by Brockhaus, 63–78.
Hoch, Gerhard. *Das Scheitern der Demokratie im ländlichen Raum. Das Beispiel der Region Kaltenkirchen Henstedt-Ulzburg 1870–1933*. Kiel: Neuer Malik Verlag, 1988.
Höcke, Björn. "Auf bestem Weg zur Volkspartei." *The European*, May 21, 2015. Available online: https://www.theeuropean.de/bjoern-hoecke/10074-afd-in-der-mitte-der-gesellschaft (accessed May 18, 2020).
Hocke, Peter. "Auswahlkriterien von Massenmedien bei der Berichterstattung über lokalen Protest. Eine Prüfung der Nachrichtenwert-Theorie anhand medienunabhängiger Demonstrationsdaten." In *Politische Akteure in der Mediendemokratie. Politiker in den Fesseln der Medien?*, edited by Heribert Schatz et al., 203–22. Opladen: Westdeutscher Verlag, 1998.

Hodenberg, Christina von. *Das andere Achtundsechzig. Gesellschaftsgeschichte einer Revolte*. München: C.H. Beck, 2018.
Hodenberg, Christina von. "Die Journalisten und der Aufbruch zur kritischen Öffentlichkeit." In *Wandlungsprozesse*, edited by Herbert, 278–311.
Hodenberg, Christina von. "Konkurrierende Konzepte von 'Öffentlichkeit' in der Ordnungskrise der 60er Jahre." In *Demokratisierung*, edited by Frese et al., 205–26.
Hodenberg, Christina von. *Konsens und Krise. Eine Geschichte der westdeutschen Medienöffentlichkeit 1945–1973*. Göttingen: Wallstein Verlag, 2006.
Hodenberg, Christina von and Detlef Siegfried (eds.). *Wo '1968' liegt. Reform und Revolte in der Geschichte der Bundesrepublik*. Göttingen: Vandenhoeck & Ruprecht, 2006.
Hoeres, Peter. "Aneignung und Abwehr der Demoskopie im intellektuellen Diskurs der frühen Bundesrepublik." In *zweite Gründung*, edited by Kersting et al., 69–84.
Hoffmann, Peter. *The History of the German Resistance, 1933–1945*. Trsl. by Richard Barry. Cambridge: MIT Press, 1979.
Hoffmann-Lange, Ursula. "Das rechtliche Einstellungspotential in der deutschen Jugend." Falter et al. (eds.). *Rechtsextremismus*, 121–37.
Hoffmann-Lange, Ursula et al. "Jugend und Politik in Deutschland." In *Kultur*, edited by Niedermayer and von Beyme, 140–62.
Hoffmann-Riem, Wolfgang. "Die Spiegel Affäre—ein Versagen der Justiz?" In *Spiegel*, edited by Doerry and Janssen, 130–49.
Hoffrogge, Ralf. *Working-Class Politics in the German Revolution. Richard Müller, the Revolutionary Shop Stewards and the Origins of the Council Movement*. Trsl by Joseph B. Keady. Leiden: Brill, 2014.
Holtmann, Everhard. "Subject Political Culture as Heritage? Continuities and Changes in the Early Postwar Years." In *Political Culture*, edited by Berg-Schlosser and Ralf, 78–87.
Hoppe, Bernd. *Von der parlamentarischen Demokratie zum Präsidialstaat. Verfassungsentwicklung am Beispiel der Kabinettsbildung in der Weimarer Republik*. Berlin: Duncker & Humblot, 1998.
Hosemann, Henriette. "Die Reform der Kriegsopferversorgung (1959) als Gegenstand von Protesthandlung." In *Ordnung und Protest. Eine gesamtdeutsche Protestgeschichte von 1949 bis heute*, edited by Martin Löhnig et al., 64. Tübingen: Mohr-Siebeck, 2015.
Hotzel, Curt. "Die großen Frontsoldatentage." In *Der Stahlhelm*. Bd. 1, edited by Franz Seldte. Berlin: Stahlhelm Verlag, 1932–33, 104–28.
Huber, Ernst Rudolf. *Verfassungsrecht des Großdeutschen Reiches*. Hamburg: Hanseatische Verlagsanstalt, 1939.
Huber, Josef. *Wer soll das alles ändern. Die Alternativen und die Alternativenbewegung*. Berlin: Rotbuch Verlag, 1984.
Hübner, Peter. "Arbeitskonflikte in Industriebetrieben in der DDR nach 1953." In *Selbstbehauptung*, edited by Poppe et al., 178–91.
Hübner, Peter. *Konsens, Konflikt und Kompromiß. Soziale Arbeiterinteressen und Sozialpolitik in der SBZ/DDR 1945–1970*. Berlin: Akademie Verlag, 1995.
Hucko, Elmar M. *The Democratic Tradition: Four German Constitutions*. Oxford: Berg Publishers, 1987.
Hughes, H. Stuart. *Consciousness and Society. The Reorientation of European Social Thought 1890–1930*. New York: Vintage Books, 1958.
Hughes, Michael L. "Civil Disobedience in Transnational Perspective: American and West German Anti-Nuclear-Power Protesters, 1975–1982." *Historical Social Research* 39, no. 1 (2014): 236–53.

Hughes, Michael L. "'The Knife in the Hands of the Children'? Debating the Political Mass Strike and Political Citizenship in Imperial Germany." *Labor History* 50, no. 2 (May 2009): 113–38.

Hughes, Michael L. *Paying for the German Inflation*. Chapel Hill: University of North Carolina Press, 1988.

Hughes, Michael L. "Reason, Emotion, Pressure, Violence: Modes of Demonstration as Conceptions of Political Citizenship in 1960s West Germany." *German History* 30, no. 2 (2012): 222–46.

Hughes, Michael L. "Rechtsstaat and *Recht* in West Germany's Nuclear Power Debate, 1975-1983." *Law and History Review* 33, no. 2 (2015): 411–34.

Hughes, Michael L. "Restitution and Democracy in Germany after Two World Wars." *Contemporary European History* 4, no. 1 (1994): 1–18.

Hughes, Michael L. *Shouldering the Burdens of Defeat. West Germany and the Reconstruction of Social Justice*. Chapel Hill: University of North Carolina Press, 1999.

Hughes, Michael L. "Splendid Demonstrations: The Political Funerals of Kaiser Wilhelm I and Wilhelm Liebknecht." *Central European History* 41 (2008): 229–53.

Hughes, Michael L. "'Through No Fault of Our Own.' West Germans Remember Their War Losses." *German History* 18, no. 2 (2000): 193–213.

Hürtgen, Renate. "'Keiner hatte Ahnung von Demokratie, im Betrieb sowieso nicht' Vom kollektiven Widerstand zur Eingabe oder Warum die Belegschaften 1989 an Anfang eines Neubeginn standen." In *Aufbruch*, edited by Gehrke and idem, 183–204.

Hürtgen, Renate. "Thesen zu Betriebs Wende." In *Aufbruch*, edited by Gehrke and Hürtgen, 24–31.

Hüttenberger, Peter. "Natioinalsozialistische Polykratie." *Geschichte und Gesellschaft* 2, no. 5 (1976): 417–42.

Imhoof, David. *Becoming a Nazi Town. Culture and Politics in Göttingen between the World Wars*. Ann Arbor: University of Michigan Press, 2013.

Inglehart, Ronald. *The Silent Revolution. Changing Values and Political Styles among Western Publics*. Princeton, NJ: Princeton University Press, 1977.

Inglehart, Ronald. "Values Ideology and Cognitive Mobilization in New Social Movements." In *Challenging*, edited by Dalton and Kuechler, 43–66.

Isensee, Josef. "Staatshoheit und Bürgerinitiativen." In *Staatsführung*, edited by Biedenkopf and v. Voss, 138–54.

Isensee, Josef. "Widerstand und demokratische Normalität." In *Jurist und Staatsbewußtsein*, edited by Peter Eisenmann et al., 41–52. Heidelberg: V. Decker und Müller, 1987.

Jäckel, Hartmut. "Die Verfassungsdebatte: Kein Abschied vom Grundgesetz." In *Die neue Bundesrepublik*, edited by idem, 127–45. Baden-Baden: Nomos Verlag, 1994.

Jander, Martin et al. "DDR-Opposition in den 70er und 80er Jahren. Ein Beitrag zu Geschichte und Forschungszustand." In *Geschichte und Transformation des SED-Staates: Beiträge und Analyse*, edited by Klaus Schröder, 233–50. Berlin: Akademie Verlag, 1994.

Jander, Martin. "Formierung und Krise der Opposition in der DDR. Die 'Initiative für unabhängige Gewerkschaften.'" In *Selbstbehauptung*, edited by Poppe et al., 284–300.

Jander, Martin. "Opposition in einer totalitären (Um-)Erziehungsdiktatur." In *Macht*, edited by Neubert and Eisenfeld, 77–87.

Jarausch, Konrad. *After Hitler. Recivilizing Germans, 1945–1995*. Oxford: Oxford University Press, 2006.

Jarausch, Konrad. "Amerikanische Einflüsse und deutsche Einsichten. Kulturelle Aspekte der Demokratisierung Westdeutschlands." In *Demokratiewunder*, edited by Bauerkämper et al., 57–81.

Jarausch, Konrad H. "Care and Coercion. The GDR as Welfare Dictatorship." In *Dictatorship*, edited by Jarausch, 47-69.
Jarausch, Konrad H. (ed.). *Dictatorship as Experience. Towards a Socio-Cultural History of the GDR*. New York: Berghahn Books, 1999.
Jarausch, Konrad et al. (eds.). *Different Germans, Many Germanies. New Transatlantic Perspectives*. New York: Berghahn Books, 2017.
Jarausch, Konrad. "Implosion oder Selbstbefreiung." In *Weg*, edited by Jarausch and Sabrow, 15-40.
Jaspar, Gotthard. *Die gescheiterte Zähmung*. Frankfurt/M: Suhrkamp, 1986.
Jasper, Gotthard. *Der Schutz der Republik. Studien zur staatlichen Sicherung der Demokratie in der Weimarer* Republik *1922-1930*. Tübingen: J.C.B. Mohr, 1963.
Jesse, Eckard. *Wahlrecht zwischen Kontinuität und Reform. Eine Analyse der Wahlsystemdiskussion und der Wahlrechtsänderungen in der Bundesrepublik Deutschland 1949-1983*. Düsseldorf: Droste Verlag, 1985.
Jesse, Eckhard. "Zwei verschiedene politische Kulturen in Deutschland?" In *neue Bundesrepublik*, edited by Jäckel, 97-125.
Joas, Hans and Frank Adloff. "Transformations of German Civil Society: Milieu change and Community Spirit." In *Civil Society*, edited by Keane, 103-38.
Jochheim, Gernot. *Protest in der Rosenstraße*. Stuttgart: Hoch-Verlag, 1990.
Johnson, Eric. *Nazi Terror. The Gestapo, Jews, and Ordinary Germans*. New York: Basic Books, 1999.
Jones, Larry Eugene. "Conservative Antisemitism in the Weimar Republic. A Case Study of the German National Peoples Party." In *The German Right in the Weimar Republic. Studies in the History of German Conservatism, Nationalism, and Antisemitism*, edited by idem, 79-107. New York: Berghahn Books, 2014.
Jones, Larry E. *German Liberalism and the Dissolution of the Weimar Party System, 1918-1933*. Chapel Hill: University of North Carolina Press, 1988.
Jones, Larry Eugene. "Nazis, Conservatives, and the Establishment of the Third Reich, 1932-1934." *Tel Aviver Jahrbuch für deutsche Geschichte* XXIII (1994): 41-64.
Jones, Larry and James Retallack (eds.). *Elections, Mass Politics, and Social Change in Modern Germany*. Cambridge: Cambridge University Press, 1992.
Jones, Mark. "The Crowd in the November Revolution, 1918." In *Germany 1916-1923. A Revolution in Context*, edited by Klaus Weinhauser, 37-57. Bielefeld: Transcript Verlag, 2015.
Jones, Mark. *Founding Weimar. Violence and the German Revolution of 1918-1919*. Cambridge: Cambridge University Press, 2016.
Jonsson, Stefan. *Crowds and Democracy. The Idea and Image of the Masses from Revolution to Fascism*. New York: Columbia University Press, 2013.
Joppke, Christian. *East German Dissidents and the Revolution of 1989. Social Movements in a Leninist Regime*. New York: NYU Press, 1995.
Joshi, Vandana. *Gender and Power in the Third Reich. Female Denouncers and the Gestapo*. New York: Palgrave Macmillan, 2003.
Juchler, Ingo. *Die Studentenbewegungen in den Vereinigten Staaten und der Bundesrepublik Deutschland der sechziger Jahre*. Berlin: Duncker & Humblot, 1996.
Jung, Otmar. "Wahlen und Abstimmung im Dritten Reich." In *Wahlen in Deutschland*, edited by Eckhard Jesse and Konrad Löw, 69-92. Berlin: Duncker & Humblot, 1998.
Kaase, Max. *The Development of Political Participation and Political Action Repertoires in West Germany, 1974-1978*. Frankfurt: Sonderforschungsbereich 3, Mikroanalytische Grundlagen der Gesellschaftspolitik, 1986.

Kaase, Max. "Partizapatorische Revolution—Ende der Parteien?" In *Bürger*, edited by Raschke, 173–89.

Kaase, Max. "Politische Beteiligung in den 80er Jahren: Strukturen und Idiosynkrasien." In *Politische Willensbildung und Interessenvermittlung*, edited by Jürgen Falter et al., 338–50. Opladen: Westdeutscher Verlag, 1984.

Kaase, Max and Alan Marsh. "Political Action Repertory. Changes over Time and a New Typology." In *Political Action*, edited by Barnes and Kaase, 137–66.

Kalb, Martin. *Coming of Age. Constructing and Controlling Youth in Munich, 1942-1973*. New York: Berghahn Books, 2016.

Kämper, Hedrun. "Demokratisches Wissen in der frühen Weimarer Republik. Historizität—Agonalität—Institutionalisierung." In *Demokratiegeschichte als Zäsurgeschichte. Diskurse der frühen Weimarer Republik*, edited by idem et al., 19–96. Berlin: de Gruyter, 2014.

Karapin, Roger. *Protest Politics in Germany. Movements on the Left and Right since the 1960s*. University Park: Pennsylvania State University Press, 2007.

Karcher, Katharina. *Sisters in Arms. Militant Feminisms in the Federal Republic of Germany since 1968*. New York: Berghahn Books, 2017.

Kater, Michael H. *The Nazi Party. A Social Profile of Members and Leaders 1919-1945*. Cambridge: Harvard University Press, 1983.

Katsiaficas, Georg. "Preface." In *The City Is Ours. Squatting and Autonomous Movements in Europe from the 1970s to the Present*, edited by Bart van der Steen et al., ix–xii. Oakland, CA: PM Press, 2017.

Kaufmann, Arthur. "Rechtsphilophie und Nationalsozialismus." In *Recht, Rechtsphilosophie und Nationalsozialismus* edited by Hubert Rottleuthner, 1–19. Wiesbaden: Franz Steiner Verlag, 1983.

Kautsky, Karl. "Die Aktion der Masse" [*Neue Zeit* 30, no. 1]. In *Die Massenstreikdebatte*, edited by Antonia Grunenberg, 261. Frankfurt: Europäische Verlagsanstalt, 1970.

Keßler, Mario and Thomas Klein. "Repression and Tolerance as Methods of Rule in Communist Societies." In *Dictatorship*, edited by Jarausch, 109–21.

Keil, Silke I. "Parteiidentifikation als der 'Pudels Kern?' Zum Einfluß unterschiedlicher Formen der Parteineigung auf die Einstellungen der Bürger zu den politischen Parteien." In *Wächst*, edited by Gabriel, 91–127.

Kempf, Udo. "Bürgerinitiativen—Der empirische Befund." In *Bürgerinitiativen*, edited by Guggenberger and idem, 295–317.

Kershaw, Ian, "Alltägliches und Außeralltägliches: ihre Bedeutung fur die Volksmeinung 1933-1939." In *Reihen fast geschlossen*, edited by Detlef Peukert and Jürgen Reulecke, 273–92.

Kershaw, Ian. *The End. The Defiance and Destruction of Hitler's Germany, 1944–45*. New York: Penguin, 2011.

Kershaw, Ian. *Hitler. 1889-1936: Hubris*. New York: W. W. Norton & Co., 1999.

Kershaw, Ian. *The 'Hitler Myth.' Image and Reality in the Third Reich*. Oxford: Oxford University Press, 1989.

Kershaw, Ian. "Persecution of the Jews and German Popular Opinion." *Yearbook of the Leo Baeck Institute* XXVI (1981): 261–89.

Kershaw, Ian. *Popular Opinion and Political Dissent in the Third Reich. Bavaria 1933-1945*. Oxford: Clarendon Press, 1983.

Kershaw, Ian. "Widerstand ohne Volk? Dissens und Widerstand im Dritten Reich." In *Widerstand*, edited by Schmädeke and Steinbach, 779–98.

Kersting, Franz-Werner. "'Unruhediskurs' Zeitgenössische Deutungen der 68er Bewegung." In *Demokratisierung*, edited by Frese et al., 715–40.
Kessel, Martina. "Demokratie als *Grenzverletzung*. Geschlecht als symbolisches System in der Weimarer Republik." In *Geschlechter(un)ordnung*, edited by Metzler and Schumann, 81–108.
Kettenacker, Lothar. *Germany since 1945*. Oxford: Oxford University Press, 1997.
Kettenacker, Lothar. "Sozialpsychologische Aspekte der Führer-Herrschaft." In *Der 'Führerstaat': Mythos und Realität. Studien zur Struktur und Politik des Dritten Reiches*, edited by Gerhard Hirschfeld and idem, 98–132. Stuttgart: Klett-Cotta, 1981.
Kießling, Friedrich. *Die undeutschen Deutschen. Eine ideengeschichtliche Archäologie der alten Bundesrepublik 1945–1972*. Paderborn: Schöningh, 2012.
Kieseritzky, Wolther v. and Klaus-Peter Sick. "Der lange Weg zur Demokratie in Deutschland. Zur Einleitung." In *Demokratie in Deutschland: Chancen und Gefährdungen im 19. und 20. Jahrhundert*, edited by idem, 9–28. München: Beck, 1999.
Kitschelt, Herbert. "New Social Movements and the Decline of Party Organization." In *Challenging*, edited by Dalton and Kuechler, 179–208.
Kittlaus, Manfred. "Straßengewalt und Terrorismus in Berlin—Erfahrungen eines Staatsschutzbeamten." In *Wege zur Bürgergesellschaft. Gewalt und Zivilisation in Deutschland Mitte des 20. Jahrhunderts*, edited by Beckenbach, Niels, 181–207. Berlin: Duncker & Humblot, 2005.
Klages, Helmut. *Traditionsbruch als Herausforderung. Perspektiven der Wertewandelsgesellschaft*. Frankfurt: Campus Verlag, 1993.
Kleßmann, Christoph. "Das Problem der 'Volksbewegung' im deutschen Widerstand." In *Der Widerstand gegen den Nationalsozialismus*, edited by Jurgen Schmädeke and Peter Steinbach, 822–37. München: Piper, 1985.
Kleßmann, Christoph. *Die doppelte Staatsgründung. Deutsche Geschichte 1945–1955*. Göttingen: Vandenhoeck & Ruprecht, 1989.
Kleßmann, Christoph and Bernd Stöver. "Einleitung: Das Krisenjahr 1953 und der 17. Juni in der DDR in der historischen Forschung." In *1953—Krisenjahr des Kalten Krieges in Europa*, edited by idem, 9–28. Köln: Bohlau Verlag, 1999.
Kleßmann, Christoph and Peter Friedemann. *Streik und Hungermärsche im Ruhrgebiet 1946–1948*. Frankfurt: Campus Verlag, 1977.
Klein, Ilona K. *Die Bundesrepublik als Parteienstaat: zur Mitwirkung der Parteien an der Willensbildung des Volkes 1945–1949*. Frankfurt/M: Peter Lang, 1990.
Kleinknecht, Thomas. "Demokratie als Staat- oder Lebensform." In *1970er Jahre*, edited by Livi, 113–29.
Klemperer, Klemens von. "'What Is the Law That Lies behind These Words?' Antigone's Question and the German Resistance against Hitler." In *Resistance against the Third Reich 1933–1990*, edited by Michael Geyer and John Boyer, 141–50. Chicago: University of Chicago Press, 1994.
Klenke, Olaf. *Kampfauftrag Mikrochip. Rationalisierung und sozialer Konflikt in der DDR*. Hamburg: VSA-Verlag, 2008.
Klikauer, Thomas. "Germany's New Populist Party: The AfD." *German Politics and Society* 36, no. 4 (December 2018): 78–97.
Klimke, Martin. *The Other Alliance. Student Protest in West Germany and the United States in the Global Sixties*. Princeton: Princeton University Press, 2010.
Klingemann, Hans D. "Ideological Conceptualization and Political Action." In *Political Action*, edited by Samuel Barnes and Max Kaase, 279–303.

Klingemann, Hans-Dieter. "Mapping Political Support in the 1990s: A Global Analysis." In *Critical Citizens. Global Support for Democratic Government*, edited by Pippa Norris, 31–56. Oxford: Oxford University Press, 1999.
Klingemann, Hans Dieter et al. (eds.). *Zwischen Wende und Wiedervereinigung. Analysen zur politischen Kultur in West- und Ost-Berlin*. Opladen: Leske + Budrich, 1995.
Klönne, Arno. "Jugendprotest und Jugendopposition. Von der HJ-Erziehung zum Cliquenwesen der Kriegszeit." In *Bayern in der NS-Zeit*. Vol. 4, edited by Martin Broszat et al., 527–620. München: Oldenbourg, 1981.
Klötzer, Sylvia and Siegfried Lokatis. "Criticism and Censorship. Negotiating Cabaret Performance and Book Production." In *Dictatorship*, edited by Jarausch, 241–63.
Klueting, Hans. "'Vernunftrepublikanismus' und 'Vertrauensdiktatur': Friedrich Meinecke in der Weimarer Republik." *Historische Zeitschrift* 242, no. 1 (February 1986): 69–98.
Knabe, Hubertus. "Der lange Weg zur Opposition—unabhängige politische Bestrebungen 1983 bis 1988." In *Opposition*, edited by Kuhrt et al., 139–55.
Knabe, Hubertus. "Kirche, Intellektuelle, unorganisierter Protest. Unabhängige politische Bestrebungen in der DDR in den 60er und 70er Jahren." In *Zum Hebst '89. Demokratische Bewegung in der DDR*, edited by Bernd Lindner et al., 22–37. Leipzig: Forum Verlag, 1994.
Knabe, Hubertus. "Neue Soziale Bewegungen im Sozialismus. Zur Genesis alternativer politischer Orentierungen in der DDR." *Kölner Zeitschrift für Soziologie und Sozialpsychologie* 40, no. 3 (1988): 551–69.
Knabe, Hubertus. "Samisdat—Gegenöffentlichkeit in den 80er Jahren." In *Opposition in der DDR*, edited by Eberhard Kuhrt et al., 299–314.
Knoch, Habbo. "Bewegende Momente. Dokumentarfotografie und die Politisierung der westdeutschen Öffentlichkeit vor 1968." In *Die Politik der Öffentlichkeit—Die Öffentlichkeit der Politik. Politische Medialisierung in der Bundesrepublik*, edited by Bernd Weisbrod, 97–124. Göttingen: Wallstein Verlag, 2003.
Knoch, Habbo. "'Mündige Bürger,' oder: Der kurze Frühling einer partizipatorischen Vision. Einleitung." In *Bürgersinn*, edited by idem, 9–53.
Kocka, Jürgen. *Facing Total War: German Society 1914–1918*. Trsl. by Barbara Weinberger. Cambridge: Cambridge University Press, 1984.
Kocka, Jürgen. "Zivilgesellschaft in historischer Perspektive." *Forschungsjournal neue soziale Bewegungen* 16, no. 2 (2003): 29–37.
Koelges, Barbara. *Der Demokratische Frauenbund. Von der DDR-Massenorganisation zum modernen politischen Frauenverband*. Wiesbaden: Westdeutscher Verlag, 2001.
Kogon, Eugen. "Das Recht auf den politischen Irrtum." *Frankfurter Hefte* 2, no. 6 (1947): 641–55.
Kolb, Eberhard. *The Weimar Republic*. Trsl. by Paul Stephen Falla. London: Unwin Hyman, 1988.
Kolinsky, Eva. *Parties, Opposition and Society in West Germany*. New York: St. Martin's Press, 1984.
Kommers, Donald P. "Building Democracy: Judicial Review and the German Rechtsstaat." In *The Postwar Transformation of Germany. Democracy, Prosperity, and Nationhood*, edited by John S. Brady et al., 94–121. Ann Arbor: University of Michigan Press, 1999.
Könke, Günter. *Organisierter Kaptialismus, Sozialdemokratie und Staat. Eine Studie zur Ideologie der sozialdemokratischen Arbeiterbewegung in der Weimarer Republik*. Stuttgart: Franz Steiner Verlag, 1987.
Koonz, Claudia. "Ethical Dilemmas and Nazi Eugenics: Single-Issue Dissent in Religious Contexts." In *Resistance*, edited by Geyer and Boyer, 15–38.

Koonz, Claudia. *The Nazi Conscience*. Cambridge: Belknap Press of Harvard University Press, 2003.
Koopmans, Ruud. *Democracy from Below. New Social Movements and the Political System in West Germany*. Boulder, CO: Westview Press, 1995.
Koopmans, Ruud and Dieter Rucht. "Rechtsradikalismus als soziale Bewegung?" In *Rechtsextremismus*, edited by Falter et al., 265–87.
Köpcke-Duttler, Arnold. "Ziviler Ungehorsam. Einige verfassungsrechtliche Versuche seiner Behinderung und ihre Kritiker." In *Ziviler Ungehorsam*, edited by Narr et al., 307–18.
Kopstein, Jeffrey. *The Politics of Economic Decline in East Germany, 1945–1989*. Chapel Hill: University of North Carolina Press, 1997.
Korioth, Stefan. "Rettung oder Überwindung der Demokratie—Die Weimarer Staatslehrer im Verfassungsnotstand 1932/33." In *Denken*, edited by Gusy, 505–31.
Koshar, Rudy. *Social Life, Local Politics, and Nazism. Marburg, 1880–1935*. Chapel Hill: University of North Carolina Press, 1986.
Kössler, Till. "Die Grenzen der Demokratie. Antikommunismus als politische und gesellschaftliche Praxis in der frühen Bundesrepublik." In *"Geistige Gefahr" und "Immunisierung der Gesellschaft": Antikommunismus und politische Kultur in der frühen Bundesrepublik*, edited by Stefan Creuzberger and Dierk Hoffmann, 229–50.
Kowalczuk, Ilka-Sascha. *Endspiel. Die Revolution von 1989 in der DDR*. Munich: C.H. Beck, 2009.
Kowalczuk, Ilko-Sascha. "Von der Freiheit, Ich zu sagen. Widerständiges Verhalten in der DDR." In *Selbstbehauptungen*, edited by Poppe et al., 85–115.
Kracht, Klaus Große. "Campaigning against Bolshevism: Catholic Action in Late Weimar Germany." *Journal of Contemporary History* 53, no. 3 (2018): 550–73.
Kramer, Nicole. *Volksgenossinnen an der Heimatfront. Mobilisierung, Verhalten, Erinnerung*. Göttingen: Vandenhoeck & Ruprecht, 2011.
Kramer, Nicole and Armin Nolzen. "Einleitung." In *Ungleichheiten im "Dritten Reich." Semantiken, Praktiken, Erfahrungen*, edited by idem, 9–26. Göttingen: Wallstein, 2012.
Kraushaar, Wolfgang. "Die Furcht vor einem 'neuen 33.' Protest gegen die Notstandsgesetzgebung." In *Streit um den Staat. Intellektuelle Debatten in der Bundesrepublik 1960–1980*, edited by Dominick Geppert and Jens Hacke, 135–50. Göttingen: Vandenhoeck & Ruprecht, 2008.
Kraushaar, Wolfgang. *Die Protest-Chronik 1949–1959. Eine illustrierte Geschichte von Bewegung, Widerstand und Utopie*. Vol. I: 1949–1952. Hamburg: Rogner & Bernhard, 1996.
Kraushaar, Wolfgang. "'Good Vibrations.' Ein Gespräch mit Wolfgang Kraushaar über Popkultur und Protestbewegung." *Mittelweg* 36 (2016): 50–80.
Kraushaar, Wolfgang. "Ordnung und Protest in der Ära Adenauers." In *Ordnung und Protest. Eine gesamtdeutsche Protestgeschichte von 1949 bis heute*, edited by Martin Löhnig et al., 13–27. Tübingen: Mohr-Siebeck, 2015.
Kreikenbom, Henry and Maxi Stapelfeld. "Steine auf dem Weg zum politischen Alltag. Vorgeprägte Orientierungen und aktuelle Erfahrungen der ehemaligen DDR-Bürger mit dem Interessenvermittlungssystem der Bundesrepublik." In *Politische Kultur*, edited by Niedermayer and von Beyme, 162–84.
Krimmel, Iris. "Politische Beteiligung in Deutschland—Strukturen und Erklärungsformen." In *Wirklich*, edited by Falter et al., 613–39.
Kroll, Frank-Luther. *Das geistige Preußen: zur Ideengeschichte eines Staates*. Paderborn: Schöningh, 2001.

Küchenhoff, Erich. "Ziviler Ungehorsam als aktiver Verfassungsschutz." In *Widerstand*, edited by Schleker, 71–81.
Kuechler, Manfred. "The Road to German Unity: Mass Sentiment in East and West Germany." *Public Opinion Quarterly* 56, no. 1 (Spring 1992): 53–76.
Kuhn, Armin. "Zwischen gesellschaftliche Intervention und radikaler Nischenpolitik. Häuserkämpfe in Berlin und Barcelona am Übergang zur neoliberalen Staat." In *All We Wanted*, edited by Balz and Friedrichs, 37–52.
Kühne, Jorg-Detlef. "Demokratisches Denken in der Weimarer Verfassungsdiskussion—Hugo Preuß und die Nationalversammlung." In *Demokratisches Denken in der Weimarer Republik*, edited by Christoph Gusy, 115–33. Baden-Baden: Nomos Verlagsgesellschaft, 2000.
Kühne, Thomas. *Belonging and Genocide. Hitler's Community, 1918–1945*. New Haven, CT: Yale University Press, 2010.
Kühne, Thomas. "Die Jahrhundertwende, die 'lange' Bismarckzeit und die Demokratisierung der politischen Kultur." In *Otto von Bismarck und Wilhelm II: Repräsentanten eines Epochenwechsels?* edited by Lothar Gall, 85–118. Paderborn: Schöningh, 2001.
Kühne, Thomas. *Dreiklassenwahlrecht und Wahlkultur im Preußen 1867–1918. Landtagswahlen zwischen korporativer Tradition und politischer Massenmarkt*. Düsseldorf: Droste Verlag, 1994.
Kühnel, Stefan. "Kommt es auf die Stimme an? Determinanten von Teilnahme und Nichtteilnahme an Wahlen." In *Partizipation*, edited by Koch et al., 11–42.
Kuhrt, Eberhard et al. (eds.). *Opposition in der DDR von den 70er Jahren bis zum Zusammenbruch der SED-Herrschaft*. Opladen: Leske + Budrich, 1999.
Kukutz, Irene. "'Nicht Rädchen, sondern Sand im Getriebe, den Kreis der Gewalt zu durchbrechen.' Frauenwiderstand in der DDR in den 80er Jahren." In *Selbstbehauptungen*, edited by Poppe et al., 272–83.
Kulka, Otto Dov. "The German Population and the Jews: State of Research and New Perspectives." In *Probing*, edited by Bankier, 275–76.
Kuller, Christiane. "The Demonstrations in Support of the Protestant Provincial Bishop Hans Meisner. A Successful Protest against the Nazi Regime?" In *Protest*, edited by Stoltzfus and Maier-Katkin, 38–54.
Kurz, Achim. *Demokratische Diktatur? Auslegung und Handhabung der Weimarer Verfassung 1919–1925*. Berlin: Duncker & Humblot, 1992.
Küster, Thomas. "Das Erlernen des Dialogs. Veränderungen des gesellschaftlichen Klimas nach 1968 am Beispiel eines Gütersloher Gymnasiums." In *Demokratisierung*, edited by Frese et al., 683–705.
Kutscha, Martin. "Der Kampf um ein Bürgerrecht. Demonstrationsfreiheit in Vergangenheit und Gegenwart." In *Demonstrationsfreiheit*, edited by idem, 13–70.
Kvistad, Gregg O. "Building Democracy and Changing Institutions: The Professional Civil Service and Political Parties in the Federal Republic of Germany." In *Transformation*, edited by Brady et al., 63–93.
Kvistad, Gregg O. *The Rise and Demise of German Statism. Loyalty and Political Membership*. Providence: Berghahn Books, 1999.
Lammersdorf, Raimund. "'Das Volk ist streng demokratisch.' Amerikanische Sorgen über das autoritäre Bewusstsein der Deutschen in der Besatzungszeit und frühen Bundesrepublik." In *Demokratiewunder*, edited by Bauerkämper et al., 85–103.
Lampe, Gerhard. *Panorama, Report und Monitor. Geschichte der politischen Fernsehmagazine 1957–1990*. Konstanz: UVK Medien, 2000.

Langenbacher, Erich. "The Mastered Past? Collective Memory Trends in Germany since Unification." In *From the Bonn to the Berlin Republic. Germany at the Twentieth Anniversary of Unification*, edited by Jeffrey J. Anderson and Erich Langenbacher, 63–89. New York: Berghahn Books, 2010.

Langewiesche, Dieter. *Liberalism in Germany*. Trsl. by Christiane Banerji. Princeton, NJ: Princeton University Press, 2000.

Langguth, Gerd. *Protestbewegung—Entwicklung, Niedergang, Renaissance. Die Neue Linke seit 1968*. Köln: Verlag Wissenschaft und Politik, 1983.

Large, David Clay. *Contending with Hitler. Varieties of German Resistance in the Third Reich*. Cambridge: Cambridge University Press, 1991.

Ledford, Kenneth. "Formalizing the Rule of Law in Prussia: The Supreme Administrative Law Court, 1876-1914." *Central European History* 37 (2004): 203–24.

Leggewie, Claus. "Bloß kein Streit! Über die Sehnsucht nach Harmonie und die anhaltenden Schwierigkeiten demokratischer Streitkultur." In *Demokratische Streitkultur. Theoretische Grundpositionen und Handlungsalternativen in Politikfeldern*, edited by Ulrich Sarcinelli, 52–62. Bonn: Bundeszentrale für politische Bildung, 1990.

Lehnert, Detlef. "Sozialdemokratie und Parlamentarismus. Von der Reichsgründungszeit zur neuen deutschen Einheit." In *SPD und Parlamentarismus. Eintwicklungen und Problemfelder 1871-1990*, edited by idem, 9–34. Köln: Böhlau Verlag, 2016.

Lehnert, Detlef. *Sozialdemokratie zwischen Protestbewegung und Regierungspartei 1848-1983*. Frankfurt/M: Suhrkamp, 1983.

Lehnert, Detlef. "Von der politisch-kulturellen Fragmentierung zur demokratischen Sammlung?" In *Pluralismus*, edited by idem and Megerle, 77–129.

Lehnert, Detlef and Christoph Müller. "Zur Einführung: Perspektiven und Problemen einer Wiederentdeckung Hugo Preuß." In *Vom Untertanenverband zur Bürgergenossenschaft*, edited by idem, 11–48. Baden-Baden: Nomos Verlagsgesellschaft, 2003.

Lemke, Christiane. "Crossing Borders and Building Barriers: Migration, Citizenship and State Building in Germany." In *European Integration in Social and Historical Perspective, 1850 to the Present*, edited by Jytte Klausen and Louise Tilly, 85–102. Lantham: Rowman & Littlefield, 1997.

Lemke, Christiane. *Die Ursachen des Umbruchs. Politische Sozialisation in der ehemaligen DDR*. Opladen: Westdeutscher Verlag, 1991.

Lemke, Christiane and Helga A. Welsh. *Germany Today. Politics and Policies in a Changing World*. Lanham: Rowman & Littlefield, 2018.

Lenk, Kurt. "Zum westdeutschen Konservatismus." In *Modernisierung*, edited by Schildt and Sywottek, 636–45.

Lenz, Ilse. "Das Private ist politisch? Zum Verhältnis von Frauenbewegung und alternativem Milieu." In *Alternative*, edited by Reichardt and Siegfried, 375–404.

Leopold, John A. *Alfred Hugenberg. The Radical Nationalist Campaign against the Weimar Republic*. New Haven, CT: Yale University Press, 1977.

Lepsius, M. Rainer. "Parteiensystem und Sozialstruktur: zum Problem der Demokratisierung der deutschen Gesellschaft." In *Deutsche Parteien vor 1918*, edited by Gerhard A. Ritter, 56–80. Köln: Kiepenheuer & Witsch, 1973.

Lepsius, Oliver. "Staatstheorie und Demokratiebegriff in der Weimarer Republik." In *Denken*, edited by Gusy, 366–414.

Lepsius, Oliver. "Versammlungsrecht und gesellschaftliche Integration." In *Brokdorf Beschluss*, edited by Doering-Manteuffel, 113–65.

Lepsius, Oliver and Anselm Doering-Manteuffel. "Die Richterpersönlichkeit und ihre protestantische Sozialisation." In *Brokdorf Beschluss*, edited by idem, 167–224.

Leugers, Antonia. "Der Protest in der Rosenstraße und die Kirchen." In *Berlin, Rosenstraße 2-4: Protest in der NS-Diktatur*, edited by idem, 47–80. Annweiler: Plöger, 2005.
Levinger, Matthew. "The Prussian Reform Movement and the Rise of Enlightened Nationalism." In *The Rise of Prussia: 1700–1830*, edited by Philip G. Dwyer, 259–77. Harlow, England: Longman, 2000.
Lidtke, Vernon L. *The Alternative Culture*. New York: Oxford University Press, 1985.
Lidtke, Vernon. *The Outlawed Party. Social Democracy in Germany, 1878–1890*. Princeton, NJ: Princeton University Press, 1966.
Liehr, Dorothee. *Von der Aktion gegen den SPIEGEL zur SPIEGEL Affäre. Zur gesellschaftspolitischen Rolle der Intellektuellen*. Frankfurt: Peter Lang, 2002.
Limbach, Jutta. *Die Demokratie und ihre Bürger. Aufbruch zu einer neuen politischen Kultur*. München: C.H. Beck, 2003.
Lindemann, Albert S. *A History of European Socialism*. New Haven, CT: Yale University Press, 1983.
Lindenberger, Thomas. "Die Diktatur der Grenzen. Zur Einleitung." In *Herrschaft und Eigen-Sinn in der Diktatur. Studien zur Gesellschaftsgeschichte der DDR*, edited by idem, 13–44. Köln: Bohlau Verlag, 1999.
Lindenberger, Thomas. "Eigen-Sinn, Domination and No Resistance." *Docupedia-Zeitgeschichte*. Available online: https://docupedia.de/zg/Eigensinn__english_version_ (accessed August 11, 2017).
Lindner, Bernd. *Die demokratische Revolution in der DDR 1989/90*. Bonn: Bundeszentrale für politische Bildung, 2010.
Lindner, Werner. *Jugendprotest seit den fünfziger Jahren: Dissens und kultureller Eigensinn*. Opladen: Leske + Budrich, 1996.
Llanque, Marcus. "Massendemokratie zwischen Kaiserreich und westlicher Demokratie." In *Denken*, edited by Gusy, 38–73.
Loberg, Molly. *The Struggle for the Streets of Berlin: Politics, Consumption, and Urban Space, 1914–1945*. Cambridge: Cambridge University Press, 2018.
Löhnig, Martin et al. (eds.). *Ordnung und Protest. Eine gesamtdeutsche Protestgeschichte von 1949 bis heute*. Tübingen: Mohr-Siebeck, 2015.
Longerich, Peter. *"Davon haben wir nichts gewusst!" Die Deutschen und die Judenverfolgung*. München: Siedler, 2006.
Lorenz, Astrid. *Demokratisierung in Ostdeutschland. Verfassungspolitische Weichenstellungen in den neue Ländern und Berlin*. Wiesbaden: Springer VS, 2013.
Lösche, Peter and Franz Walter. *Die FDP. Richtungsstreit und Zukunftszweifel*. Darmstadt: Wissenschaftliche Buchgesellschaft, 1996.
Loth, Wilfried. *Das Kaiserreich. Obrigkeitsstaat und politische Mobilisierung*. München: Deutscher Taschenbuch Verlag, 1997.
Lübbe, Hermann. "Der Nationalsozialismus im deutschen Nachkriegsbewußtsein." *Historische Zeitschrift* 236 (1983): 579–99.
Lübbe-Wolff, Gertrude. "Safeguards of Civil and Constitutional Rights—The Debate on the Role of the *Reichsgericht*." In *German and American Constitutional Thought: Contexts, Interaction, and Historical Realities*, edited by Hermann Wellenreuther, 353–72. New York: Berg Publishers, 1990.
Lüdtke, Alf. "The Appeal of Exterminating 'Others': German Workers and the Limits of Resistance." In *Resistance*, edited by Geyer and Boyer, 53–74.
Lüdtke, Alf. "'… den Menschen vergessen?'—Oder: Das Jahre im Blick von MfS, SED, FDGB und staatlicher Leitung." In *Akten*, edited by Lüdtke and Becker, 189–222.

Lüdtke, Alf. "'The Honor of Labor': Industrial Workers and the Power of Symbols under National Socialism." In *Nazism and German Society 1933-1945*, edited by David Crew, 67-109. London: Routledge, 1994.
Lüdtke, Alf. "Practices of Survival—Ways of Appropriating 'The Rules': Reconsidering Approaches to the History of the GDR." In *Power*, edited by Fulbrook, 181-93.
Lüdtke, Alf. "Wo blieb die rote Gefahr? Arbeitererfahrungen und deutscher Faschismus." In *Alltagsgeschichte. Zur Rekonstruktion historischer Erfahrungen und Lebensweisen*, edited by idem, 224-83. Frankfurt: Campus Verlag, 1989.
Ludwig, Andreas. "Fortschritt, Norm und Eigensinn. Vorwort." In *Fortschritt, Norm und Eigensinn*, edited by idem, 7-15. Berlin: Ch. Links Verlag.
Lyons, Matthew Namiroff. *The Grassroots Network. Radical Nonviolence in the Federal Republic of Germany, 1972-1985*, Western Societies Program. Occasional Paper #20. Center for International Studies, Cornell University, 1988.
Maase, Kaspar. "Amerikanisierung von unten. Demonstrative Vulgarität und kulturelle Hegemonie in der Bundesrepublik der 50er Jahren." In *Amerikanisierung*, edited by Lüdtke et al., 291-313.
Maase, Kaspar. "Establishing Cultural Democracy. Youth, 'Americanization,' and the Irresistible Rise of Popular Culture." In *Miracle Years*, edited by Schissler, 428-50.
Maase, Kaspar. *Was macht Populärkultur politisch?* Wiesbaden: VS-Verlag, 2010.
Madarász, Jeanette. "Economic Politics and Company Culture: The Problem of Routinisation." In *Power*, edited by Fulbrook, 52-75.
Madarász, Jeanette Z. *Conflict and Compromise in East Germany, 1971-1989. A Precarious Stability*. Basingstoke: Palgrave Macmillan, 2003.
Mählert, Ulrich (ed.). *Der 17. Juni 1953. Ein Aufstand für Einheit, Recht und Freiheit*. Bonn: Verlag J.H.W. Dietz Nachf, 2003.
Mai, Gunter. "'Verteidigungskrieg' und 'Volksgemeinschaft.' Staatliche Selbstbehauptung, national Solidarität und soziale Befeiung in Deutschland in der Zeit des Ersten Weltkrieges (1900-1925)." In *Der Erste Weltkrieg: Wirkung, Wahrnehmung, Analyse*, edited by Wolfgang Michalka, 583-602. München: Piper, 1994.
Maier, Charles. *Dissolution. The Crisis of Communism and the End of East Germany*. Princeton, NJ: Princeton University Press, 1997.
Maines, Mary Jo. "'Genossen und Genosseninnen.' Depictions of Gender, Militancy, and Organizing in the German Socialist Press, 1890-1914." In *Between Reform and Revolution. German Socialism and Communism from 1840-1990*, edited by David E. Barclay and Eric D. Weitz, 141-66. New York: Berghahn Books, 2009.
Majer, Diemut. "Rechtstheoretische Funktionsbestimmungen der Justiz im Nationalsozialismus am Beispiel der völkischen Ungleichheit." In *Recht, Rechtsphilosophie*, edited by Rottleuthner, 163-75.
Major, Patrick. *Behind the Berlin Wall. East Germany and the Frontiers of Power*. Oxford: Oxford University Press, 2010.
Major, Patrick and Jonathan Osmond. *The Workers' and Peasants' State. Communism and Society in East Germany under Ulbricht 1945-1971*. Manchester: Manchester University Press, 2002.
Maleck-Lewy, Eva and Virginia Primrose (eds.). *Gefährtinnen der Macht. Politische Partizipation der Frauen im vereinigten Deutschland*. Berlin: Edition sigma, 1995.
Malinowski, Stephen. "Wie zivil war der deutsche Adel? Anmerkungen zum Verhältnis von Adel und Zivilgesellschaft zwischen 1871 und 1933." In *Zivilgesellschaft als Geschichte*, edited by Ralph Jessen et al., 239-60. Wiesbaden: Verlag für Sozialwissenschaften, 2004.

Mann, Reinhard. *Protest und Kontrolle im Dritten Reich. Nationalsozialistische Herrschaft im Alltag einer rheinischen Großstadt*. Frankfurt/M: Campus Verlag, 1987.
Marsch, Alan and Max Kaase. "Measuring Political Action." In *Political Action*, edited by Barnes and Kaase, 57–96.
März, Michael. *Linker Protest nach dem Deutschen Herbst. Eine Geschichte des linken Spektrums im Schatten des "starken Staates," 1977–1979*. Bielefeld: transcript Verlag, 2012.
Mason, Tim. "The Workers' Opposition in Nazi Germany." *History Workshop Journal* xi (1981): 120–37.
Mason, Timothy W. *Sozialpolitik im Dritten Reich. Arbeiterklasse und Volksgemeinschaft*. Opladen: Westdeutscher Verlag, 1977.
Maubach, Franka. "'Volksgemeinschaft' als Geschlechtergemeinschaft. Zur Genese einer nationalsozialistischen Beziehungsform." In *Attraktion*, edited by Brockhaus, 252–68.
McCormick, John P. "Feudalism, Fascism, and Fordism: Weimar Theories of Representation and Their Legacy in the Bonn Republic." In *Liberal Democracy*, edited by Caldwell and Scheuerman, 47–73.
McElligott, Andrew. *Rethinking the Weimar Republic. Authority vs. Authoritarianism 1916–1936*. London: Bloomsbury, 2014.
McFalls, Laurence H. *Communism's Collapse, Democracy's Demise? The Cultural Context and Consequences of the East German Revolution*. New York: New York University Press, 1995.
McGuire, Kristin, "Feminist Politics beyond the Reichstag. Helen Stöcker and Visions of Reform." In *Weimar Politics/Weimar Subjects. Rethinking the Political Culture of Germany in the 1920s*, edited by Kathleen Canning et al., 138–52. New York: Berghahn Books, 2013.
Mergel, Thomas. "Dictatorship and Democracy, 1918-1939." In *The Oxford Handbook of Modern German History*, edited by Helmut Walser Smith, 423–52. Oxford: Oxford University Press, 2011.
Mergel, Thomas. "Führer, Volksgemeinschaft und Maschine. Politische Erwartungsstrukturen in der Weimarer Republik und dem Nationalsozialismus." In *Politische Kulturgeschichte der Zwischenkriegszeit 1918–1939*, edited by Wolfgang Hardtwig, 91–127. Göttingen: Vandenhoeck & Ruprecht, 2005.
Mergel, Thomas. *Parlamentarische Kultur in der Weimarer Republik. Politische Kommunikation, symbolische Politik und öffentliche Meinung im Reichstag*. Düsseldorf: Droste Verlag, 2002.
Mergel, Thomas. *Propaganda nach Hitler. Eine Kulturgeschichte des Wahlkampfs in der Bundesrepublik 1949–1990*. Göttingen: Wallstein Verlag, 2010.
Merkel, Ina and Felix Mühlberg. "Eingaben." In *Wir sind nicht die Meckerecke der Nation. Briefe an das Fernsehen der DDR*, edited by Ina Merkel, 11–46. Berlin: Schwarzkopf und Schwarzkopf, 2000.
Merritt, Anna J. and Richard L. Merritt (eds.). *Public Opinion in Occupied Germany. The OMGUS Surveys, 1945–1949*. Urbana: University of Illinois Press, 1970.
Merritt, Anna J. and Richard L. Merritt (eds.). *Public Opinion in Semisovereign Germany. The HICOG Surveys, 1949–1955*. Urbana: University of Illinois Press, 1980.
Merritt, Richard L. *Democracy Imposed. US Occupation Policy and the German Public, 1945–1949*. New Haven, CT: Yale University Press, 1995.
Merson, Allan. *Communist Resistance in Nazi Germany*. London: Lawrence and Wishart, 1985.
Meschnig, Alexander. "Die Sendung der Nation: Vom Grabenkrieg zur NS-Bewegung." In *Attraktion*, edited by Brockhaus, 29–44.

Mettele, Gisela. "The City and the *Citoyenne*. Associational Culture and Female Civic Virtues in 19th-century Germany." In *Civil Society and Gender Justice. Historical and Comparative Perspectives*, edited by Karen Hagemann et al., 112–41. New York: Berghahn Books, 2008.

Metz, Lutz. "Von den Bürgerinitiativen zu den Grünen. Entstehungsgeschichte der 'Wahlalternativen' in der Bundesrepublik Deutschland." In *Neue Bewegungen*, edited by Roth and Rucht, 263–76.

Metzler, Gabrielle. "Der lange Weg zur sozial-liberalen Politik." In *Bürgersinn*, edited by Knoch, 157–80.

Metzler, Gabriele. *Konzeptionen Politischen Handelns von Adenauer bis Brandt. Politische Planung in der pluralistischen Gesellschaft*. Paderborn: Schöningh, 2005.

Metzler, Gabriele. "Staatsversagen und Unregierbarkeit." In *Das Ende der Zuversicht? Die 70er Jahre als Geschichte*, edited by Konrad Jarausch, 243–60. Göttingen: Vandenhoeck & Ruprecht, 2008.

Metzler, Gabriele. "Stabilisierung, Normalisierung, Modernisierung: Die Bundesrepublik in den 50er Jahren." In *Lüth Urteil*, edited by Henne and Riedlinger, 25–44.

Meulemann, Heiner. "Wertwandel in der Bundesrepublik zwischen 1950 und 1980: Versuch einer zusammenfassenden Deutung vorliegender Zeitreihen." In *Wirtschaftlicher Wandel, religiöser Wandel und Wertwandel: Folgen für das politische Verhalten in der Bundesrepublik Deutschland*, edited by Dieter Oberndörfer et al., 391–411. Berlin: Duncker & Humblot, 1985.

Meuschel, Sigrid. *Legitimation und Parteiherrschaft. Zum Paradox von Stabilität und Revolution in der DDR 1945–1989*. Frankfurt: Suhrkamp, 1992.

Meyer, Birgit. "Die 'unpolitische' Frau. Politische Partizipation von Frauen oder: Habe Frauen ein anderes Verständnis von Politik?" *APZ* B25–26 (1992): 8–13.

Meyer, Gerd. "Der versorgte Mensch. Sozialistischer Paternalismus: bürokratische Bevormundung und soziale Sicherheit." In *Kultur*, edited by Wehling, 29–53.

Meyer, Gerd. "Deutschland: Ein Staat—zwei politische Kulturen." In *Länderprofile. Politische Kulturen im In- und Ausland*, edited by Hans-Georg Wehling, 13–41. Stuttgart: W. Kohlhammer Verlag, 1993.

Meyer, Karl-Heinz. *Das neue Demonstrations- und Versammlungsrecht*. 2nd ed. München: C.H. Beck, 1986.

Michael, Klaus. "Zweite Kultur oder Gegenkultur? Die Subkulturen und künstlerische Szenen der DDR und ihr Verhältnis zur politischen Opposition." In *Zwischen Verweigerung und Opposition. Politischer Protest in der DDR 1970–1989*, edited by Detlef Pollack and Dieter Rink, 106–28. Frankfurt: Campus Verlag, 1997.

Milder, Stephen. "Between Grassroots Activism and Transnational Aspirations: Anti-Nuclear Protest from the Rhine Valley to the Bundestag, 1974–1983." *Historical Social Research/Historische Sozialforschung* 39, no. 1 (2014): 191–211.

Milder, Stephen. *Greening Democracy. The Anti-Nuclear Movement and Political Environmentalism in West Germany and Beyond, 1968–1983*. Cambridge: Cambridge University Press, 2017.

Miller, Jerry Z. *The Other God That Failed. Hans Freyer and the Deradicalization of German Conservatism*. Princeton, NJ: Princeton University Press, 1987.

Millington, Richard. *State, Society and Memories of the Uprising of 17 June 1953 in the GDR*. Basingstoke: Palgrave Macmillan, 2014.

Minkenberg, Michael. "Repressionsstrategien gegen Rechtsradikalismus und Gewalt." *Forschungsjournal Neue Soziale Bewegungen* 16, no. 4 (2003): 31–42.

Mintzel, Alf. "Der akzeptierte Parteienstaat." In *Zäsuren nach 1945: Essays zur Periodisierung der deutschen Nachkriegsgeschichte*, edited by Martin Broszat, 75–94. München: Oldenbourg Verlag, 1990.
Mitchell, Maria. *The Origins of Christian Democracy. Politics and Confession in Modern Germany*. Ann Arbor: University Michigan Press, 2012.
Mitter, Armin and Stefan Wolle. *Untergang auf Raten. Unbekannte Kapitel der DDR Geschichte*. München: Bertelsmann, 1993.
Mößle, Wilhelm. "Die Verordnungsermächtigung in der Weimarer Republik." In *Demokratie in Deutschland und Frankreich 1918–1933/40. Beiträge zu einem historischen Vergleich*, edited by Horst Möller and Manfred Kittel, 269–82. Munich: R. Oldenbourg Verlag, 2002.
Moeller, Robert G. *German Peasants and Agrarian Politics, 1914–1924. The Rhineland and Westphalia*. Chapel Hill: University of North Carolina Press, 1986.
Moeller, Robert G. *Protecting Motherhood. Women and the Family in Postwar West Germany*. Berkeley: University of California Press, 1993.
Moeller, Robert G. *War Stories. The Search for a Usable Past in the Federal Republic of Germany*. Berkeley: University of California Press, 2001.
Moll, Christiane. "Acts of Resistance: The White Rose in the Light of New Archival Evidence." In *Resistance*, edited by Geyer and Boyer, 173–200.
Möller, Horst "Zwei Wege des deutschen Parlamentarismus: Preußen und Reich." In *Deutscher und Britischer Parlamentarismus*, edited by Adolf Birke and Kurt Kluxen, 135–48. München: K.G. Saur, 1985.
Mommsen, Hans. "Der Widerstand gegen Hitler und die deutschen Gesellschaft." In *Widerstand*, edited by Schmädeke and Steinbach, 3–23.
Mommsen, Hans. "Hitlers Stellung im nationalsozialistischen Herrschaftssystem." In *Führerstaat*, edited by Hirschfeld and Kettenacker, 43–72.
Mommsen, Hans. "Ist die Weimarer Republik an Fehlkonstruktionen der Reichsverfassung gescheitert? Chancen und Scheitern der ersten deutschen Republik." In *Weimar und die Republik. Geburtsstunde eines demokratischen Deutschlands*, edited by Michael Schultheiß and Julia Roßberg, 105–24. Weimar: Weimar Verlagsgesellschaft Ltd., 2009.
Mommsen, Hans. "The Origins of Chancellor Democracy and the Transformation of the German Democratic Paradigm." *German Politics & Society* 25, no. 2 (2007): 7–18.
Mommsen, Hans. *The Rise and Fall of Weimar Democracy*. Trsl by Elborg Forster and Larry Eugene Jones. Chapel Hill: University of North Carolina Press, 1989.
Mommsen, Hans. "Verfassungs- und Verwaltungsreformpläne der Widerstandsgruppen des 20. Juli 1944." In *Widerstand*, edited by Schmädeke and Steinbach, 570–97.
Mommsen, Hans. "Von Weimar nach Bonn: Zum Demokratieverständnis der Deutschen." In *Modernisierung im Wiederaufbau. Die westdeutsche Gesellschaft der 50er Jahre*, edited by Axel Schildt and Arnold Sywottek, 745–58. Bonn: Verlag J. H. W. Dietz Nachf, 1993.
Mommsen, Wolfgang J. *Imperial Germany 1867–1918. Politics, Culture, and Society in an Authoritarian State*. Trsl. by Richard Deveson. London: Arnold, 1998.
Mommsen, Wolfgang. *Max Weber and German Politics 1890–1920*. Trsl. by Michael L. Steinberg. Chicago: University of Chicago Press, 1984.
Mommsen, Wolfgang. "Zum Begriff der 'Plebiszitären Führerdemokratie' bei Max Weber." *Kölner Zeitschrift für Soziologie und Sozialpsychologie* 15 (1963): 295–322.
Mommsen-Reindl, Margarete. "Partizipation—Osteuropäische Länder." In *Wörterbuch Staat und Politik*, edited by Dieter Nohlen, 327–33. München: Piper, 1998.

Morsch, Günther. "Streik im 'Dritten Reich.'" *Vierteljahrshefte für Zeitgeschichte* 36, no. 4 (1988): 649–89.
Moses, Dirk. *German Intellectuals and the Nazi Past*. Cambridge: Cambridge University Press, 2007.
Moses, John A. "The Concept of Economic Democracy within the German Socialist Trade Unions during the Weimar Republic: The Emergence of an Alternative Route to Socialism." *Labour History* 34 (May 1978): 45–57.
Mosse, George L. *The Nationalization of the Masses. Political Symbolism and Mass Movements in Germany from the Napoleonic Wars through the Third Reich*. New York: Howard Fertig, 1975.
Mouton, Michelle. *From Nurturing the Nation to Purifying the Volk. Weimar and Nazi Family Policy, 1918–1945*. Cambridge: Cambridge University Press, 2007.
Moyn, Samuel. *Christian Human Rights*. Philadelphia: University of Pennsylvania Press, 2015.
Mühlberg, Felix. *Bürger, Bitten und Behörden. Geschichte der Eingabe in der DDR*. Berlin: Karl Dietz Verlag, 2004.
Mühlen, Patrick von zur. *Aufbruch und Umbruch in der DDR: Bürgerbewegungen, kritische Öffentlichkeit und Niedergang der SED Herrschaft*. Bonn: Verlag JHW Dietz Nachf., 2000.
Müller, Harry. "Lebenswerte und nationale Identität." In *Jugend und Jugendforschung in der DDR*, edited by Walter Friedrich and Helmut Griese, 124–35. Opladen: Leske + Budrich, 1991.
Müller, Horst. "Verwaltungsstaat und parlamentarische Demokratie: Preußen 1919–1932." In *Regierung*, edited by Ritter, 149–80.
Müller, Jan-Werner. *Contesting Democracy. Political Ideas in 20th-Century Europe*. New Haven, CT: Yale University Press, 2011.
Müller, Jan-Werner. "Introduction." In *German Ideologies since 1945: Studies in the Political Thought and Culture of the Bonn Republic*, edited by idem, 1–20. New York: Palgrave Macmillan, 2003.
Müller, Jan-Werner. "Populism (against Democracy). A Theoretical Preface and Some Episodes of a Transatlantic History." In *Transatlantic Democracy in the Twentieth Century. Transfer and Transformation*, edited by Paul Nolte, 171–88. Berlin: de Gruyter, 2016.
Müller, Jan-Werner. *What Is Populism?* Philadelphia: University of Pennsylvania Press, 2016.
Muller, Jerry Z. "German Neo-Conservativism ca. 1968–1985: Hermann Lübbe and Others." In *Ideologies*, edited by Müller, 161–84.
Müller, Tim B. "Von der 'Whig Interpretation' zur Fragilität der Demokratie. Weimar als geschichtstheoretisches Problem." *Geschichte und Gesellschaft* 44, no. 3 (2018): 430–65.
Müller, Tim B. and Hedwig Richter. "Einführung: Demokratiegeschichten. Deutschland (1800–1933) in transnationaler Perspektive." *Geschichte und Gesellschaft* 44, no. 3 (2018): 325–35.
Müller, Wolfgang C. "Politische Kultur: Konzept—Forschungsmethoden—Effekte." In *Staatsbürger oder Untertanen? Politische Kultur Deutschlands, Österreich und der Schweiz im Vergleich*, edited by Fritz Plasser and Peter A. Ulram, 3–15. Frankfurt/M: Peter Lang, 1991.
Müller-Meiningen, Ernst. *Parlamentarismus. Betrachtungen, Lehren und Erinnerungen aus deutschen Parlamenten*. Berlin/Leipzig: Verlag Walter de Gruyter, 1926.

Mushaben, Joyce Marie. "From Ausländer to Inlander. The Changing Face of Citizenship in Post-Wall Germany." In *From the Bonn to the Berlin Republic. Germany at the Twentieth Anniversary of Unification*, edited by Jeffrey J. Anderson and Eric Langenbacher, 160–82. New York: Berghahn Books, 2010.

Mushaben, Joyce Marie. *The Changing Face of Citizenship. Integration and Mobilization among Ethnic Minorities in Germany*. New York: Berghahn Books, 2008.

Mushaben, Joyce Marie. *From Post-War to Post-Wall Generations. Changing Attitudes toward the National Question and NATO in the Federal Republic of Germany*. Boulder, CO: Westview Press, 1998.

Mußgnug, Reinhard. "Bürgerinitiativen und die Mitwirkung des Bürgers an der Verwaltung." In *Staatsführung*, edited by Biedenkopf and v. Voss, 155–77.

Narr, Wolf-Dieter et al. "Den eigenen Menschenrechten, nicht dem Staat gehorchen? Von der Freiheit derjenigen, die zivilen Ungehorsam leisten." In *Ziviler Ungehorsam*, edited by idem, 21–44.

Narr, Wolf-Dieter. "Gewaltfreier Widerstand um der Demokratie und des Friedens willen." In *Demonstrationsrecht*, edited by Cobler et al., 139–69.

Narr, Wolf-Dieter et al. (eds.). *Ziviler Ungehorsam. Traditionen, Konzepte, Erfahrungen, Perspektiven*. Einhausen: hbo druck, 1992.

Nathans, Eli. *The Politics of Citizenship in Germany. Ethnicity, Utility and Nationalism*. Oxford: Berg, 2004.

Neebe, Reinhard. "Die Großindustrie und die Machtergreifung." In *Machtergreifung*, edited by Michalka, 111–23.

Negt, Oskar. "Gesellschaftliche Krise und Demonstrationsfreiheit." In *Das Demonstrationsrecht*, edited by Sebastian Cobler et al., 17–51. Reinbek bei Hamburg: Rowohlt, 1983.

Nehring, Holger. *Politics of Security. British and West German Protest Movements and the Early Cold War, 1945–1970*. Oxford: Oxford University Press, 2013.

Neidhardt, Friedhelm and Dieter Rucht. "Protestgeschichte der Bundesrepublik Deutschland 1950–1994: Ereignisse, Themen, Akteure." In *Protest in der Bundesrepublik. Strukturen und Entwicklungen*, edited by Dieter Rucht, 27–70. Frankfurt: Campus Verlag, 2001.

Neubert, Ehrhart. "Die Opposition im Jahr 1989—ein Überblick." In *Opposition*, edited by Kuhrt et al., 427–58.

Neubert, Ehrhart. "Political Culture of Protestantism in the GDR." In *Political Culture in Germany*, edited by Dirk Berg-Schlosser and Ralf Rytlewski, 153–69. Basingstoke: Palgrave McMillan, 1993.

Neubert, Ehrhart. "Was waren Opposition, Widerstand und Dissidenz in der DDR? Zur Kategorisierung politischer Gegnerschaft." In *Opposition*, edited by Kuhrt et al., 17–46.

Neubert, Ehrhardt and Bernd Eisenfeld (eds.). *Macht—Ohnmacht—Gegenmacht. Grundfragen zur politischen Geschichte in der DDR*. Bremen: Edition Temmon, 2001.

Neumann, Gerald L. "'We Are the People': Alien Suffrage in German and American Perspective." *Michigan Journal of International Law* 13 (1991–92): 259–335.

Niclauß, Karlheinz. "Der Parlamentarische Rat und das Bundesverfassungsgericht." In *Das Bundesverfassungsgericht im politischen System*, edited by Robert Chr. van Ooyen and Maring H.W. Möllers, 117–28. Wiesbaden: Verlag für Sozialwissenschaften, 2006.

Niclauß, Karlheinz. *Der Weg zum Grundgesetz. Demokratiegründung in Westdeutschland 1945–1949*. Paderborn: Schöningh, 1998.

Niclauß, Karlheinz. *Kanzlerdemokratie. Regierungsführung von Konrad Adenauer bis Angela Merkel*. 3rd ed. Wiesbaden: Springer, 2015.

Niedermayer, Oskar. *Bürger und Politik. Politische Orientierungen und Verhaltensweisen der Deutschen*. 2nd. ed. Wiesbaden: Verlag für Sozialwissenschaften, 2001.

Niedermayer, Oskar and Bettina Westle (eds.). *Demokratie und Partizipation*. Opladen: Westdeutscher Verlag, 2000.

Niedermayer, Oskar and Klaus von Beyme (eds.). *Politische Kultur in Ost- und Westdeutschland*. Opladen: Leske + Budrich, 1996.

Niemann, Heinz. *Hinterm Zaun: politische Kultur und Meinungsforschung in der DDR*. Berlin: Edition ost, 1995.

Niethammer, Lutz. "Das Volk in der DDR und die Revolution. Versuch einer historischen Wahrnehmung der laufenden Ereignisse." In *Wir sind das Volk! Flugschriften, Aufrufe und Texte einer deutschen Revolution*, edited by Charles Schüddekopf, 251–79. Reinbeck bei Hamburg: Rowahlt, 1990.

Niethammer, Lutz. "'Normalization' in the West. Traces of Memory Leading Back into the 1950s." In *Miracle*, edited by Schissler, 237–65.

Nipperdey, Thomas. "War die Wilhelminische Gesellschaft eine Untertanengesellschaft?" In *Nachdenken über die deutsche Geschichte: Essays*, edited by idem, 173–85. München: Deutscher Taschenbuch Verlag, 1991.

Noakes, Jeremy. "The Oldenburg Crucifix Struggle of November 1936: A Case Study of Opposition in the Third Reich." In *The Shaping of the Nazi State*, edited by Peter Stachura, 210–33. London: Croom Helm, 1978.

Noelle, Elizabeth and Erich Peter Neumann. *Jahrbuch der öffentlichen Meinung 1947–1955*. Allensbach: Verlag für Demoskopie, 1967.

Noelle, Elisabeth and Erich Peter Neumann (eds.). *Jahrbuch der öffentlichen Meinung 1968–1973*. Allensbach: Verlag für Demoskopie, 1974.

Noelle-Neumann, Elisabeth and Edgar Piel (eds.). *Allensbacher Jahrbuch der Demoskopie 1978–1983*. München: K.G. Saur, 1983.

Noelle-Neumann, Elisabeth and Renate Köcher (eds.). *Allensbacher Jahrbuch der Demoskopie 1984–1992*. München: K.G. Saur, 1993.

Nolte, Ernst. "Diktatur." In *Geschichtliche Grundbegriffe*. Vol. I, edited by Otto Brunner et al., 900–24. Stuttgart: Klett-Cotta, 1972.

Nolte, Paul. *Staatsbildung als Gesellschaftsreform in Preußen und den süddeutschen Staaten, 1800–1820*. Frankfurt/M: Campus Verlag, 1990.

Nord, Philip. *The Republican Moment. Struggles for Democracy in Nineteenth-Century France*. Cambridge: Harvard University Press, 1995.

Norden, Günther v. "Zwischen Teilkooperation und Widerstand. Rolle der Kirche und Konfessionen." In *Widerstand*, edited by Schmädeke and Steinbach, 227–53.

Norris, Pippa. *Critical Citizens. Global Support for Democratic Government*. Oxford: Oxford University Press, 1999.

Nowak, Kurt. "Protestantismus und Demokratie in Deutschland. Aspekte der politischen Moderne." In *Christentum und Demokratie im 20. Jahrhundert*, edited by Martin Greschat and Jochen-Christoph Kaiser, 1–18. Stuttgart: W. Kohlhammer, 1992.

Oberle, Clara M. "Antifascist Heroes and Nazi Victims. Mythmaking and Political Reorientation in Berlin, 1945–47." In *Different Germans*, edited by Jarausch et al., 107–36.

Oberreuter, Heinrich. *Notstand und Demokratie. Vom monarchischen Obrigkeits- zum demokratischen Rechtsstaat*. München: Verlag Ernst Vögel, 1978.

Oertzen, Peter von. *Betriebsräte in der November Revolution*. Düsseldorf: Droste Verlag, 1963.

Offe, Claus. "Ungovernability: On the Renaissance of Conservative Theories of Crisis." In *Spiritual Situation*, edited by Habermas, 67–88.

Ohr, Dieter. *Nationalsozialistische Propaganda und Weimarer Wahlen. Empirische Analyse zur Wirkung von NSDAP Versammlungen*. Opladen: Westdeutscher Verlag, 1997.

O'Keeffe and Patrick M. Twomey. "Union Citizenship." In *Legal issues of the Maastricht Treaty*, edited by David O'Keefe and Patrick Twomey, 87–107. London: Chancery, 1996.

Olivo, Christiane. *Creating a Democratic Civil Society in East Germany*. Basingstoke: Palgrave, 2001.

Olsen, Jonathan. "The Left Party and the AfD: Populist Competitors in Eastern Germany." *German Politics and Society* 36, no. 1 (Spring 2018): 70–83

Opp, Klaus Dieter. "The Dynamics of the Revolution." In *Spontaneous Revolution*, edited by Opp et al., 183–209.

Opp, Klaus-Dieter. "How Could It Happen? An Explanation of the East German Revolution." In *Origins*, edited by Opp et al., 27–47.

Opp, Klaus-Dieter. "Like Hawks in a Trap: Why Wasn't the Protest Movement Crushed?" In *Origins*, edited by idem et al., 167–81.

Opp, Klaus-Dieter et al. (eds.). *Origins of a Spontaneous Revolution: East Germany, 1989*. Ann Arbor: University of Michigan Press, 1995.

Opp, Klaus-Dieter and Christiane Gern. "The Social Causes of the Revolution." In *Origins*, edited by Opp et al., 99–118.

Opp, Karl-Dieter and Steven E. Finkel. "Politischer Protest, Rationalität und Lebensstile. Eine empirische Überprüfung alternativer Erklärungsmodelle." In *Partizipation*, edited by Koch et al., 73–108.

Opp de Hipt, Manfred. "Deutsche Lust am Staat? Marxist-leninistisches Staatsverständnis und realsozialistische Wirklichkeit in der DDR." In *Politische Kultur*, edited by Wehling, 54–65.

Orlow, Dietrich. *The History of the Nazi Party: 1919–1933*. Pittsburgh, PA: University of Pittsburgh Press, 1969.

Osmond, Jonathan. "Kontinuität und Konflikt in der Landwirtschaft der SBZ/DDR zur Zeit der Bodenreform und der Vergenossenschaftlichung, 1945–1961." In *Grenzen*, edited by Bessel and Jessen, 137–69.

Osmond, Jonathan. *Rural Protest in the Weimar Republic*. New York: St. Martin's Press, 1993.

Otto, Karl A. *Vom Ostermarsch zur APO. Geschichte der außerparlamentarischen Opposition in der Bundesrepublik 1960–1970*. Frankfurt: Campus Verlag, 1977.

Palmowski, Jan. *Inventing a Socialist Nation. Heimat and the Politics of Everyday Life in the GDR, 1945–1990*. Cambridge: Cambridge University Press, 2009.

Parness, Diane. *The SPD and the Challenge of Mass Politics. The Dilemma of the German Volkspartei*. Boulder, CO: Westview Press, 1991.

Partei und Gewerkschaften. Wörtlicher Abdruck des Punktes: "Partei und Gewerkschaften" aus dem Protokoll der Konferenz der Gewerkschaftsvorstände vom 19.-23. Februar 1906 in *Economics Pamphlets*, # 31 (Duke University Library).

Partridge, Damani J. *Hypersexuality and Headscarfs. Race, Sex, and Citizenship in the New Germany*. Bloomington: Indiana University Press, 2012.

Patch, Jr., William L. *Heinrich Brüning and the Dissolution of the Weimar Republic*. Cambridge: Cambridge University Press, 1998.

Pateman, Reinhard. *Der Kampf um die preußischen Wahlreform im ersten Weltkrieg*. Düsseldorf: Droste Verlag, 1964.

Paul, Gerhard and Klaus-Michael Mallmann. *Milieus und Widerstand. Eine Verhaltensgeschichte der Gesellschaft im Nationalsozialismus*. Bonn: Verlag J.H.W. Dietz Nachfolger, 1995.

Pautz, Hartwig. *Die deutsche Leitkultur: Eine Identitätsdebatte. Neue Rechte, Neorassismus und Normalisierungsbemühungen.* Stuttgart: ibidem Verlag, 2005.
Payk, Marcus M. "Der 'Amerikakomplex.' 'Massendemokratie' und Kulturkritik am Beispiel von Karl Korner." In *Demokratiewunder*, edited by Bauerkämper, 190–217.
Payk, Marcus M. "'die Herrn fügen sich nicht; sie sind schwierig.' Gemeinschaftsdenken, Generationenkonflikte und die Dynamisierung des Politischen in der konservativen Presse der 1950er und 1960er Jahre." In *Gründung*, edited by Kersting et al., 43–67.
Payk, Marcus P. "Antikommunistische Mobilisierung und konservative Revolte. William S. Schlamm, Winfried Martini und der 'kalte Bürgerkrieg' in der westdeutschen Publizistik der späten 1950er Jahre." In *Massenmedien im Kalten Krieg. Akteure, Bilder, Resonanzen*, edited by Thomas Lindenberger, 111–37. Köln: Böhlau Verlag, 2006.
Peck, Jeffrey et al. "Natives, Strangers, and Foreigners. Constituting Germans by Constructing Others." In *After Unity. Reconfiguring German Identities*, edited by Konrad H. Jarausch, 61–102. Providence: Berghahn Books, 1997.
Pence, Katherine. "Women on the Verge. Consumers between Private Desires and Public Crisis." In *Socialist Modern*, edited by Pence and Betts, 287–322.
Pence, Katherine and Paul Betts. (eds.). *Socialist Modern. East German Everyday Culture and Politics.* Ann Arbor: University of Michigan Press, 2008.
Petzina, Dietmar et al. (eds.). *Sozialgeschichtliches Arbeitsbuch.* Vol. III. München: Verlag C.H. Beck, 1978.
Petzold, Joachim. *Franz von Papen. Ein deutsches Verhängnis.* München: Buchverlag Union, 1995.
Peukert, Detlef. *Inside Nazi Germany. Conformism, Opposition, and Racism in Everyday Life.* Trsl. by Richard Deveson. New Haven, CT: Yale University Press, 1987.
Peukert, Detlev. *The Weimar Republic. The Crisis of Classical Modernity.* Trsl. by Richard Deveson. New York: Hill and Wang, 1989.
Pew Research Center. "Democratic Rights Popular Globally but Commitment to Them Not Always Strong." February 27, 2020: Available online: https://www.pewresearch.org/global/2020/02/27/democratic-rights-popular-globally-but-commitment-to-them-not-always-strong/ (accessed May 17, 2020).
Pfaff, Steven. *Exit-Voice Dynamics and the Collapse of East Germany.* Durham, NC: Duke University Press, 2006.
Pikart, Eberhard. "Auf dem Weg zum Grundgesetz." In *Die zweite Republik. 25 Jahre Bundesrepublik Deutschland—eine Bilanz*, edited by Richard Löwenthal and Hans-Peter Schwarz, 149–76. Stuttgart: Seewald Verlag, 1974.
Pine, Lisa (ed.). *Life and Times in Nazi Germany.* London: Bloomsbury, 2016.
Planert, Ute. "Vater Staat und Mutter Germania: Zur Politisierung des weiblichen Geschlechts im 19. und 20. Jahrhundert." In *Nation, Politik und Geschlecht. Frauenbewegungen und Nationalismus in der Moderne*, edited by idem, 15–65. Frankfurt: Campus Verlag, 2000.
Planert, Ute. "Women's Suffrage and Antifeminism as a Litmus Test of Modernizing Societies. A Western European Comparison." In *Imperial Germany Revisited. Continuing Debates and New Perspectives*, edited by Sven Oliver Müller and Cornelius Torp, 107–21. New York: Berghahn Books, 2013.
Pogge von Strandmann, Hartmut "Staatsstreichpläne, Alldeutsche, und Bethmann Hollweg." In *Die Erforderlichkeit des Unmöglichen. Deutschland am Vorabend des ersten Weltkrieges*, edited by idem, 7–45. Frankfurt/M: Europäische Verlagsanstalt, 1965.
Pohl, Rolf. "Das Konstrukt 'Volksgemeinschaft' als Mittel zur Erzeugung von Massenloyalitat im Nationalsozialismus." In *"Volksgemeinschaft": Mythos,*

wirkungsmächtige sociale Verheißung oder soziale Realität im "Dritten Reich?" Zwischenbilanz einer kontroversen Debatte, edited by Detlef Schmiechen-Ackermann, 69–84. Paderborn: Schoningh, 2012.

Pohl, Karl Heinrich. "Kommunen, kommunale Wahlen und kommunale Wahlrechtpolitik. Zur Bedeutung der Wahlrechtsfrage für die Kommunen und den deutschen Liberalismus." In *Modernisierung und Region in wilhelminischen Deutschland. Wahlen, Wahlrecht und Politische Kultur*, edited by Simone Lässig et al., 89–126. Bielefeld: Verlag für Regionalgeschichte, 1995.

Poiger, Ute G. *Jazz, Rock, and Rebels. Cold War Politics and American Culture in a Divided Germany*. Berkeley: University of California Press, 2000.

Pollack, Detlef. "Bedingungen der Möglichkeit politischen Protestes in der DDR. Der Volksaufstand von 1953 und die Massendemonstrationen 1989 im Vergleich." In *Verweigerung*, edited by Pollock and Rink, 303–31.

Pollack, Detlef. "Der Zusammenbruch der DDR als Verkettung getrennter Handlungslinien." In *Weg*, edited by Jarausch and Sabrow, 41–81.

Pollack, Detlef. "Kulturelle, soziale und politische Bedingungen der Möglichkeit widerständigen Verhaltens in der DDR." In *Macht—Ohmacht—Gegenmacht. Grundfragen zur politische Gegnerschaft in der DDR*, edited by Ehrhardt Neubert and Bernd Eisenfeld, 349–66. Bremen: Edition Temmon, 2001.

Pollack, Detlef. "Modernization and Modernization Blockages in GDR Society." In *Dictatorship*, edited by Jarausch, 27–45.

Pollack, Detlef. *Politische Protest. Politisch alternative Gruppen in der DDR*. Opladen: Leske + Budrich, 2000.

Pollmann, Karl Erich. *Parlamentarismus im Nordeutschen Bund 1867–1870*. Düsseldorf: Droste Verlag, 1985.

Poppe, Ulrike. "'Der Weg ist das Ziel.' Zum Selbstverständnis und der politischen Rolle oppositioneller Gruppen in der 80er Jahren." In *Selbstbehauptung*, edited by Poppe et al., 244–72.

Poppe, Ulrike et al. "Opposition, Widerstand und widerständiges Verhalten in der DDR. Forschungsstand—Grundlinien—Probleme." In *Selbstbehauptung*, edited by idem, 9–26.

Poppe, Ulrike et al. *Zwischen Selbstbehauptung und Anpassung. Formen des Widerstandes und der Opposition in der DDR*. Berlin: CH Links Verlag, 1995.

Port, Andrew I. *Conflict and Stability in the German Democratic Republic*. Cambridge: Cambridge University Press, 2007.

Port, Andrew. "The 'Grumble Gesellschaft.' Industrial Defiance and Worker Protest in Early East Germany." In *Arbeiter in der SBZ/DDR*, edited by Peter Hübner and Klaus Tenfelde, 787–810. Essen: Klartext, 1998.

Port, Andrew. "'There Will Be Blood.' The Violent Underside of the 'Peaceful' East German Revolution of 1989." In *Politische Gewalt*, edited by José Brunner, 217. Göttingen: Wallenstein Verlag, 2014.

Poscher, Ralf. "Einführung." In *Der Verfassungstag*, edited by idem, 11–50. Baden-Baden: Nomos Verlagsgesellschaft, 1999.

Poscher, Rolf. "Das Weimar Wahlrechtsgespenst." In *Schatten*, edited by Gusy, 256–80.

Pritchard, Gareth. *The Making of the GDR, 1945–1953. From Antifascism to Stalinism*. Manchester: Manchester University Press, 2000.

Pritchard, Gareth. "Workers and the Socialist Unity Party of Germany in the Summer of 1953." In *Workers' State*, edited by Major and Osmond, 112–29.

Probst, Lothar. *Bürgerbewegung und Perspektiven der Demokratie. Entstehung, Bedeutung und Zukunft*. Köln: Bund Verlag, 1993.

Pross, Helga. *Was ist heute Deutsch. Wertorientierungen in der Bundesrepublik*. Reinbek: Rowohlt, 1982.

Prowe, Diethelm. "Economic Democracy in Post-World War II Germany: Corporatist Crisis Response." *Journal of Modern History* 57, no. 3 (September 1985): 451–82.

Pulzer, Peter. *German Politics 1945–1995*. Oxford: Oxford University Press, 1995.

Pulzer, Peter. *The Rise of Political Anti-Semitism in Germany and Austria*. Rev. Ed. Cambridge: Harvard University Press, 1988.

Pyta, Wolfgang. *Dorfgemeinschaft und Parteipolitik, 1918–1933*. Düsseldorf: Droste Verlag, 1996.

Pyta, Wolfgang. *Gegen Hitler und für die Republik. Die Auseinandersetzung der deutschen Sozialdemokratie mit der NSDAP in der Weimarer Republik*. Düsseldorf: Droste Verlag, 1989.

Quint, Peter E. *The Imperfect Union. Constitutional Structures of German Unification*. Princeton, NJ: Princeton University Press, 1997.

Qvortup, Matt. "Referendums in Western Europe." In *Referendums around the World*, edited by idem, 43–64. Cham, Switzerland: Palgrave Macmillan, 2018.

Rabinach, Anson. "Organized Mass Culture in the Third Reich: The Women of the Kraft durch Freude." In *Rise*, edited by Maier et al., 97–105.

Rabinbach, Anson. "Restoring the German Spirit: Humanism and Guilt in Post-War Germany." In *German Ideologies Since 1945: Studies in the Political Thought and Culture of the Bonn Republic*, edited by Jan-Werner Müller, 23–39. Houndsmill: Palgrave Macmillan, 2003.

Rahden, Till von. "Wie Vati Demokratie lernt. Religion, Familie und die Frage der Autorität in der frühen Bundesrepublik." In *Demokratie*, edited by Fulda, 122–51.

Rapport, Mike. *1848. Year of Revolution*. New York: Basic Books, 2009.

Raschke, Joachim. "Einleitung." In *Bürger und Parteien. Ansichten und Analysen einer schwierigen Beziehung*, edited by idem, 9–31. Opladen: Westdeutscher Verlag, 1982.

Raschke, Joachim. *Soziale Bewegungen. Ein historisch-systematischer Grundriß*. Frankfurt: Campus Verlag, 1985.

Rattinger, Hans. "Parteiidentifikation in Ost- und Westdeutschland nach der Vereinigung." In *Politische Kultur*, edited by Niedermayer and von Beyme, 77–104.

Rauh, Manfred. *Die Parlamentarisierung des Deutschen Reiches*. Düsseldorf: Droste Verlag, 1977.

Reagin, Nancy R. *A German Women's Movement. Class and Gender in Hannover, 1880–1933*. Chapel Hill: University of North Carolina Press, 1995.

Rebentisch, Dieter. "Die 'politische Beurteilung' als Herrschaftsinstrument der NSDAP." In *Reihen*, edited by Detlev Peukert and Jürgen Reulecke, 107–25.

Recker, Marie-Luise and Andreas Schulz. "Parlamentarismuskritik und Antiparlamentarismus in Europa." In *Parlamentarismuskritik und Antiparlamentarismus in Europa*, edited by idem, 9–21. Düsseldorf: Droste Verlag, 2018.

Reichart, Sven. *Authentizität und Gemeinschaft. Linksalternatives Leben in den siebziger und frühen achtziger Jahren*. Berlin: Suhrkamp, 2014.

Reichardt, Sven. "Civility, Violence, and Civil Society." In *Civil Society*, edited by Keane, 139–67.

Reichardt, Sven. "Faschistische Beteiligungsdiktaturen. Anmerkungen zu einer Debatte." In *Politische Gewalt*, edited by José Brunner et al., 133–60.

Reichardt, Sven. "Gewalt, Körper, Politik. Paradoxien in der deutschen Kulturgeschichte der Zwischenkriegszeit." In *Kulturgeschichte*, edited by Hardtwig, 205–39.

Reichardt, Sven. "Große und Sozialliberale Koalition (1966–1974)." In *Die soziale Bewegungen in Deutschland seit 1945*, edited by Roland Roth and Dieter Rucht, 71–91. Frankfurt: Campus Verlag, 2008.

Reichardt, Sven and Detlef Siegfried (eds.). *Das Alternative Milieu*. Göttingen: Wallsten Verlag, 2010.

Reichardt, Sven and Detlef Siegfried. "Das Alternative Milieu." In *Alternative*, edited by idem, 9–24.

Reichel, Peter. *Der schöne Schein des Dritten Reiches. Faszination und Gewalt des Faschismus*. Frankfurt/M: Fischer Taschenbuch Verlag, 1993.

Reichel, Peter. *Vergangenheitsbewältigung in Deutschland. Die Auseinandersetzung mit der NS-Diktatur in Politik und Justiz*. München: C.H. Beck, 2007.

Repp, Kevin. *Reformers, Critics, and the Paths of German Modernity. Anti-Politics and the Search for Alternatives, 1890–1914*. Cambridge: Harvard University Press, 2000.

Requate, Jörg. "Gefährliche Intellektuelle? Staat und Gewalt in der Debatte über die RAF." In *Streit*, edited by Geppert and Hacke, 251–67.

Retallack, James. "Democracy in Disappearing Ink: Suffrage Robbery as Coup d'État." In *Germany's Second Reich: Portraits and Pathways*, edited by idem, 377–415. Toronto: University of Toronto Press, 2015.

Retallack, James. *The German Right, 1860–1920*. Toronto: University of Toronto Press, 2006.

Retallack, James. *Notables of the Right. The Conservative Party and Political Mobilization in Germany, 1876–1918*. Boston: Unwin Hyman, 1988.

Retallack, James. *Red Saxony. Electoral Battles and the Spectre of Democracy in Germany, 1860–1918*. Oxford: Oxford University Press, 2017.

Retallack, James. "'What Is to Be Done?' The Red Specter, Franchise Questions, and the Crisis of Conservative Hegemony in Saxony, 1896–1909." *Central European History* 23 (1990): 271–312.

Retterath, Jörn. "Der Volksbegriff in der Zäsur des Jahres 1918/19. Pluralistisches und holistisches Denken im katholischen, liberalen und sozialdemokratischen Milieu." In *Demokratiegeschichte als Zäsurgeschichte. Diskurse der frühen Weimarer Republik*, edited by Heidrun Kämper et al., 97–122. Berlin: deGruyter, 2014.

Retterath, Jörn. *"Was ist das Volk?" Volk- und Gemeinschaftskonzepte der politischen Mitte in Deutschland 1917–1924*. Oldenbourg: deGruyter, 2016.

Richardson-Little, Ned. "Dictatorship and Dissent: Human Rights in East Germany in the 1970s." In *The Breakthrough: Human Rights in the 1970s*, edited by Jan Eckel and Samuel Moyn, 49–67. Philadelphia: University of Pennsylvania Press, 2013.

Richardson-Little, Ned. "Human Rights, Pluralism, and the Democratization of Postwar Germany." In *Different Germans*, edited by Konrad Jarausch et al., 158–77. New York: Berghahn Books, 2017.

Richter, Claus. *Die überflüssige Generation. Jugend zwischen Apathie und Aggression*. Bodenheim: Athenäum Verlag, 1979.

Richter, Hedwig. *Moderne Wahlen. Eine Geschichte der Demokratie in Preußen und den USA im 19. Jahrhundert*. Hamburg: Hamburger Edition, 2017.

Richter, Michaela. "From State Culture to Citizen Culture: Political Parties and the Postwar Transformation of Political Culture in Germany." In *Transformation*, edited by Brady et al., 122–59.

Richthofen, Esther von. *Bringing Culture to the Masses. Control, Compromise and Participation in the GDR*. New York: Berghahn Books, 2009.

Richthofen, Esther von. "Communication and Compromise: The Prerequisites for Cultural Participation." In *Power*, edited by Fulbrook, 130–50.

Riedlinger, Arne. "Vom Boykott zur Verfassungsbeschwerde. Erich Lüth und die Kontroverse um Harlans Nachkriegsfilme." In *Lüth Urteil*, edited by idem and Henne, 147–86.
Rigoll, Dominick. *Staatsschutz in Westdeutschland. Von der Entnazifizierung zur Extremistenabwehr*. Göttingen: Wallstein Verlag, 2013.
Rink, Dieter. "Ausreiser, Kirchengruppen, Kulturopposition und Reformer. Zu Differenzen und Gemeinsamkeiten in Opposition und Widerstand in der DDR in den 70er und 80er Jahren." In *Verweigerung*, edited by Pollock and idem, 54–77.
Ritter, Gerhard A. "Der Anti-parlamentarismus und Antipluralismus der Rechts- und Linksradikalen." In *Der Überdruß an der Demokratie. Neue Lnke und alte Rechte— Unterschieden und Gemeinsamkeiten*, edited by Kurt Sontheimer et al., 43–91. Köln: Markus Verlag, 1970.
Ritter, Gerhard A. *Die deutschen Parteien 1830–1914*. Göttingen: Vandenhoeck & Ruprecht, 1985.
Ritter, Gerhard A. "Die Reichstagwahlen und die Wurzeln der deutschen Demokratie im Kaiserreich." *Historische Zeitschrift* 275, no. 2 (October 2002): 623–66.
Ritter, Gerhard A. and Merith Niehuss. *Wahlen in der Bundesrepublik Deutschland. Bundestags- und Landtagswahlen 1946–1987*. München: C.H. Beck, 1987.
Roß, Sabine. *Politische Partizipation und Nationaler Räteparlamentarismus: Determinanten des politischen Handelns der Delegierten zu den Reichsrätekongressen 1918/1919*. Köln: Zentrum für historische Sozialforschung, 1999.
Rohe, Karl. *Das Reichsbanner Schwarz Rot Gold. Ein Beitrag zur Geschichte und Struktur der politischen Kampfverbände zur Zeit der Weimarer Republik*. Düsseldorf: Droste Verlag, 1966.
Rohe, Karl. "Politische Kultur: Zum Verständnis eines theoretischen Konzepts." In *Politische Kultur*, edited by Oskar Niedermeier and Klaus von Beyme, 1–21.
Rohe, Karl. "The State Tradition in Germany: Continuities and Changes." In *Political Culture*, edited by Berg- Schlosser and Rytlewski, 215–31.
Rohe, Karl. *Wahlen und Wählertraditionen in Deutschland: Kulturelle Grundlagen deutscher Parteien und Parteiensysteme im 19. und 20. Jahrhundert*. Frankfurt/M: Suhrkamp, 1992.
Rohkrämer, Thomas. "Die fatale Attraktion der Nationalsozialismus in der Weimarer Republik." In *Attraktion*, edited by Brockhaus, 79–94.
Rohkrämer, Thomas. *A Single Communal Faith? The German Right from Conservatism to National Socialism*. New York: Berghahn Books, 2007.
Rohrschneider, Robert. *Learning Democracy. Democratic and Economic Values in Unified Germany*. Oxford: Oxford University Press, 1999.
Roos, Julia. *Weimar through the Lens of Gender. Prostitution Reform, Women's Emancipation, and German Democracy, 1919–1933*. Ann Arbor: University of Michigan Press, 2010.
Rosenbusch, Ute. *Der Weg zum Frauenwahlrecht in Deutschland*. Baden-Baden: Nomos Verlag, 1998.
Rosenhaft, Eva. *Beating the Fascists? The German Communists and Political Violence 1929–1933*. Cambridge: Cambridge University Press, 1983.
Rosenhaft, Eva. "Women, Gender, and the Limits of Political History in the Age of 'Mass' Politics." In *Elections*, edited by Jones and Retallack, 149–73.
Ross, Ronald J. *The Failure of Bismarck's Kulturkampf. Catholicism and State Power in Imperial Germany, 1871–1887*. Washington, DC: The Catholic University of American Press, 1998.

Rossol, Nadine. "Performing the Nation: Sports, Spectacles, and Aesthetics in Germany, 1926-1936." *Central European History* 43, no. 4 (December 2010): 616-38.
Roth, Roland and Dieter Rucht. "Einleitung." In *Bewegungen seit 1945*, edited by idem, 26-27.
Roth, Roland and Dieter Rucht (eds.). *Neue soziale Bewegungen in der Bundesrepublik Deutschland*. Frankfurt: Campus Verlag, 1987.
Rucht, Dieter. "Das alternative Milieu in der Bundesrepublik. Ursprünge, Infrastruktur und Nachwirkung." In *Alternative*, edited by Reichardt and Siegfried, 61-86.
Rucht, Dieter. "Die konstruktive Funktion von Protesten in und für die Zivilgesellschaft." In *Zivilgesellschaft als Geschichte. Studien zum 19. und 20. Jahrhundert*, edited by Ralph Jessen et al., 135-52. Wiesbaden: Verlag für Sozialwissenschaft, 2004.
Rucht, Dieter and Jochen Roose. "Von der Platzbesetzung zum Verhandlungstisch? Zum Wandel von Aktionen und Struktur der Ökologiebewegung." In *Protest*, edited by Rucht, 173-210.
Rucht, Dieter and Roland Roth. "Soziale Bewegungen und Protest—eine theoretische Zwischenbilanz." In *Die soziale Bewegungen seit 1945*, edited by idem, 9-36. Frankfurt: Campus Verlag, 2008.
Rüddenklau, Wolfgang. *Störenfried. DDR Opposition 1986-1989. Mit Texten aus den "Umweltblättern."* Berlin: Basis Druck Verlag, 1992.
Rudner, Thomas and Heinz Stapf. "Das Private ist politisch—Zur Entwicklung eines neuen Politikverständnisses." In *Obrigkeitsstaat*, edited by Ralf Zoll, 115-39.
Rudolph, Hermann. "Mehr als Stagnation und Revolte. Zur politischen Kultur der sechziger Jahre." In *Zäsuren nach 1945: Essays zur Periodisierung der deutschen Nachkriegsgeschicht*, edited by Martin Broszat, 141-51. München: Oldenbourg Verlag, 1990.
Ruff, Mark Edward. *The Battle for the Catholic Past in Germany, 1945-1980*. New York: Cambridge University Press, 2017.
Rupieper, Hermann-Josef. *Die Wurzeln der westdeutschen Nachkriegsdemokratie. Der amerikanische Beitrag 1945-1952*. Opladen: Westdeutscher Verlag, 1993.
Rupp, Hans Karl. *APO in der Ära Adenauer. Der Kampf gegen die Atombewaffnung in den fünfziger Jahren*. Köln: Paul Rugenstein, 1980 [1970].
Ryder, Arthur J. *The German Revolution of 1918. A Study of German Socialism in War and Revolt*. Cambridge: Cambridge University Press, 1967.
Rytlewski, Ralf. "Ein neues Deutschland? Merkmale, Differenzierungen und Wandlungen in der politischen Kultur der DDR." In *Politische Kultur*, edited by Hans Georg Wehling, 11-28.
Rytlewski, Ralf. "Soziale Kultur als politische Kultur: die DDR." Dirk Berg-Schlosser and Jakob Schissler (eds.). *Politische Kultur in Deutschland, Politische Vierteljahresschrift* Sonderheft 18 (1987): 238-46.
Sa'adah, Anne. *Germany's Second Chance. Trust, Justice, and Democratization*. Cambridge: Harvard University Press, 1998.
Sabrow, Martin. "Der Konkurs der Konsensdiktatur. Überlegungen zur inneren Zerfall der DDR aus kulturgeschichtlichen Perspektive." In *Weg*, edited by Jarausch and idem, 83-116.
Sabrow, Martin. "Der Wille zur Ohnmacht und die Macht des Unwillens." In *Macht*, edited by Neubert and Eisenfeld, 317-47.
Sabrow, Martin. "Dictatorship as Discourse. Cultural Perspectives on SED Legitimacy." In *Dictatorship*, edited by Konrad H. Jarausch, 195-211.
Saldern, Adelheid v. "Victims or Perpetrators? Controversies about the Role of Women in the Nazi State." In *Nazism*, edited by Crew, 141-65.

Sarotte, Mary Elise. *The Collapse. The Accidental Opening of the Berlin Wall*. New York: Basic Books, 2014.
Sauer, Wolfgang. *Die Mobilmachung der Gewalt*. Frankfurt/M: Ullstein Verlag, 1974.
Schäfer, Hans Dieter. *Das gespaltene Bewußtsein. Über deutsche Kultur und Lebenswirklichkeit 1933–1945*. München: Carl Hansler Verlag, 1981.
Scheck, Raffael. *Mothers of the Nation. Right-Wing Women in the Weimar Republic*. Oxford: Berg, 2004.
Schildt, Axel. "'Augstein raus—Strauß rein.' Öffentliche Reaktionen auf die *Spiegel* Affäre." In *Spiegel*, edited by Doerry and Janssen, 177–201.
Schildt, Axel. "Der Umgang mit der NS-Vergangenheit in der Öffentlichkeit der Nachkriegszeit." In *Verwandlungspolitik: NS-Eliten in der westdeutschen Nachkriegsgesellschaft*, edited by Winfried Loth and Bernd-A. Rusinek, 45–53. Frankfurt/M: Campus, 1998.
Schildt, Axel. "Die USA als 'Kulturnation.' Zur Bedetung der Amerikahäuser in den 1950er Jahre." In *Amerikanisierung. Traum und Alptraum in Deutschland des 20. Jahrhunderts*, edited by Alf Lüdtke et al., 257–69. Stuttgart: Franz Steiner Verlag, 1996.
Schildt, Axel et al. (eds.). *Dynamische Zeiten. Die 60er Jahre in den beiden deutschen Gesellschaften*. Hamburg: H. Cristians Verlag, 2000.
Schildt, Axel and Arnold Sywottek (eds.). *Modernisierung im Wiederaufbau. Die westdeutsche Gesellschaft der 50er Jahre*. Bonn: Verlag JHW Dietz Nachf., 1993.
Schirmer, Dietmar. "Politisch-kulturelle Deutungsmuster: Vorstellungen von der Welt der Politik in der Weimarer Republik." In *Gedenktage*, edited by Lehnert and Megerle, 31–60.
Schissler, Hanna (ed.). *The Miracle Years. A Cultural History of West Germany, 1949–1968*. Princeton, NJ: Princeton University Press, 2001.
Schlak, Stephan. *Wilhelm Hennis. Szenen einer Ideengeschichte der Bundesrepublik*. München: Beck, 2008.
Schletter, Christian. *Grabgesang der Demokratie. Die Debatten über das Scheitern der bundesdeutschen Demokratie*. Göttingen: Vandenhoeck & Ruprecht, 2015.
Schmädeke, Jürgen and Peter Steinbach (eds.). *Der Widerstand gegen den Nationalsozialismus. Die deutsche Gesellschaft und der Widerstand gegen Hitler*. München: Piper Verlag, 1985.
Schmid, Josef. *Kirchen, Staat und Politik in Dresden zwischen 1975 und 1989*. Koln: Bohlau Verlag, 1998.
Schmid, Thomas. "Die Wirklichkeit eines Traumes. Versuch über die Grenzen des autopoetischen Vermögens." In *Die Früchte der Revolte. Über die Veränderungen der politischen Kultur durch die Studentenbewegung*, edited by Lothar Baier et al., 7–33. Berlin: Verlag Klaus Wagenbach, 1988.
Schmiechen-Ackermann, Detlef. "Einführung." In *"Volksgemeinschaft,"* edited by idem, 13–53.
Schmiechen-Ackermann, Detlef. "Social Control and the Making of the Volksgemeinschaft." In *Visions*, edited by Steber and Gotto, 240–53.
Schmiechen-Ackermann, Detlef. *"Volksgemeinschaft": Mythos, wirkungsmächtige soziale Versheißung oder soziale Realität im "Dritten Reich?"* Paderborn: Schöningh, 2012.
Schmitt-Beck, Rüdiger and Cornelia Weins. "Gone with the Wind (of change). Neue Soziale Bewegungen und politischen Protest im Osten Deutschlands." In *Orientierungen*, edited by Gabriel, 321–51.
Schneider, Michael. *Demokratie in Gefahr? Der Konflikt um die Notstandsgesetze*. Bonn: Verlag Neue Gesellschaft, 1986.

Schneider, Michael. "Demokratisierungs-Konsens zwischen Unternehmer und Gewerkschaften? Zur Debatte um Wirtschaftsdemokratie und Mitbestimmung." In *Modernisierung*, edited by Schildt and Sywottek, 207–22.

Schneider, Michael. *Unternehmer und Demokratie. Die freien Gewerkschaften in der unternehmerischen Ideologie der Jahre 1918 bis 1933*. Bonn-Bad Godesberg: Neue Gesellschaft GmbH, 1975.

Schöbel, Carolin "Sozialisation in unterschiedlichen Systemen. Zum Profil der Persönlichkeitstypen in West- und Ost-Berlin." In *Wende*, edited by Klingemann et al., 15–39.

Schoenbaum, David. *The Spiegel Affair*. Garden City: Doubleday & Co., 1968.

Scholtyseck, Joachim. "Mauerbau und Deutsche Frage. Westdeutsche Intellektuelle und der Kalte Krieg." In *Streit*, edited by Geppert and Hacke, 69–90.

Scholz, Rupert. "Demokratie und freiheitlicher Rechtsstaat." In *Streitkultur*, edited by Sarcinelli, 304–10.

Schöneberger, Christoph. "Demokratisches Denken in der Weimarer Republik." In *Denken*, edited by Gusy, 664–9.

Schönberger, Christoph. "Die überholte Parlamentarisierung: Einflußgewinn und fehlende Herrschaftsfähigkeit des Reichstags im sich demokratisierenden Kaiserreich." *Historische Zeitschrift* 272, no. 3 (June 2001): 623–66.

Schönwälder, Karen and Triadafilos Triadafilopoulos. "A Bridge or Barrier to Incorporation? Germany's 1999 Citizenship Reform in Critical Perspective." *German Politics & Society* 30 (2012): 52–70.

Schregel, Susanne. "'Dann sage ich, brich das Gesetz.' Recht und Protest im Streit um den NATO-Doppelbeschluss." In *Ordnung*, edited by Löhnig et al., 133–48.

Schregel, Susanne. "Konjunktur der Angst. 'Politik der Subjektivität' und 'neue Friedensbewegung', 1978–1983." In *Angst im Kalten Krieg*, edited by Bernd Greiner et al., 495–520. Hamburg: Hamburger Edition, 2009.

Schröder, Richard. "Wer beherrscht den Osten?" *Deutschland Archiv*, July 7, 2019. Available online: https://www.bpb.de/geschichte/zeitgeschichte/ deutschlandarchiv/293406/wer-beherrscht-den-osten (accessed May 15, 2020).

Schroeder, Steven M. *To Forget It All and Begin Anew. Reconciliation in Occupied Germany, 1944–1954*. Toronto: University of Toronto Press, 2013.

Schulz, Kristina. *Der lange Atem der Provokation. Die Frauenbewegung in der Bundesrepublik und Frankreich 1968–1976*. Frankfurt: Campus Verlag, 2002.

Schumann, Dirk. "Einheitssucht und Gewaltakzeptanz. Politische Grundpositionen des deutschen Bürgertums nach 1918." In *Weltkrieg*, edited by Mommsen, 83–105.

Schumann, Dirk. "Political Violence, Contested Public Space, and Reasserted Masculinity in Weimar Germany." In *Weimar Publics*, edited by Canning et al., 236–53.

Schumpeter, Joseph. *Capitalism, Socialism, and Democracy*. 3rd ed. New York: Harper & Brothers Publishers, 1950.

Schüttemeyer, Suzanne S. *Bundestag und Bürger im Spiegel der Demoskopie. Eine Sekundäranalyse zur Parlamentarismusperzeption in der Bundesrepublik*. Opladen: Westdeutscher Verlag, 1986.

Schutze, Thomas and Almut Gross. *Die Autonomen. Ursprünge, Entwicklung und Profil der Autonomen*. Hamburg: Konkret Literatur Verlag, 1997.

Schwabe, Christian. *Die deutsche Modernitätskrise. Politische Kultur und Mentalität von der Reichsgründung bis zur Wiedervereinigung*. München: Wilhelm Fink Verlag, 2005.

Schwabe, Uwe. "Der Herbst '89 in Zahlen—Demonstrationen und Kundgebungen vom August 1989 bis zum April 1990." In *Opposition in der DDR*, edited by Eberhard Kuhrt et al., 719–35.

Schwartz, Michael. "Frauen und Reform im doppelten Deutschland. Zusammenhänge zu Frauenerwerbsarbeit, Abtreibungsrecht Bevölkerungspolitik um 1970." In *Ende*, edited by Jarausch, 196–225.

Schwerdtner, Peter. "Personen- und, Persönlichkeitsschutz und Rechtsfähigkeit im Nationalsozialismus." In *Recht*, edited by Rottleuthner, 82–91.

Schwörer-Roßnagel, Helmut. "Sitzblockade als Nötigung—Eine kurze Bestandsaufnahme." In *Ziviler Ungehorsam. Traditionen, Konzepte, Erfahrungen, Perspektiven*, edited by Wolf-Dieter Narr et al., 319–26. Einhausen: hbo druck, 1992.

Sedlmaier, Alexander. *Consumption and Violence. Radical Protest in Cold War West Germany*. Ann Arbor: University of Michigan Press, 2014.

Semmens, Kristin. "A Holiday from the Nazis? Everyday Tourism in the Third Reich." In *Life and Times*, edited by Lisa Pine, 131–59.

Sheehan, James J. *German History 1770–1866*. Oxford: Oxford University Press, 1989.

Sheehan, James J. *German Liberalism in the Nineteenth Century*. Chicago: University of Chicago Press, 1978.

Sichtermann, Barbara and Kai Sichtermann. *Das ist unser Haus. Eine Geschichte der Hausbesetzung*. Berlin: Aufbau Verlag, 2017.

Siegfried, Detlef. "Klingt gut, ist falsch. Legitimitätskämpfe um Popmusik in der linken Szene der 1970er Jahre." *Mittelweg* 36 (2016): 4–49.

Siegfried, Detlef. "Superkultur. Authentizität und politische Moral." In *Bürgersinn*, edited by Knoch, 251–68.

Siegfried, Detlef. "Vom Teenager zur Pop-Revolution. Politisierungstendenzen in der westdeutschen Jugendkultur 1959 bis 1968." In *Dynamische Zeiten. Die 60er Jahren in den beiden deutschen Gesellschaften*, edited by Axel Schildt et al., 582–625. Hamburg: H. Christians Verlag, 2000.

Siemann, Wolfram. *The German Revolution of 1848*. Trsl. by Christiane Banerji. New York: St. Martin's Press, 1998.

Sinn, Arndt. "Die Nötigungsstrafbarkeit von Protesthandlungen." In *Ordnung*, edited by Löhnig et al., 113–31.

Smith, Jake P. "Apathy, Subversion, and the Network Sublime: Envisioning Youth Unrest in West Germany, 1980–1987." In *A European Youth Revolt? Youth Movements, Revolt, and Transgression in the 1980s*, edited by Knud Andresen and Bart van der Steen, 231–42. Basingstoke: Palgrave, 2016.

Sneeringer, Julia. *Winning Women's Votes. Propaganda and Politics in Weimar Germany*. Chapel Hill: University of North Carolina Press, 2002.

Sontheimer, Kurt. *Antidemokratisches Denken in der Weimarer Republik. Die politischen Ideen des deutschen Nationalismus zwischen 1918 und 1933*. 2nd ed. München: Nymphenburger Verlagshandlung, 1964.

Sontheimer, Kurt. *Deutschlands Politische Kultur*. München: Piper, 1990.

Sontheimer, Kurt. *Die Adenauer Ära. Grundlegung der Bundesrepublik Deutschland*. München: dtv, 1991.

Sontheimer, Kurt. "Die politische Kultur der Weimarer Republik." In *Weimarer Republik*, edited by Karl Dietrich Bracher et al., 454–64.

Sontheimer, Kurt. *Zeitwende? Die Bundesrepublik Deutschland zwischen alter und alternativer Politik*. Hamburg: Hoffmann und Campe, 1983.

Specter, Matthew G. *Habermas. An Intellectual Biography*. Cambridge: Cambridge University Press, 2010.

Sperber, Jonathan. *The Kaiser's Voters. Electors and Elections in Imperial Germany*. Cambridge: Cambridge University Press, 1997.

Spernol, Boris. *Notstand der Demokratie. Protest gegen die Notstandsgesetzgebung und die Frage der NS-Vergangenheit*. Essen: Klartext, 2008.
Stamm, Karl-Heinz. *Alternative Öffentlichkeit. Die Erfahrungsproduktion neuer sozialen Bewegungen*. Frankfurt: Campus Verlag, 1988.
Stargardt, Nicholas. *The German War. A Nation under Arms. Citizens and Soldiers*. New York: Basic Books, 2015.
Stark, Gary D. *Banned in Berlin. Literary Censorship in Imperial Germany, 1871–1918*. New York: Berghahn Books, 2009.
Steber, Martina and Bernhard Gotto (eds.). *Visions of Community in Nazi Germany. Social Engineering and Private Lives*. Oxford: Oxford University Press, 2014.
Steber, Martina and Bernhard Gotto. "Volksgemeinschaft. Writing the Social History of the Nazi Regime." In *Visions*, edited by idem, 1–25.
Stefani, Winfried. "Mehrheitsentscheidung und Minderheiten in der pluralistischen Verfassungsdemokratie." In *Neue Bewegungen*, edited by Roth and Rucht, 344–53.
Stegmann, Dirk. "Between Interest and Radical Nationalism. Attempts to Found a New Right-Wing Party in Imperial Germany, 1887–94." In *Reform, Reaction*, edited by Jones James Retallack, 157–85.
Steinbach, Peter. "Legacies of the German Empire." In *Political Culture*, edited by Berg-Schlosser and Rytlewski, 29–42.
Steinbach, Peter. "Reichstag Elections in the Kaiserreich." In *Elections*, edited by Jones and Retallack, 119–46.
Steinbach, Peter. "Wiederherstellung des Rechtsstaats als zentrale Zielsetzung des Widerstands." In *Widerstand*, edited by Schmädeke and Steinbach, 616–38.
Steinberg, Hans-Josef. "Die Haltung der Arbeiterschaft zum NS-Regime." In *Widerstand*, edited by Schmädeke and Steinbach, 867–74.
Steiner, André. *The Plans that Failed. An Economic History of the GDR*. Trsl by Ewald Osers. New York: Berghahn Books, 2010.
Steinert, Marlis. *Hitler's War and the Germans*. Athens: Ohio University Press, 1977.
Stephenson, Jill. *Nazi Organisation of Women*. London: Croom Helm, 1981.
Stephenson, Jill. "'Resistance' to 'No Surrender': Popular Disobedience in Württemberg in 1945." In *Germans against Nazism. Nonconformity, Opposition, and Resistance in the Third Reich*, edited by Francis R. Nicosia and Lawrence D. Stokes, 351–67. New York: Berg Publishers, 1990.
Stephenson, Jill. "The Volksgemeinschaft and the Problems of Permeability: The Persistence of Traditional Attitudes in Württemberg Villages." *German History* 34, no. 1 (2016): 49–69.
Stephenson, Jill. "Women and Protest in Wartime Nazi Germany." In *Protest in Hitler's National Community. Popular Unrest and the Nazi Response*, edited by Nathan Stoltzfus and Birgit Maier-Katkin, 18–37. New York: Berghahn Books, 2016.
Stern, Fritz. "The Political Consequences of the Unpolitical German." In *The Failure of Illiberalism. Essays on the Political Culture of Modern Germany*, edited by idem, 3–25. New York: Alfred A. Knopf, 1972.
Sternstein, Wolfgang. *Überall ist Wyhl. Bürgerinitiativen gegen Atomanlagen aus der Arbeit eines Aktionsforschers*. Frankfurt: Haag+Herchen Verlag, 1978.
Steuwer, Janosch. *Ein Drittes Reich, wie ich es auffasse. Politik, Gesellschaft und privates Leben in Tagebüchern 1933–1939*. Göttingen: Wallstein Verlag, 2017.
Stibbe, Matthew. *Women in the Third Reich*. London: Arnold, 2003.
Stiller, Gabrielle. "Pädagogismus versus Unterhaltung. Zur Entwicklung der Unterhaltungskultur in der DDR." In *Kultur*, edited by Wehling, 147–57.

Stitziel, Judd. "Shopping, Sewing, Networking, Complaining. Consumer Culture and the Relationship between State and Society in the GDR." In *Socialist Modern*, edited by Pence and Betts, 253–86.

Stoltenburg, Gerhard. *Politische Strömungen im Schleswig-Holstein Landvolk 1918–1933*. Düsseldorf: Droste Verlag, 1962.

Stoltzfus, Nathan. *Hitler's Compromises. Coercion and Consensus in Nazi Germany*. New Haven, CT: Yale University Press, 2016.

Stoltzfus, Nathan. *Resistance of the Heart. Intermarriage and the Rosenstrasse Protest in Nazi Germany*. New York: W. W. Norton & Co., 1996.

Stöss, Richard. "Bestimmungen des Rechtsextremismus." In *Wende*, edited by Klingemann et al., 102–31.

Stöss, Richard. "Parteien und soziale Bewegungen. Begriffliche Abgrenzung." In *Neue Bewegungen*, edited by Roth and Rucht, 277–302.

Stöss, Richard. "Rextsextremismus in einer geteilten politischen Kultur." In *Kultur*, edited by Niedermayer and v. Beyme. 105–39.

Stöver, Bernd. *Volksgemeinschaft im Dritten Reich. Die Konsensbereitschaft aus der Sicht sozialistischer Exilberichte*. Düsseldorf: Droste Verlag, 1993.

Strenge, Irene. *Kurt von Schleicher. Politik im Reichswehrministerium am Ende der Weimarer Republik*. Berlin: Duncker & Humblot, 2006.

Ströbele, Hans-Christian. "Vorwort." In *Demonstrationsfreiheit. Kampf um ein Bürgerrecht*, edited by Martin Kutscha, 6–9. Köln: presseverlagsanstalt, 1986.

Strote, Noah Benezra. *Lions and Lambs. Conflict in Weimar and the Creation of Post-Nazi Germany*. New Haven, CT: Yale University Press, 2017.

Stürmer, Michael. "Der unvollendete Parteienstaat. Zur Vorgeschichte des Präsidialregimes am Ende der Weimarer Republik." *Vierteljahrshefte für Zeitgeschichte* 21, no. 2 (April 1971): 119–26.

Süß, Walter. "Die Stimmungslage der Bevölkerung im Spiegel von MfS Berichten." In *SED-Herrschaft*, edited by Kuhrt et al., 237–77.

Süchting-Hänger, Andrea. "'Gleichgroße mut'ge Helferinnen' in der weiblichen Gegenwelt. Der Vaterländische Frauenverein und die Politisierung konservativer Frauen 1890–1914." In *Nation, Politik und Geschlecht. Frauenbewegungen und Nationalismus in der Moderne*, edited by Ute Planert, 131–47. Frankfurt: Campus Verlag, 2000.

Suckut, Siegfried et al. "Einleitung." In *Volksstimmen. "Ehrlich aber deutlich"— Privatbriefen an die DDR-Regierung*, edited by idem, 7–18. Munich: dtv Verlag, 2016.

Suvall, Stanley. *Electoral Politics in Wilhelmine Germany*. Chapel Hill: University of North Carolina Press, 1985.

Sweeney, Dennis. "Liberalism, the Worker and the Limits of Bourgeois *Öffentlichkeit* in Wilhelmine Germany." *German History* 22, no. 1 (2004): 36–75.

Sweeney, Dennis. *Work, Race, and the Emergence of Radical Right Corporatism in Imperial Germany*. Ann Arbor: University of Michigan Press, 2009.

Switek, Niko. "Ludwig Erhard: Formierte Gesellschaft." In *"Das Wort hat der Herr Bundeskanzler": Eine Analyse der grossen Regierungserklärungen von Adenauer bis Schröder*, edited by Karl-Rudolf Korte, 117–44.

"Tausende gegen Corona-Maßnahmen." *Tagesschau.de*, May 5, 2020. Available online: https://www.tagesschau.de/inland/corona-demos-109.html (accessed May 17, 2020).

Templin, Wolfgang and Reinhard Weißhuhn. "Die Initiative Frieden und Menschenrechte." In *Opposition*, edited by Kuhrt, 171–87.

Tenfelde, Klaus. "Civil Society and the Middle Classes in Nineteenth-Century Germany." In *Civil Society before Democracy. Lessons from Nineteenth-Century Europe*, edited by

Nancy Bermeo and Philip Nord, 83–108. Lanham: Rowman & Littlefield Publishers, 2000.

Tenfelde, Klaus. "Workers' Opposition in Nazi Germany: Recent West German Research." In *Rise*, edited by Maier, 107–14.

Tenscher, Jens and Philipp Scherer. *Jugend, Politik und Medien. Politische Orientierungen und Verhaltensweisen von Jugendlichen in Rheinland-Pfalz*. Münster: LIT Verlag, 2012.

Tent, James F. *Mission on the Rhine. Reeducation and Denazification in American-Occupied Germany*. Chicago: University of Chicago Press, 1982.

Thaa, Winfried. "Das Demokratiekonzept der DDR im Umbruch?" In *Die DDR im vierzigsten Jahr. Geschichte, Situation, Perspektiven*, edited by Ilse Spittmann-Rüle and Gisela Helwig, 149–60. Köln: Deutschland Archiv, 1989.

Thaa, Winfried. "'Stuttgart 21'—Krise oder Repolitisierung der repräsentativen Demokratie?" *Politische Vierteljahresschrift* 54, no. 1 (2013): 1–20.

Thacker, Toby. "The Fifth Column. Dance Music in the Early German Democratic Republic." In *Workers' State*, edited by Major and Osmond, 227–43.

Thaidigmann, S. Isabell. "Parteien und Verbände als Vertreter von Bürgerinteressen." In *Wirklich?* edited by Falter et al., 241–73.

Thamer, Hans-Ulrich. "Die Widersprüche der 'Volksgemeinschaft' in den späten Kriegsjahren." In *"Volksgemeinschaft,"* edited by Schmiechen-Ackermann, 289–300.

Thamer, Hans-Ulrich. *Verführung und Gewalt. Deutschland 1933–1945*. Berlin: Siedler Verlag, 1986.

Thaysen, Uwe. "Bürgerinitiativen—Grüne/Alternativen—Parlament und Parteien in der Bundesrepublik." In *Bürgerinitiativen*, edited by Guggenberger and Kempe, 124–55.

Thaysen, Uwe. *Der Runde Tisch. Oder: Wo blieb das Volk? Der Weg der DDR in der Demokratie*. Opladen: Westdeutscher Verlag, 1990.

Thaysen, Uwe. "Die ausgelieferte Opposition." In *Macht*, edited by Neubert and Eisenfeld, 37–47.

Theweleit, Klaus. *Male Fantasies*. Vol. I, II. Trsl. by Chris Turner. Minneapolis: University of Minnesota Press, 1987.

Thomas, Nick. *Protest Movements in 1960s West Germany. A Social History of Dissent and Democracy*. Oxford: Berg Publishers, 2003.

Thomas, Rüdiger. "Zur Auseinandersetzung mit dem deutschen Kommunismus in der Bundeszentrale für Heimatdienst." In *"Geistige Gefahr,"* edited by Creuzberger and Hoffmann, 123–43.

Thompson, Alastair P. *Left Liberals, the State and Popular Politics in Wilhelmine Germany*. Oxford: Oxford University Press, 2000.

Tilly, Charles. *Democracy*. Cambridge: Cambridge University Press, 2007.

Tippach-Schneider, Simone. "Blumen für die Hausgemeinschaft. Kollektivformen in der DDR—ein Überblick." In *Fortschritt*, edited by Ludwig, 243–55.

Tomkins, Andrew S. *Better Active than Radioactive! Anti-Nuclear Protest in 1970s France and West Germany*. Oxford: Oxford University Press, 2016.

Topf, Richard. "Beyond Electoral Participation." In *Citizens and the State*, edited by Klingemann and Fuchs, 52–91. Oxford: Oxford University Press, 1995.

Torpey, John. *Intellectuals, Socialism, and Dissent*. Minneapolis: University of Minnesota Press, 1995.

Turek, Jürgen. "Demokratie und Staatsbewußtsein: Entwicklung der Politischen Kultur in der Bundesrepublik Deutschland." In *Politische Kultur und deutsche Frage. Materialien zum Staats- und Nationalbewußtsein in der Bundesrepublik Deutschland*, edited by Werner Weidenfeld, 233–48. Köln: Verlag Wissenschaft und Politik, 1989.

Turk, Eleanor L. "German Liberals and the Genesis of the Association Law of 1908." In *In Search of a Liberal Germany. Studies in the History of German Liberalism from 1789 to the Present*, edited by Konrad H. Jarausch and Larry E. Jones, 237–60. New York: Berg Publishers, 1990.

Uekötter, Frank. *The Greenest Nation? A New History of German Environmentalism*. Cambridge: MIT Press, 2014.

Ullrich, Sebastian. *Der Weimar-Komplex. Das Scheitern der ersten deutschen Demokratie und die politische Kultur der frühen Bundesrepublik 1945–1959*. Göttingen: Wallenstein Verlag, 2009.

Vasudevan, Alex. *The Autonomous City. A History of Urban Squatting*. London: Verso, 2007.

Vasudevan, Alex. "Autonomous Urbanisms and the Right to the City: The Spatial Politics of Squatting n Berlin, 1968–2012." In *City Is Ours*, edited by van der Steen et al., 131–51.

Verheyen, Nina. "Eifrige Diskutanten. Die Stilisierung des 'freien' Meinungsaustausches zu einer demokratischen Kulturtechnik in der westdeutschen Gesellschaft der fünfziger Jahren." In *Demokratie*, edited by Fulda et al., 99–121.

Verheyen, Nina. *Diskussionslust: eine Kulturgeschichte des "besseren Arguments" in Westdeutschland*. Göttingen: Vandenhoeck & Ruprecht, 2010.

Virchow, Fabian. "Post-Fascist Right-Wing Social Movements." In *The History of Social Movements in Global Perspective. A Survey*, edited by Stefan Berger and Holger Nehring, 619–46. London: Palgrave/Macmillan, 2017.

Vogel, Meike. "'Außerparlamentarisch oder antiparlamentarisch?' Mediale Deutungen und Benennungskämpfe der APO." In *Neue Politikgeschichte. Perspektiven einer historischen Politikforschung*, edited by Ute Frevert and Heinz-Gerhard Haupt, 140–65. Frankfurt: Campus Verlag, 2005.

Vogel, Meike. *Unruhen im Fernsehen. Protestbewegung und öffentlich-rechtliche Berichterstattung in der 1960er Jahren*. Göttingen: Wallstein Verlag, 2010.

Vogt, Martin. "Das 'Versagen' der politischen Parteien in der Weimarer Republik." In *Die nationalsozialistsiche Machtergreifung*, edited by Wolfgang Michalka, 60–73. Paderborn: Schöningh, 1984.

Vogt, Stefan. *Nationaler Sozialismus und Soziale Demokratie. Die sozialdemokratische Junge Rechte 1918–1945*. Bonn: Dietz Verlag, 2006.

Volkl, Kerstin. "Fest verankert oder ohne Halt? Die Unterstützung der Demokratie im vereinigten Deutschland." In *Wächst*, edited by Gabriel et al., 249–84.

Volkov, Shulamit. "On the Primacy of Political Violence—The Case of the Weimar Republic." In *Gewalt*, edited by José Brunner et al., 55–68.

Volkov, Shulamit. *The Rise of Popular Antimodernism in Germany. The Urban Master Artisans, 1873–1896*. Princeton, NJ: Princeton University Press, 1978.

Vollmer, Johann. "Vom 'Denkmal des mündigen Bürgers' zur Besetzungsromantik. Die Grenzen symbolischer Politik in der frühen anti-AKW Bewegung." In *Bürgersinn*, edited by Knoch, 271–93.

Vollnhals, Clemens "Einleitung." In *Entnazifizierung. Politische Säuberung und Rehabilitierung in den vier Besatzungszonen 1945–1949*, edited by idem, 7–64. München: dtv dokumente, 1991.

Voss, Peter. "Citizens against the State: Political Protest in the GDR." In *Origins*, edited by Opp and Voss, 9–26.

Voss, Peter. "The Goals of the Revolution." In *Origins*, edited by Opp et al., 49–70.

Voss, Peter. "The Role of the Church." In *Origins*, edited by Opp et al., 119–36.

Voss, Peter. "Why Were the Protests Peaceful?" In *Origins*, edited by Opp et al., 91–97.
Voss, Peter and Klaus-Dieter Opp. "'We Are the People!' A Revolution without Revolutionaries?" In *Origins*, edited by Opp et al., 155–66.
Wahl, Rainer. "Lüth und die Folgen." In *Lüth Urteil*, edited by Thomas Henne and Arne Riedlinger, 371–97. Berlin: Berliner Wissenschafts-Verlag, 2005.
Waite, Robert. *Vanguard of Nazism. The Free Corps Movement in Postwar Germany 1918–1923*. New York: W. W. Norton & Co., 1952.
Walkenhorst, Peter. *Nation—Volk—Rasse. Radikaler Nationalismus im Deutschen Kaiserreich 1890–1914*. Göttingen: Vandenhoeck & Ruprecht, 2007.
Walter-Rogg, Melanie. "Politsches Vertrauen ist gut—Misstrauen ist besser? Ausmaß und Ausstrahlungseffekte des Politiker- und Institutionsvertrauens im vereinigten Deutschland." In *Wächst*, edited by Gabriel, 129–86.
Warneke, Tim. "Aktionsformen und Politikverständnis der Friedensbewegung. Radikaler Humanismus und die Pathosformel des Menschlichen." In *Alternative*, edited by Reichert, 445–72.
Warneken, Bernd Jürgen et al. *Als die Deutschen demonstrieren lernten. Das Kulturmuster "friedliche Straßendemonstration" im preußischen Wahlrechtskampf 1908–1910*. Tübingen: Tübingen Vereinigung für Volkskunde, 1986.
Warner, Michael. *Publics and Counterpublics*. New York: Zone Books, 2002.
Wassermann, Rudolf. "Ist der Rechtsstaat noch zu retten? Zur Krise des Rechtsbewußtseins in unserer Zeit." In *Widerstand—Protest—Ziviler Ungehorsam*, edited by Manfred Schleker, 33–64. Sankt Augustin: COMDOK Verlagsabteilung, 1988.
Weßels, Bernhard. "Vermittlungsinstitutionen und Interessenvertretung: Zur Performanz von Mitgliederorganisationen in Deutschland." In *Politische Partizipation*, edited by Koch et al., 221–46.
Wehler, Hans-Ulrich. *The German Empire 1871–1918*. Trsl. by Kim Traynor. Leamington Spa: Berg Publishers, 1985.
Wehler, Hans Ulrich. *Deutsche Gesellschaftsgeschichte*, 4. durchgesehene Aufl. der broschierten Studienausgabe. Vol. 1–5. München: C.H. Beck, 2008.
Wehling, Hans Georg (ed.). *Politische Kultur in der DDR*. Stuttgart: Verlag W. Kohlhammer, 1989.
Weichlein, Siegfried. "Wahlkämpfe, Milieukultur und politische Mobilisierung im Deutschen Kaiserreich." In *Modernisierung*, edited by Lässig et al., 69–87.
Weil, Frederick D. "The Development of Democratic Attitudes in Eastern and Western Germany in a Comparative Perspective." In *Research on Democracy and Society*. Vol. I. *Democratization in Eastern and Western Europe*, edited by idem et al., 195–225. Greenwich, CT: JAI Press, 1993.
Weisbrod, Bernd. "The Crisis of Bourgeois Society in Interwar Germany." In *Fascist Italy and Nazi Germany. Comparisons and Contrasts*, edited by Richard Bessel, 23–39. Cambridge: Cambridge University Press, 1996.
Weisbrod, Bernd. "Die Politik der Repräsentation. Das Erbe des ersten Weltkrieges und der Formwandel der Politik in Europa." In *Der Erste Weltkrieg und die europäische Neuordnung*, edited by Hans Mommsen, 13–41. Köln: Böhlau Verlag, 2000.
Weisbrod, Bernd, "Gewalt in der Politik. Zur politischen Kultur in Deutschland zwischen den beiden Weltkriegen." *Geschichte in Wissenschaft und Unterricht* 43 (1992): 391–404.
Weisbrod, Bernd. "Öffentlichkeit als politischer Prozeß." In *Die Politik der Öffentlichkeit— Die Öffentlichkeit der Politik. Politische Medialisierung in der Bundesrepublik*, edited by idem, 11–25. Göttingen: Wallstein Verlag, 2003.

Weitz, Erich D. "The Ever-Present Other. Communism in the Making of West Germany." In *Miracle*, edited by Schissler, 219–32.

Welch, David. "Nazi Propaganda and the *Volksgemeinschaft*: Constructing a People's Community." *Journal of Contemporary History* 39, no. 2 (April 2004): 212–38.

Welch, David. *The Third Reich. Politics and Propaganda*. London: Routledge, 1993.

Welzel, Christian. "Modernisierung und Partizipation: Kontroversen und Befunde zur Partizipationthese." In *Bürger*, edited by Fuchs et al., 284–302.

Wengst, Udo. *Staatsaufbau und Regierungspraxis 1948–1953. Zur Geschichte der Verfasssungsorgane in der Bundesrepublik Deutschland*. Düsseldorf: Droste Verlag, 1984.

Westle, Bettina. *Kollektive Identität im vereinten Deutschland. Nation und Demokratie in der Wahrnehmung der Deutschen*. Opladen: Leske + Budrich, 1999.

Westle, Bettina. "Politische Legitimität und politische Partizipation in der Bundesrepublik Deutschland der achtziger Jahren." In *Political Participation and Democracy in Poland and West Germany*, edited by Gerd Meyer and Franciszek Ryxzka, 137–73. Warsaw: Ośrodek Badań Społecznych, 1991.

Westle, Bettina. "Politische Partizipation: Mobilisierung als Faktor geschlechtsspezifischer Ungleichheit." In *Demokratie und Partizipation*, edited by Niedermayer and Westle, 136–59.

Westle, Bettina. "Traditionalismus, Verfassungspatriotismus und Postnationalismus in vereinten Deutschland." In *Kultur*, edited by Niedermayer and v. Beyme, 43–76.

Westle, Bettina. "Zur Akzeptanz der politischen Parteien und der Demokratie in der Bundesrepublik Deutschland." In *Wahlen*, edited by Kaase and Klingemann, 253–95.

White, Dan S. *The Splintered Party. National Liberalism in Hessen and the Reich, 1867–1918*. Cambridge: Harvard University Press, 1976.

White, Hayden. "Interpretation in History." In *Tropics of Discourse*, edited by idem, 51–80. Baltimore, MD: Johns Hopkins University Press, 1986.

Whitman, James Q. *Hitler's American Model. The United States and the Making of Nazi Race Law*. Princeton, NJ: Princeton University Press, 2017.

Wickert, Christel. "Popular Attitudes to National Socialist Antisemitism: Denunciations for 'Insidious Offenses' and 'Racial Ignominy.'" In *Probing*, edited by Bankier, 282–95.

Widfeldt, Anders. "Party Membership and Party Representativeness." In *Citizens and the State*, edited by Hans-Dieter Klingemann and Dieter Fuchs, 134–82. Oxford: Oxford University Press, 1995.

Wienfort, Monika. *Monarchie in der bürgerlichen Gesellschaft Deutschlands und Englands von 1640 bis 1848*. Göttingen: Vandenhoeck & Ruprecht, 1993.

Wierling, Dorothee. "Der Staat, die Jugend und der Westen. Texte zu Konflikten der 1960er Jahre." In *Akten. Eingaben. Schaufenster. Erkundungen zu Herrschaft und Alltag*, edited by Alf Lüdtke and Peter Becker, 222–40. Berlin: Akademie Verlag, 1997.

Wierling, Dorothee. "Die Jugend als innere Feind. Konflikte in der Erziehungsdiktatur der sechziger Jahre." In *Sozialgeschichte* edited by Kaelble et al., 404–25.

Wierling, Dorothee. "How Do the 1929ers and the 1949ers Differ?" In *Power*, edited by Fulbrook, 204–19.

Wierling, Dorothee. "Youth as an Internal Enemy. Conflicts in the Education Dictatorship of the 1960s." In *Socialist Modern*, edited by Pence and Betts, 157–82.

Wiesendahl, Elmar. "Neue soziale Bewegungen und moderne Demokratie." In *Neue Bewegungen*, edited by Roth and Rucht, 364–84.

Wildt, Michael. "Die Ungleichheit des Volkes." In *Volksgemeinschaft. Neue Forschung zur Gesellschaft des Nationalsozialismus*, edited by Frank Bajohr and idem, 24–40. Frankfurt/M: Fischer Taschenbuchverlag, 2009.

Wildt, Michael. *Hitler's Volksgemeinschaft and the Dynamics of Racial Exclusion. Violence against Jews in Provincial* Germany, *1919–1939*. Trsl. by Bernard Heise. New York: Berghahn Books, 2012.
Wildt, Michael. "*Volksgemeinschaft*. A Modern Perspective on National Socialist Society." In *Visions*, edited by Steber and Gotto, 43–59.
Wildt, Michael. "Volksgemeinschaft und Führererwartung in der Weimarer Republik." In *Politische Kultur und Medienwirklickeit in der 1920er Jahren*, edited by Ute Daniel et al., 181–204. München: R. Oldenbourg Verlag, 2010.
Wildt, Michael. "'Wohlstand für alle': Das Spannungsfeld von Konsum und Politik in der Bundesrepublik." In *Die Konsumgesellschaft in Deutschland 1890–1990*, edited by Heinz-Gerhard Haupt and Claudius Torp, 305–16. Frankfurt: Campus Verlag, 2009.
Winkler, Heinrich-August. *Mittelstand, Demokratie und Nationalsozialismus. Die politische Entwicklung von Handwerk und Kleinhandel in der Weimarer Republik*. Köln: Kiepenheuer & Witsch, 1972.
Winkler, Heinrich August. "Unternehmer und Wirtschaftsdemokratie in der Weimarer Republik." In *Probleme der Demokratie heute: Tagung der Deutschen Vereinigung für Politische Wissenschaft in Berlin, Herbst 1969*, 308–22. Opladen: Westdeutscher Verl, 1971.
Winkler, Heinrich August. *Von der Revolution zur Stabilisierung. Arbeiter und Arbeiterbewegung in der Weimarer* Republik *1918–1924*. Berlin: J.H.W. Dietz Nachf., 1984.
Wirsching, Andreas. "Konstruktion und Erosion: Weimar Argumente gegen Volksbegehren und Volksentscheid." In *Schatten*, edited by Gusy, 335–53.
Witt, Peter-Christian. "Kontinuität und Diskontinuität im politischen System der Weimarer Republik." In *Regierung, Bürokratie und Parlament in Preußen und Deutschland von 1848 bis zur Gegenwart*, edited by Gerhard A. Ritter, 117–48. Düsseldorf: Droste Verlag, 1983.
"Wo die AfD erfolgreich ist." *Süddeutsche Zeitung*, September 3, 2019. Available online: https://www.sueddeutsche.de/politik/afd-wahl-auswertung-bundeslaender-1.4585616 (accessed May 15, 2020).
Woderich, Rudolf. "Mentalitäten zwischen Anpassung und Eigensinn." *Deutschland Archiv* 25, no. 1 (1992): 21–32.
Wolle, Stefan. "Es geht seinen sozialistischen Gang." In *Macht*, edited by Neubert and Eisenfeld, 307–15.
Wolle, Stefan. *Die heile Welt der Diktatur: Alltag und Herrschaft in der DDR 1971–1989*. Berlin: C.H. Links Verlag, 1998.
Woods, Roger. *The Conservative Revolution in the Weimar Republic*. New York: St. Martin's Press, 1999.
Woods, Roger. *Opposition in the GDR under Honecker 1971–1985. An Introduction and Documentation*. New York: St. Martin's Press, 1986.
Wuhs, Steven and Eric McLaughlin. "Explaining Germany's Electoral Geography." *German Politics and Society* 37, no. 1 (Spring 2019): 1–23.
Wüstemeyer, Manfred. "Re-education—die Verlierer lernen Demokratie." In *Sieger und Besiegte. Materielle und ideelle Neuorientierungen nach 1945*, edited by Holger Afflerbach and Christoph Cornelißen, 219–47. Tübingen: Francke Verlag, 1997.
Wüstenberg, Jenny. *Civil Society and Memory in Postwar Germany*. Cambridge: Cambridge University Press, 2017.
Zatlin, Jonathan. "Ausgaben und Eingaben. Das Petitionsrecht und der Untergang der DDR." *Zeitschrift für Zeitgeschichte* 10 (1997): 902–17.
Zatlin, Jonathan R. *The Currency of Socialism. Money and Political Culture in East Germany*. Cambridge: Cambridge University Press, 2009.

Zilleßen, Horst. "Bürgerinitiativen und repräsentative Demokratie." In *Bürgerinitiativen*, edited by Guggenberger and Kempf, 103–23.

Zimmermann, Friedrich. *Kabinetstücke: Politik mit Strauß und Kohl 1976–1991*. München: Herbig, 1991.

Zimmermann, Michael. "Ein schwer zur bearbeitende Pflaster: der Bergarbeiterort Hochlaumark unter dem Nationalsozialismus." In *Reihen*, edited by Peukert and Reulecke, 65–84.

Zoll, Ralf. *Vom Obrigkeitsstaat zur entgrenzten Politik. Politische Einstellungen und politisches Verhalten in der Bundesrepublik seit den 60er Jahren*. Opladen: Westdeutscher Verlag, 1999.

Zoll, Rolf. "Einleitung." In *Obrigkeitsstaat*, edited by idem, 9–13.

Zoll, Rolf. "Partizipatorische Demokratievorstellung. Eine Alternative zum obrigkeitsstaatlichen Demokratieverständnis." In *Obrigkeitsstaat*, edited by idem, 19–29.

Zollitsch, Wolfgang. "Die Vertrauensratswahlen von 1934 und 1935. Zum Stellenwert von Abstimmungen im 'Dritten Reich' am Beispiel Krupp." *Geschichte und Gesellschaft* 15, no. 3 (1989): 361–81.

Zollitsch, Wolfgang. "Modernisierung im Betrieb. Arbeiter zwischen Weltwirtschaftskrise und Nationalsozialismus." In *Anpassung*, edited by Schmiechen-Ackermann, 94–107.

Zwahr, Hartmut. *Ende einer Selbstzerstörung. Leipzig und die Revolution in der DDR*. Beucha: Sax Verlag, 2014.

Index

17 June 1953 uprising 135, 137, 142–5

acclamation 57, 60, 68, 136, 154
Adenauer, Konrad 4, 79, 82, 88–90, 92, 94, 96, 98–9, 104, 114, 116
AfD 166–7
Agnoli, Johannes 123
Ahlers, Conrad 92
Allerbeck, Klaus 117
Allies: promotion of democracy in Germany 79–81, 85, 87, 90, 93–4, 104
Alternatives (*Alternativen*) 111, 119–21, 138–40, 162
Altmann, Rüdiger 90
Anderson, Margaret 31
anti-Communism 91–2, 99, 110, 118
anti-fascism in GDR 135, 139, 141
anti-Marxism/Bolshevism 35–6, 41–2, 44, 51, 55, 57, 60, 62, 65, 67, 70, 73, 77
anti-parliamentarism 7–9, 171
  Kaiserreich 14–15, 22–3
  Weimar Republic 43, 79–80, 82, 165–6, 168
anti-political-party attitudes 1, 15, 43, 79, 86–9, 164, 166, 168
antisemitism
  FRG 99
  Kaiserreich 17, 20, 23, 31
  Third Reich 65, 73, 76
  Weimar Republic 41
anti-socialist laws 13
anti-terrorism laws 108–9, 113–14
anti-totalitarianism 91, 110
apoliticism 14–15, 30, 115
army
  FRG 85, 90–1, 150
  Kaiserreich 10, 12, 16, 29–30
  Third Reich 75
  Weimar Republic 36, 43–4, 49, 55–6
Article 23, Basic Law 156–7

Article 48, Weimar Constitution. *See* exceptional executive powers
assemblies, indoor 19, 27, 48, 98, 169
assembly/association law 19–20, 25, 38–9, 48, 121, 134, 141
associational organization and life
  FRG 86, 116, 129, 164
  GDR 144–5
  Kaiserreich 19–24, 31
  Third Reich 64, 69
  Weimar Republic 45, 47
authority/authoritarian values 1–3, 6, 169
  FRG 79–80, 85–6, 89–90, 92–3, 95, 100, 102, 106, 109–10, 114, 119–22, 125, 128
  GDR 131, 135–6, 155, 158–60, 164–6
  Kaiserreich 9–10, 12, 14, 18–19, 21, 23, 30–31
  Third Reich 65–6, 75
  Weimar Republic 33–4, 37–8, 45, 49, 53, 55–6
Autonomous and Spontis 106–7, 111, 125, 127, 167–70
autoritäre democracy 34, 45–6, 56

Basic Law (GG). *See* Constitutions, Federal Republic of Germany
Beck, Hermann 63
Berlin Wall 110, 135, 139, 143–6, 153
Berman, Sheri 47
Bernstein, Eduard 35
Berufsverbot 107–10
Bethmann Hollweg, Theobald 11, 28
Betts, Paul 143
Bevormundung. *See* infantilization, political
Biermann, Wolf 146
Bildung 15–16, 20–1
Bio-German 165
Bismarck, Otto von 10–14, 19, 23, 45
Blackbourn, David 21

bloc parties (GDR) 132–3
Borup, Allan 88
Bösch, Frank 116
Boyer, John 66
Bracher, Karl 89
Brandt, Willi 103–4, 106
bread riots 29
Brokdorf decision 107, 129
Brüning, Heinrich 53–5
Bülow, Bernhard von 11
Bundesgerichtshof (highest appeals court) 82, 106
Bundesrat
    FRG 81–2, 86, 126, 157
    Kaiserreich 11, 13
Bundestag (FRG) 82–8, 92, 97–8, 101, 103, 115, 125–6, 129, 156–7, 162, 167
Bundesverfassungsgericht, *see* Constitutional Court
Busemann, Adolf 100

Caron, Jean-Christophe 68
Center Party 12, 14–15, 18–19, 29, 34, 45–6, 50, 53–5
chaotics 111
checks and balances 4, 6, 9, 11, 37–9, 58–9, 82, 133, 142
Chickering, Roger 31
Christian Democratic Union (CDU) (GDR) 133
Christian Democratic Union/Christian Social Union (CDU/CSU) (FRG) 81–2, 86–8, 91–2, 96, 101, 103, 108–9, 114–16, 122, 155–6, 166–7
churches 73, 41, 83–4, 91
    Catholic 4, 11–14, 23–4, 54, 64, 73, 81, 91, 98, 102, 146–7
    Kulturkampf 12–13, 19, 21, 23
    Protestant 13–15, 24, 46, 64, 71, 73, 91, 98–9, 102, 126, 135, 146–7, 149
Citizens Initiatives 4, 103, 106, 112–13, 115, 118–20, 128, 162
citizenship as legal status
    European 157–8
    Federal Republic of Germany 4, 85, 105, 155, 157, 165
    general 4, 6–7

    German Democratic Republic 133
    Kaiserreich 13–15
    naturalization 13, 40, 85, 157
    Third Reich 61
    Weimar Republic 37, 40–1, 47
civil disobedience 86, 103, 106–7, 110, 121, 124–6, 163, 170
civil society 23–4, 47, 64, 140
Claß, Heinrich 22
Clinefelter, Joan L. 68
coercion (*Nötigung*) 106, 124, 152
collectivization of agriculture, GDR 145
Communists
    FRG 84–5, 97, 106–7, 110, 118, 125, 127
    GDR, *see* Socialist Unity Party (SED)
    Third Reich 58, 63, 65, 75
    Weimar Republic 23, 35–6, 40–1, 49, 51–3
compromise 3–4, 6
    FRG 79, 88, 112, 128, 142, 165
    Kaiserreich 24, 30–1
    Weimar Republic 35, 38, 43–4, 46, 55
compulsion (*Zwang*) as purpose of protest 95, 124, 170
confidence, vote of, in chancellor
    Federal Republic of Germany 82–3
    Kaiserreich 11
    Weimar Republic 38, 53
Connelly, John 62, 71
Conradt, David 101
conscience 16, 66, 75, 84, 125
Constitutional Court (FRG) 4, 82, 84–6, 88, 90, 92, 94, 99–100, 106–7, 129, 158, 169–70
constitutions 4, 7
    Federal Republic of Germany (Basic Law) 81–90, 96, 100–1, 106, 113, 115, 121–3, 126, 128–9, 156–8, 161, 166, 169
    German Democratic Republic 132–4, 142–3
    Kaiserreich 9–13, 19, 27
    Third Reich 58–60
    Weimar Republic 36–40, 43, 48, 53–4, 56
constructive no-confidence. *See* confidence, vote of, in chancellor, FRG

counterpublic 105, 120–1, 139–40
criticism, in dictatorships 65, 70, 72, 133–6, 139–41, 143, 147, 154

Dahrendorf, Ralf 88, 102, 165
Daily Telegraph Affair 12, 22
Davis, Belinda 29, 76
defining culture (*Leitkultur*) 155, 157
delivering positive outcomes 3
    FRG 79, 101, 104, 159, 167–8
    GDR 135, 154
    Kaiserreich 21
    Third Reich 62, 64, 67
    Weimar Republic 33, 43–4, 51–3, 55
democracy, forms/conceptions of 1, 4–6
    autoritäre 34, 45–6, 55–6, 169
    Chancellor 4, 89
    councils/direct 34–6, 83, 115, 136, 141, 156, 161, 166, 169
    economic 42
    leader 2, 4, 17, 33–4, 45–6, 54, 57, 59–60, 79, 86–7, 89–90, 101, 103, 156, 169
    parliamentary 4, 33, 35–9, 53–6, 79–81, 83, 101–2, 113–15, 156, 165, 169
    participatory 4, 102–3, 115–16, 128–9, 155, 162
    party 4
    will of the people 6, 22, 42–3, 45, 57–8, 60, 131, 163–4, 169
democracy that can defend itself 40, 84–5, 107–9, 158
democratization as process 1–4, 6
    FRG 79–81, 90–5, 103–4, 112–13, 116–17, 119–22, 128–9, 155–6, 158–61, 165–8, 170–1
    Kaiserreich 9, 14, 31
    Weimar Republic 33–4, 41, 44–5, 53, 56
demonstrations 169–70
    Berlin Republic 155, 167
    Bonn Republic 96–9, 102, 106–7, 123–4, 127–8
    German Democratic Republic 134, 150–2
    Kaiserreich 23, 25–6

Third Reich 73–4
    Weimar Republic 48–51
demos (the people) 4–5, 14, 61, 76, 155, 157–8, 164–5
denunciation 69–70, 134, 141
dialogue and discussion 19, 48, 87, 93–5, 111–12, 114, 116, 123–5, 128, 131–2, 137, 140, 146–7, 161
dictatorship, adaptation to 69–72, 131–2, 134, 137–41
Diewald-Kerkmann, Gisela 70
Dirke, Sabine von 100
Dutschke, Rudi 107, 123

Easter Marches 99
Ebert, Friedrich 34–6, 39–40
education and political activism 2, 4. See also *Bildung*)
    FRG 80, 88, 93, 101, 103–4, 116–17, 160–2, 164
    GDR 140
    Kaiserreich 14–15, 21, 24
election fraud, 1989 (GDR) 149, 152
Eley, Geoff 31
elites (political and economic) and democracy 2, 168
    FRG 86, 89–90, 96–7, 99, 102, 113–15, 122, 128, 152, 156, 165
    Kaiserreich 9–10, 12, 18–19, 25–8, 30
    Weimar Republic 35–6, 42, 46, 53–6
emigration. *See* flight from GDR
emotion 24, 47, 49, 95, 111, 121, 123, 155, 170
enabling acts. *See* exceptional executive powers
engagement, popular 2, 4, 6–7, 168–9
    FRG 95, 102, 114, 154
    GDR 131, 137, 140
    Kaiserreich 9–10, 17, 21, 23, 28
    Third Reich 64, 67, 69
    Weimar Republic 55–7
Environmental Library 147
environmental movements 134, 146–7
equality 5–6, 8
    FRG 83–4, 95, 110, 115, 117, 165
    GDR 133–5, 143, 148, 153
    Kaiserreich 10–12, 14–18, 20–21, 26–30

Weimar Republic 35–8, 42, 47
  Third Reich 61–2
Erhard, Ludwig 90
Erzberger, Matthais 50
eugenics 65–6, 71, 73
Euler, August-Martin 97
European Union 157–8
exceptional executive powers
  Article 48, Weimar Constitution 38–40, 54, 58
  enabling acts, Weimar Republic 39, 58–9
  state of emergency legislation, FRG 85–6, 90, 96–7, 105, 119, 126
exclusion and inclusion 4, 14, 20, 41, 61, 68, 105, 155, 158, 164–6, 171
exiters (GDR) 150–1

federalism 81–82
Fenske, Michaela 96
Finkel, Steven E. 162
First World War 12, 28–30, 45, 49, 52, 55, 57, 62, 64, 68, 76, 170
flight from GDR 134, 145–6, 149–51
Föllmer, Moritz 63
food riots 52, 76
formation of the political will. *See* will, forming political
formierte Gesellschaft (structured society) 90
Frank, Hans 60
Free Democratic Party (FDP) 81, 97, 101, 104, 106, 108–9, 114, 166
free-democratic basic order 84, 100, 129
Frei, Norbert 62, 64, 91
Freikorps 36, 49–50
Friedrich Wilhelm III 2
Fritzsche, Peter 42, 51
Führerauslese (evaluation/selection of leaders). *See* democracy, leader
funerals 18–19, 25–26, 169–70

Galen, Clemens von (Archbishop) 73
Gellately, Robert 66
German Democratic Party (DDP) 41, 45
German National People's Party (DNVP) 41, 46–7, 53
Gesamtinteresse. *See* interest, common or national

Gestapo 33, 67, 69, 72–3, 75, 92
Geyer, Michael 66
GG. *See* constitutions, Federal Republic
Gleichschaltung 64
Goebbels, Josef 60, 66, 73–4, 99
Gorbachev, Mikhail 148, 150
Greens 101, 112, 114–15, 117, 147, 156, 161, 166
Groener, Wilhelm 36
Gruner, Wolf 72
Gundelach, Peter 129

Habermas, Jürgen 24, 102, 111, 129
Haffner, Sebastian 128
Halbstarken 100, 139
Hamilton, Richard 54
happenings 121–3
Hardenberg, Karl-August von 2, 76
Harlan, Veit 99–100
hatred of foreigners (*Ausländerfeindlichkeit*) 155, 160, 165–6, 169
Helsinki Accords 147
here-stayers 151
hierarchy 14–15, 17–21, 30–1, 34, 42, 61–2, 90, 97, 153
Hindenburg, Paul von 39–40, 45–6, 51, 53–6, 58–9
Hitler, Adolf 1–2, 4, 6
  FRG 80, 83, 89, 95, 101, 109, 126
  GDR 133, 135, 137
  Weimar Republic 33, 50, 54–6
  Third Reich 57–61, 64–8, 71–6
Hochhuth, Rolf 98
Hodenberg, Christina von 104–5
Holocaust 60, 65–6, 73–4, 95, 98, 104–5
Honecker, Erich 134–5, 139, 142, 146, 150, 152
Huber, Ernst Rudolf 59
Hugenberg, Alfred 53, 56

ideals 14, 17, 30, 47, 56, 168
immigration 13, 127, 155, 157, 165–6
IMs. *See* unofficial collaborators (GDR)
inclusion. *See* exclusion and inclusion
infantilization, political (*Bevormundung*) 2, 131, 137–8
Initiative for Peace and Human Rights 142, 147

interests
  common or national (*Gesamtinteresse*) 3–4, 6–7, 14, 22, 24, 30, 42–3, 53, 59–60, 63, 66, 77, 86–7, 90, 118, 128, 132–4, 136, 142, 154, 163, 165–6, 168–9, 171
  egotistical, materialistic 3, 7, 14–15, 17–19, 21, 38, 42–4, 46, 55, 62, 66, 87, 136, 164, 168
  individual and group 3–5, 14–15, 17–18, 20–2, 26, 31, 33, 37, 42–3, 47, 73, 79, 87–90, 96, 98, 101–2, 112–13, 115, 118, 122–4, 137, 140, 164, 168, 170
  as moral claims 42, 51, 55, 62
irrationalism 33, 161, 170

Jarausch, Konrad 154
Jones, Larry 53
judicial review 39–40, 82, 84, 133
judiciary 168
  FRG 82–4, 86, 91, 106–7, 109, 124, 129, 164
  GDR 133
  Kaiserreich 11, 13, 36, 39–40
  Third Reich 59

Kaas, Ludwig 53
Kaase, Max 122
Kapp Putsch 41, 49–50
Kapp, Wolfgang 49
Kautsky, Karl 9
Kershaw, Ian 63, 66
Kießling, Friedrich 81
King, Dr. Martin Luther, Jr. 125
Klein, Ilona 87, 89
Kogon, Eugen 90
Kohl, Helmut 116, 153
Koonz, Claudia 66
Kowalczuk, Ilko-Sascha 138
KPD. *See* Communists
Krenz, Egon 152
Kulturkampf (persecution of Catholics). *See* churches, *Kulturkampf*

Laepple decision 106
LeBon, Gustav 27
Legien, Carl 36
Leipzig Trade Fair 149

Leitkultur. See defining culture
Lenin, Vladimir 9, 30, 132
Lepsius, M. Rainer 24
lèse-majesté legislation 12
Liebknecht, Karl 35, 149
Liebknecht, Wilhelm 25
Ludendorff, Erich 50
Lüth decision 99–100, 106–7, 129
Lüth, Erich 99–100
Luther, Hans 40
Lüttwitz, Walther von 49
Luxemburg, Rosa 27, 149

Maase, Kaspar 88, 91
Mann, Heinrich 30
Marxism 25, 41, 105
masculinity 47–8
mass strike 9, 27–8, 124
masses/massification 4
  FRG 83, 90–1, 95, 97, 99, 102, 113, 121–3, 132, 168
  Kaiserreich 11, 16–17, 22, 26–7, 31
  Weimar Republic 33, 35, 38, 42, 45, 48, 52
  Third Reich 57
mastering the past 90, 104–5
Max of Baden 29, 34
McFalls, Laurence 141, 153
media 99, 105, 111, 116, 120–1, 138, 147, 150, 153, 159
  broadcast 94, 111, 139–40, 149, 151–3, 155, 166
  press 13, 18, 43, 58, 91–2, 94, 100, 120, 127, 141, 166
Merritt, Richard L. 80
Meuschel, Sigrid 137
milieus and camps 18–19, 24, 46, 75
militant democracy. *See* democracy that can defend itself
ministerial government 10, 54
minority rights 5–6, 12, 27, 34, 76, 112–13, 124–5, 164
Mitchell, Maria 91
Mommsen-Reindl, Margarete 137
monarchical sovereignty 7, 10, 12, 17, 22, 43

National Front (GDR) 133, 149
National Liberal Party 12, 14

naturalization. *See* citizenship, naturalization
Naumann, Friedrich 18
Nazis
    aftermath 79–86, 88, 90–1, 94–6, 98–9, 101, 104–5, 110–11, 113, 123, 126–7, 134–5, 137, 155, 160, 166, 169–70
    in power 57–77
    in Weimar Republic 33, 38, 40–1, 43, 45–56
Neubert, Ehrhart 140
New Forum 143
new social movements (NSMs) 112–13, 127
niches 69, 138, 140, 159
Niclauß, Karlheinz 80, 87
Nipperdey, Thomas 30–1
non-compliance, in dictatorships 70–1
nonviolence 126–7, 150–2
Nuremberg Laws 61, 76

objectivity. *See* reason and objectivity in politics
Ohr, Dieter 56
Operation Valkyrie 75
Opp, Karl-Dieter 162
order 3
    FRG 77, 89, 95–7, 100, 102, 104, 109–10, 121–2, 125, 163, 165–6
    GDR 134, 136
    Kaiserreich 19, 21, 26, 30–1
    Third Reich 57, 65–6
    Weimar Republic 33–40, 49–50, 52
outcomes. *See* delivering positive outcomes

Pan-German League 19, 21–2, 31
Papen, Franz von 54–6
paramilitaries 36, 47–8, 50–2, 170
parliamentary absolutism 9, 11, 37–9, 80, 82, 133, 169
Parliamentary Council 81–3, 85, 87–8, 98
parliamentary government 3–4, 169, 171
    FRG 77, 79–82, 87–8, 99, 101–3, 113–15, 118, 129, 166
    GDR 141
    Kaiserreich 9–12, 14–15, 22, 25, 28–30

    Third Reich 60, 62
    Weimar Republic 33–41, 43–5, 49, 51–56
Passport-Germans 165
PEGIDA 165–7, 170
people's or racial community. *See Volksgemeinschaft*
persecution. *See* repression
personalities (men of character) 15, 45–6, 87
petitioning 7, 170
    FRG 71, 73, 84, 96, 98, 107, 118, 122–3, 125, 157–8, 162–4
    GDR 139–44, 147–8, 154
    Kaiserreich 21
    Third Reich 48
    Weimar Republic 39
Peukert, Detlef 63
Pius XII 98
plebiscitary elements 1, 16
    FRG 76, 83, 90, 99, 113, 156, 161, 166
    GDR 137, 152, 154
    Third Reich 67–8
    Weimar Republic 39, 59–60
pluralism 3, 6, 43–4, 79, 86, 88, 90, 93, 112–13, 142, 154, 165, 168–71
Poiger, Uta 100
political vs. private 119–20
Pollock, Detlef 136–7
polycracy 60
post-material values 104, 118–19, 138, 160, 162, 166
Prague Spring, Czechoslovakia 145
presidential decrees. *See* Art. 48
pressure as purpose of protest 48, 86, 95, 103, 105, 118, 121, 123–5, 144, 147, 170
pressure from the streets as unacceptable 4, 96–7, 102, 123, 127, 152
Preuß, Hugo 38
proportional representation 37–8, 46, 83, 87, 133, 158
protests 2, 169–70
    FRG 96–100, 115–16, 120–9, 163–4, 167
    GDR 136, 138–40, 144–52, 154–5
    Kaiserreich 21–6, 29–31
    Third Reich 72–5
    Weimar Republic 51–2

provocation 52, 123
public sphere 21, 24–5, 79, 117, 120, 131, 138–9, 143

radicals decree. *See Berufsverbot*
Rathenau, Walter 50
Rauh, Manfred 11
reason and objectivity in politics 33, 48–9, 95, 97, 110–12, 123
Rechtsstaat (rule of law) 3, 6–7
    FRG 82, 84, 92, 97, 101, 106–10, 113, 120, 125, 142, 156
    GDR 133
    Kaiserreich 11–13
    Third Reich 58–9, 70
    Weimar Republic 39, 45
Reichsbanner 50–2
Reichsrat 38–9, 41, 59
Reichstag. *See* parliamentary government
repression 11–13, 58–9, 63–4, 73, 75, 132–4, 137–9, 143, 145, 150
resignation from groups (GDR) 143–6, 148
resistance
    FRG 86, 113, 126
    GDR 138, 151
    Ruhr, 1923 49
    Third Reich 58, 69–71, 74–5
Retallack, James 22
reunification 136, 143, 153–8, 161, 163–4
revolutions
    1848 7–8
    1918 4, 29–30, 34–6, 41–4, 48, 51–2
    1989 136, 146, 148–54, 160, 167
rights 5–6
    FRG 4, 82–6, 92, 98–101, 104, 106–7, 110, 112, 114, 120–2, 129
    GDR 132, 134, 141–3, 146–7, 156–8, 161, 164
    Kaiserreich 4, 12–15, 19–21, 27–8
    Third Reich 4, 58–9, 61–2, 64, 76
    Weimar Republic 4, 37–9, 45, 48, 56
Ritter, Gerhard A. 30
Rohe, Karl 24
Rohrschneider, Robert 141
Rosenstraße protests 73–4
Rousseau, Jean-Jacques 22, 43, 132
rule of law. *See* Rechtsstaat
Rupieper, Hermann-Josef 93

SA. *See* Storm Troopers
Sabrow, Martin 153
Sauckel, Fritz 60
Schabowski, Günter 153
Schäffer, Fritz 96
Scheidemann, Philipp 27, 34, 124
Schelsky, Helmut 95
Schiller, Karl 101
Schleicher, Kurt von 54–6
Schroeder, Gerhard (Interior Minister, 1953–1961) 85–6
Schumacher, Kurt 88
Second World War 57, 64, 66–76, 101, 156–7
security 101, 104, 109, 114, 136, 160
SED. *See* Socialist Unity Party
Sedlmaier, Alexander 119
Simons, Walter 40
skeptical generation 95
social Darwinism 65–6
Social Democratic Party of Germany
    FRG 81–2, 84–8, 91–2, 96, 98–9, 101, 103, 106–9, 113–14, 166–7
    GDR 132
    Kaiserreich 9, 14–18, 20–1, 25–8, 170
    Weimar Republic 34–7, 39, 41–3, 45–6, 48–50, 53–4
    Third Reich 63, 65
Socialist Unity Party (SED) 4, 131–40, 142–53, 159–60, 162
socialization 71, 116, 159–60
Sontheimer, Kurt 161
SPD. *See* Social Democratic Party of Germany
Speer, Albert 60
Spiegel affair 86, 92
Spontis. *See* Autonomous and Spontis
squatting 107, 120
Staatsstreich (coup), in *Kaiserreich* 12, 27
stab-in-the-back legend 43–4
Stahlhelm 51–2, 55–6
Stasi (Ministry for State Security, GDR) 77, 134, 138, 141, 144, 147, 149–51
state of emergency legislation. *See* exceptional executive powers
Stauffenberg, Berthold von 33
Steinbach, Peter 31
Stinnes, Hugo 36
Stöcker, Adolf 20

Stoltzfus, Nathan 74
Storm Troopers 47, 50–3, 59, 64–5, 76
Strasser, Gregor 55–6
Strauß, Franz-Josef 92, 99, 122
strikes
    FRG 86, 97, 124, 163
    GDR 143–5
    Kaiserreich 9, 25–9
    Third Reich 72–3
    Weimar Republic 35, 41–2, 48–53, 55
structured society 90
student movement 92, 97, 101, 104–5, 107, 111, 117–20, 122–4, 127
suffrage
    1815–1870 7–8
    Federal Republic of Germany 83, 158
    German Democratic Republic 133
    Kaiserreich 10–12, 14–17, 25–30
    legal aliens 158
    Third Reich 61
    Weimar Republic 35–9, 48
Suvall, Stanley 20
Sweeney, Dennis 24

technocracy 110–11
Thoreau, David 125
trade unions 9, 14, 19, 21, 36, 42, 47, 49, 55–6, 64–5, 86–7, 93, 96–9, 113, 115, 133
tutelage 9, 21, 25, 27, 35, 113, 137

Ulbricht, Walter 135, 142
unemployment insurance, Weimar Republic 53
ungovernability 106, 109, 118, 163, 168
unions. *See* trade unions
unofficial collaborators (GDR) 134, 147, 150

valley of the clueless 140
Verheyen, Nina 93
Versailles Treaty 44, 47, 50–2, 57, 64, 67
Vesper, Michael 124
violence 170
    FRG 94–5, 105–7, 109–11, 114, 116–17, 119–23, 125–7, 129, 155, 160, 163–4, 167
    GDR 134, 150–3
    Kaiserreich 25–6
    Third Reich 58–9, 63, 65–6, 76
    Weimar Republic 33, 35–6, 39–40, 48–53
Volksgemeinschaft (people's or racial community) 33, 41–3, 54–5, 57–63, 67–8, 70–1, 77, 166
voter turnout 18, 95, 101, 133, 149, 161–2

Wandlitz 153
Weisbrod, Bernd 53
Western culture 91
Westle, Bettina 162
White Rose 75
White, Hayden 6
Wildt, Michael 61
Wilhelm I 18–19, 25, 169
Wilhelm II 12, 22, 28
will
    individual wills 33, 94–5, 110
    people's will 4, 6, 22, 29, 31, 37, 40, 42–3, 45–6, 56–8, 60, 70, 76, 113–15, 131, 133, 154, 163, 166, 169, 171
    political will, forming 46, 86, 89, 95–9, 107, 112, 114–15, 123, 128, 169
Wilson, Woodrow 29, 44
withdrawal. *See* niches
Wolle, Stefan 135
women
    political and social roles 19–21, 24, 26, 29, 37, 47–8, 51, 54, 61, 68–9, 72, 74, 105, 115, 117, 119–20, 135, 142, 162, 164, 170
    rights 4, 14, 19–21, 84–5, 134
    suffrage 17, 29, 37, 61
Workers and Soldiers Councils 29–30, 34–6

Zatlin, Jonathan 141, 145
Zimmermann, Friedrich 122

www.ingramcontent.com/pod-product-compliance
Lightning Source LLC
Chambersburg PA
CBHW072124290426
44111CB00012B/1768